The Junior League of Lake Charles, Inc.

Pirate's Pantry

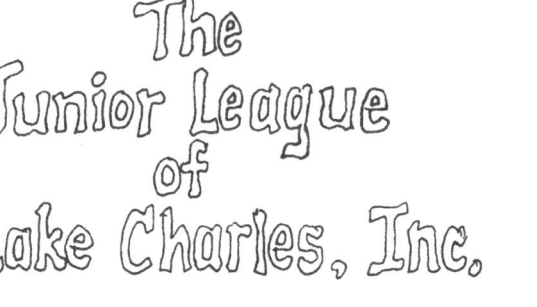

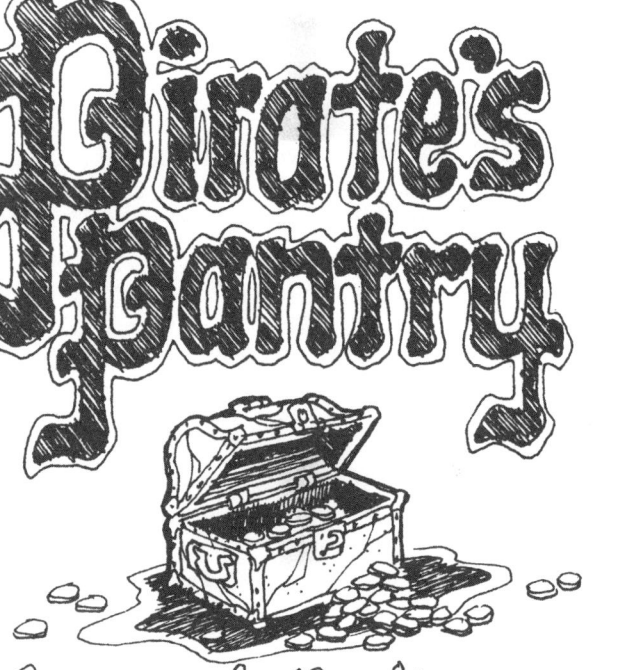

Treasured Recipes of Southwest Louisiana

PELICAN PUBLISHING COMPANY

GRETNA 2014

Copyright © 1976, 1986, 2004
The Junior League of Lake Charles, Incorporated
All rights reserved

Library of Congress Cataloging-in-Publication Data

Pirate's pantry.
    The Junior League of Lake Charles, Inc., presents pirate's pantry : treasured recipes of southwest Louisiana. - 1st Pelican ed.
    p. cm.
    Cover title: Pirate's pantry.
    Reprint. Originally published: 2nd ed. 1986.
    Includes index.
    ISBN-13: 978-0-88289-865-0
    1. Cookery, American—Louisiana style. 2. Cookery, Cajun.
3. Cookery—Louisiana. I. Junior League of Lake Charles.
II. Title.   III. Title: Pirate's pantry.
TX715.2.L68P57   1991
641.59763—dc20   91-14651
                                                                       CIP

First printing: November 1976
Second printing: May 1977
Third printing: September 1978
Fourth printing: April 1981
Fifth printing: 10th Anniversary Edition, June 1986
First Pelican edition: November 1991
Seventh printing: October 1992
Eighth printing: February 1998
Ninth printing: December 2003
Tenth printing: March 2008
Eleventh printing: May 2014

Printed in the United States of America
Published by Pelican Publishing Company, Inc.
1000 Burmaster Street, Gretna, Louisiana 70053

Table of Contents

ROUX	1
FILÉ	2
GUMBOS	3-9
SOUPS	10-20
RICE	21-33
SEAFOOD	34-84
WILDLIFE	85-104
BEVERAGES	105-114
WINE	115-117
HORS D'OEUVRES	118-142
EGGS AND CHEESE	143-150
BREADS	151-164
MEAT	165-212
POULTRY	213-233
VEGETABLES	235-269
SALADS	271-292
SAUCES	293-302
ACCOMPANIMENTS	303-308
DESSERTS	309-377
METRIC CONVERSIONS	378
FAST AND FABULOUS	379-418
INDEX	419-448

Treasure chest symbol identifies those recipes in which total preparation time is 30 minutes or less. Additional cooking or chilling time may be needed.

Cajun Cuisine

Particular emphasis has been placed on area specialties: seafood, wildlife, rice, and gumbos.

Specialties which reflect the rich natural resources of the area have remained virtually unchanged. Still served in the hunting camps, deep in the Southwest Louisiana marshes, are old favorites such as wild duck gumbo with rice, fresh filé, roast wild duck or goose with thick brown gravy, pepper jelly, boudin, dirty rice, fresh turnips and mustard greens, hot sauce, French bread, and great quantities of red wine and beer.

Featured in area restaurants are such taste tempters as "a complete crawfish dinner," including bisque, fried crawfish tails, stuffed bell peppers, etouffée and crawfish pie, or a "seafood platter" consisting of fried oysters, frog legs, shrimp, fried catfish, stuffed crab, jambalaya, fried onion rings and hush puppies, with tangy tartare and horseradish sauces on the side.

Today's guest at one of the elegant homes bordering the lake might be served a dinner of oysters Bienville or Rockefeller, French onion soup, baked quail, fresh asparagus with Hollandaise sauce, and black bottom pie, or caramel soufflé and café brûlot.

And at Sunday morning "brunch" he might find a table laden with grillades and grits; thick slices of red tomatoes or stewed okra and tomatoes; cucumbers from the garden; steaming biscuits, southern style, served with butter, mayhaw jelly, and amber figs preserved in sugar with their own juices.

Pirate's Pantry Prologue

Southwest Louisiana is an area naturally conducive to tales of mystery and romance.

A maze of moss-shadowed bayous, lush with vegetation, vines, and the ghostlike knees of bald cypress roots; of sinuous rivers and windswept marshes, it exudes mystery and the promise of hidden riches.

Whether it be the legendary Lost Mine, or the fabled gold and jewels of pirate booty, tales of buried treasure abound in Calcasieu Parish.

For more than a hundred years Lake Charles area residents have dreamed of finding Napoleon's jewels, riches purportedly buried along the shores of Calcasieu River or on the bottom of Contraband Bayou by the pirate-captain, Jean Lafitte, a frequent guest at the dinner tables of Lake Charles's wealthy Creole planters.

Inaccessible in many places, except by boat, the wetlands of Southwest Louisiana seem to inscrutably guard the secret of Lafitte's treasure trove. However, the residents are inveterate "treasure" hunters. Skilled with the pushpole and the pirogue, they harvest a rich bounty of gastronomical delights. The waters and marshes abound in the most succulent seafoods and wildlife ever to grace a table.

Perhaps it was these "natural" riches, coupled with the superb Creole cooking skills, which brought Lafitte back to the area time and again to savor the plump oysters, the rich shrimp creoles, and the crab gumbos, seasoned with spices and hot with pepper; and to relish the aroma of wild duck roasting over the coals.

We have drawn from a rich heritage of French, Spanish, and native cookery for our *Pirate's Pantry*, a treasury of family recipes, many of which have come down through the generations from Lafitte to the present.

We invite you, as our guest, to visit Southwest Louisiana — one page at a time. First, browse through the sketches and legends to steep yourself in her past. Then set sail for a culinary adventure through time — from the swashbuckling days of the pirate ships to the modern day mammoth cargo ships now harbored in the Port of Lake Charles.

You have only to open our *Pirate's Pantry* to share the treasures within!
Bon Voyage!

EDITORS

Mrs. J. J. Champeaux II
(Rosalie "Poddy" Leveque)

Mrs. William E. Shaddock
(Craig Gorham)

Mrs. Edward M. Carmouche
(Virginia Martin)

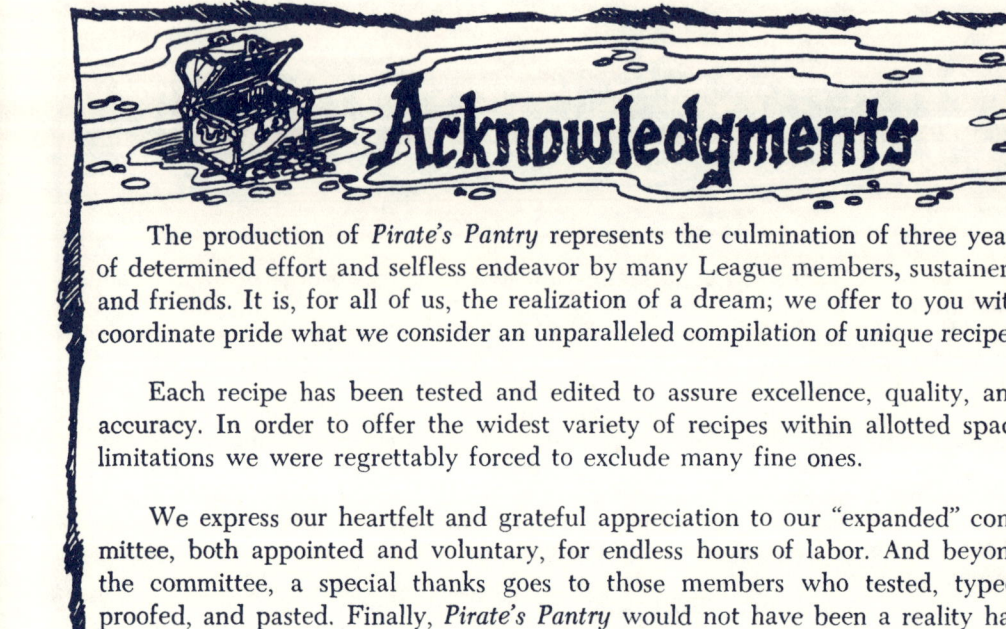

Acknowledgments

The production of *Pirate's Pantry* represents the culmination of three years of determined effort and selfless endeavor by many League members, sustainers, and friends. It is, for all of us, the realization of a dream; we offer to you with coordinate pride what we consider an unparalleled compilation of unique recipes.

Each recipe has been tested and edited to assure excellence, quality, and accuracy. In order to offer the widest variety of recipes within allotted space limitations we were regrettably forced to exclude many fine ones.

We express our heartfelt and grateful appreciation to our "expanded" committee, both appointed and voluntary, for endless hours of labor. And beyond the committee, a special thanks goes to those members who tested, typed, proofed, and pasted. Finally, *Pirate's Pantry* would not have been a reality had it not been for the generous contribution of treasured recipes by League members and friends, and for the time and patience of well-tried husbands and families who tested and tasted each of them to insure that *Pirate's Pantry* truly reflect the culinary prowess of Southwest Louisiana.

Cover design, illustrations, pen and ink sketches by
J. J. Champeaux II, FAIA

Section writers
Mrs. D. Dale Archer, Mrs. D. M. Creveling, Mrs. Donald G. Johnson,
Dr. Kalil Ieyoub, Frank N. Ingraham, Lawrence Lowery, Jr.,
William E. Shaddock

Sustaining Advisor **Publicity and Promotion**
Mrs. William E. Boyer Mrs. Richard Savoy

Food Editors
Mrs. James Boyer Mrs. David Painter
Mrs. Ben Guilbeau Mrs. James Taussig

Legends by **Title designation by**
Carolyn Stevens Moffett Mrs. Robert E. Christman

Tenth Anniversary Special Edition
Editors
Mrs. David A. Kestel
Mrs. David Brumby
Mrs. Charles R. Anderson

THE LEGEND OF JEAN LAFITTE

Some folks say that the spirit of Jean Lafitte, the pirate, still hovers over the dark waters of the Calcasieu River, with its cypress bayous and ghostlike Spanish moss. In the murky gloom of twilight, elusive swamp lights offer a phosphorescent promise of buried treasure just beyond.

It is a proven fact that the gentleman pirate and patriot came often to the Calcasieu country to trade, visit, and seek refuge; and he headquartered near here around the year 1810.

A wanted man, the dashing young pirate sought refuge here from United States war vessels. History relates that he slipped more than once under cover of darkness or fog, into safe harbor at the mouth of the Calcasieu River.[1]

Once, learning from sentinels posted down river that an attack was imminent, he sent ashore a party of his most trusted men to bury a treasure by night. Next morning, he set a large force to building an embankment, behind which he placed cannons. When the warship lay at anchor, a shot from the newly constructed fort sank the schooner and routed the accompanying gunboat.

The old fortification, known for many years as "Dead Man's Lake,"[2] can still be seen on the bank of the lake.

Another oft-told tale relates that Lafitte, pardoned by the U.S. in return for his aid in the Battle of New Orleans, sailed to France, and secretly aided Napoleon, after the Battle of Waterloo, in an attempted escape to America. Sailing with a vast amount of gold and jewels, the "Little Emperor" was apprehended and arrested, but Lafitte escaped with the treasure, which he buried along the Calcasieu River.[3]

Strange tomblike vaults, marked with iron crosses, along the shore of Big Lake[4] housed a treasure of gold Spanish doubloons, some say. Though the encroaching waters of the lake have obliterated all traces of the landmarks, the gold remains undisturbed at its bottom.

Trees marked with Roman numerals are another indication of buried treasure; and Niblett's Bluff[5] is the site where Lafitte's gold is said to be buried under 40 gum trees.

Another story places the gold at the bottom of Contraband Bayou.[6] Still another tells of a schooner, laden with gold coin and jewels gathered along the Spanish Main, which sank in the marshes south of Lake Charles.[7]

And, it is said, that the waters around Lake Charles, still provide sanctuary to the notorious pirate. Legend is that his final resting place is on the eastern shore of the lake.[8] His spirit still guards the gold of Napoleon — and casts a mighty shadow across "the Quelqueshue."

Roux

How do you make the initial *Roux* required in so many Creole and Acadian dishes? You may get as many answers as you have cooks with agreement only on the definition. A mixture of fat and flour, used to thicken sauces: a French word, derived from the Latin "Russ," meaning browned or reddish.

One accepted method of making *Roux* calls for equal parts flour and fat (oil, lard, grease, shortening, butter, or margarine), cooked very slowly in a heavy pot stirred constantly until the right shade of brown (brown-paper-bag, dark chocolate brown, brown parchment, etc.). Chopped vegetables are then added quickly to arrest the browning; the liquid, hot or cold, next.

But that's not the only way to make a *Roux*. Proportions and cooking methods can be varied with equally good results. Many good cooks use only $\frac{1}{3}$ to $\frac{1}{2}$ as much fat as flour, claiming this blends easier with the liquid without danger of separation or "curdling." Others prefer the less time-consuming oven methods. Place 2 parts flour and 1 part fat in a flat pan and cook in preheated 275°F oven until caramel color (about 2 hours), stirring 4 times during cooking. When cool, prop the pan for excess fat to drain to one corner for skimming off.

For a fat-free *Roux*, place a cast iron skillet, containing 1 inch of flour, in a 400°F oven until dark brown, stirring occasionally with a wooden spoon.

If, through experimentation, you devise a new way to make a *Roux*, simply add it to the list. Creole-Acadian cooks are notoriously individualistic!! Whichever, the *Roux* may be made ahead and refrigerated or frozen, tightly covered, for long periods of time.

Mrs. D. Dale Archer
(Valerie "Val" Grode)

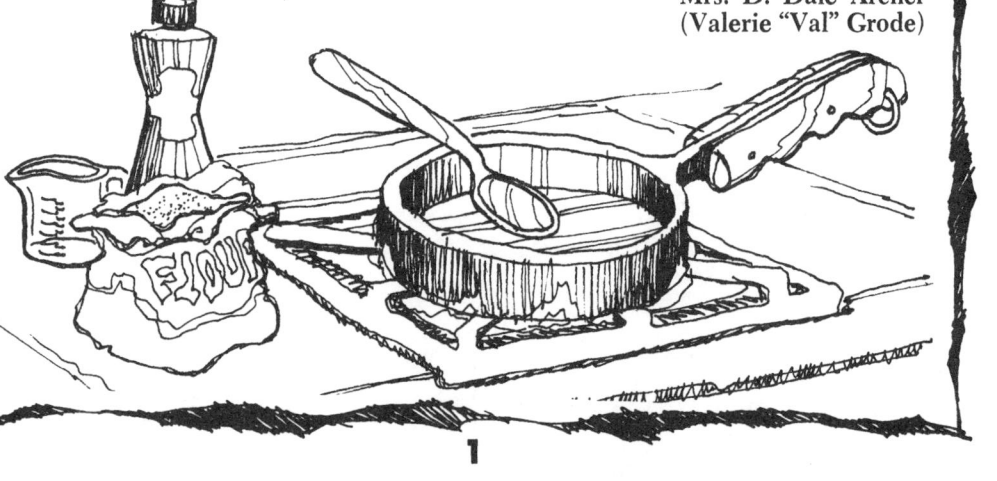

SASSAFRAS — FRESH FILÉ

Gather sassafras leaves in month of August (preferably in full moon). Pick leaves off branches and put in clean sacks (pillow case or old sheet and make into sacks). Don't fill sacks tight (about half) so you can have plenty room to shake up every day. Each morning put outdoors to dry (on dry days) *not in the sun*, under carport. Let dry till they are very brittle. On very, very dry crisp days you can grind — then and only then. Take a meat grinder and grind 1 or 2 of the sacks at a time. Don't fool with others yet. Then after grinding the 1 or 2 sacks, regrind. You'll notice it will get finer each grinding. When you get it to a powder form, then take a fine sifter and put about ½ cup in it and don't sift, but lightly tap. You only want the powder form. Then you just keep going over until you may have to throw away about ½-1 cup of the coarse sticks or small branches. Be sure to get *in no draft* or wind at all. Work with the fine powder as smooth as possible, in order for it not to fly. You may be able to do about 2 a day. So don't rush and work slow. Have clean dry jars and put it in there with a small spoon. The day you start to grind don't wash or wet anything until you finish the filé. You should only use old, dry rags. If you don't finish that day, cover leaves (that you are using, grinder and all). Be sure and don't force the filé through the sifter, after jarring your filé.

Mrs. Lena Farque
Big Lake, Louisiana

Gumbo

Gombo a la Creole, Louisiana gumbo, is perhaps the state's single most famous dish.

Like the people of South Louisiana, this native dish is a happy blending of just about everything. In fact, in the patois of the area, gumbo means "all together" or "all at once" as in the expression gumbo ya-ya, which means everyone talking at once.

The term evolved from the African "kingombo" or "ngombo," okra, a vegetable used to thicken and flavor the dish. The gombo plant was brought to Louisiana by slaves, who upon learning the French and Spanish cooking techniques of their Creole masters, combined the ingredient with a rich brown roux and spicy cayenne pepper to make a savory stew.

Gumbo may be thickened with either okra or filé, a grayish green powder derived from tender young sassafras leaves. Louisiana's Choctaw Indians discovered and used the herb long before the Acadian migration.

Characteristically, and in keeping with its diverse origins, gumbo utilizes just about anything for its base: Chicken, turkey, ham, squirrel, rabbit, crab, oyster, shrimp, fish, sausage, cabbage, or even simply herbs.

Superstitious Cajuns believed if they ate seven greens and met seven people on Good Friday they would have good luck all year — hence the origin of gumbo z'herbes (green or herb gumbo).

LOUISIANA GUMBO

½ cup Wesson oil
1 cup flour
4 quarts water
2 large onions, finely chopped
1 clove garlic, chopped
1 cup green onions, chopped
¼ cup parsley, finely chopped
⅛ cup bell pepper, chopped (optional)
⅛ cup celery, chopped (optional)
Salt and pepper to taste
Chicken, goose, duck, smoked pork sausage combination
½ teaspoon filé
Hot fluffy rice

In large gumbo pot, make a roux with oil and flour. Cook over medium heat, stirring constantly until roux is a dark caramel color. Remove from fire and add remaining ingredients, except ½ cup green onions, filé, and rice. Boil for about 2 hours, or until meat is tender and gumbo has thickened. In the last 15 minutes of boiling add reserved green onions. Remove from fire and add filé (too much will make gumbo slimy). Serve over hot rice in gumbo bowls. Serves 5-6.

Shrimp Gumbo is made the same way except that shrimp are not added until last 20 minutes of cooking time, after gumbo has preboiled for 45 minutes.

For *Seafood Gumbo*, follow same procedure as Shrimp Gumbo but add crab meat also. In the last 15 minutes of cooking, add oysters.

Mrs. Paul "Dud" Faulk
(Rena Lantz)

MRS. SOULÉ'S SEAFOOD GUMBO

1 cup oil (½ cup bacon grease and ½ cup Wesson oil)
1 full cup flour
2 large onions, finely chopped
1 clove garlic, minced
½ bell pepper, minced
1 stalk celery, finely chopped
½ bunch parsley, finely chopped
1 cup cold water
½ gallon hot water
3 Tablespoons fresh gumbo filé
1 Tablespoon cayenne pepper
Salt
3 pounds raw shrimp
1 pound crab meat
½ gallon oysters

In an iron skillet make a roux with oil and sifted flour, stirring constantly over medium heat with a wooden spoon until dark, chocolate brown. At this stage add the vegetables, stirring well, and cover skillet with an iron top. Stir frequently until vegetables are clear. Transfer to a large gumbo pot and stir in cold water at very low heat. Then add hot water, stir, and bring to a boil. Reduce heat to simmer. Add gumbo filé. Do not stir in filé, but take the spoon and dab it onto the surface so that it settles down into the gumbo. Stir around sides of gumbo pot to keep filé in the middle. Simmer for 40 minutes. Stir in salt to taste; add red pepper and turn off heat until 30 minutes before serving. Meanwhile, peel, devein, and thoroughly wash shrimp. Carefully wash the crab meat and the oysters, individually. Bring gumbo to a boil, reduce heat to a simmer, add the shrimp and crab meat, and cook 5 minutes. Stir in oysters. Immediately turn off heat, cover pot, and let stand for 10 minutes. Serve in gumbo bowls over rice. Add a small pinch of gumbo filé, a squirt or 2 of Bird's Eye Pepper sauce, and salt to taste to each bowl. Serve with French bread, mustard greens, and navy beans.

Edith Menard
Holly Beach, La.

GUMBO Z'HERBES

3 pounds lean salt meat
Cold water
4 packages frozen spinach
4 packages frozen mustard greens
1 small cabbage, if desired
1 large onion, chopped
1 clove garlic, finely minced
1 medium bell pepper, chopped
1 pound cooked ham, finely chopped
½ teaspoon black pepper

Rinse salt meat in cold water and cut into 1 inch cubes, after trimming off some of the fat. Place in a large saucepan and add cold water to 2 inches above meat. Bring to a boil and simmer until tender. Cook frozen greens as directed on package. Cool. Mix in blender the cooled greens, their cooking liquid, the onion, garlic, and bell pepper. Combine with ham and add to salt meat broth, heat, and simmer for about 20-30 minutes.

Mrs. A. J. Boudreaux
Lafayette, La.

SEAFOOD GUMBO

⅔ cup oil or bacon drippings
1 cup flour
3 large onions, chopped
3 ribs celery, chopped
5-6 cloves garlic, chopped
¼ large bell pepper, chopped
2 quarts water
3 bay leaves
Tabasco
Salt and pepper
Worcestershire sauce
2-3 pounds okra, cut
2 cans (8 ounce size) tomato sauce
1 dozen raw crabs, cleaned
1 bunch green onions, chopped
1 small bunch parsley, chopped
3 pounds raw shrimp, peeled and deveined
2 pounds crab meat
Oysters

In skillet make roux using oil and flour. Cook until it is chocolate brown color. Add chopped vegetables and stir until wilted. Transfer to large gumbo pot (not iron, as iron will make okra turn black). Add water and bring to a boil. Add seasonings, okra, and tomato sauce. Boil for approximately 1 hour. Add crabs, green onions, and parsley, continue boiling for about 20 minutes. Add shrimp 2-3 minutes after crabs. Just before serving add crab meat and oysters. Serve over hot fluffy rice in gumbo bowls. *Variation:* Omit okra or tomato sauce. Instead of seafood, use large hen, wild ducks, geese, turkey carcass, or any other type meat. Cook until tender. Add filé to individual gumbo bowls, if desired, just before serving. Serves 15.

James R. St. Dizier

WEEZE'S GUMBO

¾ cup bacon drippings
¾ cup flour
2 packages frozen cut okra, unthawed but separated
2 onions, chopped
1 bell pepper, chopped
4 ribs celery, chopped
4 green onions and tops, chopped
Parsley, chopped
2 cloves garlic, chopped
2 teaspoons black pepper
1 teaspoon paprika
2 Tablespoons salt
1 teaspoon garlic salt
4 bouillon cubes, any flavor
8 cups water
1 can (6 ounces) tomato paste
2 pounds medium shrimp, raw, peeled

In a large *heavy* iron pot or Dutch oven make roux with bacon drippings and flour. Roux will be watery at first, but it should finally be *dark* brown. Add all remaining ingredients, except shrimp. Simmer, covered (with crack), for 2 hours. Add shrimp about 10 minutes before serving. Make a chicken gumbo the same way except boil chicken in advance and use the *broth* in place of water.

Weeze Pujo

"HOT" SEAFOOD AND OKRA GUMBO FOR A CROWD

2½ cups all purpose flour
1½ cups oil
1 quart cold water
7 quarts hot water
2 pounds fresh shrimp, cleaned
5 cans Blue Plate shrimp and liquid
5 cans crab meat, fancy white and claw
2 cans cut okra and tomatoes (1 quart fresh smothered okra is better)
2 teaspoons cayenne pepper
7 teaspoons or more salt
2 teaspoons black pepper
1 can Ro-tel tomatoes with green chilies
3 medium onions, chopped
12 cloves fresh garlic, minced
1 Tablespoon dry minced garlic
3 cups bell pepper, chopped
5 cups celery, chopped
1 can (7¾ ounces) pink salmon
2 dozen fresh crabs
2 dozen hard boiled eggs, halved (optional)
2 cups green onions, chopped
2 cups parsley, chopped
Hot rice
Gumbo filé

Brown flour in oil over medium heat in a heavy pot. Stir constantly until roux is a rich, deep brown in color; then add cold water. Pour roux into very large boiling pot (about 4 gallon size). Add hot water and mix well.

Add remaining ingredients except fresh crabs, eggs, green onions and parsley to roux, cover, and boil slowly for 30 minutes. Break crabs in half and crack claws. Add crabs, eggs, green onions, and parsley and simmer for 15 minutes. Serve over hot rice with gumbo filé. Takes about 4 hours to prepare.

Mrs. Cleve LaFleur
Sulphur, La.

SQUIRREL OR DOVE GUMBO

4 squirrels, cut into 5 pieces each, or 15 doves
Salt and pepper
¼ cup bacon fat
½ cup cooking oil
¾ cup plain flour
2 quarts plus 2 cups cold water
4 ribs celery, finely chopped
⅔ cup parsley, finely chopped
⅔ cup green onion tops, finely chopped
5½ teaspoons salt
½ teaspoon black pepper
¼ teaspoon red pepper
4 dashes Tabasco
2 chicken bouillon cubes
1½ teaspoons garlic powder

Season squirrel or doves with salt and pepper. Set aside. In a heavy skillet make roux with bacon fat, oil, and flour. Stir continuously with wooden spatula over medium high heat until dark golden brown, about 1-1½ hours, depending on heat of fire. Transfer roux to heavy 6 quart pot with lid. Add water and all other ingredients. Bring to a boil. Cover, leaving a small crack in lid, and cook at a slow rolling boil until meat is very tender. Young squirrel and doves about 2½ hours, older ones longer. Serve on hot, fluffy rice in deep bowls. Serves 8.

Mrs. George Hardy Vincent
(Nina LaFleur)

GOOSE - DUCK - SAUSAGE GUMBO

1 gallon boiling water
¾ cup flour
¾ cup oil
4 large onions, chopped
6 ribs celery, chopped
3 bell peppers, chopped
4 large carrots, sliced
4 ducks
1 goose
4 pounds smoked link sausage, sliced ¼ inch thick
1 bottle Tiger sauce
⅛ cup Kitchen Bouquet
¼ cup Worcestershire sauce
2 teaspoons Tabasco
2 pounds okra, sliced
Salt and red pepper to taste
1 small can frozen orange juice concentrate
1 can mushrooms, drained
1 teaspoon each basil, oregano, crushed red pepper
1 cup red wine

Start water boiling. Make roux with flour and oil. When roux is browned, add some boiling water. Then add the roux mixture to the boiling water and stir to mix. Add onion, celery, bell pepper, and carrots to liquid. Skin the ducks and goose. Chop each in 4 or 5 pieces and add to the pot. Add sausage. Add remaining ingredients, seasoning to taste. Cover and simmer 4-6 hours. Remove bones to freeze. Serves 15-20.

Very piquant! Not the usual gumbo.

Ed McCreedy

CHAMPEAUX GUMBO

3 ducks
Salt
Garlic salt
Red and black pepper
½ cup all purpose flour
¾ cup liquid oil
1½ cups onion, chopped
1 cup celery, chopped
1 cup bell pepper, chopped
3 cloves garlic, chopped
2 quarts hot water
¼ teaspoon ground cloves
8 bay leaves
½ teaspoon filé
1 pound sausage, cooked (optional)

Clean ducks thoroughly, section, and remove skin. Season all over with salt, garlic salt, red and black pepper. Sprinkle lightly with flour. Cover bottom of large, heavy pot with ¼ cup oil. Brown meaty pieces of duck in hot oil first, adding bony pieces later. Brown well. In heavy skillet make roux with ½ cup oil and flour. When roux is golden brown, add onion, celery, bell pepper, and garlic. Cook until wilted. Add golden hot roux to hot browned ducks in large pot. Add 2 quarts hot water to large pot. This should cover ducks completely. Stir. Be sure to get all drippings loose from bottom of pot. Add cloves, bay leaves, and filé. Season to taste with salt and pepper. Simmer, covered, on low heat for 3 hours. Check periodically to see if meat is fork tender. If desired, add warm sausage to gumbo 30 minutes before serving. Filé may also be added to individual taste. Skim grease and remove bay leaves before serving. Serves 6-8.

J. J. "Joe" Champeaux II

Mrs. Matilda Geddings Gray *always served a peeled baked yam in the gumbo bowl with duck gumbo. This was standard fare for guests at her Vinton duck camp.*

Try a Cajun baked yam in your gumbo. To prepare, scrub potatoes and dry. Bake on cookie sheet at 350°F, turning every 30 minutes, until very soft. Test for doneness by gently squeezing. Serve in shell, or peeled, with butter. Leftover baked yams are good peeled, sliced ½ inch thick, and fried in 2 inches of hot cooking oil (about 4 minutes). Drain and sprinkle with granulated sugar. C'est si bon!

HEN GUMBO

½ cup oil
¾ cup flour
1 cup cold water
1 quart boiling water
1 Tablespoon file'
4 large onions, chopped
4 ribs celery, scraped and chopped
1 bell pepper, seeded and chopped
3 cloves garlic, chopped
2 Tablespoons salt
1 Tablespoon seasoned black pepper
6 shakes Tabasco
2 bay leaves *(always remove before serving)*
1 chicken bouillon cube
1 large hen, cut into serving pieces
3 quarts boiling water
½ cup parsley, chopped
½ cup green onion tops, chopped
Hot rice
¼ teaspoon file'

Make a *dark* brown roux with oil and flour in iron skillet. Add cold water (stirring constantly to stop cooking process when roux is desired color. Transfer to a large gumbo pot and add boiling water, stirring constantly. Boil 15 minutes; then add filé (preferably fresh) and stir. Add chopped vegetables and seasonings and cook 30 minutes. Remove excess fat from hen pieces, salt lightly, pepper liberally, then flour lightly. Brown hen pieces in oil (preferably peanut oil) and add to gumbo. Pour in additional boiling water and cook, covered, slowly 3-4 hours, or until hen is tender. Adjust seasonings if necessary. About 30 minutes before serving, add parsley and green onion tops. Serve over rice in gumbo bowl, adding ¼ teaspoon filé to each just before serving.

A cold night, fire in fireplace, hot gumbo, French bread, green salad, good bottle of red wine — this is South Louisiana living!!

William E. Shaddock

FRENCH ONION SOUP

- 4 Tablespoons butter
- 2 Tablespoons olive oil
- 2 pounds onions, thinly sliced (about 7 cups)
- 1 teaspoon salt
- 3 Tablespoons flour
- 2 quarts beef stock, fresh or canned, (or beef and chicken stock, combined)

CROÛTES
- 12-16 thick (1 inch) slices French bread
- 2 teaspoons olive oil
- 1 clove garlic, cut
- 1 cup imported Swiss cheese (or ½ cup each Swiss and Parmesan), grated

VARIATION: ONION SOUP GRATINÉE
- A little melted butter

In a heavy 5 quart saucepan, melt butter with olive oil over moderate heat. Stir in onions and salt and cook, uncovered, over low heat, stirring occasionally, until onions are a rich, golden brown. Sprinkle flour over onions and cook, stirring, for 2-3 minutes. Add heated stock and simmer, partially covered, for 30-40 minutes. Occasionally skim off fat. Add salt and pepper if needed.

CROÛTES:
While the soup simmers, preheat oven to 325°F. Bake bread, in 1 layer, on baking sheet for about 15 minutes. Lightly coat both sides of each slice with olive oil. Turn slices over and bake for another 15 minutes, or until bread is completely dry and lightly browned. Rub each slice with garlic and set aside. To serve, place the croûtes in a large tureen, or individual soup bowls, and ladle soup over them. Pass grated cheese. Soup may be made days ahead, but croûtes should be fresh. May be doubled. Freezes. Serves 6-8.

VARIATION: ONION SOUP GRATINÉE:
Preheat oven to 375°F. Ladle soup into ovenproof tureen or individual soup bowls. Top with croûtes and sprinkle with grated cheese. Pour melted butter over. Bake for 10-20 minutes, or until cheese melts. Slide soup under a hot broiler for 1-2 minutes to brown top, if desired.

Mrs. Avery Cook
(Carolyn De Jean)

FLOSSIE'S BEAN SOUP

4 pounds dried Great Northern beans
2 gallons cold water
6 quarts warm water
1½ pounds salt pork, cubed (remove rind)
1 cup bell pepper, chopped
10 cups onions, chopped
5 cups celery, chopped
2 cups carrots, chopped
1 Tablespoon garlic, finely chopped
8 cups canned tomatoes with juice
Pepper to taste
2-3 pounds cooked ham, cut in ¾ inch cubes
2 pounds wieners, sliced ⅛ inch thick
2 cups green onions, finely chopped
2 cups parsley, finely chopped

Wash beans and cull to remove bad ones; then place in 5 gallon kettle and cover with 2 gallons cold water. Soak overnight. Next morning, drain off water; then add 6 quarts warm water. Bring to a full boil and cook over medium heat until beans are very tender but not mushy. This takes 1½-2 hours. Remove half the cooked beans, drain well, and set aside. Add remaining ingredients, except ham, wieners, green onions, and parsley. Bring to a boil; reduce heat to medium to prevent beans from sticking and scorching. Cook, covered, stirring frequently. When vegetables and beans have become quite soft and slightly mushy (usually after 2 hours or more), add reserved beans, ham, wieners, green onions, and parsley. Let simmer for 30 minutes. If soup is to be refrigerated or frozen, let it cool to room temperature first. Freezes. Serves 40-50.

Hint: When reheating soup, never cover the kettle until soup has reached boiling point, or it will sour. Use medium heat and stir frequently until hot. Do not add salt as cured meats are usually salty enough.

Mrs. Edward H. Taussig
(Florence Streater)

MEXICAN BLACK BEAN SOUP

2 pounds black beans
1½-2 quarts water
2 cups onion, chopped
1 cup bell pepper, chopped
2 cups celery, chopped
2 cloves garlic, crushed
1 pound bacon, finely chopped
2 cans (8 ounce size) tomato sauce
2 teaspoons each oregano, Accent, cumin
4 teaspoons sugar
4 teaspoons chili powder
Salt and pepper to taste

Wash beans thoroughly. In a large pot, cover beans with 1½-2 quarts water and cook, covered, 1 hour. Add other ingredients. Cook 3 more hours. Salt and pepper to taste. Let soup cool slightly. Place in blender and blend until smooth. Heat as needed. Serve with fresh chopped onions and lemon wedges. Freezes. Serves 12.

Very delicious! Men love it!

Mrs. James H. deCordova
Jennings, La.

BEAN SOUP

Leftover ham bone
Small package (1 pound) white Navy beans
1 onion, chopped
2 ribs celery, chopped
1 can whole tomatoes
4 quarts water
2 carrots, grated
4 wieners, sliced
Salt and pepper to taste

Cut ham from bone. Boil ham bone, ham, beans, onion, celery, and tomatoes in about 4 quarts water, slowly for 3 hours. Add carrots and wieners. Cook 30 more minutes, or until beans are cooked. Season with salt and pepper to taste. Freezes. Serves 8-10.

Mrs. Charles S. Ware, Jr.
(Jan Allen)

FRESH CORN SOUP

12 ears fresh corn
1 teaspoon paprika
½ cup salad oil
2 quarts water
10 chicken bouillon cubes
1 medium onion, chopped
½ can Ro-tel tomatoes with green chilies
2 cans shoe peg white corn
1 can cream style corn
1½ pounds brisket (optional)
Salt and pepper

Cut kernels off ears of corn and scrape milk from cob. In a heavy pot, slowly cook half the corn with paprika in oil until light brown (about 15 minutes). Stir often. Add water and remaining ingredients and simmer for 30 minutes. Add salt and pepper if necessary. Add browned brisket if desired.

Mrs. Cleve LaFleur
Sulphur, La.

CHEESE SOUP

1 medium onion, chopped
2 Tablespoons butter
1-2 Tablespoons flour
1-2 cups chicken broth
½ pound American cheese, grated (3 generous fluffy cups)
1 bell pepper, cut in strips
1 can (15 ounces) red kidney beans, drained
1 healthy shot Worchestershire sauce
Seasonings to taste

Brown onion in butter; add flour to thicken and stir until smooth. Add 1-2 cups chicken broth depending on how thick a soup is desired. Add cheese and heat, stirring, until it melts. Add bell pepper, kidney beans, Worcestershire sauce, and seasonings to taste. Heat, gently stirring, until flavors blend. Serves 5.

Mrs. Leonard Knapp, Jr.
(Ann Hall)

SOUPS

HEARTY CORN CHOWDER

1 can (10¼ ounces) frozen condensed cream of potato soup, thawed (if frozen not available, use canned)
1 can (17 ounces) golden cream style corn
1 cup milk
½ teaspoon salt
⅛ teaspoon cracked black pepper
1¼ cups ham, finely chopped
3 Tablespoons fresh parsley, snipped

Combine potato soup, corn, milk, salt, and pepper in medium saucepan. Heat to serving temperature, stirring frequently. Add ham and parsley; heat thoroughly. Makes 4½ cups. Serves 6.

Mrs. Frank E. Gault
(Ruth Kelly)

OLD FASHIONED JEWISH PENICILLIN
(Chicken Soup)

1 young hen (4-5 pounds)
3 quarts water
1 Tablespoon salt
1 whole onion
1 bay leaf
2 carrots, peeled
4 tops of celery ribs
White pepper to taste

Wash hen thoroughly and trim off excess fat. Cut into halves or quarters and place in salted water in a deep heavy pot or kettle. Cover; bring to a boil on high heat. Uncover and reduce to low heat. Add onion, bay leaf, carrots, and celery tops. Simmer until hen is tender (about 3 hours). Season to taste. Skim when necessary; add extra water if needed. When done, remove hen to platter and strain soup until clear. When cooled, refrigerate for a few hours until fat has formed on top surface. Skim fat. Freeze soup in containers until ready to use. Reheat before serving. Serves 8-10.

This cures most aches, pains, and colds — and anything else that requires this type of medication.

Mrs. Hal Goldman

SOUP VERDE
(Spinach Soup)

1 package frozen chopped spinach
¼ cup parsley, chopped
¼ cup green onion tops, chopped
1 small clove garlic, mashed
1½ cups milk
1 can Campbell's cream of chicken soup
Salt, black and red pepper

Mix thawed spinach, parsley, onions, garlic, and milk in blender. Add to soup in a saucepan. Cook, uncovered, slowly until hot. Add salt and pepper to taste. May be served hot or cold and used as an appetizer or a main dish. May be prepared a day in advance. Does not freeze. Serves 4-5.

Mrs. James A. Hooper, Jr.
(Mary Ann Leveque)

SPLIT PEA SOUP

2½ quarts (10 cups) cold water
1 package (16 ounces) dried green split peas
4-8 ounce ham hock
1 large onion, chopped
3 ribs celery, chopped
2 cloves garlic (put through press, mashed, or finely chopped)
Salt and black pepper
2 Tablespoons Lea & Perrins
Tabasco

Combine first 6 ingredients in large container. Bring to boil, cover, let simmer 1½ hours, or until peas begin to get soft. Add salt, pepper to taste. Replace cover, continue simmering 30 minutes. Stir in Lea & Perrins and Tabasco to taste.

This is a very nourishing, high protein soup. It has been used for many years for friends and family members who have been ill.

Mrs. Samuel Wilmore Plauche'
(Cornelia Lane)

PELICAN HOOK SOUP

1 can (11½ ounces) green pea soup
1 can (11½ ounces) tomato soup
6 ounces crab meat, fresh or canned
½ cup milk
Sherry to taste

Place all ingredients in a 2 quart saucepan. Heat, uncovered, on medium heat until piping hot, stirring occasionally. Does not freeze. Serves 6.

Very good, 'specially on a cold day for a luncheon.

Mrs. William G. Akins, Jr.
(Kay Mishler)

VEGETABLE BEEF SOUP

5-6 pounds heavy beef shanks
4 pound chuck roast
2½ gallons cold water
3 Tablespoons salt
4 cups celery, coarsely chopped
6 cups onion, coarsely chopped
1 teaspoon garlic, finely chopped
1½ teaspoons black pepper
2 cans (8 ounce size) tomato sauce
2 cups turnips, diced
8 cups canned tomatoes, chopped into small pieces, and juice
1 bell pepper, finely chopped
2½ pounds frozen mixed vegetables
1 package (9 ounces) frozen baby lima beans
1 package (9 ounces) frozen cut corn
3 packages (9 ounce size) frozen cut green beans
4 cups okra, sliced (fresh or frozen)
2 cups cabbage, chopped
4 cups fresh greens, chopped (either mustard, spinach, or swiss chard)
1 cup parsley, chopped
1 cup medium width noodles, broken in inch long pieces
Tabasco (optional)

Place meat in a 4-5 gallon soup kettle with cover. Add water and salt. Bring to full boil, reduce to medium boil, and cook for 30 minutes. Skim off scum as it surfaces. Add ½ the celery, ½ the onions, garlic, pepper, and tomato sauce. Cook, covered, on medium heat until the meat is very tender, probably 2-3 hours. Remove meat from broth; set aside until cool enough to handle; then remove all fat, gristle, and bones. Cut meat into bite sized pieces, or larger if desired. The meat will be returned to soup later. As soon as meat is removed, add rest of onions and celery, turnips, and tomatoes. Cook for about 30 minutes; then add rest of vegetables except greens, parsley, and noodles. When vegetables are tender, but not mushy, add greens, parsley, and noodles. Boil for 10 minutes; add reserved meat. Turn off heat and correct seasonings if necessary. Add Tabasco if desired. Makes 3 gallons.

The meat may be cooked a day ahead and refrigerated with broth, completing soup later. Fresh vegetables may be used instead of frozen ones, but take a longer time to cook.

Mrs. Edward H. Taussig
(Florence Streater)

BOUILLABAISSE SOUP

¾ pound fresh striped sea bass or mackerel
1½ pounds red snapper
¼ cup carrots, chopped
2 onions, sliced
¼ cup oil
3 fresh tomatoes, sliced (or 2 cups canned)
5 cloves garlic, minced
2 Tablespoons parsley, chopped
¼ teaspoon each saffron and thyme
½ teaspoon salt
2 quarts water
1 pound fresh shrimp, raw, peeled, deveined
1½ pounds fresh crawfish tails, raw, peeled
12 fresh oysters, culled for shells

Cut fish in 1 inch slices. Sauté carrots and onion in oil for 10 minutes in large pot. Add tomatoes, garlic, and other seasonings. Add water and bring to boil. Reduce heat and simmer 15 minutes. Add fish and cook 10 minutes. Add shellfish and cook 8 minutes more. Serves 6 amply.

Mrs. Wayne Woods
Grand Chenier, La.

BIENVENU'S COURT BOUILLON

1 cup flour
1 cup oil
3 cups onions, chopped
1 cup celery, chopped
1 cup bell pepper, chopped
6 cloves garlic, chopped
1 can (16 ounces) whole tomatoes
1 can (8 ounces) tomato sauce
3 quarts water
2 Tablespoons salt
½ teaspoon each red and and black pepper
3½ pounds firm fish (red fish, red snapper, gaspergou, or drum)
1 cup onion tops, finely chopped
½ cup parsley, finely chopped

Make a roux by mixing flour and oil in a large pot, preferably one of cast iron. Cook over medium heat, stirring constantly, until mixture is medium brown. Fry onions in roux until wilted. Add celery, bell pepper, garlic, whole tomatoes, and tomato sauce. Simmer 30 minutes, stirring frequently. Oil should be separating from the mixture. Add water, salt, red and black pepper. Bring to a boil and simmer for 1 hour. Add fish, again bring to a boil, and simmer for 30 minutes. Add onion tops and parsley 5 minutes before serving. Serve in soup plates. Serves 8.

Stephanie Labbe Bienvenu
Father Ken Bienvenu

MORGANS POINT CRAB CHOWDER

3 slices bacon, diced
1 large onion, chopped
2 large potatoes, diced
1 quart water
1 can (16 ounces) tomatoes
1 Tablespoon pickling spice, tied in bag
3 bay leaves
4 slices lemon
8-10 raw dressed crabs and claws
1 quart water
Salt, pepper, Tabasco to taste

Brown bacon in 4 quart stew pot or Dutch oven. Add onion and sauté until yellow. Add potatoes and 1 quart water, cooking 10 minutes. Add tomatoes, pickling spice, bay leaves, lemon, cooking 5 more minutes. Add crabs and 1 quart water, or more if necessary, to cover crabs, and cook about 20 minutes. Add salt, pepper, and Tabasco to taste. Since picking out crab meat at the table is a messy matter, it is nicer for the cook to do this, returning just the meat to the chowder. This dish is improved by allowing to stand and reheating at serving time. Serves 4.

F. M. Simpson

FISH CHOWDER

½ cup each green onions, celery, bell pepper, chopped
4 large fresh fish fillets, skinned (trout, red snapper, or other white meat fish)
½ teaspoon each thyme and red pepper
Salt to taste
1 can (10 ounces) tomatoes
1 large potato, thinly sliced
Fish bones and tails
1½ quarts water

In an oiled, heavy enameled saucepot sprinkle onions, celery, and bell pepper. Arrange fillets on top of vegetables. Sprinkle with thyme, red pepper, and salt. Cover with tomatoes and potato. Sprinkle with more salt. Meanwhile, cover fish bones and tails with water and boil until reduced to 1 quart of liquid. Strain broth and add to fish mixture. Cover pot and simmer 1 hour. Correct seasonings and serve in gumbo bowls with French bread. Serves 4.

Absolutely essential that fish be fresh.

Mrs. D. Dale Archer
(Valerie "Val" Grode)

OYSTER SOUP

½ cup flour (¾ cup for thicker soup)
1 stick butter, melted
1 bunch green onions, finely chopped (both the white and green parts)
6 ribs celery, finely chopped
4 pints oysters and juice
Salt and pepper to taste
2 Tablespoons butter
½ cup parsley, chopped
2¼ quarts milk

In large skillet brown flour a little in butter. Add onions and celery and cook until soft and starting to brown. Add oysters and juice, cooking until oysters curl around edge. Add salt and pepper to taste. Place butter and parsley in tureen. Scald milk in separate pot and add a little to the soup. Then pour oyster mixture into tureen, adding rest of milk. Stir well. Add more salt and pepper, if needed. Does not freeze. Serves 12.

From the recipes of
Della Goos Bel

TURTLE SOUP

2 pounds turtle meat
Water to cover
Salt
⅓ cup oil
⅓ cup all purpose flour
1 cup onion, chopped
1 cup celery, chopped
2 bay leaves
2 large cloves garlic, finely chopped
½ teaspoon ground cloves
1 teaspoon salt
1 teaspoon red pepper
½ teaspoon black pepper
Eggs, turtle, if available; if not, chicken
⅓ cup cooking sherry (optional)

In large pot cover washed turtle meat with water, add a little salt, and boil until tender. Skim off foam as needed. Keep meat covered with water as it boils. While meat is boiling, make a rather dark roux with oil and flour, cooking onion and celery in it until wilted. When meat is quite tender, remove from liquid and allow to cool. Add boiling liquid (from which meat has been removed) to roux a ladleful at a time to cook flour, stirring continuously. When skillet is about half full, transfer all of roux mixture at once to boiling liquid and stir. Add bay leaves, garlic, cloves, salt, and pepper. Remove turtle meat from bones; cut in serving pieces and add to liquid. Simmer for ½ hour. Turtle eggs enhance the soup flavor. There are 2 kinds of turtle eggs. One kind is yellow and resembles the yolk of a chicken egg. Remove the membrane covering the eggs gently, as they are quite soft. Drop into soup and cook a short while. The other kind of egg has a shell. If it is the latter kind, boil for ½ hour, and, when cool, carefully break shell. Separate yolk from white and drop *just the yolk* into the soup. (The white never solidifies.)

Never freeze turtle eggs uncooked as they will become as hard as marbles and will be useless. If you cook the eggs first, they will freeze very nicely. If the turtle does not have eggs, add 2 hard boiled chicken egg yolks to each serving. Do not use the whites. If desired, add ⅓ cup cooking sherry to soup.

Dr. J. Malcolm Leveque

AVOCADO BISQUE

2 ripe avocados, peeled
1 can Campbell's cream of chicken soup
1 green onion, bulb only
1 soup can of milk
Salt, black and red pepper to taste

Reserve half of 1 avocado for garnish. Mix remaining ingredients in a blender. Better if made a day in advance and refrigerated no less than 2 hours before serving. Place a small piece of avocado on top of Bisque for garnish. Does not freeze. Serves 5-6.

Mrs. James A. Hooper, Jr.
(Mary Ann Leveque)

COLD CURRIED MUSHROOM SOUP

1 bunch green onions, sliced (white part) (reserve green tops)
3 Tablespoons butter
2½ Tablespoons flour
½ Tablespoon curry powder
1 cup water
1 cup milk
1 pound mushrooms, finely chopped
2 teaspoons salt
2 egg yolks
1 carton whipping cream

Sauté white part of onions in butter over low heat for 7-8 minutes, or until soft. Add flour and curry powder and cook over moderate heat while stirring. Add water, milk, mushrooms, and salt. Simmer, partially covered, for 30 minutes. In a bowl, beat egg yolks with cream, and beat in, pouring slowly, some of the mushroom mixture. Transfer mixture to saucepan and cook over moderately low heat, stirring, for 5 minutes until it thickens. Allow to cool, stirring several times, and chill for several hours. Serve in chilled bowls sprinkled with snippings of green onion tops. May be doubled. Serves 8.

Mrs. Robert W. Fenet

QUICK GAZPACHO SOUP

1 large can V-8 juice
½ bell pepper, chopped
2 medium tomatoes, chopped
2 ribs celery, chopped
1 cucumber, chopped
1 green onion, chopped
1 Tablespoon salad or olive oil
1½ teaspoons Worchestershire sauce
1 teaspoon Tabasco
Dash each of salt and black pepper

Pour juice into large bowl. Add all other ingredients; stir well. Cover and chill for at least 4 hours. Stir occasionally while chilling. May be prepared a day in advance and is better when it stands longer than 4 hours. Serves 6-8.

Mrs. Philip D. Burris
(Gerd Archenholtz)

CHILLED CUCUMBER SOUP

4 small cucumbers, peeled and sliced
½ cup green onions with tops, chopped
½ teaspoon salt
¼ teaspoon pepper
1 cup water
2 Tablespoons flour
¼ cup water
2 cups boiling water
½ teaspoon Accent
Dash cayenne pepper
½ Tablespoon dried chervil (absolutely necessary)
1 cup whipping cream
1 small cucumber, unpeeled, reserved for garnish

Place cucumbers, green onions, salt, pepper, and water in medium saucepan. Bring to boil, reduce heat to simmer, cover, and cook for 15 minutes. Cucumbers will be soft. Remove from heat. Slowly stir flour into about ¼ cup water to form a smooth paste. Add paste slowly, stirring, to cooked cucumbers. Add 2 cups boiling water; bring entire mixture to boil. Reduce heat to simmer, add Accent and cayenne, and taste for salt. Cover and let simmer for 10 minutes. Remove from heat and purée in blender. Pour into bowl, stir in chervil, and refrigerate. As soup chills, stir from time to time. When cold, add unwhipped cream and more salt if needed. Stir occasionally until serving time. Garnish each cup with 1 slice of unpeeled cucumber. This appetizer may be served in usual bouillon cup or in a paper cup at a camp or picnic. Serves 12.

Mrs. Everett Scott
(Zippy Connella)

MY VICHYSSOISE

4 leeks (or green onions), white part, sliced
1 inch of leeks or green onions, sliced (green part)
4 generous Tablespoons butter, melted
1 medium onion, sliced
5 medium Idaho potatoes (6 cups), peeled and sliced
3 cans (13¾ ounce size) chicken broth
1 teaspoon salt
⅛ teaspoon white pepper
2 cups milk
2 cups heavy cream
Chives, finely chopped

In 6 quart Dutch oven sauté leeks and onions in butter over medium heat for 10 minutes, stirring frequently. Add potatoes, chicken broth, salt, and pepper. Bring to boil, cover, reduce heat slightly, and allow to boil 20 minutes until potatoes are very tender. Purée mixture, 2 cups at a time, in blender until very smooth. Pour into 3 quart bowl, stir in milk and cream, and beat with wire whisk. Cover and refrigerate several hours or overnight. Beat with wire whisk just before serving. If too thick, add ½-1 cup cold milk or half and half cream. Add salt and pepper if needed. Ladle into chilled bowls and sprinkle each with 2 teaspoons chives.

*May be served as **warm** Potato Soup by heating in a Crock Pot.*

Britt Armstrong

BOREALIS REX

A stately sternwheeler, the "Borealis Rex" was for many years the only means of transportation between Lake Charles and Cameron.

Carrying mail, passengers, and freight the steamer's arrival each Wednesday created quite a stir in the coastal town. Settlers paddled their pirogues, rode horses, or walked to greet the "Rex" on "Boat Day."

Built before 1900, the riverboat once plied the waters between Natchez, Mississippi, and New Orleans. But in 1910 it was purchased by Calcasieu Captains Ben Moss and A. B. McCain, who put it into service between Cameron and Lake Charles.

Fed with pine knots, the steamer had elegant staterooms, a dining room, and an upper and lower deck. Since Cameron had few trees, wood was an important cargo.

The boat made three trips a week, arriving in Cameron on Saturdays, Wednesdays, and Mondays with intermediate stops at Vincent's Settlement, the Calcasieu Post Office, Hackberry, and Big Lake.

Church groups and parties frequently chartered the "Rex" for pleasure excursions, and no trip to Lake Charles was complete without an outing on the old steamer.

On August 6, 1918, the "Rex" sank at a point below Prien Lake, victim of the same hurricane which demolished the city of Lake Charles. When it was raised, divers found that the upper deck had been swept away in the storm.

Repaired and returned to service, the sternwheeler continued to transport mail and passengers until completion of the Sulphur-Cameron highway in 1931.

Anchored for many years at the foot of Pujo Street, the old riverboat was finally sold at a sheriff's sale for delinquent taxes to a wrecking company for $110.

Rice

Gumbo with rice, crawfish etouffée over rice, rice dressing, red beans and rice, "dirty" rice, green rice, Spanish rice, and good old rice and gravy are a few of the nourishing, economical Creole-Acadian delights featuring that versatile little grain. No Southwest Louisiana cookbook would be complete without a few hints about it.

TIPS FOR COOKING RICE:

Wash in large strainer until water runs clear.
Add a little butter or oil to pot to prevent boiling over or sticking.
If brown rice is used instead of white, cook 10 minutes longer.
Rice can be frozen in recipe form — keeps 3-6 months.
When cooking by the covered pot method, do not peek!
1 cup raw white regular rice yields 3 cups cooked.
1 cup brown yields 4 cups cooked.
1 cup parboiled rice yields 4 cups cooked.

COOKING METHODS:
COVERED-POT FLUFFY METHOD

2 cups raw rice
3 cups cold water
2 teaspoons salt

Wash rice, drain, and place in heavy 4 quart saucepan with water and salt. Bring to hard boil, cover tightly, reduce heat to low, and cook about 30 minutes. Do not lift cover during cooking. When cooked, liquid should be completely absorbed. Fluff with fork.

BOILED RICE

4 quarts water
2 cups rice
2 Tablespoons salt

Wash rice thoroughly until water runs clear. Boil water with salt and add rice gradually so that water does not stop boiling. Boil, uncovered, 15 minutes. *Do not overcook* or rice will be gummy. When cooked, drain thoroughly, and dry out in 1 of the following ways:

(1) Pour into colander and rinse with hot water. Steam over boiling water that does not touch colander. Stir to fluff.
(2) Return to pot and dry out over very low heat, stirring occasionally with fork to fluff.
(3) Place in casserole in very low oven, fluffing with a fork. Remove immediately when dry.

STEAMED RICE

1 cup rice
Butter or oil to grease pot
½ teaspoon salt, or more to taste
Water or broth

Wash rice and place in a heavy, lightly greased skillet. Season with salt and add just enough water or broth to cover rice by ½ inch. Cover tightly and bring to boil over high heat. Lower heat and cook slowly until rice is completely dry and all liquid absorbed, about 20 minutes. Fluff with fork.

BAKED RICE

1 cup rice
4 Tablespoons butter or margarine
Water or broth
½ teaspoon salt, or more to taste

Wash rice and toss with butter on top of stove for 5 minutes in heavy casserole, stirring often. Do not brown. Boil water or broth with salt and pour over rice to cover by ½ inch. Cover casserole tightly and bake at 350°F about 30 minutes, or until dry and all liquid is absorbed. Any vegetable may be sautéed with the rice in the butter and baked.

RICE

> Boudin, or blood sausage, made from pig's blood, is a great favorite among the Cajuns of South Louisiana. Boudin blanc, a variant, is made from pork without the blood. One popular version of the Louisiana recipe also contains rice and various spices.

"BOUNTY" BOUDIN

8 pounds fresh pork, ground (6 pounds *lean* pork, 2 pounds *fatty* pork)
2 pounds pork liver, ground
6 onions
3 bell peppers
12 ribs celery
6 cloves garlic
2 cups green onion tops, chopped
1 cup parsley, chopped
Boiled rice, 2 cups cooked rice for each 1 cup meat mixture
6 Tablespoons salt
5 Tablespoons black pepper
3 Tablespoons Accent
3 teaspoons red pepper
Hog casings

Place ground mixture in large pot and cover with water. Bring to a boil, cover, and simmer for 3-4 hours, or until well cooked. Pour off excess liquid and reserve. Grind onions, peppers, celery, and garlic using grinder or blender. Mix cooked meat with ground vegetables and add cooked rice. Use 1 large or 2 small bowls. Combine salt, pepper, and Accent, and mix well with other ingredients, sampling at random to assure uniformity of seasoning. If too dry, add reserved meat liquid. Fill hog casings using either a sausage stuffer or a meat grinder attachment. Twist casing every 6-10 inches (first flip to right, then to left) to make links. Tie the ends. To heat, place either in boiling water for 30 minutes or in microwave oven for about 15-30 seconds. Freezes. Makes a ton!

Mrs. William E. Shaddock
(Craig Gorham)

RICE DRESSING

2 pounds ground pork
1 pound ground beef
2 pounds giblets, ground
¼ cup cooking oil
2 large onions, finely chopped
1 cup celery, finely chopped
1 bell pepper, finely chopped
2 Tablespoons roux
1 can chicken broth
Salt, black and red pepper
1 cup green onions, chopped
3 cups cooked rice

Brown pork, beef, and giblets in oil. Add onions, celery, and bell pepper to meat mixture. Cook for 30 minutes. Add roux and chicken broth. Season with salt, black and red pepper to taste. Cook 1 hour. Add green onion and cooked rice. Serve hot. This dressing may also be used for stuffing a turkey.

Mrs. Wilmer Boudreau
(Opal LeBlanc)

CREOLE JAMBALAYA

1 Tablespoon shortening
2 Tablespoons flour
1 pound pure pork sausage, smoked, or loose uncased sausage
½ cup bell pepper, chopped
3 cups raw shrimp, peeled, deveined, and chopped
5 cups tomatoes, diced and peeled
2½ cups water
1 large onion, chopped
1 clove garlic, chopped
2 Tablespoons parsley, chopped
2 cups raw rice
2 Tablespoons Worcestershire sauce
1¼ teaspoons salt
½ teaspoon thyme
¼ teaspoon red pepper

Melt shortening in large heavy Dutch oven. Add flour and stir until blended; then add sausage (cut into bite sized pieces) and bell pepper. Cook 5 minutes. Add shrimp, tomatoes, water, onions, garlic, and parsley. Bring to a boil; add rice; and stir in Worcestershire sauce, salt, thyme, and red pepper. Cover and simmer for 30 minutes, or until rice is tender. Stir occasionally. Sprinkle with parsley. Does not freeze well. Serves 8.

Typical South Louisiana dish.

Pat Tessier
Baton Rouge, La.

Aliska Castel *of New Orleans uses 1 cup ham chopped instead of sausage in her jambalaya.*

DIRTY RICE

1 pound giblets (wild fowl, chicken, or turkey), finely chopped
½ pound pork pan sausage
1 cup onion, chopped
½ cup bell pepper, chopped
½ cup celery, chopped
2 cloves garlic, chopped
½ cup fresh parsley, chopped
½ cup green onion tops, chopped
2 cups raw rice
Salt and pepper to taste

Boil the giblets in salted water until very tender. Reserve this liquid for cooking rice (adding more water if necessary). In heavy, deep skillet start pork sausage on low heat, and as soon as fat begins to cook out, add onion, bell pepper, celery, and garlic. Continue cooking on low heat, stirring occasionally, until all vegetables are soft. Add cooked rice, giblets, green onion tops, parsley, salt, and pepper, and stir all together thoroughly, but lightly. If possible, add some drippings from the fowl or meat which you are serving. Do not let parsley and green onion tops become scorched. Better when prepared a day ahead. Freezes. Serves 10-12.

A must for every Cajun's table!

Mrs. Jake Haxthausen
(Bobbie Hopkins)

WILD RICE CASSEROLE

2 packages (6 ounce size) Uncle Ben's long grain and wild rice
2 Tablespoons butter
2 bouillon cubes
2½ cups water per package
1 cup green onion, finely chopped
½ cup celery, finely chopped
1½ cups parsley, chopped
½ stick margarine
½ cup slivered almonds, toasted
2 cans (3 ounce size) mushrooms, sliced
1 small can water chestnuts, sliced
Pats of butter

Add packets of rice, butter, and bouillon cubes to boiling water. Cover tightly and cook over low heat for about 25 minutes, or until water is absorbed. Meanwhile, sauté the green onion, celery, parsley in margarine until wilted. When rice is done, combine it, almonds, mushrooms, and water chestnuts with sautéed vegetables. Place in casserole, dot with pats of butter. May be made a day ahead and refrigerated. Bring to room temperature and heat at 350°F for 30 minutes before serving. Good party dish. Serves 8-10.

Great with any type of game.

Mrs. James E. Taussig
(Alice House)

RED BEANS AND RICE

1 pound red kidney beans
1 meaty ham bone
2 large onions, chopped
1 bell pepper, chopped
2 ribs celery, chopped
2 cloves garlic, finely chopped
Salt and pepper to taste
Pinch of sugar
1 bay leaf (optional)
2 pounds Owen's spicy sausage links
¼ cup parsley, chopped
Rice

Soak beans overnight. Rinse. Cover with water and cook with ham bone (fat trimmed off), onion, bell pepper, celery, garlic, salt, pepper, sugar, and bay leaf. While beans are cooking, boil sausage in skillet. Drain, fry until crisp, and set aside. Cook beans until fork tender; then add fried sausage. *Just* before serving, remove bay leaf and add parsley. Freezes. Serves 8.

Serve with mustard greens and corn bread — a South Louisiana specialty.

Mrs. Robert Christman
Mrs. Stephen Carter

INDONESIAN RIJSTTAFEL
(Rice Feast or Rice Table)

12-14 pounds of round steak (veal or beef)
Seasoned flour
Oil
2 large onions, chopped
Curry powder

CONDIMENTS

3 pounds shrimp, cooked
3 pounds ground beef (for small meat balls)
1 pound bacon, cooked and crumbled
3 bottles chutney
2 large cans peanuts, chopped
4 large cans mushrooms, sautéed
2 pounds coconut, toasted
3 cans pineapple tidbits, drained
12 hard boiled eggs, chopped
3 cans French fried onion rings, crumbled
2 jars pickles, drained
Chicken livers, sautéed
Cucumbers, beets, raw onions, bell peppers, diced
Mandarin oranges, drained
Fig preserves
Bananas, either sliced or baked
Sausage balls
Sardines
3 jars hot sauce
Raisins
3 pounds raw rice

Cut meat into bite sized pieces and shake in seasoned flour. Brown in oil. When brown, cover with water; add onions and curry powder to taste; cover and cook until fork tender. Serve over cooked rice with any or all of listed condiments in separate dishes. The meat may be prepared ahead of time and frozen as it is time consuming. Then on day of party all condiments may be prepared. This dish is well worth the time and expense. Serve in a bowl with tablespoon or soup spoon. Serves 35-40.

This is an American version of the ceremonial feast of the Dutch colonists in Indonesia. The people of Indonesia and Louisiana share a common bond since the heart and soul of their cuisine is rice. The "rice table" makes this meal an exciting event for the diner, with an impressive array of 25-30 different dishes. Starting with a soup bowl heaped with steaming rice, one samples each dish — a mingling of flavors and spices, cooled by fruits and raw vegetables. The best drink to "put out the fire" is ice cold beer.

Mrs. Emile Winterhaler
(Millicent Watkins)

RISOTTO CON MELANZANE
(Eggplant and Rice Casserole)

Olive oil
1-2 large eggplants, pared, sliced
1 Tablespoon margarine
1 thin slice salt pork, diced
1 medium onion, minced
1 can (6 ounces) tomato paste
2 cans (8 ounce size) tomato sauce
1 cup water
1 teaspoon salt
¼ teaspoon pepper
4 cups chicken broth
1½ cups raw rice
¼ cup margarine
¼ pound Mozzarella cheese, grated
¼ cup Parmesan cheese, grated
1 teaspoon dried basil

Preheat oven to 400°F. In a little hot olive oil, in skillet, sauté eggplant on both sides until golden brown; remove. In Dutch oven heat 1 Tablespoon olive oil and 1 Tablespoon margarine. Sauté salt pork and onion until pork is crisp. Add tomato paste, tomato sauce, water, salt, and pepper, and simmer, covered, for 40 minutes. Add chicken broth and rice. Bring to boil, simmer, covered, for 45 minutes, stirring occasionally. Stir in remaining margarine. In greased 3 quart casserole arrange ½ each rice, eggplant, Mozzarella; repeat. Top with Parmesan cheese and basil. Bake, uncovered, for 25 minutes in preheated oven.

Mrs. Terrell Woosley, Jr.
(Evelyn Shaddock)

SPANISH MEAT RICE

1 pound ground beef
2 Tablespoons bacon drippings
1 cup onions, chopped
1 bell pepper, diced
1 cup celery, finely chopped
1 can (4 ounces) sliced mushrooms and juice
1 can (14½ ounces) whole tomatoes, chopped
3½ teaspoons salt
¼ teaspoon black pepper
Dash of red pepper
¾ cup raw rice, washed well
½ cup sharp Cheddar cheese, finely cubed

Brown meat in drippings in Dutch oven. Add other ingredients, except cheese, and cover lightly. After bringing to a boil, reduce heat and simmer, covered, for 30-40 minutes, or until rice is cooked. Stir occasionally to prevent sticking; add a small amount of water only if necessary. When done, stir in cheese enough to heat thoroughly but not melt. May be made ahead of time. Freezes. Serves 6.

Mrs. William E. Trimble
(Ann Courtney)

BLACK BEANS AND RICE

1 pound black beans
1 ham bone
½ cup olive oil
Salt and pepper to taste
Tabasco to taste
Garlic to taste
½ pound ham, chopped
1 large onion, chopped
Rice

Soak beans overnight. Cover ham bone with water and boil to season water. Add beans, olive oil, salt, pepper, Tabasco, and garlic. Simmer covered for 2 or more hours. About 20 minutes before the beans are done, add ham and onion. Serve over cooked rice. Serves 6.

Mrs. Leland R. Speed
Jackson, Mississippi

SPANISH RICE

½ pound bacon
1 large onion, chopped
1-2 cloves garlic, minced
½-1 bell pepper, chopped
3 Tablespoons olive oil
1 small can tomato paste
⅓ can water
2 Tablespoons Lea & Perrins
Bacon drippings
Salt to taste
2 cups cooked rice

Fry bacon until crisp. In another pot sauté onions, garlic, and bell pepper in olive oil until light brown. Add tomato paste, water, Lea & Perrins, crumbled bacon, bacon drippings, and salt to taste. Simmer slowly, uncovered, for 2 hours. Stir occasionally. Add to cooked rice. Put in double boiler and steam for at least 30 minutes, or longer. Serves 8-10.

Mrs. Eleanor Gordon

GARDEN PILAF

½ cup blanched almonds
¾ cup butter
10 cups cooked rice, unsalted
½ cup instant minced onion
½ teaspoon pepper
3 teaspoons salt
2 teaspoons dried crushed rosemary
2 medium tomatoes
Seasoned salt for tomatoes
2 cups frozen green peas, cooked

Sauté almonds in butter in a Dutch oven. When golden, add hot rice, onion, pepper, salt, and rosemary. Toss. Cut tomatoes into eight wedges, sprinkle with seasoned salt, and add along with the cooked peas. Toss. For best results, prepare just before serving. Rice and peas may be cooked a little early, but not refrigerated. Serves 12.

A pretty dish on a buffet table.

Mrs. William D. Blake
(Katherine "Kay" Krause)

RICE O'BRIAN CASSEROLE

1 cup celery, chopped
1 cup onions, chopped
1 cup bell pepper, chopped
1 stick margarine, melted
2 beef bouillon cubes
2 cups cooked rice (leftover, fresh, or frozen)
1 can artichokes, sliced
Salt and pepper to taste
Seasoned bread crumbs

Sauté celery, onion, and bell pepper in margarine until tender. Add bouillon cubes and dissolve. Add rice and artichokes. Season to taste. Place in pyrex casserole and top with seasoned crumbs. (If raw seasoning is not easily accessible, substitute an envelope of onion soup mix.) Bake, covered, at 350°F until piping hot. May be prepared ahead. Freezes. Serves 8.

Mrs. Robert D'Aquin
Jennings, La.

BAKED EGG AND RICE

1 cup cooked rice
1 egg, well beaten
1 cup milk
2 heaping Tablespoons green onions, chopped
1 Tablespoon butter
Salt to taste
½ cup Cheddar cheese, grated (optional)

Place rice in 1 quart casserole. Add egg, milk, green onions, parsley, butter (well distributed, but *not* melted), and salt. Bake, uncovered, at 325-350°F for about 45 minutes, or until firm. If browning too fast, may be covered for part of baking time. Serves 2 amply.

Good way to use leftover rice.

Mrs. Victor Lagrange
(Ruth Viallon)

RICE CASSEROLE OR RING

1 cup cooked rice
1½ cups Cheddar cheese, grated
⅓ cup parsley, chopped
2 Tablespoons onion, grated
3 cloves garlic, pressed
1½ cups milk
¼ cup sherry
¼ cup butter, melted
3 eggs, slightly beaten
½ teaspoon Worcestershire sauce
1 teaspoon salt or less
⅛ teaspoon pepper

Combine all ingredients. Pour into ring mold or 1½ quart casserole. May spray with Pam first. Bake, uncovered, at 350°F for 45 minutes, or until set. Serves 8.

Mrs. Robert McHale

RICE

EGGPLANT SAPPHIRE

5 small eggplants, peeled, finely cubed
Water with 2 Tablespoons salt
1 medium onion, chopped
1 medium bell pepper, chopped
2 Tablespoons butter
2-3 Tablespoons cooking oil
1¼ pounds ground beef
2 cups cooked rice
Salt and pepper to taste
Bread crumbs
Dots of butter

Soak eggplants in salted water for 20 minutes. Drain. Sauté onion, bell pepper, and eggplant in butter and oil until tender and wilted. Add ground beef and cook until meat is no longer red. Add cooked rice, salt, and pepper at this time. Cook until rice is hot and blended with other ingredients. Place in casserole, sprinkle lightly with bread crumbs and dots of butter. Bake, uncovered, in preheated 325°F oven for 20 minutes. Freezes. Serves 6-8.

Mrs. Lou Bonin
(Shirley Chappuis)

SPINACH RICE

½ cup onions, chopped
½ cup celery, chopped
½ stick margarine
1 package frozen chopped spinach
1 can mushroom soup
1 small jar Cheez Whiz
2 cups cooked rice
Salt and pepper to taste
1 cup American cheese, grated

Sauté onions and celery in margarine. Cook spinach as directed on package and drain. Mix spinach, sautéed onions and celery, mushroom soup, Cheez Whiz, and rice in medium sized casserole. Season with salt and pepper. Sprinkle cheese on top. Bake, uncovered, at 350°F for 30 minutes. Serves 6.

Mrs. Richard W. Calhoun
(Patsy Boudreau)

Mrs. Scott Albritton, Mrs. Marguerite Wheeler Castle, and Mrs. Fielding Woodard of Louisville, Kentucky, *use broccoli in place of spinach.*

RICE CASSEROLE

1 cup rice
4 teaspoons margarine
2 cups Swanson chicken broth
¾ cup each of parsley, green onions, carrots, celery, chopped
1 package slivered almonds (about ¾ cup)

Coat rice with melted margarine. Place in casserole and add chicken broth. Bake, uncovered, at 350°F 40 minutes. Toss in chopped vegetables. Cook 15 minutes longer.

Mabel Collette

BEER RICE

½ cup onion, chopped
½ cup bell pepper, chopped
½ cup margarine, melted
2 chicken bouillon cubes
2 cups boiling water
1 cup raw rice
¾ cup beer
½ teaspoon salt
¼ teaspoon each pepper and thyme

Sauté onion and pepper in margarine. Add bouillon dissolved in water. Stir in everything else. Cover and simmer 40 minutes, or until liquid is gone. Serves 5-6.

Good, different. Serve with barbecued chicken.

Mrs. Jimmy Deaton
Charleston, S.C.

RICE AND ARTICHOKES

1 box chicken flavored Rice-A-Roni
1 jar marinated artichoke hearts
⅓ cup mayonnaise
¼ teaspoon curry powder
4-6 green onions, chopped
1 jar (4 ounces) stuffed olives, sliced

Fix Rice-A-Roni as directed on box. Drain and chop artichokes but keep liquid. Mix all ingredients including liquid from artichokes and *refrigerate* until served. May be prepared a day ahead. Serves 6.

Mrs. Scott Pias
(Kathleen Clower)

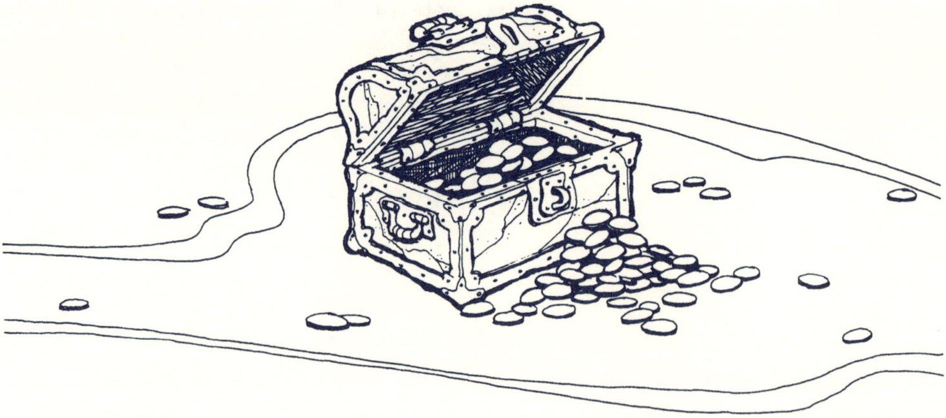

SHRIMP - RICE CASSEROLE

2 pounds shrimp
½ large onion, chopped
2 ribs celery, chopped
Garlic to taste
1 Tablespoon butter
1 can cream of mushroom soup
½ Tablespoon lemon juice
Salt and pepper to taste
1½ cups cooked rice
½ cup sour cream
¾ cup cheese, grated
Bell pepper rings

Boil shrimp and peel, devein, and cut into bite sized pieces. Sauté onion, celery, and garlic in butter. Do not brown. Add soup, lemon juice, and seasoning. Fold in rice and shrimp. Then fold in sour cream and pour into buttered pyrex casserole. Sprinkle with cheese and decorate with pepper rings. Bake at 325°F for 30 minutes. Serves 6.

Mrs. Mildred Vincent
Sulphur, La.

OYSTER AND RICE CASSEROLE

3 Tablespoons butter or margarine
½ cup onion, minced
3 Tablespoons fresh parsley, minced
1½ Tablespoons flour
2 cans (10 ounce size) frozen condensed oyster stew (soup) thawed and undiluted
1 can (8 ounces) oysters
Dash of cayenne pepper
3 cups hot cooked rice
5 hard boiled eggs, sliced
½-1 cup bread crumbs mixed with 1-2 Tablespoons melted butter

In medium saucepan melt butter over low heat. Add onion and parsley; cook until onion wilts but does not brown. Stir often. Stir in flour, oyster soup, drained oysters, and cayenne. Cook and stir constantly until thickened. Use oyster liquid with water in cooking rice. Cook rice according to package directions. Place hot cooked rice into a 1½ quart shallow baking dish (10x6x1¾ inches is a good size) and cover with sliced eggs. Pour sauce over the eggs and rice. Sprinkle with buttered crumbs. Bake, uncovered, at 350°F for about 20 minutes, or until piping hot. Serves 6.

Mrs. G. B. Hines, Jr.
(Edna McDonald)

GREEN RICE

4 cups cooked rice
2 onions, finely chopped
3 ribs celery, finely chopped
2 small cloves garlic, finely chopped
½ bunch parsley, finely chopped
1½-2 sticks butter or margarine
2 cans mushrooms, drained
2 chicken bouillon cubes
½ cup slivered almonds
1½ cups sharp Cheddar cheese, grated
Lea & Perrins
Lawry's seasoned salt

Place hot cooked rice in large casserole and mix with onions, celery, garlic, and parsley which have been sautéed in 1 stick of butter. Sauté mushrooms in ½ stick of butter and add bouillon cubes to melt in this mixture. Brown almonds in slow oven or sauté until brown in ½ stick butter on top of stove in small skillet. Add mushroom mixture, almonds, and grated cheese to rice and vegetables. Season to taste with Lea & Perrins and Lawry's seasoned salt. Bake, covered, at 325°F in a pan of warm water for 25 minutes. Freezes beautifully. May be doubled, tripled, etc.; goes well with beef, veal, or poultry. Serves 6-8.

Mrs. Barbe Goudeau
(Lou Hautot)

RICE SURPRISE

1 cup rice, cooked in 2 cups chicken broth or bouillon
1 cup sour cream
1½ Tablespoons Jalapeño pepper, minced and seeded
1½ Tablespoons Jalapeño pepper juice
⅓ cup Creamy Italian Dressing
1 can water chestnuts, drained and sliced
1 package (12 ounces) Monterey Jack cheese, grated

Grease a 2 quart casserole. Add ingredients that have been mixed well. Loosely cover casserole and bake at 350°F for 25-30 minutes. Serves 6-8.

Mrs. Thomas F. Bullock
Shreveport, La.

RICE

CURRIED RAISIN RICE

1 cup raw rice
½ cup onion, chopped
6 Tablespoons butter
1 Tablespoon curry powder
2 cups chicken broth
1½ teaspoons salt
½ cup raisins
½ cup coconut, flaked

Cook rice and onion in butter, stirring until golden. Add curry powder and mix well. Add rest of ingredients and bring to a boil. Reduce heat. Cover and cook (no stirring) 20 minutes, or until rice is done. Serves 4.

Mrs. John W. Huber
(Betty Landry)

PINEAPPLE RICE

1 can (20 ounces) crushed pineapple
1 cup sugar or less
1 stick butter or margarine
2 level teaspoons nutmeg (optional)
3 cups cooked rice
Brown sugar

Preheat oven to 350°F. Mix the pineapple, sugar, and butter in a saucepan and simmer until well mixed. Butter a 2 quart casserole and layer rice and mixture being sure the pineapple mixture is on top. Sprinkle with brown sugar if desired. Bake for 1 hour. Serves 8-10.

Miss Hannah Chalkley

GRANDMOTHER'S RICE PUDDING
(A favorite 50 years ago)

2 quarts whole milk
⅓ cup raw rice
⅛ pound butter or margarine
1 cup sugar
⅛ teaspoon salt
1 cup whipping cream (optional)

Pour milk into a 4 quart Dutch oven and bring to simmering point on top of stove. Wash rice in cold water and drain. When milk is hot, add rice, butter, sugar, and salt. Bake, uncovered, in preheated 325°F oven, stirring every 15 minutes, for 2 hours, or until pudding becomes the consistency of very thick cream. When stirring, be sure to scrape rice from bottom of container as it tends to settle and stick to it. Serve either warm or chilled with a dollop of whipped cream on top, if desired. Serves 8-10.

Mrs. Edward H. Taussig
(Florence Streater)

TIPS ON PREPARATION, CLEANING, AND COOKING FISH
PREPARATION AND CLEANING OF FISH

Since all seafood spoils quickly, remove entrails and thoroughly ice fish as soon after catching as possible. Stack with alternate layers of cracked ice rather than one on top of the other on block of ice. Upon arrival at home soak fish whole in a solution of either ⅓ white vinegar to ⅔ water, or 1 pound salt to 20-25 gallons water. The slime and oil, which give an offensive flavor, will rise to the surface. Skim it before removing the fish as it might adhere to the fish's skin.

Cut up fish, as described below, rewash in vinegar or salt solution, and remove any visible red meat, plus a little of surrounding white meat, that might create an unpleasant taste.

METHODS OF CUTTING FISH

FILLET: For proper filleting use either preferably an electric carving knife or a long, thin, flexibly bladed non-electric one. Cut just behind gills down to backbone of unscaled fish with head on; paralleling backbone, with side of knife resting against it, cut fish lengthwise to within ½ inch of tail. Flip fillet over. Cut at base of tail down to, but not through, the skin. Then work knife toward base of fillet, with blade side against the skin, to remove it from fillet. Discard skin, debone fillet, and remove rib cage. Repeat for other side.

FISH STICKS: There are 2 advantages to cutting fish into sticks: equal sizing for even cooking and the absence of bones. Any fish that lends itself to frying may be cut this way.

STEAK: For frying, cut steaks ½ inch thick; for charcoal broiling, ½-1 inch. Make cuts perpendicular to backbone, all the way through the fish, ½-1 inch apart along side of body. Divide, if desired, by cutting, paralleling backbone, to free steaks from body. Steaks may be frozen with skin on, skinning after defrosting.

ROAST: Cut roasts like steaks, but to a thickness of 4-5 inches. It is easier to skin roasts before freezing.

WHOLE: Flounder, perch, white perch, and very small bass are best cooked whole, without the head; pompanos with the head but without the eyes and gills. The oil, which gives pompano its unusually good flavor, is located in the head. Skin bass before cooking for better taste. The others need only be scaled with a wire brush or other utensil. All should be washed in either the vinegar or salt water solution described above. Score whole cooked fish with slanted cuts along the sides, about 2 inches apart.

KING MACKEREL BALLS: After many years of trial and error we learned how to change this virtually inedible fish into a gourmet's delight. The answer: to make king balls instead of conventional fillets. Ice fish, ungutted, long enough to thoroughly chill. Make a series of vertical cuts about 1½ inches apart along its side from head to tail down to the backbone, like in steaks. Place thumbs or fingers in cuts and push a ball of muscle from top and bottom of each section. Repeat for length of fish on both sides. Wash balls in salt or vinegar solution to remove slime, oil, and blood; discard fish body.

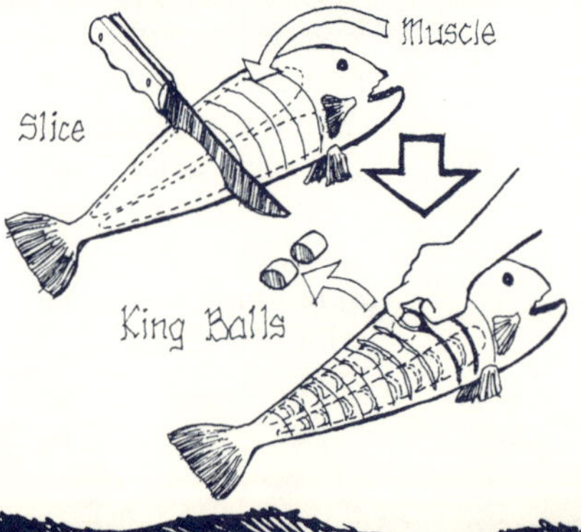

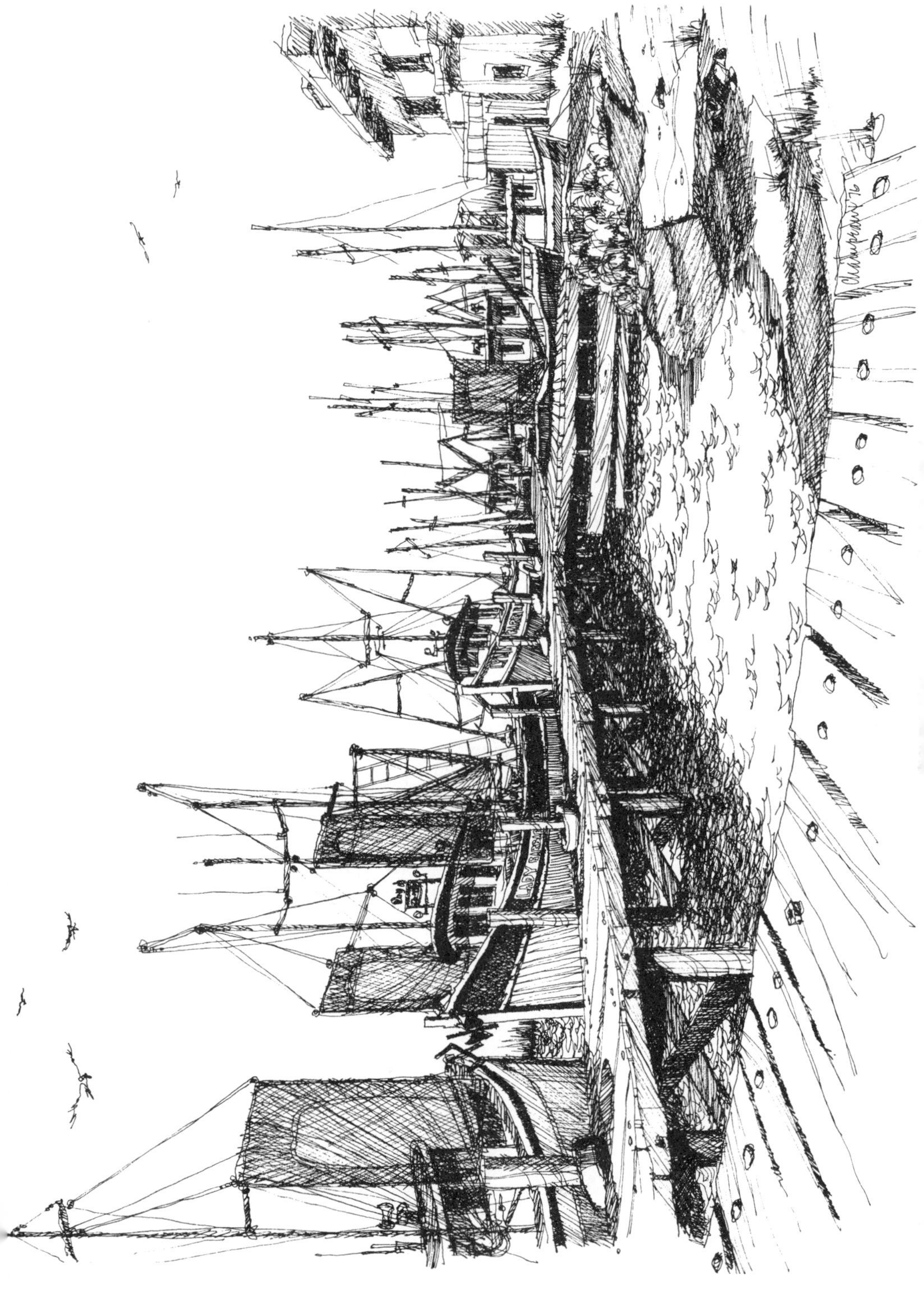

SHRIMP BOATS

The day's catch complete, a fleet of shrimp boats docks in nearby Cameron, on the Louisiana Gulf Coast. Louisiana is the nation's top producer of the delicate lobster-like seafood, netting over 80 million pounds of shrimp per year.

The shrimp are usually found within five miles of the shoreline, where rich top soil washing down from Louisiana rivers provides underwater vegetation for an ideal spawning ground. In spring and early fall trawlers ply the waters searching for the more than seven different varieties found along the coastline.

Fishing is a natural occupation for Southwest Louisiana "Cajuns," a people who trace their ancestry to the Acadians, who were expelled by the British from Canada between 1760 and 1790. Mostly fishermen and trappers by trade, these French Canadians found their way to Louisiana, settling in the bayou country.

Skilled as huntsmen and fishermen, Louisiana's "Cajuns" are also the world's best cooks. Anyone who doubts has simply to taste such famous dishes as huitres 'a la Rockefeller (oysters baked on rock salt with a spinach sauce); bouillabaisse, bisque; or pompano en papillote (pompano fish with a shrimp sauce baked in a paper bag).

HANDLING (CUTTING AND COOKING) OF SPECIFIC FISH

AMBERJACK: Cook this lean, firm-fleshed fish with seasonings that will overpower its naturally strong flavor. Cut into steaks or roasts for barbecuing or broiling, basting frequently with a basic sauce made of butter or margarine, Worcestershire sauce, Tabasco, garlic salt, and seasoned salt and pepper. A roast need not be basted if wrapped, with enough sauce, in heavy foil pierced on top for venting steam.

GULF COAST BLUE FISH: East coast blue fish are allegedly fine eating. The same is not true for the Gulf of Mexico blue fish.

COBIA OR LING: This is a good eating fish that is not strongly flavored. It is best cut into steaks or roasts for broiling or barbecuing, basting with a broiling sauce made milder by reducing the Tabasco, garlic, and Worcestershire sauce, and adding lemon juice.

CROAKER: The croaker is good freshly fried or broiled as soon after catching as possible. It does not freeze well.

DOLPHIN: For the uninitiated, we are not talking about the "Flipper" type animal, but a predominantly blue and green multicolored fish weighing from ½ to 60 plus pounds. Fried or broiled school dolphin are unequalled. Cut the large ones into steaks or fillets. For broiling use basic garlic butter sauce with less garlic for small fish, and follow instructions for Spanish mackerel.

DRUM UNDER 5 POUNDS, REDFISH OVER 10 POUNDS, AND SHEEPSHEAD: Use these fish to make "contraband crab meat" for use in stuffing other fish like flounder and smaller redfish. See recipe, p. 45. Remove head and entrails, scale, wash in salt or vinegar solution, and boil in water containing salt, red pepper, crab boil, and other seasonings. Just before fish begins to break up, remove skin with a fork and flake meat into a dish. Then proceed as per the recipe, season, and use as crab meat stuffing. This puts to good use an otherwise unappetizing fish.

FLOUNDER: Scale with wire brush, remove head and entrails, and wash in salt or vinegar solution. Excellent broiled, fried, or baked, with or without stuffing.

KING MACKEREL: Make king balls and fry in deep fat. See recipe, p. 36.

SPANISH MACKEREL: The Spanish mackerel, like the king, may be made into balls, but, unlike the king, it is also good filleted and broiled. Wash fillets first in vinegar or salt solution, salt and pepper generously, cover with alternating paper thin slices of onion and lemon, and baste with garlic-butter sauce with freshly chopped parsley added.

POMPANO: Be sure to leave head on. Great broiled with lemon and sliced almonds or with the seasoning and basting sauce used for Spanish mackerel.

REDFISH LESS THAN 10 POUNDS: Fillet redfish under 5 pounds into fish sticks for frying. Between 5 and 10 pounds bake in a highly seasoned tomato sauce. Good stuffed with shrimp, crab meat, oysters, or contraband crab meat described above.

SPECKLED TROUT: Specs are great fried (fillets or fish sticks), smoked (whole) or broiled (trout amandine). The "worms" that you might find in the meat are not really worms; according to the Louisiana Wild Life and Fisheries Commission they are not harmful. Our experience from years of spec eating indicates no adverse effect on flavor. Ignore them, or, if you must, remove them.

RED SNAPPER: The snapper is super fried as fish sticks, baked (if over 5 pounds) in a good tomato sauce, or broiled in a lemon butter sauce.

Lawrence Lowery, Jr.
William E. Shaddock

SEAFOOD

FREEZING OF FISH

Freeze fish covered with water to maintain freshness and flavor. Place fillets or sticks in large container of iced water to chill thoroughly. Remove when chilled, place in milk carton, cover with water, and tightly tape. Leave space in freezer between cartons to allow quick and even freezing. Slow freezing encourages bacterial growth and adversely affects the quality.

KING MACKEREL BALLS

METHOD I
King mackerel balls (refer to article on preparation and cleaning of seafood, p. 34)
Salt, Tabasco, black and red pepper
Milk
Egg, beaten
Corn meal
Crisco

METHOD II
King mackerel balls
Mustard, regular or hot
Salt, Tabasco, black and red pepper
Corn meal
Crisco

METHOD I
Soak fish in heavily seasoned milk and egg mixture. Remove fish and shake in bag of corn meal. Fry in hot deep fat until brown and crisp. Serve immediately as hors d'oeuvre or entree.

METHOD II
Coat fish with mustard, salt, pepper, and Tabasco. Shake in bag of corn meal. Fry in hot deep fat until brown and crisp. Serve immediately.

Jack W. Kemmerly

FRIED FISH

Fish fillets or sticks
Sour cream
Salt and garlic salt
Black and red pepper
Extra light pancake mix
Oil

Soak fish fillets or sticks in enough sour cream to coat thoroughly. Marinate for at least 2 hours. Season. Roll in seasoned pancake mix. Fry to a golden color in medium hot oil. Remove, place on absorbent paper, and eat while hot.

Lawrence Lowery, Jr.

SEAFOOD

OVEN FRIED FISH FILLETS

1 stick margarine
Fish fillets
Wesson oil
Salt and pepper
Italian bread crumbs

BASTING SAUCE
1 stick margarine, melted
Juice of 1 lemon
Dash Lea & Perrins

Melt margarine in baking pan in a 400°F oven. Do not burn. Dry fish and use hands to cover well with Wesson oil. Season with salt and pepper and roll in bread crumbs. Place in pan with margarine, skin side down. Bake, uncovered, at 400°F for 20-25 minutes, or until golden brown. Do not turn. Combine sauce ingredients. Use sauce for basting and serving with meal.

Mrs. Hal Goldman

FISH FILLETS PAYSANNE

2 medium carrots, sliced
2 medium onions, sliced
3 Tablespoons butter
½ teaspoon salt
¼ teaspoon pepper
3 Tablespoons parsley, chopped
4 fish fillets of any variety
1 cup fish stock (made by cooking fish head with 2 bay leaves, 2 sprigs parsley, ½ teaspoon salt, and enough water to cover) or 1 cup white wine
1 Tablespoon flour

Cook carrots and onions slowly in 1 Tablespoon butter. Add 1 Tablespoon butter, salt, pepper, parsley, and fish fillets. Add fish stock (or wine), bring to a boil, and cook slowly for 12 minutes. Remove fish to serving dish. Cook liquid until reduced to ½ original quantity and thicken by creaming together remaining Tablespoon butter and flour. Bring to a boil, moving pan around instead of stirring mixture to combine it. Pour over fish. Serves 4.

Mrs. Jane Porter Moon

BAKED FILLET OF FISH

Garlic salt and pepper
4 fish fillets
1 stick butter or margarine
Dash soy sauce
3 Tablespoons Worcestershire sauce

Sprinkle garlic salt and pepper on both sides of fish. Make a sauce of melted butter, soy sauce, and Worcestershire. Place fillets in baking dish and baste with sauce. Bake, uncovered, at 350°F for 30-40 minutes. Halfway through, turn over and baste again. Serves 4.

Mrs. Al James

STUFFED FLOUNDER

4 small flounders
½ cup green onions, chopped
¼ cup celery, diced
1 small clove garlic, minced
1 small can shrimp, drained
1 small can lump crab meat with liquid
½ cup bread crumbs
Salt and pepper
Oil
Lemon juice
Paprika

Prepare flounder by making slit along backbone on dark side of fish; then cut a pocket by sliding knife along ribs on both sides of backbone. Mix green onions, celery, garlic, shrimp, crab meat, bread crumbs. Salt and pepper to taste. Add enough oil to moisten and stuff ¼ of mixture into each flounder. Sprinkle with lemon juice. Wrap flounders individually in aluminum foil, slit side up. Rub skin with paprika, salt, and pepper. Bake at 350°F for 45 minutes; open foil and brown 15 minutes longer. Serve with lemon butter sauce. Serves 4.

A. R. "Buddy" Hodgkins, Jr.

FISH À LA GERD

3 flounders (about 1½ pounds each) or red snapper or combination of 2, cleaned thoroughly
Water to cover
4 Tablespoons salt
8 black peppercorns
5 medium bay leaves
5 whole allspice
Hollandaise sauce
1 small can mushrooms, drained
2 lemons, quartered

Boil fish 25-30 minutes, or until done, (testing with a fork) in water in which salt, peppercorns, bay leaves, and allspice have been preboiled slowly for 15 minutes. Remove fish and cool slightly. Carefully pick meat from bones, and place in a bowl covered with the liquid. Chill 2 hours.

MASHED POTATOES
8 medium potatoes
3 Tablespoons margarine
Milk for firm consistency
Salt and pepper to taste

MASHED POTATOES
Boil potatoes until tender, mash, and spread thinly on ovenproof platter. Drain fish and place on potatoes. Place any remaining potatoes attractively around edges of platter. Cover with Hollandaise; garnish with mushrooms. Bake, uncovered, at 325°F for 30 minutes. May be made early in the day and refrigerated. Serve with lemon wedges. Serves 4-6.

Mrs. Philip D. Burris
(Gerd Archenholtz)

SEAFOOD

COLD STUFFED RED SNAPPER

1 large (4-5 pound) red snapper
½ cup fresh pickling spice
2 Tablespoons salt
½ teaspoon ground red pepper
1 clove garlic
1 lemon, sliced

DRESSING
½ pound each lump crab meat and chopped shrimp
Bits and pieces of fish
2 hard boiled eggs, chopped
½ cup each green onions, celery, and parsley
½ cup mayonnaise
½ teaspoon tarragon
Pinch marjoram
¼ teaspoon basil
½ teaspoon each salt and red pepper
Dash Tabasco and Worcestershire sauce
Juice of ½ lemon

Remove fins, tail, and jaw bones from snapper. Parboil for 2-4 minutes, preserving intact. Carefully wrap whole fish in cheesecloth. Boil in water seasoned with remaining ingredients for about 30 minutes until just tender, not falling apart. Let cool. Carefully bone into fillets, keeping fish intact, reserving bits and pieces of fish.

DRESSING
Combine all ingredients. Mold on fish platter in shape of snapper. Carefully place fillets on top of dressing and reconstruct fish with jaws. For eye, use stuffed olive; for fins and tail, use pimiento strips and very thin slices of lemon. To garnish, surround outline of fish with stuffed deviled eggs and parsley sprigs.

Mrs. Charles Rowden

SNAPPER LUZIANNE

1 medium or large red snapper
Salt and pepper
¾ cup onion, chopped
¾ cup celery, chopped
1 clove garlic, finely chopped
1½ Tablespoons cooking oil
1 can stewed tomatoes
2 Tablespoons sugar
2 Tablespoons prepared mustard
1 Tablespoon Worcestershire sauce
¼ cup dry white wine
2 bay leaves
Pinch of thyme
½ teaspoon each orégano and pepper
½ Tablespoon salt
Dash of Tabasco
½ cup water

Scale and clean snapper. Wipe dry and rub lightly inside and out with salt and pepper. Sauté onion, celery, and garlic in oil until clear. Add remaining ingredients. Bring to a boil and simmer for 5 minutes. Spoon inside and over fish. Bake, uncovered, at 325°F for 25-30 minutes. Baste during cooking. Remove fish and thicken sauce with flour and water.

Mrs. Richard J. Chafin
(Carolyn Corley)

BARBECUED RED FISH

1 large red fish, with or without head
Salt and pepper to taste

SAUCE
2 lemons
½ cup margarine
1 Tablespoon Lea & Perrins
5 green onions, finely minced

Start charcoal pit with good hot fire at one end (325°F). Place seasoned fish, uncovered, on heavy duty foil with crimped edges. Baste liberally with sauce. Smoke 45-60 minutes with top down on cooker, maintaining a constant temperature. Need not turn. Use fork to test for doneness. Slide onto cookie sheet when done. Serves 12-15.

Mrs. Courtney A. Fenet, Jr.
(Sally Garber)

RED SNAPPER EXCELSIOR

1 stick butter
1½ cups mushrooms, sliced
3 artichoke bottoms, canned, sliced
¼ cup parsley, chopped
¼ cup red wine
Salt and pepper to taste
Flour
4 fillets of red snapper, sliced
1 Tablespoon lemon juice

In browned butter, sauté mushrooms and artichoke bottoms. Add parsley and wine; toss lightly. Season and flour snapper. Cook in hot oil until done. Pour lemon juice over fish and spoon over mushroom mixture. Serve on hot plates.

Courtesy of Maxim's
Houston, Texas

BARBECUED LING

Ling steaks
Salt and pepper
Mrs. Gill's barbecue sauce, p. 298

Saw ling steaks 1½ inches thick and season. Hold steaks together either by using 2 pieces of chicken wire threaded on either side with straightened coat hangers or with commercial cookout grill basket. Cook on barbecue grill for about 1 hour, or until done. Baste with barbecue sauce while cooking.

Mrs. Forrest Gill
(Virginia Bryan)

THELMA'S STUFFED BAKED RED FISH OR RED SNAPPER

½ stick margarine, melted
1½ cups onion, finely chopped
1 cup bell pepper, finely chopped
½ cup celery, finely chopped
1 clove garlic, finely chopped
2 cans (4 ounce size) sliced mushrooms, drained
1 cup cooked shrimp, chopped
¾ cup crab meat
2 slices bread, toasted, crumbled, and moistened
1 red fish or snapper (5 pounds), cleaned and dressed
Salt, pepper and garlic powder to taste
1 stick margarine
SAUCE
1 can (8 ounces) tomato sauce
1 can mushroom soup mixed with ½ cup water
1 Tablespoon Lea & Perrins

In saucepan sauté chopped vegetables in margarine until wilted. Add mushrooms, shrimp, crab meat, and toast. Season fish well, inside and out, with salt, pepper, and garlic powder. Place in pan or casserole containing melted margarine. Stuff cavity with stuffing. Place any left over outside of fish. Pour combined sauce ingredients over fish. Bake, covered, at 350°F for 1-1½ hours, or until fish is flaky when pricked with a fork.

Mrs. Eugene Fontenot
(Thelma Guillory)

BARBECUED FISH

1 white fish, red fish, or snapper (3 pound)
2 Tablespoons onion, chopped
1 Tablespoon margarine
2 cups ketchup
2 Tablespoons brown sugar
2 Tablespoons cider vinegar
¼ cup lemon juice
2 teaspoons Tabasco
3 Tablespoons Worcestershire sauce
½ teaspoon each salt and black pepper

Place fish in greased shallow baking pan. Brown onion lightly in margarine, add remaining ingredients, and simmer 5 minutes. Pour over fish and bake, uncovered, at 425°F for 30 minutes, or until fish is tender. Serves 6.

Mrs. Charles Carwile
(Beth Curtis)

TROUT ALEXANDER

3 large trout fillets, halved
½ stick butter or more, melted
3 green onions, chopped
¼ cup parsley, finely chopped
1 large clove garlic, minced
½ pound shrimp, peeled and deveined
¾ cup fresh mushrooms, chopped
8 ounces milk
4 Tablespoons flour
1 Tablespoon butter
½ cup sharp cheese, grated
Salt and pepper to taste
1 ounce dry white wine (optional)

Rinse fish, pat dry, place in individual baking or coquille dishes, and set aside. In skillet sauté in butter the onions, parsley, garlic, shrimp, and mushrooms until shrimp turns pink. In a saucepan boil milk, flour, butter, and cheese, stirring constantly until thick. If mixture is too thick, add milk; if too thin, add flour. Combine this mixture with that in skillet. Season to taste. Add wine. Spoon over fish, covering completely. Bake, uncovered, at 350°F 30-35 minutes, or until brown around edges. Serves 5-6.

James Alexander Hooper, Jr.

TROUT AU GRATIN

8 trout fillets
2 onions, chopped
2 cans (4 ounce size) chopped mushrooms, drained
½ pound cheese, more or less (Munster, brick, any light, mild cheese, grated)
Butter

In covered skillet cook fillets in small amount of water until tender. Fish cooks quickly. Cool, remove skin, and place in shallow baking dish. Cover with remaining ingredients, topping with butter pats. Bake, uncovered, at 350°F about 30 minutes. Cheese will be bubbly. Serves 6-8.

Mrs. David Painter
(Isabel "Bel" Thornton)

LOCK'S TROUT AMANDINE

Fillets of speckled trout or bass, skinned
1 cup almonds, slivered
Butter or margarine
2-3 cups milk (depends on number of fish)
3 ounces beer
1 teaspoon dry Coleman's mustard
2 ounces Lea & Perrins
Flour
Salt and pepper to taste

Thaw fish in advance. Cut fillets the thickness of the little finger. Brown almonds in butter. Soak first batch of fish in milk, beer, mustard, and Lea & Perrins for 10-20 minutes. Roll fish in flour, salt, and pepper. Pan fry in enough butter to cover bottom of pan, turning fish once when brown. Add butter as fish fries. Soak second batch of fish while first is frying. When fish is brown (about 4-5 minutes), remove with spatula and drain on paper towels. Place on a warm plate, spoon almonds and butter over fish, and serve immediately.

G. Lock Paret, Jr.

SEAFOOD

TROUT PLATTER

SOUP STOCK
2 quarts water
¾ bottle good dry white wine
3 carrots, sliced
1 large onion, sliced
1 small bay leaf
¼ teaspoon thyme
8-10 peppercorns
1 trout (about 8 pounds)

SAUCE
1 cup mayonnaise
8 ounces sour cream
½ cup sweet relish
2 hard boiled eggs, chopped
¼ cup parsley, chopped

GARNISH
Radishes
Watercress
Artichoke hearts
Cucumbers, sliced

Place all ingredients for soup stock in fish poacher or covered cooking vessel which will hold fish, and simmer, covered, for 10-15 minutes. Gently lower whole cleaned trout, wrapped in a large white napkin or cheesecloth, into the stock. The liquid should just barely cover the fish. Boil for 20 minutes. Transfer fish to a large platter. Carefully remove napkin. When cooled, remove skin and bones. Combine sauce ingredients and pour over cold fish just before serving. Garnish. Serves 4-6.

Mrs. Jules Reinauer
(Shirley Unger)

TROUT VERONIQUE

6 trout fillets
3 pints dry white wine
60 seedless green grapes, halved

SAUCE
5 egg yolks
1 teaspoon Accent
¼ cup wine tarragon vinegar
Dash Tabasco
4 sticks butter, melted
Salt to taste
⅛ cup tepid water

Place trout in pan, add wine, and poach about 7 minutes. Remove trout and place in individual ovenproof serving plates. Keep warm. Reduce remaining wine liquid to about 8 Tablespoons by cooking over high heat. Gradually stir wine liquid into yellow sauce. Place grapes over trout, and pour sauce over all. Glaze under broiler. Serve immediately. Serves 6.

SAUCE
Combine in mixing bowl the egg yolks, Accent, vinegar, and Tabasco. Melt butter over low heat, then gradually add to above mixture. Season with salt to taste. Add water for consistency, if needed.

Robert J. Boudreau

SKILLET TUNA CURRY

¼ cup margarine
¼ cup flour
2½ cups milk
½ teaspoon curry powder
Salt and pepper to taste
¼ cup almonds
2 cans (6 ounce size) tuna fish
2 Tablespoons sherry
2 Tablespoons butter, melted
2½ cups rice, cooked

Melt margarine in skillet on low heat. Stir in flour until blended. Gradually stir in milk. Stir constantly until thickened. Add curry powder, salt and pepper and mix well. Toast almonds in 300°F oven. Add tuna broken into large pieces, almonds, and sherry to cream sauce. Heat well, stirring frequently. Add butter to hot cooked rice. Spoon tuna sauce over rice or into center of rice ring. Serves 4.

Mrs. G. W. Swift, Jr.
(Betty Richardson)

Mrs. Lee Haugen *uses 1 can cream of mushroom soup in place of white sauce and adds 1 can pineapple tidbits, serving over rice or Chinese noodles.*

TUNA CASSEROLE

2 eggs, slightly beaten
½ cup mayonnaise
1 can cream of celery soup
1 medium onion, chopped
1 cup Pepperidge Farm dressing
1 can (4 ounces) pimiento (optional)
2 cans (7 ounce size) tuna with oil

Mix all ingredients. Bake, uncovered, in 1½ quart greased casserole at 350°F for 45 minutes. Freezes. Serves 6.

Mrs. James B. Allen
(Opal McCrary)

ALASKAN FISHERMAN STEW

2 pounds salmon, halibut, or other firm fish, fresh or frozen
1½ cups celery, sliced
½ cup onion, chopped
1 clove garlic, minced
¼ cup margarine
1 can (28 ounces) tomatoes, undrained
1 can (8 ounces) tomato sauce
2 teaspoons salt
½ teaspoon paprika
¼ teaspoon black pepper
1 package (7 ounces) spaghetti, uncooked
2 cups boiling water
¼ cup Parmesan cheese, grated

Cut fish into 1 inch chunks. Sauté celery, onion, and garlic in margarine in large heavy skillet until tender. Add tomatoes, tomato sauce, and seasonings. Cover and simmer slowly 15-20 minutes. Add uncooked spaghetti and boiling water, mix, cover, and cook slowly about 10 minutes. Add fish, cover, and cook slowly until fish flakes easily with fork, 10-20 minutes. Serve hot with cheese on top. Serves 6.

Mrs. C. C. Laborde
(Mickey Supple)

GASPERGOU

4 pounds fish
6 medium sweet potatoes, peeled and quartered
1 large onion, finely chopped
4 cloves garlic, finely chopped
Salt, red and black pepper

Dress fish leaving heads on. Rinse thoroughly and place head down in a cast iron pot. Add rest of ingredients. Place tight fitting lid on pot. Simmer 1-1½ hours until done. No water is used.

Mrs. Agnes E. Lowery
Sulphur, La.

"CONTRABAND CRAB MEAT"
(DRUM OR REDFISH)

1 fish, coarse meated, such as drum or redfish, cleaned and headed
Water
Crab boil
Salt and pepper
Lemon juice
1 onion, quartered

Place fish carefully in pot of boiling water (to cover), seasoned with remaining ingredients. (Follow package directions for crab boil.) Cook until fish is done; then carefully remove to platter and let cool. Peel off skin; then flake meat off with a fork. Be careful not to mix bones with meat.

This tastes exactly like crab meat and is delicious used in stuffing for baked fish.

Lawrence Lowery, Jr.

STUFFING FOR BAKED FISH

1 cup onions, finely chopped
¼ cup bell pepper, finely chopped
1 large clove garlic, diced
½ stick margarine
2 cups croutons, crushed, or toasted bread crumbs
¼ cup green onion tops, chopped
1 cup crab meat, "Contraband crab meat", see above, or shrimp, chopped
Salt, black and red pepper

In skillet, sauté onions, bell pepper, and garlic in margarine until cooked. Stir in croutons, green onions, and crab until mixed thoroughly. Season to taste. Excellent stuffing for fish.

Lawrence Lowery, Jr.

FILLET OF SOLE WITH SHRIMP SAUCE

1 package fillet of sole or flounder (frozen)
¼ cup milk
Salt and pepper
½ cup flour
¼ cup margarine or butter
SAUCE
2 Tablespoons flour
3 Tablespoons margarine or butter
8-10 large shrimp, cut in pieces
1½ Tablespoons onion, chopped
1 Tablespoon celery, chopped
1 cup water
1 bouillon cube
Juice of 1 lemon
1 Tablespoon Worcestershire sauce
Dash of Tabasco
Salt and pepper to taste

THAW PACKAGE OF FROZEN FISH. Prepare sauce before starting to cook the fish. In saucepan stir flour and margarine or butter until smooth. Stir in shrimp, onion, and celery. Add remaining ingredients, stirring until mixture thickens. Reduce heat to low, cover, and simmer for 20 minutes. Soak separated fillets in milk for 5 minutes, discarding milk. Salt, pepper, and lightly flour the fillets. Brown in skillet in hot melted margarine, turning only once. Handle fillets carefully when removing, and serve on warm plates. Spoon sauce over fish. Serves 4-5.

Mrs. William Storer
(Edith Mandell)

TERRELL'S PERCH

4 perch fillets, boned
Pepper
3 Tablespoons chives, chopped
1½ Tablespoons butter, melted
Salt
½ pint lump crab meat
2 ounces water

Pat fillets dry, and pepper only. In a heavy skillet sauté chives in butter. Add fillets and cook until outer rim turns white. Turn over, salt, and place ½ of crab meat around outer edge of skillet. Cook on high heat until fillets turn slightly white all over; turn fillets and crab meat, and salt. Add water, cover tightly, and cook for 1 minute. The entire cooking time should be only 3-3½ minutes. Serve immediately on hot dinner plates, spooning chives and crab meat over fillets. Serves 2.

Terrell Woosley, Jr.

BAKED FISH

1 bass (4½ pound), dressed
Butter and salt
3 bay leaves
4 onion slices
SAUCE
½ cup white wine
2 cups tomato purée

Dry fish thoroughly. Rub inside and out with butter and salt. Stuff cavity with bay leaves and onion slices. Baste fish with sauce. Bake at 350°F for 1 hour.

Mrs. Dorman Shockley
Houston, Texas

SEAFOOD

FRIED FROG LEGS

Frog legs (4 legs per person)
Buttermilk
Flour
Salt and pepper
Cooking oil

SAUCE
1 stick butter, melted
½ teaspoon Tabasco
2 Tablespoons lemon juice
1 teaspoon Worcestershire sauce
1 clove garlic, crushed

Soak frog legs in buttermilk for 1 hour. Mix flour and seasoning to taste in a paper bag. Shake 4-6 frog legs at a time in bag. Fry at a hot temperature in heavy iron pot half filled with cooking oil until golden brown (like chicken).

SAUCE
Combine all ingredients in a saucepan and heat. Serve frog legs on a large platter with sauce drizzled liberally over them.

Mrs. J. Richard Enright
(Monette Moreau)

FROG LEGS PROVENÇAL

¼ pound butter
1 small onion, thinly sliced
8 fresh mushrooms, sliced
12 frog legs
1 carrot, finely chopped
4 ripe tomatoes, cut
1 clove garlic
1 teaspoon basil
Salt and white pepper to taste

Sauté lightly in butter, onion, mushrooms, and frog legs. Remove frog legs. Add carrots, tomatoes, garlic, and basil. Simmer until thickens, about 10 minutes. Season to taste. Pour over frog legs in buttered baking dish and bake at 350°F for 15-20 minutes. Serves 4.

Jack Tullos
Sheraton Chateau Charles
Lake Charles, La.

LOBSTER TAILS

1 package (8 ounces) frozen lobster tails
1 can frozen, condensed cream of shrimp soup, thawed
¼ cup milk
1 can (3 ounces) sliced broiled mushrooms, drained
½ cup soft bread crumbs
½ cup celery, finely chopped
1 Tablespoon cooking sherry
¼ cup sharp cheese, shredded
Parsley sprigs
Lemon wedges

Drop lobster tails in boiling, unsalted water. Return to a boil. Reduce heat and simmer 15 minutes. Drain and rinse under cold water until cool to hands. Remove meat from shells and cut into bite sized pieces. Combine with soup, milk, mushrooms, bread crumbs, celery, and sherry. Divide mixture among 4 shells or individual casseroles, topped with cheese. Bake at 350°F about 25 minutes, or until hot. Trim with sprigs of parsley. Serve with lemon wedges. Serves 4.

Carolyn Stevens Moffett

CHEZ OCA'S TURTLE STEW

4 pounds turtle meat
¼ cup olive oil
½ cup butter
1 clove garlic
2 small onions
1 Tablespoon paprika
Pinch of cayenne pepper or Tabasco sauce
1 rib celery
1½ ounces flour
2 pints veal or beef stock
1 bouquet of herbs in a cheesecloth bag (consisting of 6 peppercorns, thyme, 2 bay leaves, 3 cloves, 6 corns of allspice)
Salt to taste
1 cup dry Spanish sherry
4 fresh tomatoes, scalded, skinned, and diced
1 lemon, zest, finely cut, and juice

Dice meat into 1½ inch cubes and brown in mixture of vegetable oil and butter. Add garlic, onion, paprika, cayenne, and celery. Sprinkle with flour and cook slowly for 5 minutes before adding stock. Insert bag of spices and remove in about 90 minutes, whenever meat is cooked. Correct seasoning and add sherry, tomatoes, lemon peel and juice. Garnish with shredded hard boiled eggs, bacon crumbs, and chopped parsley. Serve with steamed rice.

Fernando Oca
Chez Oca Restaurant
Lake Charles, Louisiana

PEELING OF CRAWFISH

Remove head and scoop out the yellow fat, if desired, with the top of your little finger. Squeeze sides of the shell and remove first the front 2 rings. Pinch base of tail shell with thumb and forefinger while pulling meat out with other hand. This should devein the crawfish. If not, remove meat flaps along top of tail and vein beneath it. *Do not* eat crawfish if the tail is straight and not curled under the body (this means that it was dead when boiled) unless you are *positive* that *all* were alive when placed in the boiling water.

Lawrence Lowery, Jr.
William E. Shaddock

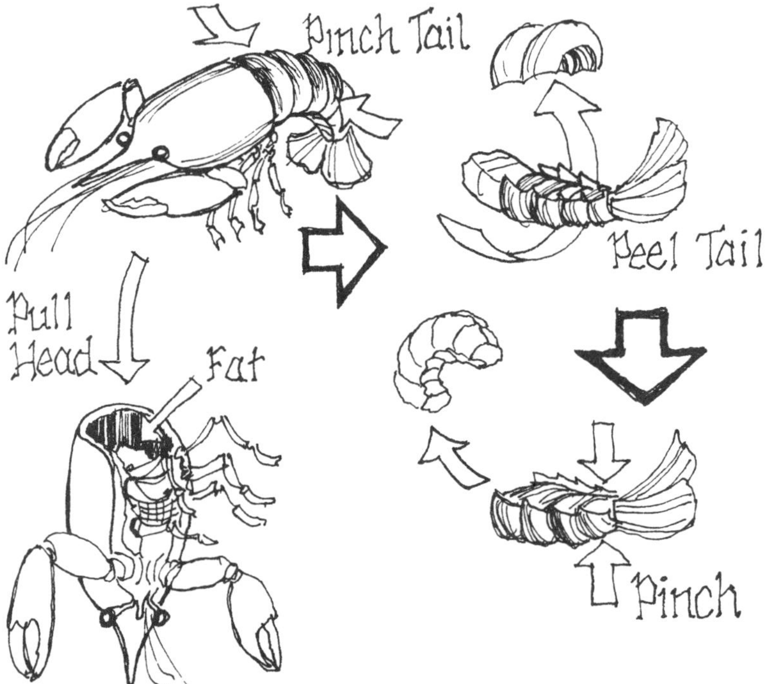

BOILED CRAWFISH

3 lemons, sectioned
3 onions, sectioned
2 cups rock salt
3 Tablespoons red pepper
1 medium jar prepared mustard
2 bags dry crab boil mix
20-30 pounds live crawfish
2 cans beer
Table salt

Place 30 quart pot ¼ filled with water over high heat. Add lemons, onions, rock salt, red pepper, and mustard. Add crab boil mix, breaking bags, and boil for 10 minutes. The aroma will knock your head off, but seasoning must be strong to permeate crawfish shell. Add crawfish. Return to boil for 7 minutes, adding beer during the last 2. Cover pot, turn off heat, and allow to simmer 3 minutes. Remove crawfish and liberally apply table salt before peeling. This only causes salt to get on fingers when peeling shells and then on the tails. Serves 10 Yankees or 3-4 Cajuns.

To serve Cajun style, heap crawfish, potatoes, and corn in middle of an old redwood table under the trees, roll up your sleeves, and dig in! When finished, hose down everyone and everything in sight.

John B. "Spike" Scofield

CRAWFISH AU GRATIN

1 medium onion, diced
1 clove garlic, diced
2 ribs celery, chopped
4 Tablespoons margarine, melted
¼ cup green onions
¼ cup pimiento
1 Tablespoon flour
¼ pound Cheddar cheese, grated
1 can (5.33 ounces) evaporated milk
1 pound crawfish tails
Salt and pepper to taste

Sauté onion, garlic, and celery in margarine until tender. Add green onions and pimiento the last 10 minutes. Mix in flour; add cheese and milk, salt and pepper, and finally the crawfish. Bake in a greased casserole at 350°F for 30-40 minutes. Sprinkle with cheese for garnish. Freezes. Serves 4.

Mrs. George B. Jourdan
Lafayette, Louisiana

CRAWFISH CASSEROLE

2 medium onions, chopped
2 ribs celery, chopped
2 bell peppers, chopped
3 sticks margarine
2 pounds crawfish tails, chopped or ground
18 slices bread, soaked in milk
Salt, red and black pepper

Sauté vegetables in margarine until tender. Add crawfish tails, and cook until well done. Remove from heat and mix well with softened bread. Season to taste with salt, red and black pepper. Place in one 9x13 inch or two 8x8 inch pans, buttered. Bake at 350°F for 20-25 minutes, or until top is brown. Freezes. Serves 6-8.

Mrs. John Hensgens

SEAFOOD

FRIED CRAWFISH TAILS

½-1 pound package crawfish tails
1 cup milk
1 egg
Flour
½ Tablespoon salt
½ teaspoon each black and red pepper
Crisco oil

Soak crawfish tails in well beaten milk and egg mixture for 1 hour or more. In paper bag, shake crawfish in flour, seasoned with salt and pepper. Heat oil to 330°F or until match lights when dropped into hot grease. Drop 2 handfuls of crawfish into grease and cook 1 minute or until golden brown. Serve hot as hors d'oeuvre or entree.

Variation — use "fish fry" or corn flour.

Dr. Richard Jones Chafin

GIULIANO'S CRAWFISH FETTUCCINE

1 heaping Tablespoon flour
1 stick butter
Pinch salt
Dash Tabasco
1 cup milk
2 cups green onions, chopped
1 pound crawfish tails and fat
½ pint whipping cream
Egg noodles (12 ounces)

Make a roux with flour and ½ stick butter, salt, and Tabasco. Cook slowly until *almost* brown; add milk, stir, and simmer. Meanwhile, sauté green onions in another pan with remaining butter until soft. Add crawfish tails and fat. Simmer for about 8 minutes; then add to roux with the cream. Simmer for another few minutes while stirring. Cook noodles in lots of boiling salted water until they are "al dente" (just barely done). Drain and serve with crawfish mixture. Serves 4-6.

Giuliano Ceseri
Florence, Italy
Lafayette, La.

CRAWFISH PIE

2 pounds crawfish tails, cleaned
Salt and red pepper
1 cup onions, finely chopped
½ cup celery, chopped
½ cup cooking oil
2 containers crawfish fat
3 Tablespoons cornstarch
1½ cups water
Green onion tops, chopped
2 pie shells (9 inch) and tops

Season crawfish tails with salt and red pepper and set aside; sauté onions and celery in oil in heavy pot until onions are tender; add crawfish tails and fat and cook 15-20 minutes. Dissolve cornstarch in water and add to crawfish mixture; cook until thick, stirring constantly. Add onion tops, season to taste, and set aside. Fill pie shells, top with crust, cut with several random slits. Bake at 350°F for 15 minutes, reduce heat to 300°F and bake an additional 15 minutes, or until crust is golden brown. Freezes. Serves 6-8.

Mrs. Howard V. Smythe
(Jennabeth Powdrill)

CRAWFISH PIE

Pie crust
6 ribs celery, finely chopped
4 green onions, finely chopped
2 white onions, finely chopped
1 bell pepper, finely chopped
Cooking oil
1 pound crawfish tails
1 can cream of mushroom soup
1 soup can water
1 small jar pimientos
2 cups cooked rice
Salt and pepper to taste

Make pie crust; place in small individual pie pans. Sauté vegetables in small amount of cooking oil. Add remaining ingredients, and season to taste. Pour into pie pans; cover or strip the tops with remaining dough. Bake at 375°F about 30 minutes, or until brown. Serve immediately. Serves 4.

Mrs. Reese J. Broussard
Jennings, La.

CRAWFISH ETOUFFÉE

3 large onions, chopped
1½ sticks butter
2 pounds crawfish tails, cleaned
Crawfish fat
Salt and red pepper to taste
Parsley, finely chopped
Green onion tops, finely chopped

Sauté onions in butter until clear. Do not use black iron pot. Add crawfish tails. Cook, covered, over low heat about 15-20 minutes. Add crawfish fat and seasonings. Add parsley and onion tops and a small amount of hot water for desired consistency. Simmer for 20 minutes. Set aside before serving for about 20 minutes. Serve over rice. May be made ahead and frozen, but is better made just before serving. Serves 5-6.

Mrs. Louis J. Bonin
(Shirley Chappuis)

CRAWFISH ETOUFFÉE

1 stick margarine
1 pound crawfish tails,
   (or shrimp) peeled
1 medium onion, chopped
2 ribs celery, chopped
½ bell pepper, chopped
1 Tablespoon paprika
½ teaspoon salt
¼ teaspoon black pepper,
   coarsely ground
Pinch thyme
1 bay leaf
1 cup chicken broth
Hot fluffy rice
1 Tablespoon parsley, chopped
1 Tablespoon green onion tops,
   cut with scissors

Melt margarine in deep, heavy frying pan. Do not use black iron pot; it will discolor the crawfish. Add crawfish and cook for 2-3 minutes. Remove crawfish with slotted spoon and set aside. Add onion, celery, bell pepper, and seasonings. Sauté for at least 10 minutes, removing bay leaf after about 5 minutes. Return crawfish tails to pan and add chicken broth. Stir and cook slowly, covered, for about 40 minutes. Serve on boiled rice and sprinkle with parsley and green onion tops. Freezes. Serves 4.

Mrs. Arthur Hollins, Jr.
(Mary Muth)

G. Lock Paret, Jr. *likes to season his etouffée with a little garlic and beer.*

FRIED STUFFED BELL PEPPER

2 large onions, finely diced
1 clove garlic, finely diced
2½ sticks margarine
1 pound crawfish tails and fat (if large, dice)
1 pound crab meat, fresh, preferably, or frozen
4 cups bread crumbs
1 Tablespoon salt
1 teaspoon black pepper
¼ teaspoon red pepper
1 cup green onions and tops, finely diced
½ cup parsley, chopped
5 large bell peppers
BATTER
2 eggs, beaten
6 ounces milk
1 cup cracker meal
1 cup corn flour
Oil

In heavy iron pot sauté onions and garlic in margarine until wilted and transparent. Add crawfish tails, fat, and crab meat. Cook 5 minutes. Add bread crumbs, salt, pepper, onions, and parsley. Cook another 10 minutes. Let stand until cool. Cut bell peppers into 3 parts lengthwise. Remove seeds and stems and parboil for 3 minutes. Mound cold stuffing on each ⅓ bell pepper and form into a ball. Make batter by beating eggs and milk together in bowl. Mix cracker meal and corn flour together in separate bowl. Roll stuffed peppers in meal mixture, then in egg mixture, and back again in meal. Fry in oil at 375°F until golden brown and hot throughout. Freezes. Serves 15.

Superb!

Soileau's Dinner Club
Opelousas, La.

CAROL'S CRAWFISH

2 pounds onions, finely ground
1 can (16 ounces) tomato sauce
¼ pound butter or margarine
1 large dill pickle, ground
Crawfish fat
1 can (21 ounces) cream of mushroom soup, condensed
5 pounds crawfish tails, peeled
1¼ teaspoons salt
1 teaspoon black pepper,
½ teaspoon red pepper
4 cloves garlic, finely chopped
1½ cups green onion tops, finely chopped
1 cup parsley, finely chopped

Boil onions in small amount of water for about 2 hours, covered, or sauté in margarine if preferred. Add tomato sauce, simmer for 30 minutes, add butter, pickle, crawfish fat, and soup, and simmer 30 minutes or longer. Add crawfish tails and remaining ingredients, adjusting seasonings to taste. Cook about 30 minutes until crawfish tails are done but not spongy. Serve over rice. Freezes. Serves 10-12.

Dr. C. B. McCauley

CRAWFISH BISQUE

1 bag cleaned crawfish shells, about 60-80 (available at seafood market)

STUFFING FOR SHELLS
2 pounds cleaned crawfish tails
4 containers crawfish fat
1 medium onion, chopped
5 large cloves garlic
⅓ cup each parsley and green onion tops, chopped
1 Tablespoon each salt and red pepper
1 teaspoon black pepper
¼ teaspoon ground cloves
1 egg
6 slices bread, dried in oven until crisp, and pulverized with a rolling pin

WATER
3 bay leaves
½ teaspoon ground cloves

ROUX
¼ cup oil
½ cup flour
½ medium onion, chopped
1 large rib celery, chopped

STUFFED HEADS
Cooking oil
1 teaspoon salt

CROUTONS
1 loaf sandwich bread

STUFFING
Using a meat grinder, grind together crawfish tails, fat, onion, garlic, parsley, and green onion. Add salt, red and black pepper, and ground cloves, and knead with hands, mixing thoroughly in large bowl. Add egg and bread crumbs and blend to a firm consistency. Pretest for consistency and seasoning by frying in advance several small patties in a little oil. If, after testing, the stuffing seems too soft, pulverize 5-6 crackers with a rolling pin, add to contents of bowl, and mix. Fill each cleaned head tightly with mixture and set aside.

WATER
In a 4 quart heavy pot, half filled with water, add bay leaves and cloves, bring to a slow boil, then simmer.

ROUX
In a large heavy skillet, make a roux. Mix oil and flour and cook slowly on low heat until dark golden brown. Sauté onion and celery. Slowly pour 1½ cups boiling water from large pot into roux, stirring constantly, and simmering for 3 minutes. Add roux to large pot of boiling water. Stir gently and let simmer very slowly.

STUFFED HEADS
In a large heavy skillet place ½ inch oil and fry stuffed heads until exposed stuffing is a dark golden brown. Remove from skillet with slotted spoon and immediately add to pot containing roux and boiling water. Reduce heat, add salt, and simmer 2-3 hours. Adjust seasoning. Skim any excess grease from top.

CROUTONS
To make croutons, cut each slice of bread into fourths and place on cookie sheets. Toast in oven at 300°F. When toasted, reduce heat to warm and leave in oven until ready to serve. Freezes. Serves 6-8.

There are about as many ways of making bisque as there are cooks. This bisque is an old family recipe passed down through the years. A lot of trouble, but with the first spoonful the taste is so deliciously satisfying, you forget all the work and enjoy the pleasure.

Dr. J. Malcolm Leveque

OPENING RAW OYSTERS

Place on firm surface such as lead shield or box containing damp salt or sand covered with a damp towel. With a thickly gloved hand holding the oyster shell flat side up, insert oyster knife into hinged end, twisting, not prying, about ¼ turn until hinge breaks. Run knife along flat shell of oyster, cutting abductor muscle at the top which attaches it. Flip off top shell, cut muscle attaching oyster to bottom shell, and it is ready to eat. CAUTION: Use a heavy leather glove to avoid slicing your hand.

A second, or lazy man's, method of opening oysters is to place them, flat side up, on a barbecue grill above hot bed of coals. When the shells pop open shortly, remove from grill and finish opening with oyster knife. Eat with desired sauce. Always check oysters for rocks or "pearls" before eating!

Lawrence Lowery, Jr.
William E. Shaddock

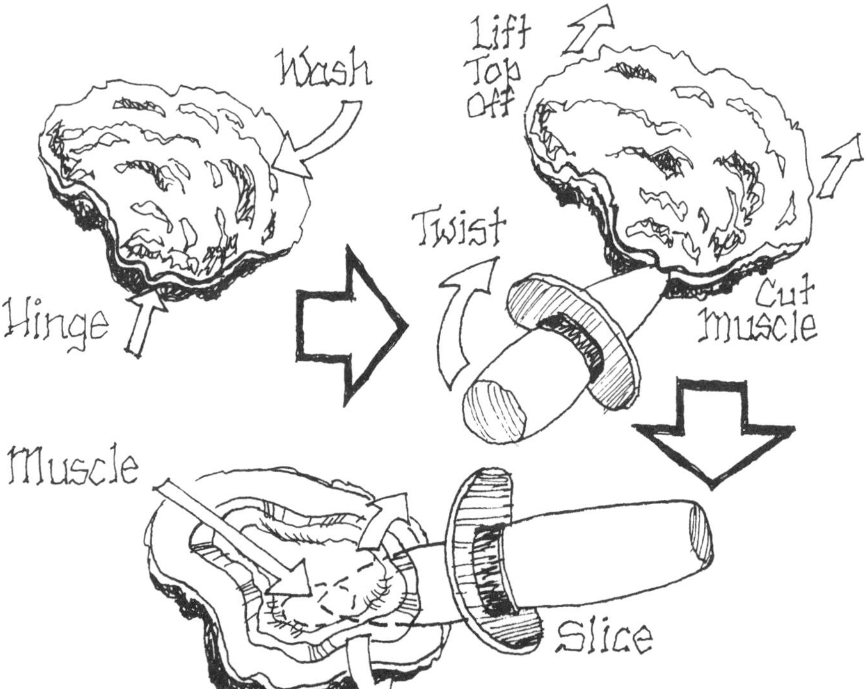

OYSTERS BIENVILLE

2 slices bacon, minced
1 small can mushrooms, minced*
4 green onions, minced
1 Tablespoon butter
2½ Tablespoons flour
½ cup whole milk
¼ pound shrimp, cooked, peeled, minced
5 Tablespoons oyster liquid
1 Tablespoon fresh lemon juice
1 Tablespoon sherry
1 teaspoon parsley, chopped
½ slice American cheese
Tabasco and salt to taste
Few drops yellow food coloring
24 oysters on half shell
Dry white wine
Rock salt

Fry bacon in heavy skillet until brown; add mushrooms and green onions, and cook until wilted. Add butter and when melted, add flour. Cook 5 minutes stirring constantly. Do not brown flour. Add milk and cook until thick. Add shrimp, oyster liquid, lemon juice, sherry, and parsley. Cook a few minutes, stirring. Add cheese, Tabasco, salt, and food coloring, and continue cooking until smooth and thick. Correct seasonings. Meanwhile, poach oysters in a little wine to cover, just until the edges curl. Arrange oysters on half shells and top with a spoonful of sauce. Place shells on a bed of rock salt and broil until sauce bubbles and just begins to brown. Serves 4.

*Everything must be minced or it will be lumpy.

Mrs. D. Dale Archer
(Valerie "Val" Grode)

OYSTERS BIENVILLE CASSEROLE

¼ cup green onions, chopped
4 Tablespoons butter, melted
¼ cup flour
¾ cup oyster liquid
¼ cup white wine
1 egg yolk
Salt and red pepper
1 cup shrimp, chopped
½ cup mushrooms, chopped
1 Tablespoon parsley, chopped
Worcestershire sauce
24 oysters, freshly shucked
Butter

Sauté onions in butter in large saucepan. Blend in flour and cook for 5 minutes, stirring constantly. Remove from heat. Blend in oyster liquid, wine, and egg yolk. Add salt, red pepper, shrimp, mushrooms, parsley, and Worcestershire. Cook on low heat for about 15 minutes. Arrange oysters in 2 casseroles, place half of shrimp mixture on top, dot with butter, cover with other half shrimp mixture. Bake, uncovered, at 400°F for 15-20 minutes. Serves 2.

Mrs. David Painter
(Isabel "Bel" Thornton)

LOCK'S OYSTER ROCKEFELLER SAUCE

1 pound butter, melted
1 bunch parsley, chopped
1 bunch green onions with tops, chopped
1 rib celery, chopped
2 packages frozen spinach, cooked and cooled
¼ cup fresh mint leaves
½ teaspoon anise seeds
2 teaspoons lemon juice
3 ounces Lea & Perrins
2 ounces absinthe
½ cup toasted bread crumbs
2 Tablespoons anchovy paste
2 dashes Tabasco
Salt and pepper to taste

Mix butter and vegetables thoroughly in blender. Add remaining ingredients and blend. This is enough sauce for 4-6 dozen oysters. Broil oysters in shells on rock salt in pan for 10 minutes, or until the edges curl. Drain juice off oysters and add Rockefeller sauce. Continue to broil until sauce bubbles and becomes slightly brown. Sauce keeps refrigerated for weeks.

G. Lock Paret, Jr.

OYSTERS ROCKEFELLER

4 packages frozen spinach
3 bunches green onions
1 small rib celery, scraped
1 bunch parsley
1 head lettuce
1 pound butter, melted
1 cup bread crumbs
3 Tablespoons Worcestershire sauce
1 Tablespoon anchovy paste
2 ounces Pernod
Salt and Tabasco to taste
12 dozen oysters
25 pounds rock salt
Parmesan cheese

Purée vegetables. Mix with butter and handful of bread crumbs. Mix Worcestershire sauce, anchovy paste, and Pernod and add to vegetable mixture. Season with salt and Tabasco. Place oysters on half shell on bed of rock salt in pie pans and cover with sauce. Sprinkle with Parmesan cheese and remainder of bread crumbs. Bake, uncovered, at 450°F for 15 minutes, or until oysters begin to curl. Serve immediately. Sauce will freeze. Serves 12.

Mrs. A. W. Noland, Jr.
(Heitie Richard)

CREOLE FRIED OYSTERS

1 egg, beaten
¾ cup tomato ketchup
2 Tablespoons Worcestershire sauce
1¼ teaspoons Tabasco
1 teaspoon celery salt
½ teaspoon each black and red pepper
1 quart oysters, drained
Corn meal
Oil for deep frying

In a deep bowl mix well the egg, ketchup, Worcestershire, Tabasco, celery salt, and pepper. Soak oysters in this sauce for 1 hour in refrigerator. Roll oysters in corn meal and fry, uncovered, in deep hot oil. Serves 4.

Mrs. L. Ron Futrell
(Sandra Allen)

FRIED OYSTERS, LOUISIANA STYLE

Oysters
Corn meal
Salt
White pepper
Cooking oil

Cull oysters carefully to remove any bits of shell. Drain and pat dry with absorbent towel. Roll in corn meal seasoned to taste. Guard against oversalting as some oysters are naturally salty. Deep fat fry to a golden brown. Do not crowd in the skillet. Drain on paper towels and serve hot with preferred seafood sauce.

Miss Maude Reid

FRENCH LOAF (OYSTER STUFFED)

1 loaf French bread (bakery)
½ cup butter
3 cloves garlic, crushed
8 slices bacon, fried
Flour
12 large oysters, more if small
8 slices fresh tomato
Mayonnaise
Horseradish

Cut loaf in half, hollow out, and save top. Melt butter and add garlic. Brush insides of loaf with mixture. Place fried bacon in cavity. Flour oysters lightly and fry very quickly. Place on top of bacon. Sear tomato slices and place on top of oysters. Replace top on bread and wrap in foil. Cook 10 minutes at 350°F. Serve hot, sliced, with mayonnaise seasoned to taste with horseradish drizzled on.

Mrs. R. Wayne Vincent
(Katherine "Kitty" Thornton)

DEVILED OYSTERS

1 cup celery, chopped
2 pounds onions, chopped
1 stick butter
1 loaf bread
100 oysters with juice
Salt and pepper to taste
2 Tablespoons parsley, chopped

Brown celery and onions in butter. Soak loaf of bread in water, squeeze it dry, and break into small pieces. Add bread to celery and onions and combine with oysters and juice. Season with salt and pepper. Bake in casserole at 325°F, 30-45 minutes just before serving. Sprinkle with parsley.

**From the recipes of
Mrs. S. A. Knapp**

OYSTERS EN BROCHETTE

1 quart raw oysters
6-8 slices bacon, cut in 1½ inch squares
2 large cans whole mushroom caps
Salt and pepper
Parmesan cheese
BASTING SAUCE
¼ stick margarine
2 Tablespoons lemon juice
2 Tablespoons Worcestershire sauce
2 Tablespoons oyster liquid

On small skewers alternate oysters, bacon squares, and mushroom caps. Place skewers on broiler pan. Lightly salt and pepper. Make sauce by combining margarine, lemon juice, Worcestershire, and oyster liquid. Place skewers under broiler and cook until bacon browns and oysters curl. Turn skewers over and repeat cooking. Baste with sauce while broiling. Just before serving, sprinkle with cheese. Serve remaining sauce with oysters. Serves 4-6.

**Mrs. Everett Schneider
(Elizabeth "Libby" Storer)**

SCALLOPED OYSTERS

1 cup each cracker and toast crumbs
½ cup butter, melted
1 quart oysters, drained
½ liquid reserved from oysters
¼ cup cream
1 teaspoon Lea & Perrins
2 Tablespoons sherry
Cayenne pepper
½ teaspoon salt
¼ teaspoon pepper
Tabasco
Paprika

Mix crumbs with butter. Place ½ crumb mixture in buttered 1½ quart oblong pyrex casserole. Mix liquids and seasonings, except paprika, and pour over oysters which have been arranged on crumbs in casserole. Cover with remaining crumbs and paprika. Bake, uncovered, at 400°F for 20 minutes, or until brown. Serves 8-10.

**Mrs. Emile R. Winterhaler
(Millicent Watkins)**

OYSTER SPAGHETTI

2 cups flour
1 cup cooking oil
4 large onions, finely chopped
4 large cloves garlic, finely chopped
1 bell pepper, finely chopped
4 ribs celery, finely chopped
1 gallon oysters, drained and checked for shells
Salt, red and black pepper
3-4 dashes Lea & Perrins
2 packages (10 ounce size) cut elbow spaghetti
½ stick butter
1 small jar pimientos, chopped
Green onion tops, chopped
Parsley, chopped

Make a roux by browning flour in oil until medium brown. Add vegetables and sauté on very low heat until wilted. Add oysters that have been seasoned with salt, pepper, and Lea & Perrins. Cook slowly. When oysters curl, add hot boiled spaghetti and mix. [Peeled, raw shrimp (5-8 pounds) may be substituted for oysters. Use only 1½ cups flour instead of 2 for roux.] Just before heat is turned off, add pimientos, onion tops, and parsley. Serve immediately. Serves 12-15.

Spaghetti should be cooked at the last minute in boiling salted water and be very hot when added to oysters. Add butter to water to prevent sticking.

Mrs. John Paul Crain

WILD RICE AND OYSTER CASSEROLE

1 box Uncle Ben's long grain and wild rice
2 bell peppers, chopped
2 onions, chopped
½ cup parsley, chopped
Margarine or butter
1 can (4 ounces) sliced mushrooms, drained
1 package blanched almonds, sliced
1 pint oysters (reserve liquid) (cut in half)
1 cup *cooked* Uncle Ben's converted rice
Salt and red pepper to taste

Cook wild rice according to package directions. Sauté bell pepper, onion, and parsley in margarine or butter. Combine all ingredients. Bake at 300°F for 30 minutes. Serves 8-10.

Mrs. Lehrue Stevens, Jr.
(Betty Scheib)

OYSTERS CRAIG-PODDY

24 homemade toast rounds (large enough to hold an oyster)
¼ cup onion, chopped
2 Tablespoons butter
1 teaspoon parsley, minced
2½ Tablespoons flour
1 cup heavy cream
¼ roll (6 ounce roll) Jalapeño pepper cheese
1 teaspoon garlic salt
1 cup dry white wine (use small amount in sauce and reserve remainder)
1 cup fresh lump crab meat
Cayenne pepper (optional)
24 fresh raw oysters
Butter, softened
Parsley
Lemon wedges

First: cut day old white bread into 24 rounds with cutter. Butter tops and bake at 300°F on cookie sheet about 45 minutes, or until dry and very light brown. Do not overbrown. Set aside.

Second: Make sauce. Sauté onion in butter until soft but not brown; add parsley and flour and cook until smooth; add cream and cook until bubbly and smooth; add cheese and garlic salt to taste and cook until cheese is melted and bubbly. Thin sauce with a little white wine until desired consistency, but still thick. Gently fold in crab meat and correct seasonings. If desired, add a little cayenne pepper to taste.

Third: Combine drained oysters and remaining white wine in saucepan and poach oysters just until edges curl.

Fourth: Arrange toast rounds on baking sheet and lightly butter with soft butter. Place an oyster on each round and top with sauce. Broil a good distance from heat until bubbly. Or arrange 4 rounds with oysters and sauce in individual, heat proof shells or plates and broil as directed. Garnish with parsley and lemon wedges. Serves 6.

A unique variety of ingredients which will hold up well under pressure.

Mrs. D. Dale Archer
(Valerie "Val" Grode)

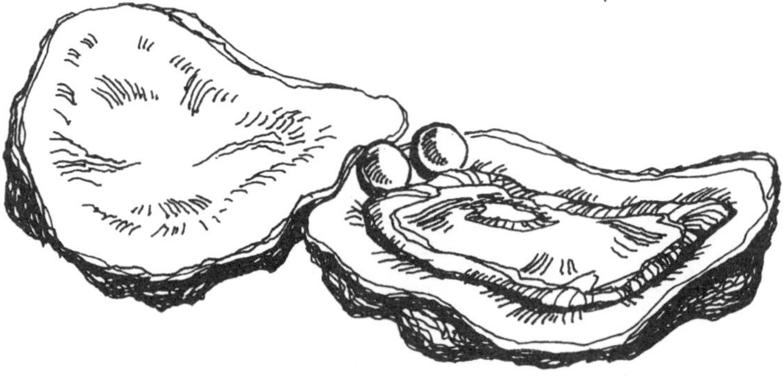

HOW TO EAT HARD SHELL CRABS

Place your right thumb on top of crab's right swimmer, which is the flat back "leg" of the crab, and the left thumb under the right tip of crab shell. Press up with left thumb and down with right thumb to remove shell. Remove lungs (dead men) and stomach and break in half. Do not remove legs or swimmers. Then follow 1 of the 2 following procedures: (a) Squeeze the halves to break down the crab section, pull swimmer out and towards back of crab. A large section of meat will adhere to swimmer. Repeat with each leg and claw. (b) Pull out each swimmer and claw separately (prying out any remaining meat with table knife).

Lawrence Lowery, Jr.
William E. Shaddock

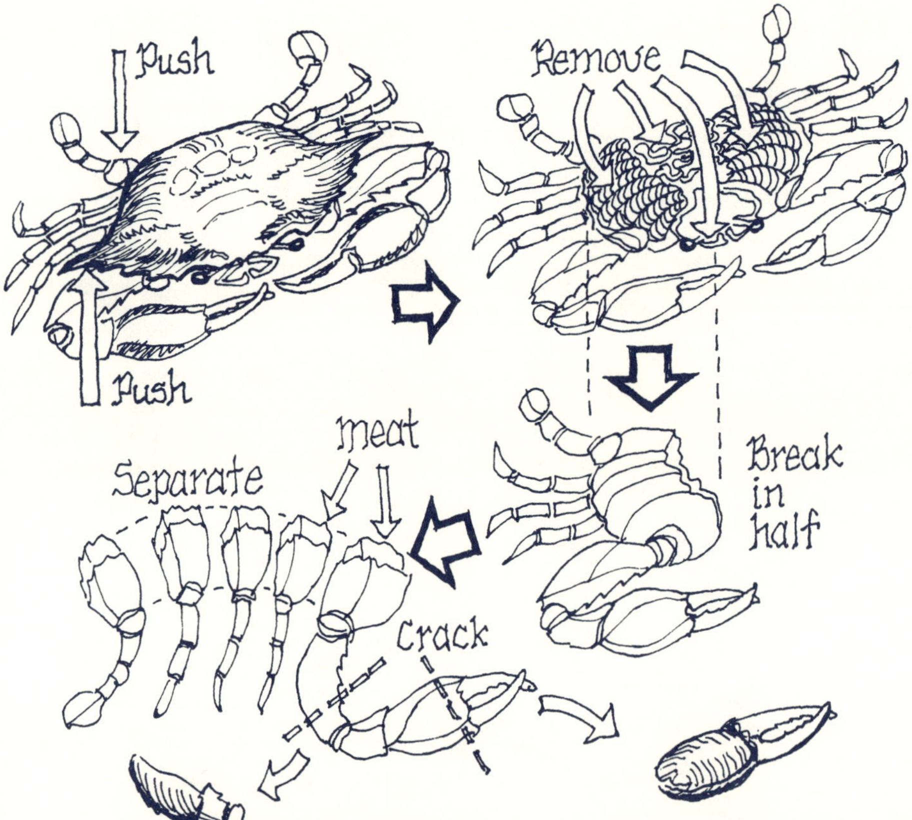

Crabs

CLEANING AND COOKING OF CRABS

SOFT SHELL

Clean soft shell crabs by raising the tips of the "shell", removing lungs and other inedible parts, and finally lifting the back of the "shell" and removing stomach and other parts between the halves. Then remove the eyes and mouth, rinse cleaned crab in vinegar or salt solution (described in section on fish), and place on ice immediately to avoid deterioration.

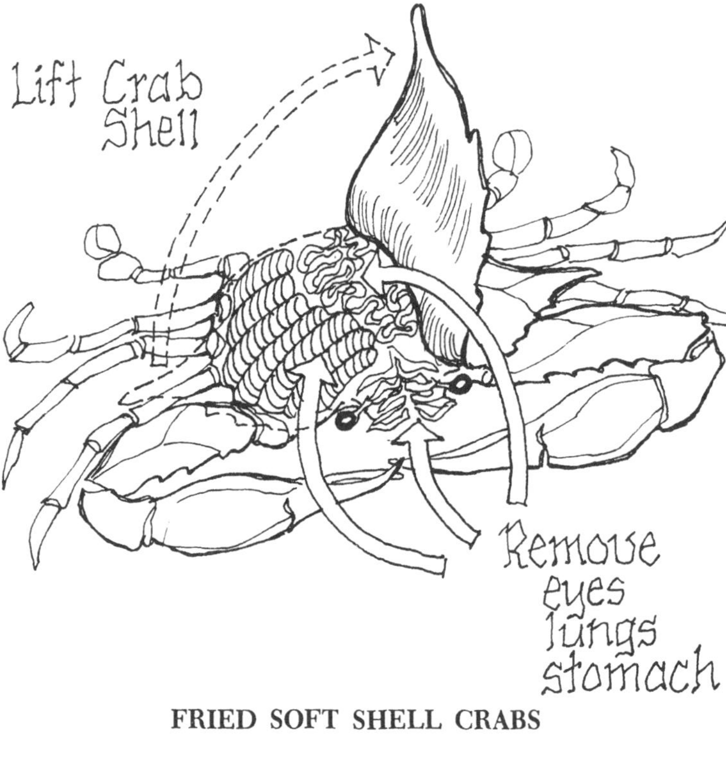

Lift Crab Shell

Remove eyes lungs stomach

FRIED SOFT SHELL CRABS

Soft shell crabs
2 cups milk
2 eggs, slightly beaten
Flour
Salt, black and cayenne pepper to taste
Oil for deep frying

Clean crabs. Soak in milk and egg mixture for 1 hour before frying. Mix flour and seasonings in brown paper bag. Shake crabs in seasoned flour. Redip crabs in milk mixture and reflour. Fry in deep hot oil until golden brown. Serve 1 large or 2 small crabs per person.

Mrs. Charles S. Ware, Jr.
(Jan Allen)

FREEZING OF CRABS

HARD SHELL

To prepare hard shell crabs for freezing proceed in the following manner: parboil in salted water just long enough to kill, remove shell, remove and discard lungs and stomach, break body in half, wash and scrub thoroughly, and cut off (do not pull off) legs and swimmers. Chill edible pieces in iced water until thoroughly cold, place in milk carton, cover with chilled water, and tightly tape. Place in freezer, allowing adequate space between containers for quick freezing.

SOFT SHELL

Clean as described p. 63, chill in iced water, place in milk carton, cover with chilled water, and tightly tape. Place in freezer, allowing adequate space between containers for quick freezing.

BOILED CRABS — OUTSIDE

Live crabs
Water
4 boxes salt
1 bottle (4 ounces) cayenne pepper
6 lemons, halved, juice and peel
4 onions, quartered
8 cloves garlic
1 box crab boil

In washtub, cover crabs with water. Add 2 boxes salt to purge. Remove after 20 minutes and wash. Meanwhile, fill large pot (50-60 quarts) ¼ full of water. Add remaining ingredients, bring to a boil, cover, and cook on butane burner for 15 minutes.* Place crabs either in a strainer or a nylon mesh laundry bag and immerse in seasoned water. Cook, covered, for 10 minutes after returning to a boil. Immediately remove crabs, spread on table, salt shells liberally (so salt will get on your hands while eating), and eat to your heart's content. Leave seasoned water in pot to use for remaining crabs. The most important thing to remember is not to overcook crabs.

**For a superb, complete meal add small, whole new potatoes, unpeeled, to seasoned water and cook until tender. Also add fresh or frozen ears of corn and cook just a few minutes until done. Serve immediately.*

William E. Shaddock

SEAFOOD

CRAB MEAT AU GRATIN*
*(Snapper Pastor Sauce Base Also)

3 cups onions, chopped
½ cup celery, chopped
3 sticks margarine
3 teaspoons seasoning mix
1½ Tablespoons flour
3 egg yolks
1 can (5.33 ounces) Carnation evaporated milk
2 cans (6.3 ounce size) drained crab meat

Sauté onions, celery, and seasoning mix in margarine until wilted. Add flour; stir in well. Mix egg yolks well into evaporated milk and slowly pour this mixture into above mixture, stirring all the while. Cook until sauce thickenes. Set aside to cool. *After* sauce cools combine with well drained crab meat and stir well, being careful not to break crab meat. Put into casserole dishes; sprinkle top with grated cheese. Bake at 350°F until bubbly. Serves 8-10.

Pat and Maugie Pastor
Chez Pastor Restaurant
Lafayette, La.

CRAB MEAT MOUSSE

1 Tablespoon gelatin
3 Tablespoons cold water
¼ cup mayonnaise
2 Tablespoons each lime and lemon juice
1 Tablespoon each parsley and chives, chopped
1 Tablespoon prepared mustard
Salt and pepper to taste
2 cups flaked cooked crab meat
¾ cup whipping cream, whipped
Slices of lime
2 avocados, mashed

Soften gelatin in cold water and dissolve in double boiler over hot water. Mix gelatin with mayonnaise, lime and lemon juice, parsley, chives, mustard, salt, and pepper to taste. Fold in crab meat and whipped cream. Pour mixture into buttered ring mold and chill until set. Unmold on serving dish. Garnish with slices of lime. Fill center with mashed avocado and sprinkle with chopped chives. May be prepared in individual molds or served as an hors d'oeuvre.

Mrs. Robert W. Fenet

COMMANDER'S FAMOUS IMPERIAL CRAB SPECIALTY

1 pound backfin lump crab meat
½ bell pepper, minced
1 small jar pimientos, minced
1 egg, beaten
⅓ cup mayonnaise
1 teaspoon dry mustard
¼ teaspoon black pepper
½ teaspoon salt

Preheat oven to 350°F. Carefully cull any shell pieces from crab meat. Mix all ingredients and toss lightly. Put in shells and bake for 15 minutes. Serves 4.

J. Gilbert Scheib

STUFFED ARTICHOKES WITH CRAB MEAT

¼ pound butter
½ cup chives, chopped
1½ cups rich cream sauce, p. 296
½ teaspoon Tabasco
1 teaspoon Lea & Perrins
½ teaspoon dry mustard
Salt and pepper to taste
¼ cup bread crumbs
1½ pounds lump crab meat
4 cooked artichokes

In browned butter, sauté chives. Add cream sauce, seasonings, bread crumbs, and mix thoroughly. Add crab meat and cook 2 minutes. Stuff artichokes with crab meat and serve hot.

*Courtesy of Maxim's
Houston, Texas*

STUFFED CRABS

1 large onion, chopped
3 ribs celery, scraped and chopped
4 cloves garlic, minced
1 Tablespoon oil
2 pounds crab meat
1 bunch green onion tops, chopped
4 slices bread, dampened, mashed
½ cup cracker meal
Butter

Sauté onion, celery, and garlic in oil about 15 minutes or until they become clear. Add crab meat, cover, and cook about 25-30 minutes. Add onion tops and bread and cook 5 minutes more. Place mixture in shells, sprinkle with cracker meal, and dot with butter. Bake at 350°F until tops are slightly brown. Freezes. Serves 8-10.

*Mrs. Don Siebarth
(Jeannie Hart)*

CRAB MEAT QUICHE

½ white onion or 2 green onions, thinly sliced
¼ bell pepper, finely chopped
1 Tablespoon margarine or butter
1 frozen pastry shell (9 inch)
3 eggs, slightly beaten
½ teaspoon Worcestershire sauce
¾ teaspoon salt
¼ teaspoon each dry mustard and red pepper
1 cup milk, light or sour cream
1 cup Colby cheese, coarsely grated
½ pound fresh crab meat

Sauté onion and bell pepper in margarine or butter, and place in pie shell which has been brushed with a little of the beaten egg. Blend well the remaining ingredients and pour into pie shell. Bake, uncovered, at 300°F for 50-60 minutes, or until custard is set and a silver knife inserted in center comes out clean. Do not slice for 10-15 minutes. Serves 6.

*Mrs. Patrick Unkel
(Barbara Perez)*

SEAFOOD

CRAB SOUFFLÉ

½ bell pepper, finely chopped
4 Tablespoons flour
3 Tablespoons butter
1¼ cups milk or chicken broth
8 egg yolks
1 cup crab meat
1 Tablespoon sherry
Salt and pepper
8 egg whites, stiffly beaten, with a pinch of salt and ⅛ teaspoon cream of tartar added
¼ cup Parmesan cheese, finely grated

Preheat oven to 400°F. Grease and dust with flour a 1½ quart soufflé dish. Simmer bell pepper in water for 10 minutes. Drain, and immediately cover with cold water to retain the green color. In saucepan add flour to melted butter until well mixed, but not brown. Gradually add milk or chicken broth. Remove from heat, and add egg yolks 1 at a time, stirring after each addition. Add bell pepper, crab meat, sherry, salt and pepper to taste. Fold this sauce into stiff egg whites and pour into soufflé dish. Dust surface with cheese. Place soufflé in oven and *immediately reduce heat to 375°F.* Bake 25 minutes. Serve immediately with a green salad and crusty bread to 4-6 people.

Mrs. William Mixon
(Debi Kramer)

CRAB MEAT SOUFFLÉ

8 slices bread
2 cups crab meat
½ cup mayonnaise
1 onion, chopped
1 bell pepper, chopped
1 cup celery, chopped
1 can mushrooms, drained
4 eggs
3 cups milk
½ pound cheese, grated
Paprika

Place 4 slices of bread into a 9x15 inch pyrex baking dish. Mix crab meat, mayonnaise, onions, bell pepper, celery, and mushrooms, and spread over sliced bread. Trim crust from remaining slices of bread and place over crab mixture. Mix eggs and milk and pour over mixture. Place dish in refrigerator for at least 2 hours. Bake, uncovered, at 325°F for 15 minutes. Remove from oven and sprinkle with cheese and paprika. Bake 1 hour more at 325°F. Serves 12.

Mrs. Sam Puckett
(Jimmy Lee Bishop)

CRAB STEW

2 bell peppers, finely chopped
2 onions, finely chopped
2 cloves garlic, finely chopped
4 ribs celery, finely chopped
1 quart water
¾ cup olive oil
¾ cup flour
1 quart tomato juice
1 can (4 ounces) mushrooms
2 pounds crab meat, white lump
Tabasco and salt to taste

Boil first 4 ingredients in water until tender. Make a roux using olive oil and flour. To the roux add the boiled vegetables and water, tomato juice, mushrooms, and crab meat. Season highly with Tabasco and salt to taste. Simmer slowly 1 hour or more. This dish may be prepared in advance and frozen before adding mushrooms and crab meat.

From the recipes of
Della Bel Krause

CRAB MEAT CASSEROLE

7-8 green onions, chopped
1 small can mushrooms, sliced
1 stick margarine
Flour
½ cup half and half cream
1 Tablespoon parsley
3 drops hot sauce (Dr. Garber's, p. 303)
Salt and pepper to taste
Pinch garlic powder
1 teaspoon Lea & Perrins
1 pound crab meat
1 cup bread crumbs, stale
Paprika

Sauté onions and mushrooms in margarine. Remove from skillet. Add enough flour to skillet to absorb remaining margarine, making white sauce by adding half and half, parsley, hot sauce, salt, pepper, garlic powder, and Lea & Perrins. Mix white sauce with crab meat, onions, mushrooms, and bread crumbs. Place in casserole and sprinkle with bread crumbs and paprika. Bake, uncovered, at 350°F for 20-30 minutes, or until thoroughly warmed. Serves 4.

Mrs. Courtney A. Fenet, Jr.
(Sally Garber)

DEVILED CRAB

1 pound crab meat, fresh, frozen, or canned
2 ribs celery, finely chopped
4-6 green onions, finely chopped
1 medium bell pepper, finely chopped
2 cloves garlic, pressed
¼ pound butter or margarine
1 tube Premium saltine crackers, finely crushed
2 Tablespoons Lea & Perrins
3 drops Evangeline Hot sauce
Salt and black pepper
Crab liquor or water
Lemon slices
½ cup parsley, chopped
Tartare sauce (optional)

Drain crab meat if canned or frozen. Save liquor. In heavy skillet over low flame, sauté vegetables in butter, cover, and simmer 15-20 minutes until tender. Stir in crackers until they are moist and butter is absorbed. Add crab meat and mix thoroughly. Season with Lea & Perrins, and hot sauce, salt and pepper to taste. "Pepper" taste should not overpower crab meat taste. Add crab liquor or small amount of water until mixture is moist. Spoon into baking shells, buttered ramekins or casserole. Bake at 325°F for 20-25 minutes, or until bubbly. Garnish with lemon slices and parsley and serve with tartare sauce if desired. Serves 4-6.

I prefer a ½ white (fresh, canned, or frozen) and ½ claw meat mixture of Louisiana crab meat.

Mrs. Locke A. Plauché
(Dorothy Smith)

Shrimp

Shrimp are extremely perishable. It is *vital* to ice them thoroughly after they are caught. Even a few minutes' delay will alter the odor and flavor. When possible, also head speedily. Local shrimpers frequently head and ice them while continuing to trawl.

Even a beginner can head shrimp. Simply pinch off head with thumb and forefinger and discard, saving tails. Lift shrimp by their "whiskers" to avoid pricks from the needlelike nose and tail.

TO FREEZE: Headless shrimp may be frozen raw (unsalted) with or without shell. For peeled shrimp, a 1 quart plastic container is best; for unpeeled, a 1 quart milk carton holds 2 pounds. Cover with iced water, shake to pack contents, seal with freezer tape, label with date, quantity, and size. Allow space between cartons for faster freezing.

Shrimp that are netted, headed, iced, and frozen the same day will keep perfectly for a year if not allowed to defrost. If they have a "pinkish" color and *slight* odor, eat as soon as possible or discard.

TO PEEL: Of the many inexpensive shrimp peelers available most are plastic, tapered, blunted at one end, and curved to conform to the back of the shrimp. Beginning from the head end and on opposite side from feelers, insert blunt end between shell and meat, running it down the "backbone" to split shell in half for easy removal with the fingers. The small black line which runs down the back of most shrimp beneath the outer shell, is the intestinal tract; clear water will wash it away. However, it is completely harmless in cooked shrimp.

TO BOIL: To a large pot of boiling water add generous amounts of salt, ½ bell pepper, 1 onion, 1 celery rib, small red hot peppers, Tabasco, juice and rind of lemon, or similar seasonings to taste and boil for 30 minutes. Add crab or shrimp boil. Add shrimp. After 3 minutes of rapid boil, remove 1 shrimp and taste for doneness. Another test for doneness is a slight wrinkling of the shell. Length of boiling time varies with size of shrimp, but a general estimate is 5 minutes. Remove from heat immediately when done to stop the cooking process, pour into a colander, reserving the liquid, and chill shrimp. Overcooking makes peeling difficult. Shrimp that are not eaten at once should be returned to cooled cooking liquid and refrigerated. So processed, they may be safely kept for 6-7 days. One final suggestion: In removing refrigerated shrimp use a slotted spoon to prevent contamination of juice.

Mrs. D. M. Creveling
(Ellanora Gorham)

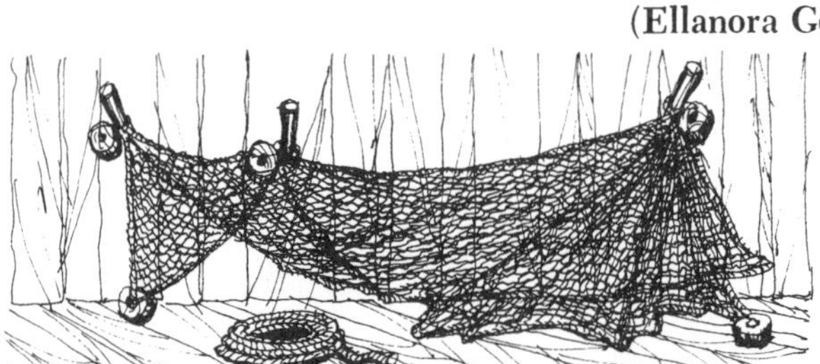

FRIED SHRIMP

2 egg yolks
⅔ cup milk
¾ cup flour
¼ teaspoon salt
1 teaspoon shortening, melted
Shrimp, raw, peeled, deveined
Cooking oil

To make batter, beat egg yolks in milk and add flour, salt, and shortening. Dip shrimp in batter 1 at a time and deep fat fry until golden brown. Drain on paper towels and serve with favorite sauce.

Miss Maude Reid

TEMPURA

1½ pounds shrimp, peeled and deveined
Flour
Tempura batter
1 quart corn oil

TEMPURA BATTER
¾ cup flour
¼ cup cornstarch
½ teaspoon baking powder
¼ teaspoon baking soda
1 cup water
1 egg

Dust shrimp lightly with flour; dip into batter. Deep fry over medium heat 1-2 minutes in sturdy 3 quart saucepan or deep fryer, filling no more than ⅓ full. Turn as needed. Drain. Serve with rice and soy sauce. Serves 4.

TEMPURA BATTER: Sift together all dry ingredients. Stir in water; then egg. Beat until smooth and frothy. (May also use 1 pound fish or boned chicken, cut in 1 inch strips, or vegetables, such as, green beans, broccoli, carrots, cauliflower, mushrooms, onion rings.)

Mrs. John B. Caire
(Peggy Huber)

FRIED SHRIMP

1 cup flour, sifted
½ teaspoon each sugar and salt
Dash of red pepper
¼ teaspoon nutmeg
1 teaspoon baking powder
1 egg, beaten
1 cup beer
1 pound shrimp, peeled
Cooking oil

Mix all ingredients, except shrimp, in a bowl. Dry peeled shrimp on paper towel, add to batter, and soak for 1 hour or more. Drop into deep, hot fat and fry about 5 minutes until golden brown. Drain on paper towels and serve immediately. Serves 4.

Mrs. Robert E. Doland
(Cheryl Grimm)

SHRIMP PATTIES

1½ pounds raw shrimp, peeled
1 medium onion, finely chopped
¼ bell pepper, finely chopped
1 rib celery, finely chopped
1 egg
1 teaspoon salt
½ teaspoon or more black pepper
1 teaspoon baking powder
½ cup green onions and parsley, mixed and finely chopped
½ cup flour
Cooking oil

Cut shrimp into 3-4 pieces. Mix with onion, bell pepper, and celery. Stir in remaining ingredients and mix well. Cover bowl and refrigerate for 1-2 hours. In skillet spoon shrimp mixture into about 1 inch hot oil and fry until brown, turning once. Makes about 27 medium sized patties.

Mrs. Clarence "Patin" Faulk
(Irene Croker)

SYBIL'S SHRIMP FRITTERS

1 egg, beaten
¼ cup milk
½ cup flour
1 cup raw shrimp, peeled and chopped
½ cup green onions, chopped
Garlic powder
2 teaspoons baking powder
½ teaspoon sugar
1 cup cooked rice
Lots of salt and pepper to taste
Fat for deep frying

Mix beaten egg with remaining ingredients. Drop by teaspoonfuls into hot oil in deep fat fryer. Mixture may be made in advance and refrigerated, but do not fry until ready to serve. Serves 4-6 as main dish and 8-12 as hors d'oeuvre.

Mrs. Jerry Wilburn

BEER BATTER FOR SHRIMP

1 can (12 ounces) beer
1½-2 cups all purpose flour
1 Tablespoon salt
1 Tablespoon paprika
Red pepper to taste

Combine all ingredients and beat with wire whisk until frothy. Batter may be used immediately or stored in refrigerator for several days. Whichever, use whisk freely to assure smoothness and uniformity.

Mrs. David Buttross, Jr.
(Joyce Abraham)

BARBECUED SHRIMP

10 pounds raw shrimp (jumbo), with or without heads
½ cup garlic juice
1 dozen bay leaves, finely crumbled
2 Tablespoons ground thyme
1-1½ cups olive oil
3 pounds butter
½ cup black pepper
½ cup seasoned salt
¼ cup plain salt
½ cup sherry
1 cup each celery, parsley, and onion, ground

Combine all ingredients and bake at 350°F for about 10 minutes. Stir mixture and then broil for 10-15 minutes. Exact cooking time depends on size of shrimp.

Edward M. Carmouche

LEMON-GARLIC BROILED SHRIMP

2 pounds raw shrimp, headless, peeled
2 cloves garlic, finely chopped
¼ cup butter or margarine, melted
3 Tablespoons lemon juice
½ teaspoon salt
Pepper, freshly ground
Tabasco, few drops
1 Tablespoon Lea & Perrins
Parsley, chopped

Rinse shrimp with cold water. Drain and dry on paper towels. Cook garlic in butter until tender. Remove garlic from pan and add remaining ingredients. Arrange shrimp in a single layer in a 15x10x1 inch pan. Cover with sauce. Broil 4 inches from heat for 8-10 minutes, depending on their size. Do not overcook. Baste with sauce once during broiling. Sprinkle with parsley just before serving. Serves 3-4.

Mrs. Emile R. Winterhaler
(Millicent Watkins)

SEAFOOD

BAKED SHRIMP

1 stick butter or margarine, melted
4 lemons
2 ounces ground black pepper
1 bottle (16 ounces) Wishbone Italian dressing
5 pounds raw shrimp, headless, unpeeled
Salt to taste
Hot French bread

Melt butter or margarine. Thinly slice 2 lemons and squeeze juice from remaining two. Combine all ingredients with shrimp and place in a 3 quart pyrex dish. Bake, tightly covered, at 350°F for 45 minutes. Serve warm unpeeled shrimp with some of the sauce. Use French bread for dipping in the sauce. Serves 5-6.

These are a bit messy to eat, but are delicious!

Mrs. Allen J. Rhorer
(Mildred Hamilton)

BAKED STUFFED SHRIMP

24 shrimp (16-20 count) with tail unpeeled and butterflied
8 ounces lump crab meat
½ stick butter
½ pound mild Cheddar cheese, grated
8 ounces mushroom soup
4 ounces cream
Bread crumbs, very fine
Garlic powder
Salt and white pepper
Paprika

Lightly sauté crab meat in butter; add cheese, soup, cream, and bread crumbs. Season. Increase bread crumbs if necessary to mold stuffing into shrimp. Sprinkle with paprika. Bake at 350°F about 10 minutes. Serves 4.

Jack Tullos
Sheraton Chateau Charles
Lake Charles, La.

SHRIMP MOSCA

3 pounds raw, headless shrimp, peeled
½ teaspoon garlic or plain salt
3 Tablespoons McCormick Italian seasoning
Dash Accent
Juice of 2 lemons
6 drops Tabasco
6 Tablespoons Italian bread crumbs
3 Tablespoons Italian cheese
1½ sticks butter
¾ cup water

In baking pan salt shrimp and cover with Italian seasoning. Mix thoroughly, rearrange in pan, and sprinkle with a blend of Accent, lemon juice, and Tabasco. Sprinkle bread crumbs and cheese over shrimp. Dot with butter. Pour water into corner of baking pan. *Do not pour over shrimp.* Bake, covered with foil, at 350°F for 30 minutes. If shrimp are extra large, bake 10-15 minutes longer. Reserve sauce for pouring over Italian bread. Serves 10-12.

Mrs. W. P. Fuller
Kinder, La.

> To make shrimp stock, peel shrimp, boil shells in seasoned water; strain. Freeze liquid and use as needed in making gumbos, seafood soups, etouffées, creoles, etc., for added flavor.

BOILED SHRIMP

3 pints cold water
1 can (8 ounces) tomatoes
3 ribs celery
3 onions, chopped
3 lemons, sliced
¾ cup salt
1 cup Wesson oil
1 Tablespoon red pepper
5 pounds shrimp

In a large kettle, combine all ingredients except shrimp and bring to a boil. Add shrimp and continue boiling 10-15 minutes until shrimp are bright pink and tender. Drain in colander. New potatoes may be boiled in seasoned water after shrimp are removed.

This is from a fishing boat captain in Cameron.

Rudolph Krause

SHRIMP MORNAY

1 small onion, diced
6 Tablespoons butter or margarine, melted
7 Tablespoons flour
1½ cups half and half
3 Tablespoons pimiento, diced
1 Tablespoon monosodium glutamate
Salt, pepper and Tabasco to taste
Slivered almonds
⅓ pound Gruyère cheese, grated
¼ pound Parmesan cheese, grated
1-1½ pounds shrimp, cooked
2 small cans mushrooms, drained

In skillet sauté onions in butter, but do not brown. Slowly add flour followed by half and half, stirring constantly to make a smooth white sauce. Add remaining ingredients, *except* cheeses, mushrooms, and shrimp. Cook, uncovered, on medium heat, stirring constantly until thick. Add cheeses, and cook, stirring constantly, until melted. Add shrimp and mushrooms about 5 minutes before serving. Serve over rice or in pastry shells. May be made ahead, frozen, and reheated slowly on low heat when time to serve. Serves 6-8.

Mrs. Mike Saloom

SEAFOOD

SHRIMP AU GRATIN

2 pounds shrimp
½ pound crab meat
1 teaspoon prepared mustard
1 teaspoon Worcestershire sauce
1 teaspoon hot sauce
1 cup cheese, grated
2 Tablespoons sherry
1 teaspoon onion, grated
Salt, red and black pepper
½ cup parsley, chopped

Wash shrimp. Boil in salted water for 10 minutes or until done. Remove shell and vein. Make a basic white sauce, p. 296, and to it add remaining ingredients except parsley. Fold in shrimp. Pour into greased baking dish and bake, uncovered, at 350°F for 25 minutes. Sprinkle with parsley before serving.

Two pounds crab meat may be substituted for shrimp, or 1 pound of each used.

Mrs. Marcus Pierson
(Gladys Daly)

SHRIMP DELIGHT

1 can artichoke hearts
1 pound shrimp, cooked, peeled
1 can (18 ounces) mushrooms, drained
Dash each Lea & Perrins and soy sauce
½ cup dry sherry
1½ cups basic white cream sauce, p. 296
½ cup Parmesan cheese, grated
Salt, pepper, paprika to taste
Parsley, green onions, chopped to garnish

Arrange artichokes, shrimp, and mushrooms in 4 individual greased baking dishes. Mix Lea & Perrins, soy sauce, sherry, and cream sauce. Pour over ingredients in baking dishes. Sprinkle with cheese, salt, pepper, and paprika. Bake at 350°F for 30-40 minutes and serve garnished with parsley and green onions. Serves 4.

Mrs. Beulah M. Breaux

SHRIMP THERMIDOR

1 cup celery, scraped and chopped
½ cup bell pepper, chopped
1 can (8 ounces) button mushrooms, drained
¼ pound butter
4 Tablespoons flour
3 cups milk
Salt and red pepper to taste
1 pound shrimp, boiled, well seasoned and peeled
Cheddar and Parmesan cheese

Sauté celery, bell pepper, and mushrooms in butter. Add flour and mix well. Slowly stir in milk and cook until thickened. Season to taste with salt and pepper. Add cooked shrimp and pour mixture into casserole. Cover top of casserole well with both cheeses. Bake, uncovered, at 375°F for 15-20 minutes or until bubbly. Serves 6-8.

Mrs. James Welsh
(Bernice Puckett)

SHRIMP CREOLE

4 Tablespoons flour
5 Tablespoons shortening
1 large onion, chopped
6-8 green onions, chopped
1 small clove garlic, chopped
½ cup celery, chopped
¼ cup bell pepper, chopped
1 can (8 ounces) tomato sauce
1 can water
Salt, red and black pepper
1 Tablespoon Worcestershire sauce
1 teaspoon hot sauce
3-4 pounds raw shrimp, peeled, deveined

Add flour to shortening in preheated deep skillet or cooker kettle and cook on medium heat until a rich, dark brown, stirring constantly to prevent scorching. Add remaining ingredients, except shrimp, seasoning to taste. Simmer for 30 minutes, cover, bring to boiling point, and add shrimp. Cook for 15-20 minutes. Serve over steamed rice. Freezes. Serves 4-6.

Mrs. Allen J. Rhorer
(Mildred Hamilton)

SHRIMP CREOLE FOR A CROWD

5 pounds all purpose flour
1 gallon corn oil
9 cups onions, chopped
8 cloves garlic (optional)
7 cans (10 ounce size) Ro-tel tomatoes
3 cans (6 ounce size) tomato paste
5 gallons water
Salt and pepper to taste
30 pounds shrimp, cleaned and deveined
3 cups green onions, chopped

Brown flour in oil until tan (about 2½-3 hours). Add onions and garlic, and sauté until wilted, stirring constantly to avoid scorching or overbrowning. Add tomatoes, tomato paste, and 4 gallons of water (or more for desired consistency). Season to taste. When all ingredients are cooked, add shrimp and cook until tender. Add green onions 30 minutes before serving. Serve over hot rice. Serves 60-80.

A. Harold Mires
Sulphur, La.

SEAFOOD

SHRIMP ETOUFFÉE

¼ cup cooking oil
½ cup flour
1½ pounds raw shrimp, peeled
1 onion, finely chopped
½ cup green onions, chopped
2 cloves garlic, finely chopped
½ bell pepper, chopped
2 ribs celery, chopped
4-5 sprigs parsley, chopped
1 large tomato, peeled and finely chopped
Salt and red pepper to taste

Make a roux with the oil and flour. Cook only to a light brown color. Add remaining ingredients. Cover pot and cook over very low heat for 30-40 minutes, or until there is sufficient gravy and shrimp are done. Stir occasionally. Since no water is added, this dish must be cooked slowly to avoid sticking. Serves 6.

This makes a beautiful gravy! Serve over hot fluffy rice.

Mrs. Paul "Dud" Faulk
(Rena Lantz)

SHRIMP SAUCE PIQUANTE

1 cup onions, finely chopped
½ cup salad oil or bacon drippings
1 cup water
2 cloves garlic, finely chopped
1 cup celery, finely chopped
1 can (16 ounces) whole tomatoes
1 can (8 ounces) tomato sauce
1 teaspoon salt
¼ teaspoon each red and black pepper
2 pounds raw shrimp, peeled and deveined
3 thin slices lemon, quartered
¼ cup each parsley and green onion tops, finely chopped

In heavy iron pot, sauté onions in heated oil or drippings until light brown. Add water, garlic, and celery, cover, and cook until tender. Add tomatoes, tomato sauce, salt, and pepper and simmer, uncovered, 30-40 minutes until slightly thickened. Add shrimp and lemon slices, cover, and cook slowly 15 minutes. Just before serving, add parsley and green onion tops. Serve on hot rice. Serves 6.

VARIATION: This recipe is equally as good as a shrimp soup. Modify by adding 1 can (6 ounces) tomato paste, more water, salt, and pepper. Serve in soup bowls with hot rice.

Mrs. William E. Trimble
(Ann Courtney)

Camarón

SHRIMP AND CRAB CRÊPES ROSEMARY

CRÊPES

¾ cup pre-sifted flour
½ teaspoon salt
4 eggs, well beaten
2 cups milk
3 Tablespoons butter, melted
1 teaspoon bourbon

CRÊPES

Sift flour and salt into bowl. Add mixture of remaining ingredients and beat until smooth. Cover and refrigerate at least 1 hour. For each crêpe, pour 2 Tablespoons batter into a well greased, preheated 6-7 inch skillet. Rotate pan to spread. Cook until brown, turn, and brown other side. Makes about 16 crêpes.

First crêpe is usually not too pretty, but don't give up — from then on the pan seems to adjust to the batter nicely!

FILLING

1 can (4-6 ounces) mushrooms, drained, sliced lengthwise
2 Tablespoons onion, finely chopped
7 Tablespoons butter
½ cup regular all purpose flour
1 teaspoon rosemary leaves, crushed
½ teaspoon seasoned salt
Few grains pepper
1½ cups chicken broth
1½ cups dairy sour cream
1 Tablespoon parsley, snipped
1 pound crab meat
1 pound cooked shrimp, chopped
1 cup Swiss cheese, shredded
Paprika
Parsley sprigs
1½ cups avocado chunks (optional)

FILLING

Prepare crêpes in advance and keep warm, or prepare and freeze. In large saucepan cook mushrooms and onions in 1 Tablespoon heated butter until lightly browned. Remove mushrooms with slotted spoon and keep warm. Heat remaining butter in the same pan with the onions and blend in flour, rosemary, salt, and pepper. Gradually add broth, stirring constantly until smooth. Bring to boiling; stir and cook about 2 minutes. Remove from heat. Blend in sour cream in small amounts and mix in parsley, cooked mushrooms, crab meat, and shrimp.

Spoon about ¼ cup filling along center line of each crêpe and roll up. Arrange in single layer in shallow baking dish. Sprinkle with cheese and paprika.

Heat at 350°F for 10-15 minutes, or until cheese is melted and crêpes are heated thoroughly. Garnish with parsley sprigs.

If desired, gently mix 1½ cups avocado chunks into the filling sauce while preparing filling. Serves 8.

Mrs. Charles Mackey
(Gail Barré)

SHRIMP POMME DE TERRE

1½ pounds shrimp, peeled and deveined
2 Tablespoons Italian salad dressing
2 Tablespoons Worcestershire sauce
Garlic salt, salt, and pepper
Hot sauce
1 small bell pepper, finely chopped
1 large green onion, finely chopped
1 large rib celery, finely chopped
1 stick butter
2 cans mushroom soup
1 cup dry sherry
6 large white potatoes, peeled
Milk, salt, butter
1 cup Cheddar cheese, shredded
Paprika

Marinate shrimp in salad dressing, Worcestershire, garlic salt, salt, pepper, and hot sauce in refrigerator for 3 hours or overnight. Sauté vegetables in butter until soft. Add shrimp, saving the marinade, and simmer until pink. Stir in soup, marinade, sherry, and simmer for 15 minutes. Boil potatoes in salted water until done. Drain and mash, beating in milk, salt, and butter until fluffy. Line 9x12 inch glass baking dish around the edges with mashed potatoes. Fill center with shrimp mixture. Top with cheese and bake, uncovered, at 350°F until bubbly. Sprinkle with paprika and serve. May be made ahead of time and heated when needed.

Mrs. Steve F. Price

SHRIMP DE JONGHE

2 cups green onions with tops, finely chopped
2 small cloves garlic, chopped or crushed
1 cup butter or margarine
2 pounds raw shrimp, peeled
3 cups bread crumbs, very fine
1 teaspoon salt
¼ teaspoon freshly ground pepper
¼ teaspoon Worcestershire sauce

In a large skillet, sauté the green onions and garlic in butter until lightly browned. Add whole shrimp; cook 3 minutes, turning several times. Add bread crumbs and cook until browned, stirring constantly. Add seasonings. Serve hot on toast points or steamed white rice. May be prepared ahead of time and frozen. Serves 8.

Mrs. C. J. Lloyd
(Claire Fore)

SAN FRANCISCO SEAFOOD QUICHE

1 package of 2 frozen pie shells (9 inch)
1 package (6 ounces) frozen king crab meat, thawed and drained
1½ cups shrimp, cooked, peeled, deveined, and chopped (fresh or canned)
1 package (8 ounces) natural Swiss cheese, chopped
½ cup celery, finely chopped
½ cup green onions, finely chopped
1 cup mayonnaise
2 Tablespoons flour
1 cup dry white wine
4 eggs, slightly beaten

Preheat oven to 350°F. Separate frozen pie shells. Combine crab meat, shrimp, cheese, celery, and onions. Divide in 2 and pour into pie shells. Combine remaining ingredients. Divide and pour evenly over seafood in pie shells. Bake, uncovered, 35-40 minutes, or until a silver knife inserted into middle comes out clean. Serve immediately, or cool, cover and refrigerate. If refrigerated, bring to room temperature before reheating. Reheat, uncovered, at 300°F for 15 minutes. If quiche is to be frozen, do not bake before freezing. Cover with plastic wrap until hard; remove, wrap in foil, and return to freezer for indefinite storage. When ready to serve, remove foil and bake frozen pie, uncovered, in preheated 350°F oven for 50 minutes. Cut in wedges to serve. Each pie serves 4-5 as a main dish, 18-20 as an hors d'oeuvre. Other seafoods may be substituted.

Mrs. John D. Hines
(Jere James)

EASY SHRIMP CURRY

1 large onion, chopped
2 Tablespoons butter or margarine
3-4 pounds raw shrimp, peeled
1 large apple, chopped
1 cup raisins
2 Tablespoons curry powder
4 cans Campbell's cream of shrimp soup
1 can Campbell's cream of mushroom soup
CONDIMENTS
Chutney
Peanuts, chopped
Hard boiled eggs, chopped
Coconut flakes, toasted
Fried bacon, crumbled

Sauté onion in margarine until soft. Add shrimp and sauté until pink for 3-5 minutes, depending on size. Remove shrimp from pan. In same pan simmer apple and raisins until apple is tender. Mix curry powder with soups and add. Add shrimp and heat, but do not overcook. Serve over hot rice with any condiments desired. Freezes. Serves 10-12.

Mrs. Emile R. Winterhaler
(Millicent Watkins)

SZECHUAN SHRIMP

1 pound small shrimp, peeled, deveined
1½ Tablespoons cornstarch
1 egg white
¼ cup bamboo shoots, finely diced
½ cup green onions, tops and bottoms, finely chopped
¼ cup hot green pepper, chopped
½ teaspoon hot red pepper flakes
1 Tablespoon garlic, minced
1 Tablespoon fresh ginger, grated
½ cup chicken broth
5 Tablespoons tomato ketchup
¼ teaspoon monosodium glutamate (optional)
½ teaspoon soy sauce
2 Tablespoons dry sherry wine
½ teaspoon sesame oil
2 cups plus 2 Tablespoons peanut oil
Salt

Rinse shrimp in cold water and pat dry. Beat cornstarch into lightly beaten egg white. Add shrimp and stir to coat. Let stand 5 hours. Combine the bamboo shoots, green onions, hot pepper, pepper flakes, garlic, and ginger and set aside. Blend the chicken broth, ketchup, MSG, soy sauce, sherry, and sesame oil. Set aside. Have ready for use a small deep-fish fryer (or casserole) and a wok or skillet. In the deep fish fryer, heat 2 cups of oil to medium hot, but not too hot. Lower shrimp, in a sieve or small wire basket, into the oil and cook for about 1 minute, without browning. Lift sieve from oil. Next, cook the shrimp and the bamboo shoot mixture quickly in 2 Tablespoons of hot oil in the wok over high heat, stirring constantly. Add the ketchup mixture and cook quickly until shrimp are coated and piping hot. Add salt to taste and serve with rice. Serves 2-4.

Mrs. Thomas B. Shearman
(Flora Inglis)

SHRIMP STROGANOFF

2 onions, minced
1 stick margarine
1 pound raw shrimp, peeled
2 Tablespoons flour
1 teaspoon salt
¼ teaspoon red pepper
1 clove garlic, mashed
1 can (4 ounces) button mushrooms, drained
1 can cream of mushroom soup
1 cup sour cream
Hot rice
½ cup chives, chopped

Sauté onions in margarine until golden brown. Add shrimp and cook until pink. Stir in flour and mix well. Add salt, pepper, garlic, mushrooms, and soup. Simmer for 15-20 minutes. Add sour cream just before serving over hot rice. Garnish with chives. Serves 4-6.

Mrs. Preston L. Savoy
(Ethel Cole)

SHRIMP FLAMBÉ

¼ cup 101-proof Kentucky bourbon
2 Tablespoons soy sauce
4 Tablespoons oil
1 clove garlic, crushed
1 Tablespoon candied ginger, minced, *or* ¼ Tablespoon each powdered ginger and sugar
1 pound raw shrimp, peeled and deveined
White or brown rice

Combine 1 Tablespoon bourbon, soy sauce, 2 Tablespoons oil, garlic, and ginger. Pour over shrimp and let marinate 5-10 minutes. Heat remaining 2 Tablespoons oil in skillet or chafing dish and add shrimp mixture. Cook, stirring occasionally, for about 5 minutes, or until shrimp turn pink. Warm remainder of bourbon, ignite, pour over shrimp, and stir slowly until flame dies. Serve with freshly cooked hot white or brown rice. Serves 2 amply.

The trick is to use a high proof liquor and warm it in a ladle over a flame before igniting it.

Mrs. William E. Trimble
(Ann Courtney)

SHRIMP LOAF

½ cup water
½ stick margarine
½ cup bread crumbs taken from center of French bread loaf, stale
2 pounds raw shrimp, peeled
⅓ cup green onions, chopped
1 can (8 ounces) tomato sauce
½ teaspoon sugar
¼ cup oil
Garlic to taste
3 eggs, beaten
1 Jalapeño pepper, chopped

Heat water, add margarine and crumbs and mix well. Add remaining ingredients and seasonings to taste. Remove top of bread loaf and scoop out center with a fork, leaving a layer on the sides. Brush inside with butter, fill with dressing. Replace top, wrap in heavy foil, and place on center rack of oven (not in a pan). Bake at 450°F for 45 minutes. Open foil last 15 minutes. Slice loaf into servings.

Mrs. George Hardy Vincent
(Nina LaFleur)

SHRIMPARAGUS

2 cans (15 ounce size) all green asparagus spears
2 Tablespoons butter, melted
2 Tablespoons flour
½ teaspoon salt
¼ teaspoon white pepper
¾ teaspoon sugar
Red pepper to taste
1 cup light cream
1 can (4½ ounces) large shrimp, drained and rinsed (or equal amount fresh cooked shrimp)
1 teaspoon lemon juice
1 egg yolk, beaten
2 Tablespoons sherry
3 Tablespoons Swiss cheese, grated
2 Tablespoons Parmesan cheese, grated

Heat asparagus spears in medium saucepan. In separate pan, blend butter, flour, salt, peppers, and sugar. Gradually stir in cream. Cook over medium heat, stirring constantly until thickened and smooth. Reduce heat and add shrimp. Combine remaining ingredients in a bowl. Stir egg mixture into sauce and heat through. Do not boil. Arrange drained asparagus in oblong baking dish and cover with sauce. Heat, uncovered, at 400°F until hot. May be served on toast as main dish. Serves 6-8.

Mrs. George Hardy Vincent
(Nina LaFleur)

BLEND OF THE BAYOU SEAFOOD CASSEROLE

1 package (8 ounces) cream cheese
1 stick margarine or butter
1 pound shrimp, peeled
1 large onion, chopped
1 bell pepper, chopped
2 ribs celery, chopped
2 Tablespoons butter
1 can mushroom soup
1 can mushrooms, drained
1 Tablespoon garlic salt
1 teaspoon Tabasco
½ teaspoon red pepper
1 pint crab meat
¾ cup cooked rice
Sharp cheese, grated
Cracker crumbs

Melt cream cheese and butter using double boiler. Sauté shrimp, onion, pepper, and celery in 2 Tablespoons butter. Add to the first mixture. Add soup, mushrooms, seasonings, crab meat, and rice. Mix well, place in 2 quart casserole, and top with cheese and cracker crumbs. Bake at 350°F about 20-30 minutes until bubbly. Freezes. Serves 8.

Mrs. W. Edgar Percy, Jr.
Mrs. R. J. Pumpelly

SHRIMP AND EGGPLANT DRESSING

1-1½ pounds shrimp, cleaned, deveined
1 large or 2 small eggplants, peeled
1½ cups water to cook eggplant
1 onion, finely chopped
1 cup celery, chopped
1 stick butter
1 clove garlic, minced
Green onions, parsley, canned mushrooms to taste
4-5 slices bread (less if desired)
1 egg (optional)
Salt, red and black pepper
Cracker crumbs

Cut shrimp into small pieces. Peel eggplant. If shells are to be used for stuffing later, scoop out eggplant, cut into small chunks, and reserve shells. Simmer eggplant over low heat in water. Reserve liquid. Sauté onion and celery in butter and add shrimp. When shrimp become pink, add garlic, green onions, parsley, and mushrooms. Add eggplant to shrimp mixture. Soak bread in cooled liquid from eggplant until all is absorbed. (Add more bread if needed.) Combine shrimp and bread mixtures, using egg for adherence, if desired. Season to taste with salt and peppers, and mix well. Pour into greased baking dish or stuff eggplant shells. Top with cracker crumbs. Bake, uncovered, at 350°F for 45-60 minutes, or until bubbly around edges. Serves 4.

Mrs. James A. Hooper
(Mary Ann Leveque)

SHRIMP CORN BREAD STUFFING FOR FISH

½ cup each onion and celery, chopped
½ stick margarine
2 cups shrimp, parboiled and peeled
1½ cups water
½ teaspoon lemon juice
¼ cup bell pepper, chopped
1 can cream of mushroom soup
1½ cups shrimp stock
2 cups cooked corn bread
2 teaspoons salt
½ teaspoon pepper
¾ cup Cheddar cheese, grated
Dash of orégano

Wilt onion and celery in margarine. Parboil shrimp in water and lemon juice for 2 minutes. Drain, reserving stock. Mix onion, celery, bell pepper, soup, stock, shrimp, corn bread, salt, pepper, and ½ *cup* of cheese. Add orégano. Stuff fish. Pour remaining dressing into greased 1½ quart casserole. Sprinkle rest of cheese on top. Bake, covered, at 350°F for 45 minutes. Serves 6.

One cup raw rice may be used instead of the corn bread with chicken and rice soup for stock.

Mrs. Robert O. Boudreaux

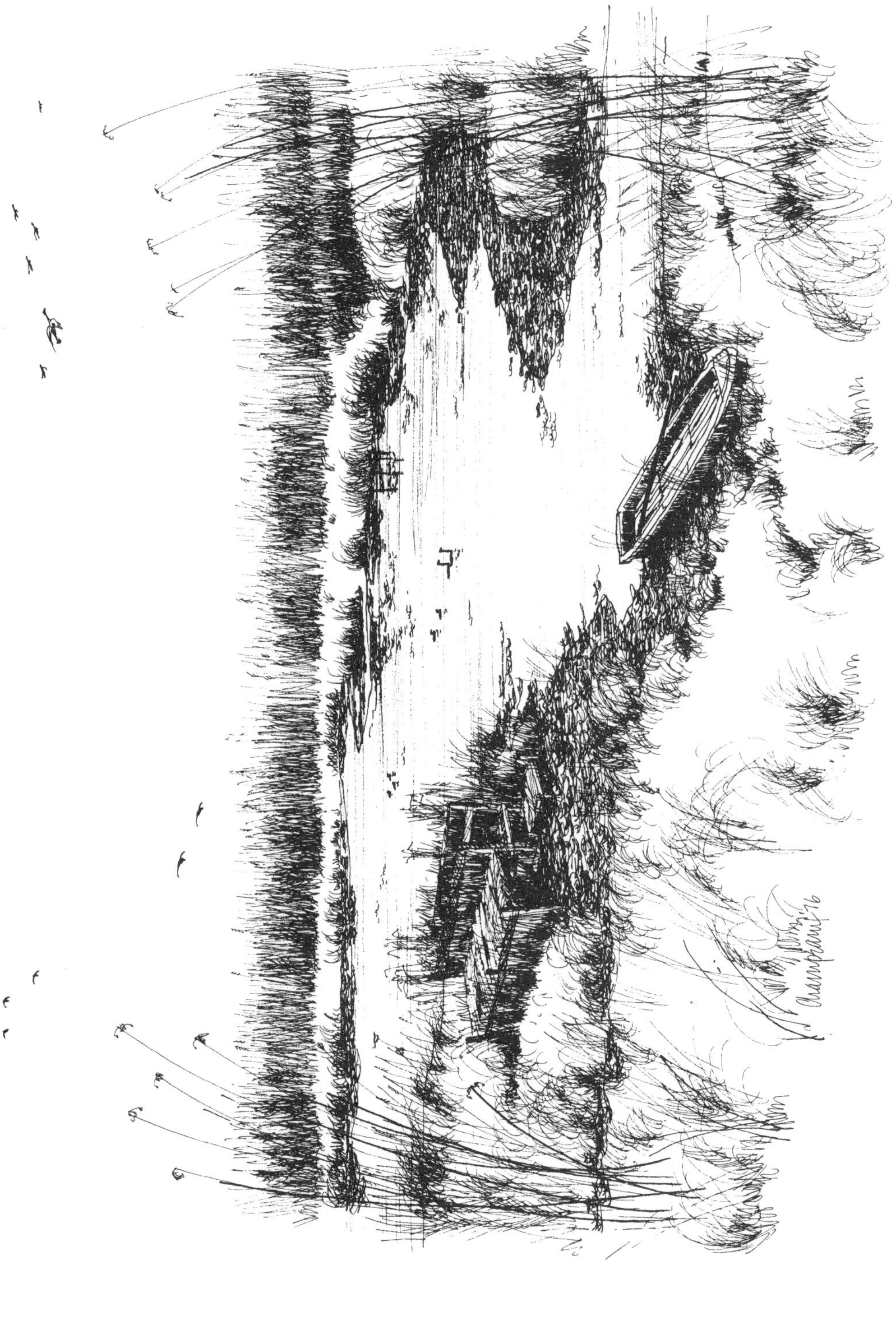

MARSHES AND DUCK BLIND

Louisiana hunters pushpole their flat-bottomed pirogues to well-concealed duck blinds deep in Southwest Louisiana's marshlands.

The playground of hunters and fishermen, Louisiana has nearly five million acres of marshland bordering its coastline and extending inward from 10 to 60 miles.

This vast treeless area of ponds and rhythmically swaying grasses provides the most extensive nursery and refuge for fish, crustaceans, and water fowl to be found anywhere on the North American continent.

In these wetlands over 100 species of fish either spawn or live, almost a third of all North American bird species either winter or permanently reside, and more than 170,000 alligators and millions of crawfish make their home.

Muskrats, blue and snow geese feed on the fat roots of the three cornered grasses in winter. Some 411 varieties of birdlife have been sighted in Louisiana, most in the southern bayou country. More than 96 species live in and near the marshes year round.

Area residents sometimes refer to the marshland as "la prairie tremblante," the trembling prairie.

Wildlife

CLEANING AND PREPARING WILDLIFE

Proper cleaning and care of deer, squirrels, rabbits, and game birds is the key to tasty meat. It is imperative, especially in warmer climates, that game animals be field dressed and cooled immediately upon killing to prevent spoilage. They should be skinned before day's end. After skinning large game, prop chest cavity open; pepper to repel flies, if it is to remain outside; place in a securely tied deer bag and hang in shade, transferring to a freezer locker as soon as possible. With smaller game, cool rapidly in an ice chest after cleaning and skinning. DO NOT wash large game after field dressing or skinning unless it is shot in the intestines. (The taste of clean killed, still hunted animals far exceeds that of either gut shot deer or those run by dogs.) If it is gut shot, wash immediately, remove all tainted meat, dry, generously sprinkle with pepper, and handle as described above. DO NOT haul game strapped on top of the car. DO NOT leave small game and birds uncleaned in warm weather.

To prepare deer for cooking or freezing, trim off tough outer membrane and remove all fat. Cooking of deer and small game is easy. Since there is little or no fat, lubricate with bacon or fat larded into meat. Cook slowly until tender. DO NOT cook deer beyond medium as further cooking will dry and toughen it.

DUCKS, DOVES, SNIPE, QUAIL, WOODCOCK, AND OTHER GAME BIRDS

Remove entrails and chill as soon as possible after killing. This reduces bacterial action, that adversely affects the taste, and prevents spoiling. However, if they are to be plucked with hot wax, chill without removing entrails.

PLUCKING DUCKS WITH WAX

Remove wings, but not the head. Melt paraffin in a pail in equal amount of boiling water. Fill a separate tub with iced water. Grasp ducks by the bill, dip into melted paraffin, then into iced water, and set them out until wax is cool. Split cooled wax coating and pull off in strips. Feathers will come off with it.

CLEANING DUCKS AFTER PLUCKING

Remove windpipe and entrails. Either remove the tail or the oil glands from it. Wash duck in baking soda and water until thoroughly clean. To freeze, chill in tub of iced water, remove head (which has been left on, according to law, for identification purposes), place in milk carton or other container, cover with iced water, tape tightly, label properly, and place in freezer, allowing enough space between cartons for quick freezing.

COOKING DUCKS AND GEESE

Teal, pintail, mallards, widgeon (in that order), and white fronted or "specklebellied" geese are good roasted or baked. A skinned duck should be pot roasted or used in gumbo or jambalaya, not baked.

Although the above listed ducks can be used for gumbo, ducks of inferior quality — gadwall "gray ducks", ring neck, scaup, spoonbills (if skin is not red) — serve as well. The red skinned duck is usually fishy tasting and should be discarded. Scaup, spoonbill, and gray ducks are better with skin and fat removed. Blue and snow geese, which are usually tough, are best in jambalaya or gumbo. Use properly cleaned hearts and gizzards in dirty rice and jambalaya. To clean gizzards the hard way, halve, remove inside sand, and peel off tough inside lining; the easy way, cut off and use tips only, discarding the middle $1/3$. The tips are tender and need no further cleaning.

William E. Shaddock
Lawrence Lowery, Jr.

Wildlife

POT ROASTED GAME
DOVE, QUAIL, SNIPE, DUCK, SQUIRREL, PHEASANT, OR RABBIT

Clean and prepare game. Cut up ducks, pheasant, squirrels, and rabbit like chicken. Split backs of dove, quail, and snipe.

The secret to good wild game cookery is in browning the meat! Make a seasoning mixture of salt, black pepper, red pepper, and garlic powder. Generously rub seasoning over entire surface of game and inside cavity. If thick gravy is desired, flour game. If natural French style gravy is desired, do not flour.

Cover the bottom of a very heavy pot with cooking oil. When hot, add game. Brown on all sides, turning often. Turn heat to medium; cover, and continue turning for about 30-40 minutes until entire surface is a succulent golden brown. If game starts to boil while browning with lid on, open lid slightly.

Now you may add a small chopped onion and a very little water, but this is not necessary. Cover tightly; reduce heat to low and continue cooking, adding a little water at a time until meat is very tender. Sprinkle with fresh minced parsley. Serve on hot rice.

Enjoyed from marshes to mansions!

Mrs. George Hardy Vincent
(Nina LaFleur)

BREAST OF DUCK AND DUCK WELLINGTON

6 ducks
Salt and pepper to taste
Onion, celery, and bacon as needed
1 cup good red wine (approximately)
¼ pound fresh mushrooms, sliced
3 Tablespoons butter
1 small onion, finely chopped
3 Tablespoons (or more) fresh parsley, chopped
¾ pound pork sausage
Liver and gizzards of ducks
1 teaspoon sage (approximately)
¼ pound cooked ham, shredded
2 Tablespoons blanched almonds or pistachio nuts, shredded (optional)
Deboned duck *(not* the whole breast)
1 egg, beaten
¼ cup sherry (approximately)
⅓ cup brandy (approximately)
Salt and pepper to taste
Bread crumbs (Pepperidge Farm herb seasoned stuffing)

PASTRY

4 cups all purpose flour
1 teaspoon salt
⅓ cup butter
½ cup shortening
1 egg, slightly beaten
¼ cup ice water (approximately)

Day before serving: Season ducks with salt and pepper. Place small piece of onion and celery in each cavity and a slice of bacon across breasts. Bake in roaster (or shallow pan) at 425°F for 20 minutes. Remove and add red wine. Cover, reduce heat to 300°F, and cook 1-1½ hours, or until tender. Cool and debone, removing duck breasts in whole sections, and reserving remaining meat on separate plate. Reserve stock.

Day of serving: Sauté mushrooms in ½ of butter. Remove, add onions and rest of butter, and cook until soft. Add parsley and remove from heat. Brown pork sausage quickly and save liquid. Cook livers and gizzards. Chop fine. Combine all with sage, ham, nuts, and deboned duck (not the breasts) and mix well. Add sherry and brandy to beaten egg, and mix with other ingredients after correcting seasoning. Add bread crumbs sparsely to achieve a consistency that shapes easily into a loaf. Add reserved stock if needed for more moisture. Cover and refrigerate all day or overnight.

Pastry: Mix flour, salt, butter, and shortening in a bowl and blend with fingers or pastry knife. Add egg and enough ice water to make a dough. Wrap in waxed paper and refrigerate for 2 hours or longer. (This may be done in advance on day of serving.) About 2 hours prior to cooking, roll out dough into a ¼ inch thick rectangle. Place duck mound in center and fold long sides up and overlap on bottom. Brush with beaten egg to seal. Trim ends of pastry and make an envelope fold, brushing with egg to seal. Place on baking sheet, cover, and refrigerate until ready to cook. The top of the Wellington may be decorated with remaining dough using cookie cutter and sealing with egg.

To cook: Preheat oven to 425°F. Brush entire surface with remaining egg and bake for about 30 minutes, or until brown.

To serve: Remove from oven, slice, and serve with heated duck breasts, toasted large mushrooms, and a good brandy and chicken stock gravy. Serves 10-12.

Mrs. Charles E. Schwing
Baton Rouge, Louisiana

BAKED WILD GOOSE OR DUCK

Goose or duck
Salt
½ apple
Wedge of onion
Strip of bacon
½ cup water
Flour

Salt inside of bird. Put apple and onion inside. Lay strip of bacon on breast. Bake, covered, at 500°F in roaster for 20 minutes. Add water and cover. Lower heat to 325°F. Bake duck for 2 hours; goose for 3 hours. Thicken drippings with flour for gravy.

Hunting camp specialty!

Mary Walters
Manhattan, Kansas

POT ROASTED STUFFED DUCK OR GOOSE

1 duck or goose
1½ medium onions, chopped
½ bell pepper, chopped
½ cup green onions, chopped
½ cup parsley, chopped
1 teaspoon black pepper
1 teaspoon salt
Garlic, if desired
1 cup cooking oil
2-3 cups water

Prepare duck. Slit top of breast, following breastbone to bottom, but not cutting through the bottom. Mix together next 7 ingredients and stuff alongside of breast. Place cooking oil in pot and brown duck, turning several times. When well browned, add 2-3 cups water. Cover and cook on medium heat 1½-2 hours, or until tender, adding more water if needed. This yields a good gravy.

Mrs. Clarence "Patin" Faulk
(Irene Croker)

Jack Kemmerly *adds chopped Jalapeño peppers and chopped bacon to the stuffing.*

THELMA'S STUFFED TEALS

1 teal per person
Salt and pepper
¼ cup each onions, bell pepper, celery, canned mushrooms, chopped (There will be an excess for 1 teal)
1 Tablespoon French's mustard
½ teaspoon Kitchen Bouquet
Margarine

Season teal with salt and pepper inside and out. Stuff with mixture of next 4 ingredients. Rub outside with mixture of French's mustard and Kitchen Bouquet. Place breast side down in baking dish with small amount of melted margarine. Place any remaining stuffing on sides of teal. Bake, covered, at 350°F until tender, or pot roast on top of stove. Make gravy with drippings.

Mrs. Eugene Fontenot
(Thelma Guillory)

IRON POT DUCK

2 mallards or pintails
Salt and pepper
½ cup Crisco
STUFFING
1 large bell pepper, chopped
2 large yellow onions, chopped
1 large apple or potato, chopped
3 generous Tablespoons ketchup
2 Tablespoons Worcestershire sauce
1 teaspoon red pepper
1½ teaspoons salt
2 teaspoons black pepper

Clean ducks well, seasoning outside liberally with salt and pepper. Mix stuffing ingredients together and stuff each duck. To hold stuffing inside, use toothpicks or steel rods to close cavity. Brown ducks in oil over medium heat in a large iron pot for about 40 minutes, or until brown on all sides. Add enough water to cover bottom ⅓ of duck. Cover and simmer until ducks are tender, 3-4 hours. Add water if necessary. Adjust seasonings. *Variation:* Add ½ cup red wine or small amount of flour to gravy to make a roux; then add more water, salt and pepper to taste. Does not freeze. Serves 6.

Why ketchup? It takes away the wild taste!

Mrs. Ray Hines
San Francisco, California

SHERRY SPICE DUCK OR GOOSE

2 ducks or 1 goose
2 Tablespoons olive oil
1 Tablespoon salt
½ teaspoon each pepper, orégano, and garlic powder
2 onions — 1 halved, 1 chopped
1 rib celery, halved
1 apple, halved
1 cup water
1 cup Taylor's cream sherry
¼ cup water
1 Tablespoon flour
½ teaspoon Kitchen Bouquet (for color)
3 Tablespoons green onions, chopped
3 Tablespoons parsley, chopped

Rub thawed ducks, inside and out, with olive oil and a mixture of salt, pepper, orégano, and garlic powder. In each duck cavity place ½ onion, celery, and apple. In large Dutch oven brown ducks, uncovered, in oven at 400°F for about 1 hour, or until brown. Put chopped second onion around ducks. Add water and sherry. Reduce heat to 350°F, cover, and cook until tender (goose, 3-3½ hours; ducks, 2½ hours). Baste and add more liquid if necessary. When ducks are done (tender when pricked with fork), make a paste with water, flour, and Kitchen Bouquet. Add this to drippings. Add green onions and parsley. Stir until blended and right consistency. Add more sherry if needed. Freezes. Serves 6.

I usually don't look for 2 hours; ducks stay moist when covered.

Mrs. Paul Comeaux
(Jane Landry)

WILD DUCK WITH OLIVE SAUCE

6 small ducks
3 small onions, halved
Salt
Water
½ cup vinegar
Red peppercorns or red pepper
¼ teaspoon thyme
¼ cup Worcestershire sauce
3 bay leaves
Salt and pepper
6 strips bacon
2 Tablespoons sugar
3 Tablespoons cornstarch
1 can (6 ounces) frozen orange juice concentrate
2 cups water
½ cup black olives, chopped

Clean ducks; put ½ onion inside each and salt generously inside and out. To tenderize, place ducks in a large pot half full of water, adding vinegar, peppercorns or red pepper, thyme, Worcestershire sauce, and bay leaves. Boil until tender, 15-30 minutes depending on size, but not falling apart. Remove ducks from vinegar solution and wash, removing onion. Arrange breast side down in deep roasting pan. Sprinkle with salt and pepper and put a strip of bacon on each duck. Mix sugar and cornstarch and blend in orange juice concentrate. Slowly add water, cooking over low heat until hot. Add olives. Pour over ducks. Bake, covered, at 350°F for about 1 hour, basting often. Does not freeze. Serves 4-6.

Mrs. M. A. Quilty, Jr.

WILD DUCK À LA CREOLE

3 wild ducks
Salt
Black and red pepper
Flour
2 cups green onions, chopped
2 cups parsley, chopped
Bread (optional)
Corn oil
1 Tablespoon flour

Clean ducks thoroughly. Season, roll in flour, and stuff with onions and parsley. Close cavity with a slice of bread (optional). Place ducks in hot oil in Dutch oven. Brown and lower heat. Remove excess oil. Add flour and stir constantly to make a roux, using a small amount of water if necessary. Cover and steam until tender, about 40-50 minutes. Remove onions and parsley; serve with steamed rice and old fashioned potato salad. Serves 6-8.

Mrs. J. Malcolm Leveque
(Marjorie Helen Schepp)

JIM'S BARBECUED DUCK

2 large ducks
1 clove garlic, quartered
Vinegar
Salt and pepper
1 bell pepper, halved
1 onion, halved
1 rib celery, cut in chunks
1 small bottle of Jack Miller's barbecue sauce or substitute

Clean ducks thoroughly. Slit both sides of breast and put ¼ clove of garlic in each side. Rub duck with vinegar, salt, and pepper. Stuff cavities with bell pepper, onion, and celery. Wrap tightly in foil and place in baking pan. Bake at 250°F for 7 hours. Open foil and add barbecue sauce. Rewrap and bake 1 more hour. Serves 4.

James H. Boyer

WILD DUCK LA FLEUR

1 medium or large wild duck
8 slivers of garlic (about size of grain of corn)
Salt
Red and black pepper
1 large turnip, peeled
3 slices bacon

Punch four holes in *each* side of the breast (down to the breastbone) and insert one sliver of garlic into each hole. Liberally apply salt, red and black pepper. Insert turnip into cavity of duck. Wrap each strip of bacon *completely* around the duck, so as to cover most of it. Trim raw edges of any jagged bones. Place duck in a sheet of heavy aluminum foil, wrapping carefully to make as airtight as possible, and raising ends to prevent drip. Avoid punching holes in foil. Place wrapped duck in pan and bake at 325°F for 3½ hours. Do not open foil for inspection. Serve in unopened foil, 1 duck per person.

Ernest G. LaFleur, Jr.

SPANISH WILD DUCK

Wild duck
Salt and pepper
White onions, sliced
Oil
Boiling water
1 white onion, chopped
1 bell pepper, chopped
1 clove garlic, chopped
½ cup celery, chopped
½ cup carrots, chopped
1 large can peeled tomatoes
Mushrooms, sliced
Stuffed olives, sliced
Rice, steamed

If duck is frozen and well cleaned, do not thaw. Season with salt and pepper, stuff with sliced onions, and brown in cast iron roaster. Add boiling water to the depth of ½ inch. Bake, covered, at 325°F for 1 hour. Pour off liquid to remove the wild flavor. Remove onions. Sauté in a 3 quart Dutch oven the onion, bell pepper, and garlic. Add celery, carrots, and tomatoes. Pour mixture over duck and bake, covered, at 350°F about 1½-2 hours until tender. About 5 minutes before serving, add mushrooms and olives. Serve sliced with tomato gravy over steamed rice. Freezes. Serves 4.

Mrs. Evelyn Chester Thompson

ORANGE GLAZED DUCK OR GOOSE

Duck or goose
Salt, black and red pepper, garlic powder
Red wine
2 slices of bread
Orange marmalade

Preheat oven to 350°F. Generously season duck or goose, inside and out. Stuff wine-soaked bread into cavity. Spread layer of marmalade on bird. Wrap tightly in heavy duty foil, avoiding puncture of foil with sharp bones. Place on cookie sheet in oven. Reduce heat to 275°F. Bake 1½ hours. Check for tenderness. Spread more marmalade on, and pour red wine over bird. Reseal and bake until meat pulls away from breast bone.

Mrs. George Hardy Vincent
(Nina LaFleur)

FRIED DUCK DELIGHT

4 ducks
Milk
1 egg, beaten
Salt and pepper
Flour
Oil for frying

Remove breast from duck and slice into bite sized pieces. Marinate in enough milk to cover for 2-3 hours. Drain. Measure 1 cup fresh milk. Add beaten egg, salt, and pepper. Dip duck into mixture, place in large plastic bag containing flour, and shake until well coated. Preheat oil and fry duck at 350°F until brown on both sides. Does not freeze.

Mrs. John E. Wood

Mrs. Fred A. Book, Jr.

APPLE-APRICOT GOOSE

1 young wild goose, thawed, 6-8 pounds
Salt and pepper
Juice of 1 lemon
¼ cup butter
¼ cup onion, chopped
1 cup tart apples, chopped
1 cup dried apricots, chopped
2 cups soft bread crumbs
½ teaspoon salt, or more, to taste
⅛ teaspoon pepper
4-6 slices bacon

Rub goose inside and out with salt, pepper, and lemon juice. Melt butter in large saucepan. Add onion and cook until tender. Stir in apple, apricots, bread crumbs, salt, and pepper. Put mixture inside goose. Cover goose with strips of bacon. Lay cheesecloth soaked in melted butter over goose. Roast at 325°F for 20-25 minutes per pound, or until tender.

Mary Walters

WILDLIFE

FRICASSEED GOOSE

1 goose, cut in small pieces
Salt and pepper
¼ cup bacon drippings
4-5 Tablespoons flour
¾ cup green onions, chopped
¼ cup bell pepper, chopped
¼ cup celery, chopped
Parsley, chopped
3 cups water
¼ cup red wine
¼ teaspoon Dr. Garber's hot sauce, p. 303
Pinch garlic salt
Pinch each of Lawry's seasoned salt and pepper

Season pieces of goose with salt and pepper and place in Dutch oven in heated bacon drippings. Remove goose when brown. Make a dark brown roux with flour. Sauté onions, bell pepper, celery, and parsley. Add goose, water, red wine, and hot sauce. Season to taste with last 3 ingredients. Cook, covered, about 2 hours at slow simmer or until meat is tender. Better if prepared ahead. Freezes. Serves 4-5.

Mrs. Courtney A. Fenet, Jr.
(Sally Garber)

GOOSE IN FOIL

1 wild speckled belly goose
2 winesap apples, quartered
Salt
Pepper
Kitchen Bouquet

Clean goose. Stuff cavity with apples. Salt and pepper, rub outside completely with Kitchen Bouquet. Wrap in heavy duty foil, making sure bones do not puncture foil. Bake at 350°F for approximately 1½-2 hours, or until tender. Serves 2-4.

Mrs. Guy Williams

LARDED GOOSE L'ORANGE

1 wild goose, 3-5 pounds
1 teaspoon salt
½ teaspoon black pepper
3 strips bacon
1 medium turnip, quartered
1 carrot, quartered
1 rib celery, cut in 2 inch pieces
1 medium seedless orange (grate the skin, then juice the orange)

Wash and pat goose dry. Sprinkle cavity with salt and pepper. With sharp knife carefully separate breast skin from breast. Cut 1 strip bacon in half crosswise and insert between skin and breast. Stuff cavity with turnip, carrot, and celery. Lay 2 pieces of bacon lengthwise on goose. Bake, uncovered, at 350°F for 1½ hours. Pour off juices into saucepan and add orange rind and juice. Baste goose liberally. Return goose to oven and bake another 1½ hours, or until tender, basting frequently. Serves 4.

Mrs. Richard E. Earle
(Georgia Baumgardner)

SMOKED WILD TURKEY

Wild turkey
Garlic
Onions
Butter, melted

Stuff breast with garlic and onions. Smoke on outdoor smoker, basting occasionally with melted butter. Cook approximately 45 minutes per pound with temperature not to exceed 250°F until tender. Wild turkey is tougher than domesticated and requires long, slow cooking.

If turkey has been grazing in areas of wild peppers, no pepper is needed for seasoning as it has its own "contraband" seasoning.

Lawrence Lowery, Jr.

TIPSY TURKEY

Wild turkey
SAUCE
2 cups Sauterne wine
1 cup soy sauce
1 cup Wesson oil
2 cloves garlic, crushed
Juice of 1 lemon

Two days before serving, begin injecting turkey with sauce, using a baster with an injector attachment. Continue injecting and basting top of turkey with sauce until ready to cook. Try not to make too many holes. The entire sauce recipe should be used by the time turkey is ready to bake. Place turkey into roasting bag and bake at 275-300°F until done.

Kay Rozell

QUAIL IN CREAM SAUCE

Salt and pepper
1 dozen quail
1 stick butter, melted
1 Tablespoon flour
1 large onion, finely chopped
½ cup bell pepper, finely chopped
¼ cup parsley, minced
1 can (8 ounces) mushrooms (reserving liquid)
1 cup table cream
¼ cup white wine
1 chicken bouillon cube

Salt and pepper birds. Brown in butter in skillet or Dutch oven on medium heat. Remove birds and place in casserole. To remaining butter, add flour, onion, and bell pepper; cover and cook slowly on low heat until onions are transparent. Add remaining ingredients, pour over birds, and bake, uncovered, at 350°F for 1 hour, or until tender. Baste twice. If gravy appears too thick, add reserved mushroom liquid. Quail are cooked when fork easily enters breast. Serve on toast or buttered noodles. Serves 6 men or 12 ladies.

From the recipes of
Mrs. Marie Bonin

QUAIL-RICE MAGNIFIQUE

4 quail, ready to cook
4 Tablespoons butter
½ teaspoon salt
Dash black and red pepper
1 cup carrot, shredded
½ cup green onion, sliced
½ cup parsley, chopped
1 cup long grain rice, raw
3 cups chicken broth
Dash Tabasco
2 slices bacon, quartered

In skillet brown birds in butter after liberally seasoning them with salt and pepper. Remove and set aside. In same skillet cook carrot, onion, and parsley until tender, stirring frequently. Add rice and stir until well mixed; add chicken broth, salt, peppers, and Tabasco. Pour mixture into greased oblong casserole and top with quail. Sprinkle with additional salt and pepper if needed and place bacon atop each quail. Cover and cook at 325°F for 1-1¼ hours, or until tender. Remove bacon slices to serve. This same recipe may be used with doves or chicken breasts.

Mrs. J. Braxton Blake
Cameron, Louisiana

BACON BAKED QUAIL

Quail
Salt
Pepper
Butter
Bacon

Prepare and season quail with salt and pepper. Place lump of butter in cavity of each bird. Wrap a strip of bacon around each bird and pin together with a toothpick. Put a little butter on top of each bird after placing them in baking dish. Add small amount of water, cover, and bake at 350°F for 2 hours or until tender. This recipe is complemented by steamed new potatoes and parsley.

From the recipes of
Mrs. J. W. Allen

PHEASANT CASSEROLE

2 pheasants, deboned
1 pound fresh mushrooms, sliced
1 bell pepper, sliced
1½ sticks butter
2 tomatoes, sliced
SAUCE
1½ sticks butter
1 medium sized bottle Heinz 57 Savory Sauce
½ pint whipping cream

Layer pheasant, mushrooms, and bell pepper in deep casserole. Combine sauce ingredients in saucepan. Heat on low, pour into casserole. Bake, uncovered, at 350°F for 1 hour. Place sliced tomatoes on top of mixture and bake about 15 more minutes. Serve over rice. Serves 6.

Mrs. Robert Foster
Sioux Falls, South Dakota

CHEZ OCA'S PHEASANT IN BRANDY SAUCE

6 small pheasants (1 pound each)
Salt and pepper to taste
½ cup butter
2 carrots
2 bay leaves
2 ribs celery
2 cloves garlic
1 medium onion
6 peppercorns
12 parsley stalks
Pinch thyme
3 ounces brandy
1 pint chicken stock

Preheat oven to 450°F. Season birds with salt and pepper and seal with butter. Place in a pan over a bed of root vegetables with the brandy and stock, covering the bottom ⅓ of birds. Cook in oven, uncovered, until browned; then lower temperature to 350°F and cover. This slow cooking process may take about 1½ hours. Remove birds and thicken sauce with a little roux. Strain roux over birds and garnish, if desired, with sautéed mushrooms, diced sautéed ham or bacon, and small button onions. Serves 6.

Master Chef Escoffier said that the meat of a fresh pheasant and that of a high one are totally different things; whatever opinion may be held in regard to the gaminess of birds that live reasonably high, it is tender, full of taste, and of incomparable flavor. In general, sautéed and deep fried pheasant are always dry. The best way of cooking it is what we call, in American culinary terms, pot roasting. This means to seal it with clarified butter on top of the stove and to finish cooking it in an earthenware container with a hermetically sealed lid.

Fernando Oca
Chez Oca Restaurant
Lake Charles, Louisiana

SMOTHERED DOVES

12 wild doves
Salt and pepper
Flour
3 Tablespoons oil
2 slices bacon, raw
1 medium onion, sliced
2 teaspoons Lea & Perrins
½ teaspoon ground thyme
1½ cups water

Season doves with salt and pepper; dredge in flour. In deep skillet brown in oil on all sides. Add bacon, diced in ½ inch pieces, and all other ingredients. Cover and simmer on low heat until tender, about 1 hour. Serve over crisp toast points. Serves 4.

Mrs. D. E. Wheeler
(Virginia Lamkin)

DOVES IN WINE
(Quail or Snipe)

Salt and pepper
Onion powder
Seasoned salt (optional)
6 doves
Garlic powder
Cayenne pepper
½ cup flour, approximately
2 Tablespoons bacon drippings or oil
1 bunch green onions, chopped
½ cup celery, chopped
1 medium white onion, chopped
¼ bell pepper, chopped (optional)
1 Tablespoon parsley, chopped
1 cup wine or cooking sherry
1 cup water

Generously sprinkle first 4 seasonings inside and outside of doves. Lightly sprinkle garlic powder and cayenne. Roll in flour and brown in bacon drippings over medium heat in iron pot. Remove doves; add next 5 ingredients, and sauté. Add wine and water, stirring constantly. Replace doves; cook, covered, about 2 hours, or until tender. Turn periodically and add water when necessary. To enhance the flavor, add ¼ cup wine about 15 minutes before serving. Serves 2.

Mrs. Kenneth W. Wimberly
(Carol Breeches)

DOVE PIE

4 slices bacon, quartered
8 doves
3 Tablespoons flour
1⅓ cups water
1 large onion, chopped
1 small can mushrooms (stems and pieces)
Salt and pepper
TOPPING
1 cup flour
1 teaspoon baking powder
½ teaspoon salt
½ cup Crisco
⅓ cup milk

In Dutch oven fry bacon until crisp. Remove bacon and brown birds in grease. Remove birds and add flour to drippings left in pan. Stir until smooth and light brown. Make gravy by adding water. Return birds and bacon. Add onions and mushrooms, and season to taste. Cover and simmer, adding water if necessary, until birds are tender — 1-1½ hours. Place in baking dish and cover with topping. Prepare topping by stirring ingredients together until smooth. Knead several times on floured board. Roll out to about ⅛ inch thick and arrange to fit baking dish. Bake, uncovered, at 425°F for 20 minutes, or until brown on top. Serves 4.

Could also use "four and twenty" blackbirds baked in the pie.

Anne Berniard

BAKED DOVE MARTIN

Dove
Garlic salt
Salt and pepper
Bacon
Worcestershire sauce
Lemon juice

Sprinkle inside and out with garlic salt, salt, and pepper. Wrap with ½ slice bacon and secure with toothpick. Baste with 2 parts Worcestershire to 1 part lemon juice. Bake, covered, at 325°F for 1 hour, or until tender, basting regularly. Let brown last 15 minutes at 350°F.

Mrs. Edward G. Martin
(Hazel Bryant)

RABBIT SAUCE PIQUANTE

1 rabbit, cut in pieces
¼ cup wine
½ teaspoon celery salt
¼ cup oil
2 cups onion, chopped
½ can tomatoes
½ can Ro-tel tomatoes
2 cloves garlic, minced
1 cup water
1 teaspoon salt
½ bunch green onion tops, chopped
¼ cup parsley, minced

Soak rabbit overnight in mixture of wine and celery salt. Remove from marinade and drain. Save marinade. Brown rabbit in hot oil in a 4 quart heavy Dutch oven. Remove each piece as it is browned. In same oil brown onions until dark. Add tomatoes and Ro-tel tomatoes. Continue stirring until dark. Add marinade, garlic, and water. Let cook over low heat until oil rises to top. Add rabbit pieces and salt. Cover and cook slowly until rabbit is tender, usually 2 hours. Just before serving, add green onion tops and parsley. Serve over hot fluffy rice. Freezes. Serves 4-6.

Mary Abate

DRUNK SQUIRREL

Salt and pepper to taste
Flour
3 squirrels, cut in pieces
Cooking oil
2 cans beer
Comino (cumin)

Salt, pepper, and flour squirrel as for frying chicken. Fry in deep hot oil until brown. Drain on paper towels. Place in casserole, pour beer over, and sprinkle with comino. Bake, covered, at 300°F for at least 2 hours until tender. Freezes. Serves 4.

You'll never have a tough squirrel with this recipe, and the beer gravy is out of this world. This method may also be used on doves if you're not sure they are young and tender.

Mrs. Jake W. Posey
(Jerry Anderson)

"GATOR" MEAT BALLS

5¼ pounds alligator meat
1½ pounds dry onions
2 bunches green onions
2 bunches parsley
1 bulb garlic
¼ bunch celery
1 cup cooking oil
2¼ pounds mashed potatoes
2½ pounds cracker meal
8 eggs
3 ounces Nugget Savory Seasoning
2 ounces salt
1 ounce black pepper

Grind first 6 ingredients together. Cook in oil for 30 minutes. Add last 6 ingredients. Mix well, chill, and shape into 1 ounce balls. Roll in cracker meal and fry in deep fat. Yields 13 pounds. Makes 208 (1 ounce) balls.

Need to come SOUTH for a 'Gator!

Joseph Guidry
Sulphur, Louisiana

FRIED ALLIGATOR

Alligator
White vinegar or lemon juice
Salt
Red pepper
2 cups corn meal
½ cup flour
Shortening

Thinly slice alligator (¼ inch thick and 4 inches long). Remove all white fatty tissue. Place alligator slices in glass bowl and cover with vinegar or lemon juice, salt, and red pepper. Soak ½ hour (no more). Roll slices in corn meal and flour seasoned with red pepper. Fry in hot grease in iron pot or deep fat fryer until golden brown (about 5 minutes). Eat while warm.

Delicious as hors d'oeuvres or main dish!

Mrs. Robert Doland
(Cheryl Grimm)

DEER SKINNING IN 5 MINUTES

After field-dressing deer, cut through the skin from chest cavity to head. Then make incision across top of head in front of ears in a circle with ends meeting at original incision. Pull back ears and head skins down to neck. Attach strong nylon rope to neck above skin and hang deer to strong tree limb so that it does not touch ground. Place sheet or tarpaulin on ground under deer extending several feet toward direction to be pulled. With a slip knot tie small strong nylon line around head skin under ears and attach other end to motorized vehicle. Saw off forelegs at joints and hind legs just *below* joints. Make incision through front skin of each leg from body to point of severance. Drive vehicle slowly but steadily away from deer. The skin will peel off leaving almost no hair or glandular oils on meat. Remove tail bone. Sprinkle liberally with black pepper while carcass is moist; prop chest cavity open with stick; and place deer in deer bag being certain to cover mouth.

CAUTION! Use extreme caution. If neck or backbone is severed, deer may fall — hence the ground cloth.

William E. Shaddock

VENISON CHATEAUBRIAND

2 pounds venison backstrap
1 stick butter or margarine
2 teaspoons garlic powder
2 teaspoons celery salt
1 package (16 ounces) Philadelphia cream cheese
2 Tablespoons Maggi or Worcestershire sauce
¼ cup dry sherry or rosé wine (optional)
1 jigger of brandy

Preheat oven to 350°F. Remove all fat on venison. Melt butter (saving 2 Tablespoons) and add garlic powder and celery salt. Put venison in oblong cake pan and pour melted seasoned butter and Maggi sauce over meat. Bake, uncovered, for 30 minutes. Turn while cooking. While venison is baking, place the reserved butter in a large skillet. Add cream cheese and mash with a spatula over medium heat for 20 minutes, or until mixture becomes a thick gravy. Add wine and cook another 10 minutes. **IMPORTANT:** Carefully watch gravy to prevent burning. Remove backstrap from oven and cut into ½ inch steaks. Pour juices from venison into gravy and mix. Add venison and cook another 5 minutes. If wine was omitted earlier, 1 jigger of brandy may be added at this time, ignited and served flaming at the table. Serve over noodles tossed in butter, parsley, and Parmesan cheese. Does not freeze. Serves 4.

Very definitely a gourmet dish. Very rich.

Don Siebarth

CHARCOALED VENISON ROAST

1 venison roast
Bacon, sliced crosswise in ¼ inch strips
Garlic, thinly sliced
Seasoned salt
1 cup wine vinegar
3 cups water
1 onion, chopped
1 Tablespoon peppercorns
3 red peppers
1 teaspoon cloves
2 ribs celery, chopped

With a sharp knife make slits in the roast and stuff with bacon and garlic. Liberally salt with seasoned salt. Mix remaining ingredients. Pour over roast in an enamel or glass pan or plastic bag. Secure the bag opening tightly and marinate 8-12 hours, turning frequently. Remove from the marinade and dry well. Brown well over a charcoal fire, insert a meat thermometer, cover, and cook slowly until desired doneness. If fire goes out, finish in oven at 350°F. Place bacon strips over meat as it cooks for a juicier roast. Serve with wild rice and hot pepper jelly.

Remember, marinated meat takes less time to cook!

Mrs. Patrick J. Unkel
(Barbara Perez)

JELLY GLAZED VENISON ROAST

Venison roast, 9 pounds
Salt to taste
Red pepper to taste
Garlic salt to taste
2 Tablespoons olive oil
1½ cups sherry or wine vinegar
4-6 strips of bacon, raw
Grease from bacon
1 Tablespoon flour
¼ cup water
3-4 Tablespoons currant jelly

THE NIGHT BEFORE COOKING, trim the meat well. Make holes for seasoning, and season with salt, red pepper, and garlic salt. Make slits crosswise in meat and rub with olive oil. Pour ½ cup sherry or wine vinegar over roast. **ON DAY OF COOKING,** cover meat with bacon strips and place on rack. Bake, uncovered, at 250°F for *40 minutes per pound* (9 pound roast, 6 hours). Using bacon grease and ½ cup sherry, baste often. One hour before serving (not included in baking time), remove meat from pan. Skim off as much fat as possible from the basting sauce. Mix the flour and water together and stir in with the sauce to form the gravy. Then add 2 Tablespoons of the jelly to the gravy and mix well. Replace meat in pan with the gravy. Pour ½ cup sherry over roast and dot with remaining jelly. Continue cooking at 275°F about 1 hour, basting with gravy. Let sit a few minutes before carving. Do not let roast cook too long. It is better to undercook than overcook. Serves 8.

Daphne and Jack Knapp

VENISON CHILI

4 pounds ground venison (may be frozen)
5 large white onions, chopped
2½ quarts water
5 cans (8 ounce size) tomato sauce
3 ounces chili blend seasoning mixture
6 ounces chili powder
3 cans (15½ ounce size) chili beans
2 squares (1 ounce size) unsweetened chocolate
Salt and red pepper to taste

In large pot cook meat and onion in water until tender. Add tomato sauce, chili seasoning, and chili powder. Cook 2 hours on medium to low heat, allowing chili to slightly bubble. Add beans and chocolate squares 30 minutes before serving. Season to taste. Serving suggestion: Place Fritos or Doritos in a large bowl. Top with chili, chopped onions, and grated cheese.

No wild venison taste! Do not let ingredients scare you!

Paula Carlin
Sulphur, Louisiana

VENISON SAUSAGE

5 pounds venison
2½ pounds lean pork
2 pounds fatty pork
6 Tablespoons salt
5 Tablespoons black pepper
3 teaspoons red pepper
3 Tablespoons monosodium glutamate or Accent
Sausage casings

Grind venison and shape into large thin patties on a table. Grind lean and fatty pork together, make into patties, and place on top of venison patties. Mix seasoning in a jar and shake well. Sprinkle ¾ of seasoning as evenly as possible over patties. Work seasoned patties with hands for several minutes to evenly distribute the ingredients. Fry small patty to test seasoning and adjust if desired. For breakfast sausage, if it will be consumed within a month or 2, add honey to that portion of seasoned meat to be made into patties. Use enough honey to flavor without getting it too watery. For sausage kept longer than 2 months, buy sausage casings. Rinse casings in water to remove salt, slip onto sausage press spout, and make into link sausage. This usually takes 2 people — 1 to turn the sausage press (or meat grinder with sausage spout attachment) and 1 to guide the sausage into 1 foot links as it leaves the press. Freeze. Before cooking, puncture links several times with a fork. Sausage may be smoked, fried, or barbecued.

William E. Shaddock

FRIED VENISON LOIN

2 large onions, peeled, thinly sliced
Cooking oil for deep fat frying
1 venison loin (12-14 inches long), sliced into ⅛ inch thick "rounds"
1 cup flour
1 Tablespoon red pepper
1 Tablespoon paprika

Place onions in heavy, covered, 1 quart casserole preheated to 120-150°F and set aside, keeping warm. Heat cooking oil until almost smoking. Shake venison "rounds" in paper bag with flour, red pepper, and paprika. Drop a few at a time into hot oil. Cook until "rounds" float to top or until done to preference, about 1 minute. They should be tender, juicy, and pink. Drain briefly on paper towels, and transfer to casserole of onions. Let stand for about 15 minutes before serving. The raw onions will flavor the venison beautifully (and vice versa, if you like raw onions). Excellent with cheese grits or spoon bread and mustard. Serves 2-3.

Mrs. Benjamin English
(Margaret Whittle)

COUNTRY STYLE VENISON STEAK

Deer steak
Flour
Salt
Red pepper
Black pepper
Cooking oil
1 large onion, chopped
2 Tablespoons flour

Roll deer steak in flour that has been seasoned with salt, red and black pepper to taste. Fry meat in cooking oil until well done. While meat is cooking, sauté onion in a small amount of oil in a covered, large iron pot. Put meat aside, and pour off all but a small amount of grease. Brown 2 Tablespoons flour in the grease, stirring constantly. Add enough water to make soupy and pour this into the sautéed onions. Add enough water to make a gravy and then add the meat. Cover and let simmer 45-60 minutes, or until meat is tender. Add more water gradually, if needed, as gravy cooks down.

Don't judge a deer by only his rack!

Dan Blalock

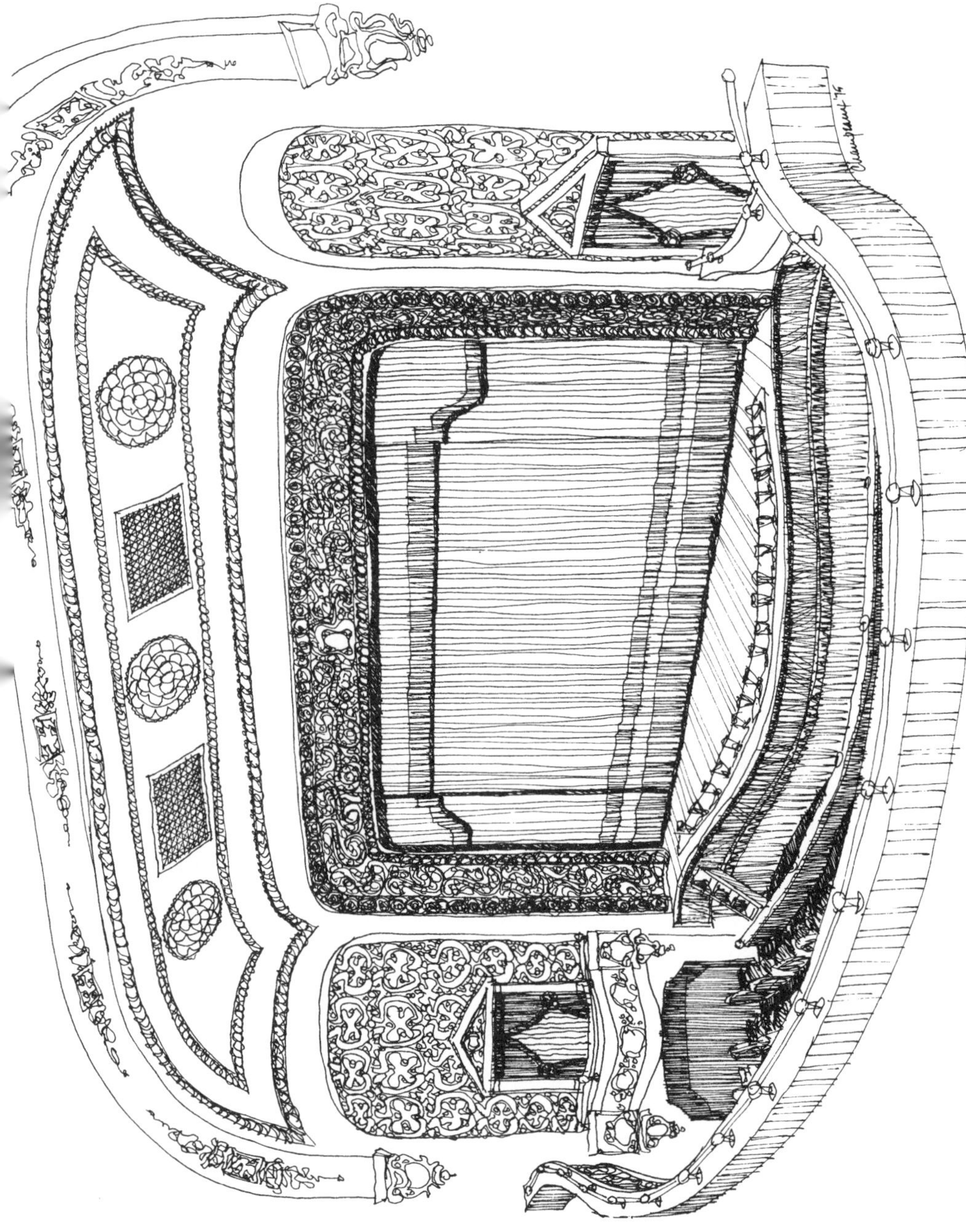

ARCADE THEATRE

Cupids and cornucopias decorated the intricately carved proscenium arch of the elegant old Arcade Theatre, once the show-place of Southwest Louisiana. Lion heads, rose garlands, and elaborate rococo motifs marked the first and second balcony rails, topped by columns with Ionic capitals.

The old theatre, which stood in the 800 block of Ryan Street, had a 50-foot stage loft and near-perfect acoustics. Its opulence was a reflection of the golden era of theatre, when the best of vaudeville, music, and drama came to the Lake Charles area.

Erected by J. L. White in 1910, after the old Williams Opera House was condemned as unsafe, it opened on September 26 with the season's gala event: Sidney Drew starring in the comedy, "Billy."

In the years to follow, audiences stirred to the rousing marches of John Phillip Sousa; thrilled to Ethel Barrymore in "The Love Duel" and Dustin Farnum in "The Virginian." They saw Isadora Duncan dance; heard Rudolph Ganz and the St. Louis Symphony; and enjoyed the first of the silent classics, D. W. Griffith's "Birth of a Nation."

This tradition was to continue for 75 years. But with the advent of television and the decline of theatre, the Arcade fell into disrepair. However, the community rallied to its support, and it was placed on the National Register of Historic Places on July 7, 1978. Although restoration efforts had begun in 1979, they were never completed. The theatre was destroyed by fire on Thanksgiving night, November 28, 1985.

It was an ironic ending for a place which had served not only as the city's entertainment center, but as a community meeting place for such events as city-wide Thanksgiving services, high school graduations, dance reviews, and amateur theatre productions. The flames were the final curtain for the old theatre, a long-standing landmark of a by-gone age.

COWBOY KICKER

5 parts milk
1 part vodka
3 parts Irish Mist
2 parts Kahlua
6 parts Coca Cola

Mix all ingredients and serve over ice. Ingredients may be mixed in a blender with crushed ice if so desired.

For a less potent drink use 7 instead 6 parts Coca Cola.

McNeese Cowboys———Fight!

Monte Hurley

THE GREEN WAVE

Crushed ice
6 ounces gin
3 ounces frozen limeade (no water)
Juice of 1 lemon
Juice of 1 lime
10 leaves fresh mint

Fill blender with crushed ice. Add all ingredients. Blend well.

Give a Hullabaloo — Rah — Rah, and consume!

Mrs. Robert J. Boudreau
(Margaret Field)

TIGER'S TAIL

1½ ounces tequila
2 ounces orange juice
Juice of ½ lemon
1 teaspoon orange flower water
1 teaspoon simple syrup, p. 106

Shake in cocktail shaker with crushed ice. Serve in double old-fashioned glass. Serves one.

Gooooo Ti———gers!!!

Dr. F. W. Raggio, Jr.

SUGAR OR SIMPLE SYRUP

1 cup sugar
1 cup water

Mix ingredients in pot; bring to a boil and boil 1 minute or until sugar is completely dissolved. Pour into bottles, cap, and place in refrigerator. Keeps indefinitely.

This is the basis for many drinks.

Karl Boellert

BLINI

1 ripe peach, peeled, pitted, and chopped
½ bottle (1/5) non vintage champagne, chilled
1 jigger peach brandy

Mix all ingredients in blender until peach is puréed. Serve in champagne glass. Serves 4.

This is an altered version of the Blini served at Harry's Bar in Venice, a popular rendezvous spot for the international jet set.

Edward M. Carmouche

BLOODY MARY

1 large can Libby's tomato juice
Juice of 4 lemons, strained
4-6 heaping Tablespoons Lea & Perrins
Salt to taste
Small pinch red pepper and black pepper as desired
Pinch of sugar
Vodka

Mix all ingredients except vodka in a large jar. Place in refrigerator until ready to serve. Will keep indefinitely. When preparing a Bloody Mary, fill glass with ice; add 1-2 ounces vodka and fill with tomato juice mixture.

Mrs. Gray Little

BLOODY MARY BY THE GALLON

2 cans (46 ounce size) tomato juice
3 Tablespoons horseradish
Juice of 1 lemon
4 Tablespoons Worcestershire sauce
Tabasco
Salt and pepper to taste
Vodka

Mix, in gallon plastic jug with top, 24 hours in advance. Taste and adjust seasoning, if needed. Keeps in refrigerator for a week without vodka. Just before serving time add 1/5 vodka and shake well. Pour in a large pitcher to serve; place celery or carrot stick in each glass. Makes 32 drinks.

David Painter

CHERRY BOUNCE

Wild Louisiana cherries
Vodka
Simple syrup

Pick and wash wild Louisiana cherries. Cover with vodka. Put in jars and forget it for a minimum of 6 months! Strain and sweeten with simple syrup to taste.

Nothing in the world like it!

Mrs. W. E. Gorham, Sr.
(Mary Tucker)

DAIQUIRI OLD-FASHIONED

2 ounces gold or dark (as distinguished from light) rum
1 heaping teaspoon sugar
2-3 dashes Angostura bitters
⅓ lime

Chill rum and a 5-7 ounce old-fashioned glass. Place sugar and bitters in glass and stir. Slice lime, place in glass and twist thoroughly to release "zest" from peel and juice. Rub peel against sides of glass. Leave peel and juice in glass. Fill glass about ⅔ full with cracked ice. Add rum and stir slowly until thoroughly chilled. Serves 1.

Frank M. Brame

BANANA DAIQUIRI

3 medium or 2 large ripe bananas
½ can frozen lemon juice
6 jiggers rum
1 small refrigerator tray of ice

Place bananas, frozen lemon juice, and rum in blender. Blend until mixed. Add ice, a small amount at a time if not precrushed. Makes a full blender of daiquiris. Serves 6.

Mrs. Edith C. Viccellio

STRAWBERRY DAIQUIRI

1 can frozen lemonade, thawed
1 small package frozen strawberries, thawed
1½ lemonade cans rum
Crushed ice

Place all ingredients in blender. Blend well and serve in chilled glasses.

Mrs. James McInnis
(Judy Coe)

EGGNOG

6 eggs, separated
¾ cup bourbon
¾ cup sugar
1 pint whipping cream, whipped
Nutmeg

Separate eggs when cold. Beat egg yolks. Add bourbon slowly to yolks, beating continuously. Refrigerate. Let egg whites warm to room temperature. Beat whites, adding sugar 2 Tablespoons at a time. Fold cream, egg yolks, and bourbon into beaten whites. Sprinkle with nutmeg. Serve in sherbet dishes. Serves 6.

Mrs. Walter House
Mrs. Nellie C. Cagle

MILK PUNCH

Ice
1 rounded teaspoon sugar
⅛ teaspoon vanilla
6 jiggers bourbon
2 jiggers dark rum
2 jiggers Kahlua
Milk
Nutmeg

Fill blender with ice to 1 inch from top. Add other ingredients in order except nutmeg, filling blender only to 1 inch from top. Put lid on and blend until ice is fine. Let sit a few minutes before pouring. Sprinkle nutmeg on top of each serving. Serves 6.

Jim Watson

NEW ORLEANS MINT JULEP

Fresh mint
1 bottle (1/5) sour mash bourbon (preferably Jack Daniels or Ezra Brooks)
1½ cups sugar or less

Early in the day to be used, fill pyrex bowl with 2-3 inches of fresh mint. Mash mint with fork. Pour bourbon over it. Add sugar. Stir and cover. Refrigerate for 8 hours. Strain over ice into julep cups or frosted glasses and garnish with cherry and sprig of fresh mint. Serves 8-10.

Mrs. Karl E. Boellert
(Kathleen Martin)

OLD-FASHIONED

2 dashes Angostura bitters
1 jigger sugar (or simple) syrup
2 jiggers bourbon
1 teaspoon cherry juice
Crushed or chipped ice
1 orange slice

In each glass mix first 4 ingredients. Add crushed ice. Stir and serve garnished with orange slice.

Charles M. Milburn

ORANGE ODYSSEY

Dash of rum — Myers
Dash of egg white
½ ounce Falernum*
1 ounce vodka
2 ounces orange juice
½ teaspoon simple syrup, p. 106
Crushed ice

Mix in blender. Serves 1.

Edward M. Carmouche

*Distributed by The Sazerac Company of New Orleans.

PINK SQUIRREL

½ ounce white crème de cacao
½ ounce light cream
½ ounce crème de noyau
Cracked ice

Shake all ingredients well and strain into 3 ounce cocktail glass. Serves 1.

Mrs. Thomas L. Raggio
(Beverly Barry Crook)

RAMOS GIN FIZZ

1-2 cups crushed ice
1 egg white
1 Tablespoon confectioners sugar
Dash vanilla
3 dashes orange flower water
2 ounces half and half
1 ounce lemon juice
2 ounces gin

Place crushed ice and remaining ingredients in shaker. Shake. (Blender may be used instead of shaker.) Serves 1.

A very old New Orleans recipe.

Britt Armstrong

"MISS TOP'S" RUM COCKTAIL

1 large can (46 ounces) pineapple juice
1½ cups lemon juice
Fifth of rum
Grenadine

Mix first 3 ingredients. Add small amount of grenadine for color and to sweeten. Place in freezer until mushy and serve.

"Miss Top" always served this in small silver stemmed glasses.

**From the recipes of
Mrs. Charles O. Noble, Sr.**

SANGRELLA

Slices of fresh peaches and oranges (or strawberries)
Juice of 2 oranges
Juice of 1 lemon
2 Tablespoons sugar syrup
1 ounce maraschino
1 ounce Cointreau
¾ bottle white wine (Spritzinger Mosel)
1 bottle red wine (Beaujolais)

Marinate fresh fruit in fruit juices, sugar syrup, and maraschino for 12 hours. Add Cointreau and wines and chill for 12-24 hours. Serves 10-12 in wine glasses.

Delightful but potent. Delicious served before or after dinner on a hot summer evening. Also good served with cheese.

Karl Boellert

SAZERAC COCKTAIL

3 dashes absinthe
1 lump sugar
1 dash orange bitters
1 dash Sazerac or Angostura bitters
Pernod or Herbsaint
2 jiggers 100 proof bourbon or rye
Lemon twist

Rim glass with absinthe. Muddle sugar with bitters and a dash of water. Fill large old-fashioned glass with cubed ice, cover with whiskey, and stir until ice cold. Remove ice and garnish with a lemon twist. Makes 1 double drink.

Mrs. John Armstrong
(Gayle Smith)

24 HOUR COCKTAILS

1 quart whiskey
1 quart water
1½ cups sugar
1 dozen lemons

Combine whiskey, water, and sugar. Squeeze lemons and add juice and rinds to mixture. Store, covered, in refrigerator 24 hours. Remove; squeeze rinds well and discard them. Serve in punch cups or old-fashioned glasses. Very potent. More water may be added if desired. Inexpensive bourbon may be used without affecting the taste.

Mrs. W. Kent Cutrer
(Linda Arnold)

VELVET HAMMER

Vanilla ice cream
2 jiggers (1 ounce size) brandy
2 jiggers vodka
1 jigger triple sec
1 jigger crème de cacao

Fill blender with vanilla ice cream. Add other ingredients and blend lightly.

Mrs. Stacy W. Smith

BEVERAGES

CREOLE COFFEE

1½ cups strong New Orleans ground coffee
Boiling water
2 Tablespoons dry cocoa or chocolate (optional)

Place dry coffee in top part of French drip coffee pot (the dripper). Pour 1 Tablespoon boiling water every 3-4 minutes over coffee until there is about a pint. Do not allow coffee to boil. Coffee may be kept and reheated.

In some French restaurants 2 Tablespoons dry cocoa or chocolate (carefully dissolved) is added to every pint of coffee.

Mrs. John Armstrong
(Gayle Smith)

CAFÉ BRÛLOT

Peel of 1 orange, sliced into narrow strips
Peel of 1 lemon, sliced into narrow strips
2 pieces (2 inches each) of stick cinnamon
12 whole cloves
6 small cubes sugar (or about 6 teaspoons)
6-8 ounces brandy
3-4 cups strong hot black coffee

Place all ingredients except last 2 in top of chafing dish or café brûlot bowl. Rub ingredients gently against sides and bottom with spoon. Add brandy. Heat until very hot, directly over flame, without bringing to a boil. Fill ladle with liquid, ignite, and lower into chafing dish. Ladle up and down gently so flame does not go out (about ½-1 minute). Gradually add coffee and stir gently. If flame has not gone out, continue stirring until it does. Serve in café brûlot or demitasse cups. Serves 8-12.

Frank M. Brame

IRISH COFFEE

Brim decaffeinated coffee
Honey
Irish whiskey
Cool Whip

Perk or drip coffee. In an Irish coffee cup stir well 1 teaspoon honey, 1 jigger Irish whiskey, and Cool Whip. Add enough hot coffee to fill ¾ cup. Serves 1.

A perfect way to end the evening!

Mrs. Joseph Lowenthal
(Margaret Welsh)

COFFEE PUNCH

Small jar instant coffee
4 cups sugar
4 cups boiling water
12 quarts milk
½ gallon chocolate ice cream
½ gallon vanilla ice cream

Mix coffee, sugar, and water. (This may be kept in refrigerator indefinitely.) Stir this mixture into milk and pour over ice cream when ready to serve. Serves 75.

Mrs. G. W. Pomeroy

COCOA

4½ cups cocoa
½ Tablespoon salt
7 Tablespoons flour
8 cups sugar
13½ quarts milk
11¼ cups water

Mix all dry ingredients. Slowly add liquids, stirring constantly until smooth. Heat, but do not boil. Serves 100.

Mrs. Clarence T. Doan

NECTAR ICE CREAM SODA

NECTAR SYRUP
2½ cups sugar
2 cups water
1 can condensed milk
1 teaspoon each vanilla and almond extract
Few drops red food coloring

Bring sugar and water to a boil and simmer until sugar dissolves. Remove from heat and add remaining ingredients. Stir well. Pour into bottle and cap. Keeps 4-6 weeks in refrigerator. Nectar should be dark pink.

SODA
2 Tablespoons nectar syrup
Ice cream
Soda

SODA
Put syrup in glass. Add ice cream. Top with a little more syrup. Fill glass with soda water. Stir and serve with spoon and straw.

Children, teenagers, and adults will like this treat.

Mrs. Karl Boellert
(Kathleen Martin)

BEVERAGES

PUNCH À LA CHAMPAGNE

2 cups orange juice
1½ cups lime juice
1 cup sugar
5-6 cups white grape juice, chilled
1 bottle champagne, chilled

Blend first 3 ingredients until sugar is well dissolved. Chill thoroughly. When ready to serve, pour citrus juice mixture into chilled punch bowl. Add grape juice and stir. Add champagne if desired. Float decorative ice ring in punch. Serves 24.

Mrs. William B. Baggett
(Gael Salter)

CLIFFORD'S RUM PUNCH

2 ounces each of lime juice, ginger ale, pineapple juice, and soda water
4 ounces sugar
8 ounces rum (Appleton Special)
Dash bitters

Mix ingredients in blender. Serve over ice, garnished with fresh mint. Serves 4.

Mrs. John W. Huber
(Betty Landry)

SLUSH PUNCH

6 packages strawberry Kool-Aid
6 quarts water
1 package strawberry Jello
1 can (46 ounces) pineapple juice
1 can (12 ounces) frozen orange juice
3 cans water
6 cups sugar
2 bottles ginger ale

Mix all ingredients except ginger ale. Freeze. Remove from freezer about 3 hours before serving time. When ready to serve, pour into punch bowl and pour ginger ale over it. Makes 2½ gallons.

Good for children's parties.

Mrs. Sam Liggio

"OLD VIRGINIA WASSAIL"

2 quarts sweet apple cider
2 cups orange juice
1 cup lemon juice
2 cans (16 ounce size) pineapple juice
1 stick whole cinnamon
1 teaspoon whole cloves
Sugar, or honey, to taste

Combine ingredients and bring to a simmer. Strain and serve hot.

This recipe for the traditional Old English Christmas wassail is based on that used by Virginia's famed Williamsburg Inn for more than a century.

Mrs. William G. Castle, Jr.
(Linda Morris)

VIRGINIA'S SPIKED FRUIT PUNCH

2 cans (1½ quart size) apple juice
2 cans (1½ quart size) sweetened pineapple juice
3 7-Ups (12 ounce size) or 6 7-Ups when wine and champagne are omitted
1 can (12 ounces) frozen lemonade concentrate
1 can pineapple chunks
1 large jar maraschino cherries
2 bottles (1/5 size) white wine
1 bottle (1/5 size) champagne

Combine all ingredients except wine and champagne. Refrigerate or freeze. Add wine and champagne when ready to serve. For decorative ice molds, fill molds of desired shape with liquid before wine and champagne are added. For added color and flavor include a few mandarin sections and mint leaves in mold. Serves 55-60.

Mrs. Edward M. Carmouche
(Virginia L. Martin)

WEDDING PUNCH

4 cans (6 ounce size) concentrated orange juice
2 cans (6 ounce size) concentrated lemonade
3 quarts cold water
2 packages (10 ounce size) frozen strawberry halves
2 bottles (1/5 of a gallon size) chilled champagne or
2 bottles (12 ounce size) ginger ale

Combine concentrates and cold water. Chill until serving time. Just before serving, combine with thawed strawberries and champagne or ginger ale. Pour into punch bowl. Float strawberries and frozen ring in punch. Yields 6 quarts or 48 portions of 4 ounces each.

FROZEN FRUIT RING

5 cups punch
Strawberry halves
Pineapple chunks
Lemon and orange slices
Red and green cherries

FROZEN FRUIT RING

Pour punch into 1½ quart ring mold. Add next 4 ingredients. Freeze until firm (at least 8 hours). To unmold, dip ring in hot water and invert into punch bowl. Ring will float.

Mrs. Sam Liggio

Wine

The connoisseur might ably recite the history, nomenclature, and geography of each wine, but his knowledge is not indispensable to its enjoyment. The uninformed, too, can revel in the pleasures of wine drinking. But armed with a few basic facts on selection, storage, and serving he can amplify those pleasures.

STORAGE: Improper storage can transform "good" wine into "bad" by preventing its normal maturation within the bottle. The two major storage abuses are a sudden, radical change in temperature and an oxygen leak in the cork. A constant 50°F temperature is ideal but not always realistic. Fortunately, since changes within a 10°F latitude do not cause irreparable harm, it is not difficult to find a suitable storage area. Avoid exposure to sunlight, direct or indirect. Consider wrapping the bottles in paper to partially negate the deteriorating effect of temperature change. Store the wine on its side, thereby keeping the cork moist and swollen, to prevent oxygen leaking into the bottle.

Aside from the conditions of storage, the duration is also important. First principles to remember are that red wines, since they mature more slowly, should remain in their bottles longer than white ones; that they require on an average of 5-10 years from bottle date for maturation compared with 3-5 years for white wines; that it is incorrect to always consider the older wine better.

SERVING: Although serving wines is not complicated, there are preparatory measures that upgrade its quality, by removing sediment, adjusting to proper temperature, and allowing oxygen to enhance the bouquet.

White wines need only to be chilled in preparation for serving — in the refrigerator for 45 minutes, in an ice bucket for 15. Do not use the freezer as overchilling will damage the taste.

For red wine the preparation is different. Because more of the grape is used in making red wine, a sediment tends to build up over the years. If the bottle is shaken, or served immediately from storage on its side, the sediment will make the wine "murky" and alter its taste. To avoid this, stand the bottle upright either the night before, or the day of, consumption at room temperature. The sediment will filter to the bottom and, if the wine is carefully poured, will remain there. This is the reason for the peculiarly shaped neck of the Bordeaux bottle — to provide a trap for the sediment filled remnants.

Red wine is served at room temperature without chilling. About an hour prior to use remove the cork for the wine to "breathe." As the oxygen mixes with the fermented wine, a pleasing bouquet is released. It is because of this bouquet that red wine is customarily served in a large "bowl shaped" glass with stem. The glass should be only half filled for the optimum aroma. A white wine glass needs no particular shape although a stemmed one is preferable so that the hand does not heat the wine.

Although much fanfare is made of the host's *tasting* the wine for approval, any flaw would be difficult to discern had he indulged in predinner cocktails. Since he is testing for proper maturation, in red wine he can do this as well by smelling the removed cork. If it has a sulphurous odor, like a burned match, it is damaged. White wine may be pretasted for proper temperature, remembering that the wine in the bottle neck is somewhat less chilled than the rest.

SELECTION: The key to wine selection is in recognizing that the wine must enhance and complement the accompanying food, whether it be served with one or all courses. This pliant capacity of wine is what makes it a unique beverage. The amateur's best criterion for selection is "plain common sense."

When more than one wine is served with the meal, begin with the lightest. Between one white and one red, serve the former first as white wines are lighter than reds. White wines are usually associated with salads, appetizers, fish, soup, and chicken; red ones with meat dishes or entrees.

White Wines: Three broad white wine categories are:
(1) Cocktail or aperitif — well chilled champagne, dry sherry at room temperature or any German.
(2) Dinner — Chablis, Pouilly Fuissé; California Pinot Chardonnay; Pouilly Fumé, good with fowl; Montrachet and Meursault, sweeter than Chablis.
(3) Dessert — cream sherry, Sauternes, and Port.

"White wine with white meat and red wine with red meat" is the time-honored adage that generally suffices. But what happens to the in-betweens, like ham? Use a rosé wine. Rosé is a pink wine made from the same grapes as some of the more popular reds, but with the skin removed early in the pressing before the color becomes fully red. Rosés should be drunk chilled, when they are young. Since they have little bouquet, the serving glass is unimportant. Rosés give an informal touch to the meal.

Red Wines: Unlike white wines, which are made solely from the juice of the grape, red wines are made from grapes crushed and fermented with the seeds and skins. The fermentation process gives not only the red color but also the distinctive bouquet, viscosity, and after-taste. Because they mature much more slowly than white wines, the vintage, or growing conditions of the grapes, is a weighty determination in the end quality.

The 3 primary categories of French red wine are Bordeaux, Burgundy (Beaujolais is related), and Rhone named for the areas in which the grapes are grown. The best vintage years are 1957, 1961, 1962, 1964, 1966, 1970, 1971, 1976, 1978; average, 1958, 1959, 1960; poor, 1954, 1956, 1963, 1965.

Bordeaux wines, easily recognized by their distinctive bottle with long straight sides and short neck, are made and bottled primarily at particular chateaux, the reputations of which strongly influence the ultimate retail price. The American equivalent of Bordeaux (also called Claret) is Cabernet Sauvignon. Numerous domestic vineyards market a delectable Cabernet Sauvignon.

The second major red wine of France is Burgundy. Wines from Burgundy have a greater price and taste range than those from Bordeaux, due primarily to vineyard ownership and district regulatory laws. While most Bordeauxs are made and bottled at a particular chateau, many Burgundies

(Pommard, Nuit St. George, for example) are made from grapes grown in one place and blended and bottled in another by an exporter. In Burgundy the reputation of the exporting merchant is as important as that of the chateau in Bordeaux. Burgundy differs from Bordeaux also in that it is made from a different grape — the Pinot Noir. The California Pinot Noir, harsher in taste than the Cabernet Sauvignon Bordeaux, is an excellent complement for wild game.

Among the large varieties of easily accessible Burgundies, the more famous deserve special mention. Romanee Conti, coming from a 4 acre vineyard of the same name, is understandably scarce. The owner also owns several other area vineyards that yield excellent high priced wines — La-Tache, Richenbourg, and Grands Echezeaux. From the vineyards of Gevrey-Chambertain, on the northernmost border of red wine production and with a more extreme climate, comes an excellent, plentiful product. The full-bodied Chambertain wines are a natural complement to heavier meats. Also superior are the softer Pommard and Clos de Vougeot Burgundies.

Several miles south of the main Burgundy area lie the prolific Beaujolais vineyards producing the hearty gamay grape. The California equivalent wines are marketed under the Gamay label. Beaujolais, a softer wine than most Burgundies, and mature at a much younger age, is usually ready to drink when marketed. Needing less care than the big name Burgundies and Clarets, and one of the few red wines that can be chilled, it is properly served before dinner.

Further to the south is the Rhone River Valley, the third red wine producing district of France. The Rhone wines, although not as noted for their taste as others, are hearty and require little care. They are a superb complement to a picnic or wild game meal. Chateauneuf-du-Pape, very strong in alcoholic content, almost purple in color, is a well known Rhone wine.

Increasingly popular with today's taste is the consumption of Port after the meal. Port is very sweet, fortified with alcohol, and best "sipped" in small quantities. Once opened, Port can be kept for a long time in a closed decanter. Ports take a while to mature and are at their best when they are fifteen or more years old.

Fun Ways to Learn Wines: The wine tasting party is an entertaining way to learn wines. Allot about 1½ ounces per taste; 14-16 tastes per bottle. Have maps available to show locations of vineyards being sampled.

Always start with the lighter white wines and move to the heavier red ones. In the white, champagne first, then a Chablis before a Montrachet; in the red, a Beaujolais before a Claret or Burgundy, then a heavy Burgundy, Chambertain, or Rhone. Alternate the tasting of different wines with a mild cheese (like Edam or Monterey Jack) and/or bread appetizer to clean the palate.

The use of half bottles or "splits" is another method of experimenting and enjoying wine. Wine matures faster in a smaller bottle so you will want to purchase recent vintages. Additional advantages include the fact that they chill faster and are more easily stored.

For a more individual approach to studying wines, keep a scrapbook of the bottle labels, which are easily soaked off.

Frank N. Ingraham

Hors d'oeuvres

HOG'S HEAD CHEESE

1 hog's head
4 pig's feet
1 shoulder pork roast (4 pounds), cut into pieces
6 whole cloves garlic
Salt, red and black pepper to taste
1 bunch green onions, minced
¾ bunch parsley, minced
4 cloves garlic, minced
2 hot green peppers, finely chopped
6 Tablespoons white vinegar

Have butcher clean hog's head. In an extra large loosely covered soup pot boil all meats in water to cover, seasoned to taste with salt, garlic, and pepper for about 3 hours or until meat falls from bone. Remove meat and cut in small pieces. Strain broth and skim fat. Add to the broth the chopped meat and remaining ingredients, except vinegar. Cook about 2 hours until mixture thickens. When cool, add vinegar. To set, place in 6 large ungreased molds of any shape. Must be prepared at least 2 days ahead. Freezes.

Another 5 pound pork shoulder roast may be substituted for the hog's head.

Mrs. Walter Moss
(Jo Duplechin)

CAVIAR MOUSSE

1 Tablespoon plus 1 teaspoon Knox unflavored gelatine
¼ cup cold water
4 hard boiled eggs, finely grated
1 carton (8 ounces) Borden's French onion dip
3 Tablespoons lemon juice
3 Tablespoons onion, grated, with juice
¼ teaspoon salt
1 Tablespoon Lea & Perrins
3 dashes Tabasco
1½ cups mayonnaise
8 ounces lump fish caviar
Parsley

Stir gelatine in cold water, place in pan of hot water, and stir until completely dissolved. Combine remaining ingredients, except parsley, and pour into a 1 quart decorative mold which has been lightly oiled. Chill overnight, or until firm. Unmold and garnish serving plate with parsley. Serve with crackers and thinly sliced party size Pumpernickel bread. Serves 30-40.

Mrs. Edward H. Taussig
(Florence Streater)

ARTICHOKE BALLS

1 can (14 ounces) artichoke hearts, drained, mashed
1 cup seasoned bread crumbs
2 eggs
2 Tablespoons olive oil
2 Tablespoons lemon juice
½ teaspoon garlic powder
½ cup Parmesan cheese

Combine all ingredients except cheese. Mix well. Refrigerate overnight or at least 4 hours. Form into bite sized balls. Roll in cheese. Bake, uncovered, at 400°F about 10 minutes, or until light brown. Freezes. Makes 48.

Mrs. Nolan Robichaux
(Linda Hooks)

ARTICHOKE-SPINACH APPETIZERS

1 large artichoke, boiled
2 quarts water
1 Tablespoon salt
1 package (10 ounces) frozen chopped spinach or 1 pound fresh spinach
4 green onions, chopped
4 outside green lettuce leaves
1 Tablespoon parsley, chopped
¾ cup seasoned bread crumbs
½ cup Romano cheese, grated
1 Tablespoon Pernod
Salt and pepper to taste
Paprika for garnish
1 Tablespoon water

Boil artichoke in salted water until a leaf pulls off easily. Drain and cool. Boil frozen or fresh spinach for 5 minutes. Squeeze out excess water. Blend spinach, green onions, and lettuce leaves in blender until puréed. Place in bowl and mix well with bread crumbs, ¼ cup cheese, Pernod, salt, and pepper. Separate artichoke leaves, stuff each leaf, and arrange in circle on buttered pie plate with stuffed heart in center. Sprinkle with remaining cheese and garnish with paprika. Place water in pie plate, cover with foil, and bake at 350°F for 15 minutes. Serve warm. Serves 6.

Mrs. Lucile M. Charlan
New Orleans, La.

Artichaut

BAKED STUFFED MUSHROOM CAPS

4 Tablespoons green onions, chopped
1½ cups crab meat
2 Tablespoons butter
1 cup white sauce
¼ teaspoon lemon juice
Salt and pepper to taste
18-24 mushroom caps (2 inch), brushed with butter

WHITE SAUCE
2 Tablespoons butter
3 Tablespoons flour
1 cup hot milk
Salt and pepper

Preheat oven to 350°F. Cook green onions and crab meat in butter until warm, stirring in sauce and seasonings. Sprinkle mushroom caps with salt and fill. Bake in shallow buttered baking dish for 10-15 minutes.

WHITE SAUCE
Melt butter, stir in flour, and cook 2 minutes. Blend in hot milk and simmer 2 minutes, stirring constantly. Add salt and pepper to taste.

Mrs. William Mixon
(Debi Kramer)

SUE'S MUSHROOMS

1 pound fresh mushrooms
2 teaspoons salt, (approximately)
2 teaspoons dried orégano (approximately)
⅔ cup oil
⅓ cup vinegar

Separate mushroom stems from caps. If caps are large, cut in half. In a large flat pan, sprinkle caps and stems with salt and orégano. In a separate pan, heat oil and vinegar to boiling and pour over mushrooms. Marinate for several hours. Store in covered container in refrigerator. Will keep for several weeks. Serves 15-20.

Mrs. Tom A. Flanagan, Jr.
(Sarah Nabors)

MUSHROOM CANAPÉS FONTE AI FRATI

1 pound whole fresh mushrooms
1 stick butter
1 teaspoon salt
¼ teaspoon black pepper, freshly ground
1½ jiggers bourbon whiskey
1 egg white
Sliced white bread, cut into canapé rounds or squares

Rinse mushrooms lightly, shake dry, and chop fine. Melt butter in heavy saucepan; add mushrooms, salt, and pepper, and sauté over moderate heat 5 minutes. Add bourbon and continue cooking over moderate heat until liquid is almost boiled away and mushroom mixture is a moist thick paste. When cool, add egg white and mix well. Spread fairly generously over bread and bake at 375°F until bread is lightly browned. Serve hot. May garnish with pimiento or chopped egg for color.

Ellis Palmer

CAVIAR BALL

11 ounces Philadelphia cream cheese, softened
2 heaping Tablespoons mayonnaise
1½ teaspoons Tabasco
¾ Tablespoon Worcestershire sauce
Celery salt to taste
¼ cup dried parsley flakes
1 jar (4 ounces) black lumpfish caviar

Mash softened cream cheese. Mix with all ingredients except caviar. Shape mixture into a ball and place in center of serving plate. Coat with the caviar. Refrigerate for 1 hour before serving. To serve, surround with assorted cocktail crackers.

Mrs. Jack Kemmerly
(Mary Watkins)

NEW POTATOES WITH SOUR CREAM AND CAVIAR

12 new potatoes 1-1½ inches in diameter, thoroughly scrubbed, unpeeled
2 Tablespoons green onions, finely chopped
Pepper, freshly ground
Salt
¾ cup sour cream
1 Tablespoon black caviar
1 Tablespoon parsley, finely chopped

Drop potatoes into 2 quart saucepan of boiling water. Cook, uncovered, over moderate heat, 15-20 minutes, or until easily pierced with tip of a sharp knife. Drain and pat dry with paper towels. Neatly scoop out ⅓ of each potato and sprinkle cavities lightly with salt and pepper. Fill each with ¼ teaspoon of sour cream (or a little less than the cavities will hold), top with ¼ teaspoon caviar and sprinkle with parsley. Serve warm.

Also delightful with crisp bacon.

Mrs. Avery Cook
(Carolyn DeJean)

TOASTED PECANS

2 cups pecan halves, freshly shelled
Salt to taste
4 Tablespoons margarine or butter

Spread pecans in large baking pan. Sprinkle with salt and add margarine. Bake, uncovered, at 300°F until toasty brown. Stir often to cover all sides with margarine. Recipe may be doubled easily.

Mrs. David Painter
(Isabel "Bel" Thornton)

CAJUN ONION RINGS

White onions
Flour
Salt
Red and black pepper
Garlic powder
Cooking oil

Refrigerate whole onions overnight. Peel and slice 1 onion per person. Mix flour, salt, peppers, and garlic powder in brown bag. Add onion slices a few at a time and shake until well coated. Deep fat fry in heavy pot in oil until onion rings are brown and float to top. Remove with slotted spoon and drain on paper towel. Serve immediately. If not served at once, omit salt until ready to serve to prevent rings from becoming soggy.

Let two Cajuns cut up an onion and you have a treat!

J. J. "Joe" Champeaux
Jack Kemmerly

PERFECT ONION RINGS

Vegetable oil
3 Tablespoons vinegar
1 cup evaporated milk
2 large onions, sliced
Flour as needed

Pour 1½ inches of vegetable oil in an iron Dutch oven. Heat oil to 375°F while preparing onion rings. Pour vinegar into a bowl containing the evaporated milk and stir until thick. Separate onion rings and drop 2-3 slices into the milk. Remove and shake in paper bag containing flour. Drop floured onion rings into heated vegetable oil and fry to a golden brown. Drain on paper towels. Salt and pepper to taste. Makes 5 average servings.

Kay Cryar Schuler

CAPANTTO

1 large (1½-2 pounds) eggplant
¾ cup olive oil
2½ cups onions, coarsely chopped
1 cup celery, chopped
2 cans (8 ounce size) tomato sauce
1 cup dry red wine
2 Tablespoons sugar
½ bottle olives, broken salad
1 can pitted ripe olives
½ jar capers
Salt and pepper to taste

Wash and dry eggplant. Cut into ½ inch cubes. Sauté in ½ cup hot oil until golden and tender. Remove. Add more oil and sauté onion and celery. Return eggplant to skillet with onion and celery. Add tomato sauce. Bring to a boil. Reduce heat, cover, and simmer 15 minutes. Add remaining ingredients. Cover and cook 20 minutes, stirring occasionally. Refrigerate. Will keep several days.

Serve on melba toast or with cold meats. Unusual and very tasty!

Mrs. Stanford L. Vincent
(Anita Cox)

MARINATED VEGETABLES

12 white cocktail size onions
1 small cauliflower, broken into flowerets
½ pound small fresh mushroom caps (or 2 cans, drained)
2 bell peppers, cut into thin strips
18 black olives
1 cup olive oil
1½ cups wine vinegar
2 teaspoons salt
¾ teaspoon pepper, freshly ground
4 Tablespoons sugar
1 clove garlic, minced

Prepare and wash vegetables. Drain well. In a saucepan bring remaining ingredients to a boil. Cool 5 minutes. Pour over vegetables which have been placed in a container suitable for storage. Cover and marinate for at least 24 hours in refrigerator. Serve with toothpicks.

Mrs. John Moore
(Johnnie Sue Cloyd)

BRISKET

3 cloves garlic, slivered
8 pounds brisket
3 teaspoons saltpeter
4 Tablespoons salt
5 Tablespoons allspice
5 Tablespoons sugar
Dash cinnamon

Insert garlic in meat. Mix remaining ingredients and pat on both sides of brisket. Wrap in heavy foil. Do not puncture. Refrigerate 4 days. Bake in original foil in 9x14 inch pan at 325°F for 4 hours. Pierce foil to check tenderness. Serve with rye bread, horseradish, and mustard. Freezes after being refrigerated for 4 days.

Looks strange, but a guaranteed delicious dish.

Susan Ayres

TURKISH BARBECUED BEEF

8 pounds tender or excellent beef, thinly sliced
Bacon drippings as needed
6 cloves garlic, minced
12 medium onions, thinly sliced
4½ cups ketchup
2¼ cups white vinegar
1 Tablespoon curry powder
4 Tablespoons paprika
1 teaspoon chili powder
5½ cups beef stock
4½ teaspoons dry mustard
Salt to taste
6 Tablespoons butter (more or less, according to amount of fat in meat)
1 teaspoon black pepper
3 Tablespoons sugar
4½ Tablespoons Worcestershire sauce
1½ teaspoons Tabasco
6 Tablespoons each of minced parsley, chives, and bell pepper

Brown meat in bacon drippings. Add garlic and brown. Transfer to a very large pot and add onions. In another pan, combine ketchup, vinegar, curry powder, paprika, chili powder, beef stock, mustard, and salt. Pour mixture over meat, bring to a boil, and cook, covered, about 4 hours. When done, mash with a potato masher. It should look shredded; if not, cook longer. Add remaining ingredients and simmer, covered, 1 hour or until of a consistency that spoons easily onto a split roll. Serve in chafing dish with pocketbook rolls. May be prepared ahead, especially the first part. Freezes. Serves 40.

Mrs. Mary Elizabeth Warren Ledford

GLACÉ MOLDS
(CHICKEN)

1½ cups water
2 chicken bouillon cubes
2 Tablespoons green onions, finely minced
1 Tablespoon celery, finely chopped
1 whole chicken breast, chopped
Black pepper, salt, and paprika to taste
1 envelope Knox unflavored gelatine
Green onion tops, chopped

Combine first 6 ingredients. Simmer until chicken is tender. Let cool. Skim off fat. Soften gelatine in ½ cup of cooled stock. Heat remaining stock and add gelatine to dissolve. Place a tiny piece of chicken and a few green onions in bottoms of 2 dozen miniature rounded molds. Pour stock over them and chill until firm. Serve on toast rounds.

Mrs. B. T. Dugazon
Baton Rouge, La.

HAM ROLL-UPS

1 package (8 ounces) Philadelphia cream cheese
1 well rounded Tablespoon almonds, chopped
3 dashes Tabasco
½ teaspoon Worcestershire sauce
¼ teaspoon dry mustard
¼ teaspoon Pickapeppa sauce
¼ teaspoon soy sauce
¼ teaspoon paprika
⅛ teaspoon each salt and pepper
2 level Tablespoons mayonnaise
2 teaspoons chives, fresh or frozen
1 package (4 ounces) rectangular shaped imported ham (Leo brand is good), precut into 4 slices

Bring cheese to room temperature. Mash well with a fork. Add remaining ingredients, except ham, and mix well. Put ¼ of mixture on each ham slice and spread evenly. Roll ham lengthwise and place folded side down on cookie sheet. Place in freezer for 45 minutes. Remove and slice each roll into 9-10 pieces. Return pieces to cookie sheet, cover with Saran wrap, and freeze until solid. Place in a plastic bag, then in a plastic container, and seal. May be stored up to 6 weeks in freezer. Takes 20-25 minutes to thaw. Makes about 3 dozen.

Mrs. Karl Boellert
(Kathleen Martin)

CHAFING DISH HAM BALLS

2 pounds ham, ground
1 pound pork, freshly ground
3 eggs
1 cup plain bread crumbs
1 cup milk
½ teaspoon salt

COOKING SAUCE
4 cups dark brown sugar
4 cups water
2 cups white vinegar

MUSTARD SAUCE
1 can Coleman dry mustard
½ cup white vinegar
½ cup sugar
1 egg, beaten

Mix well first 6 ingredients and roll into small cocktail size balls. Makes 94-100.

COOKING SAUCE
Divide sauce ingredients equally between 2 large pots, mix well, and bring to a boil. Place ½ of ham balls in each pot of boiling sauce and cook, uncovered, on top of stove for 1 hour. Serve in chafing dish with the following mustard sauce in a bowl. Freezes. Serves 50.

MUSTARD SAUCE
Mix first 2 ingredients and let stand overnight. Add sugar and egg. Heat to boiling on low heat and boil 1 minute.

Mrs. Karl Boellert
(Kathleen Martin)

LIVER PÂTÉ

1 pound pork liver
1 package frozen cooked spinach, squeezed dry, or cooked fresh spinach that when squeezed is about size of a small orange
2 medium onions
5 large cloves garlic
¼ teaspoon ground cloves
¼ teaspoon allspice
1 pound Crisco
1 level Tablespoon salt
2 teaspoons ground red pepper
1 teaspoon black pepper

Wash liver thoroughly and remove as much of gray membrane as possible. Grind together first 4 ingredients using fine blade. Put in large mixing bowl. Add other ingredients and blend well with large spoon. Spoon into an iron pot or casserole with tight fitting lid. Allow room for a slight swelling of pâté. Bake at 325°F for 1 hour, stirring well after 50 minutes. Return to oven for 10 minutes more. Remove from oven, spoon off excess grease, and immediately pass pâté through food mill (sometimes called a vegetable press) into another receptacle. (This produces a smooth paste and leaves behind all liver membranes.) Discard what remains in food mill. Adjust seasoning to taste, and mix thoroughly. Place in refrigerator in tightly covered containers, until set, about 1 hour. Serve cold on crackers. May be safely kept for 2 weeks, properly refrigerated.

Uniquely known as "Poddy's Pâté."

Dr. J. Malcolm Leveque

HORS D'OEUVRES

CHOPPED LIVER

3 medium onions, chopped
¼ cup chicken fat or oil
2 pounds chicken livers
4 hard boiled egg yolks, chopped
1 teaspoon salt
Black pepper to taste, freshly ground
Lettuce leaves

Sauté onion in fat until brown. Add livers, tossing until brown. Simmer, covered, on low heat 10 minutes. Remove from heat. Mix all ingredients with livers. Grind in meat grinder until smooth. Season to taste. Form into dome-shaped ball. Serve on large lettuce leaf with thin wafer crackers. Serves 12.

Mrs. Maurice Kleinman
(Jane Winner)

SWEDISH MEAT BALLS

1 pound lean ground meat
¾ cup bread crumbs
½ onion, minced
1 egg, beaten
¾ teaspoon cornstarch
Dash allspice
¾ cup hot milk
1 teaspoon salt
3-4 Tablespoons cooking oil as needed
3 Tablespoons flour
2 cups water
1 cup Burgundy wine
2 beef bouillon cubes
½ teaspoon salt
⅛ teaspoon pepper

Mix first 8 ingredients. Shape into balls and brown in enough oil to cover bottom of skillet. Remove meat balls. Add flour and make roux. Stir in remaining ingredients until smooth. Replace meat balls and simmer, uncovered, for 30 minutes. May be used as hors d'oeuvre or as main course over fluffy rice.

Mrs. James Albert Price

SWEET AND SOUR SPARERIBS

2-4 pounds meaty spareribs, cut into bite sized pieces
¼ cup soy sauce mixed with ¼ cup water
½ cup sugar
½ cup vinegar
¼ cup sherry
1 Tablespoon soy sauce
½ Tablespoon cornstarch mixed with 1 Tablespoon water
⅛ teaspoon powdered ginger

Brush spareribs with mixture of soy sauce and water. Bake, uncovered, at 350°F for 1 hour, or until brown and crisp. Drain, place in dish, and keep warm. Combine sugar, vinegar, sherry, and soy sauce and bring to boil. Stir in cornstarch paste and add ginger. Pour over spareribs; serve hot. Freezes. Serves 8-10.

Robert J. Boudreau

CRAB MORNAY

6 Tablespoons margarine
6 Tablespoons flour
2 cans (3 ounce size) chopped mushrooms
Chicken broth (canned or bouillon cube)
1½ cups cream or undiluted evaporated milk
1 small onion, chopped
3 Tablespoons pimiento or bell pepper, chopped
⅓ pound Gruyère cheese, grated or cut up
4 ounces Parmesan cheese, grated
1 Tablespoon Accent
Salt, black and red pepper
2 cans (7 ounce size) (or 1 pound fresh or frozen) crab meat
Assorted crackers

In chafing dish or double boiler, melt margarine and blend in flour. Drain liquid from mushrooms and add to chicken broth to make 1½ cups. Add chicken broth and cream to flour mixture, stirring constantly. When hot and thickened somewhat, add onion, pimiento, cheeses and Accent, stirring until cheeses are melted. Add seasonings to taste, using enough red pepper to give it a "lift." Add drained mushrooms and crab meat. Serve from chafing dish on assorted crackers. Freezes. Serves 30-35.

Mrs. Charles S. Ware, Sr.

HOT CRAB MEAT CANAPÉ

3 dozen toast beds
½ pound crab meat
6 Tablespoons mayonnaise
½ teaspoon salt
½ teaspoon Accent
1 Tablespoon onion, grated
2 Tablespoons lemon juice
1 Tablespoon Worcestershire sauce
½ cup Parmesan cheese, freshly ground
Paprika as needed

Make toast beds by cutting rounds of bread with biscuit cutter. Toast one side only by sautéing in a little butter. Mix next 8 ingredients. Pile mixture on untoasted side of bread rounds and sprinkle with paprika. Place under broiler until bubbly and slightly brown. May be made ahead, covered, and refrigerated; broil just before serving. Makes 3 dozen.

Mrs. James Crawford
(Sydalise "Sissie" Fredeman)

HORS D'OEUVRES

CHEZ OCA'S ESCARGOTS BOURGUIGNONNE

2 pounds butter, softened
½ cup shallots (small purple onions rarely used or grown in Louisiana, known in French as Echallots)
Pinch of nutmeg
2 cloves garlic
1½ ounces brandy
1 cup parsley, chopped
Salt and pepper to taste
36 canned snails and shells

Mix butter with rest of ingredients. Use some of seasoned butter in empty shells, insert snails, top with more butter. Bake at 400°F for 5 minutes. Serve very hot. Serves 6.

The name of this recipe comes from Bourgogne of the Burgundy country, the locale of some of the most delightful wines in the world. Supposedly snails from this part of France, fed on vine leaves, are fatter and tastier.

Fernando Oca
Chez Oca Restaurant
Lake Charles, Louisiana

ESCARGOT GARLIC

8 ounces butter or margarine, softened
16 cloves garlic, more or less, minced
½ teaspoon black pepper, coarsely ground
1 teaspoon parsley flakes
48 small or medium snails, canned

Preheat oven to 400°F. Combine all ingredients except snails. Place ½ teaspoon of this mixture in bottom of each snail crock or shell, insert a snail, and top with another ½ teaspoon butter mixture. Bake, uncovered, for 10-15 minutes until hot and bubbly. Serves 8.

R. Wayne Vincent

LOBSTER ROLLS

¼ pound butter
½ pound Kraft Cheez Whiz
1 pound fresh or canned lobster or crab meat
2 loaves fresh white bread, sliced
Butter, melted, or mayonnaise

Combine butter, Cheez Whiz and lobster. Trim crusts from bread. Roll slices quite thin. Spread lobster mixture on bread and roll pin wheel fashion. Freeze. To serve, roll lobster rolls in melted butter or mayonnaise. Cut each roll into 3 pieces. Bake, uncovered, at 400°F for 10-15 minutes.

Mrs. Henry S. Uchida
(Chico Sakaguchi)

OYSTER CANAPÉS

PASTRY

1 package (3 ounces) cream cheese
1 stick margarine
1 cup flour

FILLING

4 green onions, chopped
2 ribs celery, chopped
Margarine
1 can cream of mushroom soup
1 jar oysters, drained and chopped
Dash Lea & Perrins
Salt and pepper to taste
Bread crumbs
½ teaspoon paprika
1 Tablespoon Parmesan cheese

PASTRY

Mix cheese and margarine. Add flour, mix well, and chill 30 minutes. Form 24 balls and place in small tart pans, using thumb to spread. Should be thickest at the bottom.

FILLING

Sauté onion and celery in margarine. Add undiluted soup, oysters, Lea & Perrins, salt, pepper, and enough bread crumbs to hold mixture together. Fill tart shells. Mix 1 Tablespoon bread crumbs, paprika, and Parmesan cheese. Sprinkle on filled tarts. Bake at 425°F until brown. Shrimp or crab meat may be substituted for oysters.

Mrs. Robert B. Rhodes

OYSTERS MYSTIQUE

1 Tablespoon butter
2 dozen raw oysters, drained
2 Tablespoons lemon juice
24 dashes cayenne pepper
8 slices bacon, each cut lengthwise into 3 pieces
⅓ cup parsley, minced

Preheat oven to 450°F. Grease 2 metal baking pans (8½x11 inch) with butter. Marinate oysters in lemon juice 1 hour; then drain. Sprinkle each oyster with 1 dash cayenne, wrap with bacon, secured by a toothpick, and sprinkle with ¼ teaspoon parsley. Bake, uncovered, on lowest rack, 12-15 minutes, or until bacon is crisp.

This exciting dish was created by Monsieur Boudreau in commemoration of his Dukehood at the 1975 Krewe of Mystique Ball.

Robert J. Boudreau

DINO'S SHRIMP PASTE

2 pounds shrimp, boiled with crab boil, onion, and salt
1 small onion, grated
1 cup homemade mayonnaise
Salt and pepper to taste
Louisiana hot sauce to taste
Ritz crackers

Peel, devein, and shred boiled shrimp in blender (a few at a time). Add onion; then homemade mayonnaise (this is the secret). Add almost as much mayonnaise as you have shrimp. Salt and pepper to taste and add a little hot sauce. Serve with Ritz crackers.

Loved by Steve, Mary, and Nancy.

Mrs. W. E. Gorham, Sr.
(Mary Tucker)

MARINATED SHRIMP

2 quarts raw shrimp, peeled
1 bottle (12 ounces) wine vinegar
4 ounces each Wesson and olive oil
4 ounces lemon juice
2 Tablespoons each horseradish and prepared mustard
1 teaspoon French's Italian Seasoning
2 teaspoons Lea & Perrins
¼ teaspoon each mustard, celery, and dill seed
3 cloves garlic, crushed
3 teaspoons, or more, salt
2 onions, cubed
2 carrots, cut in small sticks
2 ribs celery, cut in small sticks
4 bell peppers, cut in small sticks
1 hot pepper, cubed

Boil shrimp in small amount of water until tender. Set aside to cool. Mix vinegar, oils, lemon juice, and seasonings. Add remaining ingredients. Fold in drained shrimp. Refrigerate for several hours before serving. Keeps well.

Flavor improves with age.

Mrs. June Crain Harper
Grand Chenier, La.

OYSTER PATTIES

1 medium onion, ground
1 small bunch green onions, finely chopped
½ pound butter
1 cup flour
4 dozen oysters and liquid
½ bunch parsley, finely chopped
1 Tablespoon celery, finely chopped
2 bay leaves
1 teaspoon thyme
1 teaspoon salt
Dash of red pepper
1 can (4 ounces) chopped mushrooms and liquid

Sauté onions and green onions in butter until soft. Add flour, stirring until well blended. Add remaining ingredients and simmer, uncovered, over low heat for 10 minutes. Add more flour if mixture becomes too thin. Serve in chafing dish with melba toast or tiny pastry shells.

Mrs. Avery Cook
(Carolyn DeJean)

DEVILS ON HORSEBACK

1 pound bacon
Salt, pepper, and garlic powder
Few drops Tabasco
2 pints oysters, rinsed and drained

Halve bacon strips and sprinkle lightly with seasonings. Roll each oyster in a bacon strip and secure with toothpick. Bake in shallow baking pan at 325-350°F for 15-20 minutes. Remove from oven and drain liquid. Then broil until bacon is crisp. Turn once. Serves 12.

Mrs. David Grissett
(Marilyn Miller)

JACK'S SHRIMP CURRY SPREAD

3 cans (6 ounce size) shrimp, chopped
2 ribs celery, diced
½ bell pepper, diced
5 green onions and tops, diced
6 heaping Tablespoons mayonnaise
2 heaping Tablespoons cream style horseradish
3 heaping teaspoons hot curry powder
Dash of Tabasco
Paprika
Ritz crackers

Mix first 8 ingredients. Garnish with paprika and serve with Ritz crackers. Better if made ahead and refrigerated several hours or overnight. Serves 12-15.

Dr. Jack E. Thielen

CREOLE SHRIMP TARTS

2 pounds fresh shrimp peeled, deveined, cooked, and chopped
½ cup each green onion tops and parsley, finely chopped
½ cup mayonnaise
¼ teaspoon cayenne pepper
1 teaspoon lemon juice
1 clove garlic, minced
½ cup mushrooms, finely chopped
Capers
Pimiento strips
Paprika

TART SHELLS
1 package (3 ounces) cream cheese, softened
½ cup butter or margarine, softened
1 cup all purpose flour
½ cup sesame seeds

Combine first 8 ingredients. Mix well. Spoon into baked tart shells. Garnish with a caper encircled by a pimiento strip. Sprinkle with paprika. Yield: 24 appetizers.

TART SHELLS
Blend cream cheese and butter. Add flour and sesame seeds, mixing well. Chill 1 hour. Shape into 2 dozen 1 inch balls. Press dough on bottom and sides of greased tart or muffin tins. Bake at 325°F for 20 minutes. Cool. Remove from pan. Yield: 24 tart shells.

Mrs. Tasca D. Savoie

TUNA PARTY SANDWICHES

2 cans (7 ounce size) white flaked tuna, rinsed and drained
½ can ripe olives, chopped
4 hard boiled eggs, chopped
⅔ cup mayonnaise
Salt and pepper to taste
1 regular loaf Pepperidge Farm bread

TOPPING
3 jars sharp Old English cheese spread
1½ cups butter, softened
3 raw eggs

Mix drained tuna with other ingredients (except topping) and season to taste. Trim crust from bread and spread with tuna mixture. Combine topping ingredients and beat until smooth. Ice open faced sandwich tops and sides with topping. Arrange in pyrex dishes. Cover and refrigerate 12 hours. Bake, uncovered, at 450°F for 8-10 minutes. Serves 12.

Wonderful, easy luncheon dish.

Mrs. A. J. Planchard, Jr.
Sulphur, La.

CRAB MEAT OPEN SANDWICH

1 large package cream cheese
1 cup crab meat
½ teaspoon Lea & Perrins
¼ cup mayonnaise
½ pint sour cream
Onion and garlic powder to taste
American cheese slices
English muffins
Tomato slices
Canadian bacon

Mix first 6 ingredients. Place ½ slice cheese on ½ English muffin. Add 1 slice tomato and 1 slice Canadian bacon. Top with gob of crab meat mixture. Bake at 300°F for about 30 minutes. Sprinkle with paprika.

Mrs. J. T. Thompson

AVOCADO DIP

1 large, very ripe avocado (reserve seed)
1 large slice of white onion
3 Tablespoons mayonnaise
1 Tablespoon lemon juice (if avocado is not very ripe, use 2 Tablespoons)
½-1 teaspoon salt, according to taste
3 drops Tabasco

Place all ingredients in blender. Blend at low speed until completely smooth. Remove from blender. Place in dish. Place avocado seed in dip to prevent from turning brown. Should be prepared several days ahead of time. Makes 1 cup.

Mrs. Charles Viccellio
(Joanna Steele)

DILL DIP

⅔ cup Hellmann's mayonnaise
⅔ cup sour cream
1 teaspoon Spice Islands dill weed
1 Tablespoon Spice Islands shredded green onions
1 teaspoon Spice Islands Beau Monde seasoning
1 Tablespoon dried parsley, shredded

Mix all ingredients except parsley in a small bowl. Place parsley in the palm of hand and pulverize a little. Add to dip and mix well. Add more dill weed, if desired. Serve with raw vegetables. Makes almost 1 pint. May be prepared 3-4 days ahead. Serves 15-20.

Mrs. Karl Boellert
(Kathleen Martin)

MOUSSELINE DIP

4 egg yolks
2 Tablespoons lemon juice
2 sticks butter, melted
Salt and pepper to taste
½ cup cream, whipped

Blend egg yolks in blender. Add lemon juice and blend. Gradually add butter, blending 2-3 minutes until sauce thickens. Fold in whipped cream. Serve with raw vegetables. Do not refrigerate.

Mrs. Thomas Shearman, Jr.
(Martha Hatchette)

CRAWFISH DIP

½ cup flour
1 cup oil
1 large onion, ground
2 ribs celery, ground
1 large bell pepper, ground
3 cloves garlic, ground
1 pound crawfish tails, coarsely ground
1 can cream of mushroom soup
1 cup water
Seasoning to taste
Parsley and green onions, chopped
2-3 small containers of crawfish fat (optional)

In heavy pot, add flour to preheated oil and cook until just slightly golden. Add onion, celery, bell pepper, and garlic, cooking 2-3 minutes. Add crawfish tails and cook 2-3 minutes longer. (Add fat at this time if using.) Stir in mushroom soup and water. Season to taste. Cook over low heat 10-15 minutes. Add parsley and onion. Shrimp may be substituted for crawfish. Serve with potato chips, wheat thins, or melba toast. Freezes. Serves 25.

Lili Landry

KUM BAK DIP

3 cloves garlic, minced
1 cup mayonnaise
½ cup each chili sauce and ketchup
1 teaspoon mustard
½ cup Wesson oil
1 teaspoon Worcestershire sauce
1 teaspoon black pepper
1 teaspoon paprika
1 onion, grated
Juice of 1 lemon
1 Tablespoon water
Dash of Tabasco
Salt to taste

Combine first 9 ingredients. Mix the lemon juice, water, and Tabasco. Add to dip. Salt to taste. Blend in mixer. Bottle and refrigerate. Makes 2 pints. Keeps in refrigerator for weeks. Use as dip for raw vegetables or as a salad dressing.

Carolyn Stevens Moffett

CRAB DIP

1 pound crab meat (preferably lump)
1 medium onion, chopped
1 large rib celery, chopped
1 stick butter or margarine
4 slices bread
½ cup milk mixed with ½ cup water
2 large cloves garlic, finely chopped
1 level teaspoon red pepper
½ teaspoon black pepper
¼ teaspoon ground cloves
1 egg, beaten
¼ cup parsley, chopped
¼ cup green onion tops, chopped
1 teaspoon salt

Cull crab meat to remove any shell and membranes. Wilt onion and celery in butter in heavy skillet. Soak bread in milk-water mixture, add to skillet, and mash until a smooth paste consistency. Add garlic, pepper, cloves, egg, and mix thoroughly. Add crab meat, parsley, and green onions, folding slowly to avoid breaking up crab meat. If dip is too firm add more of the milk-water liquid until right consistency. Adjust seasonings. Place in casserole or chafing dish and keep hot. To convert to a casserole, or to stuff crabs, add several crumbled crackers to absorb excess moisture.

Dr. J. Malcolm Leveque

EASY HOT CRAB MEAT DIP

1 cup white onion, chopped
3 ribs celery, finely chopped
4 Tablespoons margarine
2 Tablespoons flour
1 can cream of mushroom soup, undiluted
2 packages (6 ounce size) Alaskan king crab, defrosted and well drained
3 Tablespoons parsley flakes
2 Tablespoons Worcestershire sauce
1 Tablespoon lemon juice
4-5 drops Tabasco
Salt to taste

In skillet sauté onion and celery in margarine over low heat until clear. Gradually stir in flour, followed by mushroom soup. Separate crab meat chunks by tossing lightly, and add to mixture in skillet, stirring well. Cover and simmer over low heat for 5 minutes. Stir in parsley, Worcestershire sauce, and lemon juice. Simmer 5 minutes longer, stirring. Add Tabasco and mix well. Salt to taste. Serve in chafing dish with Dorito chips or wheat thins. Serves 25-30.

Mrs. Everett Schneider
(Elizabeth "Libby" Storer)

LUMP CRAB DIP

1 stick butter
1 package (8 ounces) cream cheese
1 pound lump crab meat
1 teaspoon Worcestershire sauce
Dash of Tabasco

Melt butter in double boiler, add cream cheese, and blend well. Fold in crab meat; add Worcestershire and Tabasco. Serve hot in chafing dish with crackers or melba toast.

Mrs. Lehrue Stevens, Jr.
(Betty Scheib)

CRAB-CLAM DIP

1 medium onion, finely chopped
1 stick margarine
½ cup water
1 clove garlic, minced
2 ribs celery, finely chopped
2 packages (4 ounce size) cream cheese, cut and mashed
2 cans (4 ounce size) minced clams (drain but reserve liquid for thinning dip)
2 cups lump white crab meat
Green onion tops, chopped
Minced parsley
Lemon juice
Cayenne pepper
Salt and pepper to taste

Slowly sauté onion in margarine but do not brown. Add water, garlic, and celery; cover, and simmer about 5 minutes until tender. Add cream cheese and stir until melted; add clams with a small amount of juice. When well heated fold in crab meat and seasonings, using clam liquor for softening to proper consistency. Serve hot in a chafing dish with crackers or chips. If used as an entree, reduce cream cheese to 1½ packages, use more clam liquor, and serve on toast squares. Makes 1½ quarts. Prepare ahead and refrigerate. Reheat slowly.

Mrs. William E. Trimble
(Ann Courtney)

HORS D'OEUVRES

SHRIMP DIP

2 pounds shrimp, boiled in seasoned water
4-5 ribs celery
2 green onions, ground
½ white onion, grated
Juice of 1-2 lemons
1 Tablespoon Worcestershire sauce, or more to taste
Mayonnaise, enough to moisten
Tabasco, salt, and pepper to taste

Grind together the shrimp, celery, and green onions. Add remaining ingredients, seasoning to taste. Serve on Ritz crackers. Better if refrigerated 2-3 hours before serving. Serves 10-15.

Mrs. Forrest Gill
(Virginia Bryan)

SPINACH DIP

1 package (10 ounces) frozen chopped spinach; uncooked, defrosted, and drained
4 Tablespoons parsley, chopped
4 green onions with white part, chopped
2 ribs celery
1 Tablespoon Worcestershire sauce
1 teaspoon salt
1 Tablespoon lemon juice
1 stick butter, melted
1 ounce Herbsainte
2 dozen oysters, chopped (reserve juice)
4 Tablespoons Progresso bread crumbs

Place all ingredients, except oysters and bread crumbs, in blender and mix until puréed. Pour into a bowl. Add oysters with a bit of juice. Add bread crumbs, as needed, if too thin. Heat mixture in a pot and transfer to chafing dish when ready to serve. Serve hot from a chafing dish with plain melba toast rounds.

Pernod or Absinthe may be used in place of Herbsainte.

Carolyn Marquez Stahler

TUNA DIP

½ stick butter
Flour as needed for roux
½ cup celery, chopped
½ cup white onion, chopped
1 medium jar of stuffed olives, chopped
Sprinkle of garlic powder
1 can button mushrooms, drained
1 can beef consommé
3 cans (6½ ounce size) tuna fish
Dash of Tabasco

Make a roux using butter and flour. Do not brown. Add celery, onion, olives, garlic powder, mushrooms, and consommé. Mix well while cooking over low heat. Add tuna and Tabasco. Mix all ingredients and let simmer until celery and onions are soft. Serve with crackers or pastry shells. Freezes.

Mrs. Richard J. Chafin
(Carolyn Corley)

SEAFOOD DIP À LA KINGWOOD

5 green onions, finely chopped
5 sprigs parsley, finely chopped
¼ bell pepper, finely chopped
¼ pound butter, melted
1 pound large shrimp
1 box crab boil
2 Tablespoons salt
1 Tablespoon pepper
1 onion, coarsely chopped
1 orange, unpeeled and quartered
1 lemon, unpeeled and quartered
5 cloves garlic, chopped
1 pound lump crab meat
1 can cream of mushroom soup, undiluted
1 can cream of celery soup, undiluted
Sliced almonds (optional)

In small pan, sauté green onions, parsley, and bell pepper slowly in butter about 10 minutes. Boil shrimp with crab boil, salt, black pepper, onion, orange, lemon, and garlic. Remove shrimp from water. Wrap crab meat in cheesecloth and boil in same water for 1 minute. Remove crab meat, peel shrimp, and finely chop both. To the sautéed vegetables add the soup and bring to boiling point, stirring frequently. Add crab meat and shrimp, cooking together about 15 minutes. Add salt to taste. Sliced almonds may be added. Place in chafing dish and serve on Fritos or small toasted bread slices. May be prepared ahead. Freezes.

Voris King

SHRIMP CON QUESO DIP

2 pounds Velveeta cheese
1 can frozen shrimp soup, undiluted, or Campbell's cream of shrimp soup
1 can Ro-tel tomatoes
1 can tomatoes, chopped
½ bottle dehydrated onion chips
2 Tablespoons cumin seed
1 teaspoon basil
½ teaspoon garlic chips
1 teaspoon Red Devil sauce or Tabasco
2 Tablespoons canned green chilies, diced
1 Tablespoon salt
½ teaspoon sugar
2 Tablespoons Worcestershire sauce
8 ounces cream cheese
1 pound cooked shrimp, cut into pieces

Place all ingredients, except shrimp, in top of a large double boiler. Add shrimp when cheeses melt and mixture is well blended. Serve in chafing dish with large Fritos. Freezes for up to 6 weeks.

Mrs. John W. Huber
(Betty Landry)

CHEESE BALL

1 large or 2 small packages cream cheese
½ pound each rat, pimiento, New York sharp cheese
1 medium onion, quartered
5 small, dried red chili peppers
Juice of 1 lemon
Paprika

Grind cheeses, onion, and peppers. Blend with pastry cutter until all 1 color. Blend in lemon juice. Mold into ball and roll in paprika. Refrigerate until ready to use.

Mrs. J. Robert Wheeldon
(Frances Schram)

WALNUT CHEESE BALL

2 packages (8 ounce size) cream cheese
1 package bleu cheese
2 Tablespoons pimiento, chopped
2 Tablespoons bell pepper, chopped
Dash garlic powder
¼ cup English walnuts, chopped

Mix all ingredients except the walnuts. Form ball. Wrap in waxed paper and chill. Roll chilled cheese ball in chopped walnuts. Serve with any type cracker.

Mrs. Richard J. Chafin
(Carolyn Corley)

CHEESE OLIVE SPREAD

1 package (3 ounces) cream cheese, softened
3 Tablespoons ripe olives, chopped
3 Tablespoons slivered almonds, toasted, salted, and chopped
1 clove garlic, crushed

Mix all ingredients well. Good served on melba rounds.

Mrs. John Polk
(Gayle Woods)

CHEESE BISCUITS

1 inch thick slices of bread
1 package (3 ounces) cream cheese
¼ pound sharp Cheddar cheese
1 stick margarine
2 egg whites, stiffly beaten

Cut bread in 1 inch cubes. Melt next 3 ingredients in double boiler. Fold cheese mixture into stiff egg whites. Dip bread cubes. Let stand in refrigerator overnight. Bake, uncovered, on cookie sheet, at 400°F for 10-12 minutes.

Katie McCary

JALAPEÑO CHEESE BALL

1 pound extra sharp cheese, finely ground
1 pound mild Cheddar cheese, finely ground
1 pound mild pimiento cheese, finely ground
1 small can (7 ounces) Jalapeño peppers, finely chopped
2 cups pecans, chopped
4 medium onions, chopped
12 cloves garlic, chopped
4 Tablespoons lemon juice
4 Tablespoons Worcestershire sauce
1 pound cream cheese, softened
Paprika
Parsley, freshly snipped

Mix well all ingredients except paprika and parsley. Chill and shape into balls. Cover with paprika and roll either in parsley or nuts. Wrap in plastic bags to freeze. Serve with sesame crackers. Freezes. Makes 4-6 small cheese balls.

Mrs. David Rodgers
(Sally Montgomery)

PIMIENTO CHEESE SPREAD

½ cup milk
1 Tablespoon butter
1 cup cheese, finely cut
2 eggs, well beaten
½ teaspoon salt
1 teaspoon mustard
2 Tablespoons pimientos, chopped

Heat milk, butter, and cheese on low heat until cheese is almost melted, stirring constantly. Remove from heat. Add eggs, salt, and mustard. Return to heat and cook until thick, stirring constantly. Remove from heat and stir in pimientos.

Mrs. Frank M. Brame
(Elizabeth Hardin)

THREE CHEESE ROLL

1 package (6 ounces) pimiento cheese, grated
1 package (6 ounces) American cheese, grated
1 package (3 ounces) Philadelphia cream cheese, grated
1 teaspoon Lea & Perrins
1 teaspoon Tabasco
½ jigger white rum
2 cloves garlic, finely minced
Paprika as needed

Bring cheese to room temperature. Mix with remaining ingredients except paprika. Shape into a ball or log and roll in paprika. Refrigerate 10 hours or more before serving.

Mrs. Ruth King White

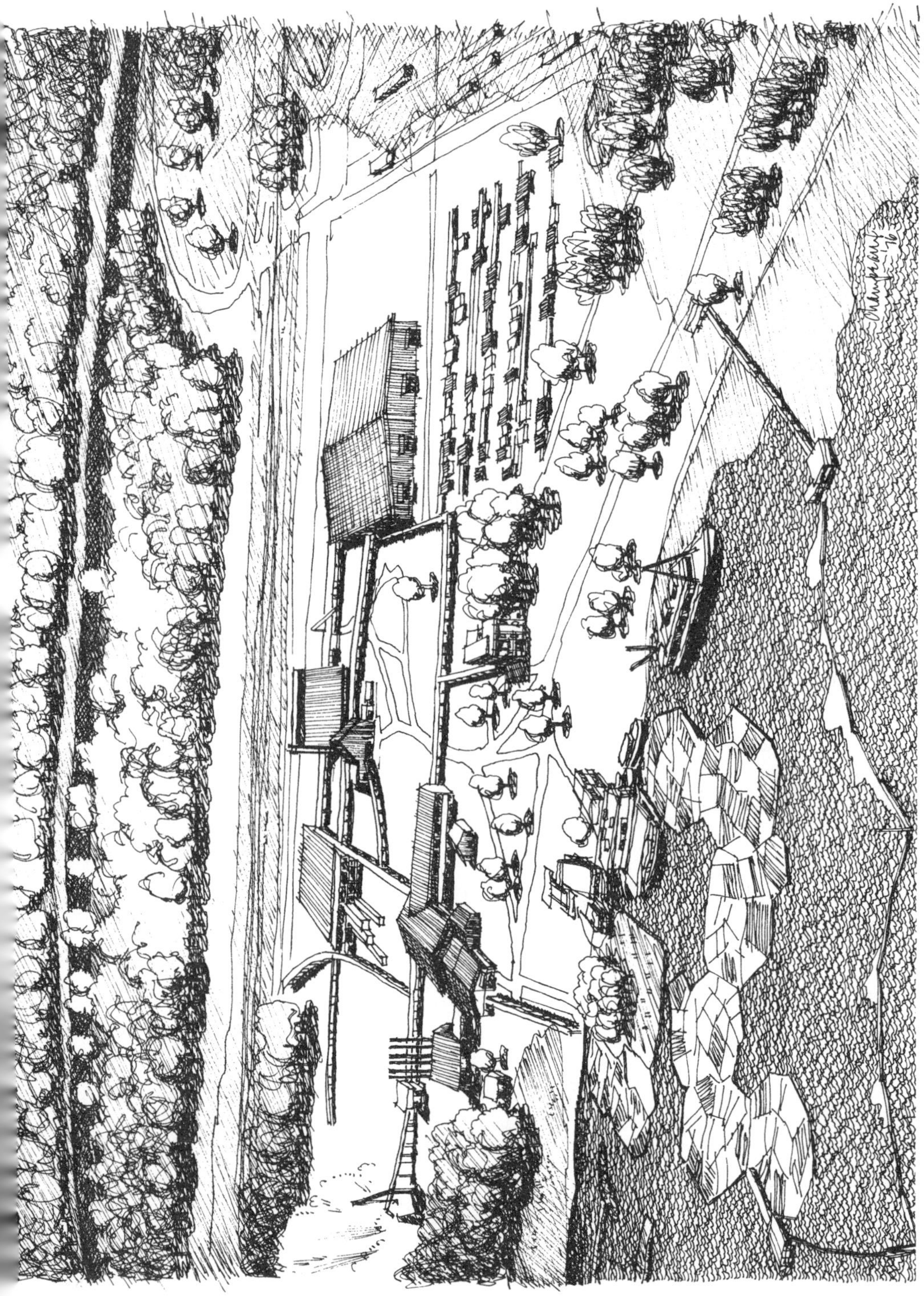

BEL LUMBER MILL

Wealth in the form of Louisiana "gold" — a vast stand of virgin longleaf yellow pine — made Lake Charles a center for the production and marketing of pine lumber following the Civil War. A magnificent longleaf pine forest stretched for 4,500 square miles west and southwest from the Red River Valley to the Sabine River and southward for about 100 miles in an irregular line from Lake Charles westward into eastern Texas.

The J. A. Bel Lumber Company, located on the northeast shore of Lake Charles, became the second largest mill in Southwest Louisiana by the turn of the century. The mill was one of 38 operating within a five-mile radius of Lake Charles between the years 1865 and 1918. It specialized in sawing long timbers that measured 70 feet in length, a record for the area.

The coming of the railroad to Southwest Louisiana in 1880 opened new markets and gave a powerful impetus to the lumber business. Prior to that time primitive sawmills located along the lower river where small schooners transported the precious cargoes of lumber to Mexico, South America, and the east coast of the United States. Some 15 to 20 schooners ran regularly, anchoring in Lake Charles and at Lockport.

By the beginning of the 20th Century and with the advent of the railroad, the lumber industry made Lake Charles a "boom" town more closely resembling a frontier village than a traditional Southern city. Special trains and boats brought the sawmill workers to Lake Charles for a night on the town. Ryan Street was lined with saloons, and it was considered "unsafe" for a lady to walk down the street on Saturday evenings when the "rowdies" came to town.

Eggs and Cheese

For a Louisiana Sunday brunch feature Bloody Marys followed by Eggs Benedict or Eggs Hussarde. Top warm Holland Rusk or crisp toast with thin slices of fried ham and a poached egg. To make Eggs Benedict, cover with Hollandaise sauce, page 293. To make Eggs Hussarde add Marchand de Vin sauce, page 295, over the Hollandaise. Serve immediately with fresh fruit and hot Louisiana coffee.

QUICHE LORRAINE

1½ cups Swiss cheese, grated
8 slices crisp bacon, crumbled
1 unbaked 9 inch pastry shell
3 eggs
1 cup heavy cream
½ cup milk
½ teaspoon salt
¼ teaspoon pepper
½ teaspoon dry mustard
2 Tablespoons onion, grated (optional)

Sprinkle cheese, bacon (and onion, if desired) in pie shell. Beat remaining ingredients and pour into shell. Bake at 375°F for 45 minutes or until brown. Serves 5-6.

Mrs. Robert W. Price, Sr.
(Betty Boedecker)

Mrs. Parker Ledbetter of France uses Gruyère cheese for a special touch in her Quiche.

MOCK QUICHE LORRAINE

8 slices bread with crusts off
Margarine or butter
4 eggs, beaten
3 cups milk
Onion to taste, finely chopped
Salt, black and red pepper to taste
1 pound sharp Cheddar cheese, grated
Ham bits (optional)

Butter bread, cut into small cubes, and arrange ½, buttered sides up, on bottom of well greased casserole. Combine eggs, milk, onion, salt and peppers. Arrange over initial bread layers ½ each of cheese and egg mixture; then remaining bread, cheese, and egg mixture. Use small ham bits between bread and cheese layers, if desired. Let stand for 3-4 hours, covered. Bake, uncovered, at 375°F for 45 minutes. If cheese topping gets too brown, cover loosely with foil the last few minutes. Serve immediately. Serves 10-12.

Great to fix ahead. Serve after the Mardi Gras Balls!

Mrs. William Janney
Houston, Texas

EASY QUICHE

½ cup mayonnaise
2 Tablespoons flour
2 eggs, beaten
½ cup milk
1⅔ cups crab meat, drained, flaked
8 ounces Swiss cheese, diced
⅓ cup green onions, sliced
1 egg white
2 pie shells

Combine mayonnaise, flour, eggs, milk until blended. Stir in crab meat, cheese, and green onions. Brush pastry shells with egg whites before filling to seal crust and prevent sogginess. Pour mixture into pastry shells. Bake at 350°F for 40-45 minutes. Serves 10-12.

1 cup chopped ham may also be used.

Mrs. William Wright
(Angell Stockwell)

Mrs. R. L. Cline, Jr.
(Geraldine Fly)

DEVILED EGGS

12 hard boiled eggs, peeled, and sliced lengthwise
½ stick margarine, melted
2 Tablespoons onion, grated
¼ cup mayonnaise
1 Tablespoon prepared mustard
1 teaspoon salt
¼ teaspoon each pepper, celery salt, and horseradish
1 teaspoon Worcestershire
5 drops Tabasco

Scoop out egg yolks and mash. In large saucepan stir onion and mashed yolks in margarine over low heat for few minutes. Remove from heat, add remaining ingredients, and mix thoroughly. Spoon into halved egg whites, sprinkle with paprika and top with olive slices or capers. Chill thoroughly before serving.

Mrs. Susan Switzer St. Dizier
Houston, Texas

STUFFED EGGS AU GRATIN

6 hard boiled eggs
½ teaspoon dry mustard
1 Tablespoon vinegar
1 teaspoon anchovy paste
½ teaspoon salt
2 Tablespoons Wesson oil

SAUCE
3 Tablespoons flour
3 Tablespoons Wesson oil
2 cups milk
1 teaspoon salt
Dash of pepper
½ teaspoon basil
Dash of Worcestershire sauce
½ cup cheese, grated

Peel eggs. Cut lengthwise. Remove yolks and mash. Add all other ingredients and mix well. Fill whites with mixture. Place in shallow baking dish which has been brushed with oil.

SAUCE
Make white sauce, cooking flour in oil. Add milk and seasonings. Pour sauce over eggs. Add Worcestershire sauce and sprinkle with cheese. Bake at 350°F for 25 minutes. To make ahead, keep, covered, in refrigerator until time to bake. Serves 6-8.

Mrs. J. R. Meek
Ponca City, Oklahoma

EGGS AND CHEESE   145

HOW TO BOIL EGGS PERFECTLY: Place eggs in tap water for 10 minutes to reduce to near room temperature. Drain, place in liberally salted cold water, cover, turn fire to medium high, and bring to a boil. Immediately reduce temperature to simmer and cook for 20 minutes. Remove eggs at once and place in ice and water to stop cooking process.

The whites are white and the yellows are yellow and never the twain shall mix!

SUNDAY NIGHT OMELETS

BASIC OMELET RECIPE

2 Tablespoons butter or margarine
6 eggs, whipped
½ teaspoon baking powder (makes eggs very light)
½ teaspoon salt
½ teaspoon white pepper

Melt butter in pan, coating sides and bottom. Pour remaining ingredients premixed into pan and cook on medium heat. When edges begin to set slightly, add desired filling in a straight line from one side to the other. Let omelet cook slowly until edges firm. With spatula lift one side over filling to the center. Center omelet in pan and flip center over side that is still open. (Flip right side over center, then center over left side.) Cook until set. Slide out on warmed platter and garnish with extra filling. Serves 3-4.

1 pound fresh chicken livers
1 onion, finely chopped
4 Tablespoons butter
Salt and pepper

CHICKEN LIVER FILLING

Sauté livers and onion in butter until done. Season to taste. Serve with ketchup if desired.

1½ cups ham, chopped
¼ pound fresh mushrooms, chopped
2 Tablespoons butter
1 cup Swiss cheese, chopped

HAM, MUSHROOM, AND CHEESE FILLING

Sauté ham and mushrooms in butter. Add cheese.

For variations follow basic omelet directions, or do your own thing.

Mrs. David Painter
(Isabel "Bel" Thornton)

CREOLE SAUCE
(Serve with a Fluffy Omelet)

¼ cup bell pepper, finely chopped
¼ cup onions, finely chopped
2 Tablespoons butter
1¼ cups canned tomatoes
¼ teaspoon Tabasco
½ teaspoon sugar
½ teaspoon salt
1 small can peas

Sauté bell pepper and onion in butter. Cook until onion is tender, but not brown. Add remaining ingredients, except peas, and continue cooking over low heat about 30 minutes or until thick. Add peas. Serve over a fluffy omelet.

Mrs. J. Malcolm Leveque
(Marjorie Helen Schepp)

BAKED DEVILED EGGS

20 hard boiled eggs
1 can cream of tomato soup
1 small can deviled ham
1 small can mushroom pieces
½ cup butter
Salt and pepper
Lea & Perrins
Chili sauce, sparingly to taste
Garlic salt, sparingly to taste
Cornstarch
1 cup sharp cheese, grated

Peel and halve eggs and place in baking dish. Mix all other ingredients, except cheese, in saucepan and thicken with a little cornstarch. Cook until thick. Pour over eggs, then sprinkle with cheese. Bake, uncovered, at 350°F for 5 minutes, or until cheese is bubbly.

Mrs. Ada Brand Shearman

EGGS À LA DEBI

¼ cup olive oil
½ cup onion, chopped
1 small clove garlic, minced
¾ cup bell pepper, diced
1½ cups tomatoes, chopped
1 teaspoon basil
1 teaspoon Tabasco
1 Tablespoon each olive oil and butter
6-8 eggs
1 cup ham, cubed
Parsley

Heat olive oil; add onions, garlic, bell pepper and cook until tender. Add tomatoes, basil, and Tabasco and cook 2 minutes longer. Keep warm. In another skillet heat oil, butter, and ham. Drain. Scramble eggs and transfer to serving platter, spread tomato mixture over, scatter ham on top, and sprinkle with parsley. Serves 3-4.

Mrs. William A. Mixon
(Debi Kramer)

CHEESE SOUFFLÉ

4 Tablespoons butter
4 Tablespoons flour
1 teaspoon salt
Dash of red pepper
1½ cups milk
½ pound cheese, grated
6 egg yolks, beaten
6 egg whites, beaten stiff but not dry

Melt butter in the top of a double boiler. Add flour, salt, and red pepper. Add milk, blending well. Cook over hot water, stirring constantly. When sauce is smooth, add cheese and stir until cheese is melted. Remove from heat and add egg yolks, stirring constantly. Cool slightly. Carefully fold this cheese sauce into egg whites. Fold in lightly until well blended. Pour into an ungreased 2 quart casserole. To make the soufflé puff up, run the tip of a teaspoon around in the mixture 1 inch from edge of casserole. Bake at 300°F for 1 hour and 15 minutes. Serve at once. Serves 6.

Mrs. Frank R. Gibson

EGGS AND CHEESE

CHEESE PUFF

2 slices bread
1 slice Swiss or American cheese
1 egg, beaten
1 cup milk
Salt and pepper to taste
Bacon, crumbled

Remove crust from bread and make sandwich by putting thick slice of cheese between. Place in greased, shallow baking dish. Beat egg and milk, adding salt and pepper. Pour over bread and refrigerate for 45 minutes. Sprinkle with bacon and bake, uncovered, at 325°F for 45 minutes, or until puffy and golden brown. Allow 1 sandwich per person.

Mrs. Cecil K. Colon
(Marion Palmer)

MACARONI-CHEESE TOMATO TANG

2 Tablespoons butter or margarine
2 Tablespoons flour
2½ cups canned tomatoes
1 small bell pepper, chopped
¼ teaspoon thyme
½ cup ripe olives, sliced
2 cups cooked macaroni (¾ cup raw)
1 small onion, minced
1½ cups Cheddar cheese, shredded
1 cup bread cubes (about 3 slices cut in 1 inch squares)
½ cup butter or margarine, melted

Melt butter; blend in flour; stir in tomatoes, bell pepper, and thyme. Cook over medium heat until thickened. Add olives, cooked macaroni, onion, and ½ of the cheese. Place in greased 1½ quart casserole. Arrange bread cubes on top. Drizzle with butter and sprinkle remaining cheese on top. Bake, uncovered, at 350°F for about 50 minutes. Freezes. Serves 6.

Mrs. James B. Allen
(Opal McCrary)

WELSH RAREBIT

1 pound sharp cheese, grated
1 teaspoon dry mustard
½ teaspoon salt
1 egg, well beaten
3 Tablespoons Worcestershire sauce
Dash of Tabasco
Enough beer to thin

Melt all ingredients in double boiler. Serve on toast with sliced tomatoes. Serves 4.

Good with cold beer!

Mrs. Thomas L. Raggio
(Beverly Barry Crook)

EGGS AND CHEESE

BAKED CHEESE GRITS

1 cup grits
2 cups water
½ stick butter
1 cup milk
2 eggs, beaten
½ cup Coon brand cheese
½ cup Cheddar cheese (Longhorn)
1 teaspoon salt
2 drops hot sauce

Cook grits; they will be stiff. Stir in butter, milk, eggs, cheese, salt, and hot sauce. Pour in baking dish. Bake, uncovered, at 350°F for 30-40 minutes. Serves 6.

Mrs. Courtney A. Fenet, Jr.
(Sally Garber)

SOUTH OF THE BORDER

4 cups water
1 stick margarine
Dash red pepper
Garlic, onion, celery powder
1 teaspoon salt, piled high
1 cup 3 minute grits
1 roll Kraft garlic cheese, diced
1 cup milk
3 whole eggs, beaten
Extra sharp or Velveeta cheese, grated

Bring water, margarine, red pepper, garlic powder, onion powder, celery powder, and salt to a boil in a large saucepan. Add grits slowly until they thicken. Reduce heat. Add garlic cheese and allow to melt. Blend milk and eggs using a mixer and add to grits. Be sure mixture is moist and soupy. If too thick, add more milk. Bake in greased casserole at 325°F for 45 minutes. When baked, sprinkle with cheese and return to oven.

If sharp cheese is not your preference, Velveeta may be substituted.

Mrs. Belvin L. Fontenot

COLORFUL PICKLED EGGS

1 dozen medium or small eggs
SOLUTION
1⅓ cups white vinegar
⅔ cup water
1 Tablespoon sugar
2 Tablespoons salt
4-5 whole cloves
½ stick cinnamon
6-7 drops food coloring

In saucepan cover eggs with water and boil slowly until hard. Meanwhile mix next 6 ingredients in another saucepan (non-metallic). Bring to a boil; reduce heat to low and keep hot until eggs are ready. Peel eggs under warm running water to keep them hot and to aid in peeling. Drop hot eggs into wide mouthed jar. Add food coloring to hot solution and stir. Pour over eggs to cover. Seal jar and rotate occasionally during first hour. This rotation circulates solution for even coloring of eggs. Refrigerate after 1 hour. Eggs are thoroughly pickled in 3 days, but may be eaten at any time before.

Mrs. B. B. Wehner
Mrs. B. Scott Wehner

TIROTRIGONA
(Greek cheese filled triangles)

1 pound feta cheese
1 pint cottage cheese
1 package (8 ounces) cream cheese
3 eggs
2 Tablespoons parsley, finely chopped
Dash pepper
¾ pound prepared fillo dough
1 cup butter or margarine, melted

Cream together cheeses. Add eggs, one at a time, beating until smooth. Mix in parsley and pepper. Lay out fillo, 1 sheet at a time, and brush with melted butter. Cut each sheet into 2 inch strips (cut across the width). Place a heaping teaspoon of cheese filling at end of pastry strip and fold over 1 corner to make a triangle. Continue folding pastry from one side to the other until the entire strip covers the filling. Repeat until all strips and filling are used. Bake triangles on buttered baking sheet in preheated 350°F oven for 15 minutes, or until golden brown. Serve hot. Makes 6 dozen. *The trick is to find the feta cheese and fillo dough. Any good import store should carry them. This recipe is tedious and time consuming but well worth it. Of all the dishes I have ever served, this has been the most sought after recipe.*

Mrs. Jake W. Posey
(Jerry Anderson)

CHILALY

2 Tablespoons onion, chopped
1 Tablespoon bell or hot pepper, chopped
2 Tablespoons butter
1 can tomatoes, strained
Salt to taste
¾ pound cheese, chopped
2 eggs, beaten
4 slices bread, toasted

Sauté onion and pepper in butter. Add tomatoes and salt and cook for 5 minutes. Add cheese and cook slowly until cheese melts. Add eggs and cook until thick. If not thick enough, add another egg. Serve over toasted bread. Serves 4.

A quick and easy money stretcher and really good.

Mrs. N. Kyle Fergerson

CREAM OF WHEAT CUSTARD

1 cup water
⅛ teaspoon salt
1 cup milk
4 Tablespoons cream of wheat (quick cooking type)
1 egg, slightly beaten
¼ cup sugar
1 teaspoon vanilla flavoring
½ teaspoon almond flavoring

Bring water to boil in saucepan. Add salt. Gradually add milk so that mixture continues to boil, reducing heat as low as possible to prevent boiling over. Sprinkle cream of wheat over boiling mixture and stir until boiling gently. Boil 5 minutes. Stir a little of the mixture into egg. Return egg mixture to saucepan and cook 1 minute more. Remove from heat and stir in sugar and flavorings. Serves 2.

Mrs. Caroline Skipper Hollins

EGGS AND CHEESE

YOGURT

4 large cans evaporated skim milk
2 cups tepid water
3 Tablespoons plain yogurt or yogurt culture

Preheat oven to 275°F. Combine all ingredients until yogurt or yogurt culture is thoroughly dissolved. Divide liquid (about 2½ quarts) between two 1½ quarts heavy pyrex or Corningware type casseroles with lids. Cover and place on center rack of oven. Close oven door and immediately turn off heat. Do not open for 8 hours. After 8 hours, if it has the consistency of sour cream, it is "made." If it is not ready, stir 2 Tablespoons more culture into each casserole. Preheat oven again and proceed as before, leaving casseroles in oven 10 hours, or until "made." Refrigerate and use with fresh fruit or as a substitute for sour cream.

Mrs. Benjamin English
(Margaret Whittle)

YOGURT POPSICLES

2-3 pints yogurt
1 large can frozen orange juice concentrate
2 teaspoons vanilla

Combine all ingredients and freeze for a delicious treat!

YOGURT DIP FOR FRUIT

Yogurt
Strawberries, crushed
Honey to taste

Combine yogurt, strawberries, and honey to taste. Dip fruit such as pineapple, watermelon, peaches, or melon into dip. Delicious!

YOGURT PIE

16 ounces creamed cottage cheese
16 ounces yogurt
4½ teaspoons unflavored gelatin
½ cup milk
½ cup sugar
1 teaspoon vanilla
1 lemon rind, grated
9 inch graham cracker crust
Nutmeg

Blend the cottage cheese and 8 ounces of yogurt in blender. Soften gelatin in milk and dissolve over hot water, stirring constantly. Add to cheese mixture and stir. Add remaining yogurt, sugar, vanilla, and lemon rind. Mix well and pour into crust, sprinkling with nutmeg. Chill 3-4 hours.

Mrs. Frederick L. Cappel
(Sally Rowden)

Place 1 batch yogurt in cheesecloth bag and allow to drip overnight for cottage cheese or cream cheese. This removes "whey." Excellent for dips.

Breads

When men gathered on the banks of Louisiana bayous and lakes to fry their freshly caught fish, the dogs would yap at their heels for a share of the catch. Spoonfuls of batter were fried in hot grease and scattered about to hush the puppies. The "Hush Puppy" was born!!

HUSH PUPPIES

1 cup yellow corn meal
2 teaspoons salt
1 cup boiling water
1 small onion, finely chopped
1 egg, slightly beaten
Flour

Combine meal and salt. Add gradually to boiling water, stirring constantly. Remove from heat and stir to smooth, thick mush. Cool. Add onion and egg. Mix thoroughly. Form into small balls, roll in flour, and fry with fish. Makes about 20 small balls.

From the recipes of
Jeanette Vitello Plauché

DOTTY'S HUSH PUPPIES

½ cup self rising flour
1½ cups self rising corn meal
1 egg
1 cup milk
1 small onion, chopped
Hot grease

Add flour to corn meal, stirring so that flour will not lump. Add remaining ingredients to dry mixture and beat lightly. Drop by teaspoonfuls into hot grease. When hush puppies float to top, they are done.

Jene Renfroe

CORN BREAD

¾ heaping cup corn meal
¾ scant cup flour
5 teaspoons baking powder
1 teaspoon salt
2 Tablespoons sugar
1 egg
1 Tablespoon oil
Milk

Mix first 5 ingredients in a bowl. Place egg and oil in a 1 cup glass measuring cup; then fill to brim with milk. Add to dry ingredients and mix well. Pour into hot, greased iron corn stick pan. Bake at 450°F until golden brown, about 10 minutes. Serves 4.

Mrs. W. R. Barnett

JALAPEÑO CORN BREAD

1 cup yellow corn meal
2 teaspoons baking powder
¼ teaspoon baking soda
1 teaspoon salt
1 cup buttermilk
2 eggs
1 cup cream style corn
1 medium onion, chopped
½ cup cheese, grated
1 clove garlic, pressed
2 small or 1 large Jalapeño pepper, chopped
2 Tablespoons bacon fat, melted
Paprika as needed

Preheat oven to 350°F. Combine dry ingredients in mixing bowl. Add buttermilk and eggs. Fold in corn, onion, cheese, garlic, and peppers. Pour into a 9x9 inch pan greased with the bacon fat. Sprinkle with paprika. Bake, uncovered, about 40 minutes or until tester comes out clean. May be prepared ahead and kept in refrigerator 2-3 days. Serve as an appetizer or with gumbo.

Mrs. Amy S. Boyd

Peggy Tilden *uses basically the same recipe but substitutes sour cream for the buttermilk.*

SPOON CORN BREAD

1 pint sweet milk
1 cup (scant) corn meal
½ teaspoon salt
2 Tablespoons sugar
1 Tablespoon butter, melted
2 teaspoons baking powder
4 eggs, separated

Scald milk. Slowly add corn meal; then cook for 2 minutes. Add salt, sugar, and butter. Cool slightly; then add baking powder and slightly beaten egg yolks. Fold in stiffly beaten egg whites. Pour into greased 1½ quart casserole or pan and bake, uncovered, at 375°F for 20-30 minutes. Serves 6.

Mrs. James B. Allen
(Opal McCrary)

ONION CORN BREAD

4 cups onion, coarsely chopped
¼ cup butter or margarine, melted
1 cup sour cream
1 cup Cheddar cheese, shredded
1 cup enriched self rising corn meal
¼ teaspoon dill weed (optional)
2 Tablespoons sugar
2 eggs, beaten
1 cup white cream style corn
¼ cup milk
¼ cup oil
Dash of Tabasco

Sauté onions in butter until soft. Add sour cream and ½ of cheese. Set aside. Stir corn meal, dill, and sugar. Mix remaining ingredients well and stir into corn meal. Pour into greased 9 inch square pan. Spoon onion mixture over corn meal and top with rest of cheese. Bake at 400°F for 25-30 minutes. Serves 8-10.

Good with fish.

Mrs. Alan Kratzer
(Carol Wise)

NANNY JEANNE'S COUSH-COUSH

1½ cups yellow corn meal
1 teaspoon salt
1 cup warm water
1 egg (optional)
2 Tablespoons cooking oil or shortening

Blend dry ingredients. Add water, and egg if desired. Stir until mixture is soft and almost runny. Cook at medium temperature on top of stove for 15 minutes. Into a heavy iron pot sprayed with "Pam," place cooking oil and batter mixture, stirring until well blended. For first 3 minutes of cooking stir occasionally to prevent burning. Then stir constantly until cereal is dry and granulated (about 15 minutes). Cover pot between stirrings. A few small lumps may remain. Serve with milk (or syrup for a sweet breakfast cereal). Serves 4.

Mrs. Fred L. Colomb
Lafayette, Louisiana

EGG BREAD

2 envelopes active dry yeast
½ cup warm water
1½ cups milk
¼ cup butter, softened
¼ cup sugar
1 Tablespoon salt
3 eggs
7½ cups flour, sifted

In a small bowl dissolve yeast in warm water. Combine milk and butter in a saucepan and scald; cool to lukewarm. In a large bowl mix sugar, salt, and eggs. Add milk and yeast mixtures to egg mixture. Slowly add sifted flour, stirring constantly. Place on floured surface, cover, and let sit 10-15 minutes. Knead until smooth and blistered, about 10 minutes. Place in greased bowl, cover, and let rise until doubled, about 1 hour. Punch down. Let rise again until almost doubled. Divide into 2 parts. Round up, cover, and let sit 10 minutes. Shape into 2 loaves that touch sides of greased and floured bread pans. Let rise until doubled. Bake at 425°F on center rack until loaves sound hollow when tapped, about 25-30 minutes. Remove from pans immediately and place on cooling racks or across top of bread pans. May be prepared a day ahead. May be doubled.

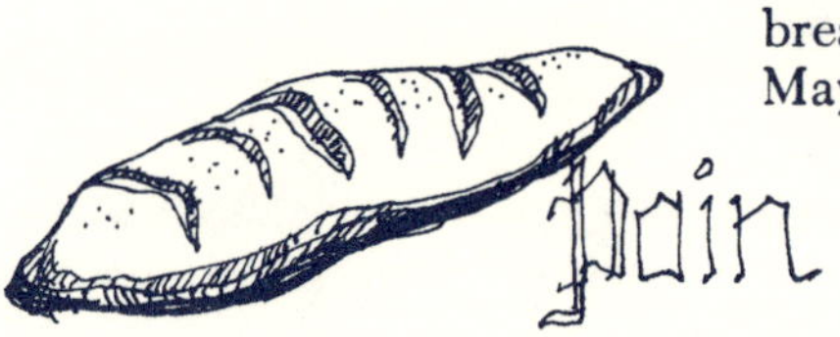

Never fails!

Mrs. James W. Crawford
(Sydalise Fredeman)

OATMEAL RAISED BREAD

1 cup milk, scalded
½ cup butter
½ cup brown sugar
1½ teaspoons salt
2 Tablespoons honey
1 cup lukewarm water
2 envelopes dry yeast
5-6 cups flour, sifted
2 eggs
1½ cups rolled oats

Pour scalded milk over butter, brown sugar, salt, and honey; cool to lukewarm. Add water to yeast and combine with milk mixture after waiting a few minutes. Stir in 2 cups flour. Add eggs, beating with mixer to blend. Add oats and enough flour to make soft dough. Turn out on lightly floured board. Knead 10 minutes until satiny, using more flour if needed. Form dough into a ball and place in greased bowl. Cover and let rise in warm place about 1 hour. Punch down, cover, and let rest 10 minutes. Shape into 2 loaves. Place in greased loaf pans and brush with melted butter. Cover and let rise until double. Bake at 375°F for 1 hour. Freezes.

Mrs. William B. Baggett
(Gael Salter)

WHOLE WHEAT BREAD

2 envelopes active dry yeast
⅓ cup honey
1 cup water
2 cups milk
¼ cup margarine or butter
1½ Tablespoons salt
5 cups whole wheat flour
¼ cup wheat germ
2-3 cups white flour

Stir yeast and 1 teaspoon honey into cup of very warm water. (Water should feel comfortable on wrist.) Let stand until bubbly, about 10 minutes. Heat in saucepan the remaining honey, milk, margarine, and salt. Pour into a large bowl and cool to lukewarm. Add yeast mixture. Stir in whole wheat flour and wheat germ. Add enough white flour to make a soft dough. Turn out on lightly floured board and knead until smooth, about 10 minutes, using just enough flour to prevent sticking. Place dough in large buttered bowl, turning dough so buttered side is up. Cover with towel. Let rise 1 hour in a warm place. Punch dough down. Turn out on floured surface, knead a few times, and cover with inverted bowl. Let rest 10 minutes. Divide dough in half. Knead each half a few times and shape into loaves. Place in 2 buttered 9x5x3 inch loaf pans. Let rise, covered, 45 minutes. Bake 40 minutes at 400°F. When done, tops will be brown and sound hollow when tapped. Remove from pans and cool on wire racks.

**Mrs. David Painter
(Isabel "Bel" Thornton)**

BOSTON BROWN BREAD

¾ cup all bran cereal
1½ cups buttermilk
¾ cup dry oatmeal
¾ cup yellow corn meal
¾ cup all purpose flour
1 teaspoon salt
¾ cup cane syrup (Steen's is good)
1 teaspoon baking soda dissolved in 1 Tablespoon water

Soak cereal in ¾ cup buttermilk for 15 minutes. Mix oatmeal, corn meal, flour, and salt in bowl. Add syrup and mix well. Add cereal mixture plus remaining ¾ cup buttermilk and mix well. Add dissolved soda to batter. Pour into well greased 1 pound coffee can with tight lid, or seal with aluminum foil. Place covered can in a tall pot which also has tight fitting lid. Fill with water to ½ depth of coffee can. Cover tightly. Bring water to slow boil, reduce to simmer, and steam until bread is moist but not soggy. It will take 4½-5 hours of slow cooking to steam bread. Best served hot with real butter. Serve with beans and wieners for a traditional Boston meal. Serves 6.

**From the recipes of
Mrs. J. H. Baumgardner**

CHEESE BREAD

2 envelopes dry yeast
2 Tablespoons sugar
2 teaspoons salt
4¼ cups flour
1 cup milk
½ cup water
2 cups sharp cheese, grated

In a large bowl stir together yeast, sugar, salt, and 1½ cups flour. Combine milk and water and heat until very warm. Add liquid to yeast mixture and stir. Add cheese and ¼ cup flour and mix well. Add remaining 2½ cups flour, ½ cup at a time, mixing well after each addition. (Best to use hands when adding the last cup.) Turn out on a lightly floured surface and knead 7-10 minutes by hand or 4-5 minutes with a dough hook. When dough is smooth and elastic, shape into a ball, place in a buttered bowl, and turn to coat all sides with butter. Cover with plastic wrap and put in a draft-free place until doubled, 1½-2 hours. Punch dough down in bowl, turn out, and knead for 1-2 minutes. Divide dough to fit 3 bread pans, 7⅝x3⅝x2½ inches. Place loaves in pans, cover, and put in a warm place until dough has again doubled in bulk, about 1½ hours. Bake in preheated 375°F oven for about 20 minutes. Bottoms of bread should sound hollow when tapped. Cool on wire racks. Freezes.

Makes great sandwiches!

Mrs. David Drez
(Judy Wolfe)

HERB STIX

4 slices bread
¼ cup butter, creamed
⅛ teaspoon thyme
⅛ teaspoon paprika
⅛ teaspoon salt
Dash cayenne pepper

Toast bread lightly on both sides. Mix creamed butter thoroughly with remaining ingredients. Spread on both sides of toast. Cut each slice into 5 strips. Bake on baking sheet at 250°F for about 20 minutes, or until crunchy. May be frozen, or kept in airtight container for several weeks. Makes 20 stix.

Good with soups, salads, or as cocktail food.

Mrs. William G. Akins
(Kay Mishler)

FRESH APPLE BREAD

4 eggs, beaten
2 cups sugar
1 cup oil
4 Tablespoons sour cream
2 teaspoons vanilla
4 cups flour
2 teaspoons baking soda
1 teaspoon salt
2 cups apples, chopped (3 apples)
1 cup pecans, chopped

Combine first 5 ingredients and beat well. Sift flour with soda and salt. Blend egg and flour mixtures. Fold in apples and pecans, mixing until blended. Pour into 2 greased and floured loaf pans. Bake at 350°F for 1 hour, or until sides pull away from pan. Freezes.

Serve warm with ice cream as a dessert.

Mrs. David Huddle
(Tucker Neilson)

BANANA NUT BREAD

¼ cup shortening
¼ cup margarine
1¼ cups white flour
½ cup whole wheat flour
1 teaspoon baking soda
1 teaspoon salt
3 small bananas, mashed
Juice of ½ lemon
1 cup white sugar
½ cup brown sugar
2 eggs
¼ cup buttermilk
½ cup pecans, chopped
1 teaspoon vanilla

Preheat oven to 325°F. Place shortening and margarine in mixing bowl. Sift the flours, soda, and salt together, using also any remnants left in sifter. Mix mashed bananas with lemon juice. Cream together the shortenings and sugars. Add eggs, 1 at a time, beating well after each. Add flour mixture and buttermilk alternately, starting and ending with flour. Add bananas, chopped pecans, and vanilla. Pour into greased and floured loaf pan and bake 1 hour and 15 minutes, or until top does not yield to finger pressure. Cool 15 minutes and turn out of pan. Freezes.

Mrs. Patrick J. Unkel
(Barbara Perez)

PUMPKIN BREAD

5 cups flour
4 cups sugar
4 teaspoons baking soda
1 teaspoon salt
1 teaspoon cloves, ground
1 teaspoon cinnamon, ground
1 cup cooking oil
1 cup raisins
½ cup pecans, chopped
1 can (1 pound 13 ounces) pumpkin

Mix ingredients as for cake. Divide into 3 loaves. Bake at 350°F for 1 hour. Test with toothpick for doneness. Let cool before removing from pans. May be served cold or warm with a little butter. Freezes.

Mrs. Margaret Streater Conover

REFRIGERATOR ROLLS

1 package dry yeast
¼ cup lukewarm water
¾ cup evaporated milk
½ cup boiling water
2 eggs, beaten
¼ cup sugar
1 teaspoon salt
¼ cup shortening, margarine, or butter, melted
4½ cups flour, sifted

Soak yeast in lukewarm water for 10 minutes. Mix milk and boiling water. Cool to lukewarm. Combine all ingredients, knead on floured board until smooth. (Do not work in additional flour.) Place in greased bowl; cover with waxed paper. When dough has doubled, knead again, return to bowl, cover well, and place in refrigerator until needed. To use, pull off desired amount, make into balls and flatten, or roll out and cut. Brush with margarine and fold over for Parker House Rolls. Brush tops with margarine. Let rise until doubled. Bake at 350°F for 20 minutes.

VARIATION: ORANGE ROLLS

Rind of 2 oranges, grated
1½ cups white sugar
Margarine
½ cup orange juice
½ pound confectioners sugar

Make basic refrigerator roll recipe. Mix orange rind and sugar. Roll out dough in a rectangle to ¼ inch thickness. Spread with soft margarine and sprinkle with orange-sugar mixture. Cut dough in half, lengthwise. Roll up as for jelly roll, then cut rolls about ½ inch thick. Place, cut side down, on greased shallow pan, let rise until double in size. Bake at 325°F until brown. Mix orange juice with confectioners sugar. Spread over top of rolls. Serve at once.

VARIATION: CINNAMON ROLLS

Margarine
Brown sugar
Ground cinnamon
Seedless raisins

Use basic refrigerator roll recipe. Roll out dough into a rectangle. Spread with soft margarine. Cover generously with brown sugar. Sprinkle with cinnamon and raisins. Roll up, holding firmly in both hands. Cut into ½ inch slices. Place, cut side down, on greased cookie sheet, leaving about ¼ inch between rolls. Place in warm place. Let rise until double in size. Bake at 350°F until light brown (about 15 minutes).

Mrs. Avery L. Cook
(Carolyn DeJean)

ICE BOX ROLLS

1 yeast cake
¼ cup lukewarm water
1 teaspoon sugar
1 cup sugar
½ cup Crisco
1 egg, beaten
2½ teaspoons salt
1 teaspoon vanilla
2 cups warm water
8-9 cups flour
Butter, melted

Mix first 3 ingredients and let sit 20 minutes. Cream sugar and Crisco. Add beaten egg, salt, vanilla, and yeast mixture. Add water and flour, but do not use mixer. Let rise until double in bulk. Knead down, cover, and refrigerate. For dinner rolls, cut off desired amount of dough and place on floured board. Cut in desired sizes. Roll in hands, dip in melted butter, and place in muffin tin. Let rise until double in bulk. Bake at 375°F for 10 minutes.
Variation: For cinnamon rolls, pat out desired amount of dough on floured board to ⅛ inch thick. Cover with melted butter, sugar, and cinnamon. Roll, then cut into ½ inch thick slices. Place, cut side up, in greased pan. Let rise until double in bulk. Bake at 375°F until golden brown, 10-15 minutes. Dough stays good for 2 weeks refrigerated.

**Mrs. Robert W. Price, Sr.
(Betty Boedecker)**

BRAN ROLLS

¾ cup sugar
1 cup oil
1 cup all bran
2½ teaspoons salt
1 cup boiling water
3 eggs, beaten
1 envelope yeast, dissolved in 1 cup lukewarm water
6½ cups flour

Combine sugar and oil in bowl. Add bran, salt, and boiling water. Let cool to lukewarm. Add eggs and dissolved yeast. Add ½ of flour, stir, add remaining flour. When well blended, knead on floured board several times. Return to bowl; rub with cooking oil. To make rolls, pinch off desired size, roll in oil, and place in oiled pyrex dish. Let rise 2 hours. Bake from 17-20 minutes at 425°F. May be kept, covered, in refrigerator up to 5 days. When ready to bake, just pinch off desired amount, let rise, and bake. Does not freeze. Makes about 30 rolls.

**Mrs. George Hardy Vincent
(Nina LaFleur)**

ICE BOX ROLLS

1 cup (scant) Crisco shortening (do not substitute)
6 cups flour, sifted
1 Tablespoon salt
½ cup sugar
2 cups milk, scalded
1 package yeast dissolved in 1 cup warm water
Butter, melted (do not substitute)

Cut shortening into sifted flour to which salt and sugar have been added. Alternately add milk and yeast mixture. Let rise for 2 hours. Refrigerate at least overnight or a maximum of 4 days. Place dough on floured surface and knead slightly. Roll out, cut with biscuit cutter, fold in half as for Parker House rolls, place in pan. Let rise 2 more hours. Prebake at 275°F about 15 minutes, and just before browning, remove from oven. Rolls may be refrigerated no longer than 2 days or frozen for later use. When ready to bake, remove from refrigerator or freezer and bring to room temperature. Brush tops with melted butter. Bake at 400°F for 10 minutes. Makes 6-7 dozen.

Recipe may not be doubled. Use bowl large enough to allow for rising. This recipe is not limited as to the type of roll to bake. Equally good for Cloverleaf, etc.

Mrs. Virgil Junk
(Renza Taussig)

PLUCKING BREAD

1 envelope active dry yeast
¼ cup warm water
1¼ cups milk, scalded and cooled
4½-5½ cups flour
4 egg yolks, well beaten
½ cup sugar
1 teaspoon salt
½ cup butter, melted and cooled

COATING MIX
½ cup butter, melted
¾ cup sugar
2 teaspoons cinnamon
½ teaspoon nutmeg
¾ cup nuts, chopped

Soften yeast in warm water for 5 minutes. Add milk and 1 cup flour. Beat and let stand 20 minutes or until light and bubbly. Blend egg yolks, sugar, salt, and melted butter. Add to yeast mixture and mix well. Knead in enough flour to make smooth and elastic. Place in greased bowl, cover, and let rise until double in bulk. Turn out on well greased surface and divide in half. Form each half into a long roll and cut into 24 pieces (total 48). Roll each piece into a ball. Dip balls into coating mix in 3 steps: melted butter, then sugar and spice mixture, then nuts. Arrange close together in a large, well greased tube pan. Let stand in a warm place 45 minutes. Bake at 350°F for 45 minutes. Cool on wire rack.

Louise Walden
Alexandria, Louisiana

ALLEN'S GOLDEN BISCUITS

2 cups flour
4 teaspoons baking powder
½ teaspoon salt
1 heaping teaspoon sugar
6 Tablespoons shortening
¾ cup milk (or 1 cup buttermilk or evaporated)

Mix together first 4 ingredients. Add shortening and cut until about consistency of corn meal. Add milk and mix in with fork. On floured cutting board knead gently, turning over several times. Roll with dusted rolling pin to ⅜-½ inch thickness. Cut to desired size with a glass. Bake, with sides touching, on ungreased cookie sheet, on high shelf in oven, at 450°F for about 10-12 minutes. Makes 16 (2½ inch) biscuits.

Allen L. Smith

EASY BUTTERMILK BISCUITS

2½ cups all purpose flour
3 teaspoons baking powder
1 teaspoon salt
½ teaspoon baking soda
⅓ cup butter, melted
1 cup buttermilk
Bacon drippings

Combine dry ingredients. Add butter and buttermilk and mix to make a sticky dough. Knead just a little on floured board. Form a smooth ball, roll to ½ inch thickness, and cut into 2 inch rounds. Place biscuits on cookie sheet or pie pan greased with bacon drippings. Bake at 450°F for 10-12 minutes. Freezes. Makes about 15 biscuits.

My grandma declares it was these that attracted my grandfather!

**Mrs. William B. Baggett
(Gael Salter)**

UNCLE BUBBER'S BISCUITS

⅔ cup milk
1 egg
⅓ stick butter or margarine, melted
3 cups Bisquick mix
⅔ teaspoon salt

Preheat oven to 350°F. Mix all wet ingredients and pour into Bisquick and salt. Roll out and cut on floured board. Bake for 8 minutes, then broil until brown on top (watch carefully). Brush tops with melted butter. Serves 6.

**Louis Cornay
Lafayette, Louisiana**

MOTHER'S DUMPLINGS

1 cup milk
1 cup (scant) flour
1 egg
¼ teaspoon salt
Soup (chicken soup best)

Heat milk to just before boiling point and add flour. Stir rapidly until mixture leaves side of pan. Remove from heat; let sit until cool, not cold. Stir in egg and salt. Beat until smooth. Drop by teaspoonfuls into simmering (not boiling) soup. Do not cover. Simmer for ½ hour. Serves 4.

Mrs. Robert W. Price, Sr.
(Betty Boedecker)

BUTTERMILK PANCAKES

1 egg
1 cup buttermilk
1 cup flour
1 teaspoon baking powder
1 Tablespoon sugar
1 teaspoon salt
3 Tablespoons liquid vegetable shortening (or melted butter)
½ teaspoon vanilla (optional)
Crisco

Beat egg in large mixing bowl and add buttermilk. Stir in dry ingredients and mix until smooth. Add shortening and blend completely. Vanilla may be added if desired. Drop by tablespoonfuls on well greased medium-hot griddle or large skillet. Makes approximately 20 pancakes.

This recipe was inspired by all those cereal breakfasts and resurrected from childhood memories of better repasts.

Allen L. Smith

PANCAKES

2 eggs
½ teaspoon salt
½ teaspoon baking soda
2 teaspoons sugar
2 teaspoons baking powder
1¼ cups flour
1 cup milk
2 Tablespoons liquid shortening

Preheat griddle to medium heat. In 1½ quart mixing bowl, beat eggs well with a spoon. Add next 4 ingredients, mixing until thoroughly blended. Then add next 3 ingredients and mix lightly, leaving lumpy. Cook on hot griddle. This recipe also makes fine crêpes using same ingredients, except reduce baking powder to 1 teaspoon.

Mrs. John D. Hines
(Jere James)

BREADS

COFFEE CAKE

3 cups flour
1 teaspoon salt
¼ cup sugar
½ cup butter, softened to room temperature
1 yeast cake
½ cup water
1 Tablespoon sugar
1 egg
½ cup milk
FILLING
1 stick margarine
1 cup nuts, chopped
½ cup brown sugar
Cinnamon
ICING
1 box confectioners sugar
1 stick butter
1 teaspoon almond extract
Warm milk to moisten

Sift dry ingredients. Add butter and work with fork or pastry blender as for pie crust. Dissolve yeast in water, add sugar and add to dry mixture. Add egg beaten with milk and mix well. Cover bowl and let dough rise 2-3 times its size. Knead on floured board several minutes. Roll with rolling pin into a rectangle about 9x12 inches until dough is ¼ inch thick. Combine margarine, nuts, and sugar, spread on dough, and sprinkle with cinnamon. Shape dough lengthwise into a roll (like a jelly roll). Grasping both ends, place on a greased cookie sheet to form a circle. With kitchen scissors space cuts 1 inch apart along outer perimeter, ¾ of way down into dough. Grasp each cut section with fingers and turn side up. Let rise for about 30 minutes. Bake at 350°F for 30 minutes. Combine ingredients for icing and spread on cake. Freezes. Serves 8-10.

Mrs. Norman Davidson
(Elaine Barnes)

SWEDISH PUFF COFFEE CAKE

PART I
1 cup flour
1 stick margarine or butter
1 Tablespoon water

PART I
Combine flour and margarine and add water, blending as for a pie crust. Place in a round tin (cake pan serves well), or divide in half and spread on baking sheet in 2 long (3x12 inch) strips, 3 inches apart.

PART II
1 cup water
1 stick margarine or butter
1 cup flour
3 eggs
1 teaspoon almond flavoring
Cardamom

PART II
Bring water and margarine to a boil, remove from heat. Add flour, beating vigorously with a wooden spoon. Add eggs, 1 at a time, beating after each. Add flavoring. Spread this over first mixture and sprinkle with cardamom. Bake at 400°F for 45 minutes.

PART III
Confectioners sugar
Almonds, toasted

PART III
While coffee cake is still warm, coat lightly with confectioners sugar and sprinkle with toasted almonds. Serve at once. Serves 8.

Makes a very showy dessert.

Mrs. Robert Smith

BAQUETTE

1 envelope yeast, dissolved in 1 cup lukewarm water
1 Tablespoon shortening
1 Tablespoon salt
2 teaspoons sugar
1 cup boiling water
6 cups unbleached flour, sifted
Egg white, slightly beaten

Set dissolved yeast aside. Combine shortening, salt, and sugar in bowl. Add boiling water; blend in dissolved yeast. Add flour, gradually, working it all in, even though the dough becomes very stiff. Knead on lightly floured board until smooth and elastic, or use dough hook on mixer. Let rise in a warm place (85-90°F) in covered, greased bowl, until doubled, about 1½ hours. Shape into 3 long oblong loaves; place on greased baking sheet and let rise until doubled again, about 1 hour. Brush with egg white. With a very sharp knife make 3 light diagonal cuts across top of each loaf. Place a pan of boiling water on bottom shelf of oven. Bake at 400°F for 15 minutes; then at 350°F for 30 minutes, or until bread is golden and sounds hollow when tapped. Serves 8.

From the recipes of Jean Lafitte

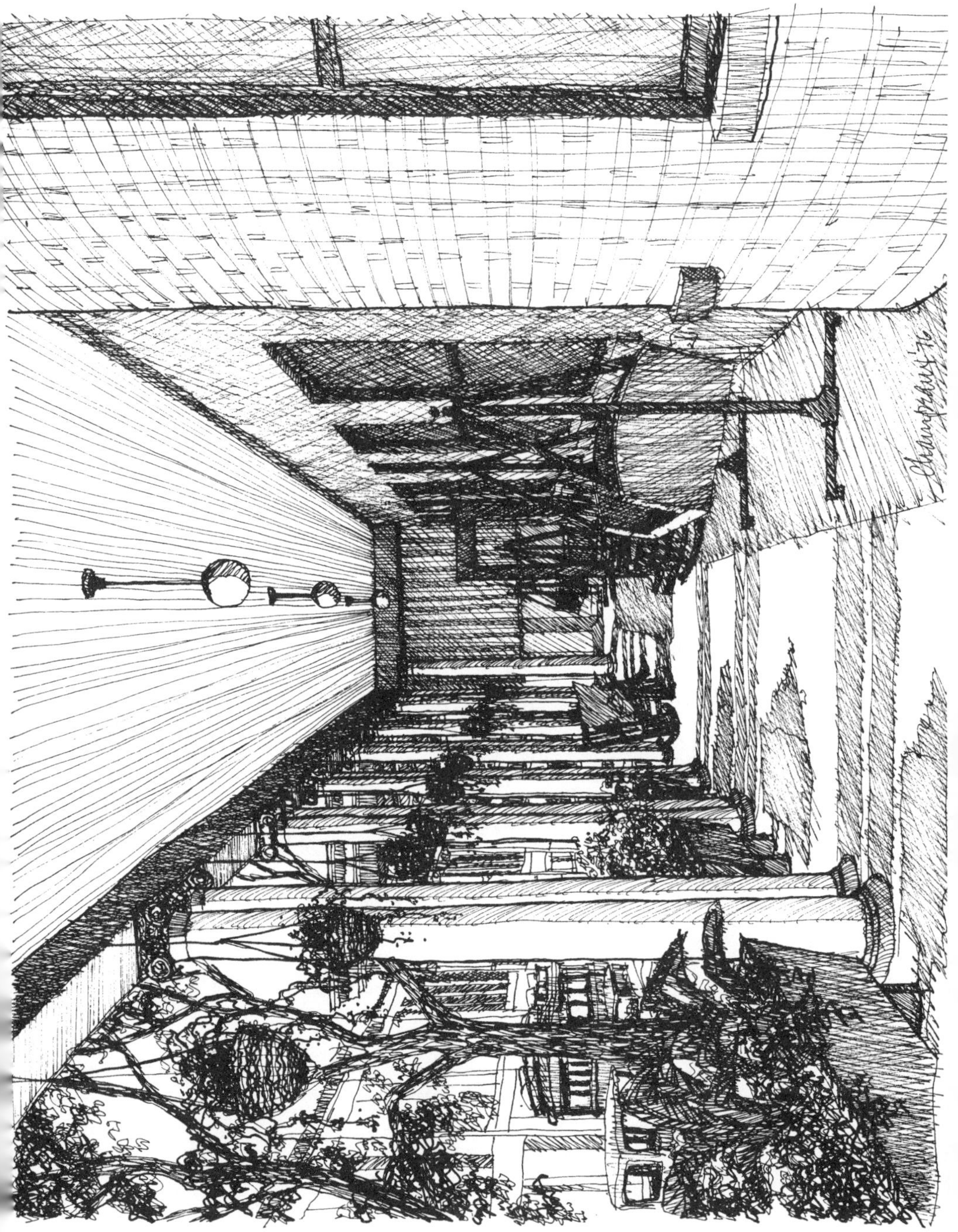

MAJESTIC HOTEL

Corinthian columns graced the portico of the old Majestic Hotel, center of the town's social life during the early 1900's.

Once located at the corner of Pujo and Bilbo Streets, the hotel's grand ballroom was one of the most spacious in the Southwest. Wainscoted with curly birch paneling and adorned with stately columns, it was the perfect backdrop for the elaborate parties, wedding receptions, and dance club affairs of the day.

Noted for its gracious hospitality, the Majestic Hotel was the stopping place for many a fashionable guest. Its registry boasted the names of such notables as Presidents Franklin D. Roosevelt and Dwight D. Eisenhower; Generals George Patton, Walter Kreuger, and Douglas MacArthur; the humorist Irvin S. Cobb; film stars Tom Mix and W. C. Fields; and sports celebrities Babe Ruth and Connie Mack.

ROAST BEEF

1 top sirloin of beef or first four ribs of a standing rib roast, at room temperature
Salt and pepper
1 cup water

SAUCE

6 large fresh mushrooms, sliced
1 Tablespoon green onions, chopped
1 Tablespoon butter
½ cup good red Bordeaux wine, reduced to ¼ cup by rapid boiling
Salt and pepper to taste
Pan juices from roast, with fat skimmed off

Rub meat with salt and pepper. Place in open roasting pan (on a rack if top sirloin cut is used). Insert meat thermometer in center without touching bone or fat. Roast at 325°F for 18 minutes per pound for rare meat (140°F on meat thermometer) or 20 minutes per pound for medium (150°F on meat thermometer). During last hour pour water over roast and baste once or twice. Let roast stand for at least 20 minutes before carving. Allow ½ pound per person.

SAUCE

Serve with following sauce: Sauté mushrooms and green onions for 1-2 minutes in butter until wilted. Combine with remaining sauce ingredients and bring to boil. For a thicker sauce, before boiling add a few balls of butter kneaded with flour.

Mrs. D. Dale Archer
(Valerie "Val" Grode)

FILET DE BOEUF WITH BÉARNAISE SAUCE

5-6 pound whole filet
½ pound butter
Béarnaise sauce, see p. 293

Have butcher trim fat from a whole filet strip. Coat filet with butter. Place on jelly roll pan or cookie sheet and refrigerate until time to cook. Place in a preheated 400°F oven for 50 minutes. Allow to sit 15 minutes before carving. Serve with Béarnaise sauce. Serves 10.

Mrs. James E. Taussig
(Alice House)

RIB ROAST OF BEEF

1 beef rib roast (2-4 ribs), 4½-12 pounds
Flour
Salt
Black pepper, freshly ground

Remove roast from refrigerator 2½-4 hours before cooking. Preheat oven to 500°F. Place roast in open shallow roasting pan, fat side up. Lightly rub a little flour into fat. Season with salt and pepper. Roast according to chart below, timing exactly. At end of cooking time *turn off heat,* but leave roast in about 2 more hours until oven is lukewarm. Do not open oven door at any time. Roast exterior will be crunchy brown. It will remain hot enough to serve for up to 4 hours. Yields 2 servings per rib.

No. of Ribs	Weight Without Short Ribs	Roasting Time 500°F
2	4½ to 5 pounds	25-30 minutes
3	8 to 9 pounds	40-45 minutes
4	11 to 12 pounds	55-60 minutes

This works out to be 15 minutes per rib, or approximately five minutes cooking time per pound of trimmed rib eye roast.

Mrs. Thomas B. Shearman
(Flora Inglis)

YORKSHIRE PUDDING

4 heaping Tablespoons flour
Pinch salt
2 eggs
1 cup liquid (¾ cup milk and ¼ cup iced water)
3 Tablespoons hot grease

Sift flour and salt together. Drop in eggs and beat mixture well. Gradually beat in just enough liquid to make stiff, smooth batter, no lumps. Let stand for a few minutes; then gradually whisk or beat in remaining liquid. Refrigerate for ½ hour. Give a final whisk before pouring into baking pan containing preheated grease. Bake, uncovered, at 400°F for 20-30 minutes. Cannot be prepared a day ahead. May be frozen, if not cooked. Serves 4-6. Serve with roast beef, gravy, and vegetables.

Don't peek, it is like a soufflé and will drop.

Mrs. Robert W. Fenet

MEATS

BOEUF À LA BLANCHE

Salt and pepper
Flour
Rump roast, 3-5 pounds, bone in
1 cup suet, crumbled
Worcestershire sauce
6 small onions
6 medium carrots
6 medium potatoes
2 Tablespoons flour
Salt and pepper to taste
Kitchen Bouquet (optional)

Salt, pepper, and flour meat. Fry suet in roasting pan on top of stove. Add meat and brown on all sides in a 450°F oven. Sprinkle with Worcestershire. Reduce heat to 400°F, cover, and cook 30-45 minutes. Add 2 cups hot water, and bake, covered, 45 minutes per pound. For last 45 minutes add seasoned vegetables, if desired, turning to cook evenly. When done, transfer meat to platter and vegetables to bowls. Discard lumps of fat. To remaining liquid add 2 cups water. Bring to boil on top of stove. Mix flour with ½ cup water until smooth and add to gravy. Salt and pepper to taste. Kitchen Bouquet darkens gravy. Freezing not recommended. Serves 4-6.

Mrs. E. Dale Dickson

SICILIAN "POT-OF-ROAST"

Shoulder roast or best quality boneless roast (15 pounds)
Seasoned tenderizer (optional)
Salt, pepper, parsley
Light flour
Worcestershire sauce
½-1 cup Spanish olives with pimientos, sliced
½-1 cup ripe black olives, sliced
2-3 cans Contadino baby tomatoes (whole), with juice
1-2 onions, sliced
2 jars sliced mushrooms with juice
1 teaspoon garlic, minced (optional)

In large deep roasting pan sprinkle roast with tenderizer, salt, pepper, and parsley. Pat with flour and add Worcestershire. Add 1-2 cups water and brown, uncovered, at 350-400°F until slightly browned. Add Spanish and black olives placing same on top of roast. Arrange remaining ingredients around and on top of roast. Cover with foil and bake at 350°F for 3 hours, or until cooked, adding more water, if necessary, to make a thin gravy. Cool in pan before slicing into small thin pieces. Freezes after cooking. Serves 50.

Excellent for buffet with individual French breads or dinner rolls. Also good with any spaghetti or macaroni dishes. Taste is enhanced if roast is frozen after cooking.

**Mrs. John L. Cocchiara
(Bonnie Harris)**

SAUERBRATEN

4 pounds boned chuck roast
Chicken fat, butter, and oil

MARINADE

1½ cups Burgundy
1½ cups cider or red wine vinegar
2 onions, sliced
1 bay leaf
1 carrot, chopped
1 rib celery, chopped
4 whole allspice
6 whole cloves
8 peppercorns
2 Tablespoons sugar
½ Tablespoon salt

Marinate roast in covered dish in refrigerator for 3-5 days. Turn occasionally. Remove from refrigerator. Pat meat dry, reserving marinade. Brown on all sides in Dutch oven with a little chicken fat, butter, and oil. Add strained marinade to browned meat. Bring to a boil, cover, and simmer for 2½-3 hours.

SAUERBRATEN GRAVY

5 Tablespoons butter
4 Tablespoons flour
1½ Tablespoons sugar
Kitchen Bouquet (optional)
Cornstarch
6 gingersnaps, pulverized

GRAVY

For the gravy make a roux with butter, flour, and sugar. Stir until dark brown in color. Add strained marinade from pot roast to achieve desired thickness. Add Kitchen Bouquet and cornstarch as needed to thicken. Add gingersnaps. Serve gravy poured over sliced sauerbraten, and separately.

Serve with a vegetable from the cabbage family.

Mrs. John W. Huber
(Betty Landry)

BAKED STEAK

1½ inch thick sirloin or round steak, trimmed
Salt to taste
Pepper, freshly ground, to taste
1 white onion, sliced
1 large or 2 small bell peppers, cut into rings
1 lemon, sliced
1 bottle chili sauce
3 Tablespoons Worcestershire sauce
1 stick butter
1 small can button mushrooms
1 small jar pimiento stuffed olives

Place steak in 9x12 inch baking pan. Salt and pepper. Cover with onion slices. Place bell pepper rings on onion and top with lemon slices. Pour chili sauce over all. Add Worcestershire. Dot with butter. Bake, uncovered, at 300°F for 3½-4 hours, or until tender, basting every 15 minutes. Add mushrooms and olives 30 minutes before meat is done. Add water while baking if gravy becomes too thick. Does not freeze.

This makes a pretty dish but must be moved to a platter very quickly because the meat is extremely tender and will tear.

Mrs. David Painter
(Isabel "Bel" Thornton)

STEAK DIANE

4 ounces butter
8 ounce beef tenderloin, cut in ¼ inch slices
1 Tablespoon Dijon mustard
2 ounces cognac or other brandy
2 ounces dry red wine
1½ cups Bordelaise sauce, p. 295
½ cup Chanterelle or fresh mushrooms, sliced
3 Tablespoons green onions, chopped
Salt and pepper to taste
Sprigs of parsley
Parsley, chopped

Melt 2 Tablespoons butter in heated chafing dish. Place steak on butter and spread top with a thin layer of mustard. Cook steak on both sides to desired doneness (not long as steak is thin). Remove pan from heat, add brandy, and ignite. When flame is almost out, add a little wine. Shake. Transfer steak to warm platter. Add Bordelaise sauce to pan juices. Cook, reducing sauce to ½. Add mushrooms, after cooking them lightly in butter with the onions. Cook a little longer, adding salt and pepper. Return steak to pan, cover with sauce, and heat. Transfer steak to platter, and garnish with sprigs of parsley on the side and chopped parsley on top.

Mrs. John W. Huber
(Betty Landry)

STEAK ROLL-UPS

2 pounds round steak, cut into 1x3 inch strips
Meat tenderizer
Red and black pepper to taste
2 eggs, beaten
Italian bread crumbs
½ cup green onions, finely chopped
½ cup bell pepper, finely chopped
3 Tablespoons parsley, finely chopped
Cooking oil

Pound steak; add meat tenderizer and pepper. Dip in eggs, then in bread crumbs. Sprinkle with green onions, bell pepper, and parsley and roll up. Secure with toothpicks. Drop in deep fat and fry until brown.

Mrs. Ray Valdetero

STEAK ZUCCHINI

3 pounds steak
½ cup margarine
3 cups fresh mushrooms, sliced
4 zucchini squash, unpeeled, quartered lengthwise, cut ½ inch thick
1 large clove garlic, finely chopped
2 medium onions, sliced lengthwise in thin wedges
2 medium bell peppers, sliced lengthwise in thin wedges
2 Tablespoons soy sauce
1 Tablespoon cornstarch mixed with ¼ cup water
Salt and pepper to taste
Lemon pepper to taste

In heavy hibachi skillet brown steaks quickly in ¼ cup margarine over high heat. Remove from heat. Remove meat and drippings and set aside. In same skillet sauté mushrooms for 3-4 minutes in ¼ cup margarine. Add zucchini, garlic, onion, and bell pepper and wilt, stirring continuously. Cut meat into bite sized pieces and add with drippings to mixture in skillet. Continue to cook, uncovered, stirring over low heat until meat is medium rare. Add soy sauce and cornstarch paste. Continue stirring. Add seasonings and sprinkle lightly with more soy sauce. Serves 6.

Lawrence Lowery, Jr.

PEPPER BEEF

1 pound lean beef, cut in ¼ inch strips
4 Tablespoons soy sauce
2 Tablespoons cornstarch
¼ teaspoon black pepper
6 bell peppers, cut in strips
6 Tablespoons oil
1 teaspoon salt
¼ teaspoon Accent

Mix beef with soy sauce, cornstarch, and pepper. Sauté bell pepper in oil in uncovered skillet until done but still crisp. Remove and set aside. Add beef mixture to oil and sauté uncovered until lightly browned. Replace bell peppers in skillet and mix gently with beef. Season. Heat uncovered. If not enough gravy, add a little cornstarch mixed with water. Serve over rice. Serves 4.

Mrs. Van H. King
(Eoline Bush)

MEATS

STEAK EMBASSY STYLE

4 tenderloin steaks, butterfly cut
Flour
¼ pound butter
1 cup onions, chopped
½ cup carrots, chopped
Salt and black pepper to taste
1 cup fresh mushrooms, chopped
¼ cup celery, chopped
¼ teaspoon garlic powder
1 teaspoon Worcestershire sauce
¼ cup fresh parsley, chopped
1 Tablespoon red wine vinegar
¼ cup red wine
1 cup sour cream

Dust tenderloins with flour and brown in butter in large heavy skillet. Remove steaks. Add remaining ingredients, except sour cream, and heat, stirring often. Return steaks to mixture. Cook, uncovered, for about 15 minutes, or until carrots are tender but not soft. Do not overcook. Before serving, add sour cream and heat. Serve on saffron rice with salad. Does not freeze. Serves 4.

Wild game, such as venison, may be substituted for the steaks.

Rev. Robert W. Seney

STUFFED BEEF ROUND

2 pounds beef round steak (½ inch thick), cut in 4 serving pieces
1 cup sharp cheese, grated
½ cup onion, chopped
½ cup celery, chopped
¼ cup parsley, snipped
¼ cup all purpose flour
1 teaspoon salt
½ teaspoon pepper
2 Tablespoons cooking oil
1 can (10½ ounces) condensed beef broth
½ teaspoon dry mustard
2 Tablespoons all purpose flour
¼ cup water

Pound steak to ¼ inch thickness. Combine cheese, onion, celery, and parsley and place about ¼ cup in center of each piece of steak, reserving remainder. Roll up each, jelly-roll fashion, secure with toothpicks, and roll in ¼ cup flour seasoned with salt and pepper. In skillet slowly brown meat in hot oil. Drain off excess fat. Combine beef broth and mustard; add to steak rolls. Cover and simmer 45 minutes. Add reserved cheese mixture to skillet; simmer 30 minutes more. Remove meat and skim fat from pan juice. Blend flour and water and add to pan. Heat and pour over meat. Serve over rice. Does not freeze. Serves 4.

This is overcooked if toothpicks burn!

Mrs. Richard E. Gerard, Jr.
(Susan Green)

BOBBY'S SEASONED STEAKS

Steaks
Celery, garlic, and onion salts
Black pepper
Worcestershire sauce
Wesson oil
Brown sugar
1 stick butter or margarine, melted
Juice of 1 lemon
Paprika
Green onions, chopped

Sprinkle steaks liberally with salts, pepper, and Worcestershire. For improved flavor season at least 1 hour before cooking. Coat with a few drops of oil and rub with brown sugar on both sides. Cook near hot charcoal fire to desired doneness, basting with sauce of melted butter, lemon juice, dash of Worcestershire, paprika, celery salt, and a handful of green onions. Does not freeze.

Robert Doland

BEEF STROGANOFF

Salt and pepper
Flour
2½ pound round steak, (¼ inch thick), cut into bite sized cubes
2 sticks butter
1 onion, finely chopped
3 beef bouillon cubes
1 can (5¾ ounces) steak sauce
1 can (5¾ ounces) mushrooms, undrained
1 steak sauce can water
1 Tablespoon cooking wine
1 pint sour cream
1 package (12 ounces) extra broad egg noodles

Season and lightly flour meat. Sauté in butter on medium heat until brown, stirring often. Add onion and bouillon and sauté lightly for a few moments, stirring constantly. Add steak sauce, mushrooms with juice, and water. Simmer 1 hour, stirring occasionally to prevent burning, or until meat is tender. Immediately before serving add wine and sour cream and mix. Serve over boiled, drained noodles. Top with freshly ground pepper, if desired. Serves 8.

Mrs. Richard J. Bono
(Meredith Hebert)

BEEF STROGANOFF

3 pounds onions (5 cups)
Cooking oil
2 pounds beef round steak, cut in thin slices
1 pound mushrooms, sliced
1 can condensed tomato soup
1 can (6 ounces) tomato paste
Few grains pepper
1 teaspoon Worcestershire sauce
1 cup sour cream
1 large jigger cognac

Put onions through food chopper, using coarse blade. Drain, reserving juice. Cook slowly for 20 minutes in oil. Add sliced steak and mushrooms. Cook until brown. Combine tomato soup, tomato paste, onion juice, and seasonings. Add to steak mixture and simmer, covered, for 1 hour. Just before serving add sour cream and cognac. Serves 8.

Very good. Serve with rice or noodles.

Mrs. Jack Thielen
(Della "Dudie" Krause)

MEATS

TUJAQUE'S BOILED BEEF

3-4 pounds short ribs of beef, cut into generous pieces
1 onion
2 carrots
3 sprigs parsley
2 ribs celery
2 Tablespoons salt

Boil meat and vegetables in large pot in 2 quarts water for 2½ hours. Add salt when water begins to boil. Remove meat when cooked. Before serving, remove bone. Serve with tomato-horseradish sauce.

SAUCE

1 cup tomato ketchup
2 teaspoons horseradish
1 teaspoon vinegar
¼ teaspoon salt

SAUCE

Combine all ingredients. Mix well and chill until ready to serve.

Murray Reiter
Memphis, Tennessee

BOILED BRISKET WITH HORSERADISH SAUCE

3 pounds fresh brisket, cut in 2 inch squares
1 onion, cut in quarters
1 clove garlic, chopped
1 rib celery, cut in bite sized pieces
2 carrots, cut in bite sized pieces
1 bay leaf, crushed
¼ teaspoon each thyme and orégano
1 teaspoon each salt and pepper

Place all ingredients in large pot, cover with water, and boil for 2 hours. Add more water if needed to keep covered. Meat is done when tender. Serve with horseradish sauce made by mixing horseradish with ketchup, salt and pepper to taste. Soup can be made from the boiling beef liquid with noodles or macaroni added.

Mrs. David Painter
(Isabel "Bel" Thornton)

BRISKET

4-5 pounds beef brisket
1 bottle Woody's barbecue concentrate, or 2 cups of any barbecue sauce, and 4 ounce bottle liquid smoke, mixed together

Marinate brisket in barbecue sauce, reserving some for serving, for at least 4 hours or overnight. Wrap in heavy duty foil and seal tightly. Bake in roasting pan at 275-300°F for 4 hours. Slice about ½ inch thick. Serve with potato salad and baked beans. May be doubled, baking 1 hour per pound. Freezes. Serves 6.

Mrs. Bill Pearson
Dallas, Texas

SHISH KABOB

3 pounds beef sirloin or top round, 1 inch thick, cut into 1 inch cubes
Wishbone Italian dressing
4 purple onions, cut in 1 inch squares
6 bell peppers, cut in 1 inch squares
Pint of cherry tomatoes

Place cubed meat in plastic container with about ¼ cup Wishbone and shake until covered with dressing. Shake onion, bell pepper, and cherry tomatoes in separate plastic container with dressing. Refrigerate both containers for 24 hours. Alternate meat, onion, pepper, and tomato on skewers, and cook on pit, or raised over hot coals, to desired doneness. For variation try pork cubes, pineapple, and bell pepper; or lamb, onion, pineapple, and bell pepper. Serve on the skewers.

Mrs. David Painter
(Isabel "Bel" Thornton)

Recipes using tomato sauce are better prepared a day ahead.

FRENCH ITALIAN SPAGHETTI

SAUCE

5 large onions, finely chopped
4 cloves garlic, finely chopped
1 Tablespoon bacon grease
1 pound hamburger meat
Salt, black and red pepper to taste
1 package (16 ounces) spaghetti
2 cans (16 ounce size) tomatoes
3 Tablespoons Worcestershire sauce
1 Tablespoon celery seed
2 Tablespoons chili powder
1 can (6 ounces) tomato paste or sauce
1 can sliced buttered mushrooms
2 Tablespoons garlic salt
½ teaspoon each sweet marjoram and basil
1 can (1½ ounces) Parmesan cheese, grated

Sauté onions and garlic in bacon grease. Brown meat and season to taste. Cook spaghetti in salted water according to package directions. Drain. Combine all ingredients, except cheese. Sprinkle with cheese. Bake, uncovered, in 3 quart casserole at 300°F for 1 hour. Flavor is better if made day ahead and left overnight in refrigerator. Sauce freezes beautifully. Serves 6.

Mrs. John W. Melton III
(Nancy LeLaurin)

PASTITSIO

1 medium onion, chopped
1 clove garlic, minced
2 Tablespoons olive oil
1½ pounds lean ground round
1½ teaspoons salt
2 dashes cinnamon
2 cans (8 ounce size) tomato sauce
5 Tablespoons butter
¼ cup flour
2 cups whole milk
Dash white pepper
Pinch nutmeg
⅓ cup Parmesan cheese, grated
1 package (8 ounces) small elbow macaroni
2 eggs
2 cups Cheddar cheese, coarsely grated

Preheat oven to 375°F. Sauté onion and garlic in oil until soft. Crumble in beef and add 1 teaspoon salt. Cook, stirring, until meat browns. Pour off oil. Stir in cinnamon and tomato sauce and set aside. Melt 3 Tablespoons butter in saucepan and whisk in flour. Add milk and cook, stirring until thickened. Add ½ teaspoon salt, pepper, nutmeg, and Parmesan cheese. Cook macaroni in boiling, salted water until tender. Drain well and return to pot. Add eggs and remaining butter. Beat briskly with wooden spoon until well mixed. In a shallow 2½ quart buttered baking dish layer ingredients as follows: ½ macaroni, layer of white sauce, all the meat, ½ Cheddar cheese; remaining macaroni, remaining white sauce (rewhisked before pouring). Shake dish gently to settle white sauce. Sprinkle with remaining Cheddar, dot with butter, and sprinkle with nutmeg. Bake, uncovered, 1 hour. If refrigerated, bring to room temperature before baking. Freezes. Serves 6.

Remarkable—everything melds into everything else, resulting in delicate, light, unique flavor.

Mrs. Kenneth L. Strauss
(Julie Ann Marx)

ITALIAN SPAGHETTI SAUCE

1¼ cups onion, chopped
¼ cup each olive oil and butter
1½ pounds ground chuck
6 strips raw bacon, chopped
3 cloves garlic, minced
4 Tablespoons parsley
1 teaspoon each salt and black pepper
½ teaspoon red pepper
⅔ cup red Chianti wine
1 cup canned tomatoes
2 cans (6 ounce size) tomato paste
2 cans (6 ounce size) tomato sauce
2 teaspoons orégano
⅔ cup Parmesan cheese
1½ cups mushrooms, sliced and sautéed

Sauté onions in olive oil and butter in large Dutch oven. Add ground chuck and bacon. Add remaining ingredients. Simmer, uncovered, for 1 hour. Serve over cooked spaghetti. Freezes. Serves 8.

Mrs. Celeste Brown Stanfield

SPAGHETTI SAUCE WITH MEAT BALLS

MEAT BALLS

1 pound ground meat
3 slices bread, soaked in water and squeezed
1 egg, beaten
½ cup cheese, grated
3 small cloves garlic, pressed
Salt and pepper to taste
Olive oil

SPAGHETTI SAUCE

1 large Bermuda onion, chopped
1 bell pepper, finely chopped
1 clove garlic, minced
2 cans tomato paste
1 rib celery and leaves, finely chopped
½ bunch green onions, finely chopped
1 Tablespoon parsley, minced
1 large can mushrooms (either whole or stems and pieces)
1 large can tomatoes, cut up
1 teaspoon orégano
¼ teaspoon thyme
1 bay leaf
3 Tablespoons Worcestershire sauce
1 Tablespoon chili sauce
1 teaspoon prepared mustard
Dash each Tabasco and paprika
Salt and pepper to taste
2 quarts water

MEAT BALLS

Mix all ingredients, except oil, thoroughly and make into balls about 1¼ inches in diameter. Brown in enough oil to cover bottom of pot. Remove and make sauce in same pot.

SPAGHETTI SAUCE

To prepare spaghetti sauce, add onion and bell pepper to olive oil left in pot. Cook on medium heat until tender. Add garlic and tomato paste and cook, stirring constantly, until tomato paste has lost its bright red color. Add remaining ingredients. Return meat balls to pot. Simmer about 2 hours until sauce is thick. Add a little water if it gets too thick. Freezes.

Serve with spaghetti and Parmesan cheese, tossed green salad, and buttered French or Italian bread. Sauce good with chicken, also.

Mrs. F. Warren Raggio, Jr.
(Mavis Cade)

NANA'S LASAGNE

1 pound ground beef
1 pound ground pork
3 eggs
1 clove garlic, minced
1 Tablespoon fresh parsley, minced
1 Tablespoon Parmesan cheese
1 Tablespoon dried sweet basil
1 teaspoon each salt and pepper
½-¾ cup Italian Progresso bread crumbs
½-¾ cup water
2 Tablespoons olive oil
2 Tablespoons butter
1 clove garlic
2 cans stewed tomatoes
1 can tomato paste
6 cloves
2 Tablespoons sugar
Salt and pepper to taste
½ pound Italian sausage, sliced
1 pound lasagne
1 pound Mozzarella cheese, sliced
1 pound Ricotta cheese

Combine beef, pork, eggs, garlic, parsley, Parmesan cheese, basil, salt, and pepper in bowl. Mix and add bread crumbs and water. Mixture should be moist and of spread consistency. Form into balls (golf ball size). In large Dutch oven sauté meat balls in olive oil and butter with garlic added. Brown on all sides. Remove garlic before it becomes brown. Add tomatoes, tomato paste, cloves, sugar, salt and pepper to taste. Simmer, covered, for 2 hours, stirring every 15 minutes. Brown sausage in small amount of butter. Set aside. Cook lasagne according to package directions and drain. In large baking dish arrange in layers the following: 1 cup of sauce, noodles, Mozzarella, sausage, meat balls, Ricotta cheese. Repeat layers until dish is almost full. Top with Parmesan cheese. Bake, uncovered, at 350°F for 30 minutes. Serves 7-10.

Mrs. Jim Johannsen
Houston, Texas

EASY LASAGNE

1½-2 pounds ground beef
2 cloves garlic, minced
1 Tablespoon hot fat
1 can (6 ounces) tomato paste
1 can (1 pound 4 ounces) tomatoes
1 teaspoon salt
¾ teaspoon oregano
1 package (8 ounces) dumpling noodles
12 ounces Swiss cheese, sliced
1 carton (12 ounces) cottage cheese

Brown beef and garlic in hot fat. Stir in tomato paste, tomatoes, and seasonings. Cover and simmer 25 minutes. While meat mixture is simmering, boil noodles according to package directions. Preheat oven to 350°F. Layer as follows in 13x9½x2 inch baking pan: meat sauce, noodles, Swiss cheese, cottage cheese, meat sauce. Bake, uncovered, 20-30 minutes. Serves 6-8.

Mrs. William L. McLeod, Jr.
(Marilyn "Cissie" Qualls)

MANICOTTI A LA ROMONA

8 manicotti shells
1 package frozen chopped spinach
1 medium onion, chopped
2 cloves garlic, chopped
2 Tablespoons butter
1 pound ground chuck
½ teaspoon salt
⅛ teaspoon ground black pepper
¼ cup Parmesan cheese, grated

Cook manicotti in large amount of boiling, salted water for 8-10 minutes. Drain and set aside. Cook spinach according to directions; drain well, squeeze dry, and chop finely. In large skillet sauté onion and garlic in butter, stirring frequently, for 7-8 minutes. Add meat and lightly brown. Remove from heat. Stir in spinach, salt, pepper, and cheese. Gently fill shells with mixture and arrange in single layer in 3 quart baking dish.

SAUCE

4 Tablespoons butter
4 Tablespoons flour
2½ cups milk, heated to boil
½ teaspoon salt
⅛ teaspoon pepper
¼ cup Parmesan cheese
Dash of nutmeg

SAUCE

In saucepan melt butter over low heat, blend in flour and cook slowly for 2 minutes. Remove from heat and pour in hot milk. Beat vigorously to blend. Return to heat and cook until sauce is smooth and thick. Add remaining ingredients.

TO ASSEMBLE DISH

1 package (8 ounces) Mozzarella cheese slices, halved
1 jar (7 ounces) whole pimiento pods, halved
Parsley, chopped

TO ASSEMBLE DISH

To assemble dish, tuck cheese slices, topped with pimiento halves between manicotti shells. Sprinkle with parsley. Cover with sauce. Bake, uncovered, at 375°F for 18-20 minutes. Freezes. Serves 8.

Mrs. John Beatty

ITALIAN LIVER

3 Tablespoons Parmesan cheese, grated
6 Tablespoons fine bread crumbs
1 Tablespoon parsley, chopped
½ teaspoon salt
Pepper, freshly ground
3 Tablespoons wine vinegar or white wine
8 slices calf liver
4 Tablespoons hot oil

Prepare a mixture of cheese, bread crumbs, parsley, salt, and pepper on a flat plate. In another plate place vinegar or wine. Quickly dip liver slices into the vinegar, then the crumb mixture, completely covering both sides. Sauté quickly in hot oil. Serves 4-6.

Mrs. Dale LeBlanc

MEAT LOAF

¾ cup rolled 1 minute oats
3 Tablespoons water
1 pound ground beef
¼ pound pork sausage
1 large onion, chopped
1 egg
2 Tablespoons Worcestershire sauce
2 teaspoons salt
½ teaspoon pepper
1 can (15 ounces) Hunt's tomato sauce with bits

Moisten oats with water. Combine ingredients (reserving ⅛ can tomato sauce) and mix well. Shape into loaf and cover with reserved tomato sauce. Bake, uncovered, at 350°F for 45-60 minutes. Freezes. Serves 6.

Mrs. James Garbo
(Connie Barnett)

MEAT LOAF

1 slice bread
1 pound ground chuck (or other cut)
½ bell pepper, diced
1 medium onion, diced
2 ribs celery, diced
1 egg, unbeaten
½ teaspoon salt, or to taste
¼ teaspoon pepper
¼ can (6 ounce size) tomato sauce
1 Tablespoon Worcestershire sauce
1 heaping teaspoon mustard
2 Tablespoons ketchup
1 teaspoon garlic salt
2 strips bacon

Dip bread in water and break into pieces. Mix well with remaining ingredients. Place in greased 8½x4½x3 inch loaf pan. Top with bacon strips. Bake, uncovered, at 375°F for 1 hour. This is also good made into meat patties.

Mrs. Soulé Smith

MEAT LOAF

1½ pounds ground beef
1 small onion, minced
½ cup seasoned bread crumbs
½ cup milk
⅓ cup chili sauce or ketchup
1 egg
1½ teaspoons salt
⅛ teaspoon black pepper, freshly ground
1 Tablespoon parsley, finely chopped

Combine all ingredients and toss lightly with a fork. Do not overmix. Place in a 9x5x3 inch loaf pan and level top. Bake, uncovered, at 350°F for 1 hour, or until done. Serve on a heated platter. Serves 8.

Mrs. Frank Daly

KIBBIE

1 teaspoon cumin
Red and black pepper and salt to taste
1 pound lean round steak, ground
3 medium onions and 2 hot peppers, ground together with ½ cup fresh mint
1 pound cracked wheat (soaked 20-30 minutes)

FILLING

1 pound ground round
2 Tablespoons butter
1 onion, chopped
Salt and pepper to taste

Add cumin, pepper, and salt to meat. Mix well. Add onion mixture. Squeeze water from wheat and discard. Mix wheat into meat mixture. Knead and squeeze between fingers about 5 minutes until of meat loaf consistency. Form into 2-3 inch balls.

FILLING

Make filling by cooking all ingredients until onions are tender. Make a deep hole in each ball, insert 1 Tablespoon of filling, close hole. Shape like a football. Fry in deep fat at 375°F. Freezes. Makes 20 balls.

Annie Saloom

KIBBIE (RAW)

1¼ cups cracked wheat, fine
1 pound lean ground lamb or beef
3 large onions, finely ground
Salt, pepper and allspice to taste
Red pepper (optional)
Mint (optional)
¾ cup ice water, more, if needed

MINCED BEEF DRESSING

½ pound ground round
1 onion, ground
1 stick butter
Salt, pepper and allspice to taste

Rinse and soak the wheat in water 10-15 minutes. Squeeze out water through cupped hands. Add to the wheat the meat, onions, seasonings, and spices to taste. Knead together, adding ice water. Put through meat grinder. Reknead. Add more water, if necessary, to soften.

DRESSING

For dressing, brown meat and onion in butter, add seasonings, and cook until onions are tender. Serves 6.

Serve Kibbie on plate, mash down, spoon beef dressing or drizzle olive oil on top. Serve onion on the side.

Mrs. David Buttross, Jr.
(Joyce Abraham)

BAKED KIBBIE

3 cups cracked wheat
2 pounds very lean heavy beef, finely ground
2 large onions, coarsely chopped
1 small Jalapeño pepper, coarsely chopped
½ cup fresh mint leaves, coarsely chopped
¼ cup fresh basil leaves (or 1-2 teaspoons dried)
4 teaspoons salt
1 teaspoon pepper
Olive oil
¼ cup butter or margarine

Wash cracked wheat several times; then soak in water for 30 minutes. Wring out and place in large bowl with beef. Purée onions, pepper, mint and basil leaves in blender. Add, along with seasoning, to cracked wheat and meat. Mix well with hands.

FILLING

1 pound ground chuck
2 onions, coarsely cut
1 teaspoon salt
½ teaspoon pepper

FILLING

For filling combine all ingredients and brown. Grease a 10x14 inch aluminum pan with generous amount of olive oil. Layer bottom with ½ cracked wheat mixture, patted down, covered with an evenly distributed layer of filling. Make meat patties from remaining cracked wheat mixture, place on filling, patting down to completely cover. Cut kibbie diagonally both ways making diamond-shaped pieces. Pour a small amount of olive oil in most of the cuts, especially around edges of pan. Dot with butter or margarine. Bake, uncovered, at 375°F for 1 hour. If not brown enough, bake 15 minutes longer at 350°F.

From the recipes of Mrs. Phillip Ieyoub

MOUSSAKA

1 large eggplant, pared, cut in ½ inch slices
1 teaspoon salt, or to taste
1 pound lean ground beef
2 medium onions, chopped
2 cloves garlic, minced
½ teaspoon thyme
¼ teaspoon each orégano and nutmeg
2 Tablespoons parsley, chopped
1 cup canned (or fresh) tomatoes
½ cup white wine
½ cup bread crumbs
Olive oil
4 teaspoons Parmesan cheese, grated

SAUCE

3 Tablespoons flour
3 Tablespoons butter, melted
1½ cups milk
2 egg yolks, well beaten
½ teaspoon salt, or to taste
Pepper to taste

Sprinkle eggplant with salt and allow to stand ½ hour. Rinse and dry thoroughly. Brown meat with onion and garlic. Drain fat. Add seasonings, parsley, tomatoes, and wine. Cover and cook slowly for 30 minutes. Cool. Add ½ the bread crumbs. Brown dry eggplant slices in olive oil. Sprinkle bottom of large rectangular casserole with remaining crumbs. Cover in sequence with layer of eggplant, meat mixture, sauce, cheese topping.

SAUCE

To prepare sauce, add flour slowly to melted butter, stirring constantly. Remove from heat. Slowly stir in milk. Return to heat and stir until sauce thickens. Add egg yolks and seasonings, stirring constantly until blended. Bake at 350°F, uncovered, 45 minutes. Freezes, but without sauce.

This dish takes time but is well worth it! Greeks use lamb instead of ground beef.

Mrs. Howard Cox
Sweetlake, La.

PICADILLO

1 medium onion, chopped
1 medium bell pepper, chopped
2 cloves garlic, finely chopped
2 Tablespoons olive oil
1 pound ground beef
1 can (8 ounces) tomato sauce
1 teaspoon capers
½ cup raisins
½ cup stuffed olives, sliced

Sauté, uncovered, onion, bell pepper, and garlic in olive oil until tender. Stir in ground beef until brown. Add tomato sauce, capers, and raisins and simmer, covered, for 10 minutes. Just before serving, add stuffed olives. Serve over rice. Freezes. Serves 4.

Penny Boelens
Opelousas, La.

CABBAGE CHOP SUEY

1 onion, chopped
1 stick margarine
1 small can mushroom pieces, drained
1 can (16 ounces) Chinese vegetables, drained (LaChoy chop suey vegetables preferable)
1 cup leftover roast, cut in small pieces
1 cup leftover gravy
1 medium head cabbage, chopped in large pieces
Salt and pepper to taste

In large covered pan sauté onions in margarine. Add mushrooms and Chinese vegetables. Stir in roast and gravy. Add cabbage pieces to top of mixture. Season to taste. Cover and steam until cabbage wilts, but is still crisp, about 3-5 minutes. Do not overcook cabbage. Serve over hot rice or Chinese noodles. Serves 4.

Easy and nobody knows that it is a "leftover."

Mrs. James W. Crawford
(Sydalise Fredeman)

ORIENTAL SPAGHETTI

½ pound each ground beef and pork
1 onion, chopped
3 Tablespoons bacon fat
1 cup cooked spaghetti
1 can Chinese vegetables
1 can water chestnuts, thinly sliced
1 can each mushrooms, bamboo shoots, and bean sprouts
1 can cream of tomato soup, undiluted
6 ounces reserved vegetable liquid
½ pound cheese, grated
Soy sauce, salt, and pepper

Cook meat and onion in bacon fat. Pour off excess fat and combine spaghetti with mixture. Drain and save juice from the vegetables, water chestnuts, mushrooms, bean sprouts, and bamboo shoots. Toss vegetable mixture with spaghetti and meat and add soup and 6 ounces of reserved liquid. In a greased casserole alternate layers of spaghetti mixture and cheese, ending with cheese. Each layer of spaghetti mixture may be seasoned with soy sauce, salt, and pepper, if desired. Bake at 425°F for 35 minutes. Serve with Jezebel sauce, p. 302.

Mrs. J. M. King
(Ruth Perkins)

KEFTETHES (STUFFED GRAPE LEAVES)

⅓ cup fine dry bread crumbs
½ cup milk
4 green onions, finely chopped
2 Tablespoons olive oil
2 pounds ground chuck
2 egg yolks
3 Tablespoons raw white rice
2 cloves garlic, minced
2 teaspoons salt
Pepper, freshly ground to taste
Grape leaves, washed well in cold water to remove brine
3 Tablespoons red wine vinegar or lemon juice
2 cups beef bouillon
½ teaspoon orégano

Soak bread crumbs in milk until soft. Sauté onion and parsley in oil until limp. Mix thoroughly with meat, egg yolks, soaked crumbs and milk, rice, garlic, salt, and pepper. With grape leaf smooth side down, place 1-2 Tablespoons of above mixture at base of stem. Fold sides to middle, then roll leaf up. Pack rolled leaves tightly, flap side down, in a 2 quart pyrex baking dish. Pour a mixture of vinegar and bouillon over keftethes. Sprinkle with orégano. Bake, covered, at 350°F 1 hour, or until rice is tender. Keftethes must be served with Avgolemono.

AVGOLEMONO (LEMON SAUCE)

2 eggs
Dash salt
Juice of 1 lemon
1 cup boiling broth or stock (take from keftethe pot)

SAUCE

To make sauce beat eggs until light. Add salt and beat in lemon juice. Gradually add hot broth, beating constantly. Heat over very low heat for a few minutes, or until sauce is thickened. Do not boil. Freezes. Serves 6.

Mrs. Jake W. Posey
(Jerry Anderson)

SWEDISH MEAT BALLS

3 pounds ground beef
Salt and pepper to taste
2 slices bread
1 can (6 ounces) evaporated milk
2 onions, chopped
1 egg
SAUCE
2 ribs celery, chopped
½ bell pepper, chopped
1 stick margarine
1 Tablespoon flour
1 can (3 ounces) mushrooms, drained
2 cans (6 ounce size) tomato sauce
½ cup ketchup
½ teaspoon mustard

In mixing bowl season meat with salt and pepper. Soak bread in milk. Mix meat with 1 onion, bread, and egg. Roll into balls and place on broiler pan. Bake, uncovered, at 350°F for 20-30 minutes. Drain. While meat balls are cooking, make sauce. Sauté celery, bell pepper, and remaining onion in margarine, stirring in flour. Add remaining ingredients and season to taste. Simmer, uncovered, about 30 minutes. During last 5 minutes add meat balls to sauce. Serve over spaghetti or rice. Freezes. Serves 6-8.

Octavia Trahan

ORIENTAL MEAT BALLS

1½ pounds ground beef
½ cup fresh bread crumbs
1 Tablespoon soy sauce
¼ teaspoon pepper
1 can (8 ounces) tomato sauce

SAUCE

¾ cup onions, finely chopped
½ bell pepper, sliced
1 can (8 ounces) tomato sauce
2 Tablespoons vegetable oil
2 Tablespoons orange marmalade
2 Tablespoons vinegar
½ teaspoon powdered ginger
2 Tablespoons cornstarch
1 cup water

Combine beef, bread crumbs, soy sauce, pepper and 1 can tomato sauce. Form into 6 large balls. Bake in shallow baking dish at 350°F for 15 minutes.

SAUCE

To make sauce sauté onion and pepper in oil. Stir in remaining ingredients including second can of tomato sauce. At end of baking time, remove excess fat from balls. Pour sauce over and return to oven for 20 minutes.

Kind of a sweet-and-sour dish.

Mrs. John E. Wood
(Sara Monticello)

LOUISIANA CREOLE OKRA WITH MEAT BALLS

2 pounds ground round steak
2 eggs
Bread crumbs
Salt and black pepper to taste
Cooking oil
2 pounds fresh okra, sliced ½ inch thick
1 large white onion, chopped
2 cloves garlic, chopped
1 small bell pepper, chopped
2 ribs celery, chopped
2 cans peeled tomatoes
Red pepper to taste

Make small meat balls from mixture of meat, eggs, bread crumbs, salt, and black pepper. Brown in cooking oil in small Magnalite roaster or fryer and drain on absorbent paper. Using drippings, cook okra until tender, stirring often. Add chopped vegetables and sauté until soft. Add tomatoes and mix well before adding meat balls. Cook slowly for about 30 minutes adding hot water as needed to keep meat balls covered. Add pepper. Freezes. Serve over rice with crowder peas, cucumber salad, and corn sticks. Serves 6-8.

A great dish in the summer when fresh vegetables are plentiful. My own original recipe for quick entertaining.

Mrs. Evelyn C. Thompson

MEAT BALLS

4 pounds ground chuck
2 pounds ground pork
1 bell pepper, finely chopped
2 large onions, finely chopped
4 cloves garlic, finely chopped
6 eggs
1 small can ripe olives, chopped (optional)
2 teaspoons each red and freshly ground black pepper
4 Tablespoons salt
1 large box corn flakes, crushed
Flour, as needed
Grease

Have butcher grind beef and pork together 3 times. In large bowl combine all ingredients, except flour and grease, and mix thoroughly. Form into balls about 2 inches in diameter. Roll in flour and fry briefly in hot grease (375°F). At this stage meat balls may be added to basic tomato sauce to serve over spaghetti or brown gravy to serve over rice. Never overcook meat balls, and they will stay moist and juicy. Freezes. Makes 68 meat balls.

W. E. Gorham, Jr.

HAMBURGER MUSHROOM QUICHE

1 pound ground meat
2 cups sharp cheese, grated
½ cup mayonnaise
½ cup milk
2 eggs
1 Tablespoon cornstarch
¼ cup green onions, chopped
2 cans mushrooms, drained (stems and pieces or sliced)
Salt and pepper to taste
1 unbaked pie shell (9½ inch)

Preheat oven to 350°F. Brown meat and drain. Combine cheese, mayonnaise, milk, eggs, and cornstarch. Stir in onion, mushrooms, and meat. Salt and pepper to taste. Pour into pie shell and bake for 40-45 minutes until puffy and golden brown. Serves 6-8.

Mrs. Ronald G. White
New Orleans, La.

HAMBURGER PIE

1 pound lean ground beef
½ cup onion, chopped
1 Tablespoon cooking oil
1 can (8 ounces) green beans, drained
1 can (10 ounces) tomato soup
1 teaspoon salt
1 Tablespoon sugar
¼ teaspoon each pepper and oregano
2 pie shells, unbaked

Brown meat and onion in oil in skillet. Stir in beans, soup, and seasonings. Pour into pie shell. Cover with second shell and seal edges. Cut slits in top. Bake at 400°F for 25 minutes, or until golden brown. Serve hot or cold.

Mrs. Pat Painter

MEATS

NATCHITOCHES MEAT PIE

FILLING

1 Tablespoon cooking oil
1 Tablespoon flour
1 large onion, chopped
1 pound ground meat
1 pound Owen's seasoned hot ground sausage
1 teaspoon salt
Dash garlic powder

CRUST

4 cups all purpose flour
2 teaspoons salt
1 teaspoon baking powder
⅔ cup shortening
1 egg, beaten
1 cup milk

FILLING

To prepare filling, cook oil and flour in heavy iron skillet over medium hot heat, stirring continuously, until light brown. Stir in onion and cook about 1 minute. Add other ingredients and mix well. Lower heat to simmer and cook until meat is done, but not dry, about 1 hour. Stir often. Drain excess fat. Remove from heat and cool to room temperature.

CRUST

To prepare crust, blend dry ingredients and cut in shortening. Add mixed egg and milk. Divide dough into 6 parts and roll each very thinly on lightly floured board. Cut into rounds using saucer as a guide. To assemble, place a heaping Tablespoon of filling in center of dough round. Fold edges together and crimp with fork dipped in water. Drop in deep fat and cook until golden brown. Drain and serve hot. Or bake, like pie crust, at 350°F until brown. Freezes. Makes 18-20 pies.

Excellent cooked directly from freezer—great "after-a-party" food.

Mrs. Tony B. Byles

MEAT PIE

Oil
1 pound ground meat
1 small bell pepper, chopped
1 large onion, chopped
1 can tomato paste
1 pie shell
1 small can black olives, chopped
1 cup cheese, shredded
Salt and pepper to taste

Sauté in oil meat, bell pepper, and onion. When almost done, add tomato paste and simmer 5-10 minutes. Pour into unbaked pie shell and cover with olives and cheese. Salt and pepper to taste. Bake at 350°F about 20 minutes, or until crust is done. Freezes. Serves 4-6.

Rev. Robert Dodwell
New Orleans, La.

MEAT POT PIE

1½ pounds beef, lamb, veal, or pork, cut into 1 inch cubes
Salt and black pepper to taste
Flour
4 Tablespoons lard or bacon drippings
1 heart of celery, chopped
1 medium onion, chopped
1 can (2 ounces) mushrooms, sliced
4 cups water
1 cup cooked carrots, cut into ½ inch pieces
½ cup cooked peas
1 cup cooked potatoes, diced, browned in lard
2 Tablespoons flour
1 teaspoon parsley, chopped

Season cubed meat with salt and pepper and roll in flour. Cook in bacon drippings, preheated in heavy kettle, until a good rich brown. Add celery, onion, and mushrooms. Add 2 cups water and simmer 1½ hours. Stir in vegetables. Blend flour with 2 cups water; stir into broth and bring to boil. Pour into 2 quart casserole, sprinkle with parsley, and cover with pie dough, slashing top to allow steam to escape. Bake, uncovered, at 425°F for 20 minutes, or until pastry is golden brown.

PIE DOUGH

1 cup flour, sifted
½ teaspoon salt
¼ cup lard
2 Tablespoons water

To prepare dough combine all ingredients. Roll out to fit top of casserole. Freezes. Serves 6.

Mrs. Marcus Pierson
(Gladys Daly)

COUNTRY PIE

CRUST

½ can (8 ounce size) tomato sauce
½ cup bread crumbs
1 pound lean ground beef
¼ cup each onion and bell pepper, chopped
1½ teaspoons salt
⅛ teaspoon each pepper and orégano (optional)

To prepare crust, combine ingredients in a bowl and mix well. Pat mixture gently onto bottom and sides of a greased 9 inch pie plate.

FILLING

1⅓ cups minute rice
1½ cans (8 ounce size) tomato sauce
½ teaspoon salt
1 cup water
1 cup Cheddar cheese, grated

To make filling, combine all ingredients, reserving ½ cup cheese. Spoon mixture into crust. Cover with foil. Bake at 350°F 25 minutes. Uncover and top with remaining cheese. Bake, uncovered, 10-15 minutes. Serves 5-6.

Mrs. C. M. Robinson III
(Barbara Best)

JOHNNY MARZETTI CHEDDAR CHEESE CASSEROLE

½ pound spaghettini
1 pound Kraft sharp cracker barrel Cheddar cheese, stick or wedge
2 pounds ground chuck
1 stick butter
2 cans (15½ ounce size) tomatoes (or 3 cans, 10 ounce size)
2 cans (6 ounce size) tomato paste
3 teaspoons salt
½ level teaspoon cayenne
¼ teaspoon each orégano and sweet basil
2 teaspoons garlic, chopped

Boil spaghettini and drain. Cut cheese into chunks. Sauté meat in iron skillet with butter until crumbly. Combine remaining ingredients. Layer in medium sized casserole or baking pan the following: ½ each of the meat, tomato mixture, and cheese. Repeat the layers. Bake, uncovered, at 350°F for 30 minutes. Freezes. Serves 6-8.

Mrs. Virginia Sigler Barnes

BEEF-BACON-MACARONI CASSEROLE

4-5 slices bacon, finely chopped
⅓ cup each onion and bell pepper, chopped
1 clove garlic, chopped
1 pound ground beef
1½ teaspoons chili powder
2 teaspoons salt
1 teaspoon sugar
3 cups water
1 cup elbow macaroni
1 can (6 ounces) tomato paste

Fry bacon, remove, and partially drain. Add onion, bell pepper, and garlic and sauté until soft. Add ground beef and sauté until brown. Add chili powder, salt, sugar, and water. Cover, cook about 20 minutes. Add macaroni, bring to a boil, and cook, covered, 5 minutes. Add tomato paste and cook, covered, 10 minutes. Adjust seasonings to taste. Serves 4.

Mrs. Henry S. Uchida
(Chico Sakaguchi)

HAMBURGER CASSEROLE

1 pound ground chuck
1 Tablespoon butter
1 clove garlic, crushed
1 teaspoon salt
¼ teaspoon pepper
1 teaspoon sugar
2 cans (8 ounce size) tomato sauce
1 small package cream cheese
1 carton sour cream
6 green onions, finely chopped
1 package (5 ounces) egg noodles
½ cup Cheddar cheese, grated

Brown meat in butter. Add remaining ingredients, except noodles and cheese, and simmer. Meanwhile, cook noodles according to package directions. Drain and add to meat mixture. Top with cheese and bake, uncovered, in Corningware skillet or baking dish at 350°F for 30 minutes, or until heated through. Serves 6.

Mrs. John J. Brooks III
(Sue Coleman)

HOLLYWOOD HASH

7 slices bacon, fried crisp
1 pound ground beef
1 large onion, chopped
1 large bell pepper, chopped
1 small can tomato paste
1 can water
1 Tablespoon Lea & Perrins
1 package (8 ounces) egg noodles, cooked
1 small can peas, drained
1 large can mushrooms, drained
Salt and pepper to taste
1 pound American cheese, grated

Brown meat in bacon grease. Add onion and bell pepper and brown. Add tomato paste and water. Simmer for 15 minutes. Add Lea & Perrins. Combine all ingredients in large casserole, reserving ½ the cheese to cover top. Bake, uncovered, at 350°F for 35 minutes. Serves 6.

Mrs. Richard W. Calhoun
(Patsy Boudreau)

TALARINI

1 clove garlic, chopped
1 large onion, chopped
1 bell pepper, chopped
2-3 Tablespoons olive oil
1 can (16 ounces) tomatoes
1 package noodles
1 pound ground meat
Salt and pepper to taste
1 large can corn
1 can ripe olives with liquid
1 pound American cheese, grated

Sauté garlic, onion, and bell pepper in olive oil until tender. Add tomatoes and cook 10 minutes. Boil noodles until tender. Fry meat in skillet. Season to taste. Pour into casserole (1 large 2½ quart or 2 small) and add corn, olives, and olive liquid. Add cheese, reserving some to sprinkle on top, and stir well. Bake, uncovered, at 325°F for 1 hour. Freezes. Serves 6-8.

Mrs. Larry Davis

TEXAS HASH

2 medium onions, chopped
1 cup celery, chopped
3 Tablespoons cooking oil
1 pound ground steak
2 cups tomato juice
1 cup uncooked spaghetti
1 teaspoon chili powder
2 teaspoons salt
½ teaspoon pepper

Cook onions and celery in oil until yellow. Add meat and cook until brown. Add remaining ingredients and mix well. Bake in greased, covered 2 quart casserole at 350°F for 45 minutes. Omit spaghetti to freeze. Serves 10.

This recipe is often used in the Texas mansion. Serve with corn bread and green salad.

Mrs. I. T. Hart
(Ruby Coats)

CHILI

2 pounds round steak, finely cubed
3 Tablespoons oil
2 Tablespoons flour
1 large onion, chopped
1 clove garlic, chopped
1 can (14½ ounces) tomatoes
4 Tablespoons chili powder
1 teaspoon salt
½ teaspoon black pepper
10 cups water
3 Tablespoons comino seeds
2 cans ranch beans

Brown meat in oil. Mix in remaining ingredients except comino seeds and beans. Add water. Tie comino seeds in cheesecloth bag and place in chili. Cook slowly, uncovered, for 2 hours. Add beans and simmer until thoroughly heated. Remove cheesecloth bag before serving. Add more water if needed. Better if prepared a day ahead. Freezes. Serves 8.

Mrs. Dan Wise
(Florence Runte)

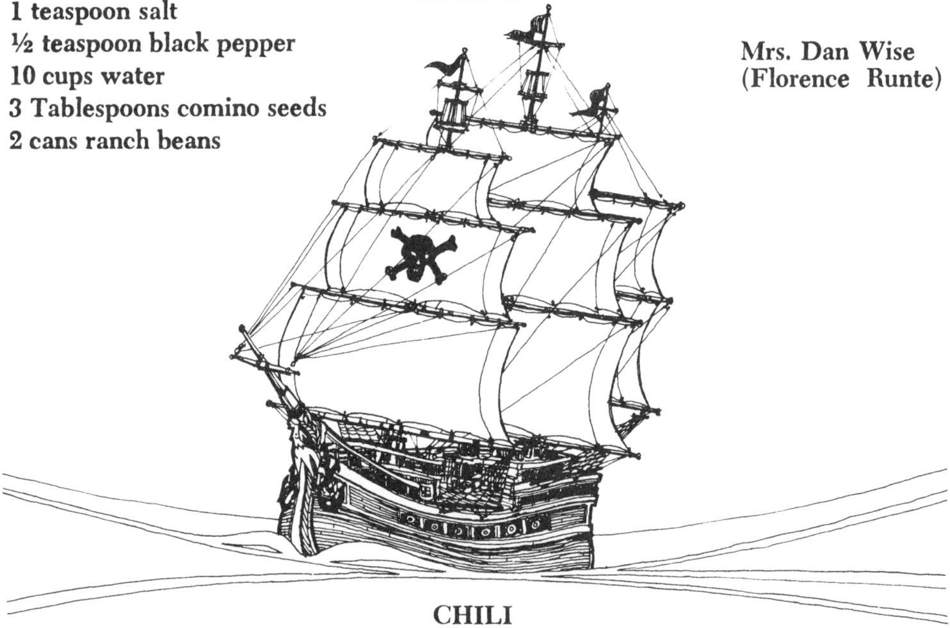

CHILI

2 pounds ground chuck
1 medium onion, finely chopped
3 cloves garlic, finely chopped
Margarine
3 teaspoons salt
1 can (8 ounces) tomato sauce
1 can (10 ounces) Ro-tel tomatoes
4 Tablespoons flour dissolved in 2 cups water
1 Tablespoon chili powder
1 teaspoon red pepper (optional)
2 cans (15 ounce size) Mexican chili beans

Brown meat, onion, and garlic in small amount of margarine. Add salt, tomato sauce, and tomatoes. Add chili powder (and, if desired, pepper). Add flour paste. Simmer about 45 minutes, stirring occasionally to prevent sticking. Add water in small amounts if needed. Add chili beans and heat thoroughly. Serves 8.

Mrs. Edith C. Viccellio

HOT CHILI

½ package red kidney beans
1 pound ground chuck
1 Tablespoon flour
1 onion, chopped
1 clove garlic, chopped
1 teaspoon salt
½ cup bell pepper, chopped
2 Tablespoons chili powder
1 can Ro-tel tomatoes
½-1 cup water

Soak beans for 1 hour. Cook as directed on package, with no seasoning except salt. Combine next 7 ingredients. Place in cold iron skillet. Cook, uncovered, over low heat until onion is wilted and meat well done and in small pieces. Stir often. Add tomatoes and simmer, adding water when necessary, until beans are ready. Add beans to meat. Freezes. Serves 4.

It's hot and brings tears to the eyes, but it's delicious and great on a cold day!

Mrs. Robert G. Dunn
(Marilyn Strait)

QUICK CHILI

2 pounds ground meat
1 medium onion, chopped
2 cans (15 ounce size) red kidney beans, drained
1 package Lawry's chili seasoning
4 cups tomato juice
1 can (8 ounces) tomato sauce
1 Tablespoon chili powder
Salt and pepper to taste

Brown meat and onion in heavy iron pot. Drain. Stir in remaining ingredients. Cook, covered, on top of stove on low heat for 3 hours. Freezes. Serves 6.

Better if prepared a day ahead.

Andrew L. "Andy" Plauché, Jr.

MEXICAN CASSEROLE

1 pound ground meat
1 onion, chopped
1 clove garlic, minced
1 can Enchilada sauce
1 can Ro-tel tomatoes
1 can cream of mushroom soup
Tortillas, quartered
1 cup sharp Cheddar cheese, grated

Sauté ground meat, onion, and garlic in skillet. Add Enchilada sauce and let bubble. Add combined tomatoes and soup and let bubble. In greased 2 quart casserole place ½ tortillas, topped with ½ meat sauce. Repeat. Top with cheese. Bake, uncovered, at 350°F for 30 minutes. Freezes, before adding cheese. Serves 6.

Jeanne Hartman

SOUTH OF THE BORDER HOT DISH

1 pound ground beef
½ cup onion, minced
1 cup kidney beans
2 cups tomatoes
1 can (8 ounces) tomato sauce
¾ teaspoon chili powder
1¼ teaspoons salt
⅛ teaspoon pepper
¼ teaspoon chilies, crushed
1 cup Cheddar cheese, shredded
1 package (6 ounces) corn chips

In saucepan sauté beef and onion until browned and tender. Add beans, undrained tomatoes, and tomato sauce. Mix well. Stir in chili powder, salt, pepper, and chilies. Heat to simmering point; continue simmering, stirring occasionally, until mixture thickens, about 20 minutes. Place in baking dish; spread cheese around edges and top with corn chips. Bake at 350°F for 8-10 minutes. Serve immediately.

Mrs. George W. Pomeroy

BEEF TACOS

1 pound lean ground beef
¼ cup cooking oil
¾ cup onion, chopped
¼ cup bell pepper, chopped
Garlic to taste
1 small can tomato sauce
Chili powder to taste
Salt and pepper to taste
1½ quarts water
Taco shells (not frozen)
Cheddar cheese, grated
Lettuce, chopped, seasoned
Raw onion, chopped
   (optional)

In large heavy pot, brown beef in cooking oil. Add onions, bell pepper, and garlic. Sauté for a few minutes, stirring frequently. Add tomato sauce, chili powder, salt, pepper, and water. Cook, uncovered, until thick enough to fill taco shells. Heat taco shells in 250°F oven until hot. Fill with thickened meat sauce. Sprinkle with cheese, lettuce, tomatoes, and onion. Freezes. Serves 4.

Children love this!

Mrs. Alford F. Elender
(Sylvia Broussard)

Mrs. Everett Schneider *uses 1 can Bloody Mary Mix in place of tomato sauce and tops with sliced avocado.*

SPANISH DELIGHT

1 large onion, chopped
1 bell pepper, chopped
1 clove garlic, chopped
3 Tablespoons olive oil
1 can (16 ounces) tomatoes
1 can (8 ounces) tomato sauce
1 Tablespoon chili powder
1 teaspoon salad herbs
¼ teaspoon orégano
Salt and pepper to taste
1 pound ground beef
1 can (15 ounces) chili without beans
1 can (14 ounces) Niblett corn, drained
1 can (4 ounces) mushroom stems and pieces, drained
1 small can pitted ripe olives, sliced or chopped
1 medium package narrow noodles
½ pound Cheddar cheese, grated
1 teaspoon paprika

Sauté onion, bell pepper, and garlic in olive oil. Add tomatoes, tomato sauce, chili powder, salad herbs, orégano, salt, and pepper. Cook for 1 hour over low heat, stirring occasionally. Brown meat separately after sauce is cooked. To sauce add meat, chili, corn, mushrooms, and olives. Boil noodles in salted water 10-15 minutes until tender, but not overcooked. Drain. Mix with meat sauce and place in casserole (1 large, 2 medium, or individual). Top with cheese sprinkled with paprika. Bake, uncovered, at 325°F for 20 minutes, or until bubbly. Freezes. Serves 6-8.

Mrs. W. Layton Stanton

BEEF BURRITOS

1 pound ground meat
1 medium onion, finely chopped
Salt, black and red peppers, and chili powder to taste
Cooking oil
1 package flour tortillas
Velveeta cheese, shredded
Jalapeno green hot sauce (optional)

Brown meat and onion together in iron skillet. Add seasoning. Meanwhile, in small frying pan, cook tortillas in hot oil a few seconds on each side, turning only once, removing when still soft enough to roll. Drain on paper towel. Place meat mixture topped with cheese on tortillas (using hot sauce here, if desired). Roll up, and secure with toothpicks. The more cheese on tortillas, the easier to hold together. Serves 4.

Dan Blalock

TAMALE AND CHILI PIE

1 jar (13½ ounces) Derby hot tamales
1 recipe chili
1 cup Fritos
¼ cup onion, chopped
½ cup sharp cheese, grated
CHILI
1 pound ground meat
1 Tablespoon oil
1 can (8 ounces) tomato sauce
1 can (15 ounces) Gebhardt's chili beans
1 package French's Chili-O-Mix

Cover bottom of 2 quart casserole with tamales. Prepare chili, using any recipe but substituting tomato sauce for tomatoes. Pour chili over tamales. Press Fritos into chili. Sprinkle with onion and cheese. Bake, uncovered, at 350°F for 20 minutes.

Very quick!

Mrs. Alan Thigpen
(Catherine Lagrange)

CHILIES RELLENOS
(Stuffed Peppers)

1 large package Monterey Jack cheese
Green chilies (canned or fresh), peeled
BATTER
Eggs (1 to each 2 whole chilies), separated and beaten
Flour (1 Tablespoon to each egg)
Cooking oil 1½ inches deep
SAUCE
½ onion, minced
1 clove garlic, minced
Cooking oil
2 cups solid pack tomatoes
2 cups stock (preferably chicken)
1½ teaspoons salt
½ teaspoon pepper
1 teaspoon orégano

Cut cheese into 1x2x½ inch thick oblongs. Wrap each in strip of peeled chili. Drop, 1 at a time, into premixed batter, remove with spoon, and fry in hot oil until golden brown on both sides. Drain on paper towels. Just prior to serving place peppers in boiling sauce just long enough to heat through, about 5 minutes. They will puff up.

Mrs. Albert Johnson
(Dixie Kingston)

HOW I COOK A HAM

½ or whole ham, smoked or cooked
Whole cloves
White granulated sugar
Louisiana sugar cane syrup
Large can (Dole's) pineapple juice
Pineapple rings
Maraschino cherries
Parsley

Boil ham for 1-2½ hours (depending on size) until tender, testing with fork. Drain, stud top surface with cloves, and cover thickly with sugar. Place in baking pan, cover with syrup, and add pineapple juice. Bake, covered, for 1 hour or more at 325°F until top is light tan and meat at the end begins to separate from bone. Should be tender enough to cut with a fork but not overcooked as it makes slicing difficult. Baste 2-3 times with juice while baking. Decorate with pineapple rings centered with cherries. Garnish serving platter with parsley.

Hams that are precooked at purchase do not have to boil as long as uncooked ones.

Mrs. Oliver Stockwell
(Roseina Holcombe)

BOILED FRESH HAM

14 pound ham
4 heaping Tablespoons salt
1 heaping Tablespoon black pepper
6 dried red peppers, or more to taste
1 teaspoon cayenne pepper

Combine all ingredients in boiling water. Boil slowly until ham is tender.

BAKED HAM

1 ham
Sliced pineapple

SAUCE

1½ cups sugar
2 Tablespoons prepared mustard
4 ounces pineapple juice
4 ounces red wine
2 ounces vinegar
2 cloves garlic, pressed

Place ham in shallow casserole topped with 3-4 pineapple slices. Combine sauce ingredients and pour over ham. Bake, uncovered, at 300°F about 20 minutes per pound, or use thermometer and bake until tender. Baste during baking.

Mrs. Edwin Deweese
Philadelphia, Miss.

HAM WELLINGTON WITH WINE SAUCE

BAKED HAM

5-8 pound fully cooked canned or boneless ham
¾ cup cherry preserves
2 Tablespoons light corn syrup

BAKED HAM

Preheat oven to 325°F. Bake ham, fat side up, for 2 hours. Combine preserves and syrup. Spoon ½ of mixture on ham. Bake 10 minutes. Spoon on rest of mixture. Bake 15 minutes longer. Cool completely.

BISCUIT CRUST

4 cups packaged biscuit mix
1 teaspoon sage
2 Tablespoons prepared mustard
¾ cup Crisco
⅔ cup milk
1 can (4½ ounces) deviled ham
1 egg yolk, beaten with 1 Tablespoon water

BISCUIT CRUST

In large bowl combine biscuit mix, sage, and mustard 2 hours before serving. Cut in shortening with pastry blender. Make well in center and add milk. Beat with fork until well mixed. Shape into ball and knead 5 minutes. On lightly floured pastry cloth, roll out 4/5 of dough to form 12x22 inch rectangle. Spread with deviled ham leaving 1½ inch margins. Encase cooled ham in dough, molding tightly, and pressing edges to seal. Refrigerate dough-covered ham on greased cookie sheet. Roll out remaining dough ⅛ inch thick and brush evenly with egg mixture. With sharp knife or cookie cutters cut out preferred shapes. Press cut-outs on dough covered ham and brush with remaining egg yolk mixture. Bake 1 hour, or until crust is golden. Let stand 10 minutes before slicing.

WINE SAUCE

3 packages (¾ ounce size) mushroom gravy sauce mix
1 cup Port wine
2 cups water
¾ cup cherry preserves

WINE SAUCE

For wine sauce make gravy according to package directions adding the Port, water, and preserves. Pass sauce with ham. Serves 10-16.

Mrs. David Buttross, Jr.
(Joyce Abraham)

CANTONESE HAM

1 center sliced ham, cut 1 inch thick
¼ cup each soy sauce, sherry, and water
½ cup green onions and tops, sliced
¼ teaspoon powdered ginger
1 Tablespoon salad oil

In a baking dish soak ham in a marinade of the remaining ingredients (except oil) for 1 hour. Remove, dry with paper towel, and brown on both sides in oil in a heavy frying pan. Pour the marinade over ham, cover, and simmer for 20 minutes. Serves 4-6, depending on size of ham slice.

Mrs. Tom A. Flanagan, Jr.
(Sarah Nabors)

CURRIED HAM IN POPOVERS

2 Tablespoons bell pepper, chopped
1 Tablespoon onion, chopped
1 Tablespoon butter or margarine
1 can condensed cream of celery soup
2 cups ham, cubed
⅓ cup mayonnaise or salad dressing
⅓ cup milk
¼-½ teaspoon curry powder

POPOVERS
2 eggs
1 cup milk
1 cup flour, sifted
½ teaspoon salt
1 Tablespoon cooking oil

In medium saucepan sauté bell pepper and onion in butter or margarine until tender but not brown. Add remaining ingredients; cook, uncovered, stirring until thoroughly heated. To prepare popovers beat eggs, milk, flour, and salt 1½ minutes with rotary or electric beater. Add cooking oil and beat 30 seconds more. Fill 6-8 well greased 5 ounce custard cups (or popover pans) ½ full. Bake, uncovered, at 475°F for 15 minutes. Reduce heat to 350°F and bake 25-30 minutes more, or until browned and firm. A few minutes before removing from oven, prick with a fork to release steam. Serve ham mixture in hot popovers, split lengthwise. Ham curry and popovers may be prepared in advance, but do not cook popovers until time to serve. Serves 6.

Mrs. Paul Kitt
(Betty Cook)

CROWN PORK ROAST

STUFFING
1 cup onions, chopped, with juice
3 cups apples, peeled, cored, and chopped
7 cups soft bread crumbs
¾ cup butter, melted
¾ cup almonds, blanched, chopped, toasted
Salt and pepper to taste
½ cup parsley, snipped
1 clove garlic, crushed
Dry white wine
Mace (optional)
ROAST
Center cut pork loin
Salt and pepper
Flour
1 cup water

To prepare stuffing, combine first 8 ingredients with a little wine to hold together. Add mace, if desired. Crown a center cut pork loin and tie securely. Cover bone ends with foil to avoid burning. Stuff with stuffing, rub generously with salt, pepper, and flour, and roast at 350°F for 30-35 minutes per pound. Pour water in pan 1 hour before removing from oven and use for basting until done. Make gravy from drippings and skim off fat. Correct seasonings. To serve, remove foil and string from bone ends and cover with paper frills. Garnish platter with parsley and glazed tiny apples. Serve with tiny new potatoes, steamed in their jackets, and a tart green salad.

Mrs. D. Dale Archer
(Valerie "Val" Grode)

PORK ROAST FOR A PARTY

20 pound fresh pork roast
1 box salt
1 jar (1½ ounces) red pepper
2 large onions, chopped in hunks
1 bulb garlic, chopped

Soak pork roast overnight in water to cover with salt and pepper. (Seasonings will penetrate.) Sprinkle onions and garlic with salt and pepper. Stuff onions and garlic in holes made in meat. Wrap roast in foil, inserting meat thermometer through the foil. In large pan, cook at 300°F for about 8-10 hours, checking thermometer to judge doneness. For last 30 minutes, unwrap, and raise heat to brown. Freezes.

Mrs. Theophile Peltier

RÔTIS DE PORC À LA BOULANGÈRE

5 pound pork loin, center cut
1 clove garlic, chopped
1 teaspoon salt
10 cups potatoes, thinly sliced
1 cup onion, coarsely chopped
2 teaspoons parsley, snipped
1 Tablespoon seasoned salt
⅛ teaspoon pepper
1 cup boiling water
3 Tablespoons butter or margarine, melted
Parsley, snipped

Preheat oven to 425°F. Trim loin of all but thin layer of fat. Rub with garlic and salt. Place pork, fat side up, on rack in shallow open roasting pan or large shallow casserole. Insert meat thermometer through fat side into center. Roast, uncovered, at 425°F for 1 hour. Reduce heat to 400°F. Remove pork and rack from pan. Pour off all fat. In roasting pan toss potatoes with onion, parsley, salt, and pepper. Pour in boiling water. Lay pork on top and brush potatoes with butter. Roast all about 1 hour, or to 185°F on thermometer gauge. On heated platter arrange roast; serve potatoes sprinkled with parsley in vegetable dish. Serves 6.

Mrs. Leo B. Kaough
(Julia Himel)

SCANDINAVIAN PORK ROAST

Deboned pork loin
Bones from roast
Salt and pepper
Pitted prunes
Peanut oil
Potatoes, peeled (optional)
Parsnips, peeled (optional)

Lay roast flat, salt and pepper to taste. Place single layer of prunes on roast. Roll and tie together in about 4 places with kitchen twine. Brush with peanut oil. Pat on salt fairly heavily. Place on rack in shallow pan (fat side up) and bake at 350°F for 25 minutes per pound plus 20 minutes. Place bones around roast for added flavor and drippings. Baste frequently. The last 40 minutes add small potatoes and baste frequently. The last 20 minutes add parsnips.

Bob Gregory

POLYNESIAN PORK ROAST 'N RICE

ROAST

½ cup soy sauce
¼ cup honey
½ cup ketchup
Deboned and rolled pork loin roast
Garlic salt

Mix soy sauce, honey, and ketchup. Pour over roast which has been seasoned with garlic salt. Bake, uncovered, at 350°F, 25 minutes per pound, basting periodically with sauce.

RICE

2 cups Uncle Ben's converted rice, raw
1 onion and bell pepper, chopped
2 Tablespoons dry parsley flakes
Cooking oil
1 can water chestnuts, chopped
1 can each mushrooms and chicken broth
1 teaspoon garlic salt
Salt and pepper to taste

To prepare rice sauté with onion, bell pepper, and parsley in oil until golden brown. Pour into casserole and add remaining ingredients. Bake at 350°F until rice is tender and fluffy.

Mrs. Heloise Braddock
Covington, La.

PORK TENDERS

2 pork tenders
Bacon strips

MARINADE

¼ cup soy sauce
1 Tablespoon onion, grated
1 clove garlic, mashed
1 Tablespoon vinegar
¼ teaspoon cayenne pepper
½ teaspoon sugar

Marinate pork tenders overnight. Place strips of bacon on tender. Bake in flat pyrex dish, uncovered, at 300°F for 1½ hours, basting several times. Serve with rice browned in butter and cooked in onion soup. Serves 4.

SAUCE

⅓ cup mayonnaise
⅓ cup sour cream
1 Tablespoon dry mustard (Spice Islands Hot Mustard)
1 Tablespoon green onions, chopped
1½ teaspoons vinegar
Salt to taste

To prepare sauce mix mayonnaise and sour cream. Add remaining ingredients. Serve on or with tenders. Also good on baked potatoes. Serves 4.

Mrs. Marion E. McDaniel
Houston, Texas

MARINADE FOR PORK TENDERLOIN

2 small pork tenders (approximately 2 pounds each)

MARINADE
1 teaspoon each thyme, sage, rosemary, chives, dry mustard, and marjoram
1 bay leaf, crumbled
Salt and pepper to taste

BARBECUE SAUCE
1 cup each brown sugar, ketchup, and water
1 cup each regular and smoky Open Pit barbecue sauce

Combine all ingredients for marinade. Spread on pork and let sit for 1 hour. Prepare sauce by combining all ingredients. Mix and pour on tenderloin. Cover with foil and roast at 325°F about 1 hour, or until done. Reserve some sauce for serving with meat later.

Mrs. W. P. Fuller
Kinder, Louisiana

BAKED PORK CHOPS

6 pork chops
1 cup ketchup
1 cup water
¼ teaspoon Tabasco
¼ teaspoon Lawry's seasoned salt
¼ teaspoon Lawry's seasoned pepper
1 Tablespoon Worcestershire sauce
¾ cup brown sugar
1 lemon, sliced

Place pork chops in pyrex casserole. Mix ketchup, water, and seasonings. Spoon over chops. Sprinkle with brown sugar and top with a lemon slice. Bake, covered, at 350°F for 1 hour. Remove cover and continue to bake for 20 minutes, or until brown.

Mrs. G. W. Swift, Jr.
(Betty Richardson)

STUFFED PORK CHOPS FINE BOUCHE

8 double pork chops, pocketed

STUFFING
2 pounds fresh spinach or 1 package (10 ounces) frozen chopped spinach
8 Italian sausages with anise
3 eggs, lightly beaten
¼ pound Parmesan or Romano cheese, finely grated
Butter
Salt and pepper to taste
1 can (10½ ounces) chicken broth (homemade preferable)

Mix cooked, chopped spinach with sausage which has been removed from casings and fried. Add eggs and cheese. Stuff the chops, secure with toothpicks, and brown lightly on both sides in butter. Place single layer in shallow casserole. Salt and pepper, add broth, and bake, uncovered, at 350°F for 1 hour. Serves 6-8.

Serve with Banana Fritters Bayou Lafourche, p. 236. Italian sausages with anise are usually delicate and mildly seasoned.

Mrs. Karl E. Boellert
(Kathleen Martin)

PORK CHOPS IN RED WINE

4 large loin chops
Salt and pepper
Paprika
1 Tablespoon butter
6 green onions, finely chopped (white and green parts)
1 cup dry red wine
Basil
Thyme

Trim fat from chops, sprinkle with salt, pepper, and paprika, and place in iron skillet sizzling with butter. Fry quickly on both sides until brown. Place in a casserole, sprinkle with onions, and add wine. Sprinkle with basil and thyme. Cook, covered, at 350°F for 30 minutes, adding more wine if necessary. Serve with Garden Pilaf, p. 27. Serves 4.

Mrs. William D. Blake
(Katherine "Kay" Krause)

SPANISH OLIVE-PORK CHOP CASSEROLE

4 loin chops, about ¾ inch thick
2 Tablespoons cooking oil
¼ cup onions, finely chopped
1 cup raw rice
2 cups chicken stock or bouillon
⅓ cup pimiento-stuffed olives, sliced
Salt and pepper to taste

Lightly brown chops on both sides in preheated oil. Remove and lightly brown onion. Combine remaining ingredients with onion and place in 13x9x2 inch pan. Top with chops. Bake, covered, at 350°F for 1 hour, or until chops and rice are tender. Serves 4.

Jene J. Renfroe

PORK RIBS SWEET AND SOUR

8 pounds pork ribs
Cooking oil
4-5 onions, finely chopped
3 cloves garlic, minced
⅓ cup sugar, or more to taste
3 ounces vinegar
4 Tablespoons soy sauce, or to taste
2 heaping Tablespoons cornstarch dissolved in ½ cup water

Have butcher cut ribs in 3 inch strips. Cut between each rib to separate. Cook in hot oil until ribs are evenly browned, stirring often to prevent sticking. Add the onions and garlic, stirring often. When ribs are well browned, add well blended sugar and vinegar mixture. In a minute add soy sauce. Slowly add cornstarch paste 15 minutes before serving.

From the recipes of
Della Bel Krause

COUNTRY PORK RIB AND TURNIP STEW

6-8 country back pork ribs
Salt
Black and red pepper
Flour
Cooking oil
1 large onion, chopped
½ cup celery, chopped
2 cloves garlic, minced
4 medium turnips, peeled and cubed, with tops

Season ribs, roll in flour, and brown in oil. Remove from pan. Add 1 Tablespoon flour to oil and stir until golden. Add onion and celery and sauté 5-10 minutes. Add garlic and pork ribs. Cover with water and simmer. When ribs are tender, add turnips. Simmer until fork tender. Serve over steamed rice. Serves 6-8.

Mrs. J. Malcolm Leveque
(Marjorie Helen Schepp)

COUNTRY-STYLE BACK RIBS AND SAUERKRAUT

3 pounds country style pork back ribs or pork chops
4 medium onions, sliced
1 can (27 ounces) sauerkraut
¼ teaspoon pepper

Layer meat over onion and ½ the sauerkraut in a 2½ quart casserole. Cover with remaining sauerkraut. Add pepper. If sauerkraut juice does not cover bottom of pan, add water. Bake, tightly covered, at 350°F for 1½-2 hours, or until meat is tender enough to come off ribs. May be cooked in Dutch oven on top of range. Stir once while cooking; spoon liquid over top. Serves 4-6.

Mrs. Louis J. Bonin
(Shirley Chappuis)

CHOUCROUTE À L'ALSACIENNE
SAUERKRAUT AND KNOCKWURST DELIGHT

2 cans (1 pound 11 ounce size) sauerkraut
1 cup carrots, finely chopped
1 cup onion, chopped
½ stick butter or margarine
1 can condensed beef broth
1 cup dry vermouth
2 pounds knockwurst or frankfurters
2 teaspoons black pepper
1 Tablespoon dried parsley
1 bay leaf

Drain and soak sauerkraut 5 minutes in cold water. Change water twice. Drain well. Sauté carrots and onion until soft in butter or margarine in large skillet with cover. Stir in drained sauerkraut. Toss to blend well. Add broth and vermouth. Score sausages and place over sauerkraut. Sprinkle with pepper and parsley. Push bay leaf to bottom of skillet. Bake, covered, at 350°F for 2 hours, or until liquid is absorbed. Discard bay leaf. Serves 8.

Mrs. Charles I. McElroy
(Verna Mae Snow)

WEENIE JAM

1 medium onion, chopped
1 small bell pepper, chopped
1 small rib celery, chopped
½ cup cooking oil
1 can (8 ounces) tomato sauce
1 package wieners, cut in ½ inch pieces
1 bay leaf
2 each cloves and whole allspice
3 cups water
1 heaping teaspoon salt
½ teaspoon red pepper
3 cups raw rice

In Dutch oven sauté onion, bell pepper, and celery in oil until clear. Add tomato sauce and cook, uncovered, 10 minutes over medium or low heat. Add wieners, spices, and 2 cups water. Cook 30 minutes more. Add remaining ingredients. Cook, covered, 30 minutes or until rice is done, stirring periodically to prevent sticking. Freezes. Serves 8.

Serve with salad, vegetable, and hot bread. Children love this!

Dr. L. J. Bonin

SWARTZ BRATS
(BRATWURST)

10 pounds pork butt
2 Tablespoons coarse pepper
4 cups water
2 ounces salt
1 teaspoon nutmeg, ground
Hog casings (see hints)

Debone pork but remove excess fat and grind coarsely. Mix all ingredients well, put through stuffer attached to meat grinder, without cutters, and into casings knotted at end. Knot both ends and twist into links every 6-8 inches. Grill over charcoal until well browned. To keep warm until serving, and to use as a sauce, slice a large onion and simmer in a can of beer. Add brats as they come off grill. Serve plain or in hot dog bun with onions, sauerkraut, and hot brown mustard. Freezes. Count on serving 1-2 links per person with Bohemian cabbage or cole slaw and German potatoes.

Hog casings may be obtained at any meat market that makes its own sausage. Extra casings may be stored for months, in a heavy salt and water solution, in lightly closed container, in refrigerator.

Edward C. Swartz

SAUSAGE STRADA

Bread slices (trim crusts)
Dried onions and parsley flakes
1 pound loose pork sausage
6 eggs
3 cups milk
Tabasco to taste
1-2 teaspoons Worcestershire sauce
Salt and pepper to taste
Cheddar cheese, grated

Line 3 quart buttered casserole with bread and sprinkle with onion and parsley. Fry sausage and drain. Sprinkle sausage over bread. Blend remaining ingredients except cheese. Pour over sausage and bread. Sprinkle on grated cheese and bake, uncovered, at 350°F for 30-40 minutes. Serves 8.

Rev. Robert W. Seney

TASSO SAUCE PIQUANTE

1½ cups flour
4 pounds Tasso, cut into 3 inch lengths
3 large onions, finely chopped
5 large cloves garlic, finely chopped
2 Tablespoons cayenne pepper, or to taste
2 cans tomato paste
4 lemons, quartered
Salt to taste, *after* cooking

In large Dutch oven with a cover, deeply brown flour. Add remaining ingredients, except tomato paste and lemons. Fill pot with water and cook, covered, at a slow boil for about 2½ hours, stirring occasionally. Add tomato paste and lemons and cook about 30 minutes more. Salt to taste. Serve over rice. Freezes. Serves 12-14.

Variation: May be made with 3 pounds of any meat or fowl plus 1 pound of smoked sausage, or with 4 pounds of smoked sausage instead of Tasso.

From the recipes of
K. Ramsey MacLeod

ROAST LEG OF LAMB

5-6 pound leg of lamb
1 teaspoon seasoned salt
1 teaspoon garlic salt
¼ teaspoon black pepper
2 Tablespoons lemon juice
1 Tablespoon Worcestershire sauce
¼ cup soy sauce
1 Tablespoon dried mint flakes, crushed
½ cup wine (sherry, white, or red)
1 cup consommé
3 Tablespoons cornstarch mixed with ¼ cup cold water
Water

Have butcher remove gland from lower part of lamb leg. Remove as much fat as possible; then rub entire surface with salt and pepper. Bake, uncovered, in small roaster with 1 cup water, at 375°F for 40 minutes. Add another cup of water if pan dries. When roast starts to brown, pour lemon juice, Worcestershire and soy sauce over it. Sprinkle with mint flakes and add another cup of water. Cover, reduce heat to 300°F, and roast 2½-3 hours. Baste with pan juices every 30 minutes; add more water, if necessary, to maintain 2 cups of liquid in roaster. Add wine and consommé the last 30 minutes of cooking. Add cornstarch paste to pan juices and stir until it reaches a full boil. Skim off any fat from surface of gravy. Makes 3 or more cups of gravy. Freezes. Serves 8.

Prepared this way lamb has a mild flavor and is very tender. Serve with mint jelly.

Mrs. Edward H. Taussig
(Florence Streater)

STUFFED LEG OF LAMB

STUFFING
2½ cups soft bread crumbs
¾ cup blanched almonds, toasted and finely chopped
¾ cup celery (leaves and ribs), ground
½ cup onion, finely chopped
3 Tablespoons butter, melted
1 egg, beaten
1½ teaspoons salt
¼ teaspoon each pepper and thyme
Dry white wine

LAMB
5-6 pound leg of lamb, deboned, at room temperature
Garlic, finely slivered
Salt and pepper
Crisco
1 cup water
Onion, celery, carrot
1 small bay leaf

STUFFING
For stuffing mix all ingredients together and correct seasonings. Use just enough wine to moisten and hold mixture together.

LAMB
Bone leg of lamb, stuff, and tie securely. Insert garlic slivers in small cuts in meat. Rub meat liberally with salt and pepper and coat with thin layer of Crisco. Place in large roasting pan with remaining ingredients and insert meat thermometer. Brown, uncovered, at 450°F; then reduce heat to 350°F. Bake, uncovered, about 20 minutes per pound. Baste every 30 minutes, adding more water if necessary. When done, skim fat from pan juices; add salt and pepper, if necessary, and a little wine. Strain gravy and serve with lamb. Serve with au gratin potatoes, mint jelly or sauce, p. 301, and green salad. Serves 8-10

This is great for a dinner party.

Mrs. D. Dale Archer
(Valerie "Val" Grode)

ITALIAN LAMB CHOPS

Lamb chops, cut from end of leg, at least 1 inch thick, deboned
Salt and pepper to taste
Onion, sliced
1 can tomatoes with juice
Sharp cheese, grated
Bread crumbs

Brown chops quickly on both sides. Place in greased casserole and season. Layer with onion, tomatoes, and a mixture of cheese and bread crumbs. Add juice from tomatoes. Bake at 375°F for 1½ hours. Cover for last half of cooking time. This may be prepared but not cooked a day ahead. Allow 1 chop per person.

Mrs. Arthur Hollins III
(Gloria Guerry)

MUTTON MARINADE

Leg of lamb
2 lemons, thinly sliced
2 cloves garlic or more to taste
1 bottle Riesling wine
1 Tablespoon peppercorns
2 bunches tarragon

Marinate lamb for 3 days in mixture of remaining ingredients. Turn often. Roast, uncovered, in marinade at 250°F for 3 hours, turning meat periodically.

Mrs. Robert W. Fenet

Mrs. Howard V. Smythe *marinates lamb or venison in Italian salad dressing for 12-24 hours before cooking.*

VEAL ROAST

6-8 pound veal rump roast
4 Tablespoons fat
3 carrots, chopped
3 onions, chopped
1 bay leaf
Thyme
Parsley, chopped
2 green celery leaves, chopped
2 whole cloves
Salt and pepper to taste
2 cups beer
1 cup chicken stock
¼-½ cup Marsala wine
Mushrooms, thinly sliced (optional)

Sear roast in fat. Add next 10 ingredients. Cover and bake in standard roasting pan at 325°F for 5 hours. Baste as it cooks. When done, remove from pan, strain stock, and make gravy with chicken stock and wine. If mushrooms are added to gravy cook about 5 minutes. Roast should be sliced very thin. Serves 6-8.

Mrs. Arthur Hollins III
(Gloria Guerry)

OSSO BUCCO

2 medium onions, chopped
2 medium carrots, chopped
2 ribs celery, chopped
3 large cloves garlic, chopped
½ stick butter
Salt and pepper to taste
Flour
3 pounds veal or heavy calf shanks
Thyme to taste
Bay leaf
1 cup tomato sauce
1 cup wine (dry red or white)
1 cup beef bouillon or beef stock
2 Tablespoons parsley, chopped
1 small strip lemon peel

Slightly brown onions, carrots, celery, and garlic in butter in large Dutch oven. Lightly salt, pepper, and flour meat. Add meat to pot and brown on all sides. Add thyme, bay leaf, tomato sauce, and wine mixed with bouillon. Salt and pepper to taste. Cook, covered, very slowly for 1¼-1½ hours. About 10 minutes before meat is done (tender but not falling off bone), add parsley and lemon peel. Remove peel before serving. Serves 4-6, depending on size of meat bones.

This is a popular Italian dish served like our stew.

Mrs. Karl Boellert
(Kathleen Martin)

BRUCCULUNI WITH SPAGHETTI

SAUCE

¼ cup olive oil
2 Tablespoons butter
1 cup onions, finely chopped
1 bouillon cube, dissolved in 1 cup water
4 cloves garlic, minced
3 Tablespoons parsley, finely chopped
1 teaspoon orégano
1 pinch red pepper
Black pepper to taste
1 teaspoon salt
2 medium tomatoes, diced (canned or fresh)
1 cup tomato juice
3 cups tomato purée
1 can tomato paste

SAUCE

Warm olive oil in Dutch oven or large pot with lid. Add butter and simmer until melted. Add onion and sauté until golden brown. Add bouillon, garlic, parsley, orégano, red and black pepper, and salt. Bring to boiling point and mix in tomatoes and tomato juice, purée, and paste. Cook, covered, on medium heat, stirring occasionally.

STUFFING

Salt and pepper
8 tenderized veal cutlets
½ pound ground beef
4 slices bacon, fried, crumbled
1 clove garlic, finely chopped
1 green onion, finely chopped
2 Tablespoons parsley, finely chopped
½ cup Italian flavored bread crumbs
½ cup plain bread crumbs
1 hard boiled egg, finely chopped
1 egg, raw

STUFFING

Salt and pepper cutlets. Combine remaining ingredients. Spread on cutlets, roll, and secure with toothpicks. Place cutlet rolls in sauce and cook on low heat until sauce is thick and meat is tender, about 1½ hours. Serve with spaghetti. Sprinkle with Parmesan cheese. Excellent meal with a tossed green salad and French or Italian bread. Freezes. Serves 8.

Mrs. F. Warren Raggio, Jr.
(Mavis Cade)

> To obtain clarified butter, melt butter and allow sediment to sink to bottom. Pour off clear butter. This is clarified and will cook without burning.

SCALLOPS OF VEAL IN WINE

8 scallops of veal
Parmesan cheese
Salt
¼ pound clarified butter
2 Tablespoons onion, grated
¼ pound fresh mushrooms, sliced
1 cup very good dry white wine
1 cup strong beef broth, well seasoned
1 Tablespoon flour mixed with a little water

Pound veal scallops until very thin. Coat with cheese and salt to taste. Sauté in butter until light brown. Transfer, with little overlapping, to a large flat pyrex dish. In the same butter sauté onion and mushrooms until wilted. Add white wine and broth and reduce liquid by boiling for several minutes. Correct seasonings. Pour over scallops, topping with grated cheese. Cover tightly with aluminum foil and bake at 350°F for 40-45 minutes. Remove foil and add flour mixed with a little water to pan juices, stirring until slightly thickened. Return dish, uncovered, to oven and bake until veal browns a little more and sauce is cooked, 10-15 minutes. Serve with buttered noodles and Italian salad. Does not freeze. Serves 4.

Mrs. D. Dale Archer
(Valerie "Val" Grode)

GRILLADES AND GRITS

1¼-1¾ pounds round of veal or beef, cut into 2 inch square pieces
2 teaspoons salt
1 teaspoon black pepper, freshly ground
⅛ teaspoon cayenne pepper
1 Tablespoon garlic, finely minced
2 Tablespoons flour
1½ Tablespoons lard
1 cup onion, chopped
1 large ripe tomato, coarsely chopped
1 cup water, more if necessary
2½-3 cups cooked grits

Trim all fat from meat, remove any bones, and pound with mallet until 2 inch squares are 4 inch squares. Rub meat all over with salt, pepper, and garlic; then rub in flour. In large skillet brown grillades well on both sides in melted lard over medium heat. Reduce heat and add remaining ingredients, except grits. Simmer, covered loosely, over low heat for about 30 minutes, uncovering to turn meat over every 10 minutes. If gravy becomes too thick, add a little water gradually. Remove to heated platter when done and place in preheated 200°F oven to keep warm. Prepare grits according to package directions. Just before serving, reheat gravy in skillet and pour over both meat and grits.

Makes a hearty inexpensive supper or a grand old fashioned Sunday breakfast.

Kathleen Malloy

VEAL PARMIGIANA

SAUCE

3 cloves garlic, minced
1 onion, minced
3 Tablespoons olive or salad oil
2½ cups tomatoes
1¼ teaspoons salt
¼ teaspoon pepper
1 can (8 ounces) tomato sauce
¼ teaspoon each thyme and orégano

SAUCE

Sauté garlic and onion in preheated oil in saucepan. Add tomatoes, breaking with a spoon, salt, and pepper. Simmer, uncovered, for 10 minutes. Add remaining ingredients. Simmer 20 minutes.

VEAL

¼ cup dry bread crumbs
¼ cup Parmesan cheese, grated
1 egg, beaten with small amount of water
1 pound veal cutlets (4)
3 Tablespoons olive or salad oil
½ pound Mozzarella or Muenster cheese
¼-½ cup Parmesan cheese, grated

VEAL

Combine bread crumbs and Parmesan cheese on waxed paper. Dip each cutlet into beaten egg and then into crumbs. Sauté in oil until brown. Place browned cutlets in 11x8x2 inch baking dish. Spoon ⅔ of prepared sauce over them. Arrange Mozzarella on top. Add remaining sauce and sprinkle with Parmesan cheese. Bake, uncovered, at 350°F for 30 minutes. Serve with spaghetti as there is plenty of sauce. Serves 4.

Mrs. Van H. King
(Eoline Bush)

VEAL CUTLETS PARMESAN

Salt and pepper to taste
2 eggs, well beaten
1 cup bread crumbs
3 Tablespoons Parmesan cheese
4 medium veal cutlets
6 Tablespoons Crisco oil
1 large can tomato sauce
4 slices Mozzarella cheese

Salt and pepper eggs to taste. Mix bread crumbs and Parmesan cheese. Dip cutlets into eggs, then into bread crumbs. Fry in hot oil for 5 minutes on each side or until golden brown. Place browned cutlets in baking pan, 13x9x2 inches, and pour tomato sauce over them. Cover with Mozzarella cheese. Bake, uncovered, at 325°F for 20 minutes, or until cheese is slightly brown. Serves 4.

Mrs. Max E. Jones
(Barbara Kunze)

STUFFED BAKED BEEF TONGUE

2½-3 pound fresh tongue
1 large onion, thinly sliced
1 large bell pepper, thinly sliced
4-5 cloves garlic, peeled, thinly sliced
1½ teaspoons salt
½ teaspoon black pepper
4 Tablespoons cooking oil
1 Tablespoon cornstarch dissolved in ¼ cup cold water

Wash tongue thoroughly, place in large kettle, cover with water, and bring to full boil. Cook, covered, on medium heat for about 45 minutes. Remove tongue but reserve cooking liquid to use in baking. Place tongue in cold water until cool enough to skin. With a sharp knife scrape or peel outer white skin. Cut slits 1 inch wide and deep over entire surface, spaced 1½ inches apart. Stuff sliver of onion, bell pepper, and garlic into each slit, reserving remainder of the vegetables for baking. Rub tongue with salt and pepper and place in heavy metal Dutch oven or small roaster with cover. Pour cooking oil over entire surface. Bake, uncovered, at 400°F, about 30 minutes, turning several times until nicely browned. Place 2 cups of reserved broth and remaining vegetables in roaster, cover, and reduce temperature to 325°F. Turn tongue several times while baking and add more broth as needed to maintain about 2 cups liquid. Bake 2 hours. Test with fork for tenderness. Should test very tender. When ready to serve, thicken broth by stirring in cornstarch paste and boiling a couple of minutes. Slice tongue into ½ inch slices and serve with gravy. Freezes. Serves 4.

Boiled potatoes and creamed spinach are especially nice with tongue.

Mrs. Edward H. Taussig
(Florence Streater)

PICKLED TONGUE

1½-2 pound tongue
½ teaspoon saltpeter
1 clove garlic
½ teaspoon mixed spices
⅛ teaspoon each red pepper and ginger
⅓ pod red pepper
¼ teaspoon allspice
1 Tablespoon salt

Rub tongue well with saltpeter. Place in earthen crock and season with remaining ingredients. Cover and refrigerate. Turn every other day for 10 days. Rinse, boil about 2½ hours, and skin when cured.

Mrs. Dan Woodring
(Laura Noland)

SMOKEHOUSE SPECIALS

8 ground meat patties
1 bottle Cattleman's Smoky Bar-B-Que sauce
1 can (10 ounces) Gebhardt's Chili Hot Dog sauce
8 large hamburger buns with seeds
2 cups sharp Cheddar cheese, grated

Barbecue patties over a charcoal fire, basting with Cattleman's sauce. Meanwhile, warm chili sauce. To assemble hamburgers pour Cattleman's sauce liberally on both sides of bun and rub together to spread evenly. Place meat on bun, top with chili sauce, and sprinkle with cheese. Top with other half of bun and wrap tightly in foil. Place in preheated 300°F oven to warm completely through and melt cheese.

M. A. "Andy" Pierson III

CHIPPED BEEF ON MUFFINS

1 Tablespoon cooking oil
1 Tablespoon flour
1 teaspoon green onions or chives, chopped
1 cup milk
1 jar chipped beef, separated
2 hard boiled eggs, chopped
Dash Tabasco
Salt and pepper to taste
2 English muffins, split and toasted

Heat oil; quickly stir in flour. Add onions and milk gradually. Cook until thick. Stir in remaining ingredients. Cook, uncovered, 3 minutes. Serve at once on toasted muffins. Serves 2-4.

Mrs. Gail Montgomery Lloyd

BACON, CHEESE, AND ONION SANDWICHES

12 slices bacon, crisply fried
4 slices American cheese
4 hamburger buns spread with mayonnaise
4 thin slices large Bermuda onion
Lettuce and tomato (optional)

Blot cooked bacon. Place cheese on 1 side of bun and run under broiler until bubbly. Remove and add onion and bacon slice. Put top on; cut and serve.

Mrs. Terry Barnett Nelson

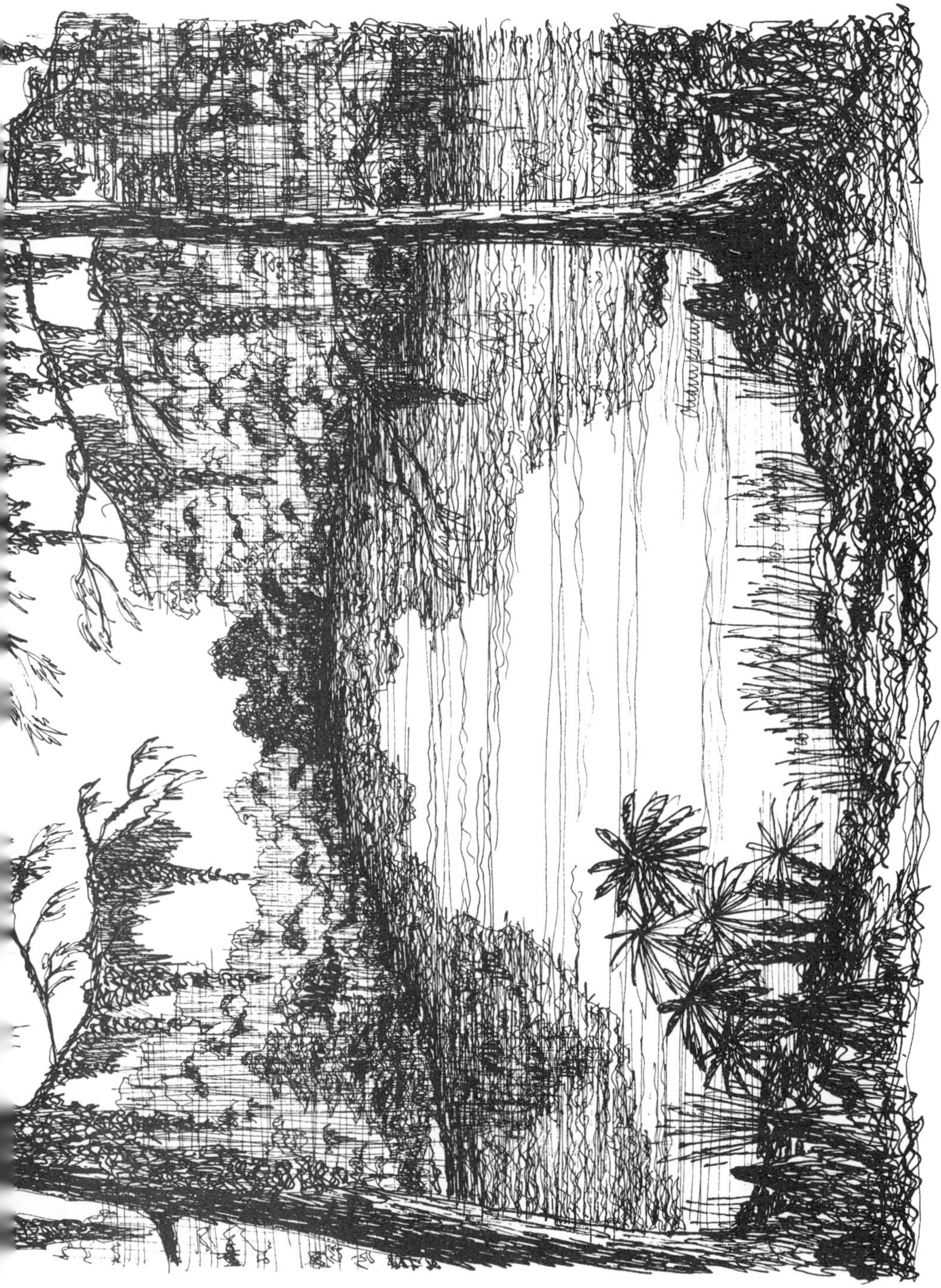

CONTRABAND BAYOU

Contraband Bayou, its banks lined with centuries-old cypress trees; trailing Spanish moss; yellow and blue swamp iris; water hyacinths and wild honeysuckle, is a romantic setting for tales of derring-do and legends of buried treasure. Smuggling was a lucrative trade in the South Louisiana area in the late 1700's and early 1800's, and Contraband Bayou, with its two entrances, seems to have been strategically situated for it. After Louisiana was ceded to Spain in 1762, the mother country enjoined the American colonies from trading with other nations, a mandate which infuriated the French population. So smuggling, in retaliation, became accepted practice, particularly after the development in 1795 of a commercially feasible method for granulating sugar, which in turn gave rise to a class of wealthy sugar planters who needed large work forces — slaves — and had a taste for fine wines, tobaccos and brandies.

According to local legend, the pirate Jean Lafitte traded contraband goods here in return for fresh meats and vegetables. It is a fact that one of Lafitte's captains, Arsene LeBleu, lived near Lake Charles on English Bayou, a branch of the Calcasieu River.

Legend has it, Lafitte's captives, left behind to guard treasure buried on the banks of Contraband Bayou, can still be seen on dark, misty nights.

CHICKEN BREAST WITH TUNA SAUCE
PETTI DI POLLO TONNATO

4 large whole chicken breasts, boned and skinned
2 Tablespoons butter
3 Tablespoons olive oil
1 can (7 ounces) high quality tuna, packed in olive oil
2 lemons
3 Tablespoons small capers, finely chopped
2 cups mayonnaise, preferably homemade
½ teaspoon white pepper
Salt to taste
1 Tablespoon parsley, finely chopped

Pull chicken breasts apart at natural divisions to make smaller sub-sections. Salt and pepper lightly and sauté in the butter and 1 Tablespoon olive oil over medium heat until lightly browned. Do not overcook. When cool, lay flat on carving board, and, holding down with palm of hand, slice through to divide each piece of breast into two portions. Blend tuna (with oil in which it was packed), juice of 1 lemon, and remaining olive oil in blender to a fairly smooth consistency. Add blended mixture and capers to mayonnaise. Add white pepper, mix well, and check for seasoning. Additional salt may be needed depending on saltiness of mayonnaise and tuna. The mixture should have a good, but not excessive, salt and lemon tang. Cover breasts with sauce and store several hours (or even a day or two) in the refrigerator. When ready to serve, arrange cold breasts on a large platter. Cover thinly with sauce and decorate with lemon slices and a sprinkling of parsley. Does not freeze. Serves 6.

This is a variant of a classic Italian dish, Roast Veal in Tuna Sauce, or Vitello Tonnato, in which slices of a well seasoned veal roast are used instead of the chicken breasts. The variant is offered because of the difficulty of finding good veal in America.

Ellis Palmer

OCTAVIA'S FRIED CHICKEN

1 medium fryer
4 eggs, well beaten
½ cup milk or water
1 teaspoon each salt and red pepper
½ teaspoon black pepper
1 teaspoon Accent
½ teaspoon garlic powder
2 cups flour seasoned with:
  1 Tablespoon baking powder
  1 or more teaspoons red pepper
  1½ teaspoons salt or more to taste
  ½ teaspoon black pepper
  ½ teaspoon Accent
Vegetable oil

Cut up fryer. Mix well eggs, milk or water, salt, red and black pepper, Accent, and garlic powder. Soak chicken in mixture for 1 hour or longer. Roll chicken in seasoned mixture. Fry, uncovered, at 400°F with vegetable oil deep enough to cover chicken. If browning too fast, reduce temperature to 350°F. When chicken is well browned, drain thoroughly. Chicken is done if tender when pierced with fork. Should be golden brown. If milk is used with seasoned egg mixture, the color is darker; if water is used, the color is lighter. Serves 4.

Southern fried chicken at its best!

                              Octavia Trahan

GEORGIA FRIED CHICKEN WITH CREAM GRAVY

2 cups flour
½ teaspoon red or black pepper
1 teaspoon salt
½ teaspoon paprika
1 large fryer, cut up, salted and cooled overnight
Shortening or corn oil

CREAM GRAVY
Drippings from fried chicken
2 cups, or more, milk

Shake flour, pepper, salt, and paprika in a paper bag. Drop in several pieces of chicken at a time and shake to coat thoroughly. Heat 4 inches of shortening in iron skillet until very hot. Cook chicken pieces about 15-20 minutes, until brown on both sides, turning only once. Use tongs, not a fork, to turn chicken. After chicken has been removed from skillet, pour off excess fat, leaving only the drippings, which should be golden brown, not burned. Add 2 cups milk, or more if necessary, stirring constantly until desired thickness.

                            Mrs. G. Lock Paret, Jr.
                            (Beverly Bowers)

CLEMENTS CHICKEN

8 single chicken breasts
   (2 per person)
½ pound unsalted
   butter, melted
Juice of 1 lemon
2 cups Progresso Italian
   bread crumbs

Skin and debone chicken breasts. Dip into butter seasoned with lemon juice; then roll thoroughly in bread crumbs. Bake, uncovered, on cookie sheet or shallow pan at 400°F for 35-40 minutes. Do not turn. Place on serving platter and pour more lemon butter over chicken. Serves 4.

Mrs. Robert W. Clements
(Gay Nell McDonnold)

STUFFED CHICKEN BREAST WITH SOUR CREAM SAUCE

8 chicken breasts
Salt and lemon juice
2 Tablespoons margarine
1 large onion, finely
   diced
1 rib celery, finely diced
1 pound Tennessee plain
   sausage
2 Tablespoons margarine
2 small cans mushrooms,
   drained
2 cups bread crumbs
1 carton sour cream
½ pint whipping cream

Bone chicken breasts but do not separate from skin. Sprinkle breasts with salt and lemon juice. To make dressing brown onion, celery, and sausage in margarine. Add 1 can mushrooms and bread crumbs. Mix together and shape to fit center of chicken. Place in chicken, folding chicken over dressing and pressing edges together. Bake, uncovered, at 325°F for 30-45 minutes, or until brown. Heat sour cream, remaining mushrooms, and whipping cream together. Serve chicken on platter, spooning with sauce as it is served on individual plates. Serves 8.

Mrs. Charles McElroy
(Verna Mae Snow)

CHICKEN WITH SHERRY

6-8 chicken breasts
Salt and pepper
Butter
1 Tablespoon flour
¼ cup sherry
1½ cups water
2 onions, cut in rings
2 bell peppers, cut in rings
Garlic powder

Season chicken with salt and pepper. Place in shallow pan with enough water to cover bottom. Dot generously with butter. Bake at 450°F for about 1 hour or until brown. Remove chicken from pan. Make gravy by stirring flour into drippings and browning. Add remaining ingredients. Return chicken to pan of gravy and cook at 350°F for 1 hour.

Mrs. David Buttross, Jr.
(Joyce Abraham)

CHICKEN VERMOUTH

6 deboned chicken breasts
Salt to taste
6 slices ham
6 slices Swiss cheese
1 cup flour
1 bag pork skins, crumbled
1 stick butter
2 Tablespoons flour
1 cup milk
½ cup vermouth

Season the chicken breasts well with salt. Wrap breasts around ham and cheese. Roll in flour and pork skins. Brown in butter. Remove breasts. Make a white sauce by adding 2 Tablespoons flour to drippings; add milk and vermouth gradually. Stir until thick. Place breasts in pyrex casserole. Pour sauce over all (saving some). Bake, uncovered, at 325°F for 20 minutes. Serve additional sauce with meal (optional). Serves 6.

Pork skins may be hard to find outside of Louisiana, but they make the dish.

Mrs. Kenneth Wimberly
(Carole Bruchis)

CHICKEN SPAGHETTI

1 large hen (5-6 pounds)
1 medium onion, peeled, halved
1-2 ribs celery
1 carrot, halved
1 bay leaf
Salt and pepper to taste

SAUCE

1 large onion, chopped
¼ cup olive oil
2 cans tomato paste
1-2 cups chicken broth, strained
1 large can (or more) mushroom pieces, drained
Salt, pepper, Tabasco, Worcestershire sauce, thyme, bay leaf
1-1½ packages (10 ounce size) spaghetti
1-1½ cups Cheddar cheese, grated
Parmesan cheese
½ cup dry sherry (optional)

Cover hen (barely) with water, add remaining ingredients, bring to boil, reduce heat to simmer, cook until hen is tender. When tender, remove from pot, cover lightly with foil or waxed paper to prevent drying. Raise heat under broth and continue cooking until reduced by ⅓ to ½. Strain and reserve. When hen cools, skim, remove meat from bones, cut in large chunks.

SAUCE

Fry onion in oil until clear. Add tomato paste and fry slowly until it darkens slightly. Add broth, mushrooms, and seasonings, sampling for taste. Cook very slowly until seasonings blend for at least 30 minutes. Remove bay leaf after about 5 minutes.

Cook spaghetti and drain well. In 3 quart greased casserole place alternate layers of spaghetti, chicken, sauce and Cheddar cheese. Continue layering, ending with sauce and cheese. Sprinkle liberally with Parmesan cheese. Add sherry, if desired, before baking. Bake, uncovered, at 325-350°F for 35-45 minutes. If at anytime the casserole seems to be drying, add reserved chicken stock; it should be quite moist but not soupy. Serves 8-10.

Mrs. Arthur Hollins, Jr.
(Mary Muth)

CHICKEN ITALIEN

2 large fryers
1 onion, chopped
1 rib celery, chopped
Salt to taste
SAUCE
3 large onions, chopped
2 bell peppers, chopped
¼ cup olive oil (do not substitute)
2 cans (15 ounce size) tomato sauce
2 medium cans or 1 large can mushrooms, drained (stems and pieces)
1 small can (2-4 ounces) ripe olives, sliced
1 small can (8½ ounces) petit póis peas, drained
Salt and pepper to taste
1 package (12 ounces) wide egg noodles
Parmesan cheese

Boil chickens in water with onion, celery, and salt. Remove from heat and let cool. Save broth. This may be done a day ahead. Remove chicken from bones and cut in large chunks with scissors.

SAUCE
In heavy pot or large skillet, sauté the onions and bell peppers in olive oil until wilted. Add tomato sauce and cook slowly, uncovered, for about 45 minutes. Add mushrooms, olives, peas, salt and pepper to taste. Boil noodles in chicken broth for 10-15 minutes. Drain and wash in hot water to remove starch. Mix chicken, sauce, and noodles together. Place in 1 large or 2 medium casseroles and top with Parmesan cheese. Bake, uncovered, at 350°F until hot. Freezes. Serves 10-12.

Mrs. W. E. Gorham, Sr.
(Mary Tucker)

COQ AU VIN

2 chickens (2 pounds each), disjointed
¼ pound butter
8 small pearl onions
¼ pound salt pork, cooked, diced
¼ pound fresh mushrooms, quartered
1 clove garlic, chopped
1½ cups dry red wine
½ cup meat glaze (or ¼ cup Bovril broth and seasoning base; when shopping look in gourmet food section)
Salt and pepper to taste

Brown chicken on both sides in butter. Place chicken in 325°F preheated oven for 10 minutes. Return to burner. Add onions, salt pork, mushrooms, garlic, and red wine. Simmer for 15 minutes, or until chicken is done. Add glaze and season to taste. Serves 4.

Murray Reiter
Memphis, Tennessee

CHICKEN, MEAT, AND SAUSAGE SPAGHETTI

6 chicken breasts
4 cups fresh or canned chicken broth
3 sweet or hot Italian sausages
6 Tablespoons butter
4 Tablespoons flour
¾ cup heavy cream
3½ cups tomato sauce
Worcestershire sauce and Tabasco to taste
6 Tablespoons olive oil
1 cup onion, chopped
1 cup bell pepper, chopped
1 cup celery, chopped
1-2 Tablespoons garlic, finely minced
1 pound round steak, ground
1½ cups mushrooms, thinly sliced
Salt and freshly ground pepper to taste
1 pound vermicelli or spaghettini
1 cup peas, cooked
1 pound sharp Cheddar cheese, cubed

Preheat oven 450°F. Simmer chicken in broth about 20 minutes. Drain, saving broth. Debone and shred chicken. Bake the sausages in oven until done, about 15 minutes. Drain and set aside. Melt 4 Tablespoons of butter and add flour, stirring until blended. Add 2 cups of reserved broth and stir rapidly until thickened and smooth. Stir in cream and tomato sauce. Season with Worcestershire and Tabasco to taste. Meanwhile, heat the oil in a large skillet and cook the onion, bell pepper, and celery until crisp-tender. Add garlic and beef, and cook, stirring, until meat browns. Add tomato and cream sauce, salt and pepper to taste. Cook mushrooms in remaining 2 Tablespoons of butter and add to sauce. Cook vermicelli or spaghettini in large quantity of salted water until half done, about 5 minutes. Drain in colander and run cold water over. Assemble dish as soon as possible. First, slice sausages into ¼ inch rings. Spoon a thin layer of sauce over bottom of a deep baking dish, add ½ pasta, chicken, sausage, peas, and cheese. Repeat with remaining ingredients, ending with a layer of cheese. Stir lightly with a 2 pronged fork to blend ingredients and add about 2 cups of remaining broth. Bake, uncovered, at 325°F about 30 minutes, or until cheese is bubbling and melted. If necessary, add more broth as casserole bakes, but do not make soupy. Best if prepared a day ahead. Freezes.

Worth the effort!

Mrs. Kenneth L. Strauss
(Julie Ann Marx)

COQ AU QUICHE

Pastry (plain) for a 10 inch pie pan
1 cup Swiss cheese, grated
½ medium onion, finely chopped
1 cup cooked chicken (about 1 chicken breast), diced
½ cup cooked ham, diced
½ cup bell pepper, coarsely chopped
3-5 large, fresh mushrooms, sliced and sautéed
3 eggs
1 cup milk
½ teaspoon salt
⅛ teaspoon black pepper
Generous dash of nutmeg

Line a glass or earthen pie pan with pastry. Put Swiss cheese, onion, chicken, ham, bell pepper, and mushrooms in pastry shell. (This much may be done a day ahead.) Beat eggs lightly with milk, salt, pepper, and nutmeg. Pour into pastry shell. Bake at 450°F for 10 minutes; then reduce heat to 350°F and bake for 30 minutes longer, or until set. Test as for baked custard. Remove from oven and allow to cool for 15 minutes or so before cutting. Does not freeze. Serves 6.

Mrs. William G. Akins
(Kay Mishler)

PRINCESS CHICKEN

2 pounds chicken thighs
½ cup mushrooms, chopped
½ cup bamboo shoots, chopped
5 slices fresh ginger (optional)
¼ cup cooking oil
⅓ cup soy sauce
⅔ cup Sauterne
1 Tablespoon sugar
3 green onions, sliced diagonally
½ cup pecans or walnuts

Chop chicken thighs into bite sized pieces after skinning and boning. Place in bottom of heavy saucepan; add mushrooms, bamboo shoots, and ginger. Preheat oil over low heat. Combine soy sauce, Sauterne, and sugar; add to oil. Cover, bring to a boil, and pour over chicken in saucepan. Cover and cook over high heat for about 15 minutes. Reduce heat to simmer and cook 10-15 minutes more. Add green onions and pecans; stir. Serve hot with rice. If ginger is used, remove before serving; it is not pleasant to bite into. Serves 4-6.

This recipe is good for both the beginner oriental cook and for the adventurous. The preparation and cooking are easy, and the dish lends itself well to experiments. Try substituting sliced white onions, turnips, or squash; or add them to the mushrooms and bamboo shoots. Have fun!

Mrs. C. C. Laborde
(Mickey Supple)

ORANGE WALNUT CHICKEN

3 teaspoons salt
2 Tablespoons curry powder
8 chicken breasts
⅔ cup butter, melted
4 teaspoons orange peel, grated
1½ cups orange juice
2 cups pineapple tidbits with juice
⅔ cup walnuts
1 cup raisins
½ teaspoon cinnamon
¼ teaspoon allspice
4 oranges, peeled, sliced
2 Tablespoons flour
¼ cup water
2 teaspoons soy sauce

Preheat oven to 400°F. Mix salt and curry powder and rub into chicken. Dip seasoned chicken into butter and place, skin side down, in a shallow, uncovered baking pan. Bake 10 minutes, turn, and bake 10 minutes longer. While chicken is baking, combine orange peel, orange juice, pineapple, walnuts, raisins, cinnamon, and allspice in a saucepan. Bring to a boil. Reduce oven temperature to 375°F. Pour boiling mixture over chicken and bake 30 minutes longer. Pour the pan juices into a saucepan. Arrange the chicken in a serving dish, garnish with orange slices, and keep warm. Combine the flour, water, and soy sauce and stir into the pan juices. Bring to a boil, stirring, and cook 2 minutes. Pour over garnished chicken. Does not freeze. Serves 8.

Mrs. Michael Sarver

Mabel Collette *uses orange juice, honey, and mustard for her sauce.*

WALNUT CHICKEN HAWAIIAN

1 cup walnuts, broken pieces
Cooking oil
2½ cups chicken, cubed
⅓ cup soy sauce
⅛ cup sherry
1 Tablespoon sugar
1 teaspoon salt
1 Tablespoon salad oil
1 cup mushrooms, diced
1¼ cups water chestnuts, diced
1¼ cups bamboo shoots
1 Tablespoon monosodium glutamate
1 cup chicken broth
2 Tablespoons cornstarch

Deep fry walnuts in oil until light brown. Drain on paper towels. Mix chicken with soy sauce, sherry, sugar, and salt. Pan fry in oil for 1 minute. Combine chicken mixture with vegetables, MSG, and chicken broth. Cover and cook until chicken is tender. Thicken mixture with cornstarch which has been mixed with a little water. Add walnuts to chicken and serve over rice. Blanched almonds, cashews, or pecans may be substituted for walnuts. Freezes. Serves 12.

Mrs. Charles S. Ware, Jr.
(Jan Allen)

CHICKEN À SEVILLE

3 Tablespoons butter or margarine
½ pound fresh mushrooms, cleaned, and halved or quartered
3-4 teaspoons olive or other cooking oil
3 pounds chicken fryer parts
Cooking oil for frying chicken
Flour
Salt and pepper
1 cup long grain white raw rice
1 large clove garlic, minced
2 cups chicken broth
12 very small white onions
1 cup small pimiento-stuffed olives
¾ teaspoon orégano
1 cup dry white wine
½ cup slivered blanched almonds, toasted

Heat butter or margarine in a large skillet and stir in mushrooms. Cook until lightly browned, stirring occasionally. Remove from skillet and set aside. Pour oil in skillet and heat. Coat chicken pieces with a blend of flour, salt, and pepper. Fry in hot oil until browned on all sides. Remove chicken and keep warm. Mix rice and garlic with oil in skillet and stir in 1 cup of the chicken broth. Turn contents of skillet into a shallow baking dish. Place onions, browned chicken, mushrooms, and olives into dish. Pour remaining broth and the wine over all. Sprinkle with orégano. Bake, covered, at 375°F for 45 minutes until rice is tender. Remove from oven and top with almonds. Does not freeze. Serves 4-6.

Good for a bridge luncheon.

Miss Lena Clausell

CHICKEN ENCHILADA CASSEROLE

4-5 single chicken breasts
Celery salt
Onion flakes
1 can cream of mushroom soup
1 can cream of chicken soup
½ cup sour cream
½ cup onion, chopped
1-2 Jalapeños, seeded and chopped
12 tortillas
4 ounces each Cheddar and Swiss cheese, grated

Season chicken breasts with celery salt and onion flakes. Wrap in foil and bake at 325°F for 1 hour. Cut chicken into bite sized pieces, reserving the liquid in the foil. Add soups, sour cream, reserved liquid, onion, and Jalapeño to chicken and mix. Tear tortillas into quarters. Layer tortillas, chicken mixture, and cheeses (mixed) twice, ending with the cheese. Bake at 350°F for 30-45 minutes or until bubbly. Serves about 4.

Mrs. J. T. Thompson

CHILI CHICKEN CASSEROLE

1 package (12 ounces) fine noodles
½ cup onion, chopped
2 Tablespoons butter
3 cans cream of mushroom soup
1 can (4 ounces) pimientos, chopped
4 Tablespoons hot green chili peppers, seeded, finely chopped
Tabasco, salt and pepper to taste
4-5 cups chicken or turkey, diced
2-3 cups sharp Cheddar cheese, grated

Preheat oven to 350°F. Cook noodles by package directions and drain. Sauté onion in butter. Stir in soup, pimiento, chili pepper, Tabasco, salt, and pepper. Layer noodles, soup mixture, chicken, and cheese in a 4 quart casserole. Bake, uncovered, at 350°F for 45 minutes. Freezes. Serves 12.

Mrs. Leonard K. Knapp, Jr.
(Ann Hall)

CHICKEN AND SHRIMP CURRY

1 large onion, chopped
1 cup celery, chopped
¼ cup cooking oil
⅓ cup flour
2 cups chicken stock (canned or fresh from boiled chicken)
1½ cups tomato juice
½ teaspoon Worcestershire sauce
1 can (8 ounces) mushrooms, drained
Salt to taste
1 Tablespoon curry powder
3-4 cups chicken or turkey, diced
1 pound shrimp, boiled, peeled

Lightly brown onions and celery in oil. Add flour and mix well. Add chicken stock and cook until thick. Add tomato juice, Worcestershire sauce, and mushrooms. Add salt if needed. Mix curry powder with a little water to make a paste. Add to above mixture. Simmer, uncovered, for 30 minutes, stirring occasionally. Before serving add chicken and shrimp and simmer. Serve over rice. Have in separate dishes: chopped peanuts, hard boiled eggs, chutney, raisins, and shredded coconut. Freezes. Serves 8.

May also be served in a chafing dish for cocktail party dip. Dee-licious!

Mrs. R. Poinsett Johnson, Jr.
(Dee Tannehill)

CURRIED CHICKEN AND BROCCOLI

2 packages frozen broccoli spears
4-5 whole chicken breasts, cooked and cut into bite sized pieces
2 cans cream of chicken soup
¾ cup mayonnaise
Juice of ½ lemon, scant
½ cup water
1 heaping teaspoon curry powder

Heat broccoli until thawed and place in bottom of 2 quart casserole. When cool, layer with chicken. Combine remaining ingredients to make sauce. Mix well and pour over broccoli and chicken. Bake, uncovered, at 350°F for 35 minutes, or until bubbly. Serves 8-9.

Mrs. Thomas B. Shearman, Sr.
(Flora Inglis)

CHICKEN CASSEROLE

1 roasting chicken, 4½-5 pounds
2 ribs celery
2 Tablespoons onion, chopped
1 bay leaf
Salt and pepper to taste
½ teaspoon nutmeg
2 cups bread crumbs, firmly packed
2 cups rice, cooked
2 Tablespoons pimientos, minced
3 cups chicken broth or milk
1 can cream of mushroom soup
5 eggs, separated, both yolks and whites beaten well

Boil chicken with celery, onion, bay leaf, salt, pepper, and nutmeg. Remove and let cool. Cut into small pieces and combine with other ingredients, adding egg whites last. Bake, uncovered, for 45 minutes at 325-350°F. Serves 12.

Mrs. James F. Newell

RED GILL'S BARBECUED CHICKEN

4 fryers, halved
Salt and pepper
Salad oil
Mrs. Gill's Barbecue Sauce, p. 298

Season fryers with salt and pepper and brush with salad oil. When coals are ready, place chicken on pit and sear on each side. Turn damper down and cook about 1½ hours, turning when necessary, and basting with barbecue sauce. Freezes. Serves 8-10.

From the recipes of
Forrest "Red" Gill

HOT CHICKEN SALAD

2 cups cooked chicken, diced
3 hard boiled eggs, chopped
1 cup celery, diced
½ cup mayonnaise
1 Tablespoon lemon juice
1 can undiluted cream of
   chicken soup
1 cup water chestnuts, sliced
Salt and pepper to taste
Corn flakes

Combine ingredients except the cereal. Place in a greased casserole and top with crushed corn flakes. Bake, uncovered, at 400°F for 20 minutes. This dish may also be served in patty shells. Serves 6.

From the recipes of
Mrs. J. W. Allen

OPELOUSAS BAKED CHICKEN

6 fryer halves
Tony's Brand Creole
   Seasoning
1 cup vegetable oil
1 cup water
1 ounce paprika

Preheat oven to 275°F. Rub washed and dried chicken halves generously with seasoning. Arrange skin side up, in large, shallow (2 inches) baking pan containing the oil and water. Place in oven, uncovered, for 30-40 minutes until hot. Remove and baste. Sprinkle with paprika. Replace in oven, still uncovered, for another 4½-5 hours. Baste every 30 minutes. The chicken will be very dark and very tender when done.

Feeds 6 good eaters or 12 children.

Dr. Sam Emerson

ROAST CHICKEN

1½-2 pound broiler, halved
2 Tablespoons butter or
   margarine, melted
Salt and pepper to taste
1 teaspoon lemon juice
¼ cup water

Place chicken in shallow aluminum pan with skin side up, salt and pepper, and brush with 1 Tablespoon butter. Bake, uncovered, at 400°F for 25 minutes. Turn over, season, brush with butter. Bake 30 minutes longer, or until tender. Add lemon juice to drippings 10 minutes before done. To make gravy, remove chicken from drippings. Pour off all drippings but 1 Tablespoon. Place pan over low heat on top of stove and scrape sides and bottom. When hot, add water and salt to taste. Serves 2.

Mrs. Carmen Bogan Murrey

CHICKEN AND NOODLES

1 hen, 3-4 pounds
2 quarts water
1 Tablespoon monosodium glutamate
1 rib celery
Salt to taste

NOODLES

2 cups all purpose flour
1 teaspoon salt
1 egg
½ egg shell of water

In a large pot or Dutch oven boil hen with water, MSG, celery, and salt for several hours on low heat until meat begins falling from the bones. This can be done the day before. Remove celery rib. Remove hen from bones and store separately from broth. To make noodles, sift 1 cup flour and salt into mixing bowl. Make a "well" in the flour, break in 1 egg, and add ½ egg shell of water. Beat into the flour until it becomes very stiff. Knead dough with hands until egg has been well worked into flour and shape into a ball. Sift 1 cup flour onto working surface and spread. Place noodle dough on surface and flatten with palm of hand. Roll out thinly with rolling pin to make about an 18 inch circle of dough. Cut in half with a sharp knife, placing one half on top of other. Continue cutting dough in half and stacking on cutting board until all used. Slice off very thin strips with a sharp knife. Toss strips with the extra flour, mixing well so that none sticks to the other. Add raw noodles by handfuls to boiling chicken broth. Cook, covered, for 30 minutes at a slow boil; stir occasionally. Broth will thicken and noodles will swell. Chicken meat may be added to broth the last 5 minutes of cooking or served separately. Does not freeze. Serves 6-8.

This is an old German recipe passed down from Grandma Hoke. It was our favorite Sunday dinner at Grandma's house. Her recipe read "Go out to the hen house for a warm egg to make the noodles..."

Mrs. Earl Daughenbaugh
(Loretta Evans)

MUSTARD CHICKEN

1 chicken (3½ pounds), cut in 4 pieces
1 jar (3½ ounces) Dijon mustard
Pepper
1½ cups chicken broth
1 cup sour cream
1 cup rice or fine noodles

Coat chicken pieces on all sides with mustard and let stand several hours. Sprinkle with pepper only. Place in heavy casserole with tight fitting lid. Add ½ cup chicken broth. Bake, covered, at 350°F for 45 minutes or until done. With bulb baster use broth at bottom to dissolve bits of mustard clinging to chicken pieces. Stir in sour cream. Reheat for 1-2 minutes. Cook rice or noodles in the remaining chicken broth. Drain and serve with chicken pieces covered with sauce. Serves 4.

Unusual flavor! A different way to prepare chicken.

Mrs. Kenneth L. Strauss
(Julie Ann Marx)

CHICKEN IN THE LIMELIGHT

1 broiler-fryer chicken, cut up
1 lime
⅓ cup flour
1½ teaspoons salt
½ teaspoon paprika
¼ cup Crisco
2 Tablespoons brown sugar
½ cup chicken broth or bouillon
½ cup white wine
2 sprigs fresh mint (or ½ teaspoon dried mint)
For garnish; 1 avocado, 1 lime, and sprigs of fresh mint

Preheat oven to 375°F. Wash chicken and pat dry. Grate peel from lime and set aside. Squeeze lime juice over chicken pieces and shake in a bag containing flour, salt, and paprika. Melt Crisco in heavy skillet (with cover) and brown chicken on all sides. Pour off all Crisco and arrange chicken in skillet in single layer. Combine lime peel and brown sugar. Sprinkle over chicken. Add liquids. Place mint on top. Bake, covered, at 375°F for 40-45 minutes. Garnish with lime wedges, avocado slices, and fresh mint. Serves 4.

Mrs. Jim Johannsen
(Johanna Pace)

BAKED CHICKEN AND RICE CASSEROLE

1 cup wild or white rice, raw
½ cup raw brown rice
Salt and pepper to taste
6 whole chicken breasts
1 package dehydrated Lipton's onion soup
1 can cream of celery soup
2 soup cans water

Put rice in bottom of a 2 quart pyrex casserole. Salt and pepper the chicken breasts and place on top of rice. Sprinkle onion soup over all ingredients. Cover with cream of celery soup and water. Bake, uncovered, at 425°F for 20 minutes. Then cover and bake at 350°F for 1½ hours more. Serves 6.

Mrs. Frank E. Gault
(Ruth Kelly)

CHICKEN AND ASPARAGUS CASSEROLE

5 Tablespoons flour
1 teaspoon salt
¼ teaspoon onion salt
¼ cup butter, melted
2½ cups light cream
1⅓ cups minute rice
1½ cups chicken (or turkey) broth
½ teaspoon pepper
1½ cups sharp cheese, grated
1½ cups asparagus or broccoli, cooked
2½ cups (or more) chicken or turkey, sliced
2 Tablespoons slivered almonds, toasted

Sift flour, ½ of salt, and onion salt into melted butter. Stir in cream. Cook, stirring until thick. Pour rice into a 2 quart shallow baking dish. Combine broth, remaining salt, and pepper; pour over rice. Sprinkle ½ of cheese over rice. Top with asparagus; then chicken. Pour over sauce. Sprinkle with remaining cheese. Bake, uncovered, at 375°F about 30 minutes. Top with almonds. Freezes. Serves 4.

**Mrs. Richard E. Gerard, Jr.
(Susan Green)**

CHICKEN AND MUSHROOMS

1 fryer, cut up
Salt and pepper to taste
3 Tablespoons cooking oil
2 onions, chopped
1 large can button mushrooms with liquid
½ cup chicken stock (or 2 chicken bouillon cubes dissolved in ½ cup water)
¾ cup green onion tops, chopped
⅓ cup parsley, chopped (optional)

Season chicken pieces with salt and pepper. Using a Dutch oven, brown chicken in oil over high heat until very brown. Do not burn. Meanwhile, in separate pan sauté onions in small amount of oil until wilted. Add mushrooms and cook only 2-3 minutes. Remove chicken from Dutch oven, add mushrooms and onions to chicken drippings, and brown slightly. Return chicken to pot, add chicken stock, cover, and simmer 30 minutes, or until chicken is tender. During the last 15 minutes add onion tops and parsley, if desired. Correct seasonings to taste. If gravy is too thin, add mixture of 1 Tablespoon butter and 1 Tablespoon flour 10 minutes before serving. Serve over hot rice. Serves 4.

Stephen E. Plauché

CREAMED CHICKEN

1 large fryer, or 4 chicken breasts, diced
1 rib celery, quartered
½ onion
Salt and pepper
1 bell pepper, finely chopped
1 medium onion, chopped
½ stick margarine
3 teaspoons flour
1 cup milk
1 Tablespoon Lea & Perrins

Boil chicken with celery, onion, salt, and pepper until tender. Remove and let cool. Cut chicken with scissors into bite sized pieces. In separate saucepan, sauté bell pepper and onion in margarine. Add flour and cook a few seconds, stirring constantly to prevent lumping. Remove from heat and slowly stir in milk to form a smooth paste. Return to fire and cook, uncovered, until thick. Season to taste with salt, pepper, and Lea & Perrins. Add chicken. May be cooked and served in individual ramekins or served on thin toasted bread such as Pepperidge Farm. Freezes. Serves 4.

Mrs. Stephen E. Plauché
(Edith Burton)

CHICKEN LIVERS WITH MUSHROOMS

8-10 chicken livers
Salt and pepper to taste
Flour
2 chicken bouillon cubes
¾ cup boiling water
Butter
2 heaping Tablespoons green onions
1 small can mushrooms, sliced

Season livers with salt and pepper and dredge lightly in flour. Dissolve bouillon cubes in boiling water. Lightly brown livers in butter. Place in a 1 quart casserole. Sauté green onions (may have to add a little butter). Add bouillon and simmer for 3-4 minutes, stirring to loosen drippings from pan. Drain about half the liquid off mushrooms and add to bouillon. Pour over livers. Bake, uncovered, in a preheated 300°F oven for about 1 hour. Serve on thin toast. Spoon liquid over livers. Serves 2.

Mrs. Victor E. Lagrange
(Ruth Viallon)

Champignon

CHICKEN OR TURKEY CROQUETTES

1 medium onion, finely chopped or grated
½ bell pepper, finely chopped
4 Tablespoons butter
5 Tablespoons flour
1 cup cold milk, or chicken stock
Salt and pepper to taste
1 Tablespoon Lea & Perrins
Juice of ½ lemon
2 cups chicken or turkey, finely chopped or ground
1 egg, beaten with 2 Tablespoons cold water
Bread or cracker crumbs
Wesson oil
Lemon wedges

Wilt onion and bell pepper in butter. Remove from heat and stir in flour. When well blended add milk (or stock) gradually to avoid lumping. Return to stove and cook until thick, stirring constantly. Season with salt, pepper, Lea & Perrins, and lemon juice. Stir in poultry (2 cups fresh crab meat may be substituted). Correct seasoning. Pour into shallow pan and chill. When firm, cut into 6-8 squares. Mold by hand into oval balls. Dip croquettes into beaten egg mixture and coat with bread or cracker crumbs. Chill until ready to fry. Immerse frying basket containing croquettes in oil heated to 390°F. Fry, uncovered, until brown. Drain. Reheat in oven if necessary. Freezes. Use foil to reheat. Serve with lemon wedges.

Mrs. D. M. Creveling
(Ellanora Gorham)

TURKEY TETRAZZINI

2 cups cooked turkey, cut in small pieces
½ pound fresh mushrooms, thinly sliced
Butter
½ pound spaghetti
2 Tablespoons butter
2 Tablespoons flour
2 cups hot turkey or chicken broth (canned may be used if necessary)
1 cup rich cream
2 Tablespoons dry sherry
Salt and pepper to taste
Parmesan cheese

Prepare turkey. Sauté mushrooms in butter until browned. Prepare spaghetti according to package directions, using salted water. Make a cream sauce by blending butter and flour and gradually adding hot broth. When this mixture reaches boiling point, reduce heat and add the cream, sherry, salt, and pepper to taste. Divide the sauce in half. Add the turkey and mushrooms to ½ of the sauce, the spaghetti to the other ½. Place the spaghetti mixture in a ring in a well greased casserole. Place the turkey and mushroom mixture in center. Cover with cheese. Bake, uncovered, at 325°F until brown. Freezes. Serves 8.

This is definitely not the same with canned mushrooms.

Mrs. Jack Thielen
(Della "Dudie" Krause)

BAKED HEN

1 baking hen
Salt and pepper to taste
2 teaspoons rosemary
1 apple, chopped
½ stick margarine, melted
1 carrot, sliced
¼ medium sized onion, sliced
GRAVY
⅔ cup milk or cream
2-3 teaspoons flour
Water
Salt and pepper to taste

Season clean hen by rubbing salt and pepper inside and out. Sprinkle some of the rosemary in the cavity and add apple. Bake, uncovered, with skin side down at 325°F for about 2 hours, or until done. Baste at intervals with margarine mixed with remaining rosemary. About 30 minutes before hen is done place carrot and onion in bottom of pan. When done, remove the hen, and discard carrot and onion. Make the gravy by adding milk and flour (well mixed) to the drippings, stirring constantly. Add enough water for the desired consistency. Salt and pepper to taste. Serves 5-6.

Mrs. Philip D. Burris
(Gerd Archenholtz)

ROAST DUCKLING CHINESE STYLE

2 Long Island ducklings (4-5 pounds)
½ cup soy sauce
2 Tablespoons ground ginger
½ cup honey
½ cup dry sherry
1 clove garlic, quartered

Preheat oven to 325°F. Wash ducklings and dry thoroughly inside and out with paper towels. Mix 3 Tablespoons soy sauce with 1 Tablespoon ginger. Brush over duck's skin and inside cavities. Place ducks on rack of one or two shallow roasting pans; let stand at room temperature for 30 minutes to absorb ginger-soy flavor. While ducks are roasting, combine the remaining soy sauce, ginger, honey, sherry, and garlic in a saucepan. Bring to a boil, stirring until well mixed. Reduce heat and simmer 10 minutes, stirring occasionally. Remove and discard garlic pieces. Roast ducks for 2½ hours, basting well with glazing mixture after 1½ hours, then again after another ½ hour.

China was the first country to raise domestic ducks. This version, although not an authentic regional Chinese dish, uses characteristic Chinese spices and seasonings and has the extra crisp skin common to many Chinese versions.

Mrs. Terrell Woosley, Jr.
(Evelyn Shaddock)

CORNISH HEN CHASSEUR

2 Cornish hens
Salt and cayenne pepper
½ teaspoon orégano
1 cup Sauterne
¼ cup water
4 Tablespoons margarine
2 cloves garlic, minced
1 can (4 ounces) mushrooms, drained
2 tomatoes, diced
1 teaspoon cornstarch
1 cup Swiss cheese, grated
Parsley

Halve hens and place in a baking pan, cavity side up. Sprinkle well with salt, cayenne pepper, and orégano. Add wine and water. In each cavity place 1 Tablespoon margarine and minced garlic. Bake, uncovered, at 375°F for 1 hour. Remove from oven, turn hens over, and add mushrooms, diced tomatoes, and cornstarch dissolved in a little water. Sprinkle cheese over all. Return to oven and continue baking about 45-60 minutes more, or until golden. Garnish with parsley. Serves 4.

Barbara Dugazon Graham
Sioux Falls, South Dakota

CORNISH HENS STUFFED WITH WILD RICE

Frozen Cornish hens, number desired
Salt and pepper
1-2 green onions, chopped
Fresh or canned mushrooms
1 box Uncle Ben's wild rice for every 4 to 6 hens
1 stick butter for every 4 hens cooked
½ cup cooking wine

Thaw hens, remove insides, and wash. Season with salt and pepper inside and out. Sauté green onions and mushrooms in butter. Cook rice according to package instructions, but slightly undercook. Stir in mushrooms and onions. Stuff into hens and secure with toothpicks or poultry pins. Place in shallow baking pan and cover with foil. (May also use covered roaster.) Bake at 250°F 1 hour or longer, basting every 15 minutes with butter. At last basting, add wine. Then cover and bake until tender. Uncover long enough to brown.

Mrs. John W. Melton III
(Nancy LeLaurin)

CANADIAN FRENCH POTATO DRESSING

6 large Idaho potatoes, boiled, peeled, mashed thoroughly
Drippings from 1 pound bacon
3 Tablespoons leaf sage
1½ cups onion, finely chopped
1 stick butter
Salt and pepper to taste

Mix potatoes thoroughly with remaining ingredients. Crush sage leaves by rubbing through the hands. Bake, uncovered, at 325°F for 45 minutes, or until top of dressing has browned and onions are thoroughly cooked. May be prepared a day ahead and baked just before serving. Serves 10.

Good with Christmas turkey or game. This has been handed down in the Smythe family for several generations.

Mrs. Howard V. Smythe
(Jennabeth Powdrill)

CORN BREAD SAUSAGE PECAN DRESSING

1 cup celery, chopped
¾-1 cup onion, chopped
½ cup bell pepper, chopped
1 stick margarine
8 cups corn bread, crumbled
5 cups toasted white bread, cubed, or 3 cups bread crumbs
5 cups canned chicken broth
½ pound pork sausage
Giblets from turkey or chicken, finely chopped (optional)
½ teaspoon salt
¼ teaspoon black pepper
4 eggs, slightly beaten
1 cup pecans, chopped

In a heavy skillet, cook celery, onion, and bell pepper in margarine until tender. Place the corn bread and cubes or crumbs in a large bowl, and add heated chicken broth and sautéed vegetables, mixing well. Cook sausage until browned, adding giblets when almost done; add to bread mixture, along with seasonings, eggs, and chopped pecans. Toss lightly to mix well. Cook in uncovered 13x9x2 inch pan at 325°F for 45 minutes. Serves 15-20, or enough dressing for an 18-20 pound turkey.

Mrs. Charles F. Hebert
Cameron, Louisiana

TURKEY DRESSING

Gizzard, liver, and heart of turkey
1 large loaf of bread, sliced
½ rib celery
2 large white onions, peeled
¼ cup butter
2½ Tablespoons lard
2 cups pecans, chopped
Salt and pepper to taste

Boil gizzard, liver, and heart until very tender. Cut all gristle off gizzard. Save the broth. Toast each slice of bread well on both sides. Grind each of the following separately: toasted bread, celery, onions, and chicken giblets. Reserve in separate dishes. In a large frying pan sauté onions in butter until wilted. Add celery and giblets. Sprinkle in toast crumbs; then pecans. Salt and pepper to taste. Add broth but make a dry dressing.

Mrs. Oliver P. Stockwell
(Roseina Holcombe)

BAKED TURKEY AND CORN BREAD DRESSING

CORN BREAD
1 cup flour
¾ cup corn meal
3 teaspoons baking powder
¾ teaspoon salt
1 cup sweet milk
1 egg, beaten
2 Tablespoons shortening, melted (do not substitute)

DRESSING
2 separate pans of corn bread
Giblets from turkey
½ onion
Celery leaves
1-2 ribs celery, quartered
1 clove garlic
1 cup green onions, finely chopped
1 cup celery (tender inner ribs), finely chopped
1 cup parsley, finely chopped
Salt and pepper to taste
3 Tablespoons margarine
3 Tablespoons giblet stock
One 12 pound turkey
Salt and pepper

GRAVY
2 chicken bouillon cubes
2 cups water
6 Tablespoons flour
8 Tablespoons water

CORN BREAD
Sift flour once; then again with corn meal, salt, and baking powder. Gradually add milk, egg, and shortening. Pour into hot greased 8x1¼ inch cake pan. Bake at 425°F for 25-30 minutes. Make 2 separate recipes (do not double) for dressing a 12 pound turkey. Serves 5-6.

DRESSING
Make corn bread 3 days before turkey is to be cooked, crumble, and leave to dry. Defrost turkey day before cooking, remove giblets and boil in water with onion, celery leaves and ribs, and garlic until tender. (Save liver; do not cook with other giblets.) When giblets are tender, remove from stock and set aside. Run giblet stock through a sieve, pushing seasoning through with the back of a spoon and set aside. Work corn bread through a large colander. Put giblets, including liver, through a food grinder. Mix corn bread, giblets, chopped onion, celery, and parsley. Add salt and pepper to taste. Then bind together with margarine and giblet stock.

Wash turkey thoroughly, removing blood from cavity. Dry inside and out and season with salt and pepper. Stuff cavity and neck with dressing, sewing together with heavy thread. (It is easier to do this the night before.) Place stuffed turkey on a lifting rack inside of a covered roaster and refrigerate until ready to cook. Bake, covered, at 325°F for 3½-4 hours, basting every hour. If turkey is not brown enough, remove cover and cook to desired brownness.

GRAVY
Skim grease from pan drippings. Dissolve chicken bouillon cubes in water. Pour into pan, scraping pan to dissolve any brown drippings. Pour remaining giblet stock into pan. With heat on low, slowly add flour mixed well with water to thicken gravy, stirring constantly for smoothness.

Mrs. Gordon Gill
(Madora Thomas)

NUTTY FRUIT CHICKEN KIEV WITH GLAZE

8 dried apricots
⅔ cup orange juice
4 whole chicken breasts, (from 4 *large* broiler-fryers) skinned, boned, split in half
⅓ cup almonds, toasted and finely chopped
5 Tablespoons Mazola margarine

GLAZE
⅓ cup wine vinegar
1 Tablespoon orange rind
⅔ cup apricot preserves
1 teaspoon dry mustard
1 teaspoon ground ginger
¼ teaspoon salt
½ teaspoon Accent
1 Tablespoon soy sauce
Reserved orange juice (plus enough to make ⅔ cup)

⅓ cup flour
1 teaspoon salt
1 teaspoon Accent
2 eggs, slightly beaten with 1 teaspoon water and ½ teaspoon salt
1 cup fine bread crumbs
1 bottle (16 ounces) Mazola oil

GARNISH
12 canned apricot halves
3 ounces cream cheese
1 Tablespoon apricot juice
3 Tablespoons almonds, toasted

Marinate dried apricots in orange juice for 10 minutes while preparing chicken breasts. Place prepared breasts between aluminum foil and flatten with meat tenderizer or edge of saucer. Remove apricots from orange juice, *reserving* juice. Finely chop apricots and combine with toasted almonds and Mazola margarine. Divide into eight portions, roll into balls, and place in freezer while preparing glaze.

GLAZE
Combine all ingredients for glaze. Simmer in small saucepan for 30 minutes.

Remove apricot balls from freezer. Place on the wide side of each chicken breast. Roll up, folding in ends to enclose filling completely. Fasten with tooth picks. Dip rolled breasts in flour mixed with salt and Accent, then in the egg-water mixture. Coat well with bread crumbs. Fry in Mazola at 350° F until deep brown, 10-15 minutes, turning often.

GARNISH
Arrange breasts on a platter, and pour glaze over them. Garnish with 12 apricot halves stuffed with the mixture of cream cheese, apricot juice, and almonds. Serves 8.

Mrs. Eunice Surles

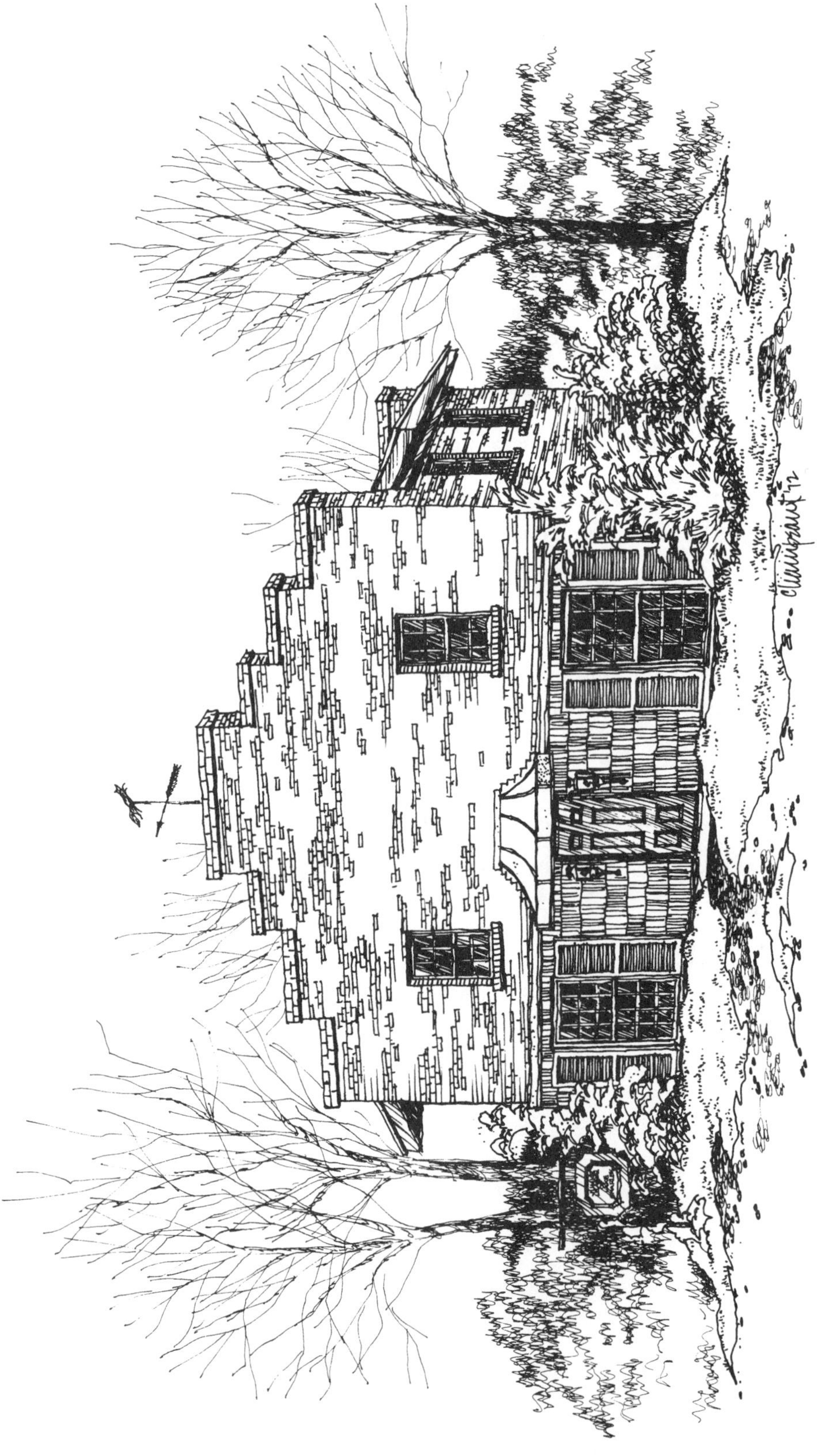

JUNIOR LEAGUE HEADQUARTERS

Spirited Percheron horses once inhabited this renovated stable, located at 1019 Front Street, which now houses The Junior League of Lake Charles. One of the oldest commercial buildings still standing in Lake Charles, the square brick structure was built in 1903 by the Waters Pierce Oil Co.

The old stable, with walls a foot thick, at one time had eight stalls to house the beautiful horses, which were bred in Normandy, France. The Percherons pulled wagonloads of empty oil barrels down to the lake front and returned them full. The oil was brought by train (from the famed Spindletop field in Beaumont, Texas, discovered in 1901) to a trestle running from Mill Street out into the lake. There it was unloaded onto the horse-drawn wagons and was subsequently delivered to the customers.

The old building has survived all manner of natural disasters including the flood of 1907, the fire of 1910, and a devastating hurricane in 1918. It now serves as a reminder of a more leisurely era, when a favorite summertime activity was a carriage ride along the lake front to picnic under huge old trees at Walnut Grove (now the site of the Lake Charles docks).

The building was renovated in 1963 and became the first home of the Imperial Calcasieu Historical Museum. It was placed on the National Register of Historical Places in December, 1980. It is currently owned by the Calcasieu Parish Police Jury and maintained by The Junior League of Lake Charles.

Vegetables

APPLE CASSEROLE

6-8 apples, peeled, sliced
1 Tablespoon lemon juice
2 Tablespoons water
¾ cup sugar
½ cup flour
1½ teaspoons cinnamon
¼ teaspoon salt
1 cup American cheese, grated
¼ cup margarine, chopped

Place apples in a 2 quart casserole. Mix lemon juice and water and pour on top of apples. In a small bowl mix sugar, flour, cinnamon, salt, and cheese. Pour on top of apples. Dot with margarine. Bake, covered, at 350°F for 30-35 minutes. Stir occasionally. Serves 4-6.

Mrs. Robert W. Clark
(Carole Lown)

ARTICHOKES

Fresh artichokes (1 per person)
Lemon as needed
Salted water to cover

Cut stem off artichoke; using scissors, cut 1 inch off top of artichoke and ½ inch off top of each leaf. Cut lemon in half and rub on all raw edges. Pry open the leaves with fingers. Using a silver spoon, dig down into the center, remove and discard the choke (hairy looking). Do not hesitate to dig and scrape hard. Close top of artichoke and boil in salted water to cover until done. Test for doneness by piercing heart with a silver fork. Remove from water, invert and drain. Serve with Hollandaise sauce for dipping.

This makes a good first course or a nice hors d'oeuvre.

Mrs. David Painter
(Isabel "Bel" Thornton)

FRESH ASPARAGUS CASSEROLE

1 bunch fresh asparagus
Salt
Italian seasoned bread crumbs
Parmesan cheese
Butter

Steam fresh asparagus until tender. Drain. Place in bottom of a casserole, sprinkle with salt, bread crumbs, and Parmesan cheese, and dot with butter. Warm in a 350°F oven for about 15 minutes. Serves 4.

Mrs. F. Lisle Peters, Jr.
(Betty Shea)

ASPARAGUS SUPREME

⅓ cup onion, minced
2 Tablespoons butter or margarine, melted
2 Tablespoons flour
1 teaspoon salt
¼ teaspoon pepper
1 cup commercial sour cream
2 cans (14 ounce size) asparagus spears, drained
½ cup sharp Cheddar cheese, grated

Sauté onion in butter, but do not brown. Add flour, salt, and pepper. Mix well and cook for 5 minutes. Add sour cream, heat well, but do not let mixture boil. Place asparagus in a shallow baking dish and cover with the sour cream mixture. Sprinkle cheese over top. Bake, uncovered, at 350°F for 10-15 minutes, or until cheese is melted and casserole is thoroughly heated. Serves 4-6.

Mrs. Walter R. House
(Catherine Hebert)

BANANA FRITTERS BAYOU LAFOURCHE

1½ cups flour
2 rounded teaspoons baking powder
½ teaspoon salt
1 Tablespoon sugar
2 eggs, beaten
Milk, if needed
4 bananas, cut into 1 inch pieces
Wesson oil, enough to make 2 inches deep in skillet

Mix dry ingredients. Pour beaten eggs into a hole in center and gradually blend into a batter. Add a little milk if needed, but the batter should be thick. Dip banana pieces into batter and drop immediately into hot oil. Fry until golden brown. Makes about 2½ dozen. Does not freeze. Serves 6-8.

Mrs. Karl Boellert
(Kathleen Martin)

BAKED BEANS FOR A CROWD

16 cans (1 pound size) beans (preferably Campbell's Home Style beans)
1 large bottle ketchup
1 package brown sugar
1 large package frozen onions, chopped
1 large package frozen bell peppers, chopped
1 small jar mustard
2 cans (16 ounce size) chili without beans
2 packages wieners, sliced
1 pound bacon

Mix all ingredients except bacon. Place bacon strips on top. Bake at 325°F for 4 hours, either in an electric roaster or a regular oven. Serves 50-80.

Great for outdoor barbecues!

Mrs. James E. Taussig
(Alice House)

BEANS WITH AN OUTDOOR FLAVOR

1 cup each onion and bell pepper, chopped
6 slices of bacon, crisply fried, chopped (reserve fat)
2 cans (1 large and 1 small) baked beans
½ cup ketchup
¼ cup brown sugar
2 Tablespoons dry mustard
1 Tablespoon salt
1 Tablespoon instant coffee
½ cup molasses
⅛ teaspoon or dash of cayenne pepper

Sauté onion and bell pepper in bacon fat about 5 minutes. Place in baking dish with combined remaining ingredients. Bake, covered, at 275°F for 2-3 hours. The longer the beans cook, the better they are.

This recipe comes from Canada.

Mrs. Lee Haugen

BASIC SOYBEANS

1 part soybeans
4 parts water
Onion, carrots, celery, chopped
Herbs
Soy sauce (Tamari)
Salt

SOYBURGERS
2 cups soybeans, cooked, mashed
1 onion, grated
1 clove garlic, minced
1 carrot, grated
1 rib celery and tops, chopped
2 eggs, beaten
3 Tablespoons oil
3 Tablespoons nutritional yeast or soy flour
½ teaspoon salt
½ cup brown rice, cooked

Soak beans overnight; then pressure cook 1 hour, or normally 2 hours. Add onion, carrot, celery or similar vegetables for flavor. Add more water if necessary. Season with a pinch of herbs and Tamari sauce to taste. Never add salt to beans until they are cooked tender, or they will take forever to cook.

SOYBURGERS
Combine all ingredients. Form patties. Broil or fry until brown. Serves 6.

Jan Schleussner Stream

GREEN BEAN CASSEROLE

2-6 Tablespoons flour
¼-½ teaspoon salt
½-1 teaspoon onion salt
½-1 teaspoon garlic powder
⅛ teaspoon black pepper
1 teaspoon sugar
2-4 Tablespoons butter, melted
2 cans (16 ounce size) or 2 packages frozen French style green beans
2 cups, or less, sour cream
Cheddar cheese, grated
Corn flake crumbs as needed

Add flour, salt, onion salt, garlic powder, pepper, and sugar to butter. Add drained green beans (if frozen beans are used, cook first); then add sour cream. Stir. Pour into a 1½ quart casserole. Cover with cheese and sprinkle with corn flake crumbs. Bake, uncovered, at 400°F for 20 minutes. Serves 4-6.

Irene Sullivan

Mrs. Harold Richard *uses 1 pint half and half soured with 2 Tablespoons vinegar instead of sour cream. She places her beans in layers and sprinkles with Parmesan cheese. She then pours sauce over all and covers with corn flake crumbs combined with ½ stick melted margarine. She bakes her casserole at 350°F for 30 minutes.*

GREEN BEAN CASSEROLE WITH CHEESE

3 packages (10 ounce size) frozen French style green beans
1 can (10½ ounces) cream of mushroom soup
1 jar (8 ounces) Cheez-Whiz
1 can (8 ounces) water chestnuts, drained and sliced
1 jar (2 ounces) chopped pimientos
1 can (4 ounces) sliced mushroom buttons, drained
1 Tablespoon Worcestershire sauce
Salt and pepper to taste
1 package (2½ ounces) slivered almonds

Cook beans according to package directions for about 3 minutes. While beans are cooking, mix all other ingredients except almonds. Drain beans well. Add to other ingredients while beans are still hot. Pour into a 3 quart casserole. Sprinkle almonds over top. Bake, uncovered, at 350°F for about 30 minutes, or until bubbling. Serves 10-12.

Mrs. Edward H. Taussig
(Florence Streater)

TEXAS BEANS

Bacon or ham to taste
1 onion, chopped
1 bell pepper, chopped
3 cans (16 ounce size) New Orleans style kidney beans
1 jar India relish
1 bottle chili sauce
Lea & Perrins and Tabasco to taste

Cook bacon or ham in bottom of large pot. Add onion and bell pepper and sauté until tender. Add beans, relish, and chili sauce. Season with Lea & Perrins and Tabasco to taste. Simmer for several hours. Serves 14-16.

Mrs. Thomas Hall
(Eunice Perkins)

HOT DOG BUTTER BEANS

1 medium onion, chopped
½ medium bell pepper, chopped
2-3 Tablespoons shortening or bacon grease
1 Tablespoon flour
1 teaspoon seasoned salt
Salt to taste
¼ teaspoon pepper
2 teaspoons prepared mustard
1 teaspoon Worcestershire sauce
2 Tablespoons brown sugar
1 can (1 pound) tomatoes
1 can (1 pound) butter beans
4 or more all beef wieners

In a skillet cook onion and bell pepper for 5 minutes in melted shortening or bacon grease. Blend in flour, salts, pepper, mustard, Worcestershire sauce, brown sugar, and tomatoes. Simmer, uncovered, for 10 minutes. Add butter beans. Cut wieners into bite sized pieces and add to mixture. Serves 4.

Children love this.

Mrs. Terry Barnett Nelson

PINEAPPLE BEETS

1 can (13½ ounces) pineapple chunks
½ cup water
⅓ cup cider vinegar
4 Tablespoons brown sugar
1 Tablespoon cornstarch
½ teaspoon salt
⅛ teaspoon ground ginger
2 cans (1 pound size) sliced beets, drained

Drain syrup from pineapple and mix with water and vinegar. Combine the brown sugar, cornstarch, salt, and ginger. Blend the 2 mixtures. Cook until thick, stirring constantly. Add beets and heat. Add pineapple chunks. Serve hot or cold.

Mrs. Mildred Vincent
Sulphur, La.

BROCCOLI MACARONI HOLLANDAISE

3 Tablespoons flour
1 teaspoon salt
⅛ teaspoon pepper
3 Tablespoons butter
1½ cups milk
¾ cup mayonnaise
1¾ cups macaroni
2 cups chopped broccoli
½ cup sharp cheese, grated

Stir flour, salt, and pepper into melted butter. Add milk gradually, stirring constantly, and cook until thickened. Fold in mayonnaise. Cook macaroni in boiling salted water until just tender. Drain, rinse, and drain again. Cook broccoli and drain well. Combine macaroni, broccoli, and sauce. Place in a 1½ quart greased casserole. Sprinkle with cheese. Bake, uncovered, at 350°F for 30 minutes. Freezes. Serves 6-8.

Mrs. William Akins
(Kay Mishler)

BROCCOLI AND CAULIFLOWER CASSEROLE

1 large onion, finely chopped
2 Tablespoons butter
1 can cream of chicken soup
1 cup Parmesan cheese
¾ small can evaporated milk
2 packages frozen whole broccoli, chopped
2 packages frozen cauliflower
½ stick butter, melted
Italian bread crumbs

Sauté onion in butter. Add soup, cheese, and milk. In separate saucepans cook broccoli and cauliflower according to package directions. Add to above mixture, stir, and pour into a 2½ quart casserole. Mix together butter and bread crumbs and sprinkle on casserole. Bake, uncovered, at 350°F until bubbly. Serves 10.

Mrs. Harold Schnauder
(Virginia Summers)

BOHEMIAN CABBAGE

1 medium head cabbage, coarsely chopped
1 large onion, sliced
Bacon drippings
1 teaspoon cider vinegar
½ cup chicken stock or 1 bouillon cube
3-4 strips bacon, fried, crumbled
½ teaspoon caraway seeds
Salt and pepper to taste
1 cup sour cream

Lightly brown cabbage and onion in bacon drippings. Add all other ingredients except sour cream. Simmer, covered, for about 30 minutes. Add sour cream just before serving and heat through. Serves 6.

Mrs. Edward C. Swartz

INTERNATIONAL GOURMET CABBAGE ROLLS

SAUCE
1 bottle (14 ounces) ketchup
1 ketchup bottle water
1 can (6 ounces) tomato paste
3 tomato paste cans water
½ teaspoon citric acid
   (or juice of 2 lemons)
7 ginger snaps
2 onions, chopped
4 ribs celery, chopped
Salt and pepper to taste
1 cup brown sugar
MEAT FILLING
2 large leafy cabbage heads
3 pounds ground chuck
½ cup rice (if desired,
   wash before using)
1 onion, grated
3 cloves garlic, minced
2 Tablespoons salt
Dash of pepper
1 heaping Tablespoon
   chicken fat or oil
2 cups raisins

Combine sauce ingredients and cook, covered, for 20 minutes. Set aside. Core cabbages and boil until tender, about 15 minutes. Drain. Mix remaining ingredients except raisins. Place small amount of this mixture into each cabbage leaf. Roll and secure with toothpick. Place cabbage rolls in large roasting pan and cover with cooked sauce. Add raisins. Bake, covered, at 350°F for 1 hour. Remove cover and baste frequently for another hour, allowing cabbage rolls to glaze. Replace cover and cook another hour, or until meat is tender. Freezes. Serves 15-20, depending on size of cabbage leaves and amount of filling.

Mrs. Hal Goldman

RED CABBAGE HEIDI

4 slices bacon
1 small onion, chopped
1 head red cabbage, shredded
½-1 cup canned chicken broth
1 teaspoon caraway seeds
Salt and pepper to taste
1-2 sour apples
½ cup dry red wine
⅛ cup lemon juice

Cut bacon into bits and brown. Add onion and sauté. Add cabbage and sauté. Add broth, caraway seeds, salt and pepper to taste. Grate the apples (including skin) into cabbage and mix. Add wine. Simmer 1½ hours. Before serving, add lemon juice so that cabbage becomes red again.

Mrs. James E. Williams
(Robyn Stewart)

SWEDISH CHRISTMAS CABBAGE

2 large, firm heads white cabbage, chopped into ½ inch pieces
2 sticks margarine
⅓ cup white vinegar
½ cup dark corn syrup
Salt and pepper to taste

Fry cabbage in generous amounts of margarine until quite brown. Browning is done in several batches, adding margarine each time. Place cabbage in large pot or Dutch oven. Pour in vinegar and syrup. Add salt and pepper to taste. Cover, leaving a small opening, and simmer for 1½-2 hours. There should be a suggestion of firmness when ready. Drain and serve. Freezes. Serves 10-12.

Mrs. Philip Burris
(Gerd Archenholtz)

BRUSSELS SPROUTS IN SOUR CREAM

2 packages frozen Brussels sprouts
1 small onion, finely chopped
1 stick margarine
1 carton (8 ounces) sour cream
Salt and pepper to taste

Boil Brussels sprouts in small amount of salted water until fork tender. Drain well. Sauté onion in margarine over low heat until transparent (not brown). Remove from burner. Stir in sour cream, salt, and pepper. Pour over Brussels sprouts; serve immediately. Serves 6.

Mrs. James G. Boyer
(Helen House)

CARROT CASSEROLE

1 bunch carrots (about 5) sliced
½ cup water
1 teaspoon salt or to taste
Dash of pepper
2 Tablespoons onion, minced
1 Tablespoon bell pepper, finely chopped
2 Tablespoons celery, finely chopped
1 egg, beaten
½ cup evaporated milk
2 slices bread, broken into small pieces
1 Tablespoon butter or margarine
4-5 saltine crackers, crumbled

Cook carrots in water with the salt, pepper, onions, bell pepper, and celery until tender. Mash. Add beaten egg to milk. Pour over the bread and soak. Add to the mashed carrot mixture. Add butter. Place mixture in a well buttered casserole or a 9 inch pie plate. Sprinkle with cracker crumbs. Bake, uncovered, at 350°F for 15-20 minutes. Serves 8.

Mrs. John Bergstedt
(Donna Giobbi)

BONIN CARROT CASSEROLE

1 bunch carrots, cut into small strips
1 cup mayonnaise
2 Tablespoons fresh horseradish, grated (or prepared horseradish)
2 Tablespoons onion, grated
Salt and pepper to taste
Buttered bread crumbs

Boil carrots until just done in small amount of water. Reserve liquid. Mix remaining ingredients, except crumbs, and moisten with some of the reserved liquid. Pour over carrot strips that have been placed in a 9 inch square baking dish. Cover with buttered bread crumbs. Bake, uncovered, at 300°F for 25-35 minutes, or until bubbly. Serves 4-5.

Mrs. Joe McIver
(Shirley Trahan)

CARROTS WITH ORANGE SAUCE

2 cans small whole carrots, drained
½ cup orange juice
½ cup sugar
1 Tablespoon cornstarch
1 teaspoon salt
1 Tablespoon orange rind, grated
2 Tablespoons butter

Preheat oven to 350°F. Place carrots in a 2 quart casserole. Combine orange juice, sugar, cornstarch, salt, and orange rind. Pour over carrots. Add butter. Bake, covered, for 30 minutes. Serves 6-8.

Mrs. Michael Miller
(Karen Mashburn)

COMPANY CAULIFLOWER

1 medium head cauliflower (or 2 boxes frozen cauliflower)
Salt and pepper to taste
1 cup sour cream
1 cup sharp American cheese, shredded
2 teaspoons sesame seed, toasted

TO TOAST SESAME SEED
Place in shallow pan in a 350°F oven for 10 minutes or until browned, shaking occasionally.

Rinse cauliflower; break into flowerets. Cook, covered, in small amount of boiling salted water until tender, 10-15 minutes. Drain well. (Or follow directions for frozen cauliflower.) Place ½ cauliflower in a 1 quart casserole; season with salt and pepper. Spread with ½ cup sour cream and sprinkle with ½ cup cheese. Top with 1 teaspoon sesame seed. Repeat layers. Bake, uncovered, at 350°F for 10 minutes, or until cheese melts and sour cream is heated through. Serves 6.

Mrs. Fred Selby
(Marjorie Lemoine)

CELERY CASSEROLE

4 cups celery, thinly sliced
4 Tablespoons butter or margarine
3 Tablespoons all purpose flour
1 teaspoon salt
1 cup milk
1 can (3 ounces) chopped mushrooms, drained
3 Tablespoons bell pepper, chopped
2 Tablespoons pimiento, chopped
1 package (4 ounces) sharp yellow cheese, grated
1 cup bread crumbs (preferably Pepperidge Farm)
2 Tablespoons butter or margarine, melted

In a skillet, sauté the celery in butter until tender. Push celery to one side and stir in flour, salt, and milk. Cook, stirring, until mixture is thick and bubbling. Stir in mushrooms, bell pepper, and pimiento. Add cheese and stir until melted. Pour mixture into a 10x6x1½ inch baking dish. Sprinkle blended bread crumbs and butter on top. Bake, uncovered, at 350°F for 20 minutes. Serves 8.

Mrs. David Buttross, Jr.
(Joyce Abraham)

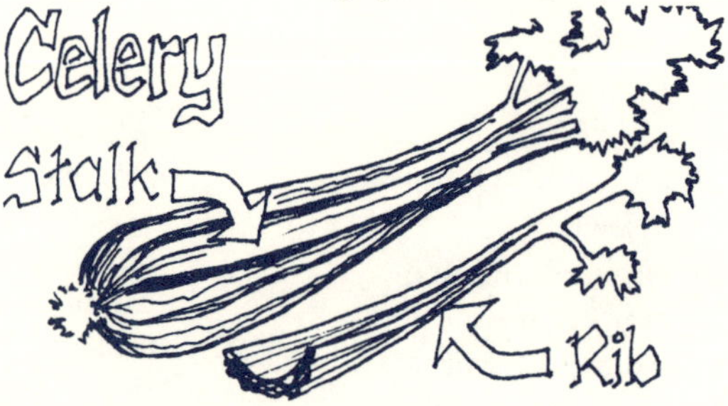

CAULIFLOWER WITH JALAPEÑO SAUCE

1 head fresh cauliflower or 2 packages frozen cauliflower
SAUCE
2 Tablespoons flour
1 teaspoon monosodium glutamate
1 teaspoon salt
¼ teaspoon black pepper
3 Tablespoons margarine, melted
1½ cups milk
4 ounces sharp Cheddar cheese
½ roll Kraft Jalapeño cheese
Paprika

Boil cauliflower in salted water until almost done but still crisp. Drain, and place in casserole dish.
SAUCE: In a saucepan, stir flour, MSG, salt, and pepper in margarine until well blended. Stir in milk and cook over low heat until thick. Cut both cheeses into small chunks and add, stirring until well blended. Pour over cauliflower, sprinkle with paprika, and bake, uncovered, at 350°F for 20 minutes, or until bubbly. Serves 6-8.

This sauce is good over everything!

Mrs. Earl Daughenbaugh
(Loretta Evans)

CHILIES STUFFED WITH BEANS

½ cup onion, minced
1 clove garlic, minced
2 Tablespoons lard
1 can (1 pound) kidney beans
Salt to taste
½ teaspoon ground cumin
2 cans (4 ounce size) California green chilies, rinsed and seeded
2 tomatoes, fresh or canned, peeled and sliced
1 Tablespoon olive oil
1 cup Monterey Jack cheese, shredded

Cook onion and garlic in lard until wilted. Drain beans and add to skillet. Mash beans well and heat. Add salt and cumin. Stuff chilies with this mixture, arrange in a baking dish, and cover with tomatoes. Drizzle olive oil over the tomatoes, sprinkle with cheese, and bake, uncovered, at 350°F for 15 minutes, or until cheese is melted and lightly browned. For microwave oven, cover with wax paper and heat for 4 minutes. Serves 4.

Mrs. Tom A. Flanagan, Jr.
(Sarah Nabors)

BAKED CORN

1 can (17 ounces) each yellow cream style corn and whole kernel corn, drained
½ cup each onion and bell pepper, chopped
2 pimientos, chopped
1 cup sharp Cheddar cheese, grated
1 cup cracker crumbs, rolled
1 egg, well beaten, with ⅔ cup milk
¼ cup butter or margarine, melted
2 Tablespoons sugar

Preheat oven to 350°F. Mix all ingredients in a 9x12x2 inch cake pan or pyrex dish. Bake in oven for 1 hour. Serves 10.

From the recipes of
Cyllene Cisco Lamkin

CORN AU GRATIN

1 pound fresh or canned whole kernel corn, drained
1½ cups (12 ounces) whipping cream
1½ Tablespoons butter
1½ Tablespoons flour
1 teaspoon salt
2 Tablespoons sugar
½ teaspoon Accent
3 Tablespoons Parmesan cheese

Combine corn and cream and bring to a boil. With a slotted spoon separate corn from cream and return cream to heat. Make a paste with butter and flour. Gradually add to cream to thicken. Simmer 5 minutes and add salt, sugar, and Accent. Return corn to cream and resume boiling over low heat. Transfer creamed corn to a casserole. Sprinkle with cheese and dot with melted butter. Brown under broiler. Serves 4.

Mrs. Mark Quilty, Jr.

SHOE PEG CORN CASSEROLE

1 large onion, chopped
1 Tablespoon margarine
1 can Ro-tel tomatoes
1 Tablespoon dried onion soup
2 cans (12 ounce size) shoe peg corn, drained
1 can (8¾ ounces) cream style corn
12 ounces sharp Cheddar cheese, grated

Sauté onion in margarine until clear. Add tomatoes and onion soup mix. Stir, cooking for 10 minutes. Add corn. Bake in uncovered casserole, at 350°F for 20 minutes. Remove from oven and sprinkle with cheese. Return to oven until cheese is melted and bubbly. May be prepared a day ahead. Serves 6-8.

This dish is very peppery because of the Ro-tel tomatoes. Cut down on the tomatoes according to taste.

Mrs. Karl Boellert
(Kathleen Martin)

CREOLE CUSHAW

1 cup sugar
¼ cup white Karo syrup
1 stick butter
3 pounds cushaw, peeled and cubed
½ teaspoon salt
¼ teaspoon powdered cloves
1¼ teaspoons each cinnamon and nutmeg

In a 4 quart heavy pot caramelize sugar until golden brown. Add syrup and then butter. Add cushaw (no water is needed), stir, and cover until liquid cooks out of cushaw, about 5 minutes. Remove cover and add salt and spices. Cook slowly, stirring carefully to prevent breaking pieces of cushaw. Cook 20-25 minutes, or until mixture is tender and syrupy. Serve as a side dish with pork roast or ham.

From the recipes of
Mrs. Eola Glasscock Schepp

CUSHAW

1 small cushaw, seeded and peeled
3 eggs, well beaten
¼ stick butter
1 Tablespoon sugar
Nutmeg

Be sure all pulp is removed from cushaw. Cut up and boil in small amount of water. Drain and mash well. Add remaining ingredients. Bake in buttered casserole at 325°F for 10 minutes.

Mrs. Thomas Raggio
(Beverly Barry Crook)

GRANDMERE'S MAQUE CHOUX

12 ears of tender corn
2 Tablespoons Crisco or other cooking oil
1 medium onion, finely chopped in blender
1 medium bell pepper, finely chopped in blender
1 Tablespoon salt or to taste
Pepper to taste
1-3 medium tomatos, peeled and chopped (optional)

Cut kernels from cobs twice, if small; 3 times if large; then lightly scrape cob. Barely heat cooking oil in a 2 quart pot. Add onion and bell pepper and cook over low heat until onions are clear, 15-20 minutes. Stir occasionally. Add salt to corn; add corn to onion and bell pepper mixture. Stir often to avoid scorching. Cook until kernels are clear. Add pepper and tomatoes. Cover mixture when it starts to bubble around edges; reduce heat to low, and cook 20-30 minutes. Freezes (when thawing add 2-3 Tablespoons milk). Serves 4.

A favorite of Renée, Cherise and Annette!

Mrs. J. J. Champeaux, Sr.
Lafayette, Louisiana

CINTRA'S EGGPLANT MANICOTTI

1 pound ricotta cheese
1 cup Romano cheese, grated
2 eggs
Salt
White pepper, freshly ground
Vegetable oil
2 medium eggplants, peeled, thinly sliced
2 cans (8 ounce size) tomato sauce

Preheat oven to 400°F. Combine the cheeses, eggs, salt, and pepper in bowl. Beat until smooth. Using a little oil in a skillet, sauté a few slices of eggplant at a time until golden. Drain on paper towels. Place tomato sauce in bottom of an 8x10 inch baking dish. Spread a Tablespoon of cheese and egg mixture on each slice of cooked eggplant and fold over. Arrange folded eggplant seamside down on top of tomato sauce. Bake in oven for 15 minutes, or until hot and bubbly. Serves 6-8.

Jan Schleussner Stream

EGGPLANT CASSEROLE

1 large eggplant, sliced in thin rounds
2 eggs, beaten
Salt and pepper to taste
1½ cups cracker crumbs, finely crushed
½-¾ cup salad oil
2 cans (8 ounce size) tomato sauce
1 teaspoon orégano
½ teaspoon Worcestershire sauce
1 package (8 ounces) American cheese slices

Dip eggplant in eggs seasoned with salt and pepper, then in cracker crumbs. Fry in hot oil until golden brown. Drain. Mix tomato sauce, orégano, and Worcestershire sauce. Layer in a 2 quart casserole ⅓ each of the eggplant, cheese, and tomato sauce. Continue the layers, ending with the tomato sauce. Bake, covered, at 350°F for 50-55 minutes. Easy and fast to prepare. May be prepared ahead and baked before serving. Serves about 6.

Mrs. Edward D. Myrick
(Laura Kaufman)

EGGPLANT CASSEROLE

4 medium eggplants, peeled
Salted water as needed
8 slices bacon, fried, crumbled
2 Tablespoons bacon grease
2 large onions, chopped
1 cup Pepperidge Farm herb seasoned bread crumbs (plus a little more as needed for topping)
Salt and pepper to taste
¼ stick butter

Place eggplant in a large container about half full of boiling salted water. Cook, covered, until tender. Drain well. Mash thoroughly. Sauté onion in bacon grease until wilted and add to eggplant. Add bacon, bread crumbs, salt and pepper to taste to eggplant. Place in 3 quart casserole. Cover with bread crumbs and dot with butter. Bake, uncovered, at 300 F until thoroughly heated. Freezes. Serves 8-10.

Mrs. Dick Watson
(Jane Stiffell)

EGGPLANT FRITTERS

1 eggplant
2 eggs
1 teaspoon baking powder
½ cup flour
½ cup milk
1 teaspoon salt

Boil eggplant until tender. Peel and remove seeds. Mash pulp. Mix remaining ingredients and add eggplant pulp. After mixing well, drop by spoonfuls into deep hot fat. Fry until golden brown. Sprinkle with sugar while still hot. Serve warm. Serves 6.

Mrs. Charles Carmouche
(Eleanor Gayle)

Eggplant should be soaked in salted water for about 20-30 minutes prior to cooking to remove bitter taste.

ESCALLOPED EGGPLANT

2 eggplants, peeled and diced
1 cup celery
1 onion, chopped
1 bell pepper, chopped
3 Tablespoons pure olive oil
½ cup water, if needed
1 chicken bouillon cube, if needed
2 cups bread crumbs
2 eggs, beaten
½ cup Parmesan cheese, grated
Salt and pepper to taste

Sauté eggplant, celery, onion, and bell pepper in olive oil until tender. If too dry, add ½ cup water and 1 chicken bouillon cube. Add bread crumbs and eggs. Place in baking dish with cheese and more bread crumbs. Bake, uncovered, at 350°F for 15-20 minutes. Serves about 6.

Mrs. Beulah M. Breaux

GUMBO GOUTER
(Eggplant and Okra)

1 large eggplant, peeled, chopped, and soaked in cold water for 1 hour
3 bell peppers, finely chopped
½ pound okra, sliced
2 large onions, finely chopped
1 clove garlic, finely chopped or mashed
1 small can tomatoes, finely chopped
½ teaspoon sugar
1 Tablespoon shortening
Salt and cayenne pepper to taste

Drain eggplant and dry. Place eggplant, bell peppers, okra, onions, garlic, tomatoes, and sugar in hot shortening in heavy skillet. Salt and pepper to taste. Simmer, tightly covered, for 1½ hours with very little water. Stir often to prevent scorching.

This can be served just so, or with the addition of cooked shrimp. Add shrimp just before removing from heat. The shrimp gives a gumbo flavor to this vegetable dish.

Cleo Wells

JHADRO
(Lebanese Lenten dish)

1 onion, chopped
¼ cup olive oil
1 cup lentils
1½ cups water
1 cup large grain cracked wheat, worked and drained
Salt to taste

Sauté onions in olive oil. Add lentils. Pour in 1 cup water and bring to boil, cooking until lentils are tender. Add wheat and salt. Add ½ cup water and steam until wheat is cooked. May be stirred a few times. The finished dish should look like cooked rice, not mushy. Approximate cooking time is 2 hours. Freezes. Serves 4-6.

Mrs. Mike Saloom

To cook greens, wash leaves thoroughly, one at a time, and remove stems. In large pot place whole onion, salt pork or ham hock, greens, and cover with water. Season to taste with salt and pepper. Cook until tender.

The liquid in which fresh leafy greens are cooked is known as "pot likker". Corn bread dunked in "pot likker" is a Cajun treat.

GRANDMA CELESTE'S STUFFED MIRLITONS

6 mirlitons (vegetable pears), halved
1 onion, chopped
1 bell pepper, chopped
Cooking oil as needed
5 slices bread, toasted
3-4 small cans deviled ham
Bread crumbs
Butter

Boil mirlitons in salted water until tender. Remove and allow to cool. Scoop out the meat with a spoon. Place shells on a cookie sheet and set aside. Sauté the onion and bell pepper in oil. Mix mirliton meat with broken toast and add to onion and bell pepper mixture. Stir, cooking down until liquid evaporates. Add deviled ham and simmer about 5 minutes. Fill shells with mixture. Sprinkle tops with bread crumbs and dot with butter. Bake, uncovered, at 350°F until brown. Freezes. Serves 12.

Mrs. Paul F. Carmouche
(Alice Moss)

STUFFED MIRLITONS

1 pound shrimp
Water, as needed, seasoned with lemon, salt, pepper, garlic salt, and bay leaves
3 large mirlitons (vegetable pears)
1 large onion, chopped
½ stick butter
½ teaspoon garlic salt
½ teaspoon seasoned salt
½ teaspoon seasoned pepper
½ teaspoon Accent
½ cup Progresso seasoned bread crumbs
½ cup sharp Cheddar cheese, grated

Boil shrimp in seasoned water. Peel, devein, and chop. Halve the mirlitons, remove seeds, and boil until soft. Scoop out meat and mash. Place shells in a baking dish. Sauté onions in butter. Add mashed mirliton, seasonings, ½ of bread crumbs, cheese, and shrimp. Stuff mixture in mirliton shells and top with remaining bread crumbs. (Grated Parmesan or Mozzarella cheese may be substituted for bread crumbs as topping.) Bake at 350°F for 25 minutes. Increase temperature to 450°F and cook 10 more minutes, or until lightly browned. Serves 6.

Mrs. George Parker

Jerry Boudreaux cooks the mirlitons, and peels, saving the juice. He sautes garlic, bell pepper, onion, and parsley stems in bacon grease; then adds peeled shrimp. When cooked, he adds this mixture to cooked mirliton and toasted bread slices soaked in juice. He seasons mixture well, places in casserole, covers with bread crumbs and dots with butter, and bakes at 350°F for 30 minutes.

JACK'S STUFFED MIRLITONS

6 mirlitons (vegetable pears)
1 small can ripe olives, chopped
1 small jar pimiento
2 Tablespoons olive oil
1½ pounds Italian sausage, browned in skillet
1 package Mozzarella cheese, grated
Salt and pepper to taste
Parmesan cheese
Italian bread crumbs
Paprika
2 Tablespoons olive oil
Water as needed

Boil mirlitons until tender. Halve and scoop insides into a bowl, discarding small hard center. Add olives, pimiento, olive oil, sausage, cheese, salt and pepper to taste. Stuff mixture into cut halves. Top with Parmesan cheese, bread crumbs, and slight sprinkling of paprika. Place olive oil and water in bottom of baking dish and add stuffed mirlitons. Bake, uncovered, at 350°F for 45 minutes.

Dr. Jack Thielen

MUSHROOM CAPS BAKED IN CHEDDAR CHEESE SAUCE

1 clove garlic, diced
3 Tablespoons butter
1 pound mushrooms, caps only
Dash of Worcestershire sauce
Salt and pepper to taste
CHEESE SAUCE
4 Tablespoons butter
4 Tablespoons flour
1 cup milk or 1½ cups light sweet cream, at room temperature
1 cup Cheddar cheese, grated
Salt and pepper to taste
Pinch of cayenne pepper
Pinch of nutmeg

Preheat oven to 350°F. Sauté garlic lightly in butter until soft; then discard garlic. Add mushroom caps and seasoning to butter; cook over low heat, covered, until tender. Prepare cheese sauce. Melt butter in a double boiler or small pan over low heat. Add flour and stir constantly with a wooden spoon. Gradually pour in milk or cream, stirring constantly until mixture thickens. Add cheese, melt thoroughly, and stir until sauce is smooth. Add seasonings. Transfer mushroom caps to a greased casserole, cover with sauce, and bake until top is lightly browned and bubbly. Serves 4.

Jan Schleussner Stream

VIENNESE FRIED MUSHROOMS

1 pound fresh mushrooms
Juice of 1 lemon
3 eggs
½ cup or more flour
1½ teaspoons salt
¼ teaspoon white pepper
1½-2 cups bread crumbs, finely crushed
Cooking oil as needed

Place washed mushrooms in bowl of cold water and lemon juice. Let stand for 5 minutes. Remove and dry with paper towels. Beat eggs, adding flour gradually to make a thick batter. Add seasoning. Cut mushrooms into bite sized pieces. Dip first into batter and then into bread crumbs. Fry in deep fat until golden brown. Serve with tartare sauce, p. 297.

*Mrs. F. Warren Raggio, Jr.
(Mavis Cade)*

SHERRIED ONIONS

4 yellow onions, thinly sliced and separated into rings
4 Tablespoons butter
1 teaspoon sugar
½ teaspoon salt
Pepper to taste
½ cup sherry

Sauté onion rings in butter over medium heat until soft. Add sugar, salt, and pepper. Add sherry at last minute and turn up heat before serving. Better when served immediately. A complement to pork. Serves 4-6.

*Mrs. M. A. Pierson III
(Caroline Abadie)*

ONIONS AU GRATIN

5 cups onions, cooked, drained, and chopped
6 Tablespoons butter or margarine
½ cup self rising flour
¼ teaspoon black pepper
½ teaspoon salt
Few drops Tabasco to taste
4½ cups Cheddar cheese, grated

Cook onions in boiling water about 5 minutes. Mix softened butter with flour and seasonings. Combine 3½ cups cheese with flour mixture and well drained onions, stirring well. Place in a 2 quart casserole and sprinkle remaining cheese on top. Bake, uncovered, at 350°F for 30 minutes. Serves 10-12.

Mrs. Garnett E. Barham
(Jane Gibson)

ONION PIE

1 cup saltine cracker crumbs
¼ cup margarine, melted
2 cups onions, thinly sliced
2 Tablespoons margarine
1 cup milk
2 eggs
¾ teaspoon black pepper
½ teaspoon salt
1-1½ cups Cheddar cheese, grated

Preheat oven to 350°F. Mix cracker crumbs with ¼ cup margarine and shape into a crust in a 9 inch pie pan. Sauté onions in 2 Tablespoons margarine over low heat about 5 minutes, until wilted. Mix milk, eggs, pepper, and salt. Add cheese and mix well. Pour over onions placed on pie crust. Bake, uncovered, for 35-40 minutes.

Mrs. Heloise Braddock
Covington, La.

OKRA ETOUFFÉE

8 cups (2 pounds) fresh okra, sliced
½ cup cooking oil
2 cups fresh tomatoes, peeled and chopped
1 cup onion, chopped
¾ cup bell pepper, chopped
2 teaspoons salt
1 teaspoon red pepper
½ cup water

Combine all ingredients in a 4 quart pot and cook, uncovered, over medium heat for 30 minutes, stirring frequently to prevent sticking. Reduce heat and continue to cook over low heat for 20-30 more minutes. Remember to stir often. Freezes. Serves 8-10.

Mrs. Joe Daigle
Baton Rouge, La.

OYSTER-PLANT FRITTERS

Salsify or oyster-plant
Butter
Salt and pepper to taste
Dash of nutmeg
All purpose flour

Cut off stem and root ends of salsify. Scrape skin off and cook. Mash, seasoning with butter, salt, pepper, and nutmeg. Shape into small round flat cakes, about 1½ inches in diameter. Dip cakes into flour. Quickly fry in butter until golden brown, turning once. Serve with meats in place of potaoes, rice, or noodles.

Mrs. Stephen E. Carter

CROWDER PEAS

2 onions, chopped
2 Tablespoons cooking oil (bacon drippings better)
1 pound crowder, purple hull, or lady cream peas, shelled
1-2 ham hocks
Salt and pepper to taste

In Dutch oven wilt onions in oil. Add peas, ham hocks, salt, and pepper to taste. Cover with water and cook in covered pot slowly until peas are tender. Stir to prevent sticking. Freezes. Serves 6-8.

Just plain ole crowder peas!

Mrs. William E. Shaddock
(Craig Gorham)

ENGLISH PEAS HASHED IN CREAM

2 pounds (unshelled weight) fresh English peas, shelled
4 large carrots, cut into 1 inch strips
4 Boston lettuce hearts, halved
2 bunches green onions, trimmed and cut into 2 inch strips
Butter and salted water as needed
16 small or 12 large new potatoes
Salt and pepper to taste
1½ cups heavy cream

Sauté vegetables in butter. Add a little salted water and cook until just tender but still crisp (most of the water will have evaporated). Meanwhile, peel a strip from circumference of potatoes and salt and steam them until tender. Combine potatoes and vegetable mixture, salt and pepper to taste. Boil cream until it thickens and pour over the mixture just before serving.

Mrs. Edwin F. Hunter, Sr.
(Shirley Kidd)

SNOW PEAS AND MUSHROOMS

1 pound fresh mushrooms, sliced
4 Tablespoons butter
½ pound snow peas
Salt and pepper to taste

Sauté mushrooms very lightly in butter. Cook snow peas in salted water until just tender. Do not overcook. Combine peas with mushrooms, season to taste. Add more butter if needed.

Mrs. John W. Huber
(Betty Landry)

STUFFED PEPPER CASSEROLE

1 pound ground round
2 Tablespoons oil
2 onions, finely chopped
1 clove garlic, chopped
4 bell peppers (cut sides in large pieces and chop ends very small)
1 cup cooked rice
2 cans (4 ounce size) tomato sauce

Brown meat in oil. Add onion and garlic. Mix in small pieces of bell pepper and cooked rice. Line sides of casserole with large pieces of bell pepper before pouring in meat and rice mixture. Top with tomato sauce. Bake, uncovered, at 350°F for 30 minutes. Add water if it looks dry.

I started making peppers this way because my children love the stuffing but not the pepper skins.

Mrs. David Painter

Mrs. Carmen Murrey *omits the rice and adds ¼ teaspoon orégano and 1 Tablespoon chopped parsley.*

STUFFED POTATOES

4 medium potatoes, peeled
1 Tablespoon parsley, finely chopped
1 Tablespoon bell pepper, finely chopped
1 clove garlic, finely chopped
Bacon drippings
½ teaspoon salt
3 slices bacon, fried, crumbled
1 cup oil

With demitasse spoon or corer, dig hole in potato, saving a piece to make a cap. Sauté parsley, bell pepper, and garlic in bacon drippings. Season with salt, add bacon, and sauté until bell pepper is soft. Stuff this mixture into hollowed potato. Cover with cap and secure with toothpick. Place potatoes in a heavy pot with heated oil, cover, and cook about 45 minutes. Check occasionally to prevent sticking. Serves 4.

**From the recipes of
J. H. Baumgardner**

STUFFED BAKED POTATOES

4 medium baking potatoes
Shortening
2 cans (7 ounce size) mushrooms, sliced
¼ cup onions, chopped
½ cup butter
1 cup sour cream
½ teaspoon each salt and pepper
1 teaspoon Beau Monde
½ cup milk, scalded
¼ cup buttered bread crumbs or ½ cup cheese, grated

Scrub, dry, and grease potatoes with shortening. Bake at 350°F for 1 hour. Remove, halve, and scoop out. Mash. In saucepan sauté mushrooms and onions in butter. Do not brown. Combine with mashed potatoes, sour cream, salt, pepper, Beau Monde, and milk. Fill potato shells and sprinkle with buttered crumbs or cheese. Bake, uncovered, on baking sheet at 400°F for 12 minutes. Serves 8.

Mrs. Mildred Vincent
Sulphur, La.

LILLIAN'S BAKED NEW POTATOES

Small new potatoes
Salt
Pepper
Garlic powder
½ stick, or more, margarine

Scrape potatoes. Place in baking dish. Sprinkle with salt, pepper, and garlic powder. Put margarine over top of potatoes. Bake, covered, at 350°F for 1 hour, or until done.

Mrs. Eugene Fontenot
(Thelma Guidry)

TEXAS POTATOES

1 large bag (2 pounds) or 3 small cartons frozen shredded hash browned potatoes, thawed
½ cup butter, melted
1 teaspoon pepper
2 teaspoons salt
½ cup onion, chopped
1 can cream of chicken soup
1 carton sour cream
2 cups corn flakes, crushed
¼ cup butter

Mix thoroughly all ingredients but the last 2. Place in a 9x13 inch baking dish, top with crushed corn flakes, and dot with butter. Bake, uncovered, at 350°F for 45 minutes. Serves 8-10.

Mrs. Glenn Doctor

POTATO PANCAKES

6 medium white potatoes, grated, drained
1 egg, slightly beaten
1 heaping Tablespoon flour
1 teaspoon salt
Crisco and butter

Blend potatoes thoroughly in mixture of egg, flour, and salt. Fry in Crisco and butter in a large uncovered skillet until golden brown. Fry quickly for crisp pancakes, slowly for soft ones. Serves 4-6.

Mrs. Jules Reinauer
(Shirley Unger)

MACARONI AND CHEESE

WHITE SAUCE
4 Tablespoons butter
4 Tablespoons flour
2 cups sweet milk
1 teaspoon each salt and pepper
Pinch red pepper
1 package (12 ounces) macaroni
3 quarts water
3 teaspoons salt
American cheese, grated

Melt butter and stir in flour. Gradually stir in milk until mixture boils and thickens. Cook 3-4 minutes longer, stirring occasionally. Add seasonings. Place over hot water and cover tightly to prevent crust from forming. If too thick, add more milk. Cook macaroni in salted water for 9-12 minutes, or until soft. Drain and rinse in cold water. Place ½ of macaroni in a buttered casserole. Pour white sauce over it and cover with cheese. Repeat. Bake, uncovered, at 375°F for 25-30 minutes, or until brown on top.

Mrs. Gray Little

POTATO PIE

10 medium potatoes, cooked
Milk
Butter
Salt and pepper to taste
1½ large onions, finely chopped
2-3 Tablespoons butter (maximum)
1½ pounds fresh mushrooms
2-3 drops fresh lemon juice
Salt and pepper
1-2 drops Worcestershire sauce
1-2 drops white wine
Dash white pepper
1 pint sour cream

This dish is better if prepared the day before final baking and serving. Mash potatoes, adding milk, butter, and seasoning, keeping them firm and not too soft. Sauté onions in butter until translucent. Add mushrooms and, with a wooden spoon, toss in butter for 3-4 minutes. Season the onion-mushroom mixture with remaining ingredients, except sour cream, to taste. Spread ½ of mashed potatoes in bottom of a large shallow casserole or pie plate. Sprinkle with a little salt and white pepper. Spread onion-mushroom mixture on top. Then spread sour cream on top of onion-mushroom mixture, using a rubber spatula. Finish with remaining mashed potatoes. Refrigerate. To serve, bring casserole to room temperature. Heat, uncovered, in a 350°F oven 25-30 minutes, turning on broiler the last 2-3 minutes to slightly brown top. Serves 8-10.

Mrs. Kenneth Strauss
(Julie Ann Marx)

SPAGHETTI A LA GIULIANO AND JOEL III
(CARBONARA)

3 eggs, beaten
½ cup heavy cream
Salt and pepper to taste
½ cup Swiss cheese, grated
Dash of Romano cheese
3 Tablespoons butter, melted
6 strips bacon, crisply fried
1 package (12 ounces) spaghetti

Have all ingredients at room temperature. Beat eggs, cream, salt, pepper, cheeses, and melted butter in large bowl. Fry bacon very crisp and crumble it in pan. Reserve grease and keep it very hot. Cook spaghetti according to directions and drain. Stir it into egg and cream mixture. Pour hot bacon and bacon grease over spaghetti and mix well. Serve immediately. Serves 6.

Joel Fletcher III
Giuliano Ceseri
Florence, Italy
Lafayette, Louisiana

FETTUCCINE ALFREDO

1 pound fettuccine noodles
8 quarts boiling water
2 Tablespoons salt
1 cup cream
1 cup butter
2 cups Parmesan cheese

Cook noodles at fast boil *al dente,* that is, tender but not mushy. Drain. Place in a heated platter or bowl. Toss with cream, butter, and cheese until the latter 2 are completely melted. Serve at once.

Mrs. Stanford Vincent
(Anita Cox)

SPINACH CASSEROLE

4 packages frozen chopped spinach, cooked
2 cans artichoke hearts
2 cans (4 ounce size) mushrooms (stems and pieces)
2 cans mushroom soup
1 cup sour cream
¾ cup mayonnaise
1 Tablespoon lemon juice
Worcestershire sauce
Tabasco
Onion and garlic powder
Salt

Drain spinach, artichoke hearts, and mushrooms. Mix with mushroom soup, sour cream, mayonnaise, and lemon juice. Season to taste with remaining ingredients. Bake, uncovered, at 350°F for 25-30 minutes. May be prepared a day ahead. Recipe may be doubled. Freezes. Serves 10.

Mrs. Leonard Knapp, Jr.
(Ann Hall)

CREAMED SPINACH

2 packages frozen spinach
2 Tablespoons margarine, melted
2 Tablespoons flour
1 cup milk
Breath of garlic powder
Salt, white and cayenne pepper
Parmesan cheese

Cook spinach according to package directions. Drain very well (mash in colander with a spoon to make as dry as possible) and place in casserole. In a small skillet mix margarine and flour with a fork. When bubbling, add milk slowly while stirring with fork until smooth. When bubbling again, add garlic powder, salt and peppers to taste. Blend this cream sauce with spinach and sprinkle top generously with cheese. Bake, uncovered, at 325°F for 25 minutes, or until bubbly and brown on top. Serves 4-6.

Even children like spinach this way!

Mrs. Arthur Hollins, Jr.
(Mary Muth)

SPINACH QUICHE BOUDREAU

1 pastry shell (10 inch) (at room temperature)
1 package frozen spinach, thawed
½ bunch green onions, chopped
2 Tablespoons butter, melted
½ teaspoon salt
Pepper
3 egg yolks
1 cup whipping cream
¼ cup Parmesan cheese, grated

Preheat oven to 450°F. Prick bottom and sides of pastry shell to prevent puffing. Cook pastry shell for 5 minutes. Remove from oven and let chill in refrigerator for at least 1 hour. Let frozen spinach thaw completely, and then squeeze out excess liquid. In skillet sauté onions in butter until tender but not brown. Then add spinach, salt, and pepper to taste, and sauté 2 minutes. Place spinach and onions in pastry shell. Beat egg yolks in cream, and pour over spinach.

Sprinkle cheese over top. Bake, uncovered, in 375°F oven for approximately 20 minutes until brown and firm. May be served warm or at room temperature.

I prefer to let it sit, then reheat in aluminum foil. Stolen from a French chef! Good served in strips as hors d'oeuvres or pie shaped as vegetable.

Robert J. Boudreau

SPINACH AND CHEESE CASSEROLE

2 pounds Polish sausage, sliced, skinned if desired
3 bags (10 ounce size) fresh spinach or 3 packages (10 ounce size) frozen spinach
½ teaspoon nutmeg
1 pound Cheshire or mild, natural yellow cheese, shredded
2 Tablespoons flour
1 teaspoon Worcestershire sauce
¾ teaspoon dry mustard
1 cup beer

Cover sausage with hot water and cook. In bottom of a shallow 8 cup baking dish arrange sausage, reserving a few slices for garnishing. Cook spinach in water clinging to washed leaves, if fresh, or according to package instructions, if frozen. Drain, pressing out all liquid with a wooden spoon. Stir in nutmeg. Spread spinach over sausage. Place cheese, flour, Worcestershire sauce, mustard, and beer in top of a double boiler over simmering water. Heat,stirring until cheese melts and forms a smooth sauce. Bring to a boil and pour over spinach and sausage. Garnish with reserved sausage slices. Run under preheated broiler to brown the cheese. May be served as a main dish with biscuits and a fruit compote. Serves 8.

Mrs. Kenneth Strauss
(Julie Ann Marx)

SPINACH RING

2 Tablespoons butter
½ cup milk
2 Tablespoons flour
3 eggs, separated
2 cups frozen chopped spinach, cooked, drained
Onion, grated
Salt, pepper, nutmeg to taste

Make sauce with butter, milk, and flour. Add beaten egg yolks, spinach, and seasonings. Fold in beaten egg whites and pour into buttered mold. Place in pan of hot water and bake, uncovered, 30 minutes at 325°F. Invert onto a hot plate. Serves 6.

Mrs. Thomas B. Shearman, Sr.
(Flora Inglis)

QUICK AND EASY SPINACH

3 packages frozen chopped spinach
1 large package Philadelphia cream cheese
Nutmeg
Tarragon
Salt

In large covered skillet place spinach in ½ cup boiling water. Cook over medium heat about 5-8 minutes until completely thawed. Drain well. Add cream cheese, stirring until melted. Add 2 shakes nutmeg and dash of tarragon. Salt to taste. Better if prepared a day ahead. Serves 8.

Mrs. Dick Watson
(Jane Stiffell)

SPINACH SUPREME

1 cup onions, chopped
¼ cup bell pepper, chopped
1 cup celery, chopped
¾ stick butter or margarine
4 packages frozen spinach, chopped
2 cans cream of mushroom soup
12 ounces Velveeta cheese, diced
Salt, pepper, and garlic powder to taste
1¼ cups bread crumbs

Sauté onions, bell pepper, and celery in butter until clear and cooked. Parboil spinach in salted water and drain. Add soup to sautéed vegetables and heat, stirring constantly. Repeat with cheese. Season with salt, pepper, and garlic powder. Add spinach and bread crumbs and mix well. Sprinkle additional bread crumbs on top. Bake, uncovered, in 3 quart casserole at 350°F for 1 hour. Freezes. Serves 8.

Mrs. Alford Elender
(Sylvia Broussard)

GLAZED ACORN SQUASH WITH PECANS

2 acorn squash
Salt to taste
4 Tablespoons maple syrup
Pecans as needed, whole or chopped
Butter

Cut squash lengthwise. Scoop out seeds and stringy pulp. Place cut side down in baking pan filled with water. Bake, uncovered, in preheated 400°F oven about 40 minutes, or until tender. Remove gently from pan to keep shells from breaking and discard water. Lightly grease pan and replace squash, cut side up. Sprinkle with salt and pour 1 Tablespoon maple syrup in each cavity. Add pecans to rim of squash. Dot with butter. Broil until pecans are toasted, being careful not to scorch. Serves 4.

Mrs. M. A. Pierson III
(Caroline Abadie)

CROOKNECK SQUASH FRITO

8 fresh crookneck squash, unpeeled, sliced
Salt
1 small onion, chopped
2 slices bacon
Black pepper
4 Tablespoons butter
1 small package Fritos, crushed
6-8 slices American cheese

Boil squash in salted water with onion and bacon until tender. Drain. Discard bacon. In casserole, place alternate layers of squash, seasoned with pepper and dotted with butter, Fritos, and cheese. Repeat layers. Bake at 350°F until bubbling hot.

Mrs. George Hardy Vincent
(Nina LaFleur)

SQUASH SUPREME

4 pounds fresh yellow squash, sliced
1 large onion, chopped
1 small bunch green onions, chopped
1 small bell pepper, chopped
Butter or oil for sautéing
2 eggs, beaten
½ stick margarine or butter
1 Tablespoon sugar
Salt and pepper to taste
½ pound Cheddar cheese, grated
1 cup seasoned bread crumbs

Cook squash until tender; drain and mash in colander until all liquid is gone. Meanwhile, sauté chopped vegetables in butter or oil until soft. Place squash, vegetables, eggs, butter, and sugar in 2 quart casserole and season to taste. Top with mixture of cheese and crumbs. Bake, uncovered, at 350°F for 30 minutes. Serves 8-10.

Mrs. William B. Pharr
(Yvonne Vidrine)

SUMMER SQUASH CASSEROLE

3-4 cups yellow squash, peeled, diced
1 teaspoon each salt and pepper
2 Tablespoons butter
5 Tablespoons cheese, grated
⅛ teaspoon paprika
½ teaspoon onion flakes
1 carton (8 ounces) sour cream
1 egg yolk, beaten
1 Tablespoon chives, chopped
Bread crumbs

Preheat oven to 375°F. Cook squash in boiling salted water until tender. Drain well and place in 2½ quart casserole. Combine salt, pepper, 1 Tablespoon butter, cheese, paprika, onion flakes, and sour cream, and stir over low heat until cheese is melted. Remove from heat. Stir in egg yolk and chives. Pour mixture over squash, sprinkle with bread crumbs, and dot with butter. Bake, uncovered, for 15 minutes. Serves 4-6.

If you haven't liked squash, you'll love it now!

Mrs. Blair Stoker
(Mickey Hall)

SQUASH DELIGHT

1½ pounds yellow or white squash
1 small onion, grated
1 medium carrot, grated
1 cup sour cream
1 can cream of chicken soup, undiluted
1 stick butter, melted
2 cups Pepperidge Farm poultry dressing

Cook squash in small amount of water until just tender. Drain, slice, and layer in a shallow baking dish alternately with onion, carrot, sour cream, and soup. Mix butter with poultry dressing and spread over squash mixture. Bake, uncovered, at 325°F for 25-35 minutes. Serves 8.

Jesselyn Oest

SQUASH STUFFED WITH SHRIMP

3 large white squash
1 large onion, chopped
2 ribs celery, chopped
½ bell pepper, chopped
2 cloves garlic, chopped
Oil as needed
1 pound raw shrimp, peeled and deveined
2-3 Tablespoons margarine
Salt and red pepper to taste
3 slices bread, soaked in water
Bread crumbs as needed

Boil squash in salted water until soft. Cool, halve, scoop out pulp and seeds, and set aside. Sauté onion, celery, bell pepper, and garlic in a little oil until soft. Add raw shrimp and margarine, cooking 10-15 minutes. Season. Add squash pulp and cook until thoroughly mixed and heated. Squeeze water from bread, break into pieces, and add to the mixture. Cook on low heat stirring until warm. Stuff into the squash halves and cover with bread crumbs. Place squash in baking dish with water covering the bottom. Bake, uncovered, at 350°F for 30 minutes, or until brown on top. Freezes. Serves 6.

Mrs. Lionel de la Houssaye (Zizi Ogden)

STUFFED WHITE SQUASH

4 large white squash
1 large onion, chopped
3 Tablespoons oil
1 pound lean ground chuck
2 teaspoons seasoned salt
1 teaspoon pepper
Bread crumbs

Boil squash in salted water until tender. Sauté onion in oil until wilted. Add ground meat and cook until slightly brown. Season to taste with salt and pepper. Cut squash in half if large; cut top off if small. Discard seeds. Carefully scoop out squash, add to ground meat mixture, and cook until blended. Stuff hollowed squash with mixture. Top with bread crumbs. Bake, uncovered, at 325°F until hot. Freezes. Serves 6-8.

Mrs. William E. Shaddock (Craig Gorham)

YELLOW OR ZUCCHINI SQUASH CASSEROLE

1 cup onions, chopped
½ stick butter
2 cups yellow or zucchini squash, cooked
3 hard boiled eggs, chopped
2 eggs, slightly beaten
1 can (small) ripe olives
Salt and pepper
2 Tablespoons sugar
1 cup American cheese, grated
½ cup each evaporated milk and half and half
½ cup cracker crumbs, or less

Sauté onions in butter. Add remaining ingredients except crumbs, and mix well. Place in greased casserole, sprinkle top with cracker crumbs, and bake at 375°F for 40 minutes. Serves 8-10.

Mrs. W. P. Fuller
Kinder, Louisiana

ZUCCHINI EGGPLANT CASSEROLE

1 cup onion, chopped
6 Tablespoons margarine
1 pound zucchini, diced
1 pound eggplant, peeled and diced
Salt and pepper to taste
2 Tablespoons parsley, chopped
2 large tomatoes, thinly sliced
½ cup Cheddar cheese, coarsely shredded
4 slices bacon, partially cooked

Preheat oven to 375°F. In skillet sauté onion in margarine. Add zucchini, eggplant, and seasoning, stirring occasionally. Cook 5 minutes and stir in parsley. Layer eggplant-zucchini mixture, tomato, and cheese in a 2 quart casserole. Cover with bacon. Bake, uncovered, for 1 hour. Serves 4-6.

Mrs. Virgil Junk

Mrs. Paul Root *parboils the zucchini, drains, and layers the zucchini, onion, and 1 can sliced tomatoes in a casserole, topped with 1 cup Mozzarella cheese.*

BAKED STUFFED TOMATOES

6 fresh tomatoes, unpeeled
Salt
½ cup broiled bacon (8-10 slices), chopped
¼ cup celery, chopped
1 small onion, minced
1 cup soft bread crumbs
½ teaspoon salt
½ cup cheese, grated
6 teaspoons butter

Preheat oven to 350°F. Cut a slice from top of each tomato, scoop out centers, and lightly salt insides. Mix tomato pulp, bacon, celery, onion, bread crumbs, salt, and ½ of cheese. Fill tomato cavities with the mixture. Cover with remaining cheese. Dot with butter. Bake in greased muffin cups or baking dish, uncovered, about 30 minutes. Serves 6.

Mrs. James Cochran
(Jacquetta Pleimann)

TOMATO CASSEROLE

2 cans stewed tomatoes
1 teaspoon salt
½ teaspoon pepper
2 Tablespoons parsley, finely chopped
2 teaspoons brown sugar
½ teaspoon dried sweet basil
1 Tablespoon lemon juice
1 Tablespoon dried onion
1 teaspoon monosodium glutamate
⅔ cup dried bread crumbs
2 Tablespoons butter

Place in 8 inch casserole all well mixed ingredients, except last 2. Brown bread crumbs in butter and spread over top of casserole. Bake, covered, in microwave oven for 4 minutes; bake, uncovered, in regular oven at 350°F for 15-20 minutes. Serves 4.

Tasty, non-fattening casserole!

Mrs. Tom Flanagan, Jr.
(Sarah Nabors)

STUFFED TOMATOES

1 pound Gulf shrimp boiled with salt, red pepper to taste, and 2 slices lemon, and peeled
6-7 slices bread, toasted
6-8 tomatoes
2 small white onions
6-7 ribs celery, chopped
1 Tablespoon butter
Salt and pepper to taste
Cracker crumbs, crushed
Butter pats

Grind shrimp and toast in meat grinder. Set aside. Slice top off tomatoes and scoop out pulp. Set aside. In a large skillet wilt the onions and celery in butter. Add shrimp and toast mixture, tomato pulp, salt and pepper to taste. Stuff into hollowed tomatoes. Pack tops of tomatoes with cracker crumbs, capping with a pat of butter. Place stuffed tomatoes in a pan with a little water in the bottom and bake at 350°F until cracker crumbs are light brown and tomatoes are done. Serves 6-8.

Mrs. Oliver Stockwell
(Roseina Holcombe)

ROMANO CASSEROLE

2 cups Progresso Italian bread crumbs
1 can artichoke hearts, drained and cut up
1 can Italian style green beans, drained
3 hard boiled eggs, chopped
½ cup Romano cheese
1 cup olive oil
¼ cup lemon juice

Combine bread crumbs, artichokes, beans, eggs, and cheese and mix lightly. Pour salad dressing and lemon juice over top and again toss lightly, moistening bread crumbs well. More salad dressing may be added if needed. Place in shallow pyrex dish and bake, uncovered, at 350°F for 20 minutes, or until hot. Freezes. Serves 6-8.

From the recipes of Helen Guchereau Caldarera

TURNIPS AND POTATOES

6 turnips, peeled
9 potatoes, peeled
1 stick butter or margarine
Salt and pepper to taste

Place turnips and potatoes in separate pots, covering with salted water (½ teaspoon to each pot). Boil until tender, drain, and mash turnips and potatoes together. Add butter or margarine, salt and pepper to taste.

Mrs. Violet King

EASY VEGETABLE SUKIYAKI

1 pound mushrooms, sliced
2 Tablespoons oil
1 pound spinach, chopped
3 celery ribs, diced
2 cups bean sprouts
1 can (6 ounces) bamboo shoots
¼ cup soy sauce
2 Tablespoons molasses
¼ cup vegetable broth
Salt and pepper to taste

In large, deep frying pan or wok brown mushrooms in heated oil. Add remaining ingredients, stirring well, and cook over medium heat for 10 minutes, or until vegetables are tender but slightly crisp. Serve immediately. (Menu suggestion: Serve with Chinese style fried rice.) Serves 4-6.

Jan Schleussner Stream

VEGETABLE CASSEROLE

1 medium eggplant
1 large red or white onion
1 green and/or 1 red pepper
2 zucchini squash
2 large fresh tomatoes
Salt and pepper to taste
3 Tablespoons margarine

Cut vegetables into slices. Place in buttered casserole, alternating vegetable slices. Season with salt and pepper, dotting at random with margarine. If recipe is doubled, baking time is doubled. Other seasonings may be added, such as olive oil, tarragon, seasoned salt, Parmesan cheese, etc. Bake, covered, at 350°F for 1 hour. Serves 4.

This is a never-fail recipe. Overcooking does not harm it.

Heidi Hansen McElroy

BUCCANEER BROCCOLI AU GRATIN

2 bunches fresh broccoli (about 4 stems per bunch)
8 cups water
1¼ Tablespoons salt
1 teaspoon lemon juice
1½ cups potato rolls (about 4; French bread may be substituted)
¾ pound creamy super sharp cheese
6 Tablespoons butter
SAUCE
¼ pound butter
1 Tablespoon flour
½ cup milk
¼ pound hot pepper cheese
8 ounces French onion dip
¼ teaspoon cayenne pepper
Bread crumbs

Prepare fresh broccoli by cutting where stem and flowerets meet. Wash and drain flowerets. Bring water, salt, and lemon juice to a vigorous boil. Add broccoli and boil, uncovered, for 2 minutes. Cover, turn off heat, and leave in pot 5 minutes. Drain. Broccoli will be firm; do not overcook. Place rolls in preheated 350°F oven. Toast 10 minutes. Rolls should be brown and crisp on outside and soft on inside. Let cool. Trim outer crust and roll with rolling pin to make bread crumbs. Cube remainder of roll into bite sized pieces.
SAUCE
Make a white sauce with butter, flour, and milk. Add hot pepper cheese and stir until melted. Add French onion dip and stir until smooth and thick. Add cayenne pepper. Remove from stove and fold in bread crumbs. Line bottom of a 3 quart casserole with a layer of broccoli and a layer of sauce, and sprinkle with ½ the super sharp cheese. Repeat layering, ending with cheese. Top with potato roll bread crumbs and dot with butter. Bake, covered, in preheated 350°F oven for 10-15 minutes, or until cheese is completely melted and bubbly. Serves 10.

Mrs. J. J. Champeaux II
(Rosalie "Poddy" Leveque)

VEGETABLES

CAJUN BAKED YAMS (OR SWEET POTATOES)

Yams or sweet potatoes
Butter

Scrub potatoes. Dry well. Bake on cookie sheet at 350°F, turning every 30 minutes, until very soft. Test for doneness by gently squeezing. Serve in shell, or peeled, with butter.

Leftover baked yams are good peeled, sliced ½ inch thick, and fried in 2 inches of hot cooking oil (about 4 minutes). Drain and sprinkle with granulated sugar. Serve with gumbo.

Mrs. George Hardy Vincent
(Nina Lafleur)

BERNIE'S CANDIED YAMS

1 cup granulated sugar
8 large yams or sweet potatoes
2 Tablespoons allspice
½ cup brown sugar
¼ pound butter

Bake yams until barely soft at 350°F for about 1 hour. Cool, peel, slice into quarters. Grease casserole and layer yams sprinkled with allspice, both sugars, and dotted with butter. Bake at 300°F for 1 hour.

Mrs. Sheldon Barré
(Bernadette Phillips)

CRANBERRIED YAMS
(Sweet Potatoes)

Dash of salt
3 cups yams, cooked and mashed with ½ cup butter and ⅓ cup milk
1 can (16 ounces) cranberry sauce
2 Tablespoons brown sugar
1 teaspoon orange rind, grated
2 Tablespoons margarine, melted
½ cup pecans or walnuts, chopped

Add dash of salt to mashed sweet potatoes and spoon into greased 4 cup casserole. Combine cranberry sauce, brown sugar, orange rind, and margarine. Spread over sweet potatoes and top with nuts. Bake at 350°F for 25-30 minutes. Serves 6.

Serve instead of cranberry sauce with turkey.

Mrs. Margaret Streater Conover

SWEET POTATO PUFFS

1 can (1 pound, 14 ounces) sweet potatoes, drained, mashed
2 Tablespoons butter, melted
3 Tablespoons orange juice
3 Tablespoons dark brown sugar
1/8 teaspoon each nutmeg and cinnamon
Salt to taste
1 can (8¼ ounces) pineapple chunks
2 cups corn flakes, crushed

Mix thoroughly all ingredients except pineapple chunks and corn flakes. Shape mixture into balls (using 1 heaping Tablespoon per ball), placing a pineapple chunk in the center of each. Roll in corn flake crumbs until completely covered. Bake on a lightly buttered baking sheet at 350°F for 30 minutes. Serves 6-8.

Mrs. Allen J. Rhorer
(Mildred Hamilton)

WHIPPED YAMS

4 medium yams (2 pounds)
Boiling water to cover
½ teaspoon ground nutmeg
¾ teaspoon salt
1/16 teaspoon ground cloves
¼ cup sugar
1 Tablespoon orange rind, grated
½ teaspoon lemon rind, grated
1 Tablespoon butter or margarine, melted
1 egg, well beaten
¼ cup heavy cream
½ cup pecans, chopped
2 Tablespoons light brown sugar

Preheat oven to 450°F. Cook whole yams in boiling water until tender 20-30 minutes. Slip skins off and mash until smooth. Add remaining ingredients, except sugar, and beat until fluffy. Place mixture in 1 quart buttered casserole. Brush with butter and sprinkle with brown sugar. Bake for 35 minutes or until brown. May top with marshmallows the last few minutes of cooking. Will not freeze. Serves 6-8.

Mrs. Charles Mackey

Mrs. Virginia Barnes *adds juice of one orange, 1 stick butter, dash of cinnamon, and raisins. Omits egg, cream, and ¼ cup sugar.*

VEGETARIAN SHISH KABOB

MARINADE
½ cup Tamari sauce
¼ cup water
1 Tablespoon curry powder
1 teaspoon ginger
1 bay leaf
1 onion, thinly sliced
2 cloves garlic, minced
VEGETABLES
5 large tomatoes, cubed, or 20 cherry tomatoes
4 bell peppers, seeded and cubed
2 large onions, cut in small chunks, or 12 whole small white onions
½ pound mushrooms, caps only

Blend all marinade ingredients well. Place vegetables in a deep bowl and cover with marinade. If more liquid is required, increase Tamari sauce and water proportionately. Cover bowl and leave in a cool place (do not refrigerate) for at least 2 hours. Remove vegetables from marinade and place alternately on skewers. Broil or barbecue, coating with marinade, until vegetables are tender and well browned. Serve hot over rice. Serves 4-6.

Jan Schleussner Stream

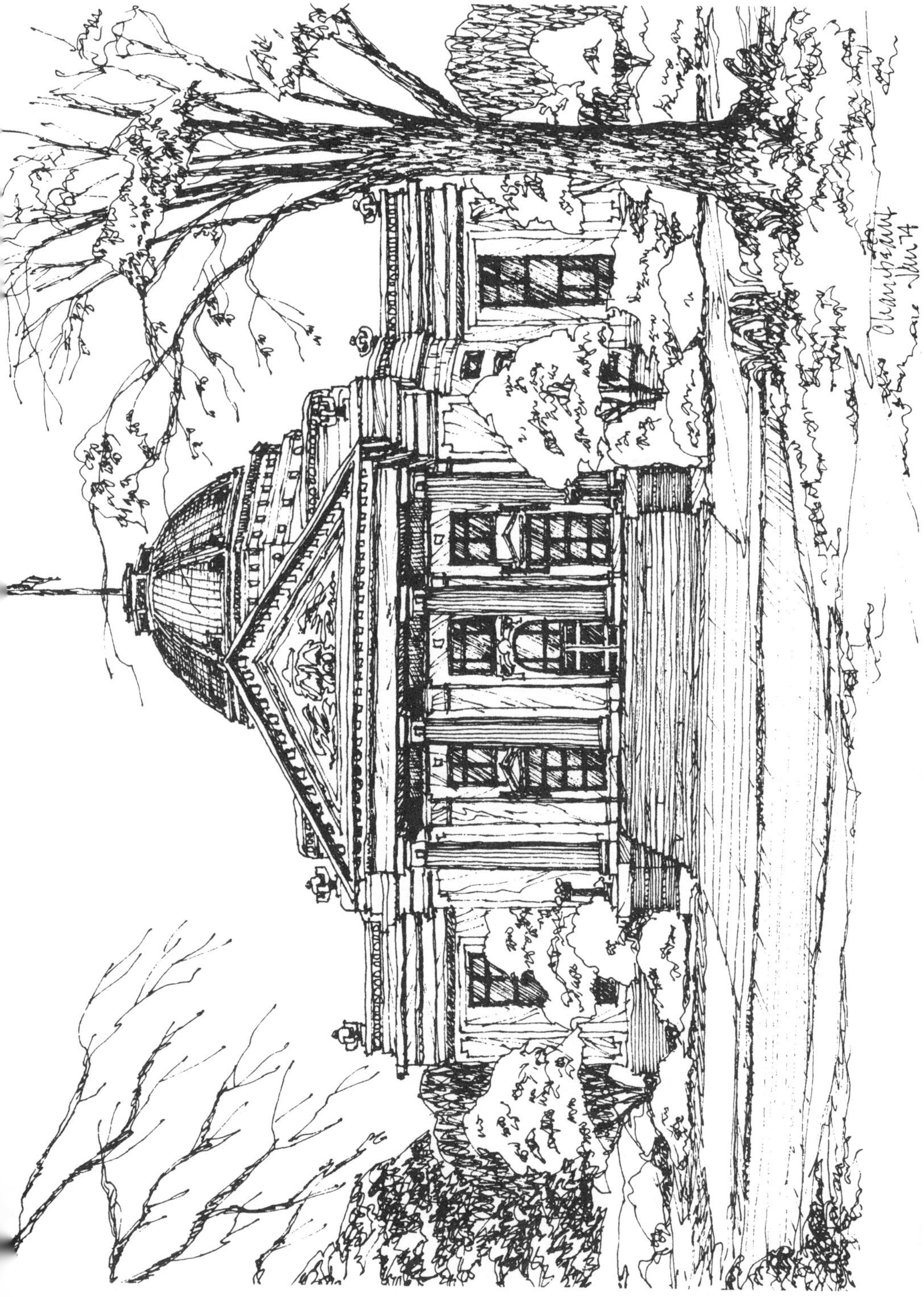

COURTHOUSE

Modeled after a famous Italian villa of the Classic period, the Calcasieu Parish Courthouse blends harmoniously with its graceful setting of stately old oak trees and flowered walkways.

The building is almost an exact copy of the renowned Villa Capra, known also as the Rotunda, which made Vicenza, Italy, a pilgrimage for architects early in the 17th century. The Villa Capra, designed by 16th Century master architect Palladio for Monsignor Paola Almerico, Referendary to Popes Pius IV and V, and begun around 1550, was not completed until after the deaths of both its architect and owner. Upon Almerico's death, his son sold it to the Capra brothers for 18,500 ducats. Completed by Vincenzo Scamozzi, a pupil of Palladio, it is a square structure with an Ionic portico on each face, a circular central hall, and a shallow dome.

Architects for the Lake Charles replica were Favrot and Livaudais of New Orleans, the same firm which designed the old Calcasieu Marine National Bank of Lake Charles, another beautiful piece of architecture. The Lake Charles Courthouse differs from the original Rotunda only in having one set of centrally located steps instead of twin ones. Constructed for the Calcasieu Parish Police Jury in 1911-12 by the Texas Building Company of Fort Worth, the two story fireproof basement brick and terra-cotta structure cost $179,887.

The present edifice is the fifth courthouse on the Ryan Street site. The first was a log building brought here from the early settlement of Marion (north of Lake Charles) in 1852, when Lake Charles became the parish seat. Several months later a larger crude building of mill timbers was erected, which was replaced in 1872 by a white frame building with green shutters. All of these structures faced North Court Street. A masonry parish courthouse, built in 1890, was the first to face Ryan Street. It was destroyed by the devastating 1910 fire which decimated a seven block area. Annexes, air conditioning, and elevators are later additions to the original structure.

SPINACH SALAD

2 bags fresh spinach
2 cans water chestnuts, thinly sliced
4 hard boiled eggs, diced
1 can bamboo shoots
½ pound bacon, fried crisp and crumbled

Chill well washed spinach. Toss together spinach, water chestnuts, eggs, and bamboo shoots. Top with bacon crumbs. Pour dressing on salad to suit taste and toss well.

SWEET AND SOUR DRESSING

1 cup salad oil
¼ cup cider vinegar
1 medium onion, finely chopped
¾ cup sugar
1 Tablespoon Lea & Perrins
⅓ cup ketchup

DRESSING

Combine all ingredients in blender. Dressing may be refrigerated in tightly closed jar for a week. Serves 15.

Mrs. Brower Dellinger

MARINATED MUSHROOM SALAD

½ pound fresh mushrooms
½ cup vinegar
½ cup olive oil
¾ teaspoon celery salt
¾ teaspoon garlic salt
¾ teaspoon onion salt
½ teaspoon white pepper
3 Tablespoons Parmesan cheese
2 heads Romaine lettuce, torn in pieces

Remove stems from mushrooms, wipe with a damp cloth, and pat dry. Cut caps into thin slices. Beat together remaining ingredients except lettuce until well blended. Marinate mushrooms in the dressing for at least 1 hour. Toss dressing with washed and dried Romaine lettuce. Correct seasoning before serving. Serves 4-6.

Mrs. D. Dale Archer
(Valerie "Val" Grode)

Champignon

ITALIAN MUSHROOM SALAD

DRESSING
¾ cup olive oil
1 tin sardines in oil
1 tube anchovy paste
2 Tablespoons garlic, chopped

SALAD
½ pound fresh mushrooms, sliced
1 head lettuce

Combine first 4 ingredients and let stand, refrigerated, at least 2 hours. Toss mushrooms and torn lettuce with salad dressing and serve immediately. Serves 6.

From the recipes of K. Ramsey MacLeod

CAESAR SALAD

2 small bunches Romaine lettuce, washed and chilled
Juice of 1 lemon
⅓ cup olive oil, flavored with garlic powder to taste
1 Tablespoon vinegar
2 teaspoons Worcestershire sauce
½ teaspoon freshly ground pepper
½ teaspoon salt
¼ cup Romano cheese, grated
2 eggs, coddled 1 minute
1 cup croutons

Tear Romaine into bite sized pieces. Combine lemon juice, olive oil, vinegar, and Worcestershire sauce. Pour over Romaine and toss with pepper, salt, cheese, egg, and croutons. Serves 4.

Irene Sullivan

GARDEN VEGETABLE SALAD

4 yellow squash, thickly cut
4 zucchini, thickly cut
3-4 ribs celery, thickly cut
1 bell pepper, chopped
½-1 purple onion, sliced
1 cucumber, sliced
Old fashioned French dressing, p. 288
Jane's Krazy Salt or seasoned salt
Tomatoes, chopped (optional)

Blanch first 3 ingredients for 5 minutes. Drain in colander with cold running water. Mix all ingredients together with Old Fashioned French dressing and lots of Jane's Krazy Salt or seasoned salt. Will keep refrigerated for several days in covered container. Tomatoes may be added before serving. Serves 12.

Mrs. Hunter Huddle (Katherine Plauché)

SPINACH SALAD

8-10 ounces raw spinach, washed and dried
Salt and pepper
2 teaspoons sugar
1 pound bacon, cooked, crumbled
4 hard boiled eggs, chopped
¾ head iceberg lettuce, washed and dried
1 Bermuda onion, thinly sliced
1 package raw Bird's Eye frozen peas, thawed
1 cup each mayonnaise and sour cream
2 ounces Parmesan cheese, grated

Using a large glass bowl, layer the following ingredients in order: Spinach, sprinkled with salt, pepper, and 1 teaspoon sugar; bacon, eggs, lettuce, sprinkled with salt, pepper, and 1 teaspoon sugar; onion, peas. Top with combined mayonnaise and sour cream. Sprinkle with Parmesan cheese. Serve with dressing on the side.

DRESSING

1 teaspoon each salt, paprika, celery seed, and dry mustard
½ cup sugar
¼ cup cider vinegar
1 cup Crisco oil

DRESSING

Mix all ingredients well in blender, except oil. Gradually add oil, blending well. Chill. Serves 8-10 people.

Mrs. Herb Krombholz
(Mary Creveling)

WILTED LETTUCE

4 slices bacon, fried, crumbled
2 teaspoons white onion, minced
Bacon drippings
1 teaspoon vinegar
½ teaspoon dry mustard
1 teaspoon sugar
Garlic salt and pepper to taste
Lettuce, bite sized (for 4 salads)
2 hard boiled eggs, minced

Fry bacon and remove from skillet. To bacon drippings, add remaining ingredients, except lettuce and eggs. Bring sauce to a boil, stirring constantly. Pour over lettuce immediately and *cover* for at least 1 minute until lettuce wilts. Sprinkle with minced eggs and crumbled bacon. Serve at once. Serves 4.

From the recipes of
Wilna Boling Mahaffey

Laitue

COLE SLAW

1 head cabbage, shredded
2-3 carrots, shredded
½ bell pepper, finely chopped
1 teaspoon celery seed
½ cup buttermilk
¾ cup mayonnaise
1 Tablespoon vinegar
1 Tablespoon sugar
½ teaspoon salt

Combine cabbage, carrots, bell pepper, and celery seed in large bowl. Mix remaining ingredients and add to vegetables. Mix well, cover, and refrigerate. Serves 6-8.

Mrs. Ed Whitaker

ICE BOX SLAW

1 medium head cabbage, shredded
2 onions, thinly sliced
¾ cup sugar
1 teaspoon celery seed
1 teaspoon prepared mustard
1 cup white vinegar
1 teaspoon sugar
1½ teaspoons salt
¾ cup salad oil

In large covered refrigerator dish, alternate layers of cabbage and onion. Sprinkle with sugar. Combine and heat the celery seed, mustard, vinegar, sugar, and salt. When hot, add the salad oil and pour over the cabbage and onions. Cover tightly and refrigerate. Keeps for *several* weeks in the refrigerator. Serves 8-10.

Variations include sliced bell pepper, carrots, and purple onion.

Mrs. Woodson Hopkins
Lafayette, Louisiana

AVOCADO COTTAGE CHEESE DELIGHT

2 pints creamed or cottage cheese, low fat
2 teaspoons Tabasco
1 teaspoon salt
2 teaspoons lemon juice
2 Tablespoons oil and vinegar salad dressing
2 medium avocados, peeled
6-8 medium tomatoes
Leaf lettuce
1 cup chives, finely chopped

In a large bowl, gently mix first 5 ingredients. Let stand. Cut avocados into small bite sized pieces. Scoop out centers of tomatoes and reserve pieces. Chill leaf lettuce well. Now add avocado and tomato pieces and ½ cup chives to cottage cheese. Toss gently to mingle all flavors. Fill tomatoes with cottage cheese mixture and sprinkle remaining chives on top. Place on bed of lettuce and chill well before serving. Serves 6-8.

Mrs. James J. Cox

MOLDED BEET SALAD

2 cans (16 ounce size) whole beets
½ cup white vinegar
½ cup brown sugar
⅛ teaspoon powdered cloves
⅛ teaspoon cinnamon
¼ teaspoon salt
1 envelope Knox gelatine
¼ cup cold water
1 package (3 ounces) lemon Jello
Wesson oil as needed
Lettuce as needed
Mayonnaise as needed

Shred beets and save juice. Combine vinegar, sugar, cloves, cinnamon, and salt in saucepan and heat. Soak gelatine in cold water in separate bowl. Heat 2 cups of beet juice; add Jello, gelatine, and vinegar mixture, and dissolve all together. Allow to chill until slightly thickened and fold in shredded beets. Pour mixture into large mold greased with Wesson oil. (Put ice water in greased mold first to close pores; then pour water off.) Cover with waxed paper and refrigerate. Unmold and serve on lettuce with mayonnaise. May also be made in individual molds. Serves 10.

Sweet and spicy flavor.

Mrs. Dan Woodring
(Laura Noland)

DIFFERENT CARROT SALAD

2 cups carrots, finely chopped
½ cup pecans, chopped
¼ teaspoon salt
⅓ cup pimiento stuffed olives, sliced
1 bell pepper, finely diced
¼ cup sweet preserved onions, chopped
½ cup Miracle Whip salad dressing
12 slices canned pineapple

Combine all ingredients except sliced pineapple and mix well. Place a slice of pineapple on lettuce leaf. Add 2 Tablespoons of carrot mixture in center of pineapple ring. Serves 12.

Mrs. Edward H. Taussig
(Florence Streater)

HARVEST SALAD

2 cups cooked rice
2 Tablespoons onion, finely chopped
1 Tablespoon vinegar
2 Tablespoons salad oil
¾ teaspoon curry powder
2 teaspoons salt
1 cup celery, chopped
1 package (10 ounces) frozen (or canned) peas, cooked, drained, and chilled
¾ cup mayonnaise

While the rice is hot, add onion, vinegar, salad oil, curry powder, and salt. Chill mixture for at least 3 hours. Just before serving, toss together with celery, peas, and mayonnaise. Serves 10.

Mrs. Edward Duff

LIMA DILL SALAD

1 package (10 ounces) frozen baby lima beans
2 Tablespoons parsley, chopped
½ cup celery, chopped
¼ cup mayonnaise
1 Tablespoon vinegar
1 Tablespoon onion, grated
½ teaspoon dill seed
½ teaspoon salt
¼ teaspoon pepper

Cook lima beans until just tender. Drain and chill. Mix chilled beans with parsley and celery. Mix remaining ingredients and pour over bean mixture. Toss well. Serve in lettuce lined bowl. Garnish as desired with tomato wedges, crumbled crisp bacon, cucumbers, or egg slices. Serves 4-5.

Mrs. Hunter Huddle
(Katherine Plauché)

PAPA JIM'S BEAN SALAD

1 clove garlic, peeled and split
3 green onion tops, finely chopped
1 rib celery, finely chopped
¼ cup bell pepper, finely chopped
Salt and pepper to taste
1 can (16 ounces) pork and beans
3 Tablespoons oil
¼ cup vinegar

Rub salad bowl with garlic. Combine onions, celery, bell pepper, salt, pepper, pork and beans. Add oil and vinegar and mix thoroughly. Serves 4-6.

This may sound wacky but it is delicious!

From the recipes of
James H. Leveque, Sr.

STRING BEAN SALAD

2 cans (16 ounce size) Blue Lake cut green beans
1 can (16 ounces) yellow wax beans
1 cup celery, finely chopped
3 hard boiled eggs, chopped in large pieces
½ cup mayonnaise
¼ cup sour cream
Juice of 1 lemon
1½ Tablespoons Lawry's seasoned salt
Pepper to taste
2 tomatoes, quartered
1 large purple onion, thinly sliced (optional)

Drain beans and rinse with water. Drain. In large bowl combine beans, celery, eggs, mayonnaise, sour cream, lemon juice, seasoned salt, and pepper. Add onion at this time if desired. After mixing, arrange tomatoes on top of salad. Chill thoroughly. Serves 8-10.

Mrs. James E. Taussig
(Alice House)

SHANGHAI SALAD

2 large heads lettuce
1½ cans bean sprouts
1-2 cans water chestnuts, sliced
1 package (2¾ ounces) almonds, toasted
1 bell pepper, thinly sliced

Combine all ingredients and toss with dressing.

DRESSING

1 pint mayonnaise
1 Tablespoon Coleman's dry mustard
Paprika
1 Tablespoon chili powder
1 medium onion, grated
1 Tablespoon vinegar
Pinch each of thyme and marjoram
Tabasco, red pepper, and salt to taste

DRESSING

Combine all ingredients and mix well.

Mrs. Austin W. Lee
(Margaret Watkins)

EASY POTATO SALAD

3 large potatoes
1 large onion, thinly sliced in rings
Mayonnaise
1 small carton creamed cottage cheese
1 carton frozen chives, thawed and drained
1 small jar chopped pimientos
Salt and pepper to taste

Boil potatoes unpared. Cool in refrigerator. Peel, thinly slice, and layer in casserole. Layer onion rings on top of potatoes. Add a scant layer of mayonnaise (better too little than too much; more can always be added later). Layer cottage cheese and top with chives and pimientos. Add salt and pepper. Cover and refrigerate. Toss before serving. Serves 6-8.

Always a hit, and men adore it!

Mrs. Lionel L. de la Houssaye
(Marie Louise "Zi Zi" Ogden)

GERMAN POTATO SALAD

5 pounds potatoes, cooked, peeled, sliced
3 onions, sliced
9 slices bacon, fried, crumbled

In a 3½ quart casserole layer the potatoes, onions, and bacon.

SAUCE

3 Tablespoons butter
3 Tablespoons flour
Bacon drippings
2¼ cups water
¾ cup vinegar
¾ cup sugar
1½ Tablespoons salt
1 teaspoon pepper

SAUCE

Add butter and flour to bacon drippings, stir, and cook 1 minute. Add remaining ingredients. Bring to a boil. Pour sauce over potato mixture. Keep warm, uncovered, in a 250°F oven. Serves 10.

Mrs. Edward C. Swartz

OLD FASHIONED POTATO SALAD

6 potatoes
4 eggs
¼ cup green onions, chopped
¼ cup parsley, chopped
3 Tablespoons vinegar
1½ teaspoons salt
½ cup oil
¼ teaspoon black pepper

Boil potatoes and eggs. Cool and cut into bite sized pieces. Combine remaining ingredients and mix with potatoes and eggs by folding over (not stirring) with a spoon. Serve chilled. Serves 6.

Mrs. J. Malcolm Leveque
(Marjorie Helen Schepp)

SALADS

POTATO SALAD

8 large Irish potatoes, cooked, finely diced
10 hard boiled eggs
Pickle mixture, made with:
  4 medium dill pickles
  4 medium sweet pickles
  3 Tablespoons salad olives
  ½ small jar pimientos
  3 ribs celery
  ¾ medium onion, grated
Mixture for egg yolks:
  5 Tablespoons mayonnaise
  2 Tablespoons prepared mustard
  Seasoned salt
  6 dashes Worcestershire sauce
  Black pepper
  1 teaspoon paprika
  Egg whites, mashed
  Salt to taste

Cover potatoes with cold water. When the water boils, reduce heat to simmer, cooking about 45 minutes. Cover eggs with water and remove from heat 10 minutes after water boils. Shell eggs and remove yolks. Save whites from about 2 eggs. Mash yolks and whites separately, reducing whites to very small pieces. Make pickle mixture, finely chopping all ingredients, and egg yolk mixture and combine in a quart container. Peel potatoes while still hot and cut into small pieces (almost like mashed potatoes). Add diced potatoes to pickle-egg mixtures. Serves 12-15.

Tartness may be varied by adding to or decreasing dill pickles and mustard.

James R. St. Dizier

MACARONI AND CHEESE SALAD

1½ cups shell macaroni
1 cup celery, sliced
1 cup carrot, shredded
¼ cup onion, chopped
1 can condensed Cheddar cheese soup
¼ cup cooking oil
2 Tablespoons vinegar
1 teaspoon sugar
1 teaspoon prepared mustard
1 teaspoon Worcestershire sauce
½ teaspoon salt
Dash of pepper

Cook macaroni according to package directions. Drain and cool. Combine macaroni, celery, carrot, and onion. In small mixer bowl combine soup, oil, vinegar, sugar, mustard, Worcestershire sauce, salt, and pepper; beat until well blended. Combine with macaroni mixture and mix well. Chill several hours. Serves 6-8.

Mrs. James M. Gunter

CHICKEN SALAD

1 whole chicken
Salt and pepper
Seasoned salt
½-1 onion
1 rib celery
2-3 hard boiled eggs, chopped
½-¾ cup celery, finely chopped
1 Tablespoon India relish
  or pickles, chopped
Mayonnaise
Parsley, chopped (optional)
Pimiento stuffed olives,
  sliced (optional)
1 teaspoon Durkee's sauce
  (optional)
Tabasco to taste
Salt and pepper

Season chicken with salt and pepper and place onion and celery rib in cavity. Boil until tender. (Stock may be frozen and used in many recipes.) Remove chicken from bone and cut into bite sized pieces with scissors. Add eggs, celery, relish, and mix all together with mayonnaise. Remaining ingredients may be added if desired.

This basic recipe may be used for shrimp, tuna fish, ground roast or ground ham. Add enough mayonnaise to hold salad together for serving either on lettuce or as sandwich spread.

Mrs. W. E. Gorham, Jr.
(May Craig Cagle)

CHICKEN BROCCOLI MOLD

2 envelopes unflavored gelatin
½ cup cold water
3½ cups boiling water
4 envelopes chicken broth mix
½ medium onion, chopped
½ teaspoon poultry seasoning
¼ teaspoon garlic powder
2 cups white meat of chicken,
  cooked and diced
1 package (9 ounces) chopped
  broccoli, cooked and drained
2 hard boiled eggs, chopped
Salt and pepper to taste

DRESSING

Mayonnaise
Lemon juice
Curry powder
Seasoned salt
Red pepper

Soften gelatin in cold water. Then add boiling water followed by broth mix, onion, poultry seasoning, and garlic powder. Cool, and stir in chicken, broccoli, and eggs. Salt and pepper to taste. Chill in ring mold until set. Unmold and serve with mayonnaise seasoned with lemon juice, curry powder, seasoned salt, and red pepper. Serves 6.

Mrs. D. E. Wheeler
(Virginia Lamkin)

CHICKEN WILD RICE SALAD

2 cups cooked chicken, cubed
1 package (6 ounces) long grain and wild rice mix
2 cups chicken broth
¼ cup bell pepper, chopped
3 Tablespoons pimiento, chopped
½ cup mayonnaise
3 Tablespoons Russian salad dressing
1 Tablespoon lemon juice
¼ teaspoon salt
2 avocados, seeded, peeled, and sliced

Boil chicken and cut into cubes. Cook rice mix with 2 cups of the chicken broth and cool. Add chicken, bell pepper, and pimiento. Combine mayonnaise, Russian dressing, lemon juice, and salt. Add to rice mixture, tossing to coat. Refrigerate until serving time. Dip sliced avocados in French dressing to prevent darkening. To serve, spoon salad mixture over avocados.

Odile Wilson

CURRIED CHICKEN AND RICE STUFFED TOMATO SALAD

8 large tomatoes, cored
2 cups cooked chicken, diced
1¼ cups mayonnaise
1½ teaspoons curry powder
1 teaspoon salt
Dash of celery salt
¼ teaspoon pepper
Lemon juice to taste
2 cups cooked rice
⅓ cup green onion, chopped
1½ cups green peas, cooked
2 Tablespoons pimiento, diced
Parsley sprigs

Scoop out tomato centers, turn upside down to drain, and chill. Boil chicken. Debone and cut into bite sized pieces. Combine mayonnaise, curry powder, salt, celery salt, pepper, and lemon juice. Add rice, chicken, green onions, peas, and pimiento. Mix well. Stuff tomatoes with mixture. Garnish with parsley sprig and chill. Does not freeze. Serves 8.

Mrs. M. A. Pierson III
(Caroline Abadie)

CRAB MEAT SALAD

1 pound crab meat, frozen or fresh
½ cup mayonnaise
2 Tablespoons onion, chopped
1 cup celery, chopped
2 Tablespoons sweet pickle, chopped
2 hard boiled eggs, chopped
½ teaspoon salt
Dash of black pepper

Remove any shell or cartilage from crab meat, being careful not to break the meat into small pieces. Combine all ingredients, chill, and serve on lettuce. Serves 6.

Mrs. Thomas B. Shearman
(Flora Inglis)

MOLDED SHRIMP SALAD

1 Tablespoon unflavored gelatin
2 Tablespoons water
2 Tablespoons lemon juice
1 bottle (2 ounces) pimiento stuffed olives, sliced
1 small jar (2 ounces) pimientos, chopped
1 Tablespoon onion, grated
2 hard boiled eggs, chopped
1½ teaspoons salt (or to taste)
¾ cup mayonnaise
¾ cup celery, chopped
1 cup cooked shrimp, peeled, chopped

Sprinkle gelatin over water and melt on low heat. Add lemon juice and pour over remaining ingredients. Mix well, adding more seasoning if needed. Pour into small ring mold (which has been dipped in cold water), cover with foil, and refrigerate. Should be made the day before serving to allow gelatin time to set. Serve on lettuce. Serves 4.

Good for a summer lunch.

Frances Hunter Heyck

SHRIMP MÉLANGE

6 pounds headless shrimp in shells
1 lemon, thickly sliced
1 onion, chopped
2 cloves garlic, chopped
Salt
Black and red pepper
1 can (16 ounces) claw crab meat
1 jar hearts of artichoke in oil
1 small jar Wishbone Italian salad dressing
2 ribs celery, finely chopped
1 teaspoon Tabasco
1 small can rolled anchovies with capers
1 head lettuce
Parsley
Olives

Boil shrimp with lemon, onion, garlic, salt, and pepper. Cool, peel, and devein shrimp. Combine remaining ingredients except lettuce, parsley, and olives. Pour over shrimp and mix gently. Top with anchovies. Cover with foil and marinate for 3-4 hours. Serve on crisp lettuce and garnish with parsley and olives. For a party, place in bowl, omitting anchovies and lettuce, and serve with crackers. Serves 8-10.

Tommy Carmouche
Napoleonville, Louisiana

Camarón

SHRIMP ASPIC

1 can consommé
1 Tablespoon Knox gelatine, dissolved
¼ cup cold water
¾ cup cold water
½ teaspoon salt
3 Tablespoons lemon juice
1 pound (about 1½-2 cups) shrimp, cooked, peeled and diced
½ cup celery, diced
1 cup canned petit pois peas, drained
1 hard boiled egg, for garnish

Dissolve gelatine in ¼ cup cold water. Combine all ingredients and mold individually or in ring. Chill. Serve on lettuce.

From the recipes of Nellie Craig Cagle

ICED SHRIMP MOLD

2 pounds shrimp, boiled and highly seasoned
2 packages (8 ounce size) cream cheese
2-3 Tablespoons mayonnaise
1-2 Tablespoons cream
Lemon juice
Worcestershire sauce, Tabasco
Red pepper
2-3 green onions, finely chopped

Peel, devein, and chop shrimp. Set aside. Use mixer to blend cream cheese, mayonnaise, cream, and lemon juice. Season to taste with Worcestershire, Tabasco, and red pepper. Add green onions. Add shrimp and mix 1 minute more. Refrigeration for 24 hours or longer enhances flavor. Serve with party crackers.

Mrs. Edmund Nagem (Helen Bishir)

BROCCOLI MOUSSE

2 packages frozen chopped broccoli
2 envelopes gelatin
1 can beef bouillon
1 quart Hellmann's mayonnnaise
4 hard boiled eggs, chopped
Salt, pepper and Tabasco to taste

Cook broccoli, drain, and set aside until needed. Stir gelatin into heated bouillon until it dissolves. Combine all ingredients. Pour mixture into a 1½-2 quart open mold and refrigerate until firm. Unmold, using a knife. Serve with crackers.

Mrs. L. M. Coleman

TUNA MOUSSE

1 envelope unflavored gelatin
2 Tablespoons lemon juice
½ cup canned chicken broth
½ cup celery, finely chopped
½ cup Hellmann's mayonnaise
¼ teaspoon black pepper
¼ cup homogenized milk
2 Tablespoons parsley, chopped
1 Tablespoon green onion, minced
1 teaspoon prepared mustard
½ teaspoon dill weed, crumbled
1 can (12½ ounces) tuna, drained and flaked
3 Tablespoons dill pickle, drained, and finely chopped

Soften gelatin in lemon juice in large mixing bowl. Add boiling chicken broth and stir until gelatin is completely dissolved. Add next 8 ingredients and beat on low speed until well mixed. Chill 30 minutes or until slightly thickened. Remove from refrigerator and stir in tuna and pickle. Mix well. Pour into a 2 cup mold, preferably fish shaped. Chill at least 6 hours before using. Serve on bed of greens. Serves 12 for luncheon; 20-25 for cocktail buffet.

Mrs. Everett Schneider
(Elizabeth "Libby" Storer)

TOMATO ASPIC

5 envelopes gelatin (1 envelope equals 1 Tablespoon)
1 can (12 ounces) Tabasco Bloody Mary Mix
1 can (46 ounces) tomato juice
1 teaspoon salt
Pepper to taste
¼ teaspoon sugar
1 Tablespoon lemon juice
1 Tablespoon Worcestershire sauce
Dash of Tabasco
1 Tablespoon onion, grated

OPTIONAL
½ cup carrot, grated
½ cup celery, finely chopped
   OR
½ cup celery
⅓ cup green olives, sliced
Mayonnaise

Place gelatin in large china or plastic mixing bowl. Pour Bloody Mary Mix over it and allow to set 10 minutes after stirring well. Pour tomato juice into a saucepan and heat, uncovered, to boiling point, but do not boil. Add salt, pepper, sugar, lemon juice, Worcestershire, Tabasco, and onion to hot juice and stir. Pour hot tomato juice over Bloody Mary and gelatin and stir well. Pour mixture into mold or large flat dish. Cool to room temperature, then refrigerate. When aspic starts to congeal, stir in desired vegetables. To serve, cut into squares and serve on lettuce leaf. Put teaspoon of mayonnaise on the top. Serves 16.

Mrs. William Storer
Edie Storer

JELLIED GAZPACHO

1 envelope unflavored gelatin
1¼ cups tomato juice
½ cup Catalina brand French dressing
¼ cup onion, finely chopped
¼ cup bell pepper, finely chopped
¼ cup celery, finely chopped
¼ cup cucumber, finely chopped
6-8 avocado halves

Soften gelatin in ¼ cup tomato juice. Stir over low heat until dissolved. Add remaining tomato juice and French dressing and mix well. Chill until slightly thickened. Fold in remaining ingredients, except avocado. Pour into 8 inch square pan and chill until firm. Spoon into avocado halves. Serves 6-8.

Mrs. Hunter Huddle
(Katherine Plauché)

GRAPEFRUIT SALAD

3 grapefruit
1 can (16 ounces) crushed pineapple
Sugar to taste
1 envelope gelatin for each 2 cups of fruit mixture
Water

CHEESE DRESSING
1 glass Kraft Old English or 1 package nippy cheese
Mayonnaise
Red pepper
Dash garlic powder

Cut grapefruit in half. Remove pulp with a grapefruit knife. Remove all sections, saving juice. Mix pineapple and sugar. In cup soak gelatin in grapefruit juice plus water (¼ cup for each envelope). Set cup in hot water until gelatin melts. Add to grapefruit. Fill grapefruit shells. Refrigerate. Cut in half to serve with cheese dressing. Serves 12.

A beautiful luncheon salad.

Mrs. G. W. Pomeroy

Fromage

FROZEN FRUIT CUP SALAD

2 cups sour cream
½ cup sugar
1 can (8 ounces) crushed pineapple, drained
1 banana, diced
⅛ teaspoon salt
2 Tablespoons lemon juice
Red food coloring
½ cup pecans, chopped
1 can large dark red cherries, drained

Mix together sour cream, sugar, pineapple, banana, salt, and lemon juice. Add food coloring to tint to desired shade of pink. Fold in pecans and cherries. Pour in paper cupcake liners in muffin tins and freeze. Remove from freezer about 15 minutes before serving time. Peel away cupcake liner and serve on lettuce leaf. After frozen, individual cups may be removed from muffin tins and stored in plastic bag or other container. Serves 8.

Mrs. William Mancuso
(Jean Guillory)

FRUIT AND WINE SALAD

2 packages (3 ounce size) raspberry Jello
2 cups boiling water
1 cup Port wine (need not be expensive)
1 can crushed pineapple
½ cup pecans, chopped
1 cup celery, finely chopped
Oil

Dissolve Jello in boiling water. Cool slightly, add wine, and continue cooling until slightly thickened. Stir in other ingredients. Pour into oiled molds and chill until firm. Serve on lettuce leaves and top with mayonnaise. Serves 10-12.

Mrs. Louise Monday Peters

ORANGE CHARLOTTE

3 Tablespoons gelatin
⅔ cup cold water
⅔ cup boiling water
2 cups sugar
6 Tablespoons lemon juice (more if not acid enough)
½ teaspoon salt
2 cups orange juice and pulp
6 egg whites, stiffly beaten
1 pint heavy cream, whipped
8 Tablespoons wine
Orange sections (optional)

Soak gelatin in cold water. Dissolve in boiling water. Add sugar, lemon juice, salt, orange juice, and pulp. Chill in pan of ice water until white and thick. Whip until frothy. Fold in stiffly beaten egg whites and whipped cream. Line mold with orange sections and pour in orange mixture. Fills large ring mold. Serves 20.

Mrs. Eugene Current-Garcia
(Alva Garrett)

SALADS

JELLO FRUIT SALAD

1 package lime Jello
1 cup heavy cream, whipped (or Cool Whip)
1 cup crushed pineapple
1 cup Velveeta cheese, cubed or grated
½ cup nuts, chopped

Follow directions on Jello package. Let it partially set. Add whipped cream (or Cool Whip); then add fruit, cheese, and nuts. Refrigerate to set before serving.

Mrs. Ronald B. Bell
(Suzanne Cagle)

RED AND WHITE FREEZE

4 cans (16 ounce size) whole cranberry sauce
4 Tablespoons lemon juice
4 cups whipped cream
½ cup powdered sugar
2 teaspoons vanilla
2 cups pecans, chopped

Thoroughly blend cranberry sauce with lemon juice and pour into 8x8x2 inch pan. Whip cream and beat in sugar. Add vanilla and pecans. Spoon over cranberry mixture and freeze. Cut in squares and thaw slightly before serving on lettuce leaf. Serves 9-12.

Mrs. Frank E. Gault
(Ruth Kelly)

STRAWBERRY-ORANGE MOLD

2 whole oranges
¼ cup celery, chopped
¼ cup pecans, chopped
6 ounces strawberry flavored gelatin
3 cups hot water
1 package (16 ounces) frozen strawberries, sliced
Mayonnaise
Lettuce

Cube oranges and remove seeds. Grind oranges, including peeling. Add celery and pecans. Dissolve gelatin in water and add strawberries. Stir until strawberries are thawed. Add orange mixture. Pour into greased mold. Refrigerate until firm. Serve with mayonnaise on crisp lettuce. Serves 10-12.

Mrs. Edwin L. Gorham, Jr.
Beaumont, Texas

VIRGINIA'S BLUEBERRY JELLO SALAD

2 boxes (3 ounce size) lemon Jello
2 cups hot pineapple juice
1 cup blueberry juice
2 pints heavy cream, whipped
1 cup blueberries
1½ cups bananas, finely chopped

Dissolve Jello in hot pineapple juice. Add blueberry juice and refrigerate until firm. Fold in whipped cream, blueberries, and bananas. Pour into mold and chill.

Mrs. William B. Baggett
(Gael Salter)

Salad Dressings

TRUE FRENCH DRESSING

1 teaspoon salt
1 teaspoon sugar
Pepper to taste
½ teaspoon each paprika and dry mustard
⅔ cup salad oil
4 Tablespoons vinegar
½ teaspoon Worcestershire sauce
Garlic powder to taste

Combine ingredients and shake well. Use over tossed salad.

Mrs. Joe Freeman
(Nancy Rose)

FRENCH-ITALIAN DRESSING

1 cup good olive oil (preferably Plagnoil)
½ cup wine vinegar
3 Tablespoons mayonnaise
2 teaspoons Zatarain's mustard
Dash each of salt, pepper, and garlic powder
Basil leaves, finely chopped (optional)

Combine ingredients in blender and blend well.

Giuliano Ceseri
Florence, Italy
Lafayette, Louisiana

OLD FASHIONED FRENCH DRESSING

½ cup salad oil
¼ cup each vinegar and sugar
⅓ cup bottled chili sauce
Juice of ½ lemon
1 teaspoon each salt and paprika

Combine ingredients and shake well. One small chopped onion or grated Roquefort cheese may be added. This makes a fairly sweet salad dressing. It is good used over tangy fruit or lettuce and tomato.

Mrs. Joe Freeman
(Nancy Rose)

AVOCADO DRESSING

2 ripe avocados, sliced
1 pint sour cream
Dash Worcestershire sauce
¼ teaspoon garlic powder
Juice of ½ lemon
Salt and pepper to taste

Blend all ingredients and refrigerate. Place avocado seed in dressing to keep dressing from turning brown.

Mrs. Fred A. Book
(Marian Monticello)

BLEU CHEESE OIL VINEGAR DRESSING

1 clove garlic, crushed
1 teaspoon salt
½ teaspoon each white pepper and celery salt
¼ teaspoon each cayenne pepper and dry mustard
¼ cup wine vinegar
1 cup salad oil
3 ounces bleu cheese, coarsely crumbled

Crush garlic with salt. Blend with remaining ingredients except oil and cheese. Mash ½ of the cheese well into blended mixture. Slowly add oil, beating constantly until thoroughly blended. Stir in remaining bleu cheese. Makes 1½ cups.

Mrs. E. K. Crosby
(Perla Baillio)

FRUIT SALAD DRESSING

½ cup sugar
1 Tablespoon flour
1 egg yolk
Juice of 1 lemon
½ cup unsweetened pineapple juice
1 cup heavy cream, whipped

Combine sugar, flour, and egg yolk in fruit juices. Cook in double boiler until thick. Cool and fold in whipped cream. Serves 12.

Mrs. Maury Riff
(Shirley Gordon)

GARLIC DRESSING

3 cloves garlic
¾ cup plus 2 Tablespoons vegetable oil
¼ cup red wine vinegar
½ teaspoon salt

Bruise garlic and let stand overnight in oil. Next day, drain oil from garlic; discard garlic. Combine oil, vinegar, and salt in a jar. Shake well. Makes about 1⅛ cups.

POPPY SEED DRESSING

1 cup white or tarragon vinegar
½ cup sugar
1 Tablespoon paprika
1½ Tablespoons dry mustard
1⅓ teaspoons ground ginger
1 Tablespoon salt
1 pinch each cayenne and white pepper
¼ cup onion juice
1 egg
1 quart oil
1⅓ cups honey
⅓ cup poppy seeds

Slowly bring to a boil the vinegar and sugar. Mix in other ingredients except last 3. Cool a little and slowly add oil, honey, and seeds. Chill well before serving over any fresh fruit combination. Keeps a long time in sealed container in refrigerator.

Especially good on grapefruit and avocado.

Mrs. Amy S. Boyd

THOUSAND ISLAND DRESSING

¾ cup mayonnaise
3 Tablespoons chili sauce
2 hard boiled eggs, chopped
1 Tablespoon sweet pickle relish
½ cup celery, chopped
Onion juice
Salt and pepper to taste

Mix first 5 ingredients and add onion juice, salt, and pepper to taste.

Mrs. William Boyer
(Monnie Watkins)

ROQUEFORT CHEESE DRESSING

1 quart mayonnaise
2 cups buttermilk
1-2 cloves garlic, pressed
1 teaspoon A-1 sauce
1 teaspoon Worcestershire sauce
1 dash Tabasco
⅛ cup wine vinegar
3 ounces Roquefort cheese, crumbled
Paprika to color

Combine all ingredients, except cheese and paprika. When well mixed, add cheese. Add paprika for desired color. Makes 1½ quarts. Bleu cheese may be substituted. Taste improves after second day. Keeps well.

Marcelle Barrios

ROTISSERIE COME BACK DRESSING

2 cloves garlic, pressed
1 small onion, grated
2 teaspoons prepared mustard
2 teaspoons paprika
1 Tablespoon Worcestershire sauce
1 cup mayonnaise
Salt to taste (about 1 Tablespoon)
2 Tablespoons water
6 dashes Louisiana hot sauce
1 Tablespoon black pepper
½ cup Wesson oil
¼ cup chili sauce
¾ cup ketchup

Combine all ingredients in blender or small mixing bowl. Will keep for weeks in refrigerator. Serve on green salad or head lettuce.

Mrs. Edwin DeWeese

MAYONNAISE

9 egg yolks
4 cups Wesson oil
1 heaping Tablespoon Lawry's seasoned salt
2 teaspoons each Lawry's seasoned pepper and black pepper
1½ teaspoons dry mustard
½ cup lemon juice
3 Tablespoons tarragon vinegar

Beat egg yolks until thick. Drip the oil slowly on yolks, beating constantly at high speed on mixer. Add seasonings and continue beating while gradually adding lemon juice and vinegar. Blend well. Refrigerate in jars.

Good on everything but vanilla ice cream!

Mrs. Yvonne Carter

SALAD OIL

2 Tablespoons pepper (coarse or ground)
1½ Tablespoons salt
1 teaspoon Accent
1 Tablespoon parsley, chopped
1 Tablespoon chives, chopped
1 teaspoon green onion, chopped
½ teaspoon garlic, chopped
1 cup salad oil
⅓ cup tarragon vinegar

Use a container that has a tight fitting lid, such as a quart size mayonnaise jar. Combine all ingredients except the vinegar, mix gently. Just before using, add the vinegar and mix gently again. Pour over salad greens, just enough to coat. Toss. Serves 12 or more.

Dr. W. E. Hunt

CHOW CHOW

1½ quarts green tomatoes
½ quart onions
1½ quarts cucumbers
12 bell peppers

BRINE
½ cup salt
3 quarts water
1 cup each flour and mustard
3 cups sugar
2 Tablespoons tumeric
2 quarts vinegar
3 Tablespoons butter

Chop tomatoes, onions, cucumbers and bell peppers and place in large crock, granite pan, or plastic container. Mix salt and water and bring to a boil. Pour over vegetables. Let stand overnight. Drain well next morning. Mix other ingredients into a paste, stirring constantly. Bring to a boil. Add vegetables and let come to a boil. Place in sterilized jars and seal while hot. Cook jars in water bath sitting on a rack for 1 hour on low heat.

Good with meat!

Mrs Sam Thornton
Boyce, La.

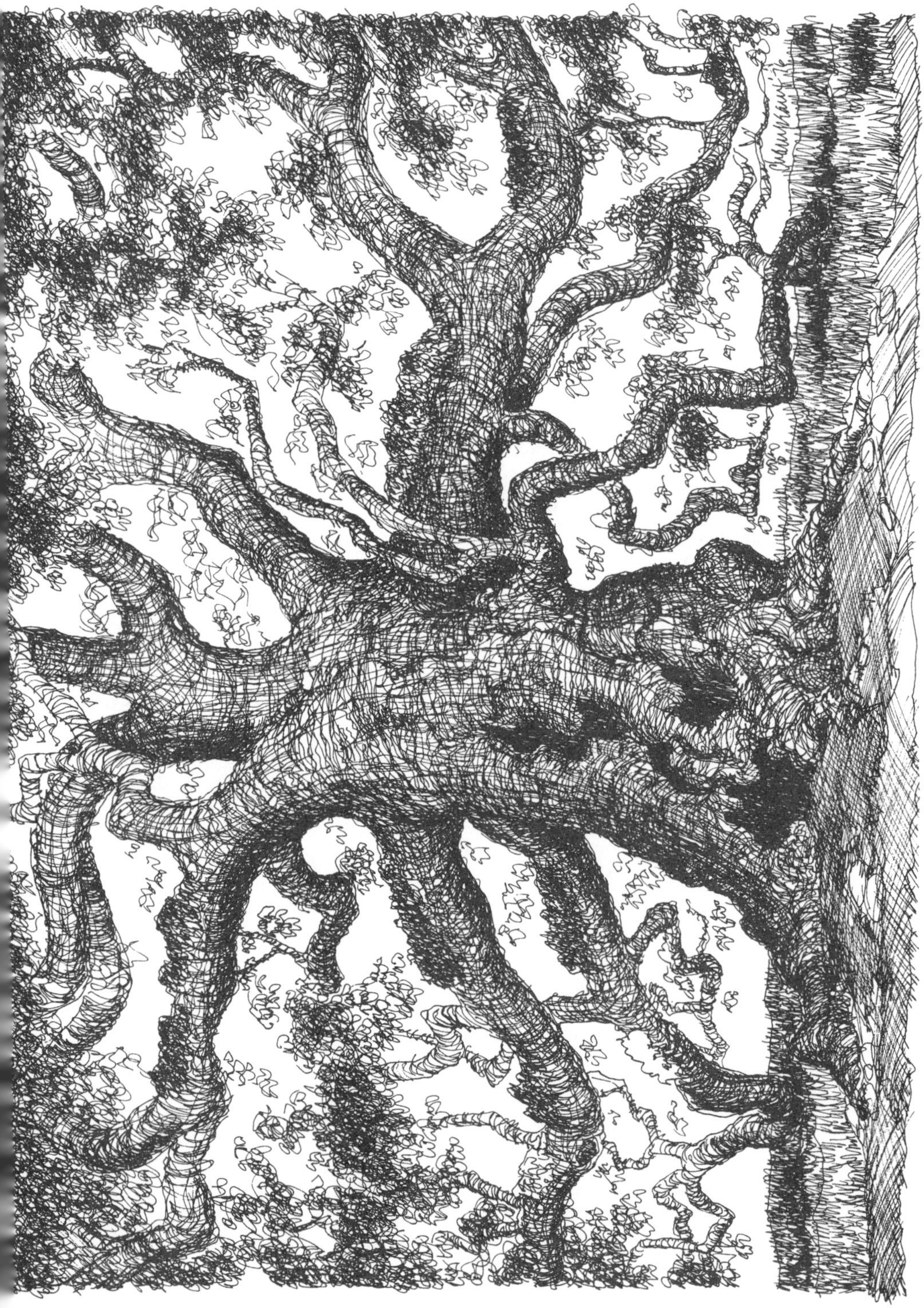

SALLIER OAK

The ancient branches of the Sallier oak, lined with resurrection fern, bend in graceful tribute to the nurturing earth.

Estimated to be more than 200 years old, this historical landmark stands on the original lands patented by the widow of Charles Sallier in 1860.

Sallier was the first settler to locate on the shores of Lake Charles. Dating back to the 1770's, the community is one of the oldest in the state of Louisiana. As time progressed the town's name evolved from "Charley's Lake" to "Charleston" and finally to Lake Charles when the city was incorporated in 1867, with a population of 430.

Descendants of Charles, and his bride Catherine LeBleu, believe the couple planted the tree when they built a cabin on the site. Ancient chains, used to bind the tree when it was split by a devastating hurricane in 1918, are still intact. Lightning struck the tree in 1938 causing extensive damage on the southwest side.

Scientifically classified "Quercus Virginiana," live oak, the beautiful old tree has a circumference of 21 feet and a limb spread of 165. It is 56 feet high, according to the Live Oak Society, in which it was registered in 1967.

Sauces

BLENDER HOLLANDAISE SAUCE

3 egg yolks
2 teaspoons to
   2 Tablespoons lemon juice
   (depending on cook's
   preference)
Dash red pepper
¼ teaspoon salt
1 stick butter

With blender on high speed, mix all ingredients but butter for 1-2 seconds. Melt butter until it bubbles. Pour into blender on high speed in steady stream. Turn blender off. The sauce is ready. To keep warm set in warm water. Serves 6.

Mrs. Emmett Sole
(Annette Bland)

BEARNAISE SAUCE

2 Tablespoons dry white wine
1 Tablespoon tarragon vinegar
2 teaspoons green onion
   tops, minced
1 teaspoon dried tarragon,
   pounded to a powder
½ teaspoon white pepper
1 cup Hollandaise sauce

Reduce first 5 ingredients over high heat until liquid is almost absorbed. Blend with Hollandaise sauce a few seconds. For broiled meats and fish.

Mrs. George Kay III
(Frances "Boo" Creveling)

MOUSSELINE SAUCE

½ cup cream, whipped
1½ cups Hollandaise sauce

Fold cream into Hollandaise. Spread over vegetables and brown lightly under broiler.

Mrs. William E. Gorham III
(Joyce Whitaker)

PARSLEY-LEMON SAUCE

1 Tablespoon parsley, finely
   minced
½ teaspoon lemon rind, finely
   grated
1 cup Hollandaise sauce

Combine ingredients thoroughly. Serve over poached or broiled fish.

Mrs. John F. Moffett
(Eleanor Greeson)

BROWN SAUCE

4 large green onions, chopped
1 cup mushrooms, chopped
½ cup butter
2 Tablespoons flour
¾ cup beef bouillion
2-3 teaspoons Kitchen Bouquet
½ cup sherry, sweet or dry
Salt, red and black pepper, Tabasco

Sauté onions and mushrooms in butter until tender not brown. Make a thin paste with flour and a little water and add. Gradually add bouillon stirring constantly. Add Kitchen Bouquet until rich brown color. Add sherry. Season to taste. Simmer 30-40 minutes.

Mrs. John B. Caire
(Peggy Huber)

SAUCE FOR BASTING ROASTS

2 Tablespoons onions, finely minced
4 ounces butter, melted
1½-2 ounces Wilson's BV (meat extract)
1 cup dry red wine
1 cup mushrooms

In saucepan sauté onions in butter until golden. Stir in BV extract with a wooden spoon until blended. Add wine. Use for basting beef tenderloin before mushrooms are added; with mushrooms use independently as sauce or gravy. Cannot be prepared ahead. Serves 8-10.

Mrs. Kenneth L. Strauss
(Julie Ann Marx)

GIBLET GRAVY

1 pound chicken gizzards and hearts (equal number of each)
1 medium onion, chopped
1 clove garlic, minced
3 Tablespoons shortening
1 quart water
2 Tablespoons paprika
½ cup flour, beaten with 1 cup water
½ cup thick sour cream
Salt and pepper to taste

Clean and wash gizzards. Sauté onion and garlic in shortening; add giblets and water. Simmer until tender. Add paprika; then simmer 7-10 minutes. Combine blended flour paste and sour cream; beat until fluffy. Stir sour cream mixture into giblets; cook over low heat for 20 minutes. Season to taste. Makes 10 servings.

Murray Reiter

BORDELAISE SAUCE JOHNSON

2 medium carrots, chopped
2 medium onions, chopped
2 sprigs parsley, chopped
¼ cup butter
2 Tablespoons flour
1 cup dry white wine
1½ cups consommé
½ teaspoon salt
½ teaspoon pepper
¼ teaspoon thyme
1 bay leaf
1 cup dry red wine
1 teaspoon lemon juice

Sauté carrots, ½ the onions, and parsley in butter in medium saucepan until golden brown. Add flour and cook until slightly brown, stirring constantly. Add white wine, consommé and seasonings. Bring to a boil; cover, and simmer 15 minutes. Meanwhile, in an 8 inch skillet, bring remaining onion and red wine to a boil and cook about 10 minutes until 2 Tablespoons of liquid remain. Combine white and red wine mixtures. Add lemon juice and cook 10-15 minutes until reduced to 1 cup. Serve warm with broiled steak.

Mrs. A. R. Johnson III
(Beverly Dupuis)

SAM'S MARCHAND DE VIN SAUCE

2 Tablespoons vegetable oil
2 Tablespoons flour
¾ cup white onion, finely chopped
2 beef cubes and 1 chicken cube in 2 cups water
3 Tablespoons tomato sauce
¼ teaspoon garlic powder
¼ teaspoon pepper, freshly ground
1 cup green onions, finely chopped
4 Tablespoons butter or margarine
½ cup red wine
1 teaspoon lemon juice
Tabasco to taste (optional)

Make a dark roux with oil and flour in an iron skillet large enough to hold about 3 cups. Wilt onion in roux for 10 minutes. Add broth, tomato sauce, garlic powder, and pepper. Cook for about 30 minutes, stirring often with wooden spoon, or until reduced to ½ original quantity (about 1½ cups). Meanwhile, in another iron skillet sauté green onions in butter for 5-10 minutes. Add wine. Cook about 20 minutes or until volume is reduced by ½ (about ¾ cup). Combine both mixtures and simmer, uncovered, 2-3 minutes. Add lemon juice and Tabasco, if desired. Serve hot with steak or chicken. Freezes. Makes 2½ cups.

Dr. Sam Emerson

CREAM OR WHITE SAUCE

2 Tablespoons butter
2 Tablespoons flour
1¼ cups light cream or milk
¼ teaspoon salt
Dash of pepper

Melt butter, preferably in top of double boiler. Add flour and stir until smooth. Add milk or cream and seasoning. Stir constantly to avoid lumping. Cook until creamy.

For a thicker sauce, add more flour. For a richer sauce, add more butter. This is a basic sauce for creamed chicken, crab meat, vegetables, etc. Cheese may be added for flavor for potatoes au gratin. Lea & Perrins for crab meat. Lemon or sherry may be added depending on the application of the sauce.

Mrs. Don Creveling
(Ellanora Gorham)

ANCHOVY BUTTER SAUCE

¼ cup butter or margarine
1 Tablespoon parsley, snipped
1 Tablespoon lemon juice
2 teaspoons anchovy paste
½ teaspoon prepared mustard
¼ teaspoon sugar
Red pepper to taste

Melt butter in saucepan over heat; add remaining ingredients and stir until well blended. Serve hot with broiled fish. Makes about ⅓ cup sauce.

Mrs. J. J. Champeaux II
(Rosalie "Poddy" Leveque)

COCKTAIL SAUCE FOR SEAFOOD

4 cups ketchup
Juice of 1 lemon (2½ Tablespoons)
1½ Tablespoons Lea & Perrins
3 heaping teaspoons cream style horseradish

Combine all ingredients and refrigerate. Serve with shrimp, crab, oysters, or crawfish.

Mrs. W. E. Gorham, Jr.
(May Craig Cagle)

MEUNIÈRE SAUCE

½ cup butter
1 Tablespoon parsley, dried or fresh
1 Tablespoon green onion tops, chopped
2 Tablespoons lemon juice
½ teaspoon each salt and pepper
1 teaspoon Worcestershire sauce

Mix all ingredients over low heat. Serve hot over fish. Especially good over trout.

Mrs. Diane Coyle Scofield

REMOULADE SAUCE

¾ cup Wesson oil
⅛ cup vinegar
¾ jar Creole mustard
2 Tablespoons paprika
2 cloves garlic, crushed
¼ small onion, minced
Dash Lea & Perrins, horseradish, and Tabasco
Salt to taste
4 green onions, chopped
Parsley, chopped

Mix all ingredients in a pint jar and shake well. Serve on iced, boiled shrimp.

Mrs. J. T. Thompson

TARTARE SAUCE

1 cup Kraft salad dressing
1 teaspoon onion
2 Tablespoons pickle relish
Dash of salt and red pepper

Mix all ingredients. Chill 1 hour before serving.

Mrs. Lawrence Lowery, Jr.
(Ammye Reeds)

WHITE REMOULADE SAUCE

½ cup Hellmann's mayonnaise
1½ Tablespoons onion, minced
½ clove garlic, pressed
Horseradish, salt and pepper to taste

Mix, cover, and chill. Correct seasoning before serving. Serve over boiled shrimp.

Mrs. Stanford L. Vincent
(Anita Cox)

BARBECUE SAUCE

1 cup onions, chopped
⅓ cup garlic, minced
2 sticks margarine
1¼ cups lemon juice
½ cup Lea & Perrins
Salt, red pepper, and Tabasco to taste
2 bouillon cubes dissolved in 1 cup water
1 Tablespoon smoke sauce (optional)

Sauté onions and garlic in margarine until transparent. Add remaining ingredients. Simmer for 10 minutes. A basic barbecue sauce for chicken, crabs, steak, and fish.

Variation: add ½ bottle of ketchup.

Mrs. Forrest Gill
(Virginia Byran)

DR. HEBERT'S GRAND CHENIER BARBECUE PLATE SAUCE

10 pounds firm fresh small yellow onions, finely diced
8 bunches green onions, finely diced
6 bell peppers (2 red and 4 green), finely diced
1 bunch celery, finely diced
8 packs frozen okra or 6 handfuls small, fresh okra, finely diced
½ pound mushrooms, sliced
Wesson oil
4 medium lemons, squeezed
6 bottles family size Del Monte ketchup
4 bottles average size hot ketchup
1 bottle "Pickapepper" (Jamaican Sauce)
1 small bottle Lea & Perrins
Powdered garlic salt, black and red pepper to taste
1 pound brown sugar
1 bottle sweet and sour sauce

Place diced vegetables in large black pot containing sparse amount of Wesson oil. Simmer slowly until wilting occurs, and sauté until golden brown. Add remaining ingredients and about 1 quart water. Bring to a boil, decrease heat to simmer, cover and stir regularly until thickening occurs to avoid sugar scorching on bottom of pot. Taste occasionally to correct seasoning, adding water, if necessary. Simmer about 2-3 hours until a smooth even texture (with "clingability" to the side of the pot) is achieved. When done, leave on stove, covered, to cool. Seal in plastic containers for freezing. Makes 3 gallons.

This is not a basting sauce. It should be prepared prior to consumption, and reheated at time of serving. It is a hot, spicy additive to such delicacies as barbecued chicken, steak, and lamb.

Dr. J. J. Hebert

SAUCES

BARBECUE SAUCE

4 onions, chopped
1 pound butter or margarine
1 cup water
2 bottles (14 ounce size) ketchup
1 bottle (10 ounces) A-1 sauce
Small can crushed pineapple
1 can (8 ounces) applesauce
Juice and sliced rinds of 3 lemons
3 bay leaves
1 Tablespoon salt
½ teaspoon each of black and red pepper
1 teaspoon each paprika and dry mustard
½-1 teaspoon garlic, or to taste
½ cup vinegar
1 large bottle Worcestershire sauce

Sauté onions in margarine. Add remaining ingredients, except vinegar and Worcestershire sauce, and bring to a boil. Simmer for 30 minutes. Add vinegar and Worcestershire and check seasonings. Simmer for 1 hour. Makes 1 quart. This is better when made the day before.

Mrs. Tom A. Flanagan, Jr.
(Sarah Nabors)

BASTING SAUCE FOR BARBECUING

½ cup cooking oil
¼ pound butter or margarine
Little less than ⅓ cup vinegar
1 teaspoon prepared mustard
2 Tablespoons Worcestershire sauce
⅓ cup fresh lemon juice, strained
1 Tablespoon garlic salt
1 Tablespoon chili powder
3 beef bouillon cubes dissolved in ½ cup boiling water
2 Tablespoons soy sauce
1 teaspoon, or more, red pepper to taste
3 teaspoons brown sugar
3 Tablespoons ketchup

Heat combined ingredients. Inject sauce into meat (large syringe is ideal) before and during cooking. Use with roasts, wild ducks, turkeys, etc., both for brushing meat and injecting with syringe.

Jim Amuny

SAUCE FOR PHEASANT

½ cup onion, minced
1 box (or can) mushrooms
4 Tablespoons butter
4 Tablespoons flour
1 cup cream
1 carton sour cream
½ teaspoon each paprika and pepper
1 teaspoon salt

Sauté onion and mushrooms in butter until done. Cook about 10 minutes at low heat. Stir in flour. Slowly stir in cream and let thicken. Add sour cream. Season with paprika, pepper, and salt. Pour on cooked pheasant and serve.

Mary Walters

VENISON BASTING SAUCE

¾ cup onion, chopped
½ cup Wesson oil
¾ cup water
¾ cup ketchup
⅓ cup lemon juice
3 Tablespoons sugar
3 Tablespoons Worcestershire sauce
2 teaspoons salt
½ teaspoon pepper

Cook onion in oil until tender. Add remaining ingredients. Simmer 15 minutes. Sear meat on both sides, then brush with sauce each time meat is turned. Serve remaining sauce. Sauce may be kept indefinitely in covered jar in refrigerator.

If you do not like venison, you will with this sauce on it. Wonderful on chicken, steak, and hamburgers, too.

Daphne and Jack Knapp

TERIYAKI MARINADE

½ inch slice ginger root
1 clove garlic
½ cup soy sauce (preferably Kikkoman)
1 Tablespoon sugar
1 Tablespoon vinegar
1 Tablespoon sherry
Monosodium glutamate (optional)

Break or cut ginger into 3-4 pieces. Drop into blender with garlic. Blend for a few seconds and add remaining ingredients. Blend until ginger and garlic are very fine. May be used on chicken, beef or pork. Overuse of MSG may jade taste buds. Since soy sauce is not a salt substitute, add salt to meat while cooking. Serve with rice or rice pilaf.

Mrs. Henry S. Uchida
(Chico Sakaguchi)

BOURBON GLAZE FOR HAM

1 cup bourbon
1 cup brown sugar, firmly packed
¼ teaspoon ground cloves
1 teaspoon orange peel

Combine all ingredients. Stir until sugar is dissolved. About 30 minutes before ham is cooked, spread ½ the glaze over it. Baste with remaining glaze until ham is done.

Mrs. John W. Huber
(Betty Landry)

HAM SAUCE

1½ teaspoons cornstarch
1 cup cherry juice
2 teaspoons ham drippings
½ cup water or pineapple juice
¼ cup lemon juice
1 teaspoon lemon peel, grated
⅛ teaspoon salt
¼ cup sugar
1 cup canned sour cherries, drained

Blend cornstarch and ¼ cup cherry juice gradually. Stir into heated remaining ingredients, except cherries. Cook and stir to prevent lumps. When thickened, add cherries and simmer 5 minutes to heat through. Serve hot with ham. Does not freeze.

Mrs. William B. Baggett
(Gael Salter)

MUSTARD SAUCE

1½ Tablespoons butter or margarine
1 egg
⅓ cup brown sugar, firmly packed
¼ cup granulated sugar
¼ cup prepared mustard
¼ teaspoon salt
⅛ teaspoon pepper
½ cup cider vinegar

Melt butter in small saucepan. Remove from heat and set aside. In small bowl, using rotary beater, beat remaining ingredients, except vinegar, until well blended. Beat in vinegar. Stir mixture into cooled butter. Mix well. Over medium heat bring to a boil, stirring. Reduce heat and simmer 3 minutes. Serve hot. Makes 1½ cups.

Good with ham or corned beef.

Dr. J. Malcolm Leveque

MINT SAUCE

1½ Tablespoons confectioners sugar
3 Tablespoons water
⅓ cup mint leaves (fresh or dried), finely chopped
½ cup white wine vinegar

Dissolve sugar in heated water, cool, and add mint leaves and vinegar. Make at least ½ hour before serving or as long as the day before. Makes 1 cup. Good with lamb.

Mrs. Robert Boling
(Judi Lee)

CORA'S CRANBERRY AND KUMQUAT SAUCE

¾ pound kumquats
1½ cups water
2½ cups sugar
1 pound fresh cranberries

Halve kumquats and remove seeds. In heavy uncovered saucepan cook with water and sugar about 8 minutes or until a thin syrup forms. Add cranberries and simmer until skins burst (takes a very short time). Pour into jars. Does not keep unless refrigerated.

Mrs. George Hardy Vincent
(Nina LaFleur)

CRANBERRY CONSERVE

1 pound cranberries
3 large oranges, washed, seeded
3 large cooking apples, washed, seeded
Sugar

Grind cranberries, unpeeled oranges and apples together. To each cup of mixture add 1½-2 cups sugar. Mix well and store in refrigerator. Do not cook.

Good with turkey, ducks, etc.

Mrs. Ruth King White

BAKED CRANBERRY SAUCE

1 pound fresh cranberries, washed and culled
2 cups sugar
1 cup orange juice
1 orange, thinly sliced

Layer ingredients in 9x13 inch pan. Bake, uncovered, at 350°F for 1 hour. Sauce will look soupy but gets firm when cold.

A delicious sauce to serve with any poultry or wild game!

Mrs. Max Farrell

ORANGE RAISIN SAUCE

¼ cup sugar
1 Tablespoon flour
1 cup boiling water
1 orange, juice and rind
⅓ cup raisins
1 Tablespoon butter

Mix sugar and flour; add boiling water and cook until clear. Add orange juice and rind, raisins, and butter. Stir. Does not freeze. Serves 8.

Mrs. E. Dale Dickson

JEZEBEL SAUCE

1 jar (16 ounces) pineapple preserves
1 jar (16 ounces) apple jelly
1 can (1½ ounces) dry mustard
1 jar (5 ounces) horseradish
Salt and pepper to taste

Combine all ingredients in mixer. Refrigerate. Delicious accompaniment to all meats. Marvelous over cream cheese served with crackers. Keeps well in refrigerator.

Mrs. David Buttross, Jr.
(Joyce Abraham)

DOC'S HOT PEPPER SAUCE

1 can whole allspice
1 can whole cloves
1 can mace
1 gallon whole hot red peppers, washed, stemmed
1 gallon cider vinegar
1 quart water
1 heaping cup garlic, chopped

Put spices in cheesecloth bag and add to other ingredients which have been premixed. Cook (out of doors, if possible) until peppers are soft. Remove spice bag. Mash mixture through a strainer or fine colander to remove skin and seeds. Keeps indefinitely in typical hot sauce bottle with shaker top.

Dr. Jared Y. Garber

HOT PEPPER SAUCE

4 cups hot peppers (½ red, ½ green)
2 cups white distilled vinegar
2 cloves garlic, thinly sliced
2 teaspoons salt

The best kind of hot pepper to use for this sauce is commonly called "ridge" or "round birds-eye" from the Grand Chenier area. If not available, use regular Tabasco peppers, chopped. Pick peppers with gloves (they burn exposed skin on contact) and wash thoroughly in colander, removing any leaves or stems. Combine all ingredients in saucepan and bring to a boil. Simmer for 4 minutes and let cool. Drain in colander, reserving juice. Place peppers in clear jar with a "shaker" top (vinegar bottles that have a cap with hole in the top are best), add juice to cover, and shake. If there is not enough liquid to cover, add more vinegar. The sauce may be used immediately, but it improves with age. Shake occasionally and add a little vinegar now and then as it depletes. However, it will eventually lose its "hot". This is a *must* for mustard greens, collards, turnips, anything—even eggs. Just leave it on the table and use when and if desired. This is a household staple in Louisiana.

William E. Shaddock

FRESH HORSERADISH

Horseradish root
Distilled white vinegar

Wash root and scrape with carrot scraper. With sharp knife, cut into ¼ inch cubes. Put 1 cup cubes and 1 cup vinegar in blender. Blend on high until mixture makes a rather smooth paste. Refrigerate in jar with tight cap. Keeps for a month or more. Serve with corned beef or roast or in red sauce for shrimp.

Mrs. J. E. Watkins
(Inez "B.C." Knapp)

HOT PEPPER JELLY

6½ cups sugar
1½ cups apple cider vinegar
¼ cup hot peppers, finely chopped
¾ cup bell pepper, finely chopped
1 bottle Certo
4-5 drops green food coloring

In large deep saucepan combine sugar and vinegar. Bring to a rolling (one which cannot be broken down by stirring) boil, stirring constantly. Add hot and bell peppers and cook 2 minutes. Remove from heat; add Certo and green food coloring. Stir continuously for 10 minutes while cooling. Pour into sterilized jars and seal with paraffin.

Warning: Wear rubber gloves when handling hot peppers! If you double this recipe, you must also double the cooling and stirring time. This prevents the chopped pepper from floating to the top.

Mrs. Susan Switzer St. Dizier
Houston, Texas

MUSTARD

1 can Coleman's dry mustard
Apple cider vinegar
2 eggs
1 cup sugar
Pinch salt

Empty mustard can and fill with apple cider vinegar. Blend vinegar and mustard and let sit overnight. The following day, beat eggs in top of double boiler with sugar and salt. Add mustard mixture and cook over boiling water until thick. Stir occasionally. Good with ham or any kind of meat!

Mrs. Paul Kitt
(Betty Cook)

How to preserve Louisiana figs: First wash, discarding broken ones. In large pot place equal weights of figs and sugar, add a little water. Simmer, lightly covered, until figs are opaque. Turn off heat; add 1 sliced lemon; let sit in pot for about 4 hours to make figs plump. Reheat and pour into sterilized Mason jars. Cool on rack. Jar tops will make a popping sound as they cool.

FIG PRESERVES FOR DIETERS

6 cups figs, peeled, mashed
½ cup water
6 small packets (.035 ounce size) artificial sweetener
2 envelopes strawberry D-zerta
1 package Knox unflavored gelatine

Cook figs with water and sweetener for 35 minutes on medium heat, stirring occasionally. Add D-zerta and cook for 10 minutes more. Just before taking off heat add the gelatine. Cool, put in small containers, and freeze. Remove containers from freezer as needed and refrigerate.

Mrs. Sam Liggio

FIG JELLO PRESERVES

6 cups peeled figs
6 cups sugar
2 packages (family size) Jello of desired flavor

Stir figs and sugar to boiling point. Add Jello, stir well, and cook 24 minutes only. Pour into jars, seal, let stand overnight, then tighten seal. Preserves assume flavor of Jello used.

Mrs. F. D. Jourdan
Lafayette, Louisiana

MAYHAW JELLY

2-4 quarts mayhaws
2 cups sugar

Wash berries thoroughly and cull. Cover with water and boil until skins pop. Reduce heat and simmer about 45 minutes. Mash berries, straining juice through a muslin cloth or stocking into a wide mouthed jar. Cover jar and let stand to cool. Combine 2 level cups sugar with 3 cups juice. Bring to a boil and cook about 20 minutes, reducing heat when mixture begins to thicken or is a little thick when dropped from a spoon. Return to boil for an instant before finishing. Ladle into sterilized jars and let stand until jelled (may take several hours). If no jelling occurs, return mixture to pot, add more sugar and recook. When jelled, seal jars with paraffin and a cap. Juice may be frozen for later use in making the jelly. Crabapples may be substituted for mayhaws.

Mrs. Lionel L. de la Houssaye
(Marie Louise "Zizi" Ogden)

BLACKBERRY PRESERVES

2½ cups sugar
½ cup water
2 quarts ripe berries, washed and sorted

Mix sugar and water in an enamel pot and bring to boil. Add berries, bring to boil, and cook 1 minute or so. Remove from heat, cover, and cool overnight. Return to stove and cook at high temperature. Bring to boil and cook rapidly until berries are plump and shiny, about 3 minutes. Remove from heat, pour into sterile jars, and seal. Makes 6-8 cups.

Joe Muth
Metairie, La.

STRAWBERRY PRESERVES

2 quarts perfect, not overripe, strawberries
8 cups granulated sugar
4 Tablespoons lemon juice
Paraffin
8 jars (8 ounce size) with lids

Make no more than 2 quarts of preserves at a time. Stem and wash strawberries. Add sugar and lemon juice, mixing gently to avoid crushing fruit (hands do the best job). Allow mixture to stand in a non-metallic bowl 3 hours or so to draw out juice. Remove to a kettle or roasting pan large enough to accommodate rapidly rising liquid when it boils. Bring to a rolling boil and cook 15 minutes. Skim off scum. Pour cooked preserves into a non-metallic bowl, cover, and let stand until next day, stirring gently from time to time. This last step is the secret of really fine-quality strawberry preserves. It plumps up the berries and counteracts their tendency to float to the top. If, after 1 day, the preserves are not yet thick enough, pour into large shallow platters and allow to dry until desired consistency, which may take several days. When ready, pour into jars and seal with 2 thin coats of paraffin and a lid. To make strawberry jam or preserves of consistently fine quality, gentle handling is a must.

Mrs. Lionel L. de la Houssaye
(Marie Louise "Zizi" Ogden)

CARROT RELISH

4 cups carrots, ground
4 cups celery, finely chopped
2 green bell peppers, slivered
2 red bell peppers, slivered
4 tart apples, ground
2 cups sugar
2 cups vinegar
2 Tablespoons salt
2 teaspoons celery seed

Mix all ingredients well. In a large pot cook, covered, until there is a color change, about 45 minutes. Pour into sterilized jars while hot and seal.

Mrs. Thomas Graham

RED RELISH

12 onions, coarsely chopped
6 cans tomatoes, chopped
12 bell peppers, coarsely chopped
3 cups sugar
3 cups white vinegar
1 heaping Tablespoon allspice
1 heaping Tablespoon cinnamon
Salt and Tabasco to taste

Sterilize 12 pint Mason jars. Cook vegetables, sugar, and vinegar about 2 hours to consistency of a thick sauce. Stir almost constantly toward the end to prevent burning. Add seasonings during last ½ hour.

Great with roast beef and duck. Good on sandwiches too! Easy to make but lots of chopping.

Mrs. Jack Thielen
(Della "Dudie" Krause)

SWEET TOMATO CHUTNEY

1 whole bulb garlic, peeled and chopped
1 piece fresh ginger (2 x 1 x 1 inch), peeled and coarsely chopped
1½ cups wine vinegar
1 can (12 ounces) whole tomatoes
1½ cups granulated sugar
1½ teaspoons salt
⅛ teaspoon cayenne pepper
2 Tablespoons blanched almonds, slivered
2 Tablespoons golden raisins

Blend garlic, ginger, and ½ cup vinegar in blender at high speed until smooth. Place undrained tomatoes, remaining vinegar, salt, and pepper into a heavy bottomed 4 quart pot with a non-metallic finish. Bring to a boil. Lower heat and simmer, uncovered, for 1½-2 hours, or until chutney thickens. (A film should cling to a spoon when dipped into the mixture.) While cooking, stir occasionally at first, more frequently as mixture thickens. Lower heat when thickening begins. The more liquid the tomatoes, the longer will be the cooking time. Add almonds and raisins when almost done and simmer for another 5 minutes, stirring constantly. Allow to cool, and bottle. Will keep for months refrigerated. Makes 2½ cups of honey-thick chutney.

Morris D. Ramsey

REFRIGERATOR DILL PICKLES

4 small to medium cucumbers
1 cup white onions (pickling onion about 1 inch in diameter)
1-2 hot peppers (about 1½ inches long)
Dill weed, 1 heaping teaspoon dried, or 1 sprig fresh (preferably fresh)
3 rounded Tablespoons salt per quart
1½ cups vinegar per quart
2 cups water per quart

Use fresh, tender, unpeeled cucumbers. Wash and remove ends. Cut lengthwise. Peel onions. Pack jar with alternate layers of cucumber and onion with dill weed on top and bottom. Add salt, vinegar, and water. Seal and refrigerate. Let pickles stand at least 24 hours before using. Will keep for weeks in refrigerator.

Mrs. E. R. Haug

PICKLED TURNIPS

Turnips, garden fresh
Apple cider vinegar
Salt and black pepper to taste
Red pepper (fresh, ground, or sauce)
Red beet juice (optional)

Wash and cut turnips in sections. Place in jars. Bring to a boil vinegar, salt, peppers and beet juice. Pour over turnips; let cool; cover jars tightly and let set a week or more before serving. Refrigerate before serving.

Tasty as an appetizer. Very different. Old family recipe.

Mrs. David Buttross, Jr.
(Joyce Abraham)

PICKLED OKRA

Young tender okra to fill 4 pint jars
Celery seed
Mustard seed
Dill seed
Red pepper, crushed
Garlic to taste
4 cups vinegar
2 cups water
½ cup salt

Separate okra according to size and soak 1 hour in cold water. Dry with terry cloth. Pack in pint jars (1 pod up, 1 down). To each jar add 1 teaspoon each of celery seed, mustard seed, dill seed, and crushed red pepper, and 1-2 garlic cloves (to taste). Bring remaining ingredients to a hard, rolling boil and pour over okra. Seal jars tightly. Let stand until cool; retighten lids. Use after 2-3 weeks. Makes 4 pints.

String beans may be substituted for okra.

Mrs. Fred L. Colomb
Mrs. F. D. Jourdan
Lafayette, La.

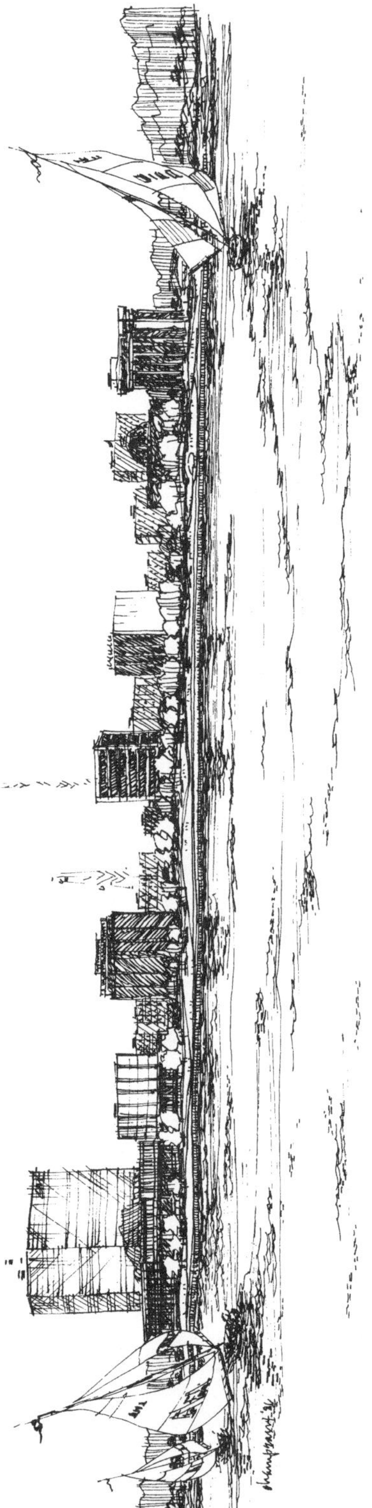

MODERN LAKE CHARLES

The blue waters of Lake Charles reflect a modern skyline. Business, recreational, and industrial complexes line the shores of the 1,000 acre lake, located in the heart of the city. Dating back to the 1770's, Lake Charles is one of the oldest communities in the state.

Blessed with an abundance of natural resources — water, oil, natural gas, salt, sulfur, and timber — and a location along a navigable river with a deep water port, Lake Charles boasts a huge petrochemical, chemical, and petroleum complex. It is the business and banking core of Southwest Louisiana as well as the center of rice production and shipping. The mild climate, beautiful waters, and white sand beaches offer year-round recreational opportunities; the Civic Center and adjacent park, peaceful retreats for leisurely pursuits.

With a population of more than 80,000, Lake Charles is both the cultural and educational hub of Southwest Louisiana. It is the home of McNeese State University, of ballet, symphony, and theater groups noted throughout the state and the nation.

Steeped in the romantic lore of the swashbuckling Jean Lafitte, and famed for its warm Cajun hospitality and fine Creole cuisine, Lake Charles is aptly called "The Treasure City" of Louisiana's Gulf Coast.

MAJESTIC HOTEL BLACK BOTTOM PIE

CRUST

20 small ginger snaps, crushed
5 Tablespoons butter, melted

FILLING

2 cups milk
1 Tablespoon cornstarch
½ cup sugar
4 egg yolks
1½ squares semi-sweet chocolate, melted
1 teaspoon vanilla
1 package gelatin
4 Tablespoons cold water
4 egg whites, beaten
½ teaspoon cream of tartar
3 teaspoons sugar
Pinch salt
3-5 teaspoons bourbon or rum whiskey
1 cup heavy cream, whipped with a little sugar
Semi-sweet chocolate shavings

CRUST: Mix ginger snaps with butter and press into pie pan. Bake 10 minutes at 325°F. Let cool.

FILLING: Cook milk, cornstarch, and sugar in double boiler over low heat until well scalded. Add egg yolks and cook until mixture coats spoon. Remove 1 cup and add melted chocolate and vanilla to it. Set aside. Soak gelatin in the cold water. Add to custard in double boiler and let cool. Beat egg whites with cream of tartar, sugar, and salt. When gelatin mixture is cool, add it to egg whites. Add bourbon. Pour chocolate mixture into pie crust, cool, and follow with custard mixture. Top with whipped cream and garnish with chocolate curls. Refrigerate for several hours until set. Serves 6-8.

Older Lake Charles residents and guests fondly recall the days of the Majestic Hotel where once "Miss Emma" Michie extended the warmest welcome and finest cuisine in Southwest Louisiana.

Mrs. Malcolm Powell
(Evelyn Knapp)

NEVER-FAIL PASTRY

2 cups all purpose flour, sifted
¼ teaspoon salt
1 teaspoon baking powder
Pinch sugar
1 cup Crisco
Ice water or cold milk (about ¼ cup) (Ice water for custard pies, milk for fruit pies)

Combine dry ingredients with Crisco, cutting well until about size of green peas. Add water or milk until pastry is right consistency. Roll out smoothly on floured pastry board. Dough will be rather soft. If it crumbles at first shape into ball and roll out again. It will still be short and not tough. Makes 2 (9 inch) shells.

NOTE: *Before* adding filling, bake about 5 minutes in preheated 400°F oven until pastry "sets." This prevents it from being soft and soggy on bottom. Then fill and bake. Freezes.

Good for beginners: It never fails and is always crisp.

Mrs. Rector Land

DUTCH APPLE CRISP

1 can apples (for pie filling)
1 cup all purpose flour, sifted
¾ cup brown sugar
1 teaspoon ground cinnamon
½ teaspoon nutmeg
¼ teaspoon salt
½ cup butter

Preheat oven to 350°F. Place apples in generously greased 1½ quart shallow baking dish. Mix remaining ingredients except butter. Cut in butter until crumbly. Sprinkle over apples. Bake 40 minutes or until topping is slightly crusty and brown. Serve warm with scoop of vanilla ice cream. Serves 6.

Yummy, quick, and easy.

Mrs. Joseph A. Brame
(Cindy Dickson)

BUTTERMILK PIE

1¾ cups sugar
¼ cup flour
½ cup buttermilk
½ cup butter, melted
3 eggs
2 Tablespoons lemon juice
1 teaspoon vanilla
Pinch of salt
1 pie shell (9 inch), unbaked

Combine all ingredients in the order given. Mix well and pour into pie shell. Bake at 350°F for 1 hour, or until brown. Filling is set when a light crust forms on top. Serves 8.

Mrs. Robert Dow
(Pat Welch)

BUTTER PIE

½ cup butter
1½ cups sugar
3 egg yolks
2 Tablespoons flour
½ cup half and half
1 teaspoon vanilla
1 pie shell, unbaked

Cream butter and sugar in mixer bowl. Add egg yolks and mix. Stir in flour, half and half, and vanilla. Pour into pie shell and bake at 425°F for 10 minutes, or until nicely brown. Reduce heat to 325°F and continue baking 30-40 minutes, or until set. Remove from oven and spread with meringue. Bake at 350°F until nicely browned.

MERINGUE

3 egg whites
⅛ teaspoon cream of tartar
Pinch of salt
1 teaspoon vanilla
8 Tablespoons sugar

MERINGUE

Make meringue by combining all ingredients except sugar, in mixer bowl. Beat until stiff and slowly add the sugar, beating well. Serves 8.

Mrs. Charles Rogers
Cameron, La.

To prevent meringue from weeping, cool it to room temperature before refrigerating. And never spread meringue on warm filling.

CHOCOLATE SWIRL PIE

½ cup sugar
1 envelope unflavored gelatin
Pinch of salt
1 cup milk
2 egg yolks, beaten
1 package (6 ounces) semi-sweet chocolate chips
⅓ cup rum
2 egg whites, beaten
¼ cup sugar
1 cup heavy cream, whipped with 2 teaspoons vanilla
1 pie shell, baked

In a heavy saucepan, combine sugar, gelatin, and salt. Stir in milk and egg yolks over low heat until thick. Remove from heat. Add chocolate and stir until melted. Add rum and chill until partially set. Beat egg whites to soft peaks; gradually add ¼ cup sugar, beating until stiff peaks form. Fold whipped cream mixture and egg white mixture together. Layer cream and chocolate mixtures in pie shell, ending with cream mixture. Use knife to swirl, getting a marble effect. Refrigerate. Serve cold. Serves 8.

Mrs. Diane Coyle Scofield

AUNTIE'S OLD TYME CHOCOLATE PIE

1 cup sugar
2 heaping Tablespoons flour
3 heaping Tablespoons cocoa or more for a deeper chocolate
1 cup milk
3 egg yolks, beaten
½ stick butter, sliced
1 Tablespoon vanilla
1 pie shell (8 inch), baked

MERINGUE

3 egg whites
¼ teaspoon cream of tartar
Pinch salt
1 teaspoon vanilla
6-7 Tablespoons sugar

Combine thoroughly first 3 dry ingredients. Add milk to beaten egg yolks and beat well. Mix dry ingredients with wet ones in saucepan or double boiler, cooking slowly over low heat until thick. Remove from heat and stir in butter and vanilla. If lumpy toward the end, beat until smooth with a hand beater or wire whisk. Pour into pie shell.

MERINGUE: Combine all ingredients except sugar. Beat until soft peaks form; then slowly add sugar 1 teaspoon at a time. Beat until stiff. Spread on pie with silver knife. Swirl in many little peaks. Brown at 325-350°F. Serves 6-8.

Mrs. William B. Baggett
(Gael Salter)

GERMAN SWEET CHOCOLATE PIE

1 package (4 ounces) Baker's German sweet chocolate, melted
¼ cup butter, melted
1⅔ cups evaporated milk
1½ cups sugar
3 Tablespoons cornstarch
⅛ teaspoon salt
2 eggs
1 teaspoon vanilla
1 pie shell (9 inch), highly fluted
1⅓ cups Baker's angel flake coconut
½ cup pecans, chopped

Melt chocolate with butter over low heat, stirring until blended. Remove from heat and gradually blend with milk. Set aside. In a bowl mix sugar, cornstarch, and salt; then thoroughly beat in eggs and vanilla. Gradually blend in chocolate mixture. Pour into pie shell. Combine coconut and pecans and sprinkle over filling. Bake at 375°F for 45-50 minutes until brown filling is soft. Serves 8.

Mrs. Odile Wilson

FUDGE PIE

2 squares bitter chocolate
2 Tablespoons butter
¾ cup flour
1 Tablespoon plus ½ teaspoon baking powder
¼ teaspoon salt
8 Tablespoons sugar
⅓ cup pecans, chopped
5½ Tablespoons milk
½ teaspoon vanilla
1 pie shell (9 inch), unbaked

TOPPING

1 square bitter chocolate
¾ cup sugar
1 cup water

Melt chocolate with butter. Sift together next four ingredients and add pecans, milk, and vanilla. Mix until smooth and add chocolate mixture. Pour into pie shell.

TOPPING

Mix topping ingredients and stir over medium heat until dissolved. Bring to boil without stirring. Pour over mixture in pie shell. Bake at 375°F for 30 minutes. Serves 6-8.

Delicious served with scoop of ice cream.

Mrs. G. W. Pomeroy

Rolling excess flour into pie dough will toughen it.

DOUBLE LEMON MERINGUE PIE

Pastry for one crust (9 inch) with 1 teaspoon grated lemon peel added to dry ingredients

FILLING

1½ cups sugar
7 Tablespoons cornstarch
¼ teaspoon salt
½ cup cold water
1 cup boiling water
3 egg yolks, slightly beaten
1 teaspoon lemon peel, grated
½ cup lemon juice

MERINGUE

3 egg whites
1 teaspoon lemon juice
6 Tablespoons sugar

Line pie pan with pastry. Bake and cool.

FILLING: Thoroughly mix dry ingredients in heavy saucepan. Stir in cold water. Add boiling water gradually, stirring constantly. Bring rapidly to boiling; reduce heat. Cook and stir about 10 minutes longer. Stir about ½ cup of hot mixture into beaten egg yolks. Immediately blend into mixture in pan. Stir and cook over low heat 3 minutes. Blend in next 2 ingredients. Cool. Pour into cooled pastry shell.

MERINGUE: Beat 3 egg whites and 1 teaspoon lemon juice until frothy. Gradually add sugar, beating constantly until stiff peaks form. Pile lightly over pie filling, sealing meringue to pastry edge. Bake at 350°F for 15 minutes, or until meringue is delicately browned. Cool on rack until ready to serve. Serves 8.

Always use real lemons and this pie will beat all other lemon pies.

Mrs. Leland Parra
(Nancy Keefe)

JAPANESE FRUIT PIE

1 stick margarine, melted
2 eggs, well beaten
½ cup each pecans, raisins, and coconut
1 cup sugar
1 Tablespoon vinegar
1 pie shell (8 inch), unbaked

Melt margarine and let cool. Add remaining ingredients. Bake in pie shell at 325°F for 40 minutes. Serves 6-8.

Delicious served hot with ice cream.

Myra Simmons

Since sugar draws juice from fruit, do not add it to filled fruit pie shell until last minute.

GRASSHOPPER PIE

15 Oreo cookies, crushed
2½-3 Tablespoons butter, melted
21 marshmallows
½ cup hot milk
3 teaspoons crème de cacao
3 teaspoons crème de menthe
Few drops green food coloring
½ pint heavy cream, whipped
German semi-sweet chocolate curls

Must be made one day ahead of time. Mix cookies with melted butter. Press into 8 inch pie plate, and chill 1 hour. Melt marshmallows in hot milk over heat. Do not boil. Let cool. Stir both liqueurs and food coloring into whipped cream. Fold whipped cream into cooled marshmallow mixture. Pour into crust. Refrigerate overnight. Garnish with chocolate curls to serve. Serves 6-8.

Mrs. Robert W. Rice
(June Arnold)

KEY LIME PIE

1 Tablespoon unflavored gelatin
1 cup sugar
¼ teaspoon salt
4 eggs, separated
½ cup lime juice
¼ cup water
1 teaspoon lime peel, grated
Few drops green food coloring
1 cup heavy cream, whipped
1 graham cracker crust (9 inch), baked

In a saucepan combine gelatin, ½ cup sugar, and salt. Beat egg yolks, lime juice, and water. Stir into gelatin. Cook and stir over medium heat until mixture comes to a boil. Remove from heat; add lime peel. Add coloring to give pale green color. Chill, stirring occasionally, until mixture mounds slightly when dropped from spoon. Beat egg whites to soft peaks; gradually add ½ cup sugar and beat to stiff peaks. Fold gelatin mixture into egg whites. Fold in whipped cream. Place in cooled graham cracker crust. Chill until firm. Top edges with whipped cream and decorate with lime peel. Serves 6-8.

Mrs. Ben J. Guilbeau
(Joanna Bertrand)

Roll out pie dough between two plastic sheets. Peel off top; invert into pie plate; peel off bottom sheet.

One spoonful of sugar added to pie dough will make the crust brown beautifully.

LITTLE PECAN TARTS

PASTRY

1 package (3 ounces) cream cheese, softened
½ cup butter, softened
1 cup flour, sifted

FILLING

1 generous cup pecans, coarsely chopped
1½ cups brown sugar
2 Tablespoons butter, softened
2 eggs
1 teaspoon vanilla
Dash of salt

PASTRY: Blend softened cream cheese and butter. Stir in flour. Chill 1 hour. Shape into 1 inch balls. Place in 1¾ inch ungreased muffin cups. (Teflon is good.) Press dough against bottom and sides.

FILLING: Place ½ of pecans in pastry lined cups. Beat remaining ingredients until smooth. Place in pastry cups and top with remaining pecans. Bake at 350°F for 25 minutes, or until filling sets. Serves 8-10.

From the recipes of
Nina Nash Sewell

CHOCOLATE PECAN PIE

1 stick butter or margarine, melted
1 cup sugar
2 eggs
½ cup flour
1 teaspoon vanilla
1 cup pecans, chopped
1 package (6 ounces) chocolate chips
1 pie shell, unbaked

Add melted butter to sugar and cream well. Add eggs one at a time and beat after each. Stir in flour, vanilla, and pecans. Mix well. Fill bottom of pie shell with the chocolate chips, and cover with filling. Bake at 350°F for 40-45 minutes. Better served warm. Freezes. Serves 8.

Mrs. Adolph S. Marx
(Mathilde Weil)

PECAN SURPRISE PIE

4 egg whites, beaten
20 Waverly crackers, or saltines, crumbled
1 pinch cream of tartar
1 cup sugar
1 cup pecans, chopped

Grease and flour pie pan. Beat egg whites until "fluffy" but not stiff. Add crumbs. Add remaining ingredients, and mix well. Bake in pie pan at 300°F until a light brown. Chill in refrigerator. Top with whipped cream before serving. Serves 6-8.

Mrs. Scott McClain
(Janice Albritton)

DESSERTS — PIES

PECAN PIE

1 pie shell (9 inch) or 6-8 individual pie shells
1 cup pecans, chopped
3 eggs
¾ cup white Karo syrup
¾ cup brown sugar, dark or light
½ stick margarine
Dash of salt

Preheat oven to 350°F. Place pecans on unbaked pie shell. Combine remaining ingredients and pour over pecans. Bake for 1 hour. Freezes. Serves 6-8.

Delicious served with vanilla ice cream.

From the recipes of
Helen Guchereau Caldarera

GRANDPA'S KARO PECAN PIE

1 cup dark Karo syrup
1 cup sugar
3 eggs, slightly beaten
1 Tablespoon cornstarch or flour
1 Tablespoon butter
¼ teaspoon each allspice and cinnamon
¾ teaspoon nutmeg
¾ cup pecans
1 pie shell (9 inch), unbaked

Mix Karo and sugar. Add remaining ingredients except pecans. Place pecans in pie shell and cover with mixture. Bake at 425°F for 10 minutes. Reduce heat to 350°F and cook for 30 minutes more or until inserted toothpick comes out clean. Freezes. Serves 6-8.

Mrs. W. Kent Cutrer
(Linda Arnold)

KENTUCKY PECAN PIE

1 cup white corn syrup
1 cup dark brown sugar
⅓ teaspoon salt
⅓ cup margarine, melted
2 teaspoons vanilla
3 eggs, slightly beaten
1 heaping cup whole pecans
1 pie shell (9 inch), unbaked

Preheat oven to 350°F. Combine syrup, sugar, salt, margarine, vanilla, and mix well. Add eggs. Pour into pie shell. Sprinkle with pecans. Bake for about 45 minutes. Freezes. Serves 8.

When cool, you may top with whipped cream or ice cream.

Mrs. Leland J. Parra
(Nancy Keefe)

GREAT PUMPKIN PIE

Whole pumpkin

FILLING

1 cup raisins
1¾ cups cooked fresh pumpkin
½ teaspoon salt
1¾ cups milk
3 eggs
⅔ cup brown sugar (packed)
2 teaspoons cinnamon
¼ teaspoon cloves
½ teaspoon each ginger and nutmeg
½ cup pecans, chopped
1 pie shell (9 inch), unbaked

PREPARATION OF FRESH PUMPKIN

Scoop out inside. Cut pumpkin into large chunks, peel off outer skin, and dice. Place in unseasoned water and cook until very tender. Mash and drain.

FILLING

In saucepan boil raisins in water to cover for 2 minutes. Drain and set aside. Blend remaining ingredients, except pecans. Add raisins and stir in pecans. Fill uncooked pie shell and bake at 425°F for 45-50 minutes or until inserted knife comes out clean. Both filling and cooked pumpkin freeze.

Must be made from the great pumpkin at Halloween! Canned pumpkin is not the same. Top with Cool Whip while warm.

Mrs. Robert E. Christman
(Louise Cornay)

DREAMY PUMPKIN PIE

⅔ cup sugar
1 envelope unflavored gelatin
1 teaspoon ground cinnamon
½ teaspoon salt
¼ teaspoon ground nutmeg
3 eggs, separated
¾ cup milk
1 cup cooked or canned pumpkin
⅓ cup sugar
1 graham cracker crust (9 inch)
½ cup heavy cream, whipped
½ cup flaked coconut, toasted

In large saucepan combine ⅔ cup sugar, gelatin, cinnamon, salt, and nutmeg. Combine slightly beaten egg yolks and milk; add to gelatin mixture. Cook, stirring constantly until slightly thickened. Stir in pumpkin. Chill until mixture mounds slightly when spooned, stirring often. Beat egg whites until soft peaks form. Gradually add ⅓ cup sugar, beating to stiff peaks. Fold chilled pumpkin mixture into egg whites. Place in graham cracker crust. Chill until firm. Just before serving, whip cream; spoon in dollops in center of pie. Sprinkle with toasted coconut. Serves 8.

Mrs. James J. Cochran
(Jacquetta Pleimann)

HARVEST SWEET POTATO JELLO PIE

1 package (3 ounces) orange Jello
1 cup boiling water
½ cup cold water
2 eggs
½ teaspoon cinnamon
1 can (16 ounces) pumpkin or sweet potatoes
¾ cup sugar
1 cup sour cream
¼ cup evaporated milk
1 teaspoon orange flavoring
1 pie shell (9 inch), baked

Dissolve Jello in hot water, stir in cold water, and chill until set. Beat eggs with cinnamon in a heavy saucepan. Add remaining ingredients and cook over low heat until thickened. Remove from heat and cool. Beat Jello mixture at high speed. Reduce to lowest speed and gradually feed in custard mixture. When thoroughly mixed, pour into baked pie shell. Refrigerate several hours. Serve with whipped cream or a non dairy topping. Freezes. Decorated like a pumpkin face it is a cute Halloween dish. Serves 8.

Mrs. Eunice Surles

HEAVENLY STRAWBERRY PIE

1½ cups sugar
5 Tablespoons cornstarch mixed with 2 Tablespoons water
1 king size 7 Up and water to fill 2¼ cups liquid (total)
1 teaspoon red food coloring
1 pie shell (9 inch), baked
1 pint fresh strawberries, halved or sliced
Whipped cream

Cook over low heat the sugar, cornstarch, and liquid mixture until thick and clear, about 30 minutes, stirring frequently. Add red food coloring and let cool. Pour ½ of mixture in pie shell. Add strawberries and pour in remaining mixture. Top with whipped cream. Serves 6-8.

Mrs. Sheldon Barre
(Bernadette Phillips)

BLACK WALNUT ROLL

ROLL

1 cup superfine sugar
8 eggs, separated
½ cup black walnuts (fresh or canned), crushed
¼ teaspoon black walnut extract
Confectioners sugar

FILLING

1½ cups heavy cream
3 Tablespoons confectioners sugar
Fresh vanilla beans, 2 inches, scraped
2 ounces cognac

SAUCE

1 cup granulated sugar
½ cup boiling water
½ cup light cream
½ cup black walnuts, chopped
Vanilla bean, 1 inch, scraped

ROLL

Add sugar to egg yolks, beat until pale yellow and ribbons string from mixer blades. Stir in walnuts, add extract. Beat egg whites until they form soft peaks. Fold egg whites and egg yolk mixture together, cutting in with a spatula; not beating. Oil a jelly roll pan, 18x12x1 inch, and cover with waxed paper extending ½ inch over ends. Do not oil top of paper. Spread the batter evenly on paper. Bake at 350°F for 17 minutes or until surface shine is gone, but do not overcook. Remove pan from oven, cover top of cake with 2 layers of paper towels wrung out in ice water, and cover these with 1 dry paper towel. Cool at room temperature 20 minutes. Peel towels off carefully, cut along sides of pan with knife to loosen, and lift ends of waxed paper to loosen. Spread out 2 overlapping pieces of waxed paper and dust top of cake with confectioners sugar, flip over on waxed paper, and gently pull other paper from the bottom.

FILLING

Pour cream into cold metal bowl and beat until it begins to thicken. Add confectioners sugar and 2 inches scraped fresh vanilla bean (split the bean and scrape out the tiny black seeds). Add the cognac and continue beating until the cream holds its shape. Spread filling over the cake and roll it up; roll top third over; then using waxed paper roll it again, dusting top with confectioners sugar to hide cracks.

SAUCE

Spread sugar in heavy frying pan and melt over low heat until a golden brown liquid. Do not burn. Slowly add boiling water, stirring continuously for 5 minutes. Remove from heat, stir in light cream. Add chopped walnuts and 1 inch scraped vanilla bean. Serve sauce warm over the cold roll. Serves 8-10.

Ed McCreedy

AMBROSIA CAKE

CAKE

1 medium orange, unpeeled, cut in chunks
1 yellow cake mix or yellow cake recipe of your choice

AMBROSIA FILLING

1½ cups sugar
3 Tablespoons cornstarch
½ teaspoon salt
1 cup water
¼ cup butter or margarine
1 can (3½ ounces) flaked coconut

FROSTING

1 or 2 packages of fluffy white frosting mix or a butter cream frosting of your own

CAKE

Blend orange chunks until almost smooth using low speed on electric blender or metal blade of food processor to make ⅔ cup ground orange. Prepare cake according to directions. Fold ⅓ cup of the ground orange into cake mix batter, reserving remaining ⅓ cup ground orange for filling. Bake, according to directions, in 2 paper lined 8 inch round pans. Cool 5 minutes. Remove from pans; cool on racks. Wrap in waxed paper or foil and refrigerate 4 hours or more.

AMBROSIA FILLING

Combine sugar, cornstarch, and salt. Slowly add water and mix well. Add butter or margarine and ⅓ cup ground orange. Cook and stir until mixture thickens and comes to a boil; cook 2 minutes. Cool; stir in coconut.

Now slice the hump off one layer and make a small notch on one side. Split layer in two and place bottom on a plate. Cover with ⅓ of ambrosia. Matching notches, replace top and cover with ½ of remaining ambrosia. Notch and split other layer; place bottom on top of already prepared layers and cover with remaining ambrosia. Top with final layer. Frost top and sides.

Mrs. Patrick J. Unkel
(Barbara Perez)

Use a fine grater to remove overly-browned edges from a cake.

ANGEL COCONUT POUND CAKE

1 cup Crisco
1 stick margarine
2½ cups sugar
5 eggs
1 cup milk
3 cups flour
¼ teaspoon salt
1 teaspoon baking powder
1 Tablespoon coconut flavoring
1 cup Angel Flake coconut

Cream Crisco and margarine. Add sugar and cream again. Add eggs, one at a time, beating after each. Combine milk with flour sifted with salt and baking powder and add gradually to sugar-egg mixture. Add coconut flavoring and fold in coconut. Bake in tube pan at 300°F for 1½ hours. Freezes. Serves 12-15, thinly sliced.

Mrs. B. S. Bell
White Castle, La.

STUFFED ANGEL FOOD CAKE

1 angel food cake
CUSTARD
⅔ cup sugar
½ teaspoon salt
6 Tablespoons flour
1 cup homogenized milk
1 cup evaporated milk
4 egg yolks, beaten
4 teaspoons vanilla
1½ pints heavy cream, whipped
Confectioners sugar

Make cake a day in advance of serving. Slice a thin layer off top of cake; set aside. Remove interior, leaving a wall thick enough to stand, and break into small pieces. Set aside to mix with custard filling.

CUSTARD: Mix together sugar, salt, and flour in saucepan. Stir in milk. Cook on low heat until thick; remove from heat. Stir a little of this mixture into beaten egg yolks, then return to custard. Return custard to stove and heat to boiling point. Cool and add 2 teaspoons of vanilla. Sweeten whipped cream to taste with confectioners sugar and 2 teaspoons vanilla. Blend 1 cup whipped cream into custard.

Put layers of custard, broken cake pieces, and whipped cream in hollowed out cake. (Save enough whipped cream to frost cake.) Replace top of cake and frost with remaining whipped cream. Place in freezer uncovered. When whipped cream frosting is hard, cover tightly with foil. Uncover to defrost. Serves 12 or more.

Agnes Y. Webb

APPLE GINGERBREAD UPSIDE DOWN CAKE

TOPPING

2 Tablespoons butter
1 cup brown sugar
1 teaspoon cinnamon
2-3 apples, cored, thinly sliced

CAKE

¼ cup shortening
¾ cup brown sugar
1 egg, well beaten
½ cup molasses
1¼ cups all purpose flour
¾ teaspoon baking soda
½ teaspoon each ginger, cinnamon, and salt
½ cup boiling water or sour milk

TOPPING

Melt butter in heavy skillet. Add brown sugar and cinnamon and arrange apples in an overlapping layer on top. Cover with cake batter.

CAKE

Cream shortening, add sugar. Add beaten egg and molasses. Sift flour with soda, spices, and salt. Add to molasses mixture alternating with hot water or milk. Bake at 350°F for 30-40 minutes in iron skillet.

Mrs. Lloyd J. Keefe

APPLE TORTE

1 cup sugar
4 Tablespoons butter
1 egg
1 teaspoon baking soda
1 cup flour
1 teaspoon cinnamon
¼ teaspoon nutmeg
2 cups apples, peeled and finely chopped
½ cup pecans
1 teaspoon vanilla

Mix in order given. Bake in a 9x9 inch greased pan at 350°F for 35 minutes. Serve warm with Spicy Sauce and whipped cream. Serves 8.

SPICY SAUCE

Mix dry ingredients thoroughly. Add boiling water and butter. Cook until thick. Add vanilla.

Mrs. James H. deCordova
Jennings, La.

SPICY SAUCE

1 cup sugar
¼ teaspoon each cinnamon and nutmeg
1½ Tablespoons cornstarch
1 cup boiling water
3 Tablespoons butter
1 teaspoon vanilla

CARAMEL NUT POUND CAKE

1 cup butter
½ cup shortening
1 box light brown sugar
1 cup granulated sugar
5 eggs
½ teaspoon baking powder
½ teaspoon salt
3 cups flour, sifted
1 cup milk
1 Tablespoon vanilla
1 cup nuts, finely chopped (black walnuts or pecans or ½ cup of each)

Cream butter, shortening, and sugar thoroughly. Gradually add granulated sugar. Continue creaming. Add eggs, one at a time, beating thoroughly after each addition. Sift baking powder and salt with flour, add alternately with milk, beginning and ending with flour. Stir in vanilla, then nuts, and blend well. Pour batter into a *well* greased and floured 10 inch tube pan, and bake at 325°F for 90 minutes, or until cake tests done. (Use long metal cake tester.) Cool in pan 15 minutes before removing.

You must use butter with this recipe, and be sure to grease your pan heavily with vegetable oil.

Mrs. J. F. Garst

For a lighter cake begin and end the batter with flour when it calls for alternate additions of flour and liquid.

CARROT CAKE

2 cups flour
2 cups sugar
2 teaspoons cinnamon
1½ teaspoons salt
2 teaspoons baking soda
4 eggs
1½ cups oil
3 cups carrots (1½ packages), grated (in blender if desired)

ICING

1 stick butter or margarine
6 ounces cream cheese
2 teaspoons vanilla
1 box (16 ounces) confectioners sugar
1 cup pecans

Preheat oven to 300°F. Mix flour, sugar, cinnamon, salt, and baking soda. Add eggs, oil, and finally, carrots. Bake 45-60 minutes in a greased and floured tube pan.

ICING

Soften butter and cream cheese at room temperature. Cream butter, cream cheese, and vanilla; add confectioners sugar gradually. Add pecans. Let cake cool about 1 hour before icing.

Marilyn Farr
Celeste Carmouche

GRAHAM CRACKER CHEESE CAKE

CRUST

½ cup granulated sugar
20 graham crackers, crushed
1 teaspoon cinnamon
1 stick butter, melted

FILLING

2 eggs
½ cup granulated sugar
1 pound Philadelphia cream cheese, room temperature
¾ stick butter, melted
1 teaspoon vanilla

TOPPING

1 pint sour cream
2 Tablespoons sugar
½ teaspoon vanilla

CRUST: Prepare 24 hours ahead. Blend sugar, cinnamon, and cracker crumbs, reserving ¼ cup for topping. Add butter to remaining crumbs and blend thoroughly. Press on bottom and part way up sides of 9 inch springside pan.

FILLING: Blend all ingredients in mixer until smooth. Pour into crust. Bake 30 minutes at 375°F.

TOPPING: Blend all ingredients. Cover cake with topping, and sprinkle with reserved crumbs. Bake for 5 minutes in preheated 475°F oven. Remove from oven. Cool slightly. Remove spring sides of pan. Cool; refrigerate and serve cold. Keeps well with airtight wraping for several days.

Mrs. Frank O. Pruitt, Jr.
(Virginia "Ginger" King)

To butter a baking pan evenly, invert it under hot running water, butter while still warm, then dust with flour.

PARTY CHEESE CAKE

2 cups graham cracker crumbs
⅓ cup confectioners sugar
¼ pound (½ cup) butter
1⅓ boxes lemon Jello (1 box and 2 Tablespoons)
⅔ cup hot water
⅔ cup ice cold water
1 cup granulated sugar
1 large package (8 ounces) Philadelphia cream cheese
1 tall can evaporated milk (ice cold)
1 teaspoon vanilla
12 maraschino cherries (optional)

Blend together crumbs, confectioners sugar, and butter in order given and mix thoroughly. Pat with hands on bottom only of a 9x13x2 inch pan, reserving enough to sprinkle on top. Dissolve lemon Jello in hot water and then add cold water. Set aside. Mix sugar with cream cheese and cream until smooth. Whip milk in electric mixer until it forms peaks. Add Jello. Whip until well blended. Add cream cheese mixture and vanilla and continue beating until smooth. Pour over crumbs in cake pan. Sprinkle with reserved crumbs. Chill until firm. Cut into oblong bars, topped with cherries. Serves 12.

Light as a cloud and simply delicious. Elegant for dessert bridge.

Mrs. C. E. Painter

SOUR CREAM CHEESE CAKE

CRUST

1 stick butter, melted
15 double graham crackers, rolled out

FILLING

3 large packages cream cheese
1 pint sour cream
1½ cups sugar
5 eggs
Juice of 1 lemon
1½ teaspoons vanilla
1 can blueberry pie filling

CRUST: Mix butter and crumbs and press in a 9 inch spring-form pan.

FILLING: Mix all ingredients except blueberry filling. Pour into unbaked pie crust. Bake at 325°F for 1 hour. Let cool in open oven for 45 minutes. Chill. Pour blueberry pie filling on top. Refrigerate.

Mrs. Lehrue Stevens, Jr.
(Betty Scheib)

Bring shortening, eggs, and milk to room temperature for easier blending.
Always sift confectioners sugar before measuring.

SWEET DOUGH CHEESE CAKE

SWEET DOUGH
6 ounces flour
4 ounces sweet butter
2 ounces granulated sugar
1 ounce milk
Pinch of salt

CHEESE CAKE
3 pounds cream cheese
12 ounces sugar (1½ cups)
6 eggs
1 teaspoon lemon rind
Pinch of salt
1 teaspoon vanilla
⅓ cup heavy sweet cream

SWEET DOUGH
Mix well ingredients for dough and line 9 inch spring form pan.

CHEESE CAKE MIXTURE: Blend cheese and sugar. Add eggs one at a time. Blend well. Blend in lemon rind, salt, and vanilla. Add sweet cream; blend. Pour into lined pan. Heat oven to 350°F. Reduce to 325°F and bake for 1-1½ hours, or until brown. Turn off heat. Leave cake in oven for 1 hour. Remove from oven, cool or refrigerate.

Mrs. Robert K. Morris

FRESH COCONUT LAYER CAKE

3 eggs, separated
1½ cups sugar
¾ cup shortening
½ teaspoon vanilla
¼ cup, or more, fresh coconut, grated
2¼ cups cake flour
2¼ teaspoons baking powder
½ teaspoon salt
¾ cup coconut milk

Beat egg whites until stiff, but not dry. Beat in ½ cup sugar, 2 Tablespoons at a time. (This procedure is very important for success of cake.) Cream shortening and add vanilla. Beat 1 cup sugar into shortening, then well beaten egg yolks. Beat thoroughly. Stir in coconut. Sift dry ingredients together and add to batter alternately with coconut milk. Fold in egg whites gently. Spoon into 2 pans (9 inch) which have been lightly greased and floured. Bake at 375°F for 25-30 minutes. Frost with 7 minute frosting and sprinkle top and sides generously with coconut.

Mrs. Stacy W. Smith
(Lois Allen)

Heat coconut in hot oven for a few minutes for easy removal from shell.

MY FAVORITE CHOCOLATE CAKE

1 cup butter, creamed with 2 cups sugar
½ cup cocoa
5 eggs, separated
2½ cups flour
1 cup sour milk or buttermilk
1 teaspoon baking soda dissolved in 1 Tablespoon hot water
1 teaspoon vanilla

To creamed butter and sugar, add cocoa and mix well. Add well beaten egg yolks, flour, and milk alternately. Add dissolved soda. Whip egg whites until light; add vanilla and fold into batter. Bake in three greased and floured round (8 inch) cake pans 20-30 minutes at 350°F. Test for doneness before removing from oven. Frost with 1½ recipes of MY FAVORITE CHOCOLATE FROSTING p. 339.

Mrs. A. L. Ducournau
Natchitoches, La.

DEVIL'S FOOD CAKE

1 cup butter
2 cups sugar
3 eggs, beaten
2½ cups Swansdown cake flour
1 teaspoon each baking soda and baking powder
¼ cup cream
½ cup buttermilk
4 heaping Tablespoons cocoa dissolved in ¾ cup boiling water and set aside
1 teaspoon vanilla

Grease 3 cake pans (9 inch) and line bottom with waxed paper. Cream butter and sugar and blend in beaten eggs. Add ½ cup flour. Combine with remaining flour, sifted with soda and baking powder. Add cream mixed with buttermilk. Add dissolved cocoa and vanilla and beat until well mixed. Bake at 350°F about 20-25 minutes. Cake will pull away from sides when done.

Variation: To make "Chocolate Spice Cake", add to this recipe: 1 teaspoon each cinnamon, allspice, and nutmeg.

Mrs. Carey J. Ellis

CHEWY FUDGE CAKE

1 box brown sugar
1 stick butter or margarine
2 eggs
2 cups all purpose flour
2 teaspoons baking powder
1 teaspoon vanilla flavoring
1 cup pecans, chopped

Melt brown sugar in saucepan with butter, cooking slowly about 10 minutes. Cool, and stir in eggs, one at a time. Add flour with baking powder. Add vanilla and pecans. Bake at 375°F in an ungreased 9x12 inch pan for 20 minutes.

Mrs. David Buttross, Jr.
(Joyce Abraham)

WHITE FRUIT CAKE

12 egg whites
1 cup butter
2½ cups sugar
2 teaspoons baking powder
4 cups flour
1 cup milk
1 pound each crystallized cherries, halved, and pineapple
1 pound citron (optional)
2 pounds pecans, shelled
2 fresh coconuts, grated

Beat eggs, not too stiff. Cream butter and sugar together. Add baking powder, flour, milk, and fruits. Mix and add coconut and pecans. Fold in beaten egg whites. Spread cake batter in buttered and floured deep bread pan and bake at 350°F for 1 hour. Enough for 3 cakes. Freezes.

Mrs. G. Lock Paret, Jr.
(Beverly Bowers)

CRANBERRY CAKE

2 cups flour
1 cup sugar
1 teaspoon each baking soda and salt
Rind of 2 oranges, grated
1 cup buttermilk
2 eggs, beaten
¾ cup Wesson oil
1 cup each nuts and dates, chopped
1 cup whole cranberries, (fresh), uncooked
¼ cup flour

Combine flour, sugar, soda, salt, orange rinds, buttermilk, eggs, Wesson oil. Dredge nuts, dates, cranberries with flour. Mix with other ingredients. Bake in greased and floured tube pan at 350°F 1 hour, or until done.

GLAZE

While still in pan, glaze with orange juice, butter and confectioners sugar mixture. Pour over cake at intervals until all glaze is used.

Mrs. James W. Crawford
(Sydalise "Sissie" Fredeman)

GLAZE

1 cup orange juice
¼ cup butter
1 cup confectioners sugar

Grease layer cake pans well, and dust with flour. Remove excess flour by gently knocking inverted pan on work surface.

Fine dry bread crumbs may be used instead of flour for dusting greased cake pan for easy removal when baked.

DATE CAKE

2 teaspoons baking soda
2 cups boiling water
1 large box (or 2 small packages) dates, chopped
4 Tablespoons butter
2 cups sugar
2 eggs
2 cups pecans, finely chopped
2¼ cups flour
1 teaspoon vanilla
CARAMEL ICING FOR DATE CAKE
2½ cups sugar
1 cup cream
1-2 teaspoons water
1 stick butter

Add soda and boiling water to chopped dates. Let cool. While date mixture is cooling, cream butter and sugar; add eggs one at a time. Add pecans, then flour and vanilla; add cooled date mixture. Bake in three 8 inch cake pans at 350°F for about 35 minutes. Ice with caramel icing.

CARAMEL ICING

Cook 2 cups sugar and cream on low heat. Brown ½ cup sugar to a light caramel; add water and combine with mixture. Boil until it forms a soft ball in water. Add butter before removing from heat. Beat with a wooden spoon or electric mixer, until right consistency to spread on cake.

Mrs. Stacy W. Smith
(Lois Allen)

FLOWER GARDEN CAKE

1 large angel food cake
6 eggs, separated
1½ cups sugar
1½ teaspoons lemon rind, grated
¾ cup lemon juice
1 package Knox gelatine dissolved in ¼ cup cold water
1½ pints heavy cream, whipped

Lightly butter tube or loaf pan. Tear cake into small pieces. Set aside. Beat egg yolks until thick and lemon colored. Pour into medium saucepan. Add ¾ cup sugar, lemon rind and juice, cook slowly, stirring constantly, until of *custard* consistency (when spoon is coated). Remove from heat and add gelatine which has been dissolved in cold water. Cool thoroughly. Beat egg whites until very stiff and add remaining sugar. Fold into cooled custard. In pan layer custard and cake pieces alternately, using custard first and last. Refrigerate until set, preferably overnight. Unmold on large cake plate and cover with sweetened whipped cream.

Mrs. Charles S. Ware, Sr.

GINGERBREAD

3 eggs
1 cup dark syrup
1 cup cooking oil
1 cup sugar
1 teaspoon each cloves, ginger, and cinnamon
2 large teaspoons baking soda dissolved in ⅛ cup hot water
2 cups flour
1 cup boiling water

Place eggs, syrup, oil, sugar, and spices in a large bowl and beat well. Add dissolved soda. Sift in flour and beat well. Add boiling water and beat lightly and quickly. Place in 9x12 inch pan lined with waxed paper. Bake at 325°F for 45 minutes. Serves 10-12.

Mrs. Charles S. Ware, Jr.
(Jan Allen)

ICE-BOX CAKE

1 cup sugar
1 stick butter
1 large can crushed pineapple, drained
1 egg
1 cup pecans, chopped
1 teaspoon vanilla
Vanilla wafers

Cream sugar and butter. Add pineapple and egg and mix well. Add pecans and vanilla. Line pan with waxed paper and cover with a layer of vanilla wafers. Cover with ½ of mixture, another layer of vanilla wafers, and top with remaining mixture. Refrigerate. Serves 10-12.

Mrs. F. W. Cayton

ITALIAN CREAM CAKE AND ICING

CAKE

1 stick margarine
½ cup Crisco
2 cups sugar
5 eggs, separated
1 teaspoon baking soda
1 cup buttermilk
2 cups flour, sifted

ICING

1 package (8 ounces) cream cheese, softened
1 stick margarine, softened
1 teaspoon vanilla
1 box confectioners sugar
1 cup pecans, finely chopped

CAKE

Cream margarine, Crisco, and sugar. Add egg yolks, beating 1 at a time, to creamed mixture. Sift flour and soda 3 times; add alternately with buttermilk to cream mixture. Beat egg whites to peaks and fold into mixture. Pour into 3 greased and floured 9 inch cake pans. Bake at 350°F for 25-30 minutes, or until done. Cool.

ICING

Combine all ingredients but pecans, beating to a spreading consistency. Add pecans. Ice cooled cake between layers and on top.

Mrs. Mildred Sims

Mrs. Logan Postell Perkins, Jr. *adds 1 teaspoon vanilla, 1 small can angel flake coconut, and 1 cup chopped nuts to creamed mixture before folding in egg whites.*

A GUTER KUCHEN

3 cups flour
2 cups sugar
3 eggs
1 cup salad oil
1 teaspoon cinnamon
½ teaspoon baking soda
½ cup hot water
1 teaspoon vanilla
½ teaspoon salt
3 raw apples, peeled, cubed
1 cup pecans, chopped

Mix thoroughly all ingredients except apples and pecans. Add apples and pecans. Bake at 325°F in large tube pan for 1 hour and 20 minutes, or until toothpick inserted in middle comes out clean.

Anne Berniard

LEMON CAKE

2 sticks butter or margarine at room temperature
1¾ cups sugar
5 eggs at room temperature
2 cups cake flour, sifted 3 times
1 Tablespoon lemon flavoring

Preheat oven to 325°F. Cream butter until light and fluffy. Add sugar and beat well. Add eggs, one at a time, beating 1 minute after each. Add sifted flour. Stir in lemon flavoring carefully. Bake in tube pan on middle rack for 1 hour. Invert pan on cake rack to cool. No frosting needed. Freezes.

Mrs. Dozier Skipper

JAM CAKE

1 cup butter, creamed
2 cups sugar
4 eggs
1 teaspoon baking soda
1 cup buttermilk
1 teaspoon each cinnamon, nutmeg, and cloves
3½ cups flour
1 cup seedless blackberry jam

To creamed butter, add sugar, then eggs one at a time. Beat well. Put soda in buttermilk. Add spices to flour and sift. Add flour and buttermilk mixtures alternately to creamed mixture. Fold in jam. Bake at 325°F. Makes one 3 layer cake plus 12 cup cakes, very moist.

FILLING

1 large can crushed pineapple
½ cup butter
1 cup sugar
1 Tablespoon cornstarch
Juice of 1 lemon

Cook filling until thick enough to spread. Spread between layers and on top.

From the recipes of Mrs. J. W. Allen

OATMEAL CAKE

1¼ cups boiling water
1 cup *quick* oatmeal
½ cup shortening
1 cup granulated sugar
1 cup brown sugar
2 eggs
1 teaspoon vanilla
1⅓ cups enriched flour
½ teaspoon salt
1 teaspoon baking soda
1½ teaspoons cinnamon
½ cup nuts, chopped

Pour boiling water over oatmeal. Let stand 20 minutes, or until cool. Cream together the shortening, sugar, brown sugar, eggs, and vanilla. Add oatmeal and mix. Sift together flour, salt, soda, and cinnamon, add to oat mixture, and mix. Stir in the nuts and pour into a 9x13x2 inch greased pan. Bake at 350°F for 30-40 minutes.

TOPPING

¾ stick soft butter
¾ cup brown sugar
⅜ cup milk
1½ cups chopped nuts and coconut, mixed
¾ teaspoon vanilla

Bring butter to room temperature and cream with sugar. Add milk, mixed nuts and coconut, and vanilla. Mix well. Spread topping on warm cake. Put in broiler and broil until bubbly.

Mrs. Henry Hoenes

PECAN TORTE

3 cups pecans
6 eggs, separated
1½ cups sugar
3 Tablespoons flour
1 teaspoon salt
2 Tablespoons Jamaica rum

FILLING

½ cup heavy cream
2 Tablespoons confectioners sugar
1 Tablespoon Jamaica rum

ICING

1 cup semi-sweet chocolate bits
½ cup sour cream

CAKE: Put pecans in blender, 1 cup at a time, until finely chopped. Beat egg yolks until very light; then beat in sugar, flour, salt, rum and pecans. Mix well, and fold in egg whites beaten stiff but not dry. Pour into three 8 inch or two 10 inch layer cake pans that have been lined with waxed paper and buttered. Bake in 350°F preheated oven about 25 minutes, or until a gentle finger pressure fails to dent. Cool well and remove from pans. A few hours before serving make filling.

FILLING: Whip cream with sugar and rum.

ICING: Melt chocolate bits and fold in sour cream. Spread over top of cake.

Mrs. Kenneth L. Strauss
(Julie Ann Marx)

PINEAPPLE UPSIDE-DOWN CAKE

TOPPING
3 Tablespoons butter or margarine
1 can (7 ounces) pineapple, crushed or sliced
Maraschino cherries
California walnuts, halved
⅔ cup dark brown sugar

CAKE
⅓ cup shortening
½ cup granulated sugar
1 egg
1 teaspoon vanilla
1¼ cups cake flour, sifted
1½ teaspoons baking powder
½ teaspoon salt

TOPPING

Melt butter in round 9 inch cake pan. Drain pineapple, reserving ½ cup syrup. Arrange cherries and walnuts in bottom of pan. Cover with brown sugar and pineapple.

CAKE

Cream together shortening and sugar. Add egg and vanilla and beat until fluffy. Sift together dry ingredients; add alternately with reserved pineapple syrup to shortening-sugar mixture, beating after each addition. Spread batter over pineapple topping. Bake at 350°F for 45-50 minutes. Let stand for 5 minutes and invert on plate.

Mrs. Stacy W. Smith
(Lois Allen)

PLUM-TAPIOCA CAKE

2 cups self rising flour
2 cups sugar
3 eggs
1 cup cooking oil
2 small jars plum with tapioca baby food
1 cup pecans, chopped
1 teaspoon each cinnamon, ground cloves, and vanilla

Mix all ingredients well and pour into greased tube pan. Bake at 350°F for 1 hour.

Jane Cook

POUND CAKE

1 pound butter
2½ cups sugar
8-10 eggs
4 cups all purpose or cake flour, unsifted
4 level teaspoons baking powder
¼ cup milk
2 teaspoons vanilla extract

Cream butter and sugar until very light. Add eggs one at a time, beating well after each addition. Gradually fold in flour, baking powder, and milk. Add vanilla. Beat well. Bake at 400°F for 50-60 minutes, or at a lesser temperature if cake browns too fast. No icing needed, but may be sprinkled with confectioners sugar.

From the recipes of
Mrs. J. A. Malloy

CHOCOLATE OR YELLOW POUND CAKE

½ pound butter
3 cups sugar
5 eggs
3 cups flour
½ cup shortening
1 cup milk
½ teaspoon each baking powder and salt
1 teaspoon vanilla

GLAZES

Lemon

Juice of 1 lemon
1 cup confectioners sugar

Chocolate

½ stick butter
3 Tablespoons cocoa
1 teaspoon vanilla

Cream butter and sugar well. Add 1 egg at a time and mix. Add remaining ingredients and blend until light. Bake at 350°F for 1 hour. For chocolate cake add 4 Tablespoons cocoa.

LEMON GLAZE: Mix lemon juice and sugar. Pour over yellow cake while still hot.

CHOCOLATE GLAZE: Mix all ingredients, and pour over chocolate cake while still hot.

Excellent all time favorite. Just remember to have ingredients at room temperature and to mix them well.

Mrs. Lorenia Pack

DESSERTS — CAKES

FOOL PROOF POUND CAKE

2 sticks butter at room temperature
½ cup shortening (or 1 stick margarine)
3 cups granulated sugar
½ teaspoon salt
5 eggs
3 cups flour, sifted
1 cup milk
½ teaspoon each vanilla and almond extract

Cream butter and shortening well. Add sugar gradually. Add salt and eggs one at a time to creamed mixture. Follow with flour added alternately ⅓ at a time with milk (start and finish with flour). Add vanilla and almond extract. Pour into large greased and floured tube pan. Start in cold oven and bake for 2 hours at 300°F.

Mrs. Robert W. Rice
(June Arnold)

SOUR CREAM POUND CAKE

1 cup butter
2½ cups sugar
3 cups flour
¾ teaspoon baking powder
¼ teaspoon soda
½ teaspoon salt
6 eggs
1 cup sour cream
1 teaspoon vanilla

Cream butter and sugar. Sift flour with other dry ingredients. Add to butter and sugar mixture alternately with eggs (2 at a time). Beat after each addition. Add sour cream and vanilla. Bake in greased tube pan at 300°F for 1½ hours.

Mrs. Ruth King White

PRALINE CAKE

1 yellow cake

PRALINE TOPPING
1 package (1 pound) light brown sugar
2 Tablespoons flour
2 eggs, beaten
½ cup butter, melted
1 teaspoon vanilla
1½ cups pecans, coarsely chopped

Pour cake batter into 2 greased and floured 13x9x2 inch pans. Bake at 350°F for about 30 minutes, or until done. Remove from oven and cool.

PRALINE TOPPING

In skillet mix light brown sugar, flour, and eggs in melted butter, and cook for 3 minutes over low heat. Remove from heat and stir in vanilla and pecans. Spread evenly over surface of cooled cakes. Bake for about 8 minutes at 400°F to set the frosting. Cool and cut into 1½ inch strips. Makes 60 bite sized servings.

Mrs. Thomas B. Shearman, Jr.
(Martha Hatchette)

DESSERTS — CAKES

PRUNE CAKE

4 eggs
1½ cups sugar
1 cup prunes, stewed, chopped
1 cup shortening, melted
1 cup sour milk
½ teaspoon each cinnamon and nutmeg
1 teaspoon each baking powder and baking soda
2 cups flour
Fudge frosting

Beat eggs thoroughly with sugar. Add prunes. Slowly stir in milk and shortening. Sift in dry ingredients and bake in three 9 inch round cake pans. Bake at 300°F for 45-60 minutes until cake tests done with straw. Fill and ice cake with fudge frosting.

Ida Tucker

PUMPKIN POUND CAKE

3 cups flour
2 teaspoons baking powder
½ teaspoon baking soda
2 teaspoons cinnamon
1 teaspoon allspice
½ teaspoon salt
1 cup salad oil
3 cups sugar
3 eggs
2 cups pumpkin

Sift first 6 ingredients, set aside. Blend oil and sugar. Add eggs, one at a time, to oil and sugar mixture. Beat well after each addition. Add pumpkin and mix well. Blend in dry ingredients and pour into greased and floured tube pan. Bake at 350°F for 1 hour. Freezes.

Mrs. A. R. Hodgkins, Jr.
(Phyllis Scripture)

SNOWBALL CAKE

2 envelopes plain gelatin
4 Tablespoons cold water
1 cup boiling water
1 can (16 ounces) crushed pineapple, undrained
1 cup white sugar
Juice of 1 lemon
2 envelopes (1 large box) Dream Whip
1 large angel food cake, torn into pieces
1 large container Cool Whip
1 large can Angel Flake coconut

Soften gelatin in cold water; add boiling water and stir until dissolved. Refrigerate. When chilled, remove, stir in pineapple, sugar and lemon juice. Refrigerate. Prepare Dream Whip according to package directions. When mixture starts to jell, fold in Dream Whip. Place as follows in 9½x3½ inch pan: ½ cake pieces, ½ gelatin mixture, ½ cake, ½ gelatin. Refrigerate 6 hours or overnight before spreading with Cool Whip and sprinkling with coconut. Leave refrigerated until ready to serve. Freezes.

Mrs. Ted Harless
(Molly Welborn)

WALNUT CAKE

3 cups sugar
1 cup butter
3 cups flour
2 cups bananas, mashed
4 eggs
8 Tablespoons buttermilk
2 teaspoons each baking soda and vanilla
2 cups Eastern Black Walnuts, chopped
¼ teaspoon salt

Cream sugar and butter. Add flour and bananas alternately with eggs. Add remaining ingredients. Bake 1 hour at 350°F in oiled and floured tube pan.

Mrs. Hugh Robinson
(Ann Birdwell)

RED VELVET CAKE

½ cup shortening
1½ cups sugar
2 eggs
1 teaspoon salt
1 Tablespoon cocoa
2 cups flour
1 cup buttermilk
1 teaspoon vanilla
1½ ounces red food coloring
1 teaspoon baking soda
1 teaspoon vinegar

FROSTING

1 cup milk
¼ cup flour
Dash of salt
½ cup shortening
1 stick margarine
1 cup sugar
1 teaspoon vanilla
Coconut, grated (optional)

Cream shortening and sugar. Add eggs. Sift salt, cocoa, and flour 3 times. Add flour mixture alternately with buttermilk to creamed mixture. Stir in vanilla and food coloring. Combine soda and vinegar and add to mixture. Pour into 2 greased and floured 9 inch cake pans. Bake at 350°F for 30-35 minutes.

FROSTING

PART 1: In saucepan combine milk, flour, and salt. Cook over low heat to pudding stage. Set aside to cool.

PART 2: Cream shortening, margarine, and sugar. Add vanilla. Add cooled pudding mixture to creamed mixture. Beat with electric mixer until smooth. Spread on cooled cake layers and top with coconut if desired. Keeps better refrigerated. Freezes.

Mrs. Charles D. Viccellio
(Joanna Steele)

To facilitate removal of cake from the pan, wrap pan in a towel and let stand for a few minutes until moisture forms to loosen it.

WHITE ICING

2 cups sugar
2 egg whites
¼ teaspoon cream of tartar
⅔ cup boiling water
Vanilla (or any) flavoring

Mix sugar, egg whites (not beaten), and cream of tartar in top of double boiler and add boiling water. Cook over boiling water, whipping constantly with electric beater until icing is fluffy and stands in peaks (from 7-10 minutes). Add flavoring. Cool before icing cake. This makes a large amount of icing and will fill and frost a 9 inch cake.

Mrs. W. E. Gorham, Sr.
(Mary Tucker)

Prevent boiled icing from becoming sugary by adding a few drops of vinegar while cooking.

ONE MINUTE ICING

3 cups sugar
¾ cup cocoa
¾ cup milk
1½ sticks margarine
½ teaspoon salt
1½ Tablespoons vanilla

Mix all ingredients except vanilla. Bring to a hard boil. Boil 1 minute. Remove and cool. Add vanilla and beat to spreading consistency. Makes a lot.

Dot Tucker
Crowley, La.

SEVEN MINUTE ICING

1 cup sugar
2 egg whites
¼ teaspoon cream of tartar
3 Tablespoons ice water
¼ teaspoon vanilla

Place sugar, unbeaten egg whites, cream of tartar, and water in top of double boiler. Place over vigorously boiling water, but do not let water touch upper pan of double boiler. Use rotary beater to beat briskly while cooking. Beat until mixture stands in a peak on beater. Remove from heat. Beat in vanilla until completely mixed.

Mrs. R. Murl Chafin
(Mildred Jones)

MOCHA ICING

1 stick butter or margarine
1 box (16 ounces) confectioners sugar
⅓ cup strong coffee, made with *heaping* teaspoon instant coffee dissolved in water
1 teaspoon vanilla
Pecans, chopped

Cream butter and sugar in electric mixer, adding coffee gradually. Add vanilla. Garnish with pecans. (Pecans are better toasted lightly in a little butter and a pinch of salt.) Use on yellow cake. Fills and ices a 9 inch square cake.

Mary Jane Gorham

MY FAVORITE CHOCOLATE FROSTING

2 squares unsweetened chocolate
1 stick butter
2 eggs, well beaten
1 box confectioners sugar
2 cups nuts, finely chopped

Melt chocolate and butter. Add eggs and sugar. Cream well and add nuts. If too stiff, add 1-2 drops hot water. Enough for top and sides of 2 layers (9 inch).

Mrs. A. L. Ducournau
Natchitoches, La.

CHOCOLATE NUT FROSTING

1 box (16 ounces) confectioners sugar
½ cup evaporated or homogenized milk
½ cup butter or margarine
¾ cup cocoa
1 teaspoon vanilla
½ cup pecans, chopped

Mix sugar and milk. Melt butter in saucepan. Stir cocoa into butter; add to sugar and milk. Add vanilla. Beat until smooth. Stir in pecans. Frost cake.

Mrs. Joseph A. Brame
(Cindy Dickson)

QUICK BROILED ICING

6 Tablespoons margarine or butter
10 Tablespoons sugar
4 Tablespoons evaporated or homogenized milk
1 can angel-flake coconut
½ cup pecans, chopped

Melt margarine or butter; add other ingredients. Spread on hot sheet cake. Broil under broiler until bubbly, *not* brown. Especially good on Devil's Food cake.

Mrs. George Hardy Vincent
(Nina LaFleur)

CARAMEL ICING

3 cups sugar
1 pint heavy cream
¼ pound butter
1 teaspoon vanilla

Caramelize ½ cup of sugar. Cook cream over low heat with remaining sugar for a few minutes. Add butter. Add caramelized sugar. (It will form lumps, but they will dissolve.) Cook until mixture forms a soft ball in ice water. Remove from heat, add vanilla, and beat until creamy. Makes enough icing for a 3 layer cake.

Mrs. Carey J. Ellis

Always add sugar to meringue gradually, beating until dissolved, to keep meringue from being grainy.
Whip cream faster and stiffer by chilling cream, bowl, and beaters.

Candy

MISS ANNABEL'S ORANGE PECANS

2½ cups brown sugar
1 scant cup milk
1 Tablespoon vinegar
1 pound whole pecans, shelled
Rind of 1 orange, grated

Cook sugar, milk, and vinegar until syrup forms a soft ball when dropped in cold water. Remove from heat and pour over pecans and rind. Beat until it begins to sugar and quickly pour into a buttered dish or on waxed paper. Separate nuts when candy has cooled.

"Miss Annabel," one of Lake Charles's "Grande Dames", was celebrated for her orange pecans. Sold nationally by mail order, the labels and hand-painted cans were designed by her dear friend, Rosa Hart.

From the recipes of
Mrs. T. A. Dees

MOTHER'S CINNAMON PECANS

1 cup sugar
½ cup water
¾ teaspoon salt
1 teaspoon vanilla
1 teaspoon cinnamon
2 cups pecan halves

Mix all ingredients, except pecans, and simmer in 2 quart heavy saucepan until mixture threads when dropped from a spoon or forms a soft ball in cold water (15-20 minutes). Remove from heat and stir in pecans. Continue stirring until all nuts are sugar coated, and break into original halves. Will last forever in plastic bags or tightly covered container.

Mrs. G. Lock Paret, Jr.
(Beverly Bowers)

BAKED PECANS

1 egg white, stiffly beaten
1 cup light brown sugar
1 pound pecan halves

Blend egg and sugar. Coat pecans well. Bake on well buttered tin at 250-275 F at least ½ hour. Will be dark tan when done.

Mrs. J. Gilbert Scheib

DESSERTS — CANDIES

CHOCOLATE FUDGE

4 strips Baker's German sweet chocolate (6 strips in a 4 ounce block)
2 cups sugar
1 cup whole milk
3 Tablespoons butter
2 teaspoons vanilla

Bring first 4 ingredients to a boil over low heat, stirring constantly. Increase to medium heat and boil until candy forms a soft ball when dropped in cold water (250°F on candy thermometer). Add vanilla and beat candy until creamy. Pour into buttered platter and cut into squares when cool.

Mrs. Oliver Stockwell
(Roseina Holcombe)

ONE HUNDRED DOLLAR CHOCOLATE FUDGE

1 stick margarine
12 marshmallows
2 cups sugar
⅔ cup evaporated milk
1½ packages (6 ounce size) chocolate chips
Nuts as desired
1 teaspoon vanilla

Melt margarine and marshmallows. Bring sugar and milk to a boil and boil for exactly 1 minute, stirring constantly. Quickly combine marshmallow and milk mixtures and pour over chocolate chips, mixing thoroughly. Add nuts and vanilla. Cool in refrigerator before cutting into squares.

Mrs. William B. Baggett
(Gael Salter)

DIVINITY FUDGE

2 cups sugar
½ cup light corn syrup
½ cup water
2 egg whites, stiffly beaten
1 teaspoon vanilla
1 cup pecans, chopped

Heat sugar, syrup, and water over low heat, stirring only until sugar dissolves. Cook until a soft ball forms in cold water. Pour ½ slowly over beaten egg whites and continue beating. Cook remaining syrup to form a hard ball. Add gradually to syrup and egg mixture while beating. Add vanilla, beating until candy is thick enough to drop from a spoon. Stir in nuts and drop by spoonfuls on buttered platter. Makes 35-40 pieces.

Marie Chavanne

CANDIED DATE LOAF

½ cup milk
¼ stick butter
⅔ cup sugar
1 cup dates, chopped
2 cups pecans, chopped

Cook milk, butter, and sugar together to soft ball stage; then add dates. Cook again, stirring constantly, until hard ball stage. Add pecans, stir until mixture turns to sugar. Wrap in damp towel, refrigerate, and slice when cool. Serves 25.

Mrs. Natolia Guilbeau
Franklin, La.

CANDIED GRAPEFRUIT PEEL

Peel (or rind) of 3-4 grapefruit
2 teaspoons salt
2 cups sugar
1 cup water
Food coloring (optional)

Prepare grapefruit peels by removing all pulp and cutting into thin strips about 2½ inches long. Cover with salted water and boil 20 minutes. Drain. Repeat this process twice more, but without salt. Drain in a colander. In small saucepan bring sugar, water, and desired food coloring to a boil (232-234°F). Add peel and simmer 30 minutes. Drain well. Roll peel in sugar to coat and shake to remove excess. Dry on racks several hours. Store in semi-airtight containers. Makes 1 quart peels. Orange peels may be substituted, but eliminate 1 boiling.

Mrs. Helen Morrow
Boyce, La.

HEAVENLY HASH

2 cups pecans, chopped
3-4 Tablespoons butter
7 level Tablespoons cocoa
4 level cups sugar
1 can (13 ounces) evaporated milk
1 stick butter
⅓ cup Karo syrup
⅛ teaspoon salt
1 jar (7 ounces) marshmallow cream
Large marshmallows, cut up

Toast pecans in butter and set aside. Combine cocoa, sugar, milk, butter, Karo, and salt. Cook on medium heat, stirring constantly, until mixture reaches a soft boil. Continue boiling until a few drops in tap water form a soft ball. Remove from heat, add marshmallow cream, and beat until gloss is gone. Add pecans and pour ½ of candy in a 10x13 inch pan. Completely cover with large marshmallows, followed by a 2nd layer of candy. Cool before cutting into squares.

Mrs. James Welsh
(Bernice Puckett)

DESSERTS — CANDIES

BUTTERMILK PRALINES

2 cups sugar
1 teaspoon baking soda
1 cup buttermilk
Pinch salt
2 Tablespoons butter
1 teaspoon vanilla
2¼ cups pecans

Cook sugar, soda, buttermilk, and salt in large heavy saucepan until a soft ball forms in cold water. Remove from heat and cool. Add butter, vanilla, and pecans. Beat until stiff and creamy. Drop by spoonfuls on waxed paper.

Mrs. Lena Farque
Big Lake, La.

HOWARD'S PECAN PRALINES

1⅓ cups milk (½ evaporated, ½ homogenized)
7 cups white sugar
⅔ cup pecans, finely chopped
1 jar Kraft caramel topping
⅔ stick butter
2½ teaspoons vanilla
2⅓ cups pecans, coarsely chopped

Mix first 4 ingredients and cook in large saucepan over medium-high heat, stirring constantly until candy thermometer reads 239°F (or few drops of mixture forms soft ball in cold water). Remove from heat and cool in pot, stirring until thermometer reads 210-200°F. Add remaining ingredients and stir until mixture begins to slightly thicken. Drop by spoonfuls on foil.

From the recipes of
Howard Cornay, Sr.

PEANUT BRITTLE

2 cups white corn syrup
1 cup water
1 cup sugar
2 cups raw peanuts, shelled
1 teaspoon baking soda
1 teaspoon vanilla
⅛ teaspoon salt

Combine syrup, water, and sugar in heavy saucepan and bring to a boil. Reduce to medium heat and boil about 20 minutes until soft ball stage is reached. Add peanuts and continue to cook about 10 more minutes, stirring often, until mixture is light brown and peanuts are popping. Remove from heat. Add soda, vanilla, and salt and beat well. Pour on heavily buttered surface and spread thin. (Cookie sheet with narrow edge is best.) Let cool and break into small pieces.

Mrs. Fred Book, Sr.

DESSERTS — CANDIES

PEANUT BUTTER BALLS

2 pounds crunchy peanut butter
3 boxes (16 ounce size) confectioners sugar
1 pound margarine
1 Tablespoon vanilla
¾ bar paraffin
2 pounds milk chocolate morsels
1 large package (12 ounces) semi-sweet morsels
1 German chocolate bar

Mix peanut butter, sugar, margarine, and vanilla. Roll into balls and refrigerate. In double boiler melt remaining ingredients. After balls have chilled, dip them in chocolate mixture. Variation: 1 cup pecans or walnuts or ½ cup dates may be added to peanut butter mixture.

Mrs. John E. Wood
(Sara Monticello)

MAMA'S SUGARED PECANS

2½ cups brown sugar (light or dark)
1 scant cup milk
1 Tablespoon vinegar
1 Tablespoon orange juice
Rind of 1 orange, grated
1 pound pecan halves

Mix all ingredients, except pecans, and boil until a few drops form a soft ball in cold water. Remove from heat and add pecans. Stir until sugared and immediately separate on waxed paper.

Mrs. W. L. Erwin
Kerrville, Texas

PECAN PUFFS

½ cup shortening (part butter)
2 Tablespoons sugar
1 teaspoon vanilla
1 cup pecans
1 cup flour
Confectioners sugar

Beat shortening until soft. Add sugar and blend until creamy. Add vanilla. Measure nuts; finely grind. Combine with flour and stir into creamed mixture. Roll into small balls and bake on ungreased cookie sheet at 300°F for 25 minutes, or until delicately browned. Roll in confectioners sugar while still hot and again when cool. Makes 2½ dozen.

Mrs. Ruth King White

To get nut meats out whole, soak overnight in salt water before cracking.

Cookies

BROWNIES

1 stick margarine
2 cups sugar, sifted
4 eggs
1 cup flour, sifted
Pinch salt
7 heaping teaspoons cocoa
1 teaspoon vanilla
1 cup nuts, chopped

Cream margarine and add sugar. Add eggs one at a time, mixing thoroughly. Add flour, salt, and cocoa and blend. Add vanilla and nuts. Bake in greased 14x8 or 9x13 inch pan at 375°F for 25 minutes, or until knife comes out clean. Makes 2 dozen.

Mrs. Dan Burkhalter
("Meg" McLachlan)

BLONDE BROWNIES

2⅔ cups flour
2½ teaspoons baking powder
½ teaspoon salt
⅔ cup butter
2¼ cups brown sugar, packed
3 eggs
1 package (12 ounces) semi-sweet chocolate chips
1 cup nuts, chopped

Preheat oven to 350°F. Sift flour, baking powder, and salt. Melt butter in large saucepan and stir in brown sugar. Cool 10 minutes. Add eggs, one at a time, beating well after each. Stir in flour mixture and chocolate chips until well blended. Spread in greased 15½x10½x1 inch pan, sprinkle with nuts, press down slightly. Bake 25-30 minutes. Do not overcook. Cool and cut into squares. Makes 3 dozen.

Mrs. Diane Coyle Scofield

EXTRA GOOD BROWNIES

2 squares semi-sweet chocolate
½ cup butter
1⅔ cups sugar
4 eggs
¼ teaspoon salt
1 cup flour
2 teaspoons vanilla

Melt chocolate and butter in saucepan. Add sugar and mix well. Add remaining ingredients and mix well, but do not beat. Bake in 9x9 inch greased and floured pan at 375°F about 45 minutes, or until brownies spring back when touched. Do not overcook. Cool and cut into squares. Makes 1 dozen.

Mrs. B. S. Bell
White Castle, La.

CREAM CHEESE COOKIES

1 cup margarine
1 package (3 ounces) Philadelphia cream cheese
1 cup sugar
1 egg yolk
2½ cups flour
⅛ teaspoon salt
1 teaspoon nutmeg

Cream margarine and cheese until smooth. Add remaining ingredients in order. Mix until smooth. Chill. Roll thinly and slice. Bake on greased cookie sheet at 350°F until golden brown. Makes 3 dozen.

Mrs. Helen Frederick

FRUIT BALLS

1 pound (2 cups) pecans, chopped
1 pound dates, finely chopped
5 ounces cherries, finely chopped
5 ounces pineapple, finely chopped
1 cup flour, sifted
1 cup sugar
¼ teaspoon salt
1 teaspoon vanilla
3 egg whites, beaten until peaked

Mix well with hands pecans and fruits. Mix flour, sugar, and salt and add to fruit mixture. Mix with hands until fruit is well covered with flour mixture. Add vanilla and mix well. Fold into beaten egg whites. Roll into balls (1 scant teaspoon per ball) and bake on greased 12x15 inch cookie sheet at 350°F for 12-15 minutes. Keeps for a month in covered container. If they dry out, add ½ apple to container. Makes 7½ dozen.

Mrs. C. D. Ballard

FRUIT CAKE COOKIES

1 stick butter
1½ cups brown sugar
4 eggs
1 cup whiskey
1 Tablespoon milk
1 teaspoon each ground cloves, allspice, nutmeg and cinnamon
3 cups flour
3 teaspoons baking soda
Dash salt
2 pounds each cherries, pineapple and pitted dates, candied
6 cups pecans, chopped

Cream butter and sugar well. Add eggs one at a time, beating well after each addition. Add whiskey and milk. Mix well. Sift all dry ingredients and add to chopped fruits and pecans. Combine the 2 mixtures. Spoon drop on cookie sheet. Bake at 350°F for 20-30 minutes.

Mrs. Gus Schram, Jr.
(Rose Burton)

HENRIETTAS

½ cup butter
1 cup sugar
2 egg yolks
1 cup flour, sifted
½ teaspoon baking powder
Pinch salt
½ teaspoon vanilla

Cream butter and sugar until light and fluffy. Add egg yolks and beat well. Gradually add remaining ingredients. Dough will be stiff. Press into 3x13x1½ inch pan. Spread with topping and bake at 325°F for 35 minutes. Cool in pan and cut into squares.

TOPPING

2 egg whites, stiffly beaten
½ cup brown sugar
1 cup pecans, chopped
1 teaspoon vanilla

TOPPING

Fold beaten egg whites into mixture of all other ingredients.

Mrs. Robert P. Howell
(Violet Hardtner)

LACE COOKIES

1 egg, beaten
1 cup sugar
2 Tablespoons plus 1 teaspoon flour
1 teaspoon salt
¼ teaspoon baking powder
1 cup quick oats
½ cup butter, melted
1 teaspoon vanilla

Combine all ingredients. Drop batter by ½ teaspoonfuls at least 2 inches apart on foil lined cookie sheet. Bake at 350°F for 13 minutes until golden brown. Leave on foil until cool. Makes 5 dozen.

Mrs. Thomas B. Shearman, Jr.
(Martha Hatchette)

MAMA'S COOKIES

1½ cups sugar
1 cup butter
2 eggs
2 teaspoons vanilla
1 teaspoon baking soda
Pinch salt
4 cups flour

Cream sugar and butter. Mix in eggs, vanilla, soda, and salt. Add flour and mix. Roll thinly and cut out cookies. (Or shape into long rolls and refrigerate until ready to use. Thinly slice cookies from roll as needed.) Bake on greased cookie sheet at 300-325°F for 12-18 minutes.

From the recipes of State Senator and Mrs. John Tom Beaty

MOTHER'S TEA CAKES

½ cup shortening
1 cup sugar
2 eggs
2¼ cups flour
¼ teaspoon salt
2 teaspoons baking powder
1 teaspoon vanilla
1 Tablespoon sweet milk

Cream shortening, sugar, and eggs in mixer. Mix remaining ingredients and add to mixer with a spoon. Mix well. Let stand overnight in refrigerator. Roll thinly on a floured bread board and cut in rounds with biscuit cutter. Bake on greased and floured cookie sheet at 375°F for 10-12 minutes until brown. Makes 2½ dozen.

Mrs. G. Lester Sadler

MOTHER'S FAVORITES

1 cup each brown and white sugar
1 cup shortening
2 eggs
1 teaspoon vanilla
½ teaspoon salt
2 cups flour
1 teaspoon baking soda
1 teaspoon baking powder
2 cups each oatmeal and corn flakes
1 cup coconut
1 cup pecans, chopped

Cream brown and white sugar with shortening. Add eggs, vanilla, salt, flour, soda, and baking powder and mix well. Mix remaining ingredients and blend well with other mixture. Drop by teaspoonfuls on greased cookie sheet and bake at 350°F for 10 minutes. Makes 7 dozen.

Mrs. Robert W. Price, Sr.
(Betty Boedecker)

OATMEAL COOKIES

1½ cups shortening
2 cups brown sugar
1 cup granulated sugar
2 eggs
½ cup water
2 teaspoons vanilla
2 cups flour
2 teaspoons salt
1 teaspoon baking soda
6 cups oatmeal

Beat shortening, both sugars, eggs, water, and vanilla. Mix together flour, salt, and soda and add oatmeal. Blend 2 mixtures together carefully. Dough will be very thick. Drop by teaspoonfuls on greased cookie sheet and bake at 350°F for 12-15 minutes.

Julie Faulk

DESSERTS — COOKIES

POTATO CHIP COOKIES

1 cup butter
½ cup sugar
1 teaspoon vanilla
½ cup potato chips, crushed
½ cup pecans, chopped
2 cups flour, sifted

Cream butter, sugar, and vanilla. Add potato chips and pecans. Stir in flour. Form into small balls, using 1 Tablespoon of dough per ball. Place on ungreased cookie sheet and flatten ball with bottom of a glass which has been dipped in sugar. Bake at 350°F for 16-18 minutes.

Mrs. J. E. Pace

CHOCOLATE PRETZELS

1 package (6 ounces) semi-sweet real chocolate morsels
2 Tablespoons corn syrup
2 Tablespoons shortening
1½ teaspoons water
1 package (9 ounces) 3 inch twisted pretzels

Combine and melt in double boiler over hot (not boiling) water all ingredients except pretzels. Remove from heat, but keep over hot water. Dip pretzels into chocolate mixture to coat thoroughly. Place on wire rack set over waxed paper. Refrigerate for 10 minutes, or until coating sets. Remove and let stand at room temperature for 1 hour, or until surface dries. Makes 2½-3 dozen.

Mrs. John W. Huber
(Betty Landry)

SLICE 'N BAKE COOKIES

3¼ cups flour
½ teaspoon salt
1 teaspoon baking soda
1 cup shortening
1½ cups sugar
3 eggs, well beaten
Flavoring
2 cups chocolate chips, pecans, or coconut

Sift together flour, salt, and soda and set aside. Cream shortening and add sugar gradually. Cream until fluffy. Add eggs and beat until smooth. Add flour mixture and mix well. Add desired flavoring and chocolate chips, pecans, or coconut. Mix well. Form into rolls in waxed paper and refrigerate until chilled. Slice and bake on cookie sheet at 400°F for 12 minutes.

Mrs. William Mancuso
(Jean Guillory)

Desserts

CARAMEL SOUFFLÉ WITH CARAMEL CUSTARD

SOUFFLÉ
2¼ cups sugar
3 Tablespoons butter
7 egg whites, stiffly beaten
Pinch salt

CUSTARD
½ cup sugar
1½ cups milk
1 Tablespoon butter
7 egg yolks, beaten
½ teaspoon caramel extract
½ pint heavy cream

Caramelize 1¼ cups sugar by cooking in skillet over low heat until a brown syrup. Pour *half* of mixture into a 2 quart soufflé dish, coating bottom and sides. Cool. Rub coating with butter. Gradually add remaining sugar and salt to beaten egg whites, beating constantly. Return skillet to stove to liquefy remaining caramel sauce. Add to egg white mixture, beating at medium speed for 5 minutes. Pour into soufflé dish. Bake in pan of hot water at 300°F about 1 hour, or until firm but light. Remove from oven. When ready to serve, bake at 350°F for 15 minutes more as soufflé must be warm to come out of dish. Invert on large serving dish and cover with custard. Soufflé will remain beautiful when prepared in the morning and reheated in the evening. (A real believe-it-or-not.)

CUSTARD: Cook sugar and milk in double boiler. When hot, add butter and egg yolks. Stir vigorously until thickened. Cool. Add caramel extract. Serves 8.

Mrs. James W. Crawford
(Sydalise "Sissie" Fredeman)

BAKED CUSTARD

2 whole eggs
2 egg yolks
1½ cups sugar
2 cups milk
Pinch of salt
1 teaspoon vanilla

Beat eggs and egg yolks with ½ cup sugar. Bring milk to boil in heavy saucepan and add to egg mixture. Set aside. Brown 1 cup sugar and pour into well buttered 1½ quart pyrex dish. Add salt and vanilla to egg-milk mixture and pour carefully over browned sugar. Set pyrex dish in pan of water and bake at 350°F about 1 hour, or until silver knife comes out clean. Individual custard cups may be used, but cooking time should be adjusted accordingly.

Mrs. J. T. Thompson

FLAN CUBANO

6 eggs, beaten
1 can evaporated milk
1 can condensed milk
1 can whole milk
2 teaspoons vanilla
1 cup sugar
¼ teaspoon salt
1 teaspoon brandy extract
12 Tablespoons sugar for caramelizing mold

Blend eggs with remaining ingredients. Pour into a cooled caramelized mold. Bake, with airtight cover, at 350°F for about 1½ hours. Test with toothpick for doneness. Remove from oven, cool at room temperature, and refrigerate. When very cold, remove from refrigerator and invert mold onto a plate. Serves 12. To caramelize the mold: In baking mold with airtight cover melt sugar over low heat. Shake so that caramel coats bottom and sides. Cool at room temperature. If such a mold is unavailable, use a regular baking dish set in pan containing water to level of flan mixture.

Gerald Morales
New Orleans, La.

SHERRY TRIFLE

EGG CUSTARD

½ cup milk
1 strip lemon rind
2 egg yolks, well beaten
1 level Tablespoon sugar

TRIFLE

1 pound cake, thinly sliced
1 jar raspberry or strawberry jam
1 can raspberries or strawberries, strained
1 cup sherry
Egg custard
½ pint heavy cream, whipped
Almonds, chopped

EGG CUSTARD

Heat milk and lemon rind together but *do not* boil. Pour into beaten egg yolks. Cook in pan over hot water until custard thinly coats back of spoon. Add sugar, strain, and cool.

TRIFLE

Spread cake slices with jam and fruit. Arrange in glass dish alternating layers of cake, jam, and fruit. Saturate with sherry and cover with cooled custard. Top with whipped cream and garnish with nuts. May be prepared a day ahead except for whipped cream topping. Does not freeze.

This is the traditional English Sherry Trifle.

Mrs. Robert W. Fenet

CRÈME BRÛLÉE

10 egg yolks at room temperature
1 quart heavy cream
2 teaspoons vanilla extract or 1 vanilla bean
12 Tablespoons sugar
1 cup light brown sugar

Whisk egg yolks with steel whisk in deep dish until light lemon colored. Heat cream with vanilla in heavy saucepan to scalding point. Add sugar and stir with wooden spoon until completely dissolved. Whisk hot cream mixture slowly, but steadily, into egg yolks. Pour custard through a fine strainer into soufflé dish, a 10x12 inch flan dish, or individual custard cups. Set in roasting pan with hot water to halfway up sides of baking dish. Do not spill water on custard. Bake at 300°F for 60-70 minutes or until silver knife inserted in center comes out clean. Refrigerate until chilled. Push brown sugar through a sieve. Spread evenly ¼ inch thick on custard. Broil 4-6 inches from broiler for 2-4 minutes, turning dish as necessary to caramelize sugar evenly. Cool slightly at room temperature before serving. To serve, crack crust with back of a spoon and serve a piece with custard. Use egg whites for meringue.

Mrs. Kenneth L. Strauss
(Julie Ann Marx)

FLOATING ISLAND

3 eggs, separated
⅔ cup sugar
2 *slightly* heaping Tablespoons flour
1 quart homogenized milk
1 teaspoon vanilla
Nutmeg

Cream egg yolks with sugar until almost white. Add flour and whip. Scald milk, stirring constantly, over medium-low heat. Pour egg mixture into *hot* milk, stirring constantly. Cook on low heat, 20-25 minutes, until thick. Remove from heat. Add vanilla. Heat a large pot of water to boiling point. Add stiffly beaten egg whites folding water over them to cook. Using a large perforated spoon, lift whites out of water, add to custard mix, and cover with custard. Sprinkle with nutmeg. Serves 4.

Mrs. B. C. de la Houssaye
Crowley, La.

FRESH APPLE NUT PUDDING WITH RUM SAUCE

1 stick butter or margarine
1⅔ cups sugar
2 eggs
2 cups flour
2 teaspoons baking soda
½ teaspoon salt
2 teaspoons cinnamon
2 Tablespoons water
2 teaspoons vanilla
½ teaspoon butter flavoring
4 apples, peeled and diced
1 cup pecans, chopped

Cream butter and sugar. Add eggs and beat until creamy. Sift dry ingredients and add to egg mixture. Add water, vanilla, and butter flavoring. Beat for 2 minutes. Mix in apples and pecans by hand. Bake in greased and floured oblong pan at 350°F for 1 hour.

RUM SAUCE

1 stick butter
1 cup water
2 Tablespoons flour
¾ cup sugar
2 teaspoons vanilla
2 teaspoons rum flavoring
¼ teaspoon butter flavoring

RUM SAUCE

In saucepan bring butter and water to a boil. Add premixed flour and sugar. Add remaining ingredients and cook until bubbly. Remove from heat and serve hot over pudding.

Mrs. Robert Clifton
(Betty Flournoy)

TRIFLING PUDDING

1 quart milk
1 heaping cup sugar
2 Tablespoons flour or cornstarch
⅛ teaspoon salt
2 eggs, beaten
1 teaspoon vanilla
1 teaspoon almond extract (optional)
1 dozen lady fingers, split
1 cup pecans, chopped
1 pint fresh strawberries, washed and hulled, *or*
1 pint frozen whole strawberries (peaches may be substituted)
1 cup heavy cream, whipped

Bring milk to boil and set aside. Add sugar, flour or cornstarch, and salt. Return to stove and add beaten eggs, stirring constantly until fairly thick. Cool and add flavorings. Chill. Line a large serving bowl with lady fingers and garnish with pecans. Layer with custard, sprinkled pecans, fruit, and whipped cream. Continue layering until all custard is used, ending with topping of whipped cream, garnished with pecans. Chill, preferably overnight. Serves 8-10 generously.

This is an original old family recipe and a great Christmas dessert.

From the recipes of
Mrs. M. A. Quilty, Sr.

BAKED BANANAS

8-9 bananas (not too ripe), peeled
1 lemon
1 cup brown sugar
½ cup honey
1 stick butter, melted

Dip peeled bananas in lemon juice and place in pyrex dish. Add sugar and honey to melted butter. Pour over bananas and bake at 325°F for about 20 minutes. Serves 6.

Mrs. Charles S. Ware, Jr.
(Jan Allen)

BANANA PUDDING

¾ cup sugar
¼ cup flour
Pinch of salt
1 cup milk
1 cup evaporated milk
2 eggs, separated
1 teaspoon vanilla
3 Tablespoons butter
Vanilla wafers
2 bananas, sliced

Combine sugar, flour, salt, milk, and egg yolks in top of double boiler. Cook, stirring constantly, until fairly thick, about 15 minutes. Add vanilla and butter. Layer vanilla wafers and sliced bananas alternately with pudding in 1 quart pyrex dish. Beat egg whites with a little sugar added to make meringue. Cover pudding with meringue and brown at 400°F for about 5 minutes. Serves 4.

This is an original and very rich.

Mrs. Wayne Kemmerly, Jr.
(Billie Jean Prescott)

GRANDMOTHER'S OLD FASHIONED BREAD PUDDING

1 quart bread crusts
4 cups whole milk
5 eggs, beaten
1½ cups sugar
1½ cups raisins or strained canned fruit
2 teaspoons vanilla
½ teaspoon nutmeg

Place bread crusts with milk in mixing bowl. Chop with spoon until well softened. Beat eggs with hand beater until light. Add to bread crusts. Add remaining ingredients. Pour into buttered 9x13 inch pyrex dish and sprinkle with nutmeg. Bake, uncovered, at 350°F for 50 minutes, or until it springs back to touch. Serve with a hard candy type sauce. Serves 20.

Has been passed down for 5 generations.

Mrs. W. Sam Vincent
Mrs. Ray Hines

BACHELOR'S MOUSSE

1 cup light cream
1 cup heavy cream
1 box instant chocolate pudding
1 cup instant whipped cream
Semi-sweet chocolate shavings

Pour light and heavy cream into mixing bowl. Add pudding mix and beat with mixer or stir until it thickens. With slotted spoon fold in instant whipped cream by cutting through cream into pudding then up and over until cream and pudding are almost, but not completely, mixed. *Do not stir.* Spoon into individual servers. Sprinkle with chocolate shavings. Refrigerate until serving time.

Willis W. Noland

CHOCOLATE MOUSSE

1 package (6 ounces) chocolate chips
2 eggs
3 Tablespoons strong hot coffee
1 Tablespoon rum or cointreau
¾ cup milk, scalded

Place first 4 ingredients in blender and add scalded milk. Blend at high speed for 2 minutes. Serve chilled in sherbet glasses. Serves 4.

Mrs. Emmett Sole
(Annette Bland)

BLENDER CHOCOLATE PÔTS DE CRÈME

1 cup semi-sweet chocolate chips
1¼ cups light cream, scalded
2 egg yolks
3 Tablespoons brandy

Place all ingredients in blender and blend until smooth. Place in creme pots or demitasse cups. Cover and chill for 3 hours. Serves 6.

Mrs. Hunter T. Huddle
(Katherine Plauché)

CHOCOLATE ICE BOX PUDDING

2 bars (4 ounce size) German sweet chocolate
3 Tablespoons water
5 eggs, separated
½ cup sugar
1 teaspoon vanilla
18 lady fingers
1 pint heavy cream, whipped

Melt chocolate with water in double boiler. Beat egg yolks with sugar for 5 minutes in electric mixer. Add to melted chocolate. Cook over boiling water 15 minutes. Cool to room temperature. Beat egg whites to form soft peaks. Add vanilla and combine with chocolate mixture. Line bottom and sides of 10x6x3 inch pyrex dish with lady fingers. Cover with chocolate, then whipped cream. Repeat layers ending with a topping of lady fingers. Should be prepared a day ahead. Serves 10-12.

Mrs. James E. Watkins
Mrs. Felix Arceneaux

GLACÉE AU CHOCOLAT

10 ounces Maillard's Eagle sweet chocolate
¼ cup strong coffee
4 eggs, separated
6 ounces sweet butter, cut in pieces
Pinch of salt
⅔ cup sugar
¼ cup water
1 cup heavy cream
½ teaspoon vanilla

In top of an enameled double boiler set over hot water, melt chocolate in coffee, stirring occasionally. Stir in egg yolks, one at a time, and cook after each addition until mixture thickens slightly. Do not allow to boil. Remove pan from hot water and stir in butter, allowing 1 piece to melt before adding next. Beat egg whites with salt until they turn opaque. Meanwhile, place sugar and water in a small, heavy saucepan, bring to a boil, stirring until sugar dissolves. Boil without stirring until thermometer registers 225°F. Start beating egg white mixture again and continue beating while pouring syrup into bowl in a steady stream. Beat meringue until shiny and firm. Using lowest speed on electric mixer, fold chocolate cream into meringue. Pour into a 2 quart stainless steel mixing bowl and chill. When well chilled, loosen with flexible knife and gently invert onto a serving plate. Pour heavy cream into a chilled bowl set on ice cubes and beat slowly until thick. Stir in vanilla. Spread top of mold wtih whipped cream. Serves 8.

Mrs. Kenneth L. Strauss
(Julie Ann Marx)

AUNT TOMMY'S CHOCOLATE DESSERT

3 squares Baker's bitter chocolate
Water
¾ cup sugar
3 eggs, separated
Pinch of salt
2 dozen, more or less, lady fingers
1 pint heavy cream, whipped

Melt chocolate in a little water until smooth. Add sugar, then egg yolks slowly. Fold in egg whites that have been beaten with a pinch of salt. Line serving dish with lady fingers. Alternate layers of chocolate mixture and whipped cream with an extra layer of lady fingers if enough. Let stand overnight. Does not freeze. Serves 8-10.

Very pretty made in a Paul Revere silver bowl.

Mrs. Jack Thielen
(Della "Dudie" Krause)

CHOCOLATE YUMMY

CRUST

1 cup flour
1 stick margarine, melted
1 cup pecans, finely chopped

FILLING

1 cup Cool Whip
1 cup confectioners sugar
1 package (8 ounces) cream cheese
1 package (3 ounces) each chocolate and vanilla instant pudding
3 cups milk
3 cups Cool Whip
1 Hershey bar, frozen grated

CRUST: Mix all ingredients well. Spread crust in a 9½x13½ inch baking dish. Bake at 350°F for 20 minutes. Cool.

FILLING: Mix Cool Whip, sugar, and cream cheese. Spread over cooled crust. Mix puddings with milk. Let set for a few minutes to thicken. Pour over cream cheese layer and top with Cool Whip. Sprinkle with Hershey. Serves 10.

A dessert men love!

Laddie Clayton

POOR MAN'S PUDDING

6 eggs, separated
1 Tablespoon cornstarch
1 quart milk, scalded
Pinch of salt

Beat egg yolks slightly and add gradually to cornstarch. Blend well. Add well beaten egg whites. Add scalded milk and salt. Slowly pour into 1½ quart casserole and bake, uncovered, at 350°F until silver knife comes out clean. Serve with hard sauce. Serves 4-6.

HARD SAUCE

¾ cup (fine granulated) sugar
½ cup butter, creamed
3 Tablespoons whiskey, or to taste

HARD SAUCE

Add sugar gradually to creamed butter. Beat until well creamed. Add whiskey a little at a time. Serve pudding hot with sauce on top.

Old family recipe.

Mrs. Eleanor Gordon

PUDDING CAKE

1 cup flour
1 stick butter or margarine
1 cup pecans, finely chopped
1 package (8 ounces) cream cheese
1 cup confectioners sugar
1 large carton Cool Whip or whipped cream
1 package (6¾ ounces) chocolate, lemon, or butterscotch instant pudding
1 package (5½ ounces) vanilla instant pudding
3 cups cold milk
1 small Hershey bar, grated

Mix flour, butter or margarine, and pecans. Spread evenly on sides and bottom of 9x12 inch baking dish and bake at 350°F for 30 minutes. Cool. Soften cream cheese and fold in sugar and 1 cup Cool Whip. Spread over crust. Beat puddings with milk at low speed until thick and creamy. Spread over cream cheese mixture. Top with remaining Cool Whip sprinkled with grated Hershey. Cool overnight. Serves 12.

Mrs. John B. Polk
(Gayle Woods)

ENGLISH TOFFEE SQUARES

1 cup vanilla wafers, crushed
1 stick butter
2 cups confectioners sugar
2 Tablespoons cocoa
2 eggs, separated
1 cup pecans, chopped, salted, and toasted
½ pint heavy cream, whipped

Line 10x7x2 inch pan with crumbs mixed with a little butter. Bake at 350°F for 7 minutes. Let cool. Cream butter and sugar. Stir in cocoa. Add egg yolks and pecans. (This mixture will be very thick.) Beat egg whites stiffly and fold into mixture. Pour over cooled crumbs. Top with whipped cream sweetened to taste. Refrigerate. Cut into squares to serve. Better if made a day ahead.

Mrs. Joan W. Johnson

LEMON PUDDING CAKE

¼ cup butter
1½ cups sugar
4 egg yolks
½ cup all purpose flour, unsifted
2 cups milk
1 teaspoon lemon rind, grated
½ cup lemon juice
4 egg whites
Whipped cream (optional)

Cream butter and sugar until well blended. Beat in egg yolks. Blend in flour and milk. Stir in lemon rind and juice. Beat egg whites until soft peaks form. Gently fold into lemon mixture. Pour into 2 quart casserole or custard cups, set in shallow pan containing 1 inch of water. Bake, uncovered, at 325°F for 1-1½ hours, or until top is brown. Let stand 30 minutes before serving. Top with whipped cream if desired. Serve hot or cold. Serves 8.

Mrs. Gene Gilbert
(Ann Richard)

LEMON CUPS

1 cup sugar
4 Tablespoons flour
⅛ teaspoon salt
2 Tablespoons butter, melted
5 Tablespoons lemon juice
Rind of 1 lemon, grated
3 egg yolks, well beaten
1½ cups milk
3 egg whites, stiffly beaten

Blend sugar, flour, and salt with butter. Add lemon juice and rind and blend well. Add to egg yolks and milk and stir well. Fold in egg whites and pour into greased pyrex custard cups. Place cups in pan of hot water and bake, uncovered, at 350°F for 45 minutes. May be served warm or chilled. Cake rises to top and custard remains on bottom. Serves 8.

Old family recipe.

Mrs. T. L. Cooper

LEMON ICE BOX DESSERT

1 package lemon or lime Jello
1 cup sugar
1 cup water
½ cup lemon juice or Real Lemon
1 large can evaporated milk, chilled

Mix all ingredients, except milk, and let stand for 35 minutes. Whip chilled milk. Mix both together, whip, and refrigerate in serving dish or parfait glasses until time to serve. Serves 4.

This dessert would be good for a ladies' luncheon, or after a heavy meal, because it is light. Serve alone or with a plain cookie.

Mrs. Charles W. Andersen
(Martha Dugas)

COLD LEMON SOUFFLÉ WITH RASPBERRY SAUCE

SOUFFLÉ

1 envelope gelatin
2 Tablespoons water
Rinds of 4 lemons, grated
½ cup lemon juice
¾ cup sugar
1 cup egg whites (7-8)
1 cup heavy cream, whipped
1½ cups Raspberry Sauce au Kirsch

RASPBERRY SAUCE au KIRSCH

1 package (10½ ounces) frozen raspberries
¼ cup sugar
2 Tablespoons kirsch

SOUFFLÉ

In a small saucepan soften gelatin in water. Add lemon rind, juice, and sugar. Stir over low heat until gelatin is thoroughly dissolved. Chill to syrupy consistency. Beat egg whites until stiff, but not dry. Fold into lemon-gelatin mixture. Fold in whipped cream. Spoon into 1½ quart soufflé dish, collared with waxed paper or foil. Chill until set, remove collar, and serve with sauce. Serves 6.

RASPBERRY SAUCE au KIRSCH

Partially defrost raspberries. Place in blender with sugar, blend at high speed for 20 seconds, strain, and stir in kirsch.

Mrs. Thomas B. Shearman, Jr.
(Martha Hatchette)

For more juice from lemons, oranges, and grapefruit heat in oven for a few minutes before squeezing.

PINEAPPLE DELIGHT DESSERT

1 Tablespoon gelatin
2 Tablespoons water
20 large marshmallows, chopped
1 large can crushed pineapple, drained
½ pint heavy cream, whipped
Large box graham crackers, crumbled
Cool Whip
Pecans, chopped
8 cherries

Soften gelatin with water in large mixing bowl. Melt marshmallows over low heat and add to crushed pineapple. Let cool while whipping cream. Fold marshmallow-pineapple mixture into whipped cream. Place ½ of crumbs in 2 quart rectangular pyrex dish. Cover with mixture and top with remaining crumbs. Refrigerate, uncovered, 24 hours before serving. Cut into squares and serve with Cool Whip, garnished with pecans and a cherry. Serves 8.

Very pretty and tasty. A family favorite.

Mrs. Evelyn Chester Thompson

PEACH CRISP

8-9 ripe peaches, peeled and sliced
1 cup flour, sifted
1 cup granulated sugar
¼ teaspoon salt
½ teaspoon cinnamon
½ cup butter, softened

Place peaches in buttered 8x8x2 inch baking dish. Sift flour with sugar, salt, and cinnamon. Cut in butter with pastry blender until mixture resembles coarse corn meal. Arrange evenly over peaches. Bake at 375°F for 45-50 minutes, or until golden brown. Serve warm with cream or ice cream.

Mrs. W. Kent Cutrer
(Linda Arnold)

PEACH KUCHEN

¼ cup butter or margarine
2 cups all purpose flour, sifted
¼ teaspoon baking powder
½ teaspoon salt
1 cup sugar
8 peach halves, canned or fresh
1 cup sour cream
2 egg yolks, beaten
1 teaspoon ground cinnamon

Work butter into flour, baking powder, and salt mixture. Add 2 Tablespoons sugar and stir until coarse corn meal consistency. Press mixture firmly over sides and bottom of 8 inch glass baking dish. Cover with peach halves. Mix sour cream and egg yolks. Pour over peaches. Combine cinnamon and remaining sugar and sprinkle on top. Bake at 400°F for 20-25 minutes, or until done. Serve hot or cold. Serves 6-8.

Mrs. M. M. Cryer, Jr.

PEACH FANTASY

1 pint sour cream
⅓ cup grenadine
1 quart vanilla ice cream, softened
1 package (12 ounces) frozen peaches, thawed

Add sour cream and grenadine to softened ice cream. Add peaches with juice. Place in individual molds and freeze. Serves 6.

Men love this dessert.

Mrs. Patrick J. Unkel
(Barbara Perez)

FRENCH CRÊPES

4 eggs
1 cup flour, sifted
1 teaspoon salt
1 cup whole milk
½ teaspoon vanilla
3 Tablespoons butter

Beat eggs, flour, and salt in bowl. Add milk, vanilla, and butter that has been melted in crêpe pan. (If made the night before serving, omit butter and part of milk from mixture until ready to cook.) For each crêpe, spoon only enough batter into hot crêpe pan to spread thinly and evenly over bottom when tilted. Brown lightly on one side. Roll with desired filling. Freezes well between sheets of wax paper.

FILLINGS

For breakfast: Cover with syrup. For brunch: Fill with creamed crab meat. For dessert: Fill with mixture of cream cheese and sour cream, roll, and top with strawberries heated in pan with sugar and a little strawberry liqueur.

Recipe has been in my family for 5 generations.

Mrs. Maurice L. Tynes
(Pam Lennox)

CRÊPES FITZGERALD FILLING

24 dessert crêpes
FILLING
2 cartons (8 ounce size) sour cream
2 packages (8 ounce size) cream cheese

STRAWBERRY TOPPING
6 cups fresh strawberries, washed, halved
Butter
Sugar to taste
1 cup kirsch
1 cup strawberry liqueur

FILLING: Mix sour cream and cream cheese. Roll crêpes with mixture in center. Crêpes may be made in advance and refrigerated and topping flamed when serving. If refrigerated, when ready to serve, allow the crêpes to sit at room temperature until center is warm if you do not like the cool center and warm topping.

STRAWBERRY TOPPING: When ready to serve, place strawberries in large bowl, dot with butter, and sweeten with sugar. Heat kirsch and strawberry liqueur in large skillet. Add strawberries. Pour over individual servings of crêpes. (May be flamed in skillet.)

Mrs. James W. Crawford
(Sydalise "Sissie" Fredeman)

CRÊPES SUZETTE

SAUCE

⅜ pound butter
12 teaspoons sugar
3 oranges (peel and juice)
1 lemon (peel and juice)
¾ ounce cointreau
¾ ounce Grand Marnier
2 ounces brandy
10-12 cooked dessert crêpes

Melt butter, add sugar, and blend. Add orange and lemon peel. Simmer 5 minutes. Add juice, simmer until peel is soft and remove with fork. Dip cooked crêpes in sauce, fold or roll and move to side of pan. Heat liqueurs and brandy and pour evenly over crêpes. Ignite. Gently slide pan back and forth over heat and spoon sauce over crêpes until flame dies. Serve at once. Makes 5-6 servings of 2 crêpes per person.

Mrs. William D. Blake
(Katherine "Kay" Krause)

CREAM PUFFS

¼ pound butter
1 cup boiling water
1 cup flour
¼ teaspoon salt
4 eggs

FILLING

1 box (3¾ ounces) instant French vanilla pudding mix prepared according to package directions

CREAMY CHOCOLATE FROSTING

¼ cup water
2 Tablespoons butter
½ teaspoon vanilla
2 squares (1 ounce size) unsweetened chocolate
1½ cups confectioners sugar

BATTER

Add butter to saucepan with the boiling water. Add flour and salt all at once and cook, stirring vigorously, until mixture is smooth and forms soft ball that does not separate. Cool mixture slightly; add eggs one at a time, beating vigorously after each until mixture is smooth. Drop batter, 1 Tablespoon per cream puff, on greased cookie sheet. Bake at 450°F for 15 minutes; then at 325°F for 25 minutes. Remove from oven and let cool. With a sharp knife slice open and remove dough from inside.

FILLING

Fill each with 1 Tablespoon instant pudding and drizzle creamy chocolate frosting over top.

CREAMY CHOCOLATE FROSTING

Heat water and butter; add vanilla and chocolate, stirring until chocolate is melted. Add confectioners sugar and beat until smooth.

Mrs. Howard Jones, Jr.
Little Rock, Ark.

PAVLOVA

4 egg whites
Pinch of salt
6 level Tablespoons sugar
1 teaspoon vanilla essence
1 teaspoon corn flour, sifted
1 teaspoon vinegar

FILLING

2 cups whipping cream
Sugar and brandy to taste
3 cups strawberries

Beat egg whites with salt in warm bowl until they stand up in peaks. Add 2 level Tablespoons of sugar, continue whisking for a minute or so, fold in remaining sugar, and whisk until very stiff. Fold in vanilla, flour, and vinegar. Pour into well greased baking dish, making sides higher than center. Bake at 325°F for 1 hour, or until crisp and slightly brown on surface and moist inside.

FILLING: Whip cream with sugar and brandy to taste until stiff. Put into cooled meringue case and pour fruit in. Serves 4-6.

You will get raves on this delicious strawberry dessert.

Mrs. Robert W. Fenet

PARFAIT (BISQUE TORTONI)

1 cup sugar
¼ teaspoon salt
½ cup water
1 teaspoon Knox gelatine
1 Tablespoon cold water
1 teaspoon vanilla
¾ cup macaroons, crushed
1¼ cups pecans, chopped
6 egg yolks, beaten
½ cup maraschino cherries, chopped
2 cups cream, whipped

Boil sugar and salt in ½ cup water until it spins a thread. Soften gelatine in 1 Tablespoon water. Pour sugar mixture over this. Add remaining ingredients. Fold in whipped cream. Chill overnight in shallow pan or parfait glasses. Top with extra whipped cream when serving. Serves 8-10.

Mrs. Thomas L. Raggio
(Beverly Barry Crook)

COLD ORANGE SOUFFLÉ

2 envelopes unflavored gelatin
1 cup cold water
10 eggs, separated
2 Tablespoons orange rind, grated
16 ounces frozen orange juice concentrate, thoroughly defrosted but with no water added
1 cup sugar
1 cup heavy cream, chilled
3 Tablespoons sugar
½ cup heavy cream, whipped

Soften gelatin in cold water for about 5 minutes. With wire whisk, rotary or electric beater, beat egg yolks until thick and lemon yellow. Beat in softened gelatin. Add orange rind. Cook in a small enameled or stainless steel saucepan over moderate heat, stirring constantly, until it thickens enough to coat a spoon lightly. Do not boil, or it will curdle. Remove pan from heat and quickly stir in orange juice. Transfer to a large mixing bowl and chill in refrigerator for about ½ hour, or until it thickens to a syrupy consistency. Beat egg whites until frothy, add 1 cup sugar slowly, and beat until whites form unwavering peaks on beater when lifted from the bowl. In another bowl whip the chilled cream until it holds its shape softly; then beat in 3 Tablespoons sugar. With a rubber spatula fold cream gently but thoroughly into orange mixture (if it has set too firmly and formed lumps, beat gently with a whisk or rotary beater until smooth); then fold in egg whites, folding until no streaks of white show. Tie a waxed paper collar around a 1½ quart soufflé dish. It should rise about 2 inches above the rim of the dish. Pour in soufflé mixture to top of collar, smooth with a spatula, and chill in refrigerator for at least 4 hours, or until firm. Carefully remove collar and pipe decorative swirls of rosettes, or whipped cream through a pastry bag, on top of soufflé. Top center with a thin slice of orange. Serves 8.

Mrs. Irving Singer
(Melba Jowers)

AMBROSIA

1 can (13½ ounces) frozen pineapple chunks, thawed
1 ripe banana, peeled
3 medium oranges, sectioned
1 cup seedless grapes, or halved grapes, seeded
⅔ cup flaked coconut
½ cup ginger ale (optional)

Drain pineapple, reserving syrup. Slice banana on bias and dip in pineapple syrup to prevent browning. Arrange ½ of each fruit in serving bowl. Top with ½ the coconut, and add remaining fruit. Pour reserved pineapple syrup over mixture. Chill thoroughly. At serving time pour ginger ale over all and top with remaining coconut. Serves 4-6.

Mrs. J. J. Champeaux II
(Rosalie "Poddy" Leveque)

CRANBERRY CRUNCH

1 cup oatmeal, uncooked
½ cup flour
1 cup dark brown sugar
½ cup butter or margarine
1 pound cranberry sauce

Mix oatmeal, flour, and brown sugar. Cut in butter until crumbly. Place ½ mixture in greased 8x8 inch pan. Cover with cranberry sauce. Spread remaining mixture over sauce. Bake at 350°F for 45 minutes.

Great served with ice cream.

Mrs. David Buttross, Jr.
(Joyce Abraham)

PRUNE WHIP

2 pounds prunes, pitted or unpitted
11 Tablespoons sugar
1 teaspoon vanilla extract
10 egg whites, stiffly beaten
1 pint heavy cream, whipped

Cover prunes with water and boil until very soft. Mash with fork to remove pits (like mush). Place in deep mixing bowl and add sugar and vanilla. Add very slowly to beaten egg whites. Line a greased tube cake pan with greased waxed paper. Pour mixture into cake pan which has been placed in pan of water. Bake at 325°F for 1 hour. (Cake will rise over cake pan when cooking, but will sink after removing from oven.) When cool, place on serving plate and refrigerate overnight. Before serving, ice entire cake with whipped cream.

Mrs. Oliver Stockwell
(Roseina Holcombe)

MR. SNOWMAN

½ cup margarine
2 cups miniature marshmallows
½ teaspoon vanilla extract
¼ teaspoon salt
3 quarts unsalted popped popcorn
Additional miniature marshamallows
Colored sugar
Toothpicks
Black construction paper
Plaid material
Small paper cup
Black crepe paper

Melt margarine over low heat; add marshmallows, vanilla extract, and salt, and stir until melted and well blended. Pour over popcorn in large bowl and toss lightly until well coated. With slightly moistened hands shape ⅓ of popcorn mixture into ball for head and ⅔ into large ball for body. Press the 2 balls together and let stand until dry. Use simple decorations on snowman. For buttons, slightly moisten miniature marshmallows, roll in colored sugar, and secure with toothpicks. Cut eyes and mouth from construction paper. Tie plaid scarf around neck. Place paper cup covered with black crepe paper on brim of black construction paper for hat.

A decorative centerpiece for a festive table and also edible.

Mrs. Ida V. Willey

SNOW ON THE MOUNTAIN

1 pound sweet chocolate
6 eggs, separated
½ pound margarine, room temperature
1 Tablespoon vanilla
7 minute icing
Coconut

Melt chocolate in double boiler over hot water. Add yolks, one at a time, beating thoroughly, over low heat. Add margarine. Beat hard so that there are no lumps. Pour into electric mixing bowl and add vanilla. Beat egg whites until stiff and fold into chocolate mixture until well mixed. Pour into greased mold. Refrigerate overnight. Unmold on serving dish and return to refrigerator. Cover with 7 minute icing and coconut. Serves 8-10.

Mrs. Harold Richard

Lightly grease top of double boiler before melting chocolate for easy removal.

DANISH PASTRY

½ pound butter (do not substitute margarine)
3 cups flour, sifted
3 Tablespoons sugar
½ cup pecans, finely chopped
1 teaspoon vanilla
Pecan halves or tart jelly for filling
Confectioners sugar

Cream butter well. Add remaining ingredients and mix well. Shape into small rounds, making a *small* impression in center. Fill with pecan half or tart jelly. Bake on ungreased cookie sheet at 275°F for 45-60 minutes. Sprinkle with confectioners sugar while pastry is still warm. Makes 5 dozen.

From recipes of
Alice B. Kelly

SHORTCAKE (FRUIT)

2 cups flour
1 teaspoon baking powder
1 teaspoon salt
2 heaping Tablespoons sugar
½ cup shortening
Milk as needed
Butter

Mix flour, baking powder, salt, and sugar. Cut in shortening with fork or pastry cutter. Add milk slowly to form dough which can be rolled. Roll dough about ¼ inch thick and cut into 3 inch rounds. Dot with butter and sprinkle with sugar. Bake on ungreased cookie sheet at 400°F until brown.

This shortcake does not overpower the fruit. An old family recipe.

Mrs. O. A. Riser, Jr.
Covington, La.

PECAN-ALMOND TARTS

1½ cups pecans, chopped
2 sticks margarine
1 cup brown sugar
1 small egg, beaten
4 Tablespoons flour
½ teaspoon almond extract
1 or more teaspoons vanilla

Place pecans on cookie sheet and toast at 350°F until light brown. Set aside to cool. Cream butter and brown sugar. Add remaining ingredients and mix until well blended. Add pecans to creamed mixture. Place in paper cups in muffin tins and freeze. Serve in paper cups.

Mrs. Thomas O. Lind
New Orleans, La.

BAKED ALASKA

CAKE

1 pound cake or sponge cake
1 quart brick style ice cream

MERINGUE

5 egg whites at room temperature
1/8 teaspoon salt
1/2 teaspoon cream of tartar
1/2 teaspoon fresh lemon juice
1 1/4 cups confectioners sugar
1 cup brandy

Slice 1/2 inch from bottom of cake lengthwise. Spread ice cream on top of cake, leaving a ridge of cake uncovered. Slice remaining cake into 1/4 inch slices and cover ice cream completely, top and sides. Reserve remaining cake for another use. Place ice cream cake in freezer while making meringue. Beat egg whites and salt until frothy (soft peaks). Add cream of tartar and lemon juice and beat slowly while adding sugar, 1 Tablespoon at a time, until stiff. Remove cake from freezer and completely cover with 1 inch thickness of meringue. Swirl remaining meringue on top. Wrap carefully and return to freezer. To serve, preheat oven to 475°F and bake cake about 3 minutes, or until brown. Heat brandy, ignite, and pour over meringue. Slice and serve on chilled plates. Serves 8.

Robert J. Boudreau

BANANAS FOSTER ON ICE CREAM

1 cup rum
1/2 cup banana liqueur
1 stick margarine
1 cup brown sugar, packed
8 bananas, peeled and quartered
Dash cinnamon
Vanilla ice cream

Heat rum and banana liqueur in saucepan. Melt margarine and brown sugar in large skillet. Add bananas and cinnamon and cook lightly. Pour rum and liqueur over bananas. *Do not stir.* Ignite; serve immediately over ice cream. Serves 10.

This is a very easy and fun dessert for a group.

Mrs. James W. Crawford
(Sydalise "Sissie" Fredeman)

ALMOND TART

PART I

1 egg white
1 Tablespoon instant coffee
2 Tablespoons sugar
½ teaspoon almond extract
1 teaspoon vanilla extract
⅛ teaspoon salt

PART II

¼ cup sugar
1 teaspoon vanilla extract
½ teaspoon almond extract
1 cup heavy cream, whipped
½ cup nuts, chopped
Vanilla wafers, crushed
Red or green cherries

PART I: Beat egg white until stiff but not dry. Add remaining ingredients and beat until stiff. Set aside.

PART II: Add sugar, vanilla and almond extracts to whipped cream. Mix well. Fold into beaten egg white and add nuts. Pour into muffin tins lined with paper cups and freeze. To serve, unmold on crushed vanilla wafers, sprinkle with a few crumbs, and top with cherry. Serves 10.

Mrs. B. T. Dugazon
Baton Rouge, La.

ANGEL FOOD CAKE ICE CREAM PIE

Angel food cake, 21 ounce size
½ gallon vanilla ice cream, softened
1 can (6 ounces) frozen lemonade, thawed
2 cartons (8 ounces) frozen strawberries, thawed

Break cake into cubes in large bowl and mix with ice cream. Pack mix in two 9 inch pie plates. Pour 3 ounces of undiluted lemonade over each. Freeze until ready to serve. When serving, spoon strawberries over each portion. Serves 16.

Mrs. Raymond Ricketts
Houston, Texas

AVOCADO CRÈME

1 pint vanilla or buttered pecan ice cream
½ cup lime sherbet
2 avocados, peeled, seeded, mashed
Juice of ½ lime or more
2 Tablespoons lemon juice
2 Tablespoons sugar
¼ teaspoon salt
1 Tablespoon light rum (optional)

Soften ice cream and sherbet. Blend all ingredients in mixer. Pour into 1½-2 quart mold or bowl and place in freezer for at least 5 hours, stirring after 1 hour. Serves 6-8.

Very unusual, tastes more like lime than avocado.

Mrs. Patrick J. Unkel
(Barbara Perez)

BUTTERSCOTCH RING FOR ICE CREAM

½ cup heavy cream
1 cup dark brown sugar
¼ cup butter
½ box (8 ounce size) corn flakes
1 cup pecans, chopped
Vanilla ice cream

Cook cream and sugar in saucepan until a soft ball can be formed. Add butter, corn flakes, and pecans. Press mixture into buttered, chilled ring mold. Cover and refrigerate until ½ hour before serving. Invert on chilled plate and fill center with mound of ice cream. Serves 8.

Mrs. Edwin L. Gorham, Jr.
Beaumont, Texas

COCONUT-PECAN MERINGUE PIE SHELL FOR ICE CREAM

4 egg whites, very stiffly beaten
1 cup graham cracker crumbs
1 cup sugar
½ cup canned coconut
½ cup pecans, chopped
Vanilla ice cream

Mix egg whites with remaining ingredients except ice cream. Bake in greased 9 inch pie plate at 350°F for 25-30 minutes. Cool and freeze. Fill with ice cream and return to freezer.

Mrs. Boyce M. Jolly
(Martha Priester)

DEE'S DESSERT

1 can (13 ounces) evaporated milk, refrigerated for several hours
Graham cracker crumbs
1 cup sugar
Juice of 2-3 lemons

Place can of milk in freezer for 30 minutes. Chill 2 quart pyrex dish and beaters. Sprinkle crumbs on bottom of pyrex dish greased with margarine. Remove milk from freezer and beat with mixer until firm. Add sugar and lemon juice and beat until very firm. Pour into pyrex dish and sprinkle with crumbs. Place, covered, in freezer for at least several hours. Serve directly from freezer. Serves 12-14.

Mrs. Audis H. Thornton
(Jane Davidson)

REFRESHING FRUIT SHERBET

3 cups sugar
1 cup lemon juice
1 can (6 ounces) frozen orange juice
1 small can crushed pineapple or desired fruit
2 quarts milk

Mix all ingredients together, pour into ice cream freezer, and freeze as directed.

This is an old family recipe.

Mrs. W. R. Barnett

ICE CREAM BOMBE

½ gallon red raspberry sherbet, softened
3 pints pink peppermint or strawberry ice cream, softened
1 cup heavy cream, whipped
¼ cup almonds, toasted
3 Tablespoons confectioners sugar
Dash salt
Rum to taste
Fruit for garnish

To mold: Line 4 or 5 quart chilled mold with softened sherbet and freeze hard. Cover with layer of ice cream and freeze hard. Add remaining ingredients, except garnish, to whipped cream and fill center of mold. Cover with a top or foil and freeze hard. May be prepared 1 or 2 days in advance.

To serve: Invert mold, wrapping with hot towels to loosen contents, on a chilled tray. Return unmolded bombe to freezer to harden for a few minutes. Garnish with fresh whole strawberries or frosted green grapes. Serves 16.

Mrs. James E. Taussig
(Alice House)

CARAMEL ICE CREAM

CRUST
2 cups flour
½ cup oatmeal
½ cup brown sugar
1 cup margarine, melted
1 cup pecans, chopped

FILLING
½ gallon vanilla ice cream
1 jar caramel ice cream topping

CRUST: Combine all ingredients and crumble on a cookie sheet. Bake at 400°F for 15-20 minutes stirring to brown evenly. Remove and press ½ of crumbs on bottom of 9x13 inch pan.
FILLING: Layer ice cream and caramel sauce on top of crumb crust. Sprinkle with remaining crumbs. Freeze. Cut into squares and top with more caramel sauce. Serves 16.

Mrs. Charles S. Mackey
(Gail Barré)

CHOCOLATE ICE CREAM

⅓ cup sugar
4 eggs, beaten
3 cups milk
4 cups heavy cream
4½ teaspoons vanilla
½ teaspoon salt
3 cups chocolate syrup

Add sugar gradually to beaten eggs. Continue to beat until very stiff. Add remaining ingredients and mix thoroughly. Pour into freezer and freeze as directed.

Mrs. G. W. Tucker
(Betty Miller)

CHRISTMAS ICE CREAM

5 eggs
1 cup sugar
1 quart heavy cream, stiffly whipped
1 Tablespoon whiskey
1 small bottle each red and green cherries, finely chopped
½ cup pecans, chopped

Beat eggs until very light. Add sugar gradually and beat until all grains are dissolved. Add whipped cream to egg mixture. Add whiskey to taste. Add cherries and pecans. Freeze in ice trays. When it begins to freeze, stir well; then return to freezing compartment. Fills 2 ice trays.

Kenneth deBlanc

HOMEMADE ICE CREAM CUSTARD

4 cups sugar
2 Tablespoons flour
Pinch salt
6 eggs, beaten
3 quarts milk
1 large can evaporated milk
1 teaspoon vanilla
Crushed fruit (optional)

Add sugar, flour, and salt to beaten eggs. Heat 1 quart milk, pour very slowly into egg mixture, and cook for about 5 minutes. Add remaining 2 quarts milk, evaporated milk, and vanilla and mix thoroughly. If desired, add crushed fruit. Pour into freezer and freeze according to instructions.

Mrs. J. E. Pace

PEPPERMINT STICK ICE CREAM

2 cups peppermint candy (½ pound)
3 cups milk
⅛ teaspoon salt
3 cups coffee cream

Dissolve candy in hot milk over heat. Add salt and coffee cream. Pour into freezer and freeze as directed.

From the recipes of Mrs. J. W. Allen

UNCOOKED HOMEMADE VANILLA ICE CREAM

9 eggs, beaten until light
3 cups sugar
¼ teaspoon salt
3 cans evaporated milk
3 milk cans water
1 pint half and half
½ pint heavy cream
3 Tablespoons vanilla

To beaten eggs add sugar and salt. Add milk, water, and both creams, continuing to beat with electric mixer. Add vanilla and beat 1 minute longer. Chill in refrigerator. Pour into ice cream freezer and freeze as directed. Serves 8.

Easy and out of this world. Don't let the raw eggs turn you off. You'll never know they are there.

Mrs. B. Howard Cox

DESSERTS — FROZEN

VANILLA ICE CREAM

6 eggs, well beaten
2 cups sugar
3 tall cans evaporated milk
¼ cup vanilla
¼ teaspoon each lemon extract and salt
4 cups milk

In large mixing bowl combine all ingredients and mix well. Pour into ice cream freezer and freeze as directed. Makes 1 gallon.

Mrs. Freda Wilson Miller

ICE CREAM MACAROON DESSERT

2 dozen almond or coconut macaroons, crumbled
1 gallon ice cream, any flavor, softened
3 Heath bars, crushed

CHOCOLATE SAUCE

½ stick butter or margarine
2 ounces (2 squares) Baker's unsweetened chocolate
1 cup sugar
1 small can evaporated milk
1 teaspoon vanilla

Line bottom of 9 or 10 inch spring form pan with crumbs. Save remaining crumbs. Layer ½ ice cream over crumbs and cover with more crumbs, drizzle with chocolate sauce. Repeat the 3 layers. Garnish top with pieces of Heath bars. Freeze and remove shortly before serving time. Remove side of form. Cut into wedges like cake. Serve with chocolate sauce. (Double sauce recipe; 1 for use in dessert; 1 to serve over it.) Serves 12.

SAUCE: Melt butter and chocolate in saucepan. Stir in sugar and cook until dissolved and mixed. Stir in milk and vanilla and cook, stirring constantly, until thick and smooth. Keeps for weeks refrigerated in container. Should not be frozen before use on this dessert.

Mrs. Adolph S. Marx
(Mathilde Weil)

SHERBET MACAROON

1 pint heavy cream, whipped
18 crisp macaroon cookies, crumbled
1 teaspoon vanilla
3 Tablespoons sugar
1 cup pecans, chopped
2 pints sherbet (2 flavors)

Mix whipped cream with remaining ingredients, except sherbet. Spread ½ mixture in 9x13 inch pan. Add sherbet by spoonfuls, alternating flavors. Spread remaining mixture. Freeze and cut into squares. Serves 6-8.

This is an Army recipe.

Mrs. Robert Welborn
(Pat Branch)

MINT ICE CREAM PIE

2 Tablespoons butter, melted
4 squares German sweet chocolate, melted
2 cups rice krispies
1 quart mint or coffee ice cream, softened
Chocolate curls

Mix butter, chocolate, and rice krispies. Spread in pie plate and freeze. Fill with ice cream and refreeze. Just before serving, sprinkle with chocolate curls. Serves 8.

This is an original recipe and is easy and good.

Mrs. Frank C. Miller, Jr.
(Angela Liggio)

To make chocolate curls, warm milk chocolate bar (4 ounces), still wrapped. Place in a warm spot just until soft, not melting. Then, pressing lightly with vegetable peeler, pare lengthwise in a long, thin stroke to form a curl. Lift with toothpick to plate; refrigerate.

WATERMELON SHERBET

2 quarts watermelon juice
1½ cups sugar
Pinch salt
1 lemon
1 egg white, beaten

Press watermelon pulp through colander to obtain 2 quarts juice. (There may be some pulp in juice.) Add sugar, salt, and lemon juice. Fold in egg white. Pour into freezer and freeze as directed. Makes nearly a gallon. Watermelon juice with sugar added may be frozen in advance.

From the recipes of
Mrs. J. W. Allen

TORTONI

1 package (8 ounces) Philadelphia cream cheese
1 cup corn syrup
1 cup milk
1 cup coconut or almond macaroons, broken
½ cup nuts, chopped
1 teaspoon vanilla
¼ teaspoon almond extract
Maraschino cherries

Mix until smooth cream cheese, corn syrup, and milk. Stir in remaining ingredients, except cherries. Spoon into paper baking cups and set in muffin pan. Freeze until firm. May be frozen for at least a week in advance of serving. Garnish with cherries. Serves 12.

Mrs. Eli Sorkow

ALOHA SAUCE

2 Tablespoons each lemon, orange, and lime juice, strained
⅓ cup water
⅔ cup sugar
2 Tablespoons rum

Mix all ingredients thoroughly. Heat until sugar is dissolved. Chill. Serve over desired fresh fruit, placed in scooped out watermelon shell or individual dishes. Makes 1½ cups.

Mrs. C. J. Lloyd
(Claire Fore)

FLUFFY BOURBON SAUCE

1 cup confectioners sugar, sifted
Pinch salt
2 egg yolks, beaten
3-4 Tablespoons bourbon
½ pint heavy cream, whipped, or Cool Whip

Beat sugar and salt into beaten egg yolks. Stir in bourbon. Gently fold in whipped cream. Chill until ready to use. Stir before using. Serves 18.

Mrs. Fannie Chitty

CARAMEL SAUCE

1¼ cups brown sugar
4 Tablespoons butter
⅔ cup light Karo syrup
¾ cup evaporated milk
½ cup nuts, chopped (optional)
½ cup maraschino cherries, finely chopped (optional)

Boil sugar, butter, and syrup until a soft ball is formed (235°F on candy thermometer). Add milk slowly to boiling sugar mixture. Add nuts and/or cherries if desired. This is a good ice cream topping.

Old family recipe.

Mrs. Lucille Coyle

CHOCOLATE SAUCE

½ stick butter or margarine
2 ounces (2 squares) Baker's unsweetened chocolate
1 cup sugar
1 small can evaporated milk
1 teaspoon vanilla

Melt butter and chocolate. Stir in sugar, cooking until melted and blended. Stir in milk and vanilla and cook until thick and smooth. Keeps for weeks refrigerated in covered container.

Mrs. Adolph Marx
(Mathilde Weil)

HARD SAUCE

½ stick butter
1 cup confectioners sugar
2 Tablespoons brandy or bourbon

Cream butter in electric mixer until soft and fluffy. Gradually add sugar beating constantly. Add brandy or bourbon and continue beating until light. Store in covered glass container in refrigerator. Serve on hot puddings or mince pie.

Mrs. Malcolm Powell
(Evelyn Knapp)

LEMON SAUCE

½ cup sugar
¼ cup lemon juice
1 cup water
2 Tablespoons cornstarch dissolved in ¼ cup cold water
1 Tablespoon corn oil margarine

Cook sugar, lemon juice, and water in small saucepan over low heat, stirring until sugar dissolves. Bring to a boil. Add cornstarch paste and, stirring constantly, cook over moderate heat until mixture thickens, clears, and begins to boil. Remove from stove and stir in margarine. Makes 1¾ cups.

Mildred Girod

RUM SAUCE

½ cup butter
1 cup granulated sugar
½ cup light cream
Dash of nutmeg
1 teaspoon vanilla extract
¼ cup (or more) light rum

Cook butter, sugar, and cream in advance in double boiler for 10-15 minutes, or until slightly thickened. Refrigerate. About 15 minutes before serving, add remaining ingredients, and reheat in double boiler. Makes 1½ cups.

This is delicious served over coconut pound cake.

Mrs. Stephen E. Plauche´
(Edith Burton)

THE METRIC SYSTEM

During this transitional period from the English system of measurement to the metric, the metric system seems to many a mystery as impenetrable as a South Louisiana swamp or as obscure as the secret of LaFitte's hidden treasure.

For example, a recipe calling for 400 milliliters might panic the bravest when faced with an equation of the following complexity to convert to cups:

$$\frac{400 \text{ ml} \times 1 \text{ liter} \times 2.113 \text{ pts.} \times 2 \text{ cups}}{1000 \text{ ml} \quad 1 \text{ liter} \quad 1 \text{ pt.}} = 1.690 \text{ cups}$$

Fortunately for the weaker minded of us, the mind-boggling equations have been transposed by Dr. Kalil Ieyoub into simple conversion tables.

APPROXIMATE CONVERSIONS FROM ENGLISH TO METRIC MEASURES

Symbol	When You Have	Multiply By	To Convert To	Symbol
oz.	ounces	28	grams	g
lb.	pounds	0.45	kilograms	kg
tsp.	teaspoons	5	milliliters	ml
Tbsp.	tablespoons	15	milliliters	ml
fl. oz.	fluid ounces	30	milliliters	ml
c	cups	0.24	liters	l
pt.	pints	0.47	liters	l
qt.	quarts	0.95	liters	l
gal.	gallons	3.8	liters	l
in.	inches	2.5	centimeters	cm
F°	Fahrenheit Temperature	5/9 after subtracting 32° from temp. reading	Celsius temp.	C°

APPROXIMATE CONVERSIONS FROM METRIC TO ENGLISH MEASURES

Symbol	When You Have	Multiply By	To Convert To	Symbol
g	grams	0.35	ounces	oz.
kg	kilograms	2.2	pounds	lb.
ml	milliliters	0.2	teaspoons	tsp.
ml	milliliters	0.067	tablespoons	Tbsp.
ml	milliliters	0.03	fluid ounces	fl. oz.
l	liters	4.17	cups	c
l	liters	2.1	pints	pt.
l	liters	1.06	quarts	qt.
l	liters	0.26	gallons	gal.
cm	centimeters	0.4	inches	in.
C°	Celsius temp.	9/5 (then add 32°)	Fahrenheit temp.	F°

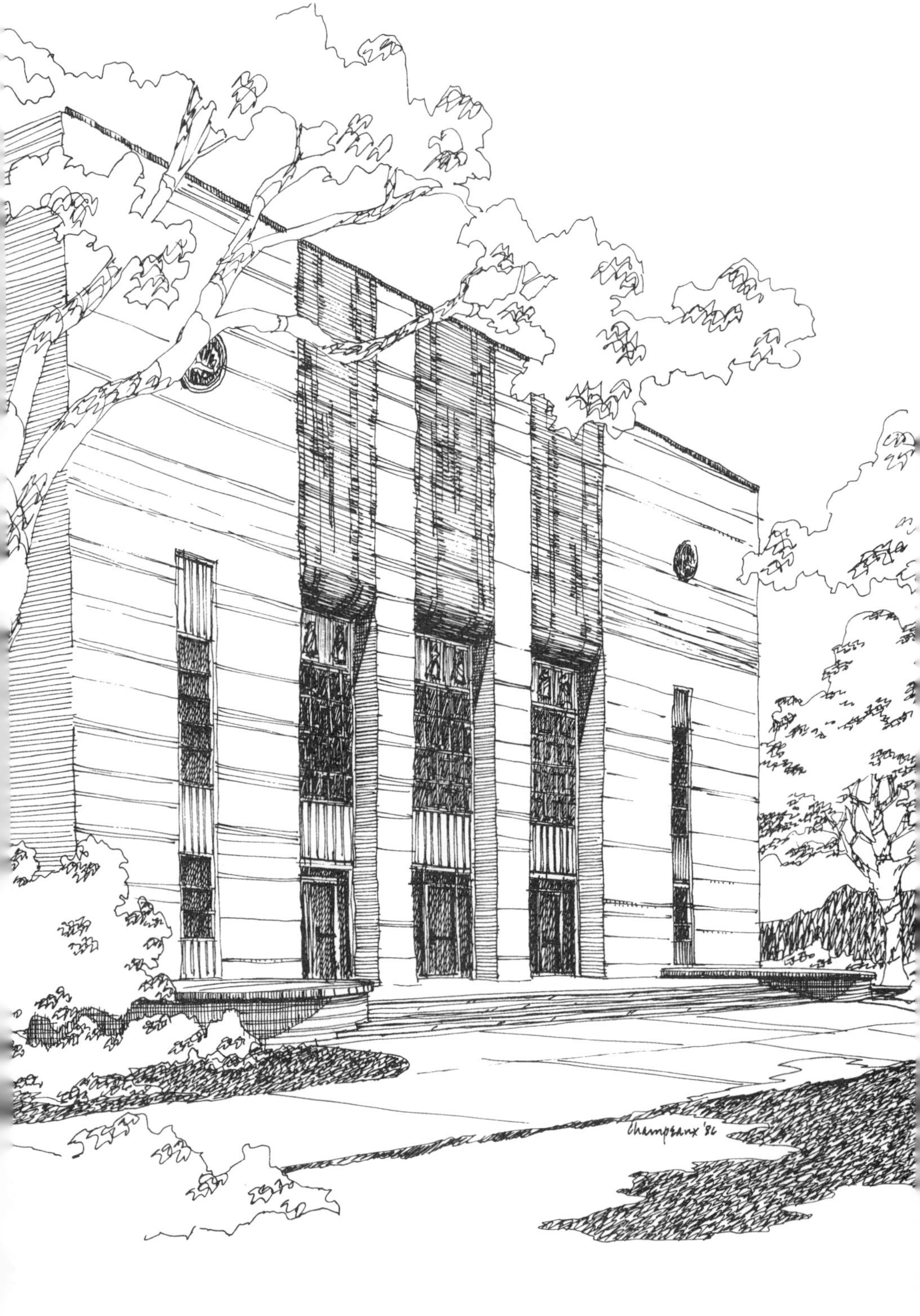
Champeaux '86

McNEESE STATE UNIVERSITY

The main auditorium is one of three original buildings still in use at McNeese State University—a reminder of its humble origins as Lake Charles Junior College. The school opened in 1939 as a division of Louisiana State University on an 86 acre tract donated by the Calcasieu Parish Police Jury. The main auditorium, completed in 1940, was still under construction when the two-year college opened its doors in the fall of 1939 with only two completed buildings, a faculty of 10 headed by Dean Joe Farrar, and a first class of 154 students.

Although discussion on how to establish an institution of higher learning had begun as early as the 20's, it was not until 1937 that funds, in the amount of $850,000, were finally appropriated, and a subsequent bond issue was passed. Gov. Richard Leche then helped secure a federal grant from the Work Projects Administration (WPA) for construction.

In 1940 the school's name was changed to the John McNeese Junior College to honor the father of Southwest Louisiana public education. McNeese had been the first superintendent of Calcasieu Parish schools. It was not long before seven new teachers were hired, a curriculum in agriculture was added, and an 80-acre farm was purchased. During the next decade the college grew in size and stature.

In July of 1950 the Louisiana legislature approved McNeese as a four-year college. On hearing the news, President Dwight D. Eisenhower sent an autographed picture and a wire of congratulations to then President Lether M. Frazar. Eisenhower had camped on McNeese property as a lieutenant colonel during the U.S. Army's Louisiana maneuvers preceding World War II.

Within five years, the college had tripled its enrollment. The first bachelor's degree was awarded in 1952, and by 1954 McNeese had been accredited by the Southern Association. In 1970 the name was changed from McNeese State College to McNeese State University denoting the school's higher status as an institution offering graduate degrees.

Academic excellence and research top the list of priorities for McNeese State University. However, the school's number one concern remains the same as it was nearly 50 years ago: the betterment of the individual student.

Fast & Fabulous

Today's cook — if truth be told —
Is adventurous, daring, smart, and bold.
The kitchen's a place for swashbuckling feats,
Thirty-minute dinners and quick-fix treats.
This section, we've added, just for your pleasure.
It's FAST AND FABULOUS, a gourmet's treasure.
Throughout this book you'll find marked with a CHEST
All that we tested and found "quickest and best."
With flagons raised high — like pirates of old:
To the fast, the fabulous, the quest, and the gold.

The Editors

SHRIMP BISQUE

1 package Knorr cream of leek soup mix
3 cups water
1 cup fresh shrimp, peeled and sautéed in 1 Tablespoon butter, or 1 can (4½ ounces) shrimp, drained
1 teaspoon Worcestershire sauce
Tabasco to taste
1 cup heavy or light cream
Parsley
Paprika

Cook soup according to package directions using only 3 cups of water instead of 4½ cups. Add shrimp, Worcestershire, and Tabasco. Remove from heat. Add cream. Season to taste. Garnish with parsley flakes and paprika.

To make crab bisque, use a small can (6½ ounces) of claw crabmeat. To make oyster bisque, use oysters and chopped artichoke hearts.

Mrs. Jeffery M. Cole
(Polly Pugh)

CHOWDER CONTRABAND

2 medium onions, chopped
1 can (4 ounces) sliced mushrooms
1 stick butter
2 cans (10½ ounce size) Swanson's chicken broth
Select 3-6 of following:
   1 package frozen hash browns
   1 package frozen or 1 fresh bunch broccoli
   1 package frozen or 1 fresh head cauliflower
   1 cup carrots, shredded
   1 can (6 ounces) artichoke hearts, drained
   1 package frozen corn
2 cans (10½ ounce size) Cheddar cheese soup
2 cups milk
Salt and pepper to taste

Sauté onions and mushrooms in butter. Add chicken broth and desired vegetables. Cook on medium high for 15 minutes. Add soup and milk. Stir well until soup is well dissolved. Season to taste. Serves 6.

Susan Elender

SAUSAGE BEAN CHOWDER

2 pounds link pork sausage
4 cups water
1 can (16 ounces) kidney beans, undrained
1 can (16 ounces) pinto beans, undrained
2 cans (16 ounce size) tomatoes, undrained
2 medium onions, chopped
2 medium potatoes, peeled and cubed
½ cup bell pepper, chopped
3 carrots, peeled and sliced
1 large bay leaf
½ teaspoon salt
½ teaspoon thyme
¼ teaspoon garlic powder
¼ teaspoon pepper

Cut sausage into 1 inch pieces. Brown and drain. Stir in remaining ingredients. Bring to a boil, cover, and reduce heat. Simmer 1 hour. Serves 6.

Faster with a food processor. Freezes well.

Mrs. Clayton Davis
(Geralyn Peace)

CRÈME D'ARTICHAUTS

3 onions, chopped
3 Tablespoons oil
2 cloves garlic, chopped
4 leeks, sliced thin
½ pound fresh mushrooms, sliced
4 cups chicken stock
4 cooked artichokes or 4 cans artichoke hearts/bottoms, puréed
Salt and pepper to taste
Juice of 1 lemon
1 teaspoon orégano
1 cup white wine
2 Tablespoons butter
2 teaspoons flour
1 cup heavy cream
Fresh parsley

Sauté onions in oil until golden. Add garlic, leeks, and mushrooms and brown. Add stock, artichokes, salt, pepper, lemon juice, orégano, and wine. Bring to boil. Reduce heat. Simmer 20 minutes. Mix butter and flour and add to liquid. Cook, stirring until thickened. Remove from heat. Add cream. Garnish with parsley. Serves 8.

Mrs. Frederick Northup
(Julie Seibels)

SQUASHBUCKLING SOUP

6 medium yellow squash, thinly sliced
1 large onion, sliced
½ stick butter
1 cup milk
1 large can evaporated milk
1 can (10½ ounces) Swanson's chicken broth
1 teaspoon sugar
1 teaspoon salt
Red pepper to taste

Sauté squash and onion in butter until tender (approximately 20 minutes). Pour half of squash and onion mixture into a blender with ½ cup of milk. Blend 45 seconds on high. Remove from blender to a separate saucepan. Repeat with remaining onion and squash mixture. Add evaporated milk and Swanson's chicken broth to saucepan. Whip with wire whisk. Add sugar, salt, and red pepper. Boil 2-3 minutes. Serves 4. Serve hot or cold.

Susan Elender

MARSH MELON SOUP

3 cantaloupes
1 small can orange juice (concentrated)
¼ cup honey
1 pint whipping cream
Dash of cinnamon

Cut up cantaloupe and place in blender with orange juice. Purée until all cantaloupe has been added. Add honey, cream, and cinnamon. Blend. (Honey may be adjusted depending on sweetness of cantaloupe.) Serve cold in glasses. Garnish with orange slice and mint. Serves 6-8 (about 5 cups).

Can be made 1 day in advance. Keeps several days. Do not freeze.

Mrs. John Van Norman
(Lee Elledge)

CARROT VICHYSSOISE

2 cups potatoes, peeled and diced
1¼ cups carrots, sliced
1 leek, sliced
3 cups chicken stock
Dash white pepper
1 teaspoon salt
1 cup heavy cream
1 raw carrot, shredded

Put potatoes, carrots, leek, and chicken stock into a saucepan. Bring to a boil and simmer for 25 minutes or until vegetables are tender. In an electric blender, purée half the vegetables and liquid at a time for 30 seconds each at high speed. Empty into mixing bowl and stir in pepper, salt, and cream. Chill. Serve in chilled bowls, garnished with shredded raw carrot. Serves 4-6.

Mrs. Frederick Northup
(Julie Seibels)

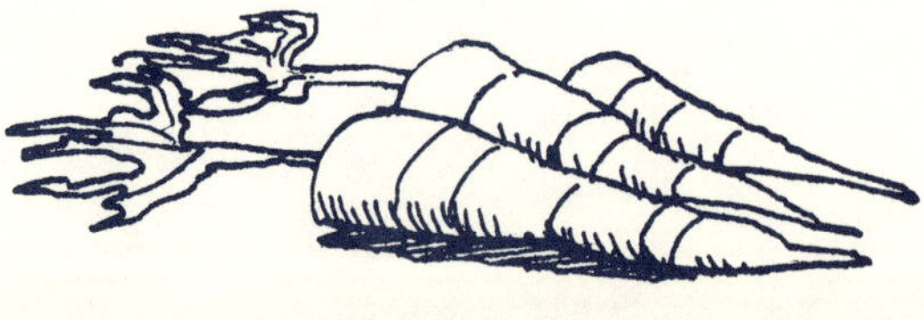

CHESTNUT MEATBALLS

2 cups soft bread crumbs (2½ slices)
½ cup milk
1 Tablespoon soy sauce
½ teaspoon garlic salt
¼ teaspoon onion powder
½ pound ground beef
½ pound bulk pork sausage
1 can (8 ounces) water chestnuts, drained and finely chopped

Combine bread crumbs, milk, soy sauce, garlic salt, and onion powder. Add ground beef, pork sausage, and water chestnuts. Mix well. Form into 1 inch balls. Bake at 350°F for 18-20 minutes. Makes about 5 dozen.

Mrs. James Henry
(Carol Williamson)

POLYNESIAN SAUSAGE

3 pounds large link smoked sausage
1 cup grape jelly
1 bottle (12 ounces) Heinz chili sauce

Cook sausage in a little water until done. When cool, cut into bite-sized pieces. In sauce pan combine jelly and chili sauce and heat over low heat until well blended. Pour over sausage pieces and serve hot with tooth pick servers. May be placed in a chafing dish. May be frozen. Serves 12.

Mrs. John McGraw, Jr.
(Mary Frances Dimmick)

SHRIMP ITALIANO

8 ounces cream cheese, softened
1 bottle (12 ounces) chili sauce
1 bunch green onions, chopped
1 can (4¼ ounces) shrimp, chopped
1 can (4¼ ounces) chopped black olives
1 bell pepper, chopped
8 ounces Mozzarella cheese, shredded

Spread cream cheese on 12 inch glass plate. Layer chili sauce, green onions, shrimp, black olives, bell pepper, and Mozzarella cheese. Serve with large corn chips. Serves 12.

Mrs. Douglas Goings
(Carol Gani)

LAST MINUTE CRAWFISH

1 bunch green onions, chopped
1 stick butter
1 package (16 ounces) crawfish tails and fat, defrosted
Lawry's seasoned garlic salt
2 Tablespoons Lea & Perrins

In a saucepan, sauté green onions in 1 stick melted butter for 3 minutes. Add crawfish tails and fat. Salt to taste. Cook 2 minutes. Add Lea & Perrins and cook on low 5 minutes. Serve immediately with crackers. Serves 6-8.

Can be served as a main dish over rice or noodles. Add 1 Tablespoon flour to the crawfish and cook for 3 more minutes, stirring frequently. Then add 1 cup or more of half-and-half slowly and cook until sauce is thickened to desired consistency.

Mrs. Keith DeSonier
(Dale Dane)

BLACKEYED PEA DIP

1 onion, chopped
2 or 3 garlic buds, mashed
1 stick margarine, melted
2 cans (16 ounce size) Jalapeño blackeyed peas, drained
1 1/3 sticks Cracker Barrel sharp cheese, grated
1 teaspoon Lea & Perrins
Dash Tabasco
Lawry's salt to taste

Sauté onion and garlic in melted margarine. Place this mixture in blender. Add remaining ingredients and cream in blender. May be served warm or cold with crackers, chips, or vegetables. Serves 20.

Perfect for those who don't like blackeyed peas to eat on New Year's Day!!

Mrs. Don Wallace
(Sylvia Van Eaton)

THISTLE DIP

1 can (14 ounces) artichoke hearts, drained
1 cup sour cream
1 cup mayonnaise
1 package Italian salad dressing mix
2 teaspoons Worcestershire sauce
Dash Tabasco
1 Tablespoon lemon juice
Paprika

Cut artichoke hearts into bite-sized pieces or mash with fork. Combine all ingredients. Cover and refrigerate at least 1 hour. Sprinkle with paprika and serve with crackers or vegetables. Makes 2 cups.

Mrs. William McCall
(Nadine Newlin)

Mrs. Michael Garber *adds 1 clove minced garlic and ¼ teaspoon onion salt.*

CURRY DIP ROYALE

1 cup mayonnaise
2 Tablespoons Durkee sauce
1 teaspoon celery seed
½ teaspoon Worcestershire sauce
Dash Tabasco
Dash black pepper
1½ Tablespoons prepared horseradish
1½ teaspoons curry powder
1 teaspoon seasoned salt
¼ teaspoon garlic powder
Juice of 1 lemon

Process in blender or food processor until well mixed. Serve with fresh vegetables. Makes 1¼ cups.

Mrs. Charles R. Anderson
(Betty Harlow)

GREEN GOODNESS DIP

6 ounces cream cheese, softened
1 cup mayonnaise
1 cup sour cream
2 Tablespoons lemon juice
2 Tablespoons tarragon vinegar
1 Tablespoon garlic salt
½ cup green onions, chopped (use more tops than bottoms)
⅔ cup fresh parsley, chopped

Mix all ingredients and serve as a dip with fresh vegetables.

Mrs. Don Wallace
(Sylvia Van Eaton)

SOMBRERO DIP

½ package dry taco seasoning
1 large can (9 ounces) bean dip
1 pint sour cream
2 containers (8 ounce size) Kraft guacamole dip
Sliced black olives
Thin tomato slices
1 can (4 ounces) chopped green chilies, drained
1 cup Cheddar cheese, grated
1 cup Monterey Jack or Mozzarella cheese, grated
1 jar (16 ounces) picante sauce

Combine taco seasoning and bean dip to make the first layer. Layer remaining ingredients in a 2 quart casserole dish in order listed. Top with picante sauce just before serving. Serve with tortilla chips. Serves 6-8.

Mrs. Mark Andrus
(Janet Crowe)

FESTIVE FLORENTINE DIP

1 package (10 ounces) chopped spinach, defrosted and drained
1 package Knorr's vegetable soup mix
1 cup mayonnaise
1 cup sour cream
1 can (8 ounces) water chestnuts, drained
¼ teaspoon red pepper

Put all the ingredients in a food processor and blend until mixed well. Chill. Serve with raw vegetables or chips. Serves 10-12.

Pretty served in a hollowed-out loaf of Hawaiian bread, head of red cabbage, or steamed artichoke.

Mary "Tootsie" Helman Parsons

CHARLIE'S PICANTE SAUCE

3 cans (14½ ounce size) stewed tomatoes, undrained
½ teaspoon salt
½ teaspoon garlic powder
3 Tablespoons oil
1½ Tablespoons white vinegar
1 can (10 ounces) Rotel tomatoes with green chilies
2 Jalapeño peppers, finely diced

In blender place juice from 1 can stewed tomatoes (no pulp), salt, garlic powder, oil, vinegar and then purée. Add Rotel, pulp from 1 can stewed tomatoes, and 1 more can stewed tomatoes. Flick blender on and off in 6-8 short pulses. Pour into large bowl. Add last can stewed tomatoes in blender. Flick blender on and off in short pulses. Pour into rest of dip. Stir in diced Jalapeños. Enjoy with tortilla chips. Stores in glass container for 2 weeks. Makes 8 cups.

Charles R. Anderson

JALAPEÑO CHEESE SPREAD

2 pounds American cheese
1 onion
1 pod garlic
4-6 Jalapeño peppers
1 pint mayonnaise

Grate cheese in food processor. Then transfer to large mixing bowl. Chop onion, garlic, and Jalapeño peppers in processor and transfer to bowl. Add mayonnaise and mix with large spoon. Beat with hand mixer until smooth. Put in jars. Makes 2 quarts.

For those less timid, increase the Jalapeño peppers.

Mrs. Louis Haxthausen
(Linda "Penny" Boelens)

STRAWBERRY PADDLE WHEEL

1 pound sharp Cheddar cheese
1 small onion
1 cup pecans
1 cup mayonnaise
Dash red pepper
Dash black pepper
1 small jar strawberry preserves

Using grating disk of processor, shred cheese, onion, and pecans. Add mayonnaise and seasonings to cheese mixture and blend with plastic blade or by hand with a fork. Form into circle and fill with strawberry preserves. Serve with crackers. Serves 15-20.

Mrs. David Brumby
(Jane Pumpelly)

SCHOONER SQUARES

6 eggs
1 pound sharp Cheddar cheese, grated
2-3 Jalapeño peppers, chopped
2 Tablespoons green chilies, chopped
Dash chili powder
Dash cumin

Beat eggs in bowl. Add grated cheese, peppers, and chilies. Add seasonings. Pour into oblong pyrex pan. Bake at 350°F for 30 minutes. Cool before cutting into squares. Makes about 35 squares.

Mrs. Adam Ortego, Jr.
(Nancy Desormeaux)

CHEESE STRAWS

½ pound butter (2 sticks)
4 ounces sharp cheese, grated
2 cups flour
¾ teaspoon salt
½ teaspoon red pepper
½ teaspoon garlic powder
2 cups Rice Krispies

Cream the butter and grated cheese. Gradually add flour, salt, red pepper, and garlic powder. Mix together well. Fold in Rice Krispies until the dough becomes stiff. (If too dry, add more butter to achieve desired consistency.) Place 2-3 inch lengths onto an ungreased cookie sheet. Flatten with a fork. Bake at 325°F for 20 minutes or until crisp. Makes about 3 dozen.

May substitute 1 package (2½ ounces) sunflower seeds for Rice Krispies.

Mrs. William McCall
(Nadine Newlin)

RYE SNACKS

1 pound hot sausage
1 pound ground beef
½ teaspoon onion salt
1 teaspoon orégano
1 Tablespoon parsley flakes
½ teaspoon garlic salt
Dash of red pepper
Dash of lemon pepper
1 pound Velveeta cheese, cubed
2 packages party rye bread

In skillet cook sausage, ground beef, and seasoning until done. Add cubed cheese and stir until melted. Spread thinly party rye bread slices while meat mixture is still hot. Place on cookie sheet under broiler until hot and bubbly, and lightly brown. Freezes well. Serves 15-20.

Mrs. Douglas Goings
(Carol Gani)

SPICE BITES

1 cup oil, heated
1 box (16 ounces) oyster crackers
1 package dry Ranch Style buttermilk dressing mix
1 teaspoon dill weed
1 teaspoon lemon pepper
1 teaspoon garlic salt
1 teaspoon Creole seasoning

Mix oil with crackers by hand in a 13x11 inch pan. Add dressing mix and spices. Toss well to coat. Bake at 275°F for 15 minutes. Store in air tight container when cool.

Great munchies. Also good in salads.

Mrs. Henry Liles
(Barbara Jenks)

BACON-WRAPPED SNACKS

1 package bacon
1 can sliced water chestnuts

Wrap ½ slice of bacon around 2 water chestnut slices. Secure with a toothpick. Place on a platter and cover with paper towels. Microwave on high for ½ minute per wrapped chestnut or until bacon is crisp. (May also be baked in conventional oven at 350°F for 15-18 minutes, or until bacon is crisp.) May be made the morning before and cooked when needed.

For added spice, marinate in soy sauce before cooking.

Mrs. Woodrow Mock
(Sharon Clayton)

MEXICAN ROLL-UPS

4 large (10 inch) flour tortillas
2 packages (8 ounce size) cream cheese, softened
1 clove garlic, minced
2 Jalapeño peppers, seeded
1 Tablespoon milk

Combine cream cheese, garlic, peppers, and milk in food processor. Spread mixture on tortillas, completely covering. Roll up jelly roll style. Wrap each roll in plastic wrap. Then roll in a damp dish towel when all are completed. Chill several hours. Slice into 12 pieces per roll. Freezes well in a freezer bag.

Good alone or dipped in picante sauce and guacamole dip.

Mrs. Henry Liles
(Barbara Jenks)

GREEK BREAD

1 loaf French bread
1 stick butter, softened
½ cup mayonnaise
Garlic powder to taste
1 small can ripe, pitted olives, drained and chopped
3 green onions, chopped
½ pound Mozzarella cheese, shredded

Cut the loaf of French bread in half lengthwise and open. Mix butter, mayonnaise, and garlic powder in a bowl. Spread on bread halves. Sprinkle olives, green onions, and Mozzarella cheese over mayonnaise mixture. Bake on a cookie sheet at 350°F for approximately 15 minutes or until cheese melts. Serves 6-8.

Mrs. David Brumby
(Jane Pumpelly)

RADIO BEER BREAD

1 can (12 ounces) beer, room temperature
2 Tablespoons sugar
3 cups self-rising flour
¼ cup butter, melted

Mix first 3 ingredients. Place in well buttered bread pan (9x4x3 inches) and pour butter on top. Bake at 350°F for 50 minutes. Bread will be crumbly if sliced hot. Serves 6-8.

Must play radio while baking bread!

Mrs. Greg Klumpp
(Susan Blake)

SWEET POPPY SEED BREAD

2 eggs
1½ cups sugar
2 cups flour
1 teaspoon baking powder
1 teaspoon salt
3 teaspoons almond extract
¾ cup cooking oil
1 cup milk
½ cup poppy seeds

Mix all ingredients well. Bake in 2 loaf pans or 4-5 small loaf pans which have been greased and floured. Bake at 350°F for 1 hour.

Mrs. John Van Norman
(Lee Elledge)

Mrs. Gregory Foreman
(Mary Patin)

STICKY BUNS

2 Tablespoons margarine
¼ cup brown sugar
¼ teaspoon cinnamon
¼ cup Karo syrup
¼ cup nuts, chopped
¼ cup raisins
1 can (8 ounces) biscuits

In a 9 inch cake pan, melt margarine. Stir in brown sugar, cinnamon, syrup, nuts, and raisins. Place biscuits on top. Bake at 400°F for 15 minutes. Let stand 5 minutes and invert on plate.

Mrs. Allen Greene
(Nelda Hesketh)

CINNAMON STICKS

1 cup sugar
2 teaspoons cinnamon
2 packages Angonoa's plain Italian style bread sticks
1 stick oleo, melted

Mix sugar and cinnamon. Roll bread sticks in melted butter, then in cinnamon-sugar mixture. Place on cookie sheet. Bake at 350°F for 10 minutes. Store in tins. Serves approximately 50.

Mrs. Joseph S. Bolton
(Jean Baldwin)

RAISIN BRAN MUFFINS

5 cups all purpose flour
3 cups sugar
12 ounces raisin bran cereal
5 teaspoons soda
2 teaspoons salt
2½ teaspoons cinnamon
1½ teaspoons allspice
4 eggs, slightly beaten
1 quart buttermilk
1 cup oil

Preheat oven to 400°F. Mix dry ingredients in large mixing bowl. Slowly add eggs, buttermilk, and oil while mixing. Place mixture in greased muffin tins or muffin papers in tins. Bake at 400°F for 15-20 minutes. Makes 5 dozen.

Store unused muffin mix in airtight container in the refrigerator. This mix lasts up to 6 weeks.

Mrs. Travis Spears
(Pam Whitehead)

Mrs. Henry Chol
(Leslie Kemmerly)

BISCUIT BITES

1 can (5 biscuits) Hungry Jack flaky biscuits
6 slices bacon, fried crisp and crumbled
½ cup cheese, grated

Spray mini-muffin pan with Pam. Separate each biscuit into 2 layers and press ½ into muffin pan. Place crumbled bacon into each biscuit. Sprinkle grated cheese over each biscuit. Bake at 375°F for 8-10 minutes. Serve hot. Makes 10 biscuits.

Use browned ground meat and barbecue sauce for a delicious hot hors d'oeuvres or an after-school snack.

Mrs. John Bradford
(Dinah Curole)

MAMMY'S FLAPJACKS

½ stick butter
⅓ cup flour
⅓ cup milk
3 eggs
Powdered sugar
Sliced lemons
Sliced limes
Sliced fruit

Melt ½ stick butter in a black iron skillet until it bubbles. Then add mixture of flour, milk, and eggs. Bake at 425°F for 20 minutes. Cut in pizza-like slices and sprinkle with powdered sugar. Garnish with lemon and lime slices and top off with sliced fruit.

Mrs. Mark Andrus
(Janet Crowe)

CRAWFISH IN A BUNDLE

2 loaves French bread
½ stick butter
1 cup celery, chopped
¼ cup onion, chopped
2 cloves garlic, chopped
1 teaspoon salt
½ teaspoon pepper
4 cups crawfish tails, boiled and peeled
½ cup black olives, chopped
½ cup mayonnaise
1 teaspoon dry mustard
½ cup Mozzarella cheese, grated
½ cup mild Cheddar cheese, grated

Carefully slice off the top third of the French bread. Hollow out the bottom portions. Save the tops. In a saucepan, melt butter on low heat and stir in celery, onion, garlic, salt, and pepper. Simmer a few minutes. Then add crawfish tails and black olives. Add mayonnaise and dry mustard. Mix well and let cool slightly. Gently add cheeses. Fill hollowed bread with mix. Put top back on bread. Baste outside with butter. Then wrap each roll in aluminum foil. Bake at 400°F for 20-30 minutes. Slice to serve. Serves 8-10.

Mrs. Bruce Kirkpatrick
(Jacqui Dyer)

EASY CRAWFISH ETOUFFÉE

1 stick butter
1 Tablespoon flour
1 onion, chopped
3 Tablespoons bell pepper, chopped
2 cloves garlic, minced
1 can cream of celery soup
1 teaspoon salt
Red pepper to taste
1 teaspoon black pepper
½ cup green onion tops
1 teaspoon parsley
1 pound crawfish tails
Paprika

Melt butter. Add flour. Stir in onions, bell pepper, and garlic. Cook until tender. Add soup. Cover and simmer for 20 minutes. Add seasonings, green onion, and parsley. Add crawfish tails. Cook over low heat. Add paprika for pink color. Serve over cooked rice. Serves 4-6.

Mrs. David Brumby
(Jane Pumpelly)

OYSTERS JEAN LAFITTE

1 cup green onions, chopped
½ cup butter, melted
3 Tablespoons flour
2 dozen oysters, 12 chopped and 12 whole (reserve liquid)
1 can (14 ounces) artichoke bottoms, drained and chopped
¾ cup oyster liquid
¾ cup Progresso Italian bread crumbs
1 teaspoon salt
½ teaspoon black pepper
1 teaspoon Lea & Perrins
¼ teaspoon dry mustard
Dash Tabasco
¼ cup Parmesan cheese

Sauté onions in butter. Blend in flour. Cook over medium heat until smooth. Add chopped oysters, artichokes, and oyster liquid. Fold in bread crumbs and seasonings. Simmer 10 minutes, stirring constantly. Place whole oysters in greased 9x12 inch casserole. Spoon dressing mixture over oysters. Sprinkle with Parmesan cheese. Bake at 350°F for 20-30 minutes or until the edges of the oysters curl. Serves 6-8.

Mrs. Charles R. Anderson
(Betty Harlow)

Mrs. David Brumby
(Jane Pumpelly)

Mrs. David Kestel
(Donna Fort)

CRAB LASAGNE

½ package (16 ounce size) lasagne noodles
1 pound lump crabmeat
1 can (10½ ounces) condensed cream of shrimp soup
1 package (8 ounces) cream cheese
1 carton (16 ounces) small curd cottage cheese
1 egg
½ cup onions, chopped
¼ cup parsley, chopped
2 teaspoons basil
½ teaspoon salt
⅛ teaspoon black pepper
3 fresh tomatoes, sliced
1 cup Cheddar cheese, grated

Cook noodles according to package directions and drain. Mix crab and soup. Combine cream cheese, cottage cheese, egg, onion, parsley, and seasonings. Layer ½ noodles in greased 11x13 inch pan. Top with ½ cream cheese mixture. Layer rest of noodles, then rest of cream cheese mixture. Arrange tomato slices on top. Sprinkle with Cheddar cheese. Bake uncovered at 350°F for 40 minutes. Remove from oven and let stand for 10 minutes. Cut into squares and serve. Serves 8-10.

Mrs. Henry Liles
(Barbara Jenks)

SHRIMP AND VEGETABLE GRILL

⅓ cup soy sauce (Kikkoman preferably)
1 medium onion, chopped
1 teaspoon ginger
2 garlic cloves, finely chopped, or ¼ teaspoon garlic powder
2 teaspoons dry mustard
1 teaspoon prepared horseradish
½ teaspoon curry powder
2 pounds large shrimp, peeled and deveined
2 pints cherry tomatoes or 4 medium tomatoes, cut in wedges
2 medium white onions, cut in wedges
2 bell peppers, cut in 1 inch squares

Combine soy sauce, onion, ginger, garlic, mustard, horseradish, and curry powder in large bowl. Blend well. Add shrimp to marinade, cover and refrigerate 15-20 minutes. Alternate shrimp, tomato, onion wedges, and bell pepper on skewers. Cook on grill over moderate fire for 8-10 minutes. Turn frequently and baste often with marinade. Serve immediately by sliding shrimp and vegetables off skewers onto bed of hot cooked rice. Serves 6.

Mrs. Clark Gunderson
(Robbie Talbert)

SHRIMP OPELOUSAS

1 pound raw shrimp, peeled
1 medium onion, chopped
1 bell pepper, chopped
Onion tops
Parsley
Salt and pepper to taste
1½ cups rice, uncooked
1 can beef broth
1 can (4½ ounces) sliced mushrooms, drained
½-1 stick margarine

Mix all ingredients in a 5 quart electric rice cooker and cook as you would plain rice. Do not add additional water. DO NOT OPEN TO STIR. Serves 6-8.

Mrs. John Bradford
(Dinah Curole)

BLACKENED REDFISH

1½ sticks butter
1½ Tablespoons paprika
1½ Tablespoons onion powder
1½ Tablespoons garlic powder
1½ Tablespoons cayenne pepper
1 Tablespoon white pepper
1 Tablespoon black pepper
1½ teaspoons thyme
1½ teaspoons rosemary
1½ teaspoons basil
1½ teaspoons cumin
1½ teaspoons salt
6 medium (7-9 ounce size) redfish fillets

Heat a large black iron skillet (no substitute) over very high heat for at least 10 minutes. Meanwhile, melt butter in a separate skillet. Combine seasonings and mix well. Pat fillets dry. Then coat both sides with melted butter. Liberally sprinkle both sides with seasoning mix. Place coated fillets in heated black iron skillet and cook, uncovered, for about 2 minutes on each side. Serves 6.

Catfish or red snapper may be substituted for redfish. Should be cooked in a well ventilated area or outdoors on a gas grill (not charcoal) because of smoke created.

Pat O'Carroll
Pat O'Carroll's Restaurant
Lake Charles, Louisiana

HOT SEAFOOD PIE

2½ cups potato chips, crushed
¼ cup margarine, melted
2 cans (6½ ounce size) crabmeat, drained and flaked
2 cans (4½ ounce size) medium shrimp, drained
1 cup celery, chopped
½ cup bell pepper, chopped
1 Tablespoon onion, grated
2 Tablespoons lemon juice
¼ teaspoon salt
¼ teaspoon pepper
¼ cup pimiento, chopped
¼ teaspoon Worcestershire sauce
1 cup mayonnaise
½ cup Cheddar cheese, shredded

Combine 1½ cups crushed potato chips and margarine. Press into a 9 inch pie plate. Bake at 375°F for 5 minutes. Cool. Combine crabmeat, shrimp, celery, bell pepper, onion, lemon juice, seasonings, pimiento, Worcestershire, and mayonnaise in a large bowl. Stir well. Spoon mixture into potato chip crust. Combine remaining crushed potato chips and cheese; sprinkle over top. Bake at 375°F for 15 minutes. Serves 8.

Mrs. Carl Joiner
(Colene Kirkpatrick)

Mrs. Michael Kent *omits the potato chip crust. She adds 1 cup cooked rice and 1 can (17 ounces) English peas, drained.*

LEMON BRANDY VEAL

4 veal cutlets, thinly sliced
Salt and pepper
½ cup flour
6 Tablespoons butter
2 Tablespoons brandy
2 Tablespoons lemon juice

Dry veal with paper towels. Season with salt and pepper. Flour both sides of veal. Heat 2 Tablespoons butter in a large skillet until bubbling and add veal. Sauté 1-1½ minutes over high heat. Turn and sauté other side, adding butter if needed. Remove veal from pan to serving platter and place in a warm oven. In the pan, melt remaining butter. Add brandy and lemon juice. Stir over medium-high heat and reduce to thicken. Pour sauce over veal and serve. Serves 2.

Kim Davey Caldarera

STEAK AU POIVRE VERT

Salt to taste
2 T-bone, rib eye, strip, or club steaks
1 Tablespoon butter
2 green onions, sliced
1 Tablespoon lemon juice
1½ teaspoons green peppercorns, mashed
1 Tablespoon La Choy brown gravy sauce
2 Tablespoons heavy cream

Heat heavy skillet. Salt it and add steaks. Cook steaks to desired doneness. Then remove to hot plates. Add butter and onions to skillet. Cook until barely limp and add lemon juice, mashed peppercorns, brown gravy sauce, and cream. Stir well, pour over steaks, and serve at once. Serves 2.

Mrs. Joseph S. Bolton
(Jean Baldwin)

STIR-FRY BEEF

1½ pounds beef tenderloin or sirloin, thinly sliced
1 Tablespoon oil
1 onion, thinly sliced
1 bell pepper, thinly sliced
½ pound fresh mushrooms, thinly sliced
½ pound bean sprouts
¼ pound snow peas, ends snipped
¼ cup soy sauce
Salt and pepper to taste

In large skillet or wok, brown beef in oil on high heat for approximately 2 minutes. Remove beef and add onions and bell pepper. Stir fry for 1½ minutes. Add remaining vegetables and stir fry for an additional 2 minutes. Add beef to mixture, along with soy sauce. Season with salt and pepper. Remove from heat immediately. (Do not overcook; vegetables should be crisp.) Serves 4.

Serve with rice—an excellent company dish since the chopping can all be done a day ahead.

Mrs. Michael Kudla
(Joellen Lee)

SPAGHETTI PIE

6 ounces spaghetti
2 Tablespoons butter
1⅓ cups Parmesan cheese, grated
2 eggs, beaten
1 cup cottage cheese
1 pound ground beef or sausage
½ cup onion, chopped
¼ cup bell pepper, chopped
1 can (8 ounces) tomatoes, chopped
1 can (6 ounces) tomato paste
1 teaspoon sugar
1 teaspoon orégano
½ teaspoon garlic salt
½ cup Mozzarella cheese, shredded

Cook and drain spaghetti. Stir in butter, Parmesan cheese, and eggs. Spread this mixture in a 9 inch pie pan as a crust. Spread cottage cheese over pasta mixture. Brown and drain ground beef. Then add onion, bell pepper, tomatoes, tomato paste, sugar, orégano, and garlic salt. Spoon meat mixture over cottage cheese layer. Bake, uncovered, at 350°F for 20 minutes. Sprinkle with Mozzarella cheese and bake for an additional 5 minutes.

Mrs. David Brumby
(Jane Pumpelly)

HAM SKILLET SUPPER

3 cups egg noodles, uncooked
2 cups cooked ham, cubed
1 Tablespoon dried onions
1½ cups milk
1 teaspoon Worcestershire sauce
1 can (17 ounces) cream style corn
4 ounces (1 cup) American cheese, cubed

In large skillet, combine all ingredients except cheese. Mix well. Heat to boiling. Cover and simmer 18-20 minutes (stirring occasionally) or until noodles are done. Stir in cheese. Heat until cheese begins to melt. Serves 4-6.

Mrs. David Kestel
(Donna Fort)

DESPERATION MEAL

4-6 medium pork chops
1 large onion, chopped
1 can (14½ ounces) whole tomatoes
½ bell pepper, chopped
1 rib celery, chopped
½ cup onion tops, chopped
½ cup parsley, chopped
Salt and pepper to taste
2 packages (6 ounce size) wild rice

Brown pork chops and onion in large skillet. Add tomatoes, bell pepper, celery, onion tops, parsley, salt, and pepper. Cook 20 minutes on low heat. Add wild rice to pork chops using ½ the water called for on the packages. Stir well and cook, covered, for 30 minutes until liquid is gone. Serves 4-6.

Chicken may be used, but should be skinned first.

Mrs. John Bradford
(Dinah Curole)

ITALIAN PORK CHOPS

1 can (8 ounces) tomato sauce
½ cup bell pepper, chopped
1 can (3 ounces) sliced mushrooms, drained
2 Tablespoons water
1 package onion gravy mix
1 teaspoon Italian herb seasoning
6 loin pork chops (½-¾ inch thick)
Salt to taste
2 Tablespoons vegetable oil

Combine tomato sauce, bell pepper, mushrooms, water, gravy mix, and Italian herb seasoning. Stir well and set aside. Season chops with salt. Brown on both sides in oil. Drain off pan drippings and discard. Pour sauce mixture over chops. Cover and simmer 45 minutes or until tender. Serves 6.

Mrs. Travis Spears
(Pam Whitehead)

FAST & FABULOUS — ENTRÉES

LEONE'S PORK AND PASTA

3 Tablespoons olive oil
½ cup butter, melted
2 cloves garlic, crushed
⅓ teaspoon black pepper
Pinch red pepper
4 lean pork chops
1 teaspoon rosemary
½ teaspoon salt
4 medium ripe tomatoes, sliced into wedges
10 fresh parsley sprigs, chopped
¾ pound spaghetti
¼ cup Parmesan cheese, grated

Heat olive oil and ¼ cup butter in large heavy skillet. Add garlic, black and red pepper. Cook slowly for 2 minutes. Sprinkle pork chops with rosemary and brown in olive oil mixture on each side for 5 minutes. Lower heat to medium and add salt, tomato wedges, and parsley. Cover and cook slowly for 25 minutes. While meat is simmering, boil pasta in salted water for 10 minutes. Drain well and put back in pot. Add remaining ¼ cup butter and mix well. Add grated cheese and a little sauce and mix. Place pasta on a hot platter. Top with meat and pour sauce over both. Serves 4.

A specialty of Mama Leone's Restaurant in New York City.

Mrs. Michael Kudla, Jr.
(JoEllen Lee)

RICE COOKER JAMBALAYA

1 pound smoked sausage
1½ cups raw rice
1 can onion soup
½ teaspoon salt
½ soup can water
½ stick butter
1 can (4½ ounces) mushrooms
½ cup bell pepper, chopped
½ cup green onions, chopped

Brown sausage. Pour off grease. Place all ingredients in electric rice cooker. Stir to blend. Cover. Press button, and when the bell rings, it's ready! Serves 4-6.

Mrs. David Brumby
(Jane Pumpelly)

CALCASIEU CHICKEN CASSEROLE

1 package (6 ounces) long grain wild rice
1 can (10 ounces) mushroom soup
1 can (10 ounces) cream of chicken soup
1 can (14 ounces) Chinese vegetables, drained
1 soup can of water
1 can (3½ ounces) mushrooms, with liquid
1 whole chicken, cut in pieces, or 6 breast halves

Mix all ingredients except chicken and put in 3 quart baking dish. Arrange chicken pieces on top. Bake at 375°F, covered, for 1 hour. Remove cover and bake ½ hour to brown. Serves 6.

Mrs. David Parnell
(Martha Allison)

CHEESE-BAKED CHICKEN BREASTS

2 cups Cheez-it cracker crumbs
1 teaspoon salt
1 teaspoon garlic salt
½ teaspoon marjoram
1 egg
1 Tablespoon water
12 chicken breast halves, boned and skinned
1 cup margarine, melted

In food processor, mix crackers, salt, garlic salt, and marjoram. Beat egg and water in a shallow dish. Dip chicken pieces in egg mixture and then coat well in crumb mixture. Place in buttered shallow dish about 1 inch apart. Drizzle with melted margarine. Bake at 350°F for 35-40 minutes or until golden brown. Serves 12.

Mrs. G. Michael Kent
(Laurie Wilson)

CHICKEN TARRAGON

1 whole chicken, cut in pieces
Salt and pepper
1 stick butter
1 onion, sliced
¼ cup Lea & Perrins
¼ cup tarragon vinegar

Salt and pepper chicken and place in a 2 quart casserole dish. Cut butter into pieces and place on top of chicken pieces. Add onion, Lea & Perrins, and vinegar. Bake, covered, at 350°F for 1½ hours. Serves 4.

Mrs. Joseph S. Bolton
(Jean Baldwin)

"PUTTIN' ON THE RITZ"

2 cups Ritz crackers, crushed
8 ounces sharp Cheddar cheese, grated
3 cans (4 ounce size) asparagus tips
1 package frozen English peas, thawed
1 can cream of mushroom soup

Reserve ½ cup Ritz crackers and ½ cup grated cheese for topping. Drain asparagus and save ½ cup juice. Layer half the following ingredients in order in a deep 1½ quart casserole: crackers, cheese, asparagus, peas, and mushroom soup. Repeat second layer. Pour in ½ cup of asparagus juice. Top with layer of cheese and crackers. Bake, uncovered, at 350°F for 30 minutes. Serves 6-8.

Allen Greene

GREEN BEANS AMANDINE

2 sticks butter
3 packages (2½ ounce size) slivered almonds
1 teaspoon fresh lemon juice
½ teaspoon salt
Pepper to taste
4 cans (16 ounce size) French style green beans, well drained

Melt butter. Stir in almonds and sauté until lightly browned over medium heat. Remove from heat. Add lemon juice, salt, pepper, and green beans. Return to burner and heat until bubbly. Serve immediately. Can be halved. Serves 16.

Mrs. Charles R. Anderson
(Betty Harlow)

GREEN BEANS MORNAY

1 Tablespoon butter
1 Tablespoon flour
¼ teaspoon dry mustard
½ teaspoon salt
1 Tablespoon onion, finely minced
⅔ cup light cream or half and half
¼ cup grated Parmesan cheese
2 cans (16 ounce size) French style green beans, drained

Over low heat, melt butter. Blend in flour, mustard, salt, and onion. Stir in cream and cook over medium heat, stirring occasionally until mixture thickens. Stir in cheese and heat one minute longer. Add drained beans to sauce; stir until heated through. Serve at once. Can be kept or reheated later in a casserole dish in oven at 325°F. Serves 10-12.

Mrs. Charles R. Anderson
(Betty Harlow)

MEI MEI'S BARBECUED GREEN BEANS

3 slices bacon
½ onion, chopped
½ cup chili sauce
1 can (16 ounces) cut green beans

Fry bacon and remove from pan. Drain and crumble. Sauté chopped onion in bacon drippings and add chili sauce. Drain half of the liquid from beans. Add remaining liquid and beans to pan. Cover and cook 45 minutes. Just before serving sprinkle bacon over beans. Serves 4-6

Mrs. Robert Dampf
(Courtney Lepick)

BIG LAKE BROCCOLI

2 small packages frozen chopped broccoli
1 stick margarine
½ pound Velveeta cheese
¼ pound Ritz crackers, crushed

Cook broccoli and drain. While hot, add ½ stick margarine and all of cheese. Stir thoroughly. Pour into buttered 8x8 inch casserole dish. Sprinkle with crushed crackers. Dot with ½ stick margarine. Bake, uncovered, at 350°F for 20-30 minutes. Serves 6-8.

Can use either 6 ounce roll of garlic cheese or Jalapeño cheese or 8 ounce jar of Jalapeño Cheez Whiz.

Mrs. James Henry
(Carol Williamson)

BROCCOLI-RICE CASSEROLE

1 small box frozen chopped broccoli
1 cup onion, chopped
1 cup celery, chopped
½ stick butter
1½ cups cooked rice
1 can cream of chicken soup
1 jar (8 ounces) Cheez Whiz or 1 roll garlic cheese
Dash of Tabasco
Salt and pepper to taste
½ teaspoon basil

Cook broccoli as directed on package. Drain well. While cooking, sauté onion and celery in butter until wilted. Combine all ingredients in a greased 2 quart casserole. Bake, uncovered, at 350°F for 45-60 minutes or until bubbly. Serves 8-10.

This casserole is better fixed the day before. It can also be fixed ahead and frozen.

**Mrs. Travis Spears
(Pam Whitehead)**

FRENCH PEAS

2 Tablespoons bacon, crumbled
2 Tablespoons onion, chopped
3 Tablespoons butter
1 can (17 ounces) early peas, drained
½ teaspoon flour
2 teaspoons sugar

Sauté bacon and onion in butter over low heat, covered, for 10 minutes. Do not brown. Add peas, flour, and sugar. Stir. Simmer 5 minutes, covered, or until heated.

Kim Davey Caldarera

HE-MAN POTATOES

½ pound Velveeta cheese
1 pint half & half
4½ ounces Cheddar cheese, shredded
1 stick margarine
Salt and pepper to taste
2 pound package frozen hash browned potatoes

Melt the first four ingredients in a saucepan over medium heat. Add a dash salt and pepper. Place frozen hash browned potatoes in a 9x13 inch dish. Pour melted cheese mixture over potatoes. Bake, uncovered, at 350°F for 1 hour. Serves 8.

Very good side dish for ham or brisket.

**Mrs. G. Michael Kent
(Laurie Wilson)**

Mrs. Peter LaFuria *adds 2 onions, thickly sliced, to potatoes.*

YELLOW SQUASH FOR SURE FIRE SQUASH HATERS

1-1½ pounds tender yellow squash
½ pound bacon
1 bunch green onions, chopped
8-10 saltine crackers
1 egg, beaten
Salt and pepper to taste

Boil squash. Drain and mash. While squash is cooking, fry bacon until crisp. Remove bacon and sauté green onions in bacon drippings until tender. Crumble bacon and saltine crackers. Combine squash, onions, bacon, and crackers with egg. Season with salt and pepper. Pour into 1½ quart ungreased casserole. Bake, uncovered, at 350°F for 20 minutes or until lightly browned. Serves 5-6.

Mrs. Michael Garber
(Karen Chaney)

NOODLES ROMANOFF

6 ounces noodles, cooked and drained
1 cup cottage cheese, small curd
1 cup sour cream
1 Tablespoon onion, minced
1 teaspoon Worcestershire sauce
½ teaspoon salt
Dash garlic salt
Dash Tabasco
1 cup Cheddar cheese, grated

Gently combine all ingredients except Cheddar cheese. Place in buttered 1½ quart casserole. Top with Cheddar cheese. Bake, uncovered, at 350°F for 30 minutes. Serves 4-6.

Excellent with beef.

Mrs. David Kestel
(Donna Fort)

ORANGE-SPINACH SALAD WITH HONEY-MUSTARD DRESSING

10 ounces fresh spinach
1 can (11 ounces) mandarin oranges, drained
1 small red onion, thinly sliced
8 ounces bacon, cooked and crumbled
8 ounces fresh mushrooms, sliced

DRESSING

¾ cup safflower oil
¼ cup red wine vinegar
¼ cup honey
¼ cup Dijon mustard
¼ cup sesame seeds, toasted
2 cloves garlic, minced, or ½ teaspoon garlic powder
2 teaspoons black pepper
2 teaspoons salt

Wash, stem, and dry spinach. Tear into pieces. Add oranges, onion, bacon, and mushrooms. Toss with enough dressing to coat. Serves 6-8.

DRESSING: Mix well and chill. Makes enough for 2 salads. Keeps for 3 weeks.

Mrs. Charles R. Anderson
(Betty Harlow)

DAVID'S SESAME SALAD

1 head lettuce
1 cup Provolone cheese, shredded
¼-½ cup sesame seed, toasted
Zesty Italian dressing

Wash and tear lettuce into bite-sized pieces. Toss lettuce, sesame seed, and generous amount of salad dressing. Place the desired amount of cheese on top. Serve the salad individually. Serves 6-8.

For instructions on how to toast sesame seed, see p.243.

David A. Kestel

THREE PESO SALAD

1 pound ground chuck
Salt and pepper to taste
1 small jar picante sauce
1 can pinto beans or kidney beans, drained
1 package (8 ounces) Fritos
½ head lettuce, chopped
2 tomatoes, diced
1 onion, chopped
1 package (10 ounces) mild Cheddar cheese, grated

Brown ground chuck with salt and pepper. Drain. Add picante sauce and beans and let simmer 10 minutes. Layer Fritos in pyrex dish and add layer of browned meat mixture, lettuce, tomatoes, onion, and cheese. Bake at 350°F, uncovered, for about 5 minutes to let cheese melt. Serves 6.

Mrs. Mark Dufrene
(Brenda Chol)

PARTY SALAD PARMESAN

1 head raw cauliflower
2 heads lettuce, washed
1 cup green onion tops, chopped
2 cups mayonnaise
2 cups Parmesan cheese
Salt to taste

Rinse cauliflower and break into flowerlets. Tear lettuce into bite-sized pieces. Add green onion. Mix mayonnaise, Parmesan cheese, and salt. Toss with salad mixture. Serves 12-16.

Mrs. David Kestel
(Donna Fort)

PICTURE-PERFECT PASTA

1 package (6 ounces) Rotini (swirly pasta)
1 package (10 ounces) frozen broccoli florets
1 can (2¼ ounces) ripe olives, sliced
1 jar (2 ounces) pimientos, chopped
3 stalks green onions, chopped
1 can (3 ounces) garbanzo beans
½ cup fresh mushrooms, sliced
1 envelope Good Seasons cheese garlic dressing
Salt and pepper to taste
Grated Parmesan cheese

Cook pasta according to directions (9 minutes). Drain and rinse. Meanwhile, blanche broccoli in microwave (3½ minutes on high). Drain. Mix pasta, broccoli, and all other salad ingredients in large salad bowl. Prepare Good Seasons cheese garlic salad dressing as directed on envelope. Pour over salad to taste. Add salt and pepper and toss. Sprinkle generously with grated Parmesan cheese. Refrigerate 2-3 hours before serving. Serves 4-6.

Mrs. David Frohn
(Mary Ward)

GREEN BEAN VINAIGRETTE

1½ cups water
1½ cups vinegar
¼ cup oil
¼ cup sugar
1 or more cloves garlic, chopped (optional)
2 cans (16 ounce size) whole green beans, drained
1 purple onion, thinly sliced

Combine water, vinegar, oil, sugar, and garlic in a 3 quart pot. Bring to a boil, stirring occasionally. In a large salad bowl, combine green beans and sliced purple onion. Pour boiling liquid over vegetables. Remove garlic. Refrigerate 2-3 hours before serving. Serves 8.

Even better if refrigerated overnight.

Mrs. William Swift
(Sheryl LeBleu)

Mrs. Charles R. Anderson *adds ½ teaspoon each of dry mustard, tarragon, and basil to green beans and onions before adding boiling liquid.*

CRAB CASHEW SALAD

2 ripe avocados
Lemon juice
1 can lump white crab meat or ½ pound lump white crab meat
2 eggs, boiled and chopped
1 can (4 ounces) sliced black olives, drained
¼ cup cashews
Lettuce
Bleu cheese dressing

Cut avocado; dice and sprinkle with lemon juice. Mix with rest of ingredients. Serve on lettuce leaves. Top with bleu cheese dressing. Serves 4-6.

Mrs. Charles R. Anderson
(Betty Harlow)

DOUBLOON DELIGHT FRUIT SALAD

1 cup crushed pineapple, drained
1 cup mandarin oranges, drained
1 cup shredded coconut
1 cup miniature marshmallows
1 small jar red maraschino cherries, drained
1 cup sour cream
¼-½ cup nuts (pecans or walnuts), chopped

Mix all ingredients gently. Cover and refrigerate several hours or preferably overnight. Serves 6-8.

Mrs. Clark Gunderson
(Robbie Talbert)

JEWELED FRUIT

1 can (21 ounces) peach pie filling
1 can (20 ounces) pineapple chunks, drained
2 cartons frozen strawberries, thawed, NOT drained
1 can (16 ounces) mandarin oranges, drained
3 bananas, sliced

Mix peach pie filling, pineapple chunks, strawberries, and mandarin oranges. Chill. Add sliced bananas just before serving. Serves 12.

"Can be made in advance. Keeps several days."

Mrs. Patrick Crawford
(Charmayne Hannie)

HOT SHERRIED FRUIT

6 cans (18 ounce size) assorted fruits, drained (pears, peaches, apricots, cherries, apple rings, pineapple chunks)
1 stick butter
2 Tablespoons flour
½ cup brown sugar
¼ teaspoon cinnamon
⅛ teaspoon nutmeg
⅛ teaspoon salt
1 cup sherry

Place drained fruit in 9x13 inch baking dish. Place apple rings on top. Melt butter. Stir in flour and sugar. Add spices and sherry. Cook sauce over low heat until thick and smooth. Pour hot sauce over fruit. Bake uncovered, at 350°F for 30 minutes.

"Even better if refrigerated overnight before baking. Keeps several days."

Mrs. Henry Liles
(Barbara Jenks)

BANANA BLUEBERRY PIE

½ cup sugar
1 package (8 ounces) cream cheese
1 container (8 ounces) Cool Whip
2 bananas
1 can (21 ounces) blueberry pie filling
2 prepared pie shells (8 inch size), regular or graham cracker

Cream sugar with cream cheese. Blend in Cool Whip. Slice bananas in bottom of pie shells. Top with cream cheese mixture. Pour the can of blueberry pie filling over top. Refrigerate.

Mrs. Michael Garber
(Karen Chaney)

HERSHEY BAR PIE

2 Hershey bars (8 ounce size) with almonds
2 Tablespoons water
1 container (12 ounces) Cool Whip
1 chocolate cookie pie crust (6 ounces)

Melt Hershey bars with water in the top of a double boiler. Pour into large bowl and mix with Cool Whip. Pour into chocolate pie crust. Freeze for at least 2 hours. May be frozen for a month. Serves 6-8.

Rich and delicious.

Mrs. Henry Chol
(Leslie Kemmerly)

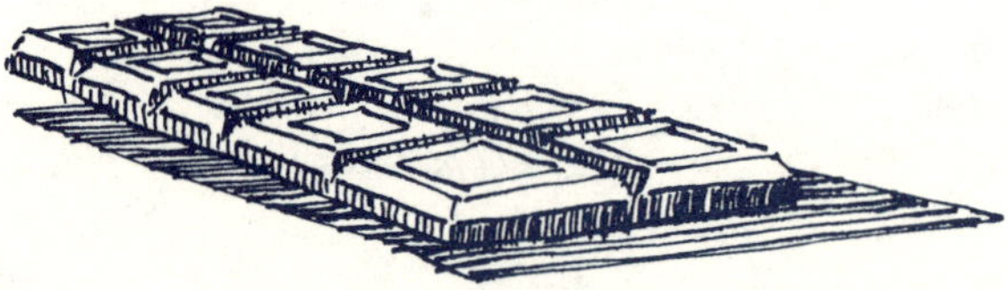

NO CRUST COCONUT PIE

2 cups milk
¾ cup sugar
½ cup biscuit mix
4 eggs
¼ cup margarine
1½ teaspoons vanilla
1 cup coconut

Combine all ingredients (except coconut) in blender. Blend on low for 3 minutes. Pour into greased 9 inch pie pan. Let stand for 5 minutes. Sprinkle with coconut. Bake at 350°F for 40 minutes. Serves 6-8.

Mrs. Robert Eakin
(Carolyn Hill)

PERFECT PEACH PIE

1 container (8 ounces) Cool Whip
1 can (14 ounces) condensed milk
½ cup lemon juice
6 fresh peaches, peeled and sliced
1 graham cracker crust

Mix Cool Whip, condensed milk, and lemon juice. Stir in peaches. Pour into prepared crust. Refrigerate until firm. Serves 8.

Can be made with fresh strawberries.

Mrs. William McCall
(Nadine Newlin)

BUTTER PECAN COFFEE CAKE

1 cup pecans, chopped
1 cup granulated sugar
1 teaspoon cinnamon
1 package Betty Crocker butter pecan cake mix
1 package instant butterscotch pudding
¾ cup water
¾ cup oil
4 eggs

Preheat oven to 350°F. Make a filling of the nuts, sugar, and cinnamon. Set aside. Combine cake mix, pudding mix, water, oil, and eggs. Stir for about 4 minutes. Put ½ cake mixture in greased and floured 9x13 inch pan. Sprinkle with ½ of filling mixture. Spread remaining cake mixture on top and sprinkle with remaining filling. Bake at 350°F for 40 minutes. Makes a big coffee cake.

Mrs. Travis Spears
(Pam Whitehead)

CHEWY BARS

1 box yellow cake mix (not pudding)
½ cup brown sugar
4 Tablespoons butter (½ stick), softened
2 eggs, large
3 Tablespoons water
4 Tablespoons flour
1 teaspoon vanilla
1 cup semi-sweet chocolate chips
½ cup nuts, finely chopped

Mix cake mix and brown sugar in large mixing bowl. Add butter, eggs, water, flour, and vanilla. Blend all ingredients well (batter will be stiff). Stir in chocolate chips and nuts by hand. Spread batter in greased 9x13 inch pan. Bake, uncovered, at 350°F for 30 minutes. Cut into squares. Makes 30 bar cookies.

Substitute spice cake and Reese's Pieces or butterscotch bits for a different taste.

Mrs. David R. Frohn
(Mary Ward)

CINDY'S PEANUT BUTTER FUDGE

2 bags (12 ounce size) butterscotch morsels
1 jar (28 ounces) crunchy peanut butter
2 cans (14 ounce size) condensed milk

Melt butterscotch and peanut butter over medium heat, stirring often. Do not scorch. After completely melted, remove from stove. Stir in milk. Mix well. Spray 13x9 inch pan with Pam. Pour mixture into pan. Refrigerate until firm. Cut into squares. Makes 100 one inch squares.

Mrs. David Crowe
(Cindy Moore)

GRAHAM CRACKER ROLL

1 box (12 ounces) graham crackers, crumbled
1 can (14 ounces) condensed milk
1 cup pecans, chopped

Mix all ingredients together. Roll into logs on waxed paper. Seal in plastic wrap. Place in refrigerator to chill. Slice and serve as cookies. Makes 30-40 cookies.

Add 1 cup chopped red and green candied cherries for Christmas cookies.

Mrs. Bill Wilson
(Patra Thies)

FUDGE MUFFINS

4 squares (1 ounce size) semi-sweet chocolate
2 sticks butter
1¾ cups sugar
Pinch salt
1 cup flour
4 eggs
1 teaspoon vanilla
2 cups pecans, chopped

Melt chocolate and butter gently in Teflon skillet. Add sugar, salt, and flour. Stir well. Add eggs, one at a time. Stir in, do not beat. Add vanilla and chopped nuts. Fill muffin pans (lined with paper baking cups) ¾ full. Bake at 325°F for 25 minutes for regular size or 20 minutes for miniature size. Makes 2 dozen regular or 6 dozen miniature muffins.

Mrs. Charles R. Anderson
(Betty Harlow)

LEMON CHEESE SQUARES

1 box lemon cake mix
1 stick margarine, softened
1 Tablespoon water
1 egg
1 package (8 ounces) cream cheese
2 eggs
1 box (1 pound) powdered sugar

Combine cake mix, margarine, water, and 1 egg. Press into a greased 9x13 inch pan. Blend together cream cheese, 2 eggs, and powdered sugar. Pour on top of cake mix layer. Bake, uncovered, at 325°F for 25 minutes. When cool, cut into squares. Garnish with fresh fruit.

Mrs. Henry Liles
(Barbara Jenks)

LEMON WHIPPERSNAPS

1 package lemon cake mix
2 cups Cool Whip
1 egg
½ cup sifted powdered sugar

Grease cookie sheets. Combine cake mix, whipped topping, and egg in a large bowl. Stir until well mixed. Drop by teaspoon into powdered sugar. Roll to coat. Place 1½ inches apart on cookie sheet. Bake at 350°F for 10-15 minutes. Makes about 4 dozen cookies.

Mrs. Robert E. Eakin
(Carolyn Hill)

MICROWAVE BROWNIES

¾ cup margarine
3 eggs
1½ cups sugar
¾ teaspoon salt
1½ teaspoons vanilla
1¼ cups flour
½ cup cocoa
½ cup nuts, chopped (optional)
6 ounces chocolate chips (optional)

Melt margarine. Stir in remainder of ingredients. Spread into greased 9x13 inch dish. Microwave on high 3 minutes. Turn ½ turn and microwave 3 more minutes. Turn ½ turn and microwave 4 minutes. Serves 24.

Mrs. Aaron Huffman
(Barbara Binder)

CHEESE CAKE FONDUE

1 package (8 ounces) cream cheese
⅓ cup sugar
1 egg
1 teaspoon vanilla

On high, microwave cream cheese in a 2-3 cup glass serving dish 1-1¼ minutes or until soft, stirring once. Blend in sugar. Beat in egg. Microwave on high, uncovered, 1½-2 minutes stirring every ½ minute. Stir in vanilla. May be served at room temperature. Do not chill before serving. If made ahead, let stand at room temperature approximately 1 hour before serving. Serve with dippers such as assorted fruits, angel food cake cubes, sugar cookies, or wafers.

Mrs. Bill Wilson
(Patra Thies)

FRESH FRUIT BAVARIAN

2 quarts fresh strawberries (reserve 6 pretty whole ones), washed, dried, and sliced
1 package (8 ounces) cream cheese
½ cup powdered sugar
1 pint whipping cream (very cold!)
1 teaspoon vanilla flavoring
Mint, optional

Arrange sliced strawberries in 6 stemmed glasses or other dessert dishes. In medium mixing bowl, blend remaining ingredients with electric mixer until smooth. Pour cream mixture over strawberries. Garnish with reserved strawberries and sprig of fresh mint, if desired. Serves 6.

May also use any other fresh fruit desired instead of strawberries.

Mrs. Clark Gunderson
(Robbie Talbert)

FROZEN BUTTER PECAN DELIGHT

1 stick margarine
1 cup brown sugar
2½ cups Rice Krispies, crushed
½ cup coconut
½ cup nuts, chopped
½ gallon butter pecan ice cream, softened

Melt margarine. Mix with brown sugar, Rice Krispies, coconut, and nuts. Press half of mixture into bottom of ungreased 9x13 inch dish. Spread ice cream over mixture. Sprinkle remaining topping mixture over ice cream. Freeze 30 minutes or longer before serving. Can be frozen up to 2 weeks. Serves 12.

Mrs. Aaron Huffman
(Barbara Binder)

SHORTCUT BANANA PUDDING

1 package (5½ ounces) instant vanilla pudding
3 cups milk
4 bananas, sliced
1 container (4 ounces) Cool Whip
Vanilla wafers

Mix pudding and milk together with mixer for about 2 minutes. Add bananas and Cool Whip. Line a 13x9 inch pyrex dish with vanilla wafers (this includes the dish sides). Add mixture and refrigerate until firm. Serves 12.

Mrs. Woodrow Mock
(Sharon Clayton)

FRUIT PIZZA

1 roll slice and bake sugar cookie dough
1 package (8 ounces) cream cheese, room temperature
⅓ container (8 ounce size) of Cool Whip
1 teaspoon vanilla
¼ cup powdered sugar
Assorted fruit (strawberries, kiwi, blueberries, banana-dipped in lemon juice, peaches, grapes, mandarin oranges)
¼ cup apricot preserves, heated and strained (optional)
1 sprig fresh mint

Slice cookies and arrange on a greased pizza pan, patting to make an even crust (they will rise). Bake at 350°F for 12 minutes until light golden. Cool. Whip cream cheese, Cool Whip, vanilla, and sugar until smooth. Spread on cookie crust. Arrange your choice of sliced fruit on top in a decorative manner. Garnish with sprig of fresh mint and chill to serve. Serves 8-10.

Mrs. Henry Liles
(Barbara Jenks)

QUICK PEACH COBBLER

1 stick margarine
1 cup flour
1 cup sugar
2 teaspoons baking powder
¾ cup water
1 large can (29 ounces) sliced peaches, drained
Cool Whip or vanilla ice cream

Melt margarine in 9x13 inch dish. Mix flour, sugar, baking powder, and water in separate bowl. Pour flour mixture into 9x13 inch dish and stir to mix with melted margarine. Pour sliced peaches on top and mix into batter. Bake, uncovered, at 350°F for 1 hour. Top with Cool Whip or vanilla ice cream. Serves 6-8.

Mrs. James Nichols
(Kay Hardin)

INDEX **419**

Accompaniments
  Blackberry Preserves 306
  Carrot Relish 307
  Chow Chow 292
  Cora's Cranberry and Kumquat Sauce 302
  Doc's Hot Pepper Sauce 303
  Fig Jello Preserves 305
  Fig Preserves for Dieters 305
  Fresh Horseradish 304
  Hot Pepper Jelly 304
  Hot Pepper Sauce 303
  How to Preserve Louisiana Figs 305
  Mayhaw Jelly 305
  Mayonnaise 292
  Mustard 304
  Pickled Okra 308
  Pickled Turnips 308
  Red Relish 307
  Refrigerator Dill Pickles 308
  Strawberry Preserves 306
  Sweet Tomato Chutney 307
  Yorkshire Pudding 166
Alaskan Fisherman Stew 44
Allen's Golden Biscuits 161
Alligator, Fried 99
Alligator, "Gator" Meat Balls 99
Almond Tart 370
Almonds, Green Beans Amandine 403
Aloha Sauce 376
Amberjack, Tips on 35
Ambrosia 366
Ambrosia Cake 321
Anchovy Butter Sauce 296
Anchovy, Shrimp Mélange 282
Angel Coconut Pound Cake 321
Angel Food Cake, Flower Garden 330
Angel Food Cake Ice Cream Pie 370
Angel Food Cake, Snowball 336
Angel Food Cake, Stuffed 322
Appetizers (See Hors d'Oeuvres)
Apple-Apricot Goose 92
Apple Bread, Fresh 157
Apple Casserole 235
Apple Crisp, Dutch 310
Apple Gingerbread Upside Down Cake 322
Apple, Guter Kuchen, A 331
Apple Nut Pudding, Fresh, With
  Rum Sauce 353
Apple Torte 323
Artichoke Balls 119
Artichoke-Spinach Appetizers 119
Artichokes 235
Artichokes, Crème d'Artichauts 381
Artichokes, Oysters Jean Lafitte 395
Artichokes, Rice and 30
Artichokes, Romano Casserole 266
Artichokes, Spinach Casserole 258
Artichokes, Stuffed with Crabmeat 66
Artichokes, Thistle Dip 385
Asparagus Casserole, Chicken and 227
Asparagus Casserole, Fresh 235
Asparagus, "Puttin' on the Ritz 403
Asparagus, Shrimparagus 83
Asparagus Supreme 236
Aspic, Shrimp 283
Aspic, Tomato 284
Aunt Tommy's Chocolate Dessert 356
Auntie's Old Tyme Chocolate Pie 312
Avgolemono (Lemon Sauce) for Keftethes ...184
Avocado Bisque 19

Avocado Cottage Cheese Delight 275
Avocado Crème 370
Avocado Dip 135
Avocado Dressing 289

Bachelor's Mousse 355
Bacon Baked Quail 95
Bacon-Beef-Macaroni Casserole 189
Bacon, Biscuit Bites 393
Bacon, Cheese, and Onion Sandwiches 212
Bacon, Hollywood Hash 190
Bacon-Wrapped Snacks 390
Baked Alaska 369
Baked Bananas 354
Baked Beans for a Crowd 236
Baked Cheese Grits 148
Baked Chicken and Rice Casserole 226
Baked Corn 245
Baked Cranberry Sauce 302
Baked Custard 350
Baked Deviled Eggs 146
Baked Dove Martin 98
Baked Egg and Rice 28
Baked Filet of Fish 37
Baked Fish 46
Baked Fish, Stuffing for 45
Baked Ham 196, 197
Baked Hen 230
Baked Kibbie 181
Baked Pecans 340
Baked Pork Chops 201
Baked Rice 21
Baked Shrimp 73
Baked Steak 169
Baked Stuffed Mushroom Caps 120
Baked Stuffed Shrimp 73
Baked Stuffed Tomatoes 265
Baked Turkey and Corn Bread Dressing 233
Baked Wild Goose or Duck 88
Baked Yams 8, 268
Bamboo Shoots, Easy Vegetable Sukiyaki 266
Banana Blueberry Pie 412
Banana Daiquiri 107
Banana Fritters Bayou Lafourche 236
Banana Nut Bread 157
Banana Pudding 354
Banana Pudding, Shortcut 417
Bananas, Baked 354
Bananas Foster on Ice Cream 369
Bananas, Shortcut Banana Pudding 417
Baquette 164
Barbecue (See also Sauces)
Barbecue, Bobby's Seasoned Steaks 172
Barbecue Sauce 201, 298, 299
Barbecue, Smokehouse Specials 212
Barbecued Beef, Turkish 124
Barbecued Chicken, Red Gill's 223
Barbecued Duck, Jim's 90
Barbecued Fish 41
Barbecued Ling 40
Barbecued Red Fish 40
Barbecued Shrimp 72
Basic Soybeans 237
Bass, Baked Fish 46
Bass, Lock's Trout Amandine 42
Bass, Tips on 34
Basting Sauce for Barbecuing 299

INDEX

Basting Sauce for Oysters en Brochette 59
Batter, Beer for Shrimp 72
Batter, Chilies Rellenos 195
Batter, Tempura 70
Bean, Green, Casserole 238
Bean, Green, Casserole with Cheese 238
Bean Salad, Papa Jim's 276
Bean Salad, String 277
Bean Soup 12
Bean Soup, Flossie's 11
Bean Soup, Mexican Black 11
Bean, Sprouts, Easy Vegetable Sukiyaki 266
Beans, Baked for a Crowd 236
Beans, Black, and Rice 27
Beans, Black, Mexican Soup 11
Beans, Butter, Hot Dog 239
Beans, Chili 191
Beans, Chilies, Stuffed with 245
Beans, Flossie's Soup 11
Beans, Hot Chili 192
Beans, Quick Chili 192
Beans, Red, and Rice 24
Beans, Soup 12
Beans, South of the Border Hot Dish 193
Beans, Texas 239
Beans with an Outdoor Flavor 237
Béarnaise Sauce 293
Beef
  Bacon-Macaroni Casserole 189
  Baked Steak 169
  Bobby's Seasoned Steaks 172
  Boeuf à la Blanche 167
  Boiled Brisket with Horseradish Sauce 173
  Brisket 124, 173
  Burritos 194
  Cabbage Chop Suey 183
  Chili 191
  Chipped on Muffins 212
  Filet de Boeuf with Béarnaise Sauce ...165
  Grillades and Grits 209
  Meat Pot Pie 188
  Minced Dressing for Kibbie 180
  Osso Bucco 207
  Pepper Beef 170
  Pickled Tongue 211
  Rib Roast of 166
  Roast 165
  Sauerbraten 168
  Shish Kabob 174
  Sicilian "Pot-of-Roast" 167
  Steak Diane 169
  Steak Embassy Style 171
  Steak Roll-ups 170
  Steak Zucchini 170
  Stroganoff 172
  Stuffed Round 171
  Tacos 193
  Tasso Sauce Piquante 205
  Tongue, Pickled 211
  Tongue, Stuffed Baked 211
  Tujaque's Boiled 173
  Turkish Barbecued 124
  Vegetable Soup 15
Beef, Ground
  Baked Kibbie 181
  Beef-Bacon-Macaroni Casserole 189
  Brucculuni with Spaghetti 208
  Burritos 194
  Chestnut Meatballs 383
  Chicken, Meat, and Sausage Spaghetti 218

Chili 191
Country Pie 188
Easy Lasagne 177
Eggplant Sapphire 29
French Italian Spaghetti 174
Hamburger Casserole 189
Hamburger Mushroom Quiche 186
Hamburger Pie 186
Hollywood Hash 190
Hot Chili 192
International Gourmet Cabbage Rolls 241
Italian Spaghetti Sauce 175
Johnny Marzetti Cheddar Cheese
  Casserole 189
Keftetches (Stuffed Grape Leaves) 184
Kibbie 180
Kibbie (Raw) 180
Louisiana Creole Okra with Meat Balls 185
Manicotti à la Romona 178
Meat Balls 127, 176, 184, 185, 186, 383
Meat Loaf 179
Meat Pie 187
Mexican Casserole 192
Minced Beef Dressing for Kibbie (Raw) ...180
Moussaka 182
Nana's Lasagne 177
Natchitoches Meat Pie 187
Oriental Meat Balls 185
Oriental Spaghetti 183
Pastitsio 175
Picadillo 182
Quick Chili 192
Rice Dressing 22
Rye Snacks 389
Smokehouse Specials 212
South of the Border Hot Dish 193
Spaghetti Sauce with Meat Balls 176
Spaghetti Pie 399
Spanish Delight 194
Spanish Meat Rice 26
Stuffed Pepper Casserole 255
Stuffed White Squash 263
Swedish Meat Balls 127, 184
Tacos 193
Talarini 190
Tamale and Chili Pie 195
Texas Hash 190
Three Peso Salad 408
Beef Liver (See Liver)
Beef Steak
  Baked Steak 169
  Beef Stroganoff 172
  Bobby's Seasoned Steaks 172
  Chili 191
  Indonesian Rijsttafel 25
  Pepper Beef 170
  Shish Kabob 174
  Steak au Poivre Vert 398
  Steak Diane 169
  Steak Embassy Style 171
  Steak Roll-ups 170
  Steak Zucchini 170
  Stir-Fry Beef 399
  Stuffed Beef Round 171
Beer Batter for Shrimp 72
Beer, Drunk Squirrel 98
Beer, Radio Bread 391
Beer Rice 30
Beet, Molded Salad 275
Beets, Pineapple 239

INDEX

Bell Pepper, Fried Stuffed 53
Bell Pepper, Stuffed Casserole 255
Bernie's Candied Yams 268
Beverages
   Banana Daiquiri 107
   Blini 106
   Bloody Mary 106
   Bloody Mary by the Gallon 106
   Bourbon Drinks
      Eggnog 108
      Irish Coffee 111
      Milk Punch 108
      New Orleans Mint Julep 108
      Old-Fashioned 108
      Sazerac Cocktail 110
      24 Hour Cocktails 110
   Brandy Drinks
      Blini 106
      Café Brûlot 111
      Velvet Hammer 110
   Café Brûlot 111
   Champagne Drinks
      Blini 106
      Punch à la Champagne 113
      Virginia's Spiked Fruit Punch 114
      Wedding Punch 114
   Cherry Bounce 107
   Clifford's Rum Punch 113
   Cocoa 112
   Coffee Drinks
      Café Brûlot 111
      Coffee Punch 111
      Creole Coffee 111
      Irish Coffee 111
   Coffee Punch 112
   Cowboy Kicker 105
   Creole Coffee 111
   Daiquiri Old-Fashioned 107
   Eggnog 107
   Frozen Fruit Ring 114
   Gin Drinks
      Green Wave 105
      Ramos Gin Fizz 109
   Green Wave 105
   Irish Coffee 111
   Liqueur Drinks
      Cowboy Kicker 105
      Milk Punch 108
      Pink Squirrel 109
      Sangrella 110
      Velvet Hammer 110
   Milk Punch 108
   "Miss Top's" Rum Cocktail 109
   Nectar Ice Cream Soda 112
   New Orleans Mint Julep 108
   Old-Fashioned 108
   "Old Virginia Wassail" 113
   Orange Odyssey 109
   Pink Squirrel 109
   Punch à la Champagne 113
   Punch, Clifford's Rum 113
   Punch, Coffee 112
   Punch, Frozen Fruit Ring 114
   Punch, Milk 108
   Punch, "Old Virginia Wassail" 113
   Punch, Slush 113
   Punch, Virginia's Spiked Fruit 114
   Punch, Wedding 114
   Ramos Gin Fizz 109
   Rum Drinks
      Banana Daiquiri 107
      Clifford's Rum Punch 113
      Daiquiri Old-Fashioned 107
      Milk Punch 108
      "Miss Top's" Rum Cocktail 109
      Strawberry Daiquiri 107
   Sangrella 110
   Sazerac Cocktail 110
   Slush Punch 113
   Strawberry Daiquiri 107
   Sugar or Simple Syrup 106
   Tequila Drinks
      Tiger's Tail 105
   Tiger's Tail 105
   24 Hour Cocktails 110
   Velvet Hammer 110
   Virginia's Spiked Fruit Punch 114
   Vodka Drinks
      Bloody Mary 106
      Bloody Mary by the Gallon 106
      Cherry Bounce 107
      Cowboy Kicker 105
      Orange Odyssey 109
      Velvet Hammer 110
   Wedding Punch 114
   Whiskey (See Bourbon)
   Wine Drinks
      Sangrella 110
      Virginia's Spiked Fruit Punch 114
Bienvenu's Court Bouillon 16
Big Lake Broccoli 404
Biscuit Bites 393
Biscuit Crust for Ham Wellington 197
Biscuits, Allen's Golden 161
Biscuits, Biscuit Bites 393
Biscuits, Cheese 141
Biscuits, Easy Buttermilk 161
Biscuits, Sticky Buns 392
Biscuits, Uncle Bubber's 161
Bisque, Avocado 19
Bisque, Crawfish 54
Bisque, Shrimp 379
Bisque Tortoni (Parfait) 364
Black Bean Soup, Mexican 11
Black Beans and Rice 27
Black Bottom Pie, Majestic Hotel 309
Black Walnut Cake 337
Black Walnut Roll 320
Black Walnuts, Caramel Nut Pound Cake ... 323
Blackberry Jam Cake 332
Blackberry Preserves 306
Blackened Redfish 397
Blackeyed Pea Dip 384
Blend of the Bayou Seafood Casserole ... 83
Blender Chocolate Pôts de Crème 355
Blender Hollandaise Sauce 293
Bleu Cheese Oil Vinegar Dressing 289
Blonde Brownies 345
Blini 106
Bloody Mary 106
Bloody Mary by the Gallon 106
Blueberry, Banana Pie 412
Blueberry Jello Salad, Virginia's 287
Bobby's Seasoned Steaks 172
Boeuf à la Blanche 167
Bohemian Cabbage 240
Boiled Brisket with Horseradish Sauce ... 173
Boiled, Crabs-Outside 64
Boiled Crawfish 50
Boiled Eggs 145

INDEX

Boiled Fresh Ham 196
Boiled Rice 21
Boiled Shrimp 74
Bonin Carrot Casserole 243
Bordelaise Sauce Johnson 295
Boston Brown Bread 155
Boudin, "Bounty" 22
Bouillabaisse Soup 16
"Bounty" Boudin 22
Bourbon Drinks (*See* Beverages)
Bourbon Glaze for Ham 301
Bourbon Fluffy Sauce 376
Bran Rolls 159
Bratwurst (Swartz Brats) 204
Bread Pudding, Grandmother's
  Old Fashioned 354
Breads
  Allen's Golden Biscuits 161
  Apple, Fresh 157
  Banana Nut 157
  Baquette 164
  Biscuit Bites 393
  Boston Brown 155
  Bran Rolls 159
  Cheese 156
  Cheese Biscuits 141
  Cinnamon Rolls 158
  Cinnamon Sticks 392
  Corn 152
  Dotty's Hush Puppies 151
  Easy Buttermilk Biscuits 161
  Egg 154
  French Loaf (Oyster Stuffed) 58
  Fresh Apple 157
  Greek 391
  Herb Stix 156
  Hush Puppies 151
  Ice Box Rolls 159, 160
  Jalapeño Corn 152
  Mammy's Flapjacks 393
  Nanny Jeanne's Coush Coush 153
  Oatmeal Raised 154
  Onion Corn 153
  Orange Rolls 158
  Plucking 160
  Pumpkin 157
  Radio Beer 391
  Raisin Bran Muffins 392
  Refrigerator Rolls 158
  Shrimp Loaf 82
  Spice Bites 389
  Spoon Corn 152
  Sticky Buns 392
  Sweet Poppy Seed 391
  Uncle Bubber's Biscuits 161
  Whole Wheat 155
Breads, Yeast
  Baquette 164
  Bran Rolls 159
  Cheese 156
  Cinnamon Rolls 158
  Coffee Cake 163
  Egg 154
  Ice Box Rolls 159, 160
  Oatmeal Raised 154
  Orange Rolls 158
  Plucking 160
  Refrigerator Rolls 158
  Whole Wheat 155
Breakfast Cereal, Nanny Jeanne's
  Coush-Coush 153

Breast of Duck and Duck Wellington 87
Brine for Chow Chow 292
Brisket 124, 173
Brisket, Boiled with Horseradish Sauce 173
Brittle, Peanut 343
Broccoli and Cauliflower Casserole 240
Broccoli Au Gratin Buccaneer 267
Broccoli, Big Lake 404
Broccoli, Curried Chicken and 223
Broccoli Macaroni Hollandaise 240
Broccoli Mold, Chicken 280
Broccoli Mousse 283
Broccoli-Rice Casserole 405
Brown Sauce 294
Brownies 345
Brownies, Blonde 345
Brownies, Extra Good 345
Brownies, Microwave 416
Brunch, Louisiana Sunday 143
Brucculuni With Spaghetti 208
Brussels Sprouts in Sour Cream 242
Buccaneer Broccoli Au Gratin 267
Burritos, Beef 194
Butter, Clarified 209
Butter Pecan Coffee Cake 413
Butter Pie 311
Butter Sauce, Anchovy 296
Buttermilk Biscuits, Easy 161
Buttermilk Pancakes 162
Buttermilk Pie 311
Buttermilk Pralines 343
Butterscotch, Cindy's Peanut Butter Fudge ..414
Butterscotch Ring for Ice Cream 371

Cabbage, Bohemian 240
Cabbage, Chop Suey 183
Cabbage, Cole Slaw 274
Cabbage, Ice Box Slaw 274
Cabbage, Red, Heidi 241
Cabbage Rolls, International Gourmet ..241
Cabbage, Swedish Christmas 242
Caesar Salad 272
Café Brûlot 111
Cajun Baked Yams (or Sweet Potatoes) ... 8, 268
Cajun Onion Rings 122
Cakes
  Ambrosia 321
  Angel Coconut Pound 321
  Angel Food Ice Cream Pie 370
  Apple Gingerbread Upside Down 322
  Apple Torte 323
  Baked Alaska 369
  Black Walnut Roll 320
  Butter Pecan Coffee 413
  Caramel Nut Pound 323
  Carrot 324
  Chewy Fudge 327
  Chocolate or Yellow Pound 334
  Coffee 163
  Coffee, Swedish Puff 163
  Cranberry 328
  Date 328
  Devil's Food 327
  Flower Garden 330
  Fool Proof Pound 335
  Fresh Coconut Layer 326
  Gingerbread 330
  Graham Cracker Cheese 324

INDEX **423**

Guter Kuchen 331
Ice Box 330
Italian Cream and Icing 331
Jam 332
Lemon 331
Lemon Pudding 359
Mother's Tea 348
My Favorite Chocolate 327
Oatmeal 332
Party Cheese 325
Pecan Torte 333
Pineapple Upside-Down 333
Plum-Tapioca 334
Pound 334
Praline 335
Prune 336
Prune Whip 366
Pudding 358
Pumpkin Pound 336
Red Velvet 337
Shortcake (Fruit) 368
Snowball 336
Sour Cream Cheese 325
Sour Cream Pound 335
Stuffed Angel Food 322
Sweet Dough Cheese 326
Walnut 337
White Fruit 328
Calcasieu Chicken Casserole 402
Calf Liver (*See* Liver)
Canadian French Potato Dressing 231
Canapés (*See* Hors d'Oeuvres)
Candied Date Loaf 342
Candied Grapefruit Peel 342
Candy and Confections (*See also* Desserts)
Baked Pecans 340
Buttermilk Pralines 343
Candied Date Loaf 342
Candied Grapefruit Peel 342
Chocolate Fudge 341
Divinity Fudge 341
Heavenly Hash 342
Howard's Pecan Pralines 343
Mama's Sugared Pecans 344
Miss Annabel's Orange Pecans 340
Mr. Snowman 367
Mother's Cinnamon Pecans 340
One Hundred Dollar Chocolate Fudge ...341
Peanut Brittle 343
Peanut Butter Balls 344
Pecan Puffs 344
Cantaloupe Soup, Marsh Melon 382
Cantonese Ham 197
Capantto 123
Caramel Ice Cream 372
Caramel Icing 339
Caramel Icing for Date Cake 329
Caramel Nut Pound Cake 323
Caramel Sauce 376
Caramel Soufflé with Caramel Custard ..350
Carbonara (Spaghetti à la Guiliano and
  Joel III) 258
Carol's Crawfish 53
Carrot Cake 324
Carrot Casserole 242
Carrot Casserole, Bonin 243
Carrot Relish 307
Carrot Salad, Different 275
Carrot Vichyssoise 382
Carrots with Orange Sauce 243

Casseroles
Apple 235
Asparagus, Fresh 235
Asparagus, "Puttin' on the Ritz" 403
Asparagus Supreme 236
Baked Chicken and Rice 226
Baked Corn 245
Baked Egg and Rice 28
Beans, Baked for a Crowd 236
Beans with an Outdoor Flavor 237
Beef-Bacon-Macaroni 189
Beef Stroganoff 172
Big Lake Broccoli 404
Black Beans and Rice 27
Blend of the Bayou Seafood 83
Bonin Carrot 243
Broccoli and Cauliflower 240
Broccoli, Big Lake 404
Broccoli Macaroni Hollandaise 240
Broccoli-Rice 405
Buccaneer Broccoli Au Gratin 267
Calcasieu Chicken 402
Canadian French Potato Dressing 231
Carrot 242
Carrots with Orange Sauce 243
Cauliflower with Jalapeño Sauce 244
Celery 244
Chicken 223
Chicken and Asparagus 227
Chicken Enchilada 221
Chicken Italien 217
Chicken Tarragon 402
Chili Chicken 222
Cintra's Eggplant Manicotti 247
Company Cauliflower 243
Corn Au Gratin 246
Country Pie 188
Country-Style Back Ribs and Sauerkraut ..203
Crab Meat 68
Crawfish 50
Crawfish Au Gratin 50
Creamed Spinach 259
Crookneck Squash Frito 261
Curried Chicken and Broccoli 223
Cushaw 247
Desperation Meal 400
Eggplant 248
Eggplant Sapphire 29
Escalloped Eggplant 249
French Italian Spaghetti 174
Green Bean 238
Green Bean with Cheese 238
Green Rice 32
Hamburger 189
Hollywood Hash 190
Hot Chicken Salad 224
Johnny Marzetti Cheddar Cheese 189
Macaroni and Cheese 257
Macaroni-Cheese Tomato Tang 147
Meat Pot Pie 188
Mexican 192
Moussaka 182
Mushroom Caps Baked in Cheddar
  Cheese Sauce 252
Onion Pie 253
Onions Au Gratin 253
Oyster and Rice 31
Oysters Bienville 56
Pastitsio 175
Pheasant 95

INDEX

Pineapple Rice 33
Potato Pie 257
"Puttin' on the Ritz" 403
Quail-Rice Magnifique 95
Quick and Easy Spinach 260
Rice 29
Rice O'Brian 28
Rice or Ring 28
Rice Surprise 32
Risotto Con Melanzane 26
Romano 266
Sausage Strada 204
Scalloped Oysters 59
Shoe Peg Corn 246
Shrimp-Rice 31
South of the Border Hot Dish 193
Spanish Delight 194
Spanish Meat Rice 26
Spanish Olive-Pork Chop 202
Spinach 258
Spinach and Cheese 260
Spinach Rice 29
Spinach Ring 260
Spinach Supreme 261
Squash Delight 263
Squash Stuffed with Shrimp 263
Squash Supreme 262
Stuffed Pepper 255
Summer Squash 262
Talarini 190
Tamale and Chili Pie 195
Texas Hash 190
Texas Potatoes 256
Tomato 265
Tuna 44
Turkey Tetrazzini 229
Vegetable 267
Weenie Jam 203
Whipped Yams 269
Wild Rice 24
Wild Rice and Oyster 60
Yellow or Zucchini Squash 264
Yellow Squash for Sure Fire Squash
  Haters 406
Zucchini Eggplant 264
Cauliflower Casserole and Broccoli ... 240
Cauliflower, Company 243
Cauliflower with Jalapeño Sauce 244
Caviar Ball 121
Caviar Mousse 118
Caviar, New Potatoes with Sour Cream and .. 121
Celery Casserole 244
Chafing Dish Ham Balls 126
Champagne, Punch à la 113
Champeaux Gumbo 8
Charcoaled Venison Roast 101
Charlie's Picante Sauce 387
Chateaubriand, Venison 101
Cheese
  Bacon and Onion Sandwiches 212
  Baked Chicken Breasts 402
  Ball 141
  Ball, Jalapeño 142
  Biscuits 141
  Bleu Oil Vinegar Dressing 289
  Bread 156
  Buccaneer Broccoli Au Gratin 267
  Chicken Enchilada Casserole 221
  Chilaly 149
  Chili Chicken Casserole 222

Chilies Rellenos 195
Chilies Stuffed with Beans 245
Cintra's Eggplant Manicotti 247
Corn Au Gratin 246
Dressing for Grapefruit Salad 285
Fettuccine Alfredo 258
Green Bean Casserole with 238
Grits, Baked 148
Grits, South of the Border 148
Ham, Mushroom Omelet 145
Hog's Head 118
Hollywood Hash 190
Jalapeño Ball 142
Johnny Marzetti Cheddar Casserole .. 189
Macaroni and 257
Macaroni Salad 279
Macaroni Tomato Tang 147
Mock Quiche Lorraine 143
Mushroom Caps Baked in Cheddar
  Sauce 252
Olive Spread 141
Onions Au Gratin 253
Pimiento Spread 142
Puff 147
Romano Casserole 266
Roquefort Dressing 291
Schooner Squares 388
Shrimp Con Queso Dip 140
Soufflé 146
Soup 12
South of the Border 148
Spaghetti à la Guiliano and
  Joel III (Carbonara) 258
Spanish Rice 27
Spinach and Casserole 260
Squares, Schooner 388
Strawberry Paddle Wheel 388
Straws 388
Sweet Dough Cake 326
Three Cheese Roll 142
Tirotrigona 149
Veal Cutlets Parmesan 210
Veal Parmigiana 210
Walnut Ball 141
Welsh Rarebit 147
Cheese Cake Fondue 416
Cheese Cake, Graham Cracker 324
Cheese Cake, Party 325
Cheese Cake, Sour Cream 326
Cheese Cake, Sweet Dough 326
Cherry Bounce 107
Chestnut Meatballs 383
Chewy Bars 414
Chewy Fudge Cake 327
Chez Oca's Escargots Bourguignonne .. 129
Chez Oca's Pheasant in Brandy Sauce .. 96
Chez Oca's Turtle Stew 48
Chicken
  à Seville 221
  and Asparagus Casserole 227
  and Mushrooms 227
  and Noodles 225
  and Shrimp Curry 222
  Baked and Rice 226
  Baked Hen 230
  Breast with Sour Cream Sauce, Stuffed .. 215
  Breast with Tuna Sauce or Petti di Pollo
    Tonnato 213
  Broccoli Mold 280
  Calcasieu Casserole 402

INDEX

Casserole 223
Cheese-Baked Breasts 402
Chili Casserole 222
Clement's 215
Coq Au Quiche 219
Coq Au Vin 217
Creamed 228
Croquettes, or Turkey 229
Curried, and Broccoli 223
Curried, and Rice Stuffed Tomato Salad ... 281
Enchilada Casserole 221
Fried, Georgia, with Cream Gravy 214
Fried, Octavia's 214
Georgia Fried with Cream Gravy 214
Glacé Molds 125
Hen Gumbo 9
Hot Salad 224
in the Limelight 226
Italien 217
Kiev, Nutty Fruit, with Glaze 234
Liver, Chopped 127
Liver Omelet 145
Livers with Mushrooms 228
Louisiana Gumbo 3
Meat, and Sausage Spaghetti 218
Mustard 226
Old Fashioned Jewish Penicillin
   (Chicken Soup) 13
Opelousas Baked 224
or Turkey Croquettes 229
Orange Walnut 220
Princess 219
Red Gill's Barbecued 223
Roast 224
Salad 280
Soup, Old Fashioned Jewish Penicillin ... 13
Spaghetti 216
Tarragon 402
Vermouth 216
Walnut Hawaiian 220
Weeze's Gumbo 5
Wild Rice Salad 281
with Sherry 215
Chilaly 149
Chili 191
Chili Chicken Casserole 222
Chili, Hot 192
Chili Pie, and Tamale 195
Chili, Quick 192
Chili, Venison 102
Chilies Rellenos 195
Chilies Stuffed with Beans 245
Chilled Cucumber Soup 20
Chinese Food (*See* Foreign Foods)
Chipped Beef on Muffins 212
Chocolate
   Bachelor's Mousse 355
   Blonde Brownies 345
   Brownies 345
   Chewy Bars 414
   Cream Puffs 363
   Creamy Frosting 363
   Dessert, Aunt Tommy's 356
   Devil's Food Cake 327
   Extra Good Brownies 345
   Fudge 341
   Fudge Muffins 415
   Glacée au Chocolat 356
   Glaze for Chocolate or Yellow
      Pound Cake 334

Hershey Bar Pie 412
Ice Box Pudding 355
Ice Cream 372
Ice Cream Macaroon Dessert 374
Majestic Black Bottom Pie 309
Microwave Brownies 416
Mint Ice Cream Pie 375
Mousse 355
My Favorite Cake 327
My Favorite Frosting 339
Nut Frosting 339
One Hundred Dollar Chocolate Fudge ... 341
or Yellow Pound Cake 334
Peanut Butter Balls 344
Pie, Auntie's Old Tyme 312
Pie, Fudge 313
Pie, German Sweet 313
Pie, Pecan 316
Pie, Swirl 312
Pôts de Crème, Blender 355
Pretzels 349
Red Velvet Cake 337
Sauce 374, 376
Snow on the Mountain 367
Yummy 357
Chopped Liver 127
Chop Suey, Cabbage 183
Choucroute à L'Alsacienne Sauerkraut and
   Knockwurst Delight 203
Chow Chow 292
Chowder Contraband 380
Chowders (*See* Soups)
Christmas Ice Cream 373
Chutney, Sweet Tomato 307
Cindy's Peanut Butter Fudge 414
Cinnamon Rolls 158
Cinnamon Sticks 392
Cintra's Eggplant Manicotti 247
Clam, Crab Dip 138
Clarified Butter 209
Clement's Chicken 215
Clifford's Rum Punch 113
Cobbler, Quick Peach 418
Cobia, Tips on 35
Cocktail Sauce for Seafood 296
Cocoa 112
Coconut, Ambrosia Cake 321
Coconut, Fresh Layer Cake 326
Coconut, German Sweet Chocolate Pie ... 313
Coconut, Japanese Fruit Pie 314
Coconut, Mother's Favorites 348
Coconut, No Crust Coconut Pie 413
Coconut-Pecan Meringue Pie Shell for
   Ice Cream 371
Coconut Pound Cake, Angel 321
Coconut, Snow on the Mountain 367
Coconut, Snowball Cake 336
Coffee, Café Brûlot 111
Coffee Cake 163
Coffee Cake, Swedish Puff 163
Coffee, Creole 111
Coffee, Irish 111
Coffee, Mocha Icing 338
Coffee Punch 112
Cold Curried Mushroom Soup 19
Cold Lemon Soufflé with Raspberry Sauce ... 360
Cold Orange Soufflé 365
Cold Stuffed Red Snapper 39
Cole Slaw 274
Cole Slaw, Ice Box 274

INDEX

Colorful Pickled Eggs 148
Commander's Famous Imperial Crab
   Specialty 65
Company Cauliflower 243
"Contraband Crab Meat" 45
Cookies
   Blonde Brownies 345
   Brownies 345
   Chewy Bars 414
   Chocolate Pretzels 349
   Cream Cheese 346
   Danish Pastry 368
   English Toffee Squares 358
   Extra Good Brownies 345
   Fruit Balls 346
   Fruit Cake 346
   Graham Cracker Roll 414
   Henriettas 347
   Lace 347
   Lemon Cheese Squares 415
   Lemon Whippersnaps 415
   Mama's 347
   Mother's Favorites 348
   Mother's Tea Cakes 348
   Oatmeal 348
   Pecan Puffs 344
   Potato Chip 349
   Slice 'n Bake 349
Coq Au Quiche 219
Coq Au Vin 217
Cora's Cranberry and Kumquat Sauce ... 302
Corn Au Gratin 246
Corn, Baked 245
Corn Bread 152
Corn Bread Dressing, Baked Turkey and . 233
Corn Bread, Hush Puppies 151
Corn Bread, Hush Puppies, Dotty's 151
Corn Bread, Jalapeño 152
Corn Bread, Nanny Jeanne's Coush-Coush . 153
Corn Bread, Onion 153
Corn Bread Sausage Pecan Dressing 232
Corn Bread, Shrimp Stuffing for Fish 84
Corn Bread, Spoon 152
Corn Soup, Fresh 12
Corn, Grand Mere's Maque Choux 247
Corn Chowder, Hearty 13
Corn, Shoe-Peg Casserole 246
Cornish Hen Chasseur 231
Cornish Hens Stuffed with Wild Rice ... 231
Cottage Cheese Avocado Delight 275
Country Pie 188
Country Pork Rib and Turnip Stew 202
Country Style Back Ribs and Sauerkraut . 203
Country-Style Venison Steak 104
Court Bouillon, Bienvenu's 16
Coush-Coush, Nanny Jeanne's 153
Cowboy Kicker 105
Crab (See also Crab Meat)
   Crab Cashew Salad 410
   Crab Chowder, Morgans Point 17
   Crab-Clam Dip 138
   Crab Crêpes Rosemary, Shrimp and ... 78
   Crab, Deviled 68
   Crab Dip 137
   Crab, Freezing of 64
   Crab Imperial, Commander's Famous
      Specialty 65
   Crab Lasagne 395
Crab Meat (See also Crabs)
   Au Gratin 65

Blend of the Bayou Casserole 83
Casserole 68
Chowder, Morgans Point 17
Clam Dip 138
   "Contraband" 45
Crab Cashew Salad 410
Crab Lasagne 395
Crêpes Rosemary, Shrimp and 78
Deviled 68
Dip 137
Dip, Lump 138
Easy Hot Dip 137
Freezing of 64
Fried Stuffed Bell Pepper 53
Gumbo, Mrs. Soulé's Seafood 4
Gumbo, Seafood 5
Hot Canapé 128
Imperial, Commander's Famous Crab
   Specialty 65
Lasagne 395
Lobster Rolls 129
Lump Dip 138
Mornay 128
Mousse 65
Mrs. Soulé's Seafood Gumbo 4
Open Sandwich 134
Pelican Hook Soup 14
Quiche 66
Quiche, Easy 144
Salad 281
San Francisco Seafood Quiche 80
Seafood Dip à la Kingwood 140
Seafood Gumbo 5
Shrimp and Crab Crêpes Rosemary 78
Soufflé 67
Soufflé, Hot 67
Stew 67
Stuffed Artichokes with 66
Stuffed Mushroom Caps, Baked 120
Crab Mornay 128
Crab Soufflé 67
Crab Stew 67
Crabs, Boiled-Outside 64
Crabs, Cleaning and Cooking of 62, 63
Crabs, How to Eat 62
Crabs, Seafood Gumbo 5
Crabs, Soft Shell, Cleaning of 63
Crabs, Soft Shell, Freezing of 64
Crabs, Soft Shell, Fried 63
Crabs, Stuffed 66
Crackers, Spice Bites 389
Cranberried Yams 268
Cranberry and Kumquat Sauce, Cora's . 302
Cranberry Cake 328
Cranberry Conserve 302
Cranberry Crunch 366
Cranberry, Red and White Freeze 287
Cranberry Sauce, Baked 302
Crawfish Au Gratin 50
Crawfish Bisque 54
Crawfish, Boiled 50
Crawfish, Carol's 53
Crawfish Casserole 50
Crawfish Dip 136
Crawfish, Easy Etouffée 394
Crawfish Etouffée 52
Crawfish, Fried Stuffed Bell Pepper 53
Crawfish, Fried Tails 51
Crawfish, Giuliano's Fettuccine 51
Crawfish in a Bundle 394

INDEX

Crawfish, Last Minute 384
Crawfish Pie 51, 52
Crawfish, Tips on Peeling 49
Cream Cheese Cookies 346
Cream Gravy, Georgia Fried Chicken with ...214
Cream of Wheat Custard 149
Cream or White Sauce 296
Cream Puffs 363
Creamed Chicken 228
Creamed Spinach 259
Creamy Chocolate Frosting 363
Crème Brûlée 352
Crème d'Artichauts 381
Crème de Menthe, Grasshopper Pie 315
Creole Coffee 111
Creole Cushaw 246
Creole Fried Oysters 58
Creole Jambalaya 23
Creole Sauce 145
Creole Shrimp Tarts 133
Crêpes Fitzgerald Filling 362
Crêpes, French 362
Crêpes, Shrimp and Crab Rosemary 78
Crêpes Suzette 363
Croaker, Tips on 35
Crookneck Squash Frito 261
Croquettes, Chicken or Turkey 229
Croutes, French Onion Soup 10
Croutons 54
Crowder Peas 254
Crown Pork Roast 198
Crusts (*See* Pastry)
Cucumbers, Chilled Soup 20
Curried Chicken and Broccoli 223
Curried Chicken and Rice Stuffed Tomato
  Salad 281
Curried Ham in Popovers 198
Curried Raisin Rice 33
Curry, Chicken and Broccoli 223
Curry, Chicken and Rice Stuffed Tomato
  Salad 281
Curry, Chicken and Shrimp 222
Curry, Cold Mushroom Soup 19
Curry Dip Royale 385
Curry, Easy Shrimp 80
Curry, Ham in Popovers 198
Curry, Jack's Shrimp Spread 133
Curry, Orange Walnut Chicken 220
Curry, Raisin Rice 33
Curry, Rice and Artichokes 30
Curry, Skillet Tuna 44
Cushaw 247
Cushaw, Creole 246
Custards and Puddings
  Aunt Tommy's Chocolate Dessert 356
  Baked Custard 350
  Banana Pudding 354
  Blender Chocolate Pôts de Crème 355
  Caramel Soufflé with Caramel Custard 350
  Chocolate Ice Box Pudding 355
  Chocolate Yummy 357
  Cold Lemon Soufflé with Raspberry
    Sauce 360
  Cold Orange Soufflé 365
  Cream of Wheat Custard 149
  Cream Puffs 363
  Crème Brûlée 352
  Custard 322
  Egg Custard, Sherry Trifle 351
  English Toffee Squares 358
  Flan Cubano 351
  Floating Island 352
  Fresh Apple Nut Pudding with Rum
    Sauce 353
  Glacée au Chocolat 356
  Grandmother's Old Fashioned Bread
    Pudding 354
  Grandmother's Rice Pudding 33
  Homemade Ice Cream 373
  Lemon Cups 359
  Lemon Ice Box Dessert 359
  Lemon Pudding Cake 359
  Parfait (Bisque Tortoni) 364
  Pineapple Delight Dessert 360
  Poor Man's Pudding 358
  Pudding Cake 359
  Sherry Trifle 351
  Shortcut Banana Pudding 417
  Snow on the Mountain 367
  Stuffed Angel Food Cake 322
  Trifling Pudding 353
  Yorkshire Pudding 166

Daiquiri, Banana 107
Daiquiri Old-Fashioned 107
Daiquiri, Strawberry 107
Danish Pastry 368
Date Cake 329
Date Loaf, Candied 342
David's Sesame Salad 407
Dee's Dessert 371
Deer (*See* Venison)
Deer, Skinning of 100
Desperation Meal 400
Desserts (*See also* Cakes, Candy, Confections,
  Cookies, Frozen Desserts, and Pies)
  Almond Tart 370
  Aloha Sauce 376
  Ambrosia 366
  Ambrosia Cake 321
  Angel Coconut Pound Cake 321
  Angel Food Cake Ice Cream Pie 370
  Apple Gingerbread Upside Down Cake ...322
  Apple Torte 323
  Aunt Tommy's Chocolate Dessert 356
  Auntie's Old Tyme Chocolate Pie 312
  Avocado Crème 370
  Bachelor's Mousse 355
  Baked Alaska 369
  Baked Bananas 354
  Baked Custard 350
  Banana Blueberry Pie 412
  Banana Fritters Bayou Lafourche 236
  Banana Pudding 354
  Bananas Foster on Ice Cream 369
  Black Walnut Roll 320
  Blender Chocolate Pôts de Crème 355
  Blonde Brownies 345
  Brownies 345
  Butter Pecan Coffee Cake 413
  Butter Pie 311
  Buttermilk Pie 311
  Butterscotch Ring for Ice Cream 371
  Caramel Ice Cream 372
  Caramel Icing 339
  Caramel Icing for Date Cake 329
  Caramel Nut Pound Cake 323

INDEX

Caramel Sauce ... 376
Caramel Soufflé with Caramel Custard ... 350
Carrot Cake ... 324
Cheese Cake Fondue ... 416
Chewy Bars ... 414
Chewy Fudge Cake ... 327
Chocolate Ice Box Pudding ... 355
Chocolate Ice Cream ... 372
Chocolate Mousse ... 355
Chocolate Nut Frosting ... 339
Chocolate or Yellow Pound Cake ... 334
Chocolate Pecan Pie ... 316
Chocolate Pretzels ... 349
Chocolate Sauce ... 376
Chocolate Swirl Pie ... 312
Chocolate Yummy ... 357
Christmas Ice Cream ... 373
Cindy's Peanut Butter Fudge ... 414
Coconut-Pecan Meringue Pie Shell for Ice Cream ... 371
Cold Lemon Soufflé with Raspberry Sauce au Kirsch ... 360
Cold Orange Soufflé ... 365
Cranberry Cake ... 328
Cranberry Crunch ... 366
Cream Cheese Cookies ... 346
Cream Puffs ... 363
Crème Brûlée ... 352
Crêpes Fitzgerald Filling ... 362
Crêpes Suzette ... 363
Danish Pastry ... 368
Date Cake ... 329
Date Loaf ... 342
Dee's Dessert ... 371
Devil's Food Cake ... 327
Double Lemon Meringue Pie ... 314
Dreamy Pumpkin Pie ... 318
Dutch Apple Crisp ... 310
English Toffee Squares ... 358
Extra Good Brownies ... 345
Flan Cubano ... 351
Floating Island ... 352
Flower Garden Cake ... 330
Fluffy Bourbon Sauce ... 376
Fool Proof Pound Cake ... 335
French Crêpes ... 362
French Apple Nut Pudding with Rum Sauce ... 353
Fresh Coconut Layer Cake ... 326
Fresh Fruit Bavarian ... 417
Frozen Butter Pecan Delight ... 417
Fruit Balls ... 346
Fruit Cake Cookies ... 346
Fruit Pizza ... 418
Fudge Muffins ... 415
Fudge Pie ... 313
German Sweet Chocolate Pie ... 313
Gingerbread ... 330
Glacée au Chocolat ... 356
Graham Cracker Cheese Cake ... 324
Graham Cracker Roll ... 414
Grandmother's Old Fashioned Bread Pudding ... 354
Grandmother's Rice Pudding ... 33
Grandpa's Karo Pecan Pie ... 317
Grasshopper Pie ... 315
Great Pumpkin Pie ... 318
Guter Kuchen, A ... 331
Hard Sauce ... 358, 377
Harvest Sweet Potato Jello Pie ... 319
Heavenly Strawberry Pie ... 319

Henriettas ... 347
Hershey Bar Pie ... 412
Homemade Ice Cream Custard ... 373
Ice-Box Cake ... 330
Ice Cream Bombe ... 372
Ice Cream Macaroon Dessert ... 374
Italian Cream Cake and Icing ... 331
Jam Cake ... 332
Japanese Fruit Pie ... 314
Kentucky Pecan Pie ... 317
Key Lime Pie ... 315
Lace Cookies ... 347
Lemon Cake ... 331
Lemon Cheese Squares ... 415
Lemon Cups ... 359
Lemon Ice Box Dessert ... 359
Lemon Pudding Cake ... 359
Lemon Sauce ... 377
Lemon Whippersnaps ... 415
Little Pecan Tarts ... 316
Majestic Hotel Black Bottom Pie ... 309
Mama's Cookies ... 347
Microwave Brownies ... 416
Mint Ice Cream Pie ... 375
Mocha Icing ... 338
Mother's Favorites ... 348
Mother's Tea Cakes ... 348
Mr. Snowman ... 367
My Favorite Chocolate Cake ... 327
My Favorite Chocolate Frosting ... 339
Never-Fail Pastry ... 310
No Crust Coconut Pie ... 413
Oatmeal Cake ... 332
Oatmeal Cookies ... 348
One Minute Icing ... 338
Parfait (Bisque Tortoni) ... 364
Party Cheese Cake ... 325
Pavlova ... 364
Peach Crisp ... 361
Peach Fantasy ... 361
Peach Kuchen ... 361
Peanut Brittle ... 343
Peanut Surprise Pie ... 316
Pecan-Almond Tarts ... 368
Pecan Pie ... 317
Pecan Puffs ... 344
Pecan Surprise Pie ... 316
Pecan Torte ... 333
Peppermint Stick Ice Cream ... 373
Perfect Peach Pie ... 413
Pineapple Delight Dessert ... 360
Pineapple Upside-Down Cake ... 333
Plum-Tapioca Cake ... 334
Poor Man's Pudding ... 358
Potato Chip Cookies ... 349
Pound Cake ... 334
Praline Cake ... 335
Prune Cake ... 336
Prune Whip ... 366
Pudding Cake ... 358
Pumpkin Pound Cake ... 336
Quick Broiled Icing ... 339
Quick Peach Cobbler ... 418
Red Velvet Cake ... 337
Refreshing Fruit Sherbet ... 371
Rum Sauce ... 353, 377
Seven Minute Icing ... 338
Sherbet Macaroon ... 374
Sherry Trifle ... 351
Short Cake (Fruit) ... 368
Shortcut Banana Pudding ... 417

INDEX

Slice 'n Bake Cookies 349
Snow on the Mountain 367
Snowball Cake 336
Sour Cream Cheese Cake 325
Sour Cream Pound Cake 335
Stuffed Angel Food Cake 322
Sweet Dough Cheese Cake 326
Tortoni 375
Trifling Pudding 353
Uncooked Homemade Vanilla Ice Cream ..373
Vanilla Ice Cream 374
Walnut Cake 337
Watermelon Sherbet 375
White Fruit Cake 328
White Icing 338
Deviled Crab 68
Deviled Eggs 144
Deviled Eggs, Baked 146
Deviled Ham, Biscuit Crust 197
Deviled Ham, Grandma Celeste's Stuffed
  Mirlitons 250
Deviled Oysters 59
Devil's Food Cake 327
Devils on Horseback 132
Diet Food, Avocado-Cottage Cheese
  Delight 275
Diet Food, Fig Preserves for Dieters .305
Different Carrot Salad 275
Dill Dip 135
Dill, Lima Salad 276
Dill Pickles, Refrigerator 308
Dino's Shrimp Paste 131
Dips
  Avocado 135
  Blackeyed Pea 384
  Crab 137
  Crab-Clam 138
  Crawfish 136
  Curry Royale 385
  Dill 135
  Easy Hot Crabmeat 137
  Festive Florentine Dip 386
  Green Goodness 386
  Kum Bak 136
  Lump Crab 138
  Mousseline 135
  Seafood à la Kingwood 140
  Shrimp 139
  Shrimp con Queso 140
  Shrimp Italiano 383
  Sombrero 386
  Spinach 139, 386
  Thistle 385
  Tuna 139
  Yogurt, for Fruit 150
Dirty Rice 23
Divinity Fudge 341
Doc's Hot Pepper Sauce 303
Dr. Hebert's Grand Chenier Barbecue
  Plate Sauce 298
Dolphin, Tips on 35
Dotty's Hush Puppies 151
Double Lemon Meringue Pie 314
Doubloon Delight Fruit Salad 410
Dough (See Pastry)
Dove, Baked Martin 98
Dove Pie 97
Dove, Pot Roasted Game 86
Dove, Squirrel Gumbo 7
Doves in Wine (Quail or Snipe) 97

Doves, Smothered 96
Dreamy Pumpkin Pie 318
Dressing (See also Stuffing)
  Dressing, Baked Turkey and Corn Bread ..233
  Dressing, Canadian French Potato ...231
  Dressing, Corn Bread Sausage Pecan .232
  Dressing, Minced Beef for Kibbie ...180
  Dressing, Rice 22
  Dressing, Shrimp and Eggplant 84
  Dressing, Turkey 232
Dressings for Salads (See Salad
  Dressings and Sauces)
Drinks (See Beverages)
Drum, "Contraband Crabmeat" 45
Drum, Tips on 35
Drunk Squirrel 98
Duck
  Baked Wild Goose or 88
  Breast of and Duck Wellington 87
  Champeaux Gumbo 8
  Cleaning 85
  Cooking 85
  Fried Delight 92
  Goose-Sausage Gumbo 7
  Iron Pot 89
  Jim's Barbecued 90
  Louisiana Gumbo 3
  or Goose, Orange Glazed 92
  or Goose, Sherry Spice 89
  or Goose, Stuffed, Pot Roasted 88
  Plucking 85
  Pot Roasted Game 86
  Roast Duckling Chinese Style 230
  Thelma's Stuffed Teals 88
  Wellington 87
  Wild à la Creole 90
  Wild, LaFleur 91
  Wild, Spanish 91
  Wild, with Olive Sauce 90
Dumplings, Mother's 162
Dutch Apple Crisp 310

Easy Buttermilk Biscuits 161
Easy Crawfish Etouffée 394
Easy Hot Crab Meat Dip 137
Easy Lasagne 177
Easy Potato Salad 278
Easy Quiche 144
Easy Shrimp Curry 80
Easy Vegetable Sukiyaki 266
Egg, Baked and Rice 28
Egg Bread 154
Egg Custard, Sherry Trifle 351
Egg Nog 108
Eggplant, Capantto 123
Eggplant Casserole 248
Eggplant Dressing, Shrimp and 84
Eggplant, Escalloped 249
Eggplant Fritters 248
Eggplant, Gumbo Gouter 249
Eggplant, How to Remove Bitter Taste .249
Eggplant, Manicotti, Cintra's 247
Eggplant, Moussaka 182
Eggplant, Risotto con Melanzane (Eggplant
  and Rice Casserole) 26
Eggplant Sapphire 29
Eggplant, Vegetable Casserole 267

INDEX

Eggplant, Zucchini Casserole 264
Eggs (*See also* Omelet)
  à la Debi 146
  Au Gratin, Stuffed 144
  Basic Omelet Recipe 145
  Benedict 143
  Boil, How to 145
  Cheese Soufflé 146
  Chicken Liver Omelet 145
  Chilaly 149
  Colorful Pickled 148
  Crab Meat Quiche 66
  Crab Soufflé 67
  Custard, Sherry Trifle 351
  Deviled 144
  Deviled, Baked 146
  Easy Quiche 144
  Egg Nog 108
  Ham, Mushroom, and Cheese Omelet 145
  Hamburger Mushroom Quiche 186
  Hot Crab Meat Soufflé 67
  How to Boil Perfectly 145
  Hussarde 143
  Louisiana Sunday Brunch 143
  Mock Quiche Lorraine 143
  Omelets 145
  Quiche Lorraine 143
  Rice, Baked 28
  San Francisco Seafood Quiche 80
  Spinach Quiche Boudreau 259
  Tirotrigona 149
Enchilada Casserole, Chicken 221
English Peas, French 407
English Peas Hashed in Cream 254
English Toffee Squares 358
Escalloped Eggplant 249
Escargot Garlic 129
Escargots Bourguignonne, Chez Oca's 129
Etouffée, Crawfish 52
Etouffée, Easy Crawfish 394
Etouffée, Okra 253
Etouffée, Shrimp 77
Extra Good Brownies 345

Fast and Fabulous Recipes
  Anchovy Butter Sauce 296
  Asparagus Supreme 236
  Avocado Dressing 289
  Bacon, Cheese, and Onion Sandwiches ...212
  Bacon-Wrapped Snacks 390
  Baked Bananas 354
  Baked Cheese Grits 148
  Baked Corn 245
  Baked Fillet of Fish 37
  Baked Pecans 340
  Baked Pork Chops 201
  Baked Shrimp 73
  Banana Blueberry Pie 412
  Banana Daiquiri 107
  Bananas Foster on Ice Cream 369
  Barbecue Sauce 298
  Barbecued Fish 41
  Barbecued Shrimp 72
  Basting Sauce for Barbecuing 299
  Beef Tacos 193
  Big Lake Broccoli 404
  Biscuit Bites 393

Blackened Redfish 397
Blackeyed Pea Dip 384
Blender Hollandaise Sauce 293
Bleu Cheese Oil Vinegar Dressing 289
Bourbon Glaze for Ham 301
Broccoli and Cauliflower Casserole 240
Broccoli-Rice Casserole 405
Brussels Sprouts in Sour Cream 242
Butter Pecan Coffee Cake 413
Buttermilk Pancakes 162
Buttermilk Pie 311
Calcasieu Chicken Casserole 402
Carrot Vichyssoise 382
Carrots with Orange Sauce 243
Cauliflower with Jalapeño Sauce 244
Charlie's Picante Sauce 387
Cheese-Baked Chicken Breasts 402
Cheese Cake Fondue 416
Cheese Olive Spread 141
Cheese Soup 12
Cheese Straws 388
Chestnut Meatballs 383
Chewy Bars 414
Chewy Fudge Cake 327
Chicken Tarragon 402
Chilaly 149
Chocolate Sauce 376
Chowder Contraband 380
Cindy's Peanut Butter Fudge 414
Cinnamon Sticks 392
Clifford's Rum Punch 113
Cocktail Sauce for Seafood 296
Commander's Famous Imperial Crab
  Specialty 65
Company Cauliflower 243
Corn Bread 152
Crab Cashew Salad 410
Crab Lasagne 395
Crab Meat Open Sandwich 134
Cranberry Crunch 366
Crawfish in a Bundle 394
Cream or White Sauce 296
Creamed Spinach 259
Crème d'Artichauts 381
Crookneck Squash Frito 261
Curry Dip Royale 385
David's Sesame Salad 407
Desperation Meal 400
Dill Dip 135
Doubloon Delight Fruit Salad 410
Dutch Apple Crisp 310
Easy Crawfish Etouffée 394
Easy Hot Crab Meat Dip 137
Easy Quiche 144
Extra Good Brownies 345
Festive Florentine Dip 386
Fettuccine Alfredo 258
French-Italian Dressing 288
French Peas 405
Fresh Asparagus Casserole 235
Fresh Fruit Bavarian 417
Fried Oysters, Louisiana Style 58
Frozen Butter Pecan Delight 417
Fruit Pizza 418
Fudge Muffins 415
Gingerbread 330
Graham Cracker Roll 414
Grandpa's Karo Pecan Pie 317
Greek Bread 391
Green Bean Casserole 238

INDEX **431**

Green Bean Casserole with Cheese 238
Green Bean Vinaigrette 409
Green Beans Amandine 403
Green Beans Mornay 404
Green Goodness Dip 386
Ham Skillet Supper 400
Hamburger Mushroom Quiche 186
Hard Sauce 377
He-Man Potatoes 405
Hearty Corn Chowder 13
Herb Sticks 156
Hershey Bar Pie 412
Hot Dog Butter Beans 239
Hot Seafood Pie 397
Hot Sherried Fruit 411
Irish Coffee 111
Italian Pork Chops 400
Jalapeño Cheese Spread 387
Japanese Fruit Pie 314
Jeweled Fruit 411
Jezebel Sauce 302
Kentucky Pecan Pie 317
Kum Bak Dip 136
Lace Cookies 347
Last Minute Crawfish 384
Lemon Brandy Veal 398
Lemon Cheese Squares 415
Lemon Whippersnaps 415
Leone's Pork and Pasta 401
Lillian's Baked New Potatoes 256
Lump Crab Dip 138
Mammy's Flapjacks 393
Marinated Mushroom Salad 271
Marsh Melon Soup 382
Meat Loaf 179
Mei Mei's Barbecued Green Beans 404
Meunière Sauce 297
Mexican Casserole 192
Mexican Roll-ups 390
Microwave Brownies 416
Milk Punch 108
No Crust Coconut Pie 413
Noodles Romanoff 406
Old Fashioned French Dressing 288
"Old Virginia Wassail" 113
One Minute Icing 338
Onion Pie 253
Orange-Spinach Salad with Honey-
   Mustard Dressing 407
Oven Fried Fish Fillets 37
Oysters Jean Lafitte 395
Pancakes 162
Papa Jim's Bean Salad 276
Party Salad Parmesan 408
Pecan Pie 317
Pelican Hook Soup 14
Perfect Peach Pie 413
Picture-Perfect Pasta..................409
Pineapple Beets 239
Pink Squirrel 109
Plum-Tapioca Cake 334
Polynesian Sausage 383
Pork Chops in Red Wine 202
Pumpkin Bread 157
"Puttin' on the Ritz" 403
Quiche Lorraine 143
Quick and Easy Spinach 260
Quick Peach Cobbler 418
Radio Beer Bread 391
Raisin Bran Muffins 392

Rice Cooker Jambalaya 401
Roquefort Cheese Dressing 291
Rotisserie Come Back Dressing 291
Rye Snacks 389
Sausage Bean Chowder 380
Schooner Squares 388
Shanghai Salad 277
Sherried Onions 252
Shoe Peg Corn Casserole 226
Shortcut Banana Pudding 417
Shrimp and Vegetable Grill 396
Shrimp Bisque 379
Shrimp Italiano 383
Shrimp Opelousas 396
Shrimp Stroganoff 81
Snow Peas and Mushrooms 255
Sombrero Dip 386
Soup Verde 14
Spaghetti Pie 399
Spanish Olive-Pork Chop Casserole 202
Spice Bites 389
Spinach Casserole 258
Spinach Dip, Festive Florentine 386
Squashbuckling Soup 381
Steak au Poivre Vert 398
Sticky Buns 392
Stir-Fry Beef 399
Strawberry Paddle Wheel 388
Sweet Poppy Seed Bread 391
Terrell's Perch 46
Texas Hash 190
Texas Potatoes 256
Thistle Dip 385
Thousand Island Dressing 290
Three Peso Salad 408
Tomato Casserole 265
True French Dressing 288
Uncle Bubber's Biscuits 161
Veal Cutlets Parmesan 210
Velvet Hammer 110
Walnut Cheese Ball 141
Welsh Rarebit 147
White Remoulade Sauce 297
Yellow Squash for Sure Fire Squash
   Haters 406
Yogurt Dip for Fruit 150
Festive Florentine Dip 386
Fettuccine Alfredo 258
Fettuccine, Guiliano's Crawfish 51
Fig Jello Preserves 305
Fig Preserves 305
Fig Preserves for Dieters 305
Figs, Louisiana, How to Preserve 305
Filé, Sassafras 2
Filet de Boeuf with Béarnaise Sauce 165
Fillet of Sole with Shrimp Sauce 46
Fish
   à la Gerd 38
   Alaskan Fisherman Stew 44
   Baked 46
   Baked Fillet of 37
   Barbecued 41
   Barbecued Ling 40
   Barbecued Red Fish 40
   Bienvenu's Court Bouillon 16
   Bouillabaisse Soup 16
   Chowder 17
   Cold Stuffed Red Snapper 39
   "Contraband Crabmeat" 45
   Fillet of Sole with Shrimp Sauce 46

INDEX

Fillets, Oven Fried 37
Fillets, Paysanne 37
Freezing of 36
Fried 36
Gaspergou 45
King Mackerel Balls 34, 36
Lock's Trout Amandine 42
Red Snapper Excelsior 40
Shrimp Corn Bread Stuffing for 84
Skillet Tuna Curry 44
Snapper Luzianne 39
Stuffed Flounder 38
Stuffing for, Baked 45
Terrell's Perch 46
Thelma's Stuffed, Baked 41
Tips on Preparation, Cleaning and
  Cooking 34, 35
Trout Alexander 42
Trout Au Gratin 42
Trout Platter 43
Trout Veronique 43
Tuna Casserole 44
Flambé, Shrimp 82
Flaming Desserts, Bananas Foster on Ice
  Cream 369
Flaming Desserts, Crêpes Fitzgerald
  Filling 362
Flaming Desserts, Crêpes Suzette 363
Flan Cubano 351
Floating Island 352
Flossie's Bean Soup 11
Flounder, Fillet of Sole with Shrimp Sauce ... 46
Flounder, Fish à la Gerd 38
Flounder, Stuffed 38
Flounder, Tips on 34, 35
Flower Garden Cake 330
Fluffy Bourbon Sauce 376
Fondue, Cheese Cake 416
Fool Proof Pound Cake 335
Foreign Foods and Beverages (See also Italian and
  Mexican Foods)
  Avgolemono (Lemon Sauce) 184
  Baked Kibbie 181
  Bohemian Cabbage 240
  Bratwurst, Swartz Brats 204
  Cabbage Chop Suey 183
  Canadian French Potato Dressing 231
  Cantonese Ham 197
  Chez Oca's Escargots Bourguignonne 129
  Chicken and Noodles 225
  Chicken and Shrimp Curry 222
  Chilaly 149
  Choucroute à L'Alsacienne Sauerkraut
    and Knockwurst Delight 203
  Chutney, Sweet Tomato 307
  Coq Au Quiche 219
  Coq Au Vin 217
  Crème d'Artichauts 381
  Curried Chicken and Broccoli 223
  Curried Raisin Rice 33
  Easy Shrimp Curry 80
  Easy Vegetable Sukiyaki 266
  Flan, Cubano 351
  French Crêpes 362
  French Loaf (Oyster Stuffed) 58
  French Onion Soup 10
  French Peas 405
  German Potato Salad 278
  Greek Bread 391
  Green Beans Mornay 404

Guter Kuchen, A 331
Indonesian Rijstaffel 25
International Gourmet Cabbage Rolls 241
Jhadro 250
Keftethes (Stuffed Grape Leaves) 184
Kibbie 180
Kibbie (Raw) 180
Moussaka 182
Noodles Romanoff 406
Nutty Fruit Chicken Kiev with Glaze 234
Old Fashioned Jewish Penicillin
  (Chicken Soup) 13
Orange Walnut Chicken 220
Oriental Meat Balls 185
Oriental Spaghetti 183
Pavlova 364
Peach Kuchen 361
Pepper Beef 170
Petti Di Pollo Tonnato 213
Pineapple Beets 239
Polynesian Pork Roast 'n Rice 200
Pork Ribs with Sweet and Sour 202
Princess Chicken 219
Red Cabbage Heidi 241
Roast Duckling Chinese Style 230
Rôtis de Porc à la Boulangère 199
Sangrella 110
Sauerbraten 168
Scandinavian Pork Roast 199
Shanghai Salad 277
Shrimp de Jonghe 79
Shrimp Pomme de Terre 79
Steak au Poivre Vert 398
Stir-Fry Beef 399
Swartz Brats (Bratwurst) 204
Swedish Christmas Cabbage 242
Swedish Puff Coffee Cake 163
Sweet and Sour Spareribs 127
Sweet Tomato Chutney 307
Szechuan Shrimp 81
Tempura 70
Tempura Batter 70
Teriyaki Marinade 300
Tirotrigona 149
Turkish Barbecued Beef 124
Walnut Chicken Hawaiian 220
Frankfurters (See Weiners)
French Food (See also Foreign Foods)
French Crêpes 362
French Dressing, Old Fashioned 288
French Dressing, True 288
French-Italian Dressing 288
French Italian Spaghetti 174
French Loaf (Oyster Stuffed) 58
French Onion Soup 10
French Peas 405
Fresh Apple Bread 157
Fresh Apple Nut Pudding with Rum Sauce ...353
Fresh Asparagus Casserole 235
Fresh Coconut Layer Cake 326
Fresh Corn Soup 12
Fresh Fruit Bavarian 417
Fresh Horseradish 304
Fricasséed Goose 93
Fried Alligator 99
Fried Crawfish Tails 51
Fried Duck Delight 92
Fried Fish 36, 37
Fried Frog Legs 47
Fried Oysters, Louisiana Style 58

INDEX **433**

Fried Shrimp ... 70
Fried Soft Shell Crabs ... 63
Fried Stuffed Bell Pepper ... 53
Fried Venison Loin ... 103
Fritters, Banana, Bayou Lafourche ... 236
Fritters, Eggplant ... 248
Fritters, Oyster-Plant ... 254
Fritters, Shrimp, Sybil's ... 71
Frog Legs, Fried ... 47
Frog Legs Provençal ... 47
Frostings (*See* Icings)
Frozen Butter Pecan Delight ... 417
Frozen Desserts
   Almond Tart ... 370
   Angel Food Cake Ice Cream Pie ... 370
   Avocado Crème ... 370
   Baked Alaska ... 369
   Bananas Foster on Ice Cream ... 369
   Butter Pecan Delight ... 417
   Butterscotch Ring for Ice Cream ... 371
   Caramel Ice Cream ... 372
   Chocolate Ice Cream ... 372
   Christmas Ice Cream ... 373
   Coconut-Pecan Meringue Pie Shell
      for Ice Cream ... 371
   Dee's Dessert ... 371
   Fruit Cup Salad ... 286
   Homemade Ice Cream Custard ... 373
   Ice Cream Bombe ... 372
   Ice Cream Macaroon Dessert ... 374
   Mint Ice Cream Pie ... 375
   Peach Fantasy ... 361
   Pecan-Almond Tarts ... 368
   Peppermint Stick Ice Cream ... 373
   Red and White Freeze ... 287
   Refreshing Fruit Sherbet ... 371
   Sherbet Macaroon ... 374
   Tortoni ... 375
   Uncooked Homemade Vanilla Ice Cream ... 373
   Vanilla Ice Cream ... 374
   Watermelon Sherbet ... 375
Frozen Fruit Cup Salad ... 286
Frozen Fruit Ring ... 114
Fruit and Wine Salad ... 286
Fruit Balls ... 346
Fruit Cake Cookies ... 346
Fruit Cake, White ... 328
Fruit Cup Salad, Frozen ... 286
Fruit, Fresh Bavarian ... 417
Fruit, Hot Sherried ... 411
Fruit, Jello Salad ... 287
Fruit, Jeweled ... 411
Fruit Pie, Japanese ... 314
Fruit Pizza ... 418
Fruit Salad, Doubloon Delight ... 410
Fruit Salad Dressing ... 289
Fruit Sauce for Barbecue ... 299
Fruit Sherbet, Refreshing ... 371
Fruit Shortcake ... 368
Fudge Cake, Chewy ... 327
Fudge, Chocolate ... 341
Fudge, Chocolate, One Hundred Dollar ... 341
Fudge, Cindy's Peanut Butter ... 414
Fudge, Divinity ... 341
Fudge Muffins ... 415
Fudge Pie ... 313

Game (*See* Wildlife)

Garden Pilaf ... 27
Garden Vegetable Salad ... 272
Garlic Dressing ... 290
Gaspergou ... 45
"Gator" Meat Balls ... 99
Gazpacho, Quick ... 19
Gazpacho, Jellied ... 285
Georgia Fried Chicken with Cream Gravy ... 214
German Potato Salad ... 278
German Sweet Chocolate Pie ... 313
Giblet Gravy ... 294
Giblets, Dirty Rice ... 23
Giblets, Rice Dressing ... 22
Gin Fizz, Ramos ... 109
Gingerbread ... 330
Gingerbread, Apple Upside Down Cake ... 322
Giuliano's Crawfish Fettuccine ... 51
Glacé Molds ... 125
Glacée au Chocolat ... 356
Glaze, Chocolate ... 334
Glaze for Cranberry Cake ... 328
Glaze for Ham, Bourbon ... 301
Glaze for Nutty Fruit Chicken Kiev ... 234
Glaze, Lemon ... 334
Glazed Acorn Squash with Pecans ... 261
Goose, Apple-Apricot ... 92
Goose, Blue, Tips on ... 85
Goose-Duck-Sausage Gumbo ... 7
Goose, Fricasséed ... 93
Goose in Foil ... 93
Goose, Larded, L'Orange ... 93
Goose, Louisiana Gumbo ... 3
Goose or Duck, Orange Glazed ... 92
Goose or Duck, Sherry Spice ... 89
Goose or Duck, Stuffed, Pot Roasted ... 88
Goose or Duck, Wild, Baked ... 88
Goose, Snow, Tips on ... 85
Goose, Speckbellied, Tips on ... 85
Graham Cracker Cheese Cake ... 324
Graham Cracker Roll ... 414
Grandma Celeste's Stuffed Mirlitons ... 250
Grandmère's Maque Choux ... 247
Grandmother's Old Fashioned Bread
   Pudding ... 354
Grandmother's Rice Pudding ... 33
Grandpa's Karo Pecan Pie ... 317
Grape Leaves, Keftethes
   (Stuffed Grape Leaves) ... 184
Grapefruit Peel, Candied ... 342
Grapefruit Salad ... 285
Grasshopper Pie ... 315
Gravies (*See* Sauces)
Gray Duck (Gadwall), Tips on ... 85
Great Pumpkin Pie ... 318
Greek Bread ... 391
Green Bean Casserole ... 238
Green Bean Casserole with Cheese ... 238
Green Bean Vinaigrette ... 409
Green Bean, String Bean Salad ... 277
Green Beans Amandine ... 403
Green Beans, Mei Mei's Barbecued ... 404
Green Beans Mornay ... 404
Green Beans, Romano Casserole ... 266
Green Goodness Dip ... 386
Green Rice ... 32
Green Wave ... 105
Greens, Gumbo Z'Herbes ... 4
Greens, How to Cook ... 250
Grillades and Grits ... 209
Grits, Baked Cheese ... 148

INDEX

Grits, Grillades and 209
Grits, South of the Border 148
Gumbo
   Champeaux 8
   Filé, Sassafras 2
   Goose-Duck-Sausage 7
   Gouter 249
   Hen 9
   History and Derivation 3
   "Hot" Seafood and Okra for a Crowd 6
   Louisiana 3
   Mrs. Soulé's Seafood 4
   Seafood 3, 5
   Shrimp 3
   Squirrel or Dove 7
   Weeze's 5
   Z'Herbes 4
Guter Kuchen, A 331

Ham
   Baked 196
   Balls, Chafing Dish 126
   Black Beans and Rice 27
   Boiled Fresh 196
   Bourbon Glaze for 301
   Cantonese 197
   Chicken Vermouth 216
   Coq Au Quiche 219
   Curried in Popovers 198
   How I Cook a 196
   Mushrooms, and Cheese Omelet 145
   Roll-Ups 125
   Sauce 196, 301
   Skillet Supper 400
   Wellington with Wine Sauce 197
Hamburger (See also Beef, Ground)
Hamburger Casserole 189
Hamburger Mushroom Quiche 186
Hamburger Pie 186
Hard Sauce 358, 377
Harvest Salad 276
Harvest Sweet Potato Jello Pie 319
Hash, Hollywood 190
Hash, Texas 190
Hearty Corn Chowder 13
Heavenly Hash 342
Heavenly Strawberry Pie 319
He-Man Potatoes 405
Hen, Baked 230
Hen, Cornish Chasseur 231
Hen Gumbo 9
Henriettas 347
Hens, Cornish Stuffed with Wild Rice ...231
Herb Stix 156
Hershey Bar Pie 412
Hog's Head Cheese 118
Hollandaise, Broccoli Macaroni 240
Hollandaise Sauce, Blender 293
Hollywood Hash 190
Homemade Ice Cream Custard 373
Hors d'Oeuvres
   Artichoke Balls 119
   Artichoke-Spinach Appetizers 119
   Artichokes 235
   Avocado Dip 135
   Bacon-Wrapped Snacks 390
   Baked Stuffed Mushroom Caps 120

   Blackeyed Pea Dip 384
   Brisket 124
   Cajun Onion Rings 122
   Capantto 123
   Caviar Ball 121
   Caviar Mousse 118
   Chafing Dish Ham Balls 126
   Charlie's Picante Sauce 387
   Cheese Ball 141
   Cheese Biscuits 141
   Cheese Olive Spread 141
   Cheese Straws 388
   Chestnut Meatballs 383
   Chez Oca's Escargots Bourguignonne ..129
   Chicken and Shrimp Curry 222
   Chopped Liver 127
   Crab-Clam Dip 138
   Crab Dip 137
   Crab Meat, "Contraband" 45
   Crab Meat Mousse 65
   Crab Meat Open Sandwich 134
   Crab Mornay 128
   Crawfish Dip 136
   Creole Shrimp Tarts 133
   Curry Dip Royale 385
   Deviled Eggs 144
   Devils on Horseback 132
   Dill Dip 135
   Dino's Shrimp Paste 131
   Easy Hot Crab Meat Dip 137
   Easy Quiche 144
   Escargot Garlic 129
   Festive Florentine Dip 386
   Fried Alligator 99
   "Gator" Meat Balls 99
   Glacé Molds 125
   Green Goodness Dip 386
   Ham Roll-Ups 125
   Herb Stix 156
   Hog's Head Cheese 118
   Hot Chicken Salad 224
   Hot Crab Meat Canapé 128
   "Hot" Seafood and Okra Gumbo for a
     Crowd 6
   Jack's Shrimp Curry Spread 133
   Jalapeño Cheese Ball 142
   Jalapeño Cheese Spread 387
   Jezebel Sauce 302
   Kum Bak Dip 136
   Last Minute Crawfish 384
   Liver Pâté 126
   Lobster Rolls 129
   Lump Crab Dip 138
   Marinated Shrimp 131
   Marinated Vegetables 123
   Mexican Roll-ups 390
   Mock Quiche Lorraine 143
   Mousseline Dip 135
   Mushroom Canapés Fonte Ai Frati ..120
   New Potatoes with Sour Cream and
     Caviar 121
   Oyster Canapés 130
   Oyster Patties 132
   Oysters Mystique 130
   Perfect Onion Rings 122
   Pickled Okra 308
   Pickled Turnips 308
   Pimiento Cheese Spread 142
   Polynesian Sausage 383
   Pork Roast for a Party 199

INDEX

Quiche Lorraine 143
Rye Snacks 389
Schooner Squares 388
Seafood Dip à la Kingwood 140
Shrimp con Queso Dip 140
Shrimp Dip 139
Shrimp Italiano 383
Skillet Tuna Curry 44
Sombrero Dip 386
Spice Bites 389
Spinach Dip 139, 386
Spinach Quiche Boudreau 259
Strawberry Paddle Wheel 388
Sue's Mushrooms 120
Swedish Meat Balls 127
Sweet and Sour Spareribs 127
Sybil's Shrimp Fritters 71
Thistle Dip 385
Three Cheese Roll 142
Tirotrigona 149
Toasted Pecans 122
Tuna Dip 139
Tuna Party Sandwiches 134
Turkish Barbecued Beef 124
Walnut Cheese Ball 141
Horseradish, Fresh 304
Horseradish Sauce, Boiled Brisket
  with 173
Hot Chicken Salad 224
Hot Chili 192
Hot Crab Meat Canapé 128
Hot Crab Meat Soufflé 67
Hot Dog Butter Beans 239
Hot Pepper Jelly 304
Hot Pepper Sauce 303
Hot Pepper Sauce, Doc's 303
"Hot" Seafood Gumbo for a Crowd 6
Hot Seafood Pie 397
Hot Sherried Fruit 411
How I Cook a Ham 196
How to. . . . .
  Boil Crabs 64
  Boil Crawfish 50
  Boil Eggs Perfectly 145
  Boil Shrimp 69, 74
  Butter Pan Evenly 324
  Clarify Butter 209
  Clean Crabs 62, 63
  Clean Fish 34, 35
  Clean Soft Shell Crabs 63
  Clean Wildlife 85
  Cook a Ham 196
  Cook a Yam 8
  Cook Crabs 63
  Cook Ducks 85
  Cook Fish 34, 35
  Cook Geese 85
  Cook Greens 250
  Cook Rice 21
  Crack Nuts Whole 344
  Eat Crabs 62
  Fillet Fish 34
  Freeze Crabs 64
  Freeze Fish 36
  Freeze Shrimp 69
  Get More Juice from Lemons 360
  Keep Soup from "Souring" 11
  Make a Cake Lighter 323
  Make a Perfect Fruit Pie 314
  Make a Roux 1
  Make an Inexpensive Crab Meat
    Substitute 45
  Make Chocolate Curls 375
  Make Filé 2
  Make Pie Crust Brown Beautifully ... 315
  Make Shrimp Stock 74
  Open Oysters 55
  Peel Crabs 62
  Peel Crawfish 49
  Peel Shrimp 69
  Pluck Ducks 85
  Pot Roast Game 86
  Prepare a Louisiana Brunch 143
  Prepare Fish 34, 35
  Prepare Wildlife 85
  Preserve Louisiana Figs 305
  Prevent Icing from Becoming Sugary . 338
  Prevent Meringue from Being Grainy . 339
  Prevent Meringue from Weeping 311
  Remove Bitter Taste from Eggplant .. 249
  Remove Brown Edges from Cake 321
  Remove Cake from Pan 337
  Remove Coconut from Shell 326
  Remove Melted Chocolate Easily 367
  Remove the Wild Taste in Duck 89
  Roll Out Pie Dough 315
  Select Wine 115
  Serve Wine 115
  Skin a Deer 100
  Store Wine 115
  Toast Sesame Seed 243
  Whip Cream Faster 339
Howard's Pecan Pralines 343
Hush Puppies 151
Hush Puppies, Dotty's 151

Ice-Box Cake 330
Ice Box Rolls 159, 160
Ice Box Slaw 274
Ice Cream (*See also* Frozen Desserts)
  Angel Food Cake Pie 370
  Baked Alaska 369
  Bananas Foster on 369
  Bombe 372
  Butterscotch Ring for 371
  Caramel 372
  Chocolate 372
  Christmas 373
  Coconut-Pecan Meringue Pie Shell for 371
  Coffee Punch 12
  Frozen Butter Pecan Delight 417
  Homemade Custard 373
  Macaroon Dessert 374
  Mint Pie 375
  Nectar Soda 112
  Peppermint Stick 373
  Refreshing Fruit Sherbet 371
  Sherbet Macaroon 374
  Uncooked Homemade Vanilla 373
  Vanilla 374
  Watermelon Sherbet 375
Iced Shrimp Mold 283
Icings (*See also* Glaze)
  Caramel 339
  Caramel for Date Cake 329
  Chocolate Nut Frosting 339

INDEX

Cream Cheese for Carrot Cake 324
Cream Cheese for Italian Cream Cake 331
Creamy Chocolate Frosting 363
Italian Cream Cake and 331
Mocha 338
My Favorite Chocolate Frosting 339
One Minute 338
Praline 335
Quick Broiled 339
Red Velvet Cake 337
Seven Minute 338
Sour Cream for Pecan Torte 333
White 338
Indonesian Rijsttafel (Rice Feast or Rice Table) 25
International Gourmet Cabbage Rolls 241
Irish Coffee 111
Iron Pot Duck 89
Italian Cream Cake and Icing 331
Italian Foods
  Bisque Tortoni 364
  Blini 106
  Brucculuni with Spaghetti 208
  Caesar Salad 272
  Capantto 123
  Carbonara 258
  Chicken à Seville 221
  Chicken Breast with Tuna Sauce (Petti Di Pollo Tonnato) 213
  Chicken Italien 217
  Chicken, Meat, and Sausage Spaghetti 218
  Chicken Spaghetti 216
  Cintra's Eggplant Manicotti 247
  David's Sesame Salad 407
  Easy Lasagne 177
  Eggs à la Debi 146
  Fettuccine Alfredo 258
  French-Italian Dressing 288
  French Italian Spaghetti 174
  Guiliano's Crawfish Fettuccine 51
  Italian Cream Cake and Icing 331
  Italian Lamb Chops 206
  Italian Liver 178
  Italian Mushroom Salad 272
  Italian Pork Chops 400
  Italian Spaghetti Sauce 175
  Johnny Marzetti Cheddar Cheese Casserole 189
  Leone's Pork and Pasta 401
  Manicotti à la Romona 178
  Marinated Vegetables 123
  Mousseline Dip 135
  Mousseline Sauce 293
  Mushrooms Canapés Fonte Ai Frati 120
  Nana's Lasagne 177
  Osso Bucco 207
  Oyster Spaghetti 60
  Pastitsio 175
  Picadilly 182
  Picture Perfect Pasta 409
  Risotto con Melanzane 26
  Romano Casserole 266
  Scallops of Veal in Wine 209
  Shrimp Italiano 383
  Shrimp Mosca 73
  Sicilian "Pot-of-Roast" 167
  Spaghetti à la Giuliano and Joel III (Carbonara) 258
  Spaghetti Pie 399
  Spaghetti Sauce with Meat Balls 176

Steak Zucchini 170
Stuffed Pork Chops Fine Bouche 201
Talarini 190
Tortoni 375
Turkey Tetrazzini 229
Veal Cutlets Parmesan 210
Veal Parmigiana 210
Italian Lamb Chops 206
Italian Liver 178
Italian Mushroom Salad 272
Italian Pork Chops 400
Italian Spaghetti Sauce 175

Jack's Shrimp Curry Spread 133
Jack's Stuffed Mirlitons 251
Jalapeño Cheese Ball 142
Jalapeño Cheese Spread 387
Jalapeño Corn Bread 152
Jalapeño Peppers, Jalapeño Cheese Spread 387
Jalapeño Peppers, Schooner Squares 388
Jalapeño, Rice Surprise 32
Jalapeño Sauce, Cauliflower with 244
Jam Cake 332
Jambalaya, Creole 23
Jambalaya, Rice Cooker 401
Japanese Fruit Pie 314
Jean Lafitte, Legend of vii
Jean Lafitte, Oysters 395
Jean Lafitte, Recipe of 164
Jellied Gazpacho 285
Jello Fruit Salad 287
Jello, Harvest Sweet Potato Pie 319
Jello, Lemon Ice Box Dessert 359
Jello, Virginia's Blueberry Salad 287
Jelly Glazed Venison Roast 102
Jelly, Hot Pepper 304
Jelly, Mayhaw 305
Jelly Roll, Black Walnut 320
Jeweled Fruit 411
Jezebel Sauce 302
Jhadro 250
Jim's Barbecued Duck 90
Johnny Marzetti Cheddar Cheese Casserole 189

Karo Pecan Pie, Grandpa's 317
Keftethes, (Stuffed Grape Leaves) 184
Kentucky Pecan Pie 317
Key Lime Pie 315
Kibbie 180
Kibbie, Baked 181
Kibbie, Minced Dressing for 180
Kibbie (Raw) 180
King Mackerel Balls 34, 36
King Mackerel, Tips on 35, 36
Knockwurst, Choucroute à L'Alsacienne Sauerkraut and Delight 203
Kuchen, A Guter 331
Kuchen, Peach 361
Kum Bak Dip 136
Kumquat Sauce, Cora's Cranberry and 302

INDEX

Lace Cookies 347
Lamb Chops, Italian 206
Lamb, Kibbie (Raw) 180
Lamb, Mint Sauce 301
Lamb, Mutton Marinade 207
Lamb, Roast Leg of 205
Lamb, Stuffed Leg of 206
Larded Goose L'Orange 93
Lasagne, Crab 395
Lasagne, Easy 177
Lasagne, Nana's 177
Last Minute Crawfish 384
Layer Cake (See Cakes)
Legend of Jean Lafitte vii
Lemon Brandy Veal 398
Lemon Cake 331
Lemon Cheese Squares 415
Lemon Cups 359
Lemon-Garlic Broiled Shrimp 72
Lemon Glaze for Chocolate or
  Yellow Pound Cake 334
Lemon Ice Box Dessert 359
Lemon, Parsley Sauce 293
Lemon Meringue Pie, Double 314
Lemon Pudding Cake 359
Lemon Sauce 377
Lemon Sauce (Augolemono) 184
Lemon Soufflé with Raspberry Sauce, Cold .. 360
Lemon Whippersnaps 415
Lentils, Jhadro 350
Leone's Pork and Pasta 401
Lettuce, Wilted 273
Lillian's Baked New Potatoes 256
Lima Dill Salad 276
Lime, Chicken in the Limelight 226
Lime Pie, Key 315
Ling, Barbecued 40
Ling, Tips on 35
Liquors (See Beverages)
Little Pecan Tarts 316
Liver, Chopped (Chicken) 127
Liver, Italian 178
Liver Omelet, Chicken 145
Liver Pâté 126
Livers, Chicken with Mushrooms 228
Lobster Rolls 129
Lobster Tails 47
Lock's Oyster Rockefeller Sauce 57
Lock's Trout Amandine 42
Louisiana Creole Okra with Meat Balls .. 185
Louisiana Gumbo 3
Louisiana Sunday Brunch 143
Lump Crab Dip 138

Macaroni (See also Pasta and Spaghetti)
Macaroni and Cheese 257
Macaroni and Cheese Salad 279
Macaroni, Beef-Bacon Casserole 189
Macaroni, Broccoli Hollandaise 240
Macaroni-Cheese Tomato Tang 147
Macaroon, Ice Cream Dessert 374
Macaroon, Sherbet 374
Mackerel Balls, King 34, 36
Majestic Hotel Black Bottom Pie 309
Mallards, Tips on 85
Mama's Cookies 347
Mama's Sugared Pecans 344

Mammy's Flapjacks 393
Manicotti à la Romona 178
Manicotti, Cintra's Eggplant 247
Marchand de Vin Sauce, Sam's 295
Marinade for Pork Tenderloin 201
Marinade for Pork Tenders 200
Marinade for Vegetarian Shish Kabob ... 270
Marinade, Mutton 207
Marinade, Sauerbraten 168
Marinade, Teriyaki 300
Marinades (See Sauces)
Marinated Mushroom Salad 271
Marinated Shrimp 131
Marinated Vegetables 123
Marsh Melon Soup 382
Marshmallow, Pineapple Delight Dessert ... 360
Mashed Potatoes, Fish à la Gerd 38
Mayhaw Jelly 305
Mayonnaise 292
Meats (See kinds, i.e., Beef, Casseroles, Ham,
  Lamb, Pork, Spareribs, and Veal)
Meat Balls 176, 186
Meat Balls, Chestnut 383
Meat Balls, "Gator" 99
Meat Balls, Louisiana Creole Okra 185
Meat Balls, Oriental 185
Meat Balls, Swedish 127, 184
Meat Loaf 179
Meat Pie 187
Meat Pot Pie 188
Mei Mei's Barbecued Green Beans 404
Meringue 311, 312, 314, 364, 369
Meringue, Coconut-Pecan 371
Metric System 378
Meunière Sauce 297
Mexican Black Bean Soup 11
Mexican Casserole 192
Mexican Foods
  Beef Burritos 194
  Beef Tacos 193
  Black Beans and Rice 27
  Cauliflower with Jalapeño Sauce 244
  Charlie's Picante Sauce 387
  Chicken Enchilada Casserole 221
  Chili 191
  Chili Chicken Casserole 222
  Chili, Hot 192
  Chili, Quick 192
  Chili, Venison 102
  Chilies Rellenos 195
  Chilies Stuffed with Beans 245
  Hot Chili 192
  Jalapeño Cheese Ball 142
  Jalapeño Cheese Spread 387
  Jalapeño Corn Bread 152
  Jalapeño, Rice Surprise 32
  Jalapeño Sauce, for Cauliflower 244
  Jalapeño, Schooner Squares 388
  Mexican Black Bean Soup 11
  Mexican Casserole 192
  Mexican Roll-ups 390
  Picadillo 182
  Quick Gazpacho Soup 19
  Sauce for Chilies Rellenos 195
  Shrimp con Queso Dip 140
  Sombrero Dip 386
  South of the Border 148
  South of the Border Hot Dish 193
  Spanish Delight 194
  Spanish Meat Rice 26

INDEX

Spanish Rice 27
Spanish Wild Duck 91
Tamale and Chili Pie 195
Texas Beans 239
Three Peso Salad 408
Venison Chili 102
Mexican Roll-ups 390
Microwave Brownies 416
Milk Punch 108
Minced Beef Dressing for Kibbie 180
Mint Ice Cream Pie 375
Mint Julep, New Orleans 108
Mint Sauce 301
Mirlitons, Stuffed 251
Mirlitons, Stuffed, Grandma Celeste's ...250
Mirlitons, Stuffed, Jack's 251
Miss Annabel's Orange Pecans 340
"Miss Top's" Rum Cocktail 109
Mr. Snowman 367
Mocha Icing 338
Mock Quiche Lorraine 143
Molded Beet Salad 275
Molded Shrimp Salad 282
Molds
  Beet Salad 275
  Broccoli Mousse 283
  Chicken Broccoli 280
  Crab Meat Mousse 65
  Frozen Fruit Cup Salad 286
  Fruit Wine Salad 286
  Glacé 125
  Ice Cream Bombe 372
  Iced Shrimp 283
  Jello Fruit Salad 287
  Orange Charlotte 286
  Peach Fantasy 361
  Red and White Freeze 287
  Shrimp Aspic 283
  Shrimp Salad 282
  Snow on the Mountain 367
  Strawberry-Orange 287
  Tomato Aspic 284
  Tuna Mousse 284
  Virginia's Blueberry Jello Salad 287
Morgans Point Crab Chowder 17
Mother's Cinnamon Pecans 340
Mother's Dumplings 162
Mother's Favorites 348
Mother's Tea Cakes 348
Moussaka 182
Mousse, Bachelor's 355
Mousse, Broccoli 282
Mousse, Caviar 118
Mousse, Chocolate 355
Mousse, Crab Meat 65
Mousse, Tuna 284
Mousseline Dip 135
Mousseline Sauce 293
Mr. Snowman 367
Mrs. Soulé's Seafood Gumbo 4
Muffins, Chipped Beef on 212
Muffins, Fudge 415
Muffins, Raisin Bran 392
Mushroom Canapés Fonte Ai Frati 120
Mushroom Caps Baked in Cheddar
  Cheese Sauce 252
Mushroom Caps, Baked Stuffed 120
Mushroom, Ham, and Cheese Omelet 145
Mushroom, Hamburger Quiche 186
Mushroom, Italian Salad 272

Mushroom, Marinated Salad 271
Mushroom Soup, Cold Curried 19
Mushrooms, Brown Sauce 294
Mushrooms, Chicken and 227
Mushrooms, Chicken Livers with 228
Mushrooms, Cold Curried Soup 19
Mushrooms, Easy Vegetable Sukiyaki 266
Mushrooms, Potato Pie 257
Mushrooms, Snow Peas and 255
Mushrooms, Spinach Casserole 258
Mushrooms, Sue's 120
Mushrooms, Viennese Fried 252
Mustard 304
Mustard Chicken 226
Mustard Greens, Gumbo Z'Herbes 4
Mustard Sauce 126, 301
Mutton Marinade 207
My Favorite Chocolate Cake 327
My Favorite Chocolate Frosting 339
My Vichyssoise 20

Nana's Lasagne 177
Nanny Jeanne's Coush-Coush 153
Natchitoches Meat Pie 187
Navy Beans, Bean Soup 12
Nectar Ice Cream Soda 112
Nectar Syrup 112
Never-Fail Pastry 310
New Orleans Mint Julep 108
New Potatoes with Sour Cream and Caviar .121
No Crust Coconut Pie 413
Noodles (See also Pasta and Spaghetti)
Noodles, Chicken and 225
Noodles, Ham Skillet Supper 400
Noodles Romanoff 406
Nuts (See kinds, i.e., Black Walnuts, Peanuts,
  Pecans, and Walnuts)
Nutty Fruit Chicken Kiev with Glaze 234

Oatmeal Cake 332
Oatmeal Cookies 348
Oatmeal Cookies, Mother's Favorites 348
Oatmeal, Cranberry Crunch 366
Oatmeal Raised Bread 154
Octavia's Fried Chicken 214
Okra Etouffée 253
Okra Gumbo for a Crowd, "Hot"
  Seafood and 6
Okra, Gumbo Gouter 249
Okra, Pickled 308
Okra with Meat Balls, Louisiana Creole .185
Old-Fashioned 108
Old Fashioned French Dressing 288
Old Fashioned Jewish Penicillin
  (Chicken Soup) 13
Old Fashioned Potato Salad 278
"Old Virginia Wassail" 113
Olive-Pork Chop Casserole, Spanish 202
Olive Sauce for Wild Duck 90
Omelet, Basic Recipe 145
Omelet, Chicken Liver 145
Omelet, Creole Sauce 145
Omelet, Ham, Mushroom, and Cheese 145
Omelets, Sunday Night 145

INDEX

One Hundred Dollar Chocolate Fudge 341
One Minute Icing 338
Onion Corn Bread 153
Onion Pie 253
Onion Rings, Cajun 122
Onion Rings, Perfect 122
Onion Sandwiches, Bacon, Cheese 212
Onion Soup, French 10
Onion Soup Gratinée 10
Onions Au Gratin 253
Onions, Sherried 252
Opelousas Baked Chicken 224
Orange Charlotte 286
Orange Glazed Duck or Goose 92
Orange, Larded Goose L'Orange 93
Orange Odyssey 109
Orange Raisin Sauce 302
Orange Rolls 158
Orange Sauce, with Carrots 243
Orange Soufflé, Cold 365
Orange-Spinach Salad with Honey-Mustard
  Dressing 407
Orange, Strawberry Mold 287
Orange Walnut Chicken 220
Oriental Meat Balls 185
Oriental Spaghetti 183
Osso Bucco 207
Oven Fried Fish Fillets 37
Oyster and Rice Casserole 31
Oyster Canapés 130
Oyster Patties 132
Oyster-Plant Fritters 254
Oyster Soup 17
Oyster Spaghetti 60
Oysters
  and Rice Casserole 31
  Bienville 56
  Bienville Casserole 56
  Canapés 130
  Craig-Poddy 61
  Creole Fried 58
  Deviled 59
  Devils on Horseback 132
  en Brochette 59
  French Loaf (Stuffed) 58
  Fried, Louisiana Style 58
  Jean Lafitte 395
  Lock's Rockefeller Sauce 57
  Mystique 130
  Patties 132
  Opening of 55
  Rockefeller 57
  Scalloped 59
  Soup 17
  Spaghetti 60
  Wild Rice and Casserole 60

Pancakes 162
Pancakes, Buttermilk 162
Pancakes, Potato 257
Papa Jim's Bean Salad 276
Parfait (Bisque Tortoni) 364
Parsley-Lemon Sauce 293
Party Cheese Cake 325
Party Salad Parmesan 408
Party Sandwiches, Tuna 134
Pasta (See also Macaroni and Spaghetti)

Beef Stroganoff 172
Chicken and Noodles 225
Easy Lasagne 177
Fettuccine Alfredo 258
Giuliano's Crawfish Fettuccine 51
Ham Skillet Supper 400
Hamburger Casserole 189
Homemade Noodles 225
Hollywood Hash 190
Leone's Pork and 401
Manicotti à la Romona 178
Nana's Lasagne 177
Noodles Romanoff 406
Pastitsio 175
Salad, Picture Perfect 409
Spaghetti Pie 399
Spanish Delight 194
Tallarini 190
Pastitsio 175
Pastry (See also Pies)
  Almond Tart 370
  Biscuit Crust for Ham Wellington ...197
  Breast of Duck and Duck Wellington . 87
  Coconut-Pecan Meringue Pie Shell
    for Ice Cream 371
  Cream Puffs 363
  Crust for Black Bottom Pie 309
  Crust for Chocolate Yummy 357
  Crust for Country Pie 188
  Danish 368
  Graham Cracker Crust 324, 325
  Guter Kuchen, A 331
  Natchitoches Meat Pie 187
  Never-Fail 310
  Oatmeal Crust for Caramel Ice Cream .372
  Pastry for Little Pecan Tarts 316
  Peach Kuchen 361
  Pecan-Almond Tarts 368
  Pie Dough 188
  Popovers 198
  Shortcake (Fruit) 368
  Sweet Dough 326
  Tart Shells for Creole Shrimp 133
Pâté, Liver 126
Pavlova 364
Peach Crisp 361
Peach Fantasy 361
Peach Kuchen 361
Peaches, Perfect Peach Pie 413
Peaches, Quick Peach Cobbler 418
Peanut Brittle 343
Peanut Butter Balls 344
Peanut Butter, Cindy's Fudge 414
Peas, Blackeyed, Dip 384
Peas, Crowder 254
Peas, English, Hashed in Cream 254
Peas, French 405
Peas, Harvest Salad 276
Peas, Snow, and Mushrooms 255
Peas, Snow, Stir-Fry Beef 399
Peas, Split, Soup 14
Pecan-Almond Tarts 368
Pecans
  Almond Tarts 370
  Baked 340
  Butter Pecan Coffee Cake 413
  Candied Date Loaf 342
  Caramel Nut Pound Cake 323
  Chocolate Nut Frosting 339
  Corn Bread Sausage Dressing 232

INDEX

Divinity Fudge 341
Fresh Apple Nut Pudding with
  Rum Sauce 353
Frozen Butter Pecan Delight 417
Glazed Acorn Squash with 261
Guter Kuchen, A 331
Heavenly Hash 342
Italian Cream Cake 331
Mama's Sugared 344
Miss Annabel's Orange 340
Mother's Cinnamon 340
Mother's Favorites 348
Pie 317
Pie, Chocolate 316
Pie, Fudge 313
Pie, German Sweet Chocolate 313
Pie, Grandpa's Karo 317
Pie, Japanese Fruit 314
Pie, Kentucky 317
Pie, Surprise 316
Pie Shell, Coconut-Pecan Meringue
  for Ice Cream 371
Praline Cake 335
Pralines, Buttermilk 343
Pralines, Howard's 343
Puffs 344
Quick Broiled Icing 339
Surprise Pie 316
Tarts, Little 316
Toasted 122
Torte 333
Pelican Hook Soup 14
Pepper Beef 170
Peppers (See Bell Pepper and Hot Peppers)
Peppermint Stick Ice Cream 373
Perch, Terrell's 46
Perch, Tips on 34
Perch, White, Tips on 34
Perfect Onion Rings 122
Perfect Peach Pie 413
Pheasant Casserole 95
Pheasant in Brandy Sauce, Chez Oca's 96
Pheasant, Hot Roasted Game 86
Pheasant, Sauce for 300
Picadillo 182
Pickled Eggs, Colorful 148
Pickled Okra 308
Pickled Tongue 211
Pickled Turnips 308
Pickles, Refrigerator Dill 308
Picture-Perfect Pasta 409
Pie Dough 188
Pie Shells (See Pastry)
Pies (See also Quiche)
  Angel Food Cake Ice Cream 370
  Auntie's Old Tyme Chocolate ..312
  Banana Blueberry 412
  Butter 311
  Buttermilk 311
  Chocolate Pecan 316
  Chocolate Swirl 312
  Coq Au Quiche 219
  Country 188
  Crawfish 51, 52
  Double Lemon Meringue 314
  Dove 97
  Dreamy Pumpkin 318
  Fudge 313
  German Sweet Chocolate 313
  Grandpa's Karo Pecan 317

Grasshopper 315
Great Pumpkin 318
Hamburger 186
Harvest Sweet Potato Jello 319
Heavenly Strawberry 319
Hershey Bar 412
Hot Seafood 397
Japanese Fruit 314
Kentucky Pecan 317
Key Lime 315
Little Pecan Tarts 316
Majestic Hotel Black Bottom 309
Meat 187
Meat Pot 188
Mint Ice Cream 375
Natchitoches Meat 187
No Crust Coconut 413
Onion 253
Pecan 317
Pecan Surprise 316
Perfect Peach 413
Potato 257
Spaghetti 399
Tamale and Chili 195
Yogurt 150
Pimiento Cheese Spread 142
Pineapple Beets 239
Pineapple Delight Dessert 360
Pineapple Rice 33
Pineapple Upside-Down Cake 333
Pink Squirrel 109
Pintail Duck, Tips on 85
Pizza, Fruit 418
Plucking Bread 160
Plum-Tapioca Cake 334
Polynesian Pork Roast 'n Rice ...200
Polynesian Sausage 383
Pompano, Tips on 34, 35
Poor Man's Pudding 358
Popcorn, Mr. Snowman 367
Popovers 198
Poppy Seed Dressing 290
Poppy Seed, Sweet Bread 391
Popsicles, Yogurt 150
Pork (See also Ham)
  Butt, Swartz Brats (Bratwurst) ...204
  Chop Casserole, Spanish Olive ..202
  Chops, Baked 201
  Chops, Desperation Meal 400
  Chops in Red Wine 202
  Chops, Italian 400
  Chops, Leone's Pork and Pasta ..401
  Country-Style Back Ribs and Sauerkraut ..203
  Hog's Head Cheese 118
  Polynesian Roast 'n Rice 200
  Rib and Turnip Stew, Country ..202
  Ribs Sweet and Sour 202
  Roast, Crown 198
  Roast for a Party 199
  Rôtis de Porc à la Boulangère ..199
  Sausage Strada 204
  Scandinavian Roast 199
  Stuffed Chops Fine Bouche 201
  Swartz Brats (Bratwurst) 204
  Sweet and Sour Spareribs 127
  Tasso Sauce Piquante 205
  Tenderloin, Marinde for 201
  Tenders 200
Pork, Ground
  "Bounty" Boudin 22

INDEX

Chafing Dish Ham Balls 126
Meat Balls 186
Nana's Lasagne 177
Oriental Spaghetti 183
Rice Dressing 22
Pot Likker 250
Pot Roasted Game 86
Pot Roasted Stuffed Duck or Goose 88
Potato Chip Cookies 349
Potato Dressing, Canadian French 231
Potato Pancakes 257
Potato Pie 257
Potato Salad 279
Potato Salad, Easy 278
Potato Salad, German 278
Potato Salad, Old Fashioned 278
Potatoes
  Dressing, Canadian French 231
  He-Man 405
  Lillian's Baked New 256
  Mashed with Fish à la Gerd 38
  New with Sour Cream and Caviar 121
  Pancakes 257
  Pie 257
  Rôtis de Porc à la Boulangère 199
  Salad 279
  Salad, Easy 278
  Salad, German 278
  Salad, Old Fashioned 278
  Shrimp Pomme de Terre 79
  Stuffed 255
  Stuffed Baked 256
  Texas 256
  Turnips and 266
  Vichyssoise, Carrot 382
  Vichyssoise, My 20
Pôts de Crème, Blender Chocolate 355
Poultry (See kinds, i.e., Chicken, Cornish Hen, Duck, Quail, and Turkey)
Pound Cake 334
Pound Cake, Angel Coconut 321
Pound Cake, Caramel Nut 323
Pound Cake, Fool Proof 335
Pound Cake, Pumpkin 336
Pound Cake, Sour Cream 335
Pound, Chocolate or Yellow Cake 334
Praline Cake 335
Pralines, Buttermilk 343
Pralines, Howard's Pecan 343
Preserves, Blackberry 306
Preserves, Fig 305
Preserves, Fig for Dieters 305
Preserves, Fig Jello 305
Preserves, Strawberry 306
Pretzels, Chocolate 349
Princess Chicken 219
Prune Cake 336
Prune Whip 366
Pudding (See Custards and Puddings)
Pudding Cake 358
Pudding Cake, Lemon 359
Pumpkin Bread 157
Pumpkin Pie, Dreamy 318
Pumpkin Pie, Great 318
Pumpkin Pie, Harvest Sweet Potato Jello 319
Pumpkin Pound Cake 336
Punch à la Champagne 113
Punch, Clifford's Rum 113
Punch, Coffee 112
Punch, Frozen Fruit Ring 114

Punch, Milk 108
Punch, "Old Virginia Wassail" 113
Punch, Slush 113
Punch, Virginia's Spiked Fruit 114
Punch, Wedding 114
"Puttin' on the Ritz" 403

Quail, Bacon Baked 95
Quail, Dove Pie 97
Quail, Doves in Wine 97
Quail in Cream Sauce 94
Quail, Pot Roasted Game 86
Quail-Rice Magnifique 95
Quiche, Coq Au 219
Quiche, Crab Meat 66
Quiche, Easy 144
Quiche, Hamburger Mushroom 186
Quiche Lorraine 143
Quiche Lorraine, Mock 143
Quiche, San Francisco Seafood 80
Quiche, Spinach Boudreau 259
Quick and Easy Recipes (See Fast and Fabulous)
Quick and Easy Spinach 260
Quick Broiled Icing 339
Quick Chili 192
Quick Gazpacho Soup 19
Quick Peach Cobbler 418

Rabbit, Pot Roasted Game 86
Rabbit Sauce Piquante 98
Radio Beer Bread 391
Raisin Bran Muffins 392
Raisin, Japanese Fruit Pie 314
Raisin, Orange Sauce 302
Raisin Rice, Curried 33
Ramos Gin Fizz 109
Raspberry Sauce au Kirsch 360
Red and White Freeze 287
Red Beans and Rice 24
Red Cabbage Heidi 241
Red Fish, Barbecued 40, 41
Red Fish, "Contraband Crab Meat" 45
Red Fish or Red Snapper, Thelma's
  Stuffed Baked 41
Red Fish or Red Snapper, Tips on 35
Red Gill's Barbecued Chicken 223
Red Relish 307
Red Snapper, Barbecued 41
Red Snapper, Cold Stuffed 39
Red Snapper, Excelsior 40
Red Snapper, Fish à la Gerd 38
Red Snapper, Luzianne 39
Red Snapper or Red Fish, Thelma's
  Stuffed Baked 41
Red Snapper, Tips on 35
Red Velvet Cake 337
Refreshing Fruit Sherbet 371
Refrigerator Dill Pickles 308
Refrigerator Rolls 158
Relish, Carrot 307
Relish, Chow Chow 292
Relish, Red 307
Relish, Sweet Tomato Chutney 307
Remoulade Sauce 297
Remoulade Sauce, White 297

INDEX

Rib, Country Pork and Turnip Stew 202
Rib Roast of Beef 166
Ribs, Country-Style Back and Sauerkraut 203
Ribs, Pork, Sweet and Sour 202
Rice (*See also* Wild Rice)
   and Artichokes 30
   Baked 21
   Baked Chicken and Casserole 226
   Baked Egg and 28
   Beer 30
   Black Beans and 27
   Boiled 21
   "Bounty" Boudin 22
   Broccoli Casserole 405
   Calcasieu Chicken Casserole 402
   Casserole 29
   Casserole or Ring 28
   Casserole, Oyster and 31
   Cooker Jambalaya 401
   Cooking of, Methods 21
   Country Pie 188
   Creole Jambalaya 23
   Curried Raisin 33
   Desperation Meal 400
   Dirty 23
   Dressing 22
   Eggplant Sapphire 29
   Garden Pilaf 27
   Green 32
   Harvest Salad 276
   Indonesian Rijsttafel 25
   O'Brian Casserole 28
   Oyster and Rice Casserole 31
   Pineapple 33
   Polynesian Pork Roast 'n 200
   Pudding, Grandmother's 33
   Quail Magnifique 95
   Red Beans and 24
   Risotto Con Melanzane 26
   Salad, Stuffed Tomato and Curried
      Chicken 281
   Shrimp Casserole 31
   Shrimp Opelousas 396
   Spanish 27
   Spanish Meat 26
   Spanish Olive-Pork Chop Casserole 202
   Spinach 29
   Steamed 21
   Stuffed Pepper Casserole 255
   Surprise 32
   Tips for Cooking 21
   Weenie Jam 203
   Wild, and Oyster Casserole 60
   Wild, Casserole 24
   Wild, Chicken Salad 281
   Wild, Cornish Hens Stuffed with 231
Ring Neck, Goose, Tips on 85
Risotto Con Melanzane 26
Roast Beef
   Boeuf à la Blanche 167
   Cabbage Chop Suey 183
   Filet de Bouef with Béarnaise Sauce 165
   Rib Roast of Beef 166
   Roast Beef 165
   Sauce 165
   Sauce for Basting 294
   Sauerbraten 168
   Sicilian "Pot-of-Roast" 167
   Veal Roast 207
Roast Chicken 224

Roast Duckling Chinese Style 230
Roast Leg of Lamb 205
Roast Pork
   Crown 198
   Polynesian 'n Rice 200
   Pork Roast for a Party 199
   Rôtis de Porc à la Boulangère 199
   Scandinavian 199
Roast, Veal 207
Roast, Venison, Charcoaled 101
Roast, Venison, Jelly Glazed 102
Rolls, Bran 159
Rolls, Cinnamon 158
Rolls, Ice Box 159, 160
Rolls, Orange 158
Rolls, Refrigerator 158
Romano Casserole 266
Roquefort Cheese Dressing 291
Rôtis de Porc à la Boulangère 199
Rotisserie Come Back Dressing 291
Roux 1, 54
Rum Drinks (*See* Beverages)
Rum Sauce, ... 353, 377
Rum Sauce for Fresh Apple Nut Pudding . . . 353
Rye Snacks 389

Salad Dressings (*See also* Sauces)
   Avocado 289
   Bleu Cheese Oil Vinegar 289
   Cheese for Grapefruit 285
   for Shanghai Salad 277
   French-Italian 288
   Fruit 289
   Garlic 290
   Italian, for Mushroom Salad 272
   Mayonnaise 292
   Old Fashioned French 288
   Poppy Seed 290
   Roquefort Cheese 291
   Rotisserie Come Back 291
   Salad Oil 292
   Sweet and Sour 271, 273
   Thousand Island 290
   True French 288
Salad Oil 292
Salads
   Avocado Cottage Cheese Delight 275
   Broccoli Mousse 283
   Caesar 272
   Chicken Broccoli Mold 280
   Chicken 280
   Chicken, Hot 224
   Chicken Wild Rice 281
   Cole Slaw 274
   Crab Cashew 410
   Crab Meat 281
   Curried Chicken and Rice Stuffed
      Tomato 281
   David's Sesame 407
   Different Carrot 275
   Doubloon Delight Fruit 410
   Easy Potato 278
   Frozen Fruit Cup 286
   Fruit and Wine 286
   Garden Vegetable 272
   German Potato 278
   Grapefruit 285

INDEX

Green Bean Vinaigrette 409
Harvest 276
Hot Chicken 224
Hot Sherried Fruit 411
Ice Box Slaw 274
Iced Shrimp Mold 283
Italian Mushroom 272
Jellied Gazpacho 285
Jello Fruit 287
Jeweled Fruit 411
Lima Dill 276
Macaroni and Cheese 279
Marinated Mushroom 271
Molded Beet 275
Molded Shrimp 282
Old Fashioned Potato 278
Orange Charlotte 286
Orange-Spinach, with Honey-Mustard
  Dressing 407
Papa Jim's Bean 276
Party, Parmesan 408
Picture-Perfect Pasta 409
Potato 279
Red and White Freeze 287
Rice and Artichokes 30
Shanghai 277
Shrimp Aspic 283
Shrimp Mélange 282
Spinach 271, 273
Strawberry-Orange Mold 287
String Bean 277
Three Peso Salad 408
Tomato Aspic 284
Tuna Mousse 284
Virginia's Blueberry Jello 287
Wilted Lettuce 273
Salmon, Alaskan Fisherman Stew 44
Salsify, Oyster-Plant Fritters 254
Sam's Marchand de Vin Sauce 295
San Francisco Seafood Quiche 80
Sandwich, Bacon, Cheese, and Onion .212
Sandwich, Cheese Puff 147
Sandwich, Crab Meat Open 134
Sandwich, Crawfish in a Bundle 394
Sandwich, French Loaf (Oyster Stuffed) 58
Sandwich, Tuna Party 134
Sangrella 110
Sardines, Italian Mushroom Salad ...272
Sassafras 2
Sauce Piquante, Rabbit 98
Sauce Piquante, Shrimp 77
Sauce Piquante, Tasso 205
Sauces
  Aloha 376
  Anchovy Butter 296
  Au Gratin 144
  Au Gratin for Buccaneer Broccoli .267
  Avgolemono (Lemon for Keftethes) .184
  Baked Cranberry 302
  Barbecue 201, 298, 299
  Basting for Barbecuing 299
  Basting for Oysters en Brochette . 59
  Basting for Roasts 294
  Béarnaise 293
  Blender Hollandaise 293
  Bordelaise Johnson 295
  Bourbon Glaze for Ham 301
  Brandy, Chez Oca's Pheasant in ... 96
  Brown 294
  Buccaneer Broccoli 267
  Caramel 376
  Cheese, Cheddar for Mushroom Caps .252
  Chocolate 374, 376
  Chow Chow 292
  Clarified Butter 209
  Cocktail for Seafood 296
  Cora's Cranberry and Kumquat 302
  Cranberry Conserve 302
  Cream or White 120, 257, 296
  Creole 145
  Doc's Hot Pepper 303
  Dr. Hebert's Grand Chenier
    Barbecue Plate 298
  Fluffy Bourbon 376
  for Baked Ham 196
  for Baked Hen 230
  for Basting Roasts 294
  for Black Walnut Roll 320
  for Bobby's Seasoned Steaks 172
  for Brucculini with Spaghetti 208
  for Buccaneer Broccoli 267
  for Chicken Italien 217
  for Chicken Spaghetti 216
  for Chilies Rellenos 195
  for Crêpes Suzette 363
  for French-Italian Spaghetti 174
  for International Cabbage Rolls ..241
  for Manicotti a la Romona 178
  for Moussaka 182
  for Oriental Meat Balls 185
  for Pheasant 300
  for Pork Tenders 200
  for Roast Beef 165
  for Stuffed Eggs Au Gratin 144
  for Swedish Meat Balls 184
  for Tujaque's Boiled Beef 173
  for Veal Parmigiano 210
  Gravy, Cream, Georgia Fried
    Chicken with 214
  Gravy, Cream with Baked Hen 230
  Gravy, for Cornbread Dressing 233
  Gravy, Giblet 294
  Gravy, Sauerbraten 168
  Ham 301
  Hard 377
  Hard for Poor Man's Pudding 358
  Hollandaise, Blender 293
  Horseradish with Boiled Brisket ..173
  Hot Pepper 303
  Italian Spaghetti 175
  Jalapeño for Cauliflower 244
  Jezebel 302
  Lemon 377
  Lemon, Avgolemono, for Keftethes .184
  Lock's Oyster Rockefeller 57
  Marchand De Vin, Sam's 295
  Marinade for Pork Tenderloin 201
  Marinade for Vegetarian Shish Kabob ..270
  Meunière 297
  Mayonnaise 292
  Mint 301
  Mousseline 293
  Mustard 126, 301
  Mutton Marinade 207
  Olive for Wild Duck 90
  Orange Raisin 302
  Orange, with Carrots 243
  Parsley-Lemon 293
  Picadillo 182
  Raspberry au Kirsch for Cold
    Lemon Soufflé 360

INDEX

Remoulade 297
Rum 353, 377
Sauerbraten Gravy 168
Sauerbraten Marinade 168
Shrimp, Fillet of Sole with 46
Sour Cream, Stuffed Chicken
  Breast with 215
Spaghetti, Italian 175
Spaghetti with Meat Balls 176
Spicy, for Apple Torte 323
Tartare 297
Teriyaki Marinade 300
Tomato Horseradish with Tujaque's
  Boiled Beef 173
Tuna with Chicken Breast 213
Venison Basting 300
White 120, 257, 296
White Remoulade 297
Wine for Ham Wellington 197
Sauerbraten 168
Sauerbraten Gravy 168
Sauerbraten Marinade 168
Sauerkraut, Country-Style Back Ribs and 203
Sauerkraut, and Knockwurst Delight,
  Choucroute à L'Alsacienne 203
Sausage
  Bean Chowder 380
  Chestnut Meatballs 383
  Goose-Duck Gumbo 7
  Jack's Stuffed Mirlitons 251
  Jambalaya, Creole 23
  Meat Loaf 179
  Nana's Lasagne 177
  Natchitoches Meat Pie 187
  Pecan Dressing, Corn Bread 232
  Polynesian 383
  Rice Cooker Jambalaya 401
  Rye Snacks 389
  Spaghetti, Chicken, Meat and 218
  Spinach and Cheese Casserole 260
  Strada 204
  Swartz Brats (Bratwurst) 204
  Tasso Sauce Piquante 205
  Venison 103
Sazerac Cocktail 110
Scalloped Oysters 59
Scallops of Veal in Wine 209
Scandinavian Pork Roast 199
Scaup Duck, Tips on 85
Schooner Squares 388
Seafood (See also specific kinds, i.e., Alligator,
  Crab Meat, Crawfish, Fish, Lobster, Oysters,
  Perch, Red Fish, Red Snapper, Shrimp, Trout,
  Tuna, Turtle, etc.)
  Baked Stuffed Shrimp 73
  Blend of the Bayou Seafood Casserole 83
  Bouillabaisse Soup 16
  Cocktail Sauce for 296
  Cold Stuffed Red Snapper 39
  Crab-Clam Dip 138
  Dip à la Kingwood 140
  Fillet of Sole with Shrimp Sauce 46
  Fried Stuffed Bell Pepper 53
  Gumbo 3, 5
  Gumbo, Mrs. Soulé's 4
  "Hot" Seafood and Okra Gumbo for a
    Crowd 6
  Hot Seafood Pie 397
  How to Clean 34, 49, 55, 62, 63, 69
  How to Cook 35, 69

Lobster Rolls 129
Lobster Tails 47
Louisiana Gumbo 3
Mrs. Soulé's Seafood Gumbo 4
Oysters Bienville 56
Oysters Bienville Casserole 56
Oysters Craig-Poddy 61
San Francisco Seafood Quiche 80
Shrimp and Crab Crêpes Rosemary 78
Shrimp Au Gratin 75
Shrimp Corn Bread Stuffing for Fish .. 84
Shrimp Mélange 282
Stuffed Flounder 38
Tartare Sauce for 297
Thelma's Stuffed Baked Red Fish or Red
  Snapper 41
Tips on Preparation, Cleaning, and
  Cooking 34, 35
Trout Alexander 42
Sesame Seed, To Toast 243
Seven Minute Icing 338
Shanghai Salad 277
Sherbet Macaroon 374
Sherbet, Refreshing Fruit 371
Sherbet, Watermelon 375
Sherried Onions 252
Sherry, Chicken with 215
Sherry Spice Goose or Duck 89
Sherry Trifle 351
Shish Kabob, Shrimp and Vegetable Grill 396
Shish Kabob, Vegetarian 270
Shish Kabob 174
Shoe Peg Corn Casserole 246
Shortcake (Fruit) 368
Shortcut Banana Pudding 417
Shrimp
  and Crab Crêpes Rosemary 78
  and Eggplant Dressing 84
  and Vegetable Grill 396
  Asparagus 83
  Aspic 283
  Au Gratin 75
  Baked 73
  Baked Stuffed 73
  Barbecued 72
  Bisque 379
  Beer Batter for 72
  Blend of the Bayou Seafood Casserole 83
  Boil, How to 69
  Boiled 74
  con Queso Dip 140
  Corn Bread Stuffing for Fish 84
  Creole 76
  Creole for a Crowd 76
  Curry, Chicken and 222
  Curry, Easy 80
  Curry Spread, Jack's 133
  de Jonghe 79
  Delight 75
  Dip 139
  Etouffée 77
  Flambé 82
  Freeze, How to 69
  Fried 70
  Gumbo Gouter 249
  Italiano 383
  Jambalaya, Creole 23
  Lemon-Garlic Broiled 72
  Loaf 82
  Marinated 131

INDEX

Mélange	282
Mold, Iced	283
Mornay	74
Mosca	73
Opelousas	396
Paste, Dino's	131
Patties	71
Peel, How to	69
Pomme De Terre	79
Rice Casserole	31
Salad, Molded	282
San Francisco Seafood Quiche	80
Sauce, Fillet of Sole with	46
Sauce Piquante	77
Squash, Stuffed with	263
Stock, How to Make	74
Stroganoff	81
Stuffed Mirlitons	251
Stuffed Tomatoes	265
Sybil's Fritters	71
Szechuan	81
Tarts, Creole	133
Tempura	70
Thermidor	75
Tips on	69
Weeze's Gumbo	5
Shrimparagus	83
Sicilian "Pot-of-Roast"	167
Simple Syrup	106
Sirloin (*See* Beef Steak)	
Skillet Tuna Curry	44
Skinning, Deer	100
Slaw, Cole	274
Slaw, Ice Box	274
Slice 'n Bake Cookies	349
Slush Punch	113
Smoked Wild Turkey	94
Smokehouse Specials	212
Smothered Doves	96
Snails (*See* Escargots)	
Snapper (*See also* Red Snapper)	
Snapper Luzianne	39
Snapper Pastor Sauce Base	65
Snipe, Dove Pie	97
Snipe, Doves in Wine	97
Snipe, Pot Roasted Game	86
Snow on the Mountain	367
Snow Peas and Mushrooms	255
Snowball Cake	336
Soda, Nectar Ice Cream	112
Soft Shell Crabs (*See* Crabs)	
Sole, Fillet of, with Shrimp Sauce	46
Sombrero Dip	386
Soufflé, Caramel with Caramel Custard	350
Soufflé, Cheese	146
Soufflé, Cold Lemon with Raspberry Sauce	360
Soufflé, Cold Orange	365
Soufflé, Crab	67
Soufflé, Hot Crab Meat	67
Soups	
Avocado Bisque	19
Bean	12
Bienvenu's Court Bouillon	16
Black Bean Soup, Mexican	11
Bouillabaisse	16
Cantaloupe, Marsh Melon	382
Carrot Vichyssoise	382
Cheese	12
Chez Oca's Turtle Stew	48
Chicken, Old Fashioned Jewish Penicillin	13
Chowder Contraband	380
Cold Curried Mushroom	19
Crab Stew	67
Crème d'Artichauts	381
Cucumber, Chilled	20
Fish Chowder	17
Flossie's Bean	11
French Onion	10
Fresh Corn	12
Hearty Corn Chowder	13
Marsh Melon	382
Mexican Black Bean	11
Morgans Point Crab Chowder	17
My Vichyssoise	20
Old Fashioned Jewish Penicillin (Chicken Soup)	13
Oyster	17
Pelican Hook	14
Quick Gazpacho	19
Sausage Bean Chowder	380
Shrimp Bisque	379
Shrimp Sauce Piquante	77
Spinach	14
Split Pea	14
Squashbuckling	381
Turtle	18
Vegetable Beef	15
Verde (Spinach Soup)	14
Sour Cream and Caviar, New Potatoes with	121
Sour Cream, Brussels Sprouts in	242
Sour Cream Cheese Cake	325
Sour Cream Pound Cake	335
South of the Border	148
South of the Border Hot Dish	193
Soybeans, Basic	237
Soyburgers	237
Spaghetti (*See also* Macaroni and Pasta)	
à la Giuliano and Joel III (Carbonara)	258
Chicken	216
Chicken, Meat, and Sausage	218
French Italian	174
Italian Sauce	175
Johnny Marzetti Cheddar Cheese Casserole	189
Leone's Pork and Pasta	401
Oriental	183
Oyster	60
Pie	399
Sauce with Meat Balls	176
Texas Hash	190
Turkey Tetrazzini	229
with Brucculuni	208
Spanish Delight	194
Spanish Meat Rice	26
Spanish Mackerel, Tips on	35
Spanish Olive-Pork Chop Casserole	202
Spanish Rice	27
Spanish Wild Duck	91
Spareribs, Sweet and Sour	127
Spice Bites	389
Spinach	
and Cheese Casserole	260
Artichoke Appetizers	119
Casserole	258
Creamed	259
Dip	139, 386
Festive Florentine Dip	386
Gumbo Z'Herbes	4
Lock's Oyster Rockefeller Sauce	57

INDEX

Orange-Spinach Salad with
  Honey-Mustard Dressing 407
Oysters Rockefeller 57
Quiche Boudreau 259
Quick and Easy 260
Rice 29
Ring 260
Salad 271, 273
Soup Verde 14
Stuffing for Pork Chops 201
Supreme 261
Split Pea Soup 14
Spoonbill, Tips on 85
Spoon Corn Bread 152
Squash
  Crookneck Frito 261
  Delight 263
  Glazed Acorn with Pecans 261
  Soup, Squashbuckling 381
  Steak Zucchini 170
  Stuffed with Shrimp 263
  Summer Casserole 262
  Supreme 262
  Vegetable Casserole 261
  White, Stuffed 263
  Yellow or Zucchini Casserole 264
  Yellow, for Sure Fire Squash Haters ..406
  Zucchini Eggplant Casserole 264
Squashbuckling Soup 381
Squirrel, Drunk 98
Squirrel or Dove Gumbo 7
Squirrel, Pot Roasted Game 86
Steak (See also Beef Steak)
Steak au Poivre Vert 398
Steak Diane 169
Steak Embassy Style 171
Steak Roll-ups 170
Steak Zucchini 170
Stew, Alaskan Fisherman 44
Stew, Country Pork Rib and Turnip 202
Stew, Crab 67
Stew, Osso Bucco 207
Stew, Turtle, Chez Oca's 48
Stir-Fry Beef 399
Sticky Buns 392
Stock, Shrimp, How to Make 74
Strada, Sausage 204
Strawberry, Angel Food Cake Ice
  Cream Pie 370
Strawberry Daiquiri 107
Strawberry-Orange Mold 287
Strawberry Paddle Wheel 388
Strawberry, Pavlova 364
Strawberry Pie, Heavenly 319
Strawberry Preserves 306
Strawberry Topping for Crêpes
  Fitzgerald 362
Strawberries, Fresh Fruit Bavarian 417
String Bean Salad 277
Stroganoff, Shrimp 81
Stroganoff, Beef 172
Stuffed Angel Food Cake 322
Stuffed Artichokes with Crab Meat 66
Stuffed Baked Beef Tongue 211
Stuffed Baked Potatoes 256
Stuffed Bell Pepper, Fried 53
Stuffed Beef Round 171
Stuffed Chicken Breast with Sour
  Cream Sauce 215
Stuffed Crabs 66

Stuffed Eggs Au Gratin 144
Stuffed Flounder 38
Stuffed Leg of Lamb 206
Stuffed Mirlitons 250, 251
Stuffed Pepper Casserole 255
Stuffed Pork Chops Fine Bouche 201
Stuffed Potatoes 255
Stuffed Squash with Shrimp 263
Stuffed Tomatoes 265
Stuffed White Squash 263
Stuffing (See also Dressing)
Stuffing for Baked Fish 45
Stuffing for Brucculuni 208
Stuffing for Crown Pork Roast 198
Stuffing for Fish, Shrimp Corn Bread 84
Stuffing for Lamb 206
Stuffing for Pork Chops 201
Sue's Mushrooms 120
Sugar or Simple Syrup 106
Sukiyaki, Easy Vegetable 266
Summer Squash Casserole 262
Sunday Night Omelets 145
Swartz Brats (Bratwurst) 204
Swedish Christmas Cabbage 242
Swedish Meat Balls 127, 184
Swedish Puff Coffee Cake 163
Sweet and Sour Dressing 271
Sweet and Sour, Pork Ribs 202
Sweet and Sour Spareribs 127
Sweet Dough Cheese Cake 326
Sweet Poppy Seed Bread 391
Sweet Potato, Harvest Jello Pie 319
Sweet Potato Puffs 269
Sweet Potatoes (See Yams)
Sweet Tomato Chutney 307
Sukiyaki, Easy Vegetable 266
Sybil's Shrimp Fritters 71
Syrup, Nectar 112
Syrup, Sugar or Simple 106
Szechuan Shrimp 81

Tacos, Beef 193
Talarini 190
Tamale and Chili Pie 195
Tapioca Plum Cake 334
Tart, Almond 370
Tart Shells 133
Tartare Sauce 297
Tarts, Creole Shrimp 133
Tarts, Little Pecan 316
Tarts, Pecan-Almond 368
Tasso Sauce Piquante 205
Teal, Tips on 85
Teals, Thelma's Stuffed 88
Tea Cakes, Mother's 348
Tempura 70
Tempura Batter 70
Teriyaki Marinade 300
Tetrazzini, Turkey 229
Terrell's Perch 46
Texas Beans 239
Texas Hash 190
Texas Potatoes 256
Thelma's Stuffed Baked Red Fish or
  Red Snapper 41
Thelma's Stuffed Teals 88
Thistle Dip 385

INDEX

Thousand Island Dressing 290
Three Cheese Roll 142
Three Peso Salad 408
Tiger's Tail 105
Tipsy Turkey 94
Tirotrigona 149
Toasted Pecans 122
Toffee Squares, English 358
Tomato Aspic 284
Tomato Casserole 265
Tomato Chutney, Sweet 307
Tomato Horseradish Sauce for Tujaque's
  Boiled Beef 173
Tomato Stuffed, Curried Chicken and
  Rice Salad 281
Tomato Tang, Macaroni-Cheese 147
Tomatoes, Baked Stuffed 265
Tomatoes, Charlie's Picante Sauce 387
Tomatoes, Quick Gazpacho Soup 19
Tomatoes, Red Relish 307
Tomatoes, Shrimp and Vegetable Grill 396
Tomatoes, Stuffed 265
Tongue, Pickled 211
Tongue, Stuffed Baked Beef 211
Torte, Apple 323
Torte, Pecan 333
Tortillas, Mexican Roll-ups 390
Tortoni 375
Tortoni, Bisque 364
Trifle, Sherry 351
Trifling Pudding 353
Trout Alexander 42
Trout Amandine, Lock's 42
Trout Au Gratin 42
Trout Platter 43
Trout Speckled, Tips on 35
Trout Veronique 43
True French Dressing 288
Tujaque's Boiled Beef 173
Tuna Casserole 44
Tuna Curry, Skillet 44
Tuna Dip 139
Tuna Mousse 284
Tuna Party Sandwiches 134
Tuna Sauce, Chicken Breast with or Petti
  di Pollo Tonnato 213
Turkey, Baked, and Corn Bread Dressing ...233
Turkey Dressing 232
Turkey or Chicken Croquettes 229
Turkey Tetrazzini 229
Turkey, Tipsy 94
Turkey, Wild, Smoked 94
Turkish Barbecued Beef 124
Turnip Stew, Country Pork Rib and 202
Turnips and Potatoes 266
Turnips, Pickled 308
Turtle Soup 18
Turtle Stew, Chez Oca's 48
Twenty-four (24) Hour Cocktails 110
Uncle Bubber's Biscuits 161
Uncooked Homemade Vanilla Ice Cream 373

Vanilla Ice Cream 374
Veal
  Brucculuni with Spaghetti 208
  Chicken Breasts with Tuna Sauce or Petti
    di Pollo Tonnato 213

Cutlets Parmesan 210
Grillades and Grits 209
Lemon Brandy 398
Osso Bucco 207
Parmigiana 210
Roast 207
Scallops of, in Wine 209
Vegetables (*See also* kinds, i.e., Broccoli, Cabbage,
  etc.)
Vegetable Beef Soup 15
Vegetable Casserole 267
Vegetable Salad, Garden 272
Vegetable Sukiyaki, Easy 266
Vegetables, Chowder Contraband 380
Vegetables, Marinated 123
Vegetables, Meat Pot Pie 188
Vegetables, Quick Gazpacho Soup 19
Vegetables, Shrimp and Vegetable Grill ...396
Vegetarian Burgers, Soyburgers 237
Vegetarian Shish Kabob 270
Velvet Hammer 110
Venison Basting Sauce 300
Venison Chateaubriand 101
Venison Chili 102
Venison, How to Skin a Deer 100
Venison Loin, Fried 103
Venison Roast, Charcoaled 101
Venison Roast, Jelly Glazed 102
Venison Sausage 103
Venison Steak, Country Style 104
Vermouth Chicken 216
Vichyssoise, Carrot 382
Vichyssoise, My 20
Viennese Fried Mushrooms 252
Vinegar Oil Dressing, Bleu Cheese 289
Virginia's Blueberry Jello Salad 287
Virginia's Spiked Fruit Punch 114

Walnut Cake 337
Walnut Cheese Ball 141
Walnut Chicken Hawaiian 220
Walnut Chicken, Orange 220
Walnut Roll, Black 320
Walnuts, Caramel Nut Pound Cake 323
"Wassail, Old Virginia" 113
Water Chestnuts, Bacon-Wrapped Snacks ...390
Water Chestnuts, Chestnut Meatballs 383
Watermelon Sherbet 375
Wedding Punch 114
Weenie Jam 203
Weeze's Gumbo 5
Wellington, Duck 87
Wellington, Ham with Wine Sauce 197
Welsh Rarebit 147
Wheat, Jhadro 250
Wheat, Kibbie, Baked 181
Wheat, Kibbie (Raw) 180
Wheat, Whole Bread 155
Whipped Yams 269
White Fruit Cake 328
White Icing 338
White Remoulade Sauce 297
White Sauce 120, 257, 296
Whole Wheat Bread 155
Widgeon, Tips on 85
Wieners, Choucroute à L'Alsacienne
  Sauerkraut and Knockwurst Delight 203

INDEX

Wieners, Hot Dog Butter Beans 239
Wieners, Weenie Jam 203
Wild Duck à la Creole 90
Wild Duck La Fleur 91
Wild Duck with Olive Sauce 90
Wild Rice and Oyster Casserole 60
Wild Rice Casserole 24
Wild Rice, Chicken Salad 281
Wild Rice, Cornish Hen Stuffed with 231
Wildlife
   Apple-Apricot Goose 92
   Bacon Baked Quail 95
   Baked Dove Martin 98
   Baked Wild Goose or Duck 88
   Breast of Duck and Duck Wellington 87
   Champeaux Gumbo 8
   Charcoaled Venison Roast 101
   Chez Oca's Pheasant in Brandy Sauce 96
   Chez Oca's Turtle Stew 48
   Cleaning and Preparing of 85
   Cooking Ducks 85
   Country Style Venison Steak 104
   Deer Skinning in Five Minutes 100
   Dove Pie 97
   Doves in Wine (Quail or Snipe) 97
   Drunk Squirrel 98
   Fricasséed Goose 93
   Fried Alligator 99
   Fried Duck Delight 92
   Fried Venison Loin 103
   "Gator" Meat Balls 99
   Goose-Duck-Sausage Gumbo 7
   Goose in Foil 93
   Iron Pot Duck 89
   Jelly Glazed Venison Roast 102
   Jim's Barbecued Duck 90
   Larded Goose L'Orange 93
   Orange Glazed Duck or Goose 92
   Pheasant Casserole 95
   Pheasant, Sauce for 300
   Plucking Ducks 85
   Pot Roasted Game 86
   Pot Roasted Stuffed Duck or Goose 88
   Quail in Cream Sauce 94
   Quail-Rice Magnifique 95
   Rabbit Sauce Piquante 98
   Sherry Spice Duck or Goose 89
   Smoked Wild Turkey 94

Smothered Doves 96
Spanish Wild Duck 91
Squirrel or Dove Gumbo 7
Thelma's Stuffed Teals 88
Tipsy Turkey 94
Turtle Soup 18
Venison Basting Sauce 300
Venison Chateaubriand 101
Venison Chili 102
Venison Loin, Fried 103
Vension, How to Skin a Deer 100
Venison Roast, Charcoaled 101
Venison Roast, Jelly Glazed 102
Venison Sausage 103
Venison Steak, Country Style 104
Wild Duck à la Creole 90
Wild Duck La Fleur 91
Wild Duck with Olive Sauce 90
Wilted Lettuce 273
Wine Sauce for Ham Wellington 197
Wines: Storage, Serving, and Selection . . 115-117

Yams, Bernie's Candied 268
Yams, Cajun Baked 8, 268
Yams, Cranberried 268
Yams, Harvest Sweet Potato Jello Pie 319
Yams, Sweet Potato Puffs 269
Yams, Whipped 269
Yellow or Zucchini Squash Casserole 264
Yellow Pound Cake, or Chocolate 334
Yellow Squash for Sure Fire Squash Haters . . .406
Yogurt 150
Yogurt Dip for Fruit 150
Yogurt Pie 150
Yogurt Popsicles 150
Yorkshire Pudding 166

Zucchini Eggplant Casserole 264
Zucchini, Steak 170
Zucchini, Vegetable Casserole 267
Zucchini, or Yellow Squash Casserole 264